THE WINSTON SPECIALS

Troopships via the Cape 1940-43

Archie Munro

Published by Maritime Books, Lodge Hill, Liskeard, Cornwall PL14 4EL,
England

Printed and bound by Biddles Ltd, King's Lynn, Norfolk

Contents

List of Illustrations

24. *Empire Pride* the only troopship to be built in Britain during WW2, running machinery trials at mouth of Loch Long, Firth of Clyde, 4 September 1941. (*TRK 4/4/84/2*) (*Glasgow City Libraries and Archives*)
25. *Stirling Castle* berthing at Singapore 30 September 1941 having arrived in WS 10. (Note lack of defensive armament) (*IWM FE 96*)
26. *Westernland* berthing at Singapore 25 September 1941 with Indian reinforcements from Bombay. (*IWMFE75*)
27. WS 17 on passage between UK and Freetown and prior to 31 March 1942, showing 14 ships of columns 1 to 4, from L to R: 43. *Dominion Monarch*; 42. *Duchess ofAtholl*; 34. *Arundel Castle*; 41. *Tamaroa*; 33. *Oronsay* with 24. *City of Lincoln* (hidden); 32. *Empress of Russia*; 23. *JV Oldenbamevelt*; 14. *Dunedin Star*; 31. *Abosso* (C); 13. *Kina II*; 22. *Samaria*; 12. *Port Wyndham*; 21. *Leopoldville*; 11. *Glaucus*. (Photo probably taken from cruiser *Shropshire*). (*Ambrose Greenway*)
28. WS 17 concurrent picture looking westward over columns 6 to 8, from L. to R: 81. *Largs Bay*; 71. *Mataroa*; 82. *Bhutan*; 72. *Sobieski*; 61. *Almanzora*; 73. *HMS Adamant*; 83. *Rembrandt* (hidden;) *HMS Illustrious* 62. *Cameronia*; 84. *City of Edinburgh*; 63. *HMS Karanja*. (*Ambrose Greenway*)
29. *Largs Bay* (left) and *Nieuw Zeeland* berthing Singapore 6 November 1941 having arrived in WS 11. (*IWM FE 307*)
30. *Duchess of Atholl* berthing in Belfast 2 March 1942 in convoy AT 12 with first US troops to land in the UK. (*IWM H 17557*)
31. *Queen Elizabeth* anchored at Suez 18 July 1942 on arrival as convoy WS 19Y. (*IWM E 14726*)
32. WS 19 columns 1,2 and 3 viewed from air escort when approaching the Cap Vert gap, morning of 19 May 1942. L. to R. *Athlone Castle, Highland Brigade, Moreton Bay* with *Ormonde* (behind). *Clan Macarthur, Monarch of Bermuda*, Ocean escort *HMS Mauritius* in foreground. (*IWM A.10615*)
33. *Pasteur* of WS 19 leaving Freetown 26 May 1942 (*IWM A.10612*)
34. *Monarch of Bermuda* of WS 19 leaving Freetown 26 May 1942 (*IWM A.10611*)
35. The Jewish Club in Durban was placed at the disposal of H.M. and Allied Forces and as a Canteen during the years 1940-45, in which period over 2 million members of the Services made use of it.
36. *Strathnaver* of WS 19 leaving Freetown 26 May 1942. (*IWM 10613*)
37. *Athlone Castle* leaving Freetown in WS 19, 26 May 1942. Note windchutes into troopdecks, boatropes rigged to each lifeboat and extensive gunpits. (*IWM A 10610*)
38. *Strathnaver* under repair at St Johns, Newfoundland, 15 September 1943, having sailed from New York for Liverpool in convoy UT 2 and put in for repairs. (*NMM 56/146*)
39. King George V Dock, Glasgow, 28 June 1943, from L to R: *Letitia, Banfora* (both embarking for KMF 19); Ocean type; *California* (pre-Faith Convoy); *Mooltan* (pre-WS 32); *Antenor* (repairing); *Nea Hellas* (embarking for KMF 19). (*Glasgow City Libraries & Archives - T-CN 19/216/1*)
40. *Monarch of Bermuda* (©*National Maritime Museum*)
41. *Rangitiki* (©*NMM*)
42. *Ruys* (©*NMM*)
43. *Sibajak* (©*NMM*)
44. *Highland Monarch* (©*NMM*)
45. *Staffordshire* 15.4.43 (©*NMM*)
46. *Orduna* (©*NMM*)
47. *Ormonde* (©*NMM*)
48. *Acquitania* (©*NMM*)

Foreword

by

Admiral Sir Nigel Essenhigh GCB DL

More than 60 years after the events described in this book and, in an era when the mass movement of people by air transport is taken for granted, it is perhaps difficult to grasp the scale and complexity of the sea borne trooping activities undertaken in the years leading up to and during the Second World War.

In the 1930s, unlike today, Britain's wider interests around the world could not be safeguarded by rapid, short notice deployment of expeditionary forces and thus British garrisons had to be maintained in widely dispersed locations overseas and supported by sea. However, the small, specialist troop ship fleet of the 1930s that maintained this overseas presence was insufficient to meet the challenge of the burgeoning requirements for much larger troop movements as Britain entered the Second World War.

Planners thus turned to the British merchant fleet which in these years was pre- eminent in the world passenger liner trade. Very quickly they requisitioned ships to transport people and equipment to and from destinations throughout the Far East, Asia, Middle East, Africa and the Mediterranean.

The strategic importance to the British war effort of oil supplies from the Middle East dictated that force levels in that region had rapidly to be built up and maintained and, naturally, the Suez Canal provided the critical artery for the troop ship routes. However, in June 1940 when Italy entered the war. Axis domination of the Mediterranean Sea lanes was such that reinforcement shipping could no longer use that route.

The alternative, passage via the North and South Atlantic, the Indian Ocean and the Red Sea was almost twice as long but there was no choice and so, with classic Churchillian doggedness, there began a 3 year long series of trooping convoys which carried over a million people around the long Cape of Good Hope route until Allied sea control was re-asserted in the Mediterranean in 1943.

This book tells the story of those voyages, known as the Winston Specials. It tells of the huge organisational feat needed to stage such a venture and, using previously untapped sources, it tells much of it from the viewpoint of the Merchant Navy mariners who made it all possible. At a time when the Royal Navy's own resources were stretched to near breaking point, the Admiralty somehow found the escorts necessary to shepherd these convoys through the most dangerous waters of their extended voyages. We read here of the outstanding cooperation between the Royal and Merchant Navies which ensured that, despite the considerable risks involved, there were remarkably few losses.

We are also given some fascinating glimpses of the impact that these long voyages had on the lives of so many people who had never travelled outside their home countries and never anywhere by sea: many of course never returned to their home countries. Significantly, even though it is now a very different world in which Britain pursues its foreign policy objectives, this book contains a lesson from the not too distant past that has relevance in the 21st Century.

It reminds us that, whilst so called "peace time" military activities beyond our shores can often be enabled and supported using strategic lift assets owned by or under regular contract to the Ministry of Defence, much as was the case with the pre-WWII trooping fleet, matters change quickly once the operation is scaled up. As soon as the requirement for troop and equipment movement escalates, planners need to be ready to charter or requisition assets that may well be in short supply due to similar demands placed on the market by allies or coalition partners.

In 1940 the Winston Specials were made feasible because British shipping companies owned and operated half of the world's passenger vessels. Today as we have seen in more recent campaigns including the Falklands War, the Gulf War and the Iraq War, the challenges are different. Over 60 years on, today's Winston Specials would likely comprise a mix of air transport and specialist shipping much of which would not be under British ownership or the British flag and no longer manned by British crews.

But perhaps most importantly of all this book and its story of the 52 Winston Special convoys is a testament to the bravery and utter determination of the Merchant Navy crews who fought their ships through a long, difficult and largely unsung campaign over 3 very dangerous years. Without them these strategically vital troop movements would not have been possible. A quotation attributed to Admiral Jackie Fisher says that "the Army is a projectile fired by the Navy". In the Winston Special years it was very much the Merchant Navy who did just that. Here they get long overdue credit for their efforts in a detailed account of this historic venture.

Admiral Sir Nigel Essenhigh
November 2005

Introduction

This is a work of previously unpublished material which begins with a precis of pre-war trooping and military needs serving overseas garrisons scattered worldwide. Six years later just over 200 ocean-going passenger ships had been adapted to serve as British troopships having a total carrying capacity of over 400,000 personnel at any one time.

The size of the British passenger fleet in 1939 proved critical to its ability for carrying large numbers of personnel to destinations wordwide in wartime. It was a fleet which had reigned supreme on ocean routes for the first three or four decades of the 20th century. By 1939 the British and Dominion passenger fleet represented 43 per cent of the world total.

The earliest wartime troop convoys were across the Indian Ocean and from the UK eastwards to strengthen overseas garrisons. These assembled even before war broke out and were followed by some reinforcement convoys including one from India to France and the movement of the Cavalry Division to Palestine; the last in a long line of horsed formations to serve with the British Army. Major movements brought the 1st Canadian Division to the UK and the Australian Corps and New Zealand Division to the Middle East.

The short campaign in Norway engaged 35,000 British and French troops in the spring of 1940 and held seventeen British liners under requisition for varying periods until the evacuation from that country three months later. Dunkirk was followed by the lesser known evacuation of the BEF from the Biscay ports involving twelve liners and the loss of *Lancastria* with 1,500 lives. The loss of western mainland Europe to Nazi domination brought the threat of invasion and diversion of the third Anzac convoy from the Middle East to the UK; the first to pass around the Cape, but soon followed by the movement of West African troops to Kenya and the return of eight regular battalions from India to add to home defences.

As Britain faced invasion from across the English Channel, Churchill and the War Cabinet had the foresight and courage to foresee, even at this critical hour, the need to reinforce and defend Egypt from an Italian Army preparing to invade its borders. The consequences of our failure to meet that threat leading to the loss of oil reserves in Iraq and eventually the Caucasus would have been catastrophic.

The Italian declaration of war in June 1940 effectively closed the Mediterranean to through-traffic and forced shipping on these routes to make the long voyage around the Cape of Good Hope with a consequent increase in the risks and length of passage to and from destinations in the Middle East, India, Singapore and beyond.

What Britain did then have, was a large fleet of suitable passenger liners with dedicated officers and crews well able to carry troops over long distances and also a Royal Navy with the resources to protect them throughout their projected voyages around the Cape. It thus came about that a series of troopship convoys began to sail from the UK in the summer of 1940 carrying personnel of all three services bound for the Middle East, but soon expanded to include destinations in West, South and East Africa, Aden, India, Burma, Ceylon, Singapore, Iraq, Madagascar, Australia and the Falkland Islands.

The first convoy, styled WS 1 and widely believed to mean 'Winston Special', comprised three of the 'Monster' Cunard liners which transhipped into smaller ships in Ceylon. A small reinforcement convoy direct from the UK to Suez was then followed by the first of the larger troop convoys around the Cape and established a pattern which lasted for the next three years.

Each convoy was elaborately planned, assembled, dispatched and proceeded throughout as a military operation rather than a trade convoy. Most of the troops had never previously left the home shores let alone sailed on a luxury liner where everything was strange and unfamiliar made even worse by blackout conditions. The stark introduction to life at sea as the liners first emerged from sheltered waters to meet the North Atlantic was only one aspect of the voyage which remained with the troops for the rest of their lives.

The steamy heat of Freetown without shore leave was made up for by a few days and nights amongst the bright lights and outstanding hospitality of the South African population in Capetown and Durban, which for many set the scene for friendships which outlasted the war. During the final section of the voyage after leaving the Cape the troops were first made aware of their destination whether it be Suez, Bombay, Basra or Singapore.

Most WS convoys spent seven weeks on passage and having twice passed through the tropics, reached their destinations and disembarked the troops who first moved to training areas before being disposed to meet the enemy.

A maximum of seventy to eighty liners were deemed suitable and available for WS service at any one time. Well over a million personnel of the armed forces were carried in these convoys during the three year period until the Mediterranean was re-opened for through troopship sailings in the summer of 1943. Aircraft several times attacked the WS convoys and caused serious damage as did the occasional U-Boat who chanced upon them while the commerce raider *Admiral Hipper* attacked and damaged two ships of WS 5A. Two of the convoys passed directly over an undetected enemy minefield laid off the South African coast, but all of the troopships escaped unscathed.

No two convoys were the same in size, composition, weather encountered or route followed. Each is described in sufficient detail to allow readers and researchers to follow the passage that fathers or grandfathers, even mothers and grandmothers took to war in a far off land from which many never returned. Despite the high class of tonnage in the WS convoys, some ships were unable to prevent making smoke, some even incessantly while others fell behind and straggled due to engine trouble or bad coal or oil fuel. Many famous regiments travelled on the WS route, some recording their experiences of an historic period in both the military and maritime life of Britain which can hardly be repeated.

The homeward voyages of all liners were made unescorted and independently and put to valuable use by loading to capacity in East or South Africa, Bombay, the Antipodes or the Argentine: all cargoes were required to help maintain the vital food and import programme into the UK.

The critical shortage of trooping tonnage in 1941 was far beyond the capacity demanded by the War Office. Every means of increasing capacity within the limited size of the fleet was explored in great depth. The end result had the effect of increasing capacity on existing tonnage by an incredible sixty per cent.

Problems abounded in berthing the liners in home ports at a time when only the Clyde, Mersey and Bristol Channel ports could be used due to enemy air raids on the south and east coasts. The shiprepair yards were short of just about everything including labour and materials, which seriously delayed time under repair. Pressure on the west coast ports increased as the war progressed but the Clyde alone had a vast and safe anchorage area adjacent to its shipbuilding and shiprepair base where more than a hundred ships were safely accommodated at any one time.

There were some unusual convoys in the series. In October 1941 WS 12X carried 18 British Division across the Atlantic to Halifax where the troops were transhipped on to American (not yet at war) transports and eventually landed in Singapore. In March 1942 WS 17 sailed with the liners and assault troops for the landings on Madagascar and in November that year with all of the Freetown escort force withdrawn for the Torch operation, WS 24 refuelled instead at Bahia (now Salvador) in Brazil. From January 1943 the WS convoys left the UK combined with the KMF series for North Africa, breaking off to the west of Gibraltar before continuing to Freetown. The last of the series carried 81 West African division to India for service in Burma.

Acknowledgements

The earliest basis of research for this work was the movement Cards maintained by the Ministry of War Transport, without which the complete story of these troopships or their convoys or homeward voyages could not have been written. Admiralty records and War Diaries held in the Public Record Office were widely consulted and much help given by the Naval Historical Branch of the MoD, as also my good friend, Arnold Hague, who in many instances, was able to help and corroborate my research.

The records of many former shipping companies were examined and Masters' reports viewed. Much assistance was given by the South African Port Authorities and many other correspondents in that country, while notes of the outstanding work undertaken by Imperial Movement Control in Capetown and Durban gave much insight into the vast transhipment organisation which operated in these two ports.

Clyde Navigation Trust records were examined for shipping in the river to Glasgow, and those of Clyde Marine Services Ltd. in Greenock for much of that which occurred in the vast Clyde Anchorages where half the liners embarked or assembled for convoy. The official war history series published by HMSO were consulted as appropriate while many regimental histories provided a useful background to life on a wartime troopship. Acknowledgement is duly given to the source of each photograph, most being from the collections held in the Imperial War Museum and National Maritime Museum.

None of this story could have been undertaken without the kindest assistance from innumerable individuals in the reference services mentioned, but most of all without the dedicated and loving support of my dear wife Emily, who always believed in the project and provided the legible manuscript from endless pages of frequently illegible script. Both of us had witnessed the assembly and departure of these great liners from the wartime Clyde Anchorages, sustained by anecdotes from our fathers who experienced the ships first hand from anxious times with the Clyde Pilotage Authority. Finally my thanks are due to a most accommodating publisher for believing in this volume as a valuable historical aspect of the war at sea not previously recorded.

Archie D Munro
Greenock, 2006

Preface

Pre-war Trooping and Military Needs

After proposing a toast to the builders, following the launch of the troopship *Devonshire* at Fairfield's Govan Shipyard on 20th December 1938, Mr. W. G. Hynard, Director of Sea Transport at the Board of Trade, said "he was afraid that neither the Fairfield nor any other company could expect further orders for troopships in the near future".   His remarks were doubtless based on the impending completion of the *Devonshire* as the fulfilment of a modernization programme for the peacetime trooping fleet. In the event, Mr. Hynard's words proved more accurate than he could ever have imagined; nearly fifteen years elapsed before another such troopship was built, and this ship together with her sister were the last in a long line to be employed in the overseas movement of British troops by sea. Apart from the Falklands conflict of 1982, military personnel have been carried almost exclusively by air transport since the demise of the trooping fleet in 1962.

In stark contrast to the actual building of troopships, however, British shipyards were soon to be involved in the conversion of passenger liners for troop-carrying on a scale that could hardly have been envisaged in 1938. In times of war, additional tonnage for trooping was simply obtained by chartering or requisitioning suitable passenger tonnage from the liner companies, of which there was a large and ready supply in the 1930s. Nearly two hundred ocean-going passenger ships were ultimately adapted for British trooping service during the Second World War to swell the carrying capacity of the 1939 peacetime trooping fleet from 14,000 to over 400,000 personnel at any one time.

Until 1935 only five ships were normally employed on regular peacetime trooping service; the fleet then consisting of *Neuralia* and *Nevasa* of British India, together with *Dorsetshire*, *Somersetshire* and *Lancashire* of Bibby Bros. They were all of modest speeds, 12.5 or 13 knots and with capacities varying from 1,428 to 1,728 troops. None of those ships had in the first instance been designed for trooping, but were adapted for the purpose at a later stage in their careers. The B.I. sisters *Neuralia* and *Nevasa* were built for their company's mail and passenger service between London and Calcutta, and following outstanding trooping work in the 1914-18 War were then employed on the London/East Africa route until converted as permanent troopships in 1925. Similarly the Bibby sisters *Dorsetshire* and *Somersetshire* had originally been cargo ships until entirely reconstructed for trooping service in 1927. The *Lancashire* of 1917 had been engaged on the Bibby Line passenger and cargo service between Liverpool and Rangoon until joining the trooping fleet in 1930. All of these ships were crewed and operated by their respective owners under long-term charter agreements with the Sea Transport Division of the Board of Trade.

Trooping Service in the 1930s primarily involved the movement and relief of military units stationed in various garrisons throughout the British Empire: the vast majority of which were in India where civil disturbances in the towns, tribal feuds on the North West Frontier, and the constant threat of Soviet aggression through neighbouring Afghanistan caused the deployment, by 1939, of 63,000 British and 205,000 Indian troops in what was largely a static defensive role. In Egypt a force of 27,000 British troops was responsible for the security of the Suez Canal and Nile Delta, whilst a further 19,000 were in Palestine on internal security duties and protection of oil pipelines. There were also British garrisons of varying strengths at Shanghai and Tientsin in Northern China, in Malaya and Singapore, in Hongkong, the Sudan, Burma, Malta, Gibraltar, the West Indies, Bermuda and Mauritius: altogether a total overseas commitment of nearly 150,000 men which had to be maintained in the normal course of events by the existing peacetime trooping fleet. There was not then, of course, the sophisticated logistical support or even the need for it that exists today. Regiments serving abroad generally completed a fifteen years tour before returning to the U.K., whilst the troops themselves served six years on foreign service before qualifying for relief. Infantry regiments on garrison duties usually began their overseas tour by spending the first two or three years acclimatizing in the Middle East, moving then to the Far East for a year or so before settling down in India for periods up to about 10 years on perhaps two or three different stations; of which one was generally on the turbulent and fabled North West Frontier. The return home was made with a short spell in Egypt, Palestine, or the Sudan. It was these frequent movements of so many individual battalions and the almost continual turnround of personnel within these units for multifarious reasons that kept the peacetime troopships so busily employed. Some 40,000 military personnel were transported annually to and from overseas stations by these vessels.

Trooping voyages were not usually made during the period of the Southwest Monsoon in the Indian Ocean as the exigencies of the summer climate in India during these months deterred all but the most necessary troop movements. The ships were then laid up in the River Fal from May to September as their spartan but functional accommodation rather precluded alternative employment, although the B.I. pair were frequently used for short Baltic cruises from east coast ports in the summer months. This restricted trading season called for shrewd economics and resulted in a class of ship rather smaller and slower than ideal for passages to India and the Far East in an age when passenger liners were offering steadily increasing facilities quite outwith the capabilities of the rapidly ageing troopships. Troop accommodation was in messdecks, naval fashion, with hammocks slung from the deckhead overnight and stowed away in daytime to allow space for eating and recreation. Conditions were indifferent and became highlighted in the 1930s as troops experienced the comparative luxury of passenger ship travel when international tension caused increased movements that simply outgrew the limited supply of troopships.

The department responsible for the supply and chartering of troopships was the Sea Transport Division of the Board of Trade, a somewhat anomalous and ancient body of Admiralty origin owing allegiance to all three fighting Services and staffed largely by ex-Naval personnel. With a view to modernizing the ageing trooping fleet this department, in conjunction with the British India S.N. Co. Ltd. drew up plans early in 1934 for the construction of two specially designed troopships to be owned and operated by that company and placed on long term charter to the Board of Trade.

The first ship was ordered from Barclay Curle's Whiteinch yard on the Clyde soon after Hitler came to power as the German Dictator in August of that year, and launched as *Dilwara* on 17th October 1935, just after war began between Italy and Abyssinia. Steadily rising tension throughout the western world dominated the construction of these ships as the power of the German and Italian military machines steadily gained momentum. The second ship was named *Dunera* at a launching ceremony in Barclay Curle's yard on 10th May 1937: Germany had then begun their re-militarisation of the Rhineland and Italian troops occupied Addis Abbaba. It was therefore no surprise when the Director of Sea Transport announced that orders were pending for two further troopships similar to the first pair.

The new ships were of course a vast improvement on previous troopers, having been specially designed for the purpose from the keel up. Of increased dimensions and tonnage, the machinery installed was the twin-screw diesel arrangement found so economical in the Bibby sisters, *Dorsetshire* and *Somersetshire*. Unfortunately the increased power of these vessels was largely absorbed by their greater displacement, which resulted in a disappointingly modest increase in speed over the older ships and later proved a severe handicap when operating under wartime conditions. They still offered hammocks rather than bunks in the troopdecks, however, although a great deal more space per man was available with much improved messing and recreational facilities than previous troopships.

The third ship of the series was also built by Barclay Curle, and took to the water as the *Ettrick* of the P & O Steam Navigation Co. Ltd. on 25th August 1938. Clydesiders were then engrossed in the spectacular Empire Exhibition while Clydebank rejoiced as the *Queen Mary* crossed the Atlantic eastbound at a speed of 31.69 knots to regain the Blue Riband for Cunard and Great Britain - a record she was to hold for the next fourteen years. The *Ettrick* sailed out of the Clyde on 16th December 1938, past the second Cunard giant *Queen Elizabeth* then in the early stages of fitting out, and arrived at Southampton on completion of sea trials just as the final ship of the quartette, Bibby's *Devonshire* slid into the water from the Fairfield yard at Govan. On delivery of this last ship in July 1939, four new ships had been added to the trooping fleet.

It seems certain that these vessels were first intended as replacements for the ageing British India and Bibby sisters in the trooping fleet. Their additional berths, however were almost immediately absorbed as military movements to the Middle East sharply increased in the second half of the 1930s due to the threatening situation resulting from the Italian conquest of Abyssinia on the one hand and growing Arab/Jewish tension in Palestine on the other. The older ships were thus reprieved and continued in service, and even with the additional new tonnage becoming available from 1936 onwards there were still insufficient berths to keep pace with demand. Passenger ships were then chartered from the liner companies to supplement the limited tonnage; notable amongst them being some of the 'Intermediate' sized North Atlantic liners of the Cunard, Anchor, and C.P.S. Companies, who thus found most welcome employment for their excess tonnage during the slack off-season months of their highly competitive trade. In this way the Anchor Line's *Cameronia* made four consecutive troop voyages between September 1935 and April 1936, while the same company's *California* made two such voyages towards the end of 1936, a further two at the end of 1937, and another in February 1938 when she arrived at Glasgow with 400 men of the Rifle Brigade from Malta; the first troopship to berth there since the end of the First World War, and proved to be the forerunner of many hundreds that arrived in the second major conflict.

During the early months of 1939 the British Army finally began to prepare and organise for the major war that now inevitably lay ahead. There were then 64 individual Infantry Regiments each of two battalions in the regular peacetime army, and together with five Guards Regiments each of three battalions made a grand total of 143 regular battalions of infantry on the active list, of which no less than 78 were serving abroad - 35 in India, 11 in Palestine, 10 in Egypt, 4 each in Malta and Malaya and the remaining 14 spread as far apart as Tientsin in China and Jamaica in the West Indies. This left only 65 battalions of infantry on home service. Each regiment, however, maintained a supplementary force of two Territorial battalions that could and did mobilize into active service in the event of emergency. In addition the Government in the spring of 1939 ordered the duplication of the Territorial Army and so by September 1939 some 250 such battalions had been formed. This effectively increased the fighting strength of the army to about 400 battalions of 300,000 men. In theory at least, these units could have been formed into the equivalent of some 40 Infantry Divisions, but in the event no more than 35 such British Divisions were in being at any one time.

In peacetime, overseas movements of complete military units were generally restricted to those of battalion strength, usually for internal security garrison duties, whereas in wartime much larger and more complex formations were moved across the oceans from one theatre of operations to another as the strategic situation required. The organisation of the British Army for war was centred around the Division, of which there was, in 1939, three distinct types - Infantry, Armoured and Cavalry. The basic unit of infantry was the Battalion with a strength of about 780 officers and men. An Infantry Brigade was a permanent grouping of three Infantry Battalions plus a Field Regiment of Artillery and a Headquarters Staff through which a Brigadier exercised control over some 2,500 officers and men. The Infantry Division was commanded by a Major-General and consisted of a Headquarters Staff, three infantry Brigades and numerous miscellaneous units such as Signals, Engineers, Transport, Medical, Sappers, etc.: the whole comprising a force of about 13,800 men and 2,000 vehicles. Similarly an Armoured Division totalled 9,500 men with 1,800 vehicles and 350 tanks, whilst a Cavalry Division was of 11,000 men and 6,000 horses. Thus, where a troopship in peacetime could comfortably accommodate and move an Infantry Battalion, several troopships were required in wartime to move a Division, and many more again to lift the multitude of miscellaneous non-combatant units required to keep the Divisional fighting troops adequately maintained in the field.

Trooping in the first half of 1939 followed much the same pattern as previous years, until the summer lay-up period was cut short when the threat of war hastened the reinforcement of many overseas garrisons. As the summer months passed, the nine peacetime troopships set out on their final pre-war voyages dressed in customary trooping paintwork: white hulls and blue ribands surmounted by buff funnels. These colours soon gave way to drab blacks and greys and even for a time stone coloured upperworks and funnels. It was to be seven years before the brilliant and distinctive peacetime colourings re-appeared.

The B.I. sisters, *Dilwara* and *Dunera* had engaged in short Baltic cruises in the summer months, but these were not undertaken in 1939 and both ships remained at Southampton and Falmouth awaiting orders. First ship out of lay-up was *Dilwara* which left Southampton on 1st July for Hong Kong, calling en route at Malta, Port Said, Aden, Bombay, Colombo, Sabang and Singapore. *Dilwara* was at Suez homeward bound when war was declared between Britain and Germany on 3rd September, and was held in the Canal area to prepare for wartime passage and await commencement of the convoy system. She left Port Said on 9th September as Commodore ship of the first westbound Mediterranean convoy, designated 'Blue One', containing one Dutch and 19 British ships steaming at the slow speed of 9 knots. When north of the Algerian coast on 16th September *Dilwara* suffered a minor collision with the Blue Funnel *Stentor* due to misinterpreted alterations of course arising from faulty convoy-signal equipment. Both ships continued in the first homeward convoy from Gibraltar; *Dilwara* arriving safely at Southampton on 6th October.

The next outward sailings were by *Lancashire* on 4th July followed a week later by the chartered Lamport & Holt liner *Voltaire*: these ships were bound for Bombay whence they returned to Southampton on 22nd and 28th August respectively. *Lancashire* remained in the Solent for the next two months pending future employment; *Voltaire* was immediately requisitioned by the Admiralty and left the following day for conversion into an Armed Merchant Cruiser, serving in this capacity until April 1941 when sunk in the South Atlantic from an action with the German raider Thor.

Leaving Southampton on 19th July, the P & O Company's *Ettrick* set off on her third and longest voyage since completion only seven months earlier. She had on board a full complement of Naval and Military drafts for Malta, Aden, Colombo, Singapore and Hong Kong. *Ettrick* left Hong Kong on 26th August for Northern China, to embark there the 1st Bn Durham Light Infantry then stationed at Chingwangtao and Tientsin, but the grave situation in Europe caused a cancellation of this movement and the ship returned to Hong Kong, arriving there on 1st September as the German Armies marched into Poland. *Ettrick* was now equipped at the Naval Dockyard with a 4-inch poop-mounted gun, the hull painted grey, the funnel black, while the upperworks were left gleaming white as if to suggest possible peaceful intentions. She remained in the Far East a further six weeks and did not return home until June 1940. Departure of *Ettrick* from Southampton was followed by the sailing of *Dorsetshire* on 25th July with reinforcement details for Mediterranean garrisons at Gibraltar, Malta, Haifa and Alexandria; the ship returning to Southampton on 18th August where she remained with *Lancashire* awaiting further orders.

Had it been known that the departure of the 26 year old *Nevasa* on 1st August 1939 was to be her last from the U.K., or that she was to spend the next eight and a half years abroad on continuous trooping service only returning home to be paid -off and scrapped at the end of 1947, there would surely have been a memorable send-off to mark the occasion. *Nevasa* was in the Arabian Sea when war was declared and arrived at Mombasa on 7th September where she was repainted and prepared for her second period of war service as a troopship.

Bibby's *Somersetshire* left the Solent on 4th August on a short voyage of three weeks duration to Port Said and back to Southampton, and remained there with her sister ship and *Lancashire* until 3rd September. The next two troopship sailings embarked reinforcements for Singapore: *Neuralia* leaving Southampton on 12th August followed by *Dunera* on the 25th. *Neuralia* reached Colombo on 3rd September and after disembarking troops at Singapore was immediately ordered to Bombay, subsequently returning to Southampton on 31st October and passing through the Mediterranean in Convoy 'Blue Four' of 30 ships. *Dunera* was outward bound in the eastern half of the Mediterranean when war was declared and reached Singapore on 24th September, whence she was employed on extended voyages in this area and like *Ettrick* did not return to the U.K. until the summer of 1940.

The last pre-war troopship sailing was appropriately made by the recently delivered *Devonshire*, which strangely had been laid-up in the Fal for five weeks following acceptance by owners. *Devonshire* was ordered to prepare for a voyage to Singapore and Hong Kong departing on 29th August, but these orders were cancelled and she sailed a day earlier with drafts and details for miscellaneous units in Gibraltar, Malta, Alexandria and Bombay. Leaving Gibraltar on 2nd September she passed through the Suez Canal during the night of 13th/14th and after bunkering at Aden arrived at Bombay on the 24th just as *Neuralia* arrived there from Singapore. *Neuralia* embarked Indian troops and sailed for the Middle East, *Devonshire* was repainted, armed and blacked-out for wartime voyaging: nearly five years elapsed before her owners viewed her again in the U.K.

Although the size and capacity of the trooping fleet had effectively doubled with delivery of the new ships by July 1939, the combined lifting capacity of the entire fleet was barely sufficient to embark a single Infantry Division of the British Army at war establishment strength. In practice of course the fleet could hardly be retained on such a combined basis. When war broke out only three troopships were immediately available in the U.K., with a total personnel capacity of 4,800. Plans had earlier been made to send out some 13,000 reservists to overseas stations whenever hostilities opened, and these personnel were embarked and sailed in one convoy of fast passenger liners two days after war was declared; such vessels immediately became the key factor in wartime trooping and were to remain the mainstay of the trooping fleet, not just for the duration of hostilities but for the next nine continuous years.

Chapter 1

The British Passenger Fleet in 1939

During the First World War passenger liners were requisitioned for trooping service more or less as the campaigns and troop movements developed. Some ships were fully converted for the purpose and made maximum use of all available space, others only temporarily taken up offered limited capacity according to the number of ordinary passenger berths on board. The system proved adequate; even allowing the large number of liners serving the White Ensign as Armed Merchant Cruisers (AMCs) and some troopship losses when the U-Boat campaign gathered momentum, no real shortage of personnel-carrying tonnage occurred during these years. The greatest mass of the military bogged down in trench warfare on the continent of Europe, was quickly served by cross-channel steamers operating as transports from south of England ports. Overseas campaigns involving British and Empire troops were restricted to the Middle East, to Gallipoli, Egypt, Mesopotamia etc., and were reasonably accessible by troopships passing directly through the Mediterranean Sea that remained open to the Allies throughout the conflict. For most of that war, only limited and infrequent bodies of troops were moved across the oceans, mainly the Empire contingents from Australia, India, Canada and New Zealand, and not until the final year of the war did the United States join the Allies when large numbers of American troops crossed the North Atlantic to fight in France. When hostilities finally ceased and servicemen returned to their native shores,

British troopships had carried over 23 million personnel of all nations: a very large proportion of which had simply made a short and relatively peaceful crossing of the English Channel.

From the time of the Munich crisis in September 1938 war loomed ever nearer almost week by week. The British Army was feverishly engaged in re-equipping the infantry on a mechanised basis, the Royal Navy taking delivery of new warships while modernizing their older ships, and the Royal Air Force fast assembling the squadrons of fighters that later won renown in the Battle of Britain. No comparable measures were, however, made to increase or even prepare the existing trooping fleet for a major war. Possibly the ready supply of passenger liners suitable for trooping was simply taken for granted; in any event it was probably recognized that the main campaign would again be fought on the continent of Europe, for which transportation could readily be arranged in cross-channel steamers, still then available in large numbers.

In the long term, no one could really say what the fighting services might need in the way of shipping to transport troops or equipment across the seas or oceans in the event of war. No one indeed could even say where the need might arise, or when, or how many troops or how much equipment might be required for any one purpose and without which no estimates of the necessary shipping could be made.

As may be seen from the accompanying table, British passenger liners had reigned supreme on ocean routes for the first three or four decades of the 20th century. The growth in numbers and size of these ships had of course begun on the North Atlantic,

Passenger Liners over 10,000 grt.

Year	British and Dominion		
	North Atlantic	Other Routes	World Total
1900	21	4	54
1914	60	67	197
1931	54	131	349
1939	36	122	369

but during the 1920s had spread gradually to all other passenger routes. The peak in actual numbers of British liners was probably reached in 1931, following which there was a great deal of rationalization due to trade recessions and a decline in emigrant traffic. Concurrent with the reduction in numbers of ships, their size generally continued to increase on nearly all routes culminating in the construction of the two Queens exceeding 80,000 grt for the North Atlantic express service, which were never subsequently surpassed in size (other than by bulkers and VLCCs) until the advent of giant cruise liners six decades later. Although by 1939 the British and Dominion share of passenger liners had then fallen to 43 per cent of the total, with a strength of 158 ships it still remained by far the largest and a most formidable fleet for moving military personnel around the world.

A major reduction of the British passenger fleet was initiated at a stroke on 25th August 1939, nine days before war was declared, when the Admiralty began to requisition liners for conversion to AMCs; 55 of these valuable ships (eight owned in the Commonwealth) were taken up within the next two months and so removed 44,000 berths from the capacity of the peacetime fleet, which, under wartime conditions, would have carried three times that number of troops. "This single event was made without protest from the Board of Trade and subsequently caused the severest shortage of personnel capacity in the years ahead".[1] In the summer of 1939, however, there was such an abundance of large passenger liners in the British Merchant fleet that difficulties soon arose in keeping them usefully employed; less than eighteen months later this situation was irretrievably reversed and never returned, indeed the zenith of the great line-voyage passenger ships had by then passed into history.

In addition to those vessels exceeding 10,000 tons gross there were, in 1939, a further 88 British ships of limited passenger capacity but nevertheless holding appropriate Passenger Certificates employed mainly on intermediate services between the United Kingdom and India, Burma, Africa, the West Indies, and the many cross-trades of the Indian Ocean between India, Africa and Asia. The Dominions of Canada, India, Australia and New Zealand contributed a further 54 passenger ships of those lesser sizes and there were also 71 smaller cross-channel steamers employed on the short-sea routes to France, Belgium, Holland and across the Irish Sea to the Isle of Man and Ireland.

The total British and Dominion passenger tonnage at that time was therefore 374 ships of 3.98mn gross tons having a combined carrying capacity for 271,676 persons.[2] However, less than half these ships were suitable for fast North Atlantic crossings or extended ocean voyages such as those demanded by the WS route going around the Cape to Suez. Deductions had also to be made for those taken up for service as AMCs, for the five largest and fastest classed as 'Monsters', and a further ten lost by enemy action before the first WS convoys set out for the Middle East in the Summer of 1940.[3]

In September 1939 the number of passenger ships, including those on cross-channel routes, represented nearly 13% of the total shipping on the British register. In terms of gross tonnage that percentage almost doubled while the proportion of crews amounted to 34% or 67,500 out of 193,500 British seamen, by then employed on passenger ships. By reason of their size, speed and superior facilities, passenger liners were obliged to carry thirty or more diverse categories of personnel, such as bakers, butchers, plumbers, waiters, etc., unheard of on smaller ships. Whereas an ordinary coal-burning tramp might carry a crew of forty, a North Atlantic liner of the intermediate size required a crew of ten or twelve times that number.

On pre-war peacetime service the regular scheduled voyages that these great ships once operated is now merely a memory. However, it is necessary to take a view of these ships and the services they operated worldwide as at September 1939, certainly of those liners which later proved capable of carrying, sustaining and safely delivering large numbers of military personnel to the Middle and Near East through three of the most difficult years of war. Although designed to carry a maximum number of passengers on certain specific routes, once requisitioned they had to be adapted to carry not hundreds but thousands of mixed personnel on any number of routes where all the inherent difficulties of fuelling, watering and storing at unfamiliar ports were often magnified by the inability of these places to meet such needs in the quantities required.

It can be seen from the table in *Appendix 1* that those liners employed on the relatively short North Atlantic routes provided the greatest personnel capacity and were therefore the most attractive for early trooping employment. However, almost all passenger liners also carried cargoes, which constituted a considerable proportion of the valuable import programme from five different continents, particularly in foodstuffs, and could not be replaced by other suitable tonnage, simply because it did not exist. There had to be a balance of requisitions from all trades to prevent denuding one or other to unacceptable levels. Nevertheless, the largest proportion of liners selected by the Admiralty for conversion to AMCs did come from the North Atlantic and Near/Far East trades.

Clearly the most prestigious passenger service in the world was the weekly, Cunard White Star express service between Southampton and New York operated by the *Queen Mary* and her ageing consort *Aquitania* (but due for replacement by the new *Queen Elizabeth* in April 1940). The last peacetime departures were made on 30th August whereupon the service was suspended and both ships temporarily laid up. From London, Cunard also had an 'intermediate' express service to New York with the new *Mauretania* and the ex-White Star motorships *Britannic* and *Georgic*; this service ceased on 11th October and all three ships transferred to Liverpool. The main intermediate service was a weekly one from Liverpool to Boston or New York, given by *Scythia*, *Samaria* and any two of *Franconia*, *Carinthia*, and *Laconia*, the vessel not so used being employed on cruising from New York. The last two named became AMCs, *Franconia* went trooping from the outset while the remaining two with support from *Britannic* continued an irregular service until all three became troopships by December 1940.

There were two Cunard services to Canada, using Quebec and Montreal in summer and Halifax with St John's (NB) in winter. This was a weekly service from London by *Ausonia*, *Aurania*, *Ascania* and *Alaunia* that ended on 11th August following which all four were taken up as AMCs. A similar but shared service with the Donaldson-Atlantic Line operated from Glasgow and Liverpool by Donaldson's *Athenia* and *Letitia*, and from Liverpool and the Clyde by the Cunard *Andania* and *Antonia*. The middle two went off as AMCs, *Athenia* was lost on 3rd September while *Antonia* continued on service until taken up for conversion to a Fleet Repair Ship in November 1940.

The two other Cunarders were *Laurentic* and *Lancastria*; the former having been laid-up since 1935 but now taken up as an AMC. *Lancastria* was a general purpose ship and was cruising from New York when ordered home in September to assist on the New York and Halifax routes until taken up for trooping in the Norway and Biscay evacuations which ended in her tragic loss at St. Nazaire.

From Glasgow the Anchor Line also maintained a weekly service to New York, from which *California* and *Transylvania* became AMCs, while an additional vessel, *Caledonia*, which had been on summer cruises from Glasgow, was similarly taken up. *Cameronia* alone continued the service until taken up for trooping in November 1940.

Canadian-Pacific was the main rival to Cunard on services to Canada. The magnificent *Empress of Britain* and lesser *Empress of Australia* provided a weekly express service in summer from Southampton to Quebec that terminated promptly on 2nd September when the former ship was laid-up and the latter went off trooping on a permanent basis and was never released until broken-up thirteen years later. The main CPS service was weekly from Liverpool to Quebec and Montreal, and St John's (NB) in winter. Four *Duchess* and three *Mont* class liners could be used on this route, but in summer 1939 *Duchess of Richmond* and *Atholl* were cruising from Canada while *Montclare* and *Montcalm* similarly operated from UK ports. *Montrose* and her two sisters soon became AMCs, while *Duchess of Bedford* made a trooping voyage to Bombay before joining *Duchess of York* and her sisters in continuing a somewhat irregular service with frequent interruptions for trooping until all four had been fully requisitioned for this purpose by November 1940.

On the western side of the Atlantic, Furness-Withy operated the luxury class 'millionaire's service' between New York and Bermuda with the *Monarch* and *Queen of Bermuda*; a mere crossing of 36 hours which terminated on 15th September due to U.S. Neutrality Laws. By this date the *Queen* was in Belfast converting to an AMC while the *Monarch* was laid-up pending trooping requisition two months later. A Furness subsidiary also operated a modest two-ship service between Liverpool and Boston but neither was of the 'WS type'.

The design of liners that traded through the tropics to the Far East, Southern Africa and the Antipodes was quite different to those employed on the North Atlantic. With a passage time of three, four or even six weeks and mostly warm weather throughout, passengers required long open promenades and extensive sports decks. On the Australian and Far East routes especially, frequent port calls helped promote holidays along the route and also allowed passengers short breaks ashore to relieve the monotony. P & O with their associated Orient Line were the principal players on the Australian route with as many as eighteen liners available, many of the newest were frequently cruising. The UK terminal for both companies was Tilbury, the P & O service being fortnightly throughout the year but Orient only during the busy season from September to January and otherwise monthly. The P & O route was via Marseilles, where European mails and passengers who wished to avoid the rigours of Biscay could embark; this service alternated with their China mail service with similar calls and frequency as far as Bombay and Colombo, thus allowing a weekly service to those destinations. From August 1939 the P & O frequency became irregular when *Maloja*, *Mooltan*, *Cathay*, and *Comorin* became AMCs, and *Narkunda* transferred to the China route in November. *Strathaird* went off trooping in September and continued on this service for the next seven years, leaving the remaining four *Straths*, with occasional interruptions, to maintain the service until they too were requisitioned in October 1940, *Strathallan* and *Strathnaver* in Liverpool while *Strathmore* and *Stratheden* were taken up in Australia.

The complementary Orient Line service was conveniently sandwiched in between the P & O sailings and so allowed travellers for Australia a weekly service. The Orient ships called at Toulon, Naples and Colombo, but otherwise the same Australian ports as far as the terminal at Brisbane. During the slack season the surplus Orient ships went cruising as in 1939 when *Orford*, *Orion* and *Orcades* were in the UK and sent off on a trooping voyage to Alexandria. The last two returned to trade for a time but *Orford* remained on requisition until bombed and sunk at Marseilles in June 1940. *Orama* was taken up to assist in the evacuation from Norway at the end of May 1940 and sunk when returning home. Meanwhile the Australian service continued almost monthly until February 1940 when it became irregular due to trooping requisitions from Australia, Canada, Madagascar and evacuations from western Europe. *Orion* was trooping continuously from January 1940 while the remainder was similarly taken up from April onwards; *Oronsay*, *Ormonde*, *Otranto*, *Orcades* and finally *Orontes* in September 1940.

The green hulled Bay class liners of the Aberdeen and Commonwealth Line, part owned by P & O and Shaw Savill, provided roughly monthly sailings from London via Suez to the five main Australian ports with accommodation for over 500 Tourist Class passengers. *Jervis Bay*, *Moreton* and *Esperance Bay* were each taken up as AMCs, while *Largs Bay* continued the service alone until she too was requisitioned for trooping but not until August 1941. There was a further service to Australia jointly operated by six elderly steamers of Blue Funnel and Shaw Savill, which used the former White-

Star route via the Cape. These were all coal burners of modest speed and unsuitable for the WS route.

A completely new service began in February with the maiden voyage of the Shaw Savill liner *Dominion Monarch*, going out from London via Madeira and Tenerife to Capetown and Durban, thence to Fremantle, Melbourne and Sydney, before reaching the terminal ports of Wellington and Auckland in New Zealand. Offering luxurious accommodation for 517 First Class passengers only, the *Dominion Monarch* was then the most powerful motorship in the world with enormous refrigerated capacity and the largest liner on the trade routes to South Africa, Australia and New Zealand. Although considered and rejected for trooping in December 1939, she continued on service and was able to complete four round voyages when finally requisitioned in August 1940. Shaw Savill also operated a monthly service for passengers between London and New Zealand via Panama, using four liners with accommodation varying from 130 to 300 passengers. From this route *Arawa* immediately became an AMC, *Akaroa* was never requisitioned while *Mataroa* and *Tamaroa* remained on service until taken up for trooping in November 1940.

The main passenger service to New Zealand was appropriately given by the P & O controlled New Zealand Shipping Company, on a monthly frequency from London and Plymouth to reach Wellington or Auckland five weeks later. Four elderly modest speed steamers and three relatively modern motorships were employed; only the latter were suitable for WS service but *Rangitane* fell victim to German raiders in November 1940, while *Rangitata* and *Rangitiki* were then about to begin conversion for trooping.

As many as nine different passenger services were available to the Near and Far East, in addition to those liners on the Australian trade which called en route at ports on the Indian coast. The main service was the 'China Mail' of P & O, which started out from London and proceeded onwards from Colombo via Penang, Singapore, Hong Kong and Shanghai before reaching Kobe and Yokohama in Japan. Eight liners were fully engaged on this service with accommodation for 300 to 500 passengers, and having the ideal Admiralty specification for conversion to AMCs were promptly requisitioned accordingly. *Rawalpindi* and *Rajputana* were lost when so employed; *Ranpura* was permanently retained by the Admiralty, while *Canton*, *Carthage*, *Corfu*, *Chitral* and *Ranchi* were not released for trooping until 1943/44. The service was only kept in being by *Narkunda* (*qv*) and *Viceroy of India*, a one-off dual purpose liner designed for cruising and providing extra Bombay sailings during the spring and autumn when the demand for passages was at its height. The calls in Japan were suspended as early as September 1939 and the service terminated when the *Viceroy* and *Narkunda* were taken up for trooping in November 1940 and April 1941 respectively.

The Blue Funnel Line also had a Far Eastern Service, offering a monthly frequency from Liverpool to ports in Malaya, Manila, Hong Kong, Shanghai and five ports in Japan. These liners carried 140-180 passengers; *Aeneas* was sunk in July 1940, *Sarpedon* was never requisitioned but *Antenor*, *Hector* and *Patroclus* all became AMCs of which only the former survived to convert for trooping at a later date.

The Burmese capital of Rangoon was particularly well served by the fortnightly schedules of both the Bibby and Henderson Lines, which alternated and thus combined to provide a weekly service from Liverpool. The Henderson ships were of modest speed and capacities unsuitable for WS service, while those of Bibby were each of 15 knots and accommodation for 200 - 200 passengers. *Shropshire*, *Cheshire*, *Derbyshire* and *Worcestershire* immediately became AMCs, *Yorkshire* was lost in October 1939,

Oxfordshire converted to a Hospital Ship and *Staffordshire* alone continued the service until taken up for trooping in December 1941.

In addition to their New York service, the Anchor Line also provided a rather irregular passenger service from Liverpool to Bombay and Karachi. Three of the ships were of 12 knots or less but the modern motorships *Cilicia* and *Circassia* had accommodation for 400 passengers and with a speed of 16 knots were immediately requisitioned as AMCs. Additionally, both Ellermans and the British India Company (B.I.) provided cargo-passenger line services to India; the latter serving Colombo, Madras and Calcutta while Ellermans had separate services to Bombay and Calcutta. Only *City of Benares* from all three routes would have been suitable for WS service but was lost carrying refugees and children to Canada in September 1940.

Almost all the passenger services to South Africa in 1939 were in the hands of the Union-Castle Line, whose distinctive red funnelled and lavender hulled liners offered splendid facilities in up to four classes over four separate routes. The principal Cape Mail service departed Southampton every Thursday afternoon and required eight liners of up to 27,000 tons with a minimum speed of 19 knots to maintain the schedule, which included arriving at Capetown within thirteen days, and thereafter coastal calls to Durban which was reached exactly three weeks after leaving Southampton. The elderly reserve ship, *Edinburgh Castle*, was saved from the breakers to languish at Freetown as a Naval Base Accommodation Ship for the duration of hostilities. *Carnarvon Castle* was taken up as an AMC and replaced by the intermediate *Durban Castle* and so allowed the mail service to continue with very little disturbance until the summer of 1940, when Southampton was abandoned in favour of Liverpool or Glasgow. Requisitions for trooping began in July 1940 when *Athlone Castle* was taken up, *Durban Castle* followed in August, *Stirling*, *Windsor* and *Warwick Castles* in October, *Capetown* and *Winchester Castles* in November and finally *Arundel Castle* on 23rd December.

Union-Castle also provided three separate intermediate services from London; one calling at nine coast ports from Lobito as far as Beira in Mozambique, whence the return voyage was made in the reverse direction. Three modern liners were on this route, of which *Durban* and *Pretoria Castles* had sufficient speed to relieve on the mail service as indeed the first named immediately transferred while *Pretoria* and *Dunnottar Castles* became AMCs. The other services operated entirely around Africa, one going clockwise outward through the Mediterranean and returning by the west coast while the other went anti-clockwise. Both the ships and services were well patronized by passengers who could enjoy a cruise round Africa visiting 21 ports in 14 countries within the space of 12 weeks. The clockwise trio were the elderly steamers *Llandovery*, *Llandaff* and *Llanstephan Castles*; the former became a Hospital Ship in September 1940, *Llandaff* a troopship for Indian Ocean service in January 1941 and *Llanstephan* concurrently requisitioned for similar service although used on a variety of other routes. The anticlockwise ships were all motorships: *Dunvegan Castle* became an AMC, *Dunbar Castle* struck a mine and sank in the Thames Estuary in January 1940, while *Llangibby Castle* remained on service, apart from three short trooping trips from Durban to Mombasa, until fully requisitioned for trooping in November 1940.

Two other companies, Ellerman and Bullard King's Natal Line provided frequent cargo-passenger services to South Africa, but only two ships of the former company, *City of Paris* and *City of London* were taken up for Indian Ocean trooping and none of the latter. To East Africa the B.I. company offered a regular service from London via the Mediterranean and going as far south as Beira, using five of their 'M' class vessels but not deemed suitable for trooping.

Elder Dempster Lines, the only British company providing passenger services to West Africa, operated a fortnightly schedule from Liverpool to Freetown, Takoradi and either Accra or Lagos. Four ships carrying up to 530 passengers were employed on the route while the reserve ship *Aba*, was taken up as a Hospital Ship. *Accra* was sunk by torpedo in July 1940, *Apapa* by bombing attack four months later and *Adda*, after short trooping trips in the autumn of 1940, was torpedoed and sunk in June 1941. The most recent and highest capacity ship, *Abosso*, continued on service until requisitioned for trooping in November 1941. Three small steamers of the Yeoward Line operated a weekly cargo and passenger service between Liverpool and the Canary Islands, none were suitable for trooping and two were lost in 1941.

Although first discovered and settled by Spain and Portugal, the importance of British investment in developing mining, the haciendas and railways, together with the necessary shipping services to the vast continent of South America is now difficult to contemplate. By the 1930s eight British companies employed nearly 40 passenger liners of various types on South American services, although by 1939 four had converted to cruising. The principal player was Royal Mail Lines whose prestigious mail service from Southampton operated roughly every three weeks, with calls at Lisbon, Pernambuco, Bahia, Rio, Santos, Montevideo and thence to the Argentine capital of Buenos Aires. Only three liners were required on the route of which *Asturias* and *Alcantara* became AMCs while *Almanzora*, almost due for replacement, was taken up for trooping in December 1939. Her sister ship *Atlantis* and by then a cruise liner, was bought by the government and converted to a Hospital Ship. Meanwhile Royal Mail, who were about to celebrate their centenary by sailing the splendid new *Andes* on her maiden voyage that September, suspended the mail ship sailings and laid up the *Andes* until she was taken up for trooping two months later.

From London's Royal Victoria Dock, the fortnightly service by Royal Mail's five *Highland* class motorships continued without disruption despite the war, except that Boulogne was omitted from the outward schedule which otherwise duplicated the mail ship ports of call. These were very popular passenger ships each accommodating 700 and had vast refrigerated capacity in 43 compartments, exceeding even that of the *Dominion Monarch* of twice their tonnage. From the beginning of 1940 the service became increasingly disrupted and by July the last two departures from London proceeded northabout via the east coast; various west coast ports were then used including Cardiff and Swansea. *Highland Patriot* fell victim to a U-Boat when approaching the Irish coast on 1st October 1940, *Highland Brigade* and *Highland Monarch* were requisitioned that same month for trooping while *Highland Chieftain* and *Highland Princess* followed on 4th November.

In competition with the Highland ships, three Blue Star Liners provided a rather irregular service from London to Rio, Santos and Buenos Aires, each carrying 150 First Class passengers. None were requisitioned and all became war loses by 1942. Another of that same class but converted for cruising in 1929, *Arandora Star* was briefly engaged in trooping from May 1940 until her tragic loss carrying German and Italian internees to Canada in July of that year. From Liverpool the Booth Line provided a limited passenger service to north Brazil, going 1,000 miles up the Amazon to Manaus on the Rio Negro. Only two ships were so employed, *Hilary* carrying 330 passengers and *Anselm* 146; both were coal-burners of modest speed and dimensions yet both were requisitioned, the former to serve as an Ocean Boarding Vessel, while *Anselm* continued to serve her owners until taken up for trooping in November 1940.

For almost two decades prior to 1930, the Liverpool company of Lamport & Holt operated a luxury passenger service between New York and the River Plate, until financial difficulties forced their withdrawal and thereafter their two largest liners *Voltaire* and *Vandyck* were converted for cruising. The former first became a Naval Accommodation Ship and later converted to AMC, *Vandyck* was assigned as Armed Boarding Vessel and both became war losses by April 1941. Possibly foreseeing the closure of the Lamport service, the Prince Line built four new motorship liners in 1929 each to carry 100 passengers on exactly the old L&H route. These ships had refrigerated spaces and in carrying mainly American passengers remained profitable until the Neutrality Laws forced their diversion elsewhere. By December 1940 *Southern Prince* became a Minelayer and by that time the others were employed on the North Atlantic, where *Western Prince* became a war loss in December 1941. *Northern Prince* was lost in the approaches to Piraeus in April 1941, *Eastern Prince* alone became a troopship in November 1940 but for service on the Indian Ocean. Two passenger-cargo services linked the U.K. with the West Indies: that of Elders & Fyffes using five ships and Harrison Line two, and while three of the former became Armed Boarding Vessels, none from either company were used for trooping.

In contrast to the many British companies serving the east coast of South America, only the Pacific Steam Navigation Company (PSNC) provided passenger and cargo services to the west coast, which stretched 4,000 miles from Panama to Cape Horn. By 1938 this Company was a subsidiary of Royal Mail and provided a rather irregular passenger service from Liverpool, with calls at La Pallice, Bermuda, Nassau, Havana and Kingston, before transiting Panama to reach Callao and Iquique in Peru and finally the Chilean capital of Valparaiso five weeks after leaving the Mersey. Four ships were on this service of which *Oropesa*, *Orbita* and *Orduna* were somewhat ageing steamers each of 14 knots and capacities of 600-900 passengers; all remained on the route until taken up for trooping between September 1940 and March 1941. The luxury class company flagship *Reina del Pacifico* of 18 knots and accommodation for 900 passengers was requisitioned for trooping as early as August 1939.

Of the many cross-trades operated by British and Dominion passenger ships in 1939, those of Canadian-Pacific linking western Canada with China, Japan and the Phillipines were easily the best known and most acclaimed. Four white-painted, three funnelled Empress liners made fortnightly crossings of the North Pacific from Vancouver via Honolulu to Yokohama, Shanghai, Hong Kong and occasionally Manila. These were fast ships of 19-20 knots each carrying 1100-1200 passengers, but the 1930s brought a gradual decline of both passengers and valuable cargoes such as tea and silk, to the extent that war only served to bring about the demise of the whole service. The largest and newest ship, *Empress of Japan*, was requisitioned for trooping at Vancouver in November 1939 and never subsequently released until November 1948. Similarly, *Empress of Canada* was taken up concurrently in Hong Kong, while the two older sisters, by then 27 years old and still burning coal, continued the service until they too were taken up for trooping: the *Empress of Russia* in November 1940 and *Empress of Asia* two months later. Fifty years of Empress liners on the Pacific came to an end.

On the Indian Ocean the British India (B.I.) Company was the prime mover on the many cross-routes linking the major ports of India to those of South and East Africa, the Seychelles, Persian Gulf, Burma, Malaya, China and Japan. At least 23 of those small to medium sized ships each carrying up to 250 passengers were requisitioned to serve as troopships or Hospital Ships on the Indian Ocean or Mediterranean. Only *Karanja* and *Kenya* were suited for WS service and requisitioned for such on reaching the U.K. in July 1940. There were also three small vessels of Blue Funnel trading between Malaya and Australia and others of Scindia and the Mogul Line with Passenger Certificates but none of these were suitable for the WS route.

Finally, there were those liners owned and crewed from Australia, New Zealand and Canada. The former had four taken up as AMCs: *Bulolo, Kanimbla, Manoora* and *Westralia* which all later served as Commissioned Assault Ships; two others became Hospital Ships to serve their own forces stationed overseas. The Union Steamship Company of New Zealand operated four notably fast liners each carrying 500-900 passengers, of which *Aorangi* and *Niagara* provided a service linking Vancouver with Honolulu, Fiji, Auckland and Sydney. The first named was taken up for trooping and sent to the U.K. in September 1941, *Niagara* was mined and sunk off New Zealand in June 1940. The other two ships were *Awatea* and *Monowai*, the former built expressly for the Trans-Tasman route between Sydney, Auckland and Wellington but from July 1940 making occasional trips to Vancouver or single trooping voyages until fully taken up and sent to the U.K. in September 1941. *Monowai* became an AMC while the smaller *Maunganui* served as the NZ Forces Hospital Ship from January 1941. Canada also had a number of both short-sea and ocean-going passenger ships, of which *Prince David, Prince Robert* and *North Star* became AMCs, *Princess Kathleen* and *Princess Marguerite* short-sea troopers, *New Northland* a coastal trooper, *Lady Rodney* for North Atlantic trooping and *Lady Nelson* a Hospital Ship for the same route.

From these worldwide trade routes came the passenger ships that now formed the bulk of the British trooping fleet. Augmented by others chartered or requisitioned from the conquered nations of Europe, these great liners, together with their officers and crews, and given safe escort by the Royal Navy, represented the means by which Britain was able to implement a successful maritime strategy by carrying her military might around the Cape of Good Hope to face her enemies afresh in the Middle and Far East, a feat scarcely comprehensible even to those who actually accomplished it.

Chapter 2

Early Troop Moves
from the UK and Dominions

Apart from the mass of over 400,000 B.E.F. personnel who crossed to France from September 1939 onwards, the early months of war saw few overseas troop movements other than reinforcement details to bring garrison units up to war establishment strength. The first group of Dominion troops from Australia, New Zealand and Canada began to cross the oceans in December 1939, but these were preceded by formations from India some weeks before war broke out.

Plans had been made as early as 1937 for sending Indian troops to Egypt, Aden, Singapore, Burma and Iran. Those for Egypt comprised 11 Indian Infantry Brigade from Ahmednagar, and 4 Field Regiment, Royal Artillery from Hyderabad, which embarked at Bombay and Karachi respectively as Heron Force on five B.I. ships and a Mogul liner on 3rd August 1939: the whole force totalling 5,275 officers and men.[1]

As was the custom then, each Indian Brigade contained one British and two Indian battalions and in this instance the British component was 2nd Queens Own Cameron Highlanders, who had been eight months in India.[2] Both groups of ships formed up as the 'Heron Convoy' on 6th August and made slow and uncomfortable progress across the Indian Ocean in the SW monsoon; the ships rolling and pitching and the troops crowded in the blacked out 'tween decks, which had been hastily adapted with inadequate ventilation provided; a vexing problem to be endured by many troops in the years ahead. On reaching the comparative shelter of the Gulf of Aden, the convoy was met and escorted halfway up the Red Sea by the cruisers *Manchester* and *Gloucester* and two sloops.[3] The troops disembarked by lighters at Suez on 17th August when the ships returned to India and reverted to trade. In a similar manner six other B.I. ships were concurrently taken up in Madras and Calcutta to carry 12th Indian Brigade (including 2nd Argylls) in three unescorted groups to land in Singapore by 11th August: the start of a prolonged though piecemeal build-up of military forces in Malaya and Singapore. Another force entitled K4, comprising 5th Indian Brigade and lst Field Regiment R.A., embarked at Bombay and Karachi on 23rd September aboard six B.I. ships (one being *Karanja* which had been in the 'Heron' convoy) and sailed across the Indian Ocean in pleasant though now wartime conditions escorted by the cruiser *Manchester* and a sloop, to disembark at Suez on 3rd October, whereupon the ships again returned to their normal trade. The requisition of B.I ships for trooping and Hospital Ship service on the Indian Ocean routes went hand in hand with the large liners taken up in the U.K., to the extent that by autumn 1940 few there remained on commercial service. Their conversion was a much more simple matter as the 'tween-deck spaces normally used for unberthed Indian deck passengers, were easily adapted for troops by fitting hooks for hammocks on the deckheads. It was then a matter of supplying tables, hammocks and blankets to accommodate the number required.[4]

On 25th August, ten passenger liners then in UK ports or due there shortly were requisitioned for despatching overseas a force of 13,000 naval and military personnel. The naval component comprised specialist crews for AMCs fitting out abroad, reservists to increase H.M. ship complements to war establishment, and both naval and military personnel to strengthen shore stations and provide reservists for garrisons serving abroad in the Mediterranean and Indian Ocean areas. Forward planning began six months earlier when arrangements were made to berth and embark half the ships in Glasgow and the remainder at the Tail of the Bank anchorage. In the event *Montcalm, Reina del Pacifico* and *Duchess of Bedford* embarked in Glasgow on 3rd September, while *Scythia, Orford* and *Durban Castle* followed next day. The remaining liners *Britannic, Orcades, Orion* and *Strathaird* embarked from Clyde steamers at the Tail of the Bank. The whole procedure of berthing, storing and embarking the ships was carried through like a military operation. Valuable experience was gained and this first wartime troop convoy, codenamed the 'Glasgow Convoy' or 'GC One', provided the basis of future planning for the main troopship movements in and out of the Clyde in the years ahead.

No time was allowed to make internal changes to the liners and few were able to disguise their peacetime colours and so the convoy made a fine sight as it sailed out of the Clyde line ahead during the evening of 5th September,[5] escorted by eight 'V' and 'W' class destroyers. As the convoy passed down the Irish Sea a broad front of five columns was formed and when northwest of the Scillies, the battleship *Ramillies* and four 'E' class destroyers joined as ocean escort. Admiralty instructions issued on 29th August had planned the convoy route around the Cape, due to the deteriorating international situation, but in the event the convoy was directed to use the Mediterranean. When passing through the Straits of Gibraltar on the 14th, *Ramillies* and her destroyers were relieved by the cruiser *Galatea* and ten other destroyers: six being French. *Scythia* also left the convoy here to disembark in Gibraltar and return home. When passing Malta on the 14th, *Durban Castle* detached to disembark at Valetta and thereafter returned home to resume sailings to the Cape. On approaching the eastern end of the Mediterranean on the 16th, the Orient liners *Orion*, *Orcades* and *Orford* detached to disembark in Alexandria and thereafter return home independently, and here also the Commodore aboard *Orion*, Rear Admiral C. A. M. Sarel (Rtd) ceased his duties. His report drew attention to some of the difficulties which had beset and plagued him and indeed many other convoy commodores in the early months of the war: much due to inexperience or misunderstanding of convoy procedures but also due to lack of equipment such as proper fog buoys.

On arrival at Port Said, *Montcalm* disembarked there and returned home to begin conversion as an AMC; the remaining four liners transited the Suez Canal and continued down the Red Sea escorted first by the sloop *Egret* and later by the cruiser *Liverpool*: all berthing at Aden on the 22nd to refuel. Later that day *Britannic*, *Duchess of Bedford* and *Reina del Pacifico*, with *Liverpool* continuing as escort, sailed onwards to cross the Indian Ocean and three days later the convoy split after being met by the aircraft-carrier *Eagle*, which thereafter detached with *Reina del Pacifico* towards the Nine Degree Channel and Colombo. A small contingent was landed at that port and *Reina del Pacifico* then continued up the Bay of Bengal, escorted now by the cruiser *Cornwall*, with personnel for the AMCs fitting out in Calcutta. The *Reina del Pacifico* anchored in Saugur Roads at the mouth of the Hooghly on 1st October, where the naval personnel were transferred to smaller ships for the remaining 80 mile passage to Calcutta. The *Reina del Pacifico* then sailed onwards to Singapore, still escorted by *Cornwall*, to land her remaining personnel and thereafter proceeded homewards via Rangoon and Colombo to reach Liverpool on 28th November. Meanwhile the two Bombay ships reached that port on 27th September and disembarked 3,000 personnel including the naval specialist crews for the four AMCs fitting out there. Both ships remained at Bombay for nearly two weeks before returning home independently to resume their respective trades on the North Atlantic. *Strathaird* had detached from the main convoy at Aden, and left there on 23rd September escorted by the sloop *Auckland*, carrying naval shore staff for Capetown and crews for the AMCs fitting out in Simonstown. She then returned home via Lagos, Takoradi, Freetown and Gibraltar, landing small naval detachments at each of these ports before arriving in Tilbury on 11th November. Naval Control staffs were now in place around the Cape route and as far east as Singapore.

A further reinforcement convoy was prepared before GC 1 had reached India, to carry the balance of reservists who had been unable to join that first convoy. These personnel were embarked on four liners at Southampton: 1300 each on *Franconia* and *Empress of Australia*, 700 on *Alcantara* about to begin conversion to AMC and some on *Athlone Castle* actually on her scheduled mail voyage to the Cape. The first two named liners were fully requisitioned for trooping; fitted with hammocks, painted grey overall and armed with single 4-inch guns. All four ships sailed from Southampton during the late evening of 28th September as convoy SO 10 (presumably as Southampton 10) escorted by two 'I' class destroyers.[6] Heavy weather was encountered on the passage to Gibraltar when both destroyers lost touch with their charges for half a day but all reached that port safely on 3rd October and where *Athlone Castle* thereafter proceeded independently for the Cape. The SOE later reported that "destroyers are not at all suitable...for fast convoys in the Atlantic during the winter months"[7] and that the "station-keeping of *Athlone Castle* was consistently bad",[7] although no particular reason was given. From Gibraltar the other liners continued into the Mediterranean and where at dusk on 5th October a serious collision occurred when *Franconia* ran into the port side of *Alcantara*. Considerable damage resulted to both vessels although the only injury was a fractured shoulder bone suffered by Captain Bissett of Franconia,[8] when thrown to the deck by the impact. The convoy reached Malta next day where both ships disembarked and *Alcantara* sailed for Alexandria to undergo hull repairs and subsequently fitted as an AMC in Malta. Repairs to *Franconia* were carried out in Malta. She then embarked 700 Polish airmen and landed them at Marseilles before returning home for major drydocking and repairs at Birkenhead.[8] *Empress of Australia* proceeded onwards to disembark her reinforcements at Bombay and Colombo before returning home via Port Sudan, Malta and Gibraltar. These two convoys completed the preliminary overseas troop movements from the UK, adequately met from the liner companies at very short notice although using ship capacities little above pre-war passenger levels. Embarkations had been smoothly effected and no enemy interference occurred throughout the passages. Meanwhile the main body of the British Army was moving across the English Channel to establish itself as the BEF in France.

There is little record of the Indian Expeditionary Force that moved to France in December 1939, other than being of brigade strength and partly equipped with mules. Embarkation was completed at Bombay on 10th December aboard *Lancashire* and four B.I. ships, of which two were fitted with 'tweendeck stalls for the mules. Some British officers and NCOs en route to the UK were also embarked: the total numbering about 4,000. These five ships sailed from Bombay as convoy K 6 with two French liners attached and escorted by the Australian cruiser *Hobart*, together with AMCs *Ranchi* and *Maloja*: the latter being on passage to the UK.[9] On reaching the Gulf of Aden, the escorts and French ships detached and allowed the five unescorted British ships to increase speed to 14 knots. Suez was reached on the 20th and Marseilles six days later where the force was soon disembarking in very cold, wintry weather, to entrain for destinations in Northern France. The four B.I. ships, supplemented by *Dilwara* and *Devonshire*, were now made ready to embark the leading (6th) Brigade of 1st British Cavalry Division, the last in a long line of horsed formations to serve with the British Army. The total strength was 9,000 men and 4,000 horses and having crossed the channel from Southampton were thereafter entrained to Marseilles for final shipment to Haifa in Palestine. The Division was a recently formed Territorial force composed mainly of Yeomanry regiments from eight English counties, whose 6th Brigade had left home on 18th December. Their six transports (*Rajula*, *Rohna*, *Talamba*, *Tairea* and two above named) sailed from Marseilles as the First Cavalry Convoy on 3rd January 1940 and reached Haifa six days later, with Captain C.A. Harris, the Master of *Devonshire* acting as Commodore; escort was provided to the west of Malta by two destroyers. On the return voyage the depot ship *Resource* accompanied the convoy for the first two days towards Malta, and when passing through the Sicilian narrows in the early morning of 16th January, the relief escort challenged from directly ahead of the convoy and caused an emergency turn to port from which *Rajula* failed to comply and was for a time left far astern, but was the only incident worthy of note.[10]

The Second Cavalry Convoy left Marseilles on 23 January carrying the 5th Brigade composed of the Yorkshire Dragoons, Yorkshire Hussars and Notts Yeomanry, all aboard the same ships except *Tairea* which was replaced by *Lancashire*. The Third Convoy left in two parts on 14th and 16th February; the first being *Dilwara* and *Devonshire*, and last of *Rajula* and *Rohna*: which latter pair left Marseilles again on 4th March with the balance of the horses. The Divisional rear elements were embarked on two later independent sailings of *Talamba*. Unfortunately, and despite the logistical effort involved of moving the Division to the Middle East, their service there was short lived. As early as September 1940, Churchill was urging their conversion to armour rather than be tethered to horses for a security role in Palestine. Four months later he was incensed to discover that nothing of the kind had happened, and heard to his horror "that the whole Division was to be carted back home, and that this was not to begin until 1st June 1941."[11] He then asked for the cost of moving the Division to and from the Middle East and of maintaining it there and "kept out of action".[11] These pressures had the desired effect: 5th Brigade was fully motorized by early May 1941 and fought with distinction in the Syrian Campaign while the other two Cavalry Brigades similarly converted to join 10th Armoured Division in the desert.

During the six months prior to the German invasion of the Low Countries in May 1940, Marseilles became the focal point for British troop moves between the UK, India, the Far East and all the numerous garrisons scattered around the Mediterranean, saving as it did the most hazardous section of the voyage between Gibraltar and the UK where U-Boats were then active. Most of these movements were made by ships of the pre-war trooping fleet, bringing from India a considerable flow of Officers, NCOs and experienced Other Ranks being combed out of overseas garrisons, to provide the nucleus of new units forming at home, while Drafts of relatively inexperienced replacements were sent by return. Five other trooping liners visited Marseilles during this period to assist these movements: *Duchess of Atholl* on 11th January to make two trooping runs to and from Alexandria, the Polish *Batory* and *Sobieski* in February and the Orient sisters *Orford* and *Otranto* late in February having previously landed Australian troops at Kantara. On 4th March the Orient ships moved to the nearby naval base at Toulon, left there on the 13th for Glasgow but were ordered back and finally left again on 9th April carrying French personnel to Madagascar and returned with French Colonial troops on 23rd May: the last British troopships to reach the port before the collapse of France. After disembarkation they were sent to an anchorage to await arrangements for an evacuation, where on 1st June, *Orford* was bombed and set on fire during a German air attack: she was beached and later completely burnt out and abandoned as a total loss. *Otranto* left next day unscathed for Gibraltar and Liverpool, the last British liner to clear the Mediterranean before its closure to through traffic. This also had the effect of dispersing the pre-war troopships to other routes and principally those of the Indian Ocean. Voyages between the UK and that area now had to take the much longer route around the Cape and ideally required much larger and faster ships, as did the North Atlantic movements from Canada or those from the far distant Antipodes.

Prior to the outbreak of war the Canadian Government authorized the organization of two Infantry Divisions and soon afterwards discussed with the War Office their deployment overseas and in particular of sending 1st Canadian Division to the UK. By late October 1939 it was agreed to send the first contingent of 7,400 troops in convoy from Halifax (NS) early in December. Three laid-up liners were earmarked accordingly: *Empress of Britain* in Quebec, *Monarch of Bermuda* in New York, and *Aquitania* in Southampton. Together with *Duchess of Bedford* and *Empress of Australia* recently returned from India, all were requisitioned during November and sent independently to Halifax where they were assembled by the first week of December. Embarkation of the Canadian troops took place on the morning of 10th December aboard all five ships conveniently berthed alongside. Major-General McNaughton and his Headquarters Staff were embarked on *Aquitania*. A large naval covering force was to accompany this first Canadian convoy, numbered TC 1 (assumed to be Troops Canadian 1), comprising the aircraft carrier *Furious*, battle-cruiser *Repulse*, cruiser *Emerald* and two H class destroyers which left the harbour early on the 10th to sweep ahead and join the convoy at a rendezvous on the eastern extremity of the Great Newfoundland Bank. The five liners were to be accompanied throughout by the battleship *Resolution*, whose Commanding Officer acted in the combined role of Convoy Commodore and Senior Officer of the Escort. The Vice Commodore was Captain G. Gibbons, RD RNR, the Master of *Aquitania*.[12]

Resolution left her anchorage at 1140 on the 10th and was followed out of the harbour with almost clockwork precision at 25 minute intervals by the liners led by *Duchess of Bedford*. Pilots were landed off Chebucto Head where four Canadian destroyers formed the head of the column, until reaching the end of the swept channel when convoy T C One formed into three columns and a zigzag pattern commenced. Next evening the convoy ran into fog when to the south of Cape Race and *Empress of Australia* lost touch. The fog continued overnight, at times very thick, and next morning (12th) the covering force failed to make contact as planned although *Emerald* successfully joined that evening. The fog persisted for 33 hours over a distance of 600 miles until 0430 on the 13th when it cleared and by daylight with no sign of *Empress of Australia*, *Emerald* was sent back to search and although this proved fruitless, some comfort was gained by making contact with an aircraft from *Furious* which confirmed the proximity of that ship.

Twelve Home Fleet destroyers sailed from the UK on the 12th to meet the convoy in longitude 25° West, but the Official History tells of another force sent to cover the convoy, "That same morning a Coastal Command aircraft sighted enemy surface forces in the central North Sea steering west...the sighting reports presented a possible threat to the approaching Canadian Troop Convoy since, if the enemy ships were trying to break out into the Atlantic"....[13] (Only three weeks had passed since the *Scharnhorst* and *Gneisenau* had been at large and sank the AMC *Rawalpindi*.) "Accordingly Admiral Forbes sailed from the Clyde with the *Warspite*, *Hood* and *Barham*"[13]. The Admiralty was taking no chances, although the enemy force turned out to be no more than a minelaying sortie.

Indifferent visibility continued to dog the passage of TC 1, and despite contact between *Emerald* and the aircraft from *Furious* on the 13th, the covering force failed to gain touch with the convoy, nor did the two flotillas of destroyers, until the morning of the 16th, when the convoy had reached a position 200 miles from the Irish Coast: *Empress of Australia* rejoined at noon that day having been out of touch for the previous five. That afternoon *Furious*, *Resolution* and *Repulse* each took station at the head of three columns of the convoy as it approached the North Channel, each one spaced five miles apart. At 0430 on the 17th when between Islay and Rathlin, disaster narrowly struck the leading group of *Furious* and *Aquitania* when the outbound Cunarder *Samaria* passed between them and was in collision with both these ships. The horizontal wireless masts on the starboard side of *Furious* were carried away, as were five outswung lifeboats on the port side of *Aquitania*, while the next two ships in line were very narrowly missed. The damage to *Samaria* was sufficient as to require her return to the Mersey where repairs lasted four weeks. "Enquiry revealed that the collision had been caused by the *Samaria* being given a route close to the inward bound convoy's track...because the routing authority in Liverpool had not been informed of the troop convoy's movements"[13] although this was known on the Clyde.

Furious led the three groups of TC 1 into the Clyde that morning where all except *Duchess of Bedford* (which proceeded to Glasgow) anchored at the Tail of the Bank.

The spectacle of four large transports, three battleships, two battlecruisers, an aircraft-carrier, three AMCs and several destroyers provided an impressive background for the Canadian troops who landed by tenders during the next two days to entrain for Aldershot and training grounds in the south of England. *Furious* later recommended that future covering forces should be sailed with North Atlantic convoys throughout, "in view of the low visibility so frequently experienced off the Newfoundland Banks".[14] Prior consultation with the Masters of the liners involved: three of whom were senior officers of the RNR, having between them 140 years of experience and knowledge of conditions on the North Atlantic, would surely have confirmed that view.

The second Canadian convoy (TC 2) carried some 8,500 men and was almost ready to leave Halifax before TC 1 dispersed from the Clyde. Seven liners were employed: *Andes* and *Orama* requisitioned from lay-up in the Clyde and Cowes Roads, *Reina del Pacifico* returned from Singapore, *Almanzora* from Buenos Aires, *Ormonde* in London and the now unemployed Polish liners *Batory* and *Chrobry* which had been made available on charter to the Ministry of Shipping. All were berthed in Halifax by 21 December where embarkation was completed next day; the convoy then left the harbour expeditiously to be escorted throughout by the battleship *Revenge* and French warships *Dunkerque* and *Gloire*. Snow squalls, sleet and low visibility were experienced during the first two days but Christmas morning brought a short respite of fine weather until a southerly wind freshened that afternoon to become a full gale overnight with gusts to Force 12. Speed had to be reduced to allow *Ormonde* "to haul out of line and refit three square ports which had been broken by the beam sea".[15] (A similar incident occurred to the P & O cruise ship *Oriana* in the same area, 60 years later.) On the morning of the 28th the convoy was met in the Western Approaches by twelve destroyers. Next morning the French warships were replaced by fleet minesweepers that continued with the convoy until arrival in the Clyde soon after daylight on the 30th; *Reina del Pacifico* and *Batory* went upriver to disembark in Glasgow while the others disembarked by tenders from the anchorage. On 31st December a luncheon was given aboard *Andes* "to celebrate the successful conclusion of her first voyage. Amongst the guests were the Secretary of State for the Dominions (Mr. Anthony Eden), the Minister of Shipping, the Canadian High Commissioner and the C-in-C Scottish Command."[16] None of the liners had further immediate employment, three lay idle in Liverpool and the Solent for almost three months, *Batory* went trooping in the Mediterranean and *Andes* sailed for the Far East: *Chrobry* alone was required for TC 3 and sailed for Halifax on the 15th January.

Convoy TC 3 from Halifax was made up of the same liners as TC 1, except that *Chrobry* was substituted for *Duchess of Bedford* that had resumed her owners' commercial service. A total of 7,400 were carried in this convoy comprising ancillary and technical troops for attachment to 1st Canadian Division, together with some units intended to serve with British formations; *Chrobry* being fully embarked with lumbermen. The convoy sailed on 30th January 1940 escorted by the battleships *Valiant* and *Malaya* and cruiser *Enterprise*, with combined post of Commodore and S.O.E. being held by Captain H.B. Rawlings on *Valiant*. Fine weather was encountered until the morning of 1st February when fog and mist set in with snowstorms and poor visibility later that day. No further incidents occurred until the afternoon of the 6th when two divisions were formed for the approach to the North Channel; here a SE'ly gale with driving rain was encountered between Inishtrahull and Rathlin Island but all ships arrived safely in the Clyde in the late afternoon of the 7th. *Chrobry* and *Empress of Australia* disembarked in Glasgow while *Aquitania*, *Empress of Britain* and *Monarch of Bermuda* remained at the anchorage. With all troops landed, a total of 23,300 Canadians were now in the UK and destined for France after initial winter training and equipping. Their 1st Brigade did in fact land at Brest on 14th June but was again almost immediately evacuated. The 2nd Brigade took part in the Spitzbergen raid in August 1941 but the Division was not otherwise engaged with the enemy until the Sicilian landings of 1943. *Aquitania* left the Clyde on 12th February, the same day as the minesweeper *Gleaner* sank *U.33* in the searched channel SE of Pladda; the Cunarder was overhauled in Southampton and thereafter sailed for Australia to take part in convoy US 3. *Empress of Britain* was moved to Southampton and also sailed for Australia and US 3. The other three liners remained idle in the Clyde until their involvement in the Norwegian campaign in April. The TC series of convoys continued with TC 4 in May and thereafter until the end of April 1941 when it was redesignated NA and finally became part of the AT series in August 1942. Two further Canadian infantry divisions and an armoured division crossed in the TC series aboard one hundred liners without loss.

The early decision of the Canadian Government in preparing forces for overseas deployment was matched by a similar resolve from that of the Australian and New Zealand Governments to raise their own Divisions. These units were in training camps by mid November 1939 and shortly after it was decided to send the Australian Division to Palestine and the NZ Division to Egypt, where each would complete their respective training and equipment. The Australian Division was numbered the 6th and a 7th was to be raised to allow an Australian Corps to be formed in the Middle East. The New Zealand Expeditionary Force was known as such until renamed 2nd NZ Division. Both countries' respective formations were to be split into smaller contingents suitable for convoying; each one containing a brigade and a proportion of base and divisional troops to be ready for embarkation at the beginning of January 1940. The requisition of liners for this movement required a positioning voyage of four or five weeks from the UK and was met in full by the due date despite coinciding with the first Canadian contingent. The slowest ship was *Dunera* which left Gibraltar for Fremantle on 16th November and was then directed to Wellington. Two Polish liners were chartered; *Pilsudski*, then fitting for trooping on the Tyne which sailed on 25th November but was mined and sunk off the Humber next morning, also *Chrobry* then in an unfinished state at Southampton and substituted by her sister-ship *Sobieski* then at Dakar, where she left on 28th November for Capetown, thence to Fremantle and finally to the New Zealand South Island port of Lyttelton. In the UK were *Orford*, *Otranto* and *Strathaird* that sailed for Sydney during the last week of November. *Orion* was taken up from trade at Sydney on the 29th of that month, *Orcades* at Gibraltar when outward bound to Brisbane and *Rangitata* of the NZS company when discharging in Auckland, although not being required for embarkation until early January was able to load a homeward cargo of refrigerated produce in the interval. From the cross-Pacific route the two largest *Empress* liners were requisitioned: *Empress of Japan* at Vancouver and *Empress of Canada* at Hong Kong. The last ship *Strathnaver* was taken up at Colombo on an outward mail voyage and sent direct to Sydney where she arrived on 4th January.

There was much excitement in Wellington when the battleship *Ramillies* arrived on 31st December, fresh from raider hunting in the Indian Ocean and now detailed as ocean escort for the Anzac convoy. Her bearded sailors lent colour to the city streets and were soon augmented by the khaki-clad New Zealand troops arriving for embarkation. On 4th January the New Zealand cruiser *Leander* left Wellington with *Dunera* for Lyttelton, where she joined *Sobieski* embarking the South Island troops of two battalions, a Field Ambulance and Field Hygiene Section plus 307 all ranks of Divisional Signals previously embarked at Wellington. These two liners were played out of the harbour by a local band on the afternoon of the 5th to join the other NZ ships in Cook Strait. In Wellington, Major-General Freyberg with his Headquarters staff and a Field Regiment were embarked on *Empress of Canada*, 19 Battalion from Wellington District on *Strathaird*, 4 Brigade HQ and 18 Auckland Battalion on *Orion*, and various base details and two squadrons of Divisional Cavalry on *Rangitata*. During the afternoon of the 5th, the liners moved away from their berths and anchored in the harbour, to sail next morning astern of the *Ramillies* and Australian cruiser *Canberra* and join with the two ships from Lyttelton. A total of 6,529 all ranks were embarked in this First Echelon which essentially comprised 4th NZ Brigade.[17]

The six New Zealand transports and escorting warships enjoyed a pleasant and uneventful passage across a relatively calm Tasman Sea. Few of the ships carried more than their peacetime passenger complements, most cabins were unchanged and dining saloons largely unaltered mainly because it was assumed the ships would be returned to trade on completion of the voyage. On the morning of 9th January, *Ramillies* and *Empress of Canada* left the convoy to proceed ahead to Sydney, where General Freyberg landed and travelled onwards by air to Egypt, while the *Empress* returned and rejoined the convoy next morning escorted by the cruiser *Australia*.

The leading formation of 6th Australian Division comprised four battalions raised and trained in New South Wales to become 16th Infantry Brigade, who embarked at Sydney on the 9th aboard *Orford*, *Otranto*, *Orcades*, and *Strathnaver*, while *Empress of Japan* had been sent ahead to Melbourne and there embarked the Divisional Headquarters and other base troops; the whole force totalling 6,571 all ranks. The *Ramillies* and liners from Sydney left that harbour in the afternoon of the 10th, "their rails and rigging crowded with troops, gazing with sentiment at the disappearing city".[18] Two hours later and out of sight of land they joined with the New Zealand section and formed three columns as Convoy US One, the first of a famous series to carry the Anzac formations to the Middle East during the next two years. The appointed Commodore, Captain M.R.B. Blackwood DSO RN had joined *Orion* at Sydney prior to her departure for Wellington and Captain F. Caffyn, the Master of *Dunera* was Vice Commodore. *Canberra* rejoined *Australia* and *Ramillies* as ocean escorts. After passing through the Bass Strait on the 12th, *Empress of Japan* joined late that evening from Melbourne. The convoy was now complete and proceeding towards Fremantle for replenishment.

Undoubtedly more was written and published on the passage of this first US convoy than any other personnel convoy at any time, much of it providing the enemy with valuable intelligence although not then able to intervene or prevent its safe arrival. Diverse newspaper reports in New Zealand, Australia, in Colombo and even Italy actually named the Divisions, some of the liners and even *Ramillies*. This incredible lapse of security was not to the advantage of the Admiralty, nor of the ships and troops under their charge or indeed the Governments of Australia and New Zealand. Escorts for the convoy had exercised the minds of the Admiralty from early in November when it became evident that one and possibly two German pocket-battleships were operating in the South Atlantic. The final arrangements were only agreed on 12th December, the eve of the Battle of the River Plate.

All the transports of the convoy were fuelled and watered in Fremantle within two days of arrival on the afternoon of the 18th, and during this time the troops enjoyed two last uproarious nights ashore, interspersed with route marches on the 19th. The warships meanwhile were either anchored in Gage Roads or patrolling to seaward. After leaving Fremantle the cruisers *Canberra* and *Australia* were relieved by the British *Kent* and French *Suffren*, and a fine ten day passage was made to the next call at Colombo, where similar arrangements were made and "caused some anxiety both to local authorities and their own officers, where Australians did not and had not seen or understood class distinctions between themselves and dark-skinned natives....many handed their haversack bundles to importunate native beggars...but otherwise evoked little criticism from local officials".[19]

The convoy left Colombo on 1st February with the two previous cruisers now relieved by *Sussex* and the carrier *Eagle*. Also attached was the French liner *Athos II* carrying French troops from Indo-China to Djibouti in French Somaliland. The escort was supplemented next day by the Australian cruiser *Hobart* which had come on from Colombo with *Otranto*, delayed there in fuelling. The convoy had a calm passage across the Indian Ocean enlivened only by aircraft carrying out patrols and flying exercises from *Eagle*. The destroyer *Westcott* joined to the NE of Socotra as anti-submarine escort, *Hobart* then detached ahead to fuel at Aden and rejoined on the 8th to go ahead with six of the transports while the remainder entered Aden for fuel and continued onwards on the 9th escorted by *Sussex* and *Westcott*. Both groups reached Suez on the 12th, the Australians then disembarked at Kantara and Port Said to move by train to Gaza in Palestine, while the New Zealanders landed by lighters at Suez and moved to Maadi Camp near Cairo. Both contingents were welcomed by Anthony Eden and General Wavell, C-in-C Middle East: both formations were to give distinguished service in the Desert Campaign from whence the New Zealand Division moved to Italy and remained for the whole of that campaign until the end of hostilities in May 1945.

As soon as the liners had disembarked, *Rangitata*, *Orion*, *Strathnaver* and *Orcades* were released from requisition and returned to the UK to resume trade voyages; *Sobieski*, *Orford* and *Otranto* went to Marseilles for further trooping. Both *Empress* liners were required for convoy US 3 from Australia and New Zealand while *Strathaird* and *Dunera* were allocated for US 2; all four were routed initially and independently to Fremantle.

The next convoy from the Antipodes had to be much larger in having to embark 14,000 Australians of their 17th and 18th Brigades, and 7,000 from 5th New Zealand Brigade; both groups being ready to leave in the first half of April, provided the necessary shipping could be found. Early in February 1940 discussions began between the Admiralty, the Australian Naval Board, the Director of Sea Transport and the Ministry of Shipping concerning the possibility of using either *Queen Mary* or *Mauretania* or both liners (then laid-up in New York), with some P&O/Orient/B.I. ships in further US convoys from Australia to the Middle East. An anchorage in Athol Bight in Sydney Harbour was deemed to be the best berth for *Queen Mary*: the D of ST said "it was desirable to use both *Queen Mary* and *Mauretania* to prevent deterioration during prolonged lay-up" but conversely felt "the loss of either would be equally great". He also pointed out that the "length, draft and bunkering arrangements for *Queen Mary* had been expressly designed for one particular trade, and would be a perpetual source of anxiety in others, quite apart from the war risk."[20] The D of ST was absolutely correct - yet the difficulties were surmounted. On 9th March 770 officers and crew left Liverpool in the *Antonia* to recommission the two 'Monsters' in New York. *Mauretania* put to sea on 20th March, transited Panama, bunkered in Honolulu and reached Sydney on 14th

April. *Queen Mary* left New York on 21st March under the command of Commodore R.B. Irving, and having refuelled at Trinidad, Table Bay outside Capetown and Gage Roads outside Fremantle, reached Sydney three days after her consort. Both ships then began to land their fine furniture and fittings, while extra bunks, hammocks and additional sanitary equipment were provided and stores loaded for 32 days. The *Queen Mary* was now able to accommodate over 4,000 troops and *Mauretania* 2,500. Meanwhile the other liners to complete the lifting had been arriving in Australia from 7th March onwards, *Strathaird, Dunera, Empress of Japan, Empress of Canada* from Suez, two other 'Monsters' *Empress of Britain* and *Aquitania* from Southampton (the former via Suez and latter via the Cape), *Andes* from Hong Kong, and B.I. troopers *Neuralia* from Bombay, *Nevasa* and P&O *Ettrick* from Marseilles. The total capacity of these twelve liners was over 23,000 but with a speed difference of 15 knots between the pre-war troopers and *Queen Mary* it was decided to split the convoy into two groups. By mid March the general plan was for US 2 to comprise *Strathaird* and the four slower ships: the remainder being US 3.

The second echelon of 6th Australian Division, comprising four battalions and Headquarters of their 17th Brigade, all raised in Victoria, embarked and sailed from Melbourne on 15th April aboard *Strathaird, Dunera, Ettrick* and *Neuralia*. Outside Port Phillip Heads *Ramillies* and *Adelaide* joined as ocean escort with the Commodore of US 2, Commander R.C. Garcia, RAN, aboard *Strathaird*. The passage to Fremantle was uneventful; the cruiser *Sydney* augmenting the escort on the latter section of the voyage which was completed at an average speed of 12.4 knots. The voyage was resumed from Fremantle on the 22nd where *Nevasa* joined carrying the West Australia battalion for 19th Brigade then forming in Palestine, and making a total 7,200 all ranks aboard the ships of US 2. *Ramillies* and *Sydney* continued as escorts towards Colombo, until the latter was relieved by the French *Suffren* well north of the equator. The possibility of encountering U-Boats in the Indian Ocean caused the convoy to make four long tacks of the route and so achieve a greater divergence from the normal. (U-Boats had not yet operated further than the English Channel).[21]

Increasing evidence of Italy entering the war caused the Admiralty to divert British ships from the Mediterranean to the Cape route from 27th April. They also believed it undesirable to pass convoys US 2 and 3 through the Red Sea, where Italian naval forces based at Massawa could threaten their safe passage, and suggested diversion to the UK. The Dominions office in London welcomed this possibility and advised the Commonwealth Governments accordingly. The situation was watched on a daily basis but in the event US 2 was allowed to continue through the Red Sea.

The ships of US 2 were berthed in Colombo for fuel and water for two nights and sailed again early on 5th May escorted by *Ramillies, Kent* and *Suffren*. The passage to Aden was made in fair weather before the onset of the SW monsoon at an average speed of 12.9 knots. Once in the Gulf of Aden two D class destroyers joined the escort and maintained an anti-submarine patrol while the convoy was berthed in Aden for six hours on the 12th. The impending threat of Italy entering the war caused the escort to be strengthened for passage through the southern half of the Red Sea, where air or submarine attack appeared most likely. Thus *Liverpool* and a sloop now joined to make a total of six warships. No Italian warships were seen, but when the convoy was near Masamirit Island on the 13th, an Italian Lloyd-Triestino liner was sighted on the port beam and caused the SOE to order a 90° starboard turn to avoid contact. When abreast of Port Sudan that night, the sloop and *Liverpool* parted company. The convoy entered the Gulf of Suez on the 16th and reached Suez next morning, where all ships including *Ramillies* and *Suffren* entered the canal; some to anchor at first in the Great Bitter Lake while others berthed and disembarked at Kantara and Port Said. The Australians entrained to Palestine and there completed the basic formation of 6th Australian Division of three complete brigades. Their first action was a successful attack on Bardia in January 1941; they later went to Greece and one brigade to Syria but were withdrawn from the Middle East for the defence of their homeland in March 1942. All five ships of US 2 were dispersed into the Mediterranean by 20th May: *Strathaird* going on to Liverpool, *Ettrick* was diverted into Bordeaux to assist the evacuation from that port, and thereafter to Glasgow, while the other three were sent to West Africa on French account for trips from Dakar to Casablanca, from where *Dunera* and *Neuralia* proceeded to Liverpool while *Nevasa* was retained at Freetown.

Chapter 3

Changes in Europe
and First Convoys Around the Cape

The short campaign in Norway that engaged 35,000 British and French troops in the spring of 1940 had its origins in the outbreak of the Russian-Finnish War in November 1939. By 19th December the Allies agreed to prepare a force of 100,000 British and 50,000 French to aid the Finns, which only began to materialize on 5th February when vague plans were made for landings at Narvik, Trondheim, Bergen and Stavanger, but using greatly reduced numbers. On 26th February the Ministry of Shipping were advised by the D of S T that thirteen transports were being used for this Special Service, (i.e. the planned expedition to Norway) of which *Aquitania*, *Empress of Britain*, *Empress of Australia*, *Reina del Pacifico*, *Franconia*, *Monarch of Bermuda*, *Orion*, *Chrobry* and *Batory* were all immediately available in UK ports, while *Orford*, *Otranto* and *Duchess of Atholl* then trooping in the Mediterranean were expected home in the next four weeks.[1] As it happened *Aquitania* and *Empress of Britain* were sent off to New Zealand for the US 2 movement while *Orford* and *Otranto* in the Mediterranean were sent to Madagascar on French account.

The entire Norwegian campaign was characterized by constantly changing plans much dictated by the enemy who held air superiority throughout which seriously endangered not only the transports but the warships involved and led to the early evacuation of the forces landed in central Norway and thereafter the entire expedition. The Allied landings were to take place about 20th March and by the 10th of that month arrangements were almost complete for the two brigades destined for Narvik to proceed to Glasgow and Gourock for embarkation on *Empress of Australia, Reina del Pacifico, Duchess of Atholl, Chrobry, Batory, Monarch of Bermuda* and *Franconia*, while a single battalion for Trondheim was to embark on *Orion* at Rosyth. Three days later the Finns agreed the terms of an Armistice with Russia and the War Office stood down the British forces being made ready and while *Duchess of Atholl* was released to trade, the other liners were kept in readiness awaiting further orders. Five liners had been held on the Clyde awaiting developments of the Norwegian position for nine weeks from early February, but these were very uncertain times and shipping had to be readily available if an expedition was to be mounted at short notice.

Less than two weeks later, the French government suddenly demanded action against the continuing flow of German iron ore traffic from Narvik and caused the Admiralty to review an earlier plan to mine the Norwegian Leads, with an associated military 'Plan R4' to take immediate advantage of the instant when German forces might react by setting foot on Norwegian soil, as they were expected to do. To this plan 24th (Guards) Brigade was assigned to Narvik, while five other battalions of 146 and 148 Brigades were to occupy Trondheim, Bergen and Stavanger. The plans were agreed on 28th March to become effective with the minelaying operations on 5th April but were later delayed to the 8th.[2] Embarkation began aboard *Batory* and *Chrobry* in Glasgow on the 3rd and on *Monarch of Bermuda, Empress of Australia* and *Reina del Pacifico* five days later but the central Norway plans were forestalled with news of the German landings in that area, and from this point onwards the plans had to be frequently amended and become increasingly complex to follow. In the event, *Batory* and *Chrobry* moved from the Clyde to Scapa Flow on the 9th, and made rendezvous with the other three liners on the 12th: the whole force proceeding as Convoy NP 1 escorted by the cruisers *Manchester* and *Birmingham* towards Narvik. Although equipped with Arctic clothing outbound for a destination as yet unknown, the troops viewed the expedition as a peacetime voyage, spreading "themselves around the decks, sunbathing, which gave the ships the appearance of being on a Mediterranean cruise".[3] The Irish Guards boarding *Monarch of Bermuda* were shown to their cabins by guides and stewards who told them "four of you in there - there was only one last time, but he was a New York stockbroker; two Sergeants in here - an actress once complained about this cabin, but you'll find it all right."[4] The 4 Bn Lincolns on *Empress of Australia* noted that "accommodation, messing and services were up to pre-war standard. Everyone was most comfortable and time passed pleasantly".[5] After crossing the Arctic Circle on the 14th, *Empress of Australia* and *Chrobry* carrying the troops of 146 Brigade, were detached south towards Namsos with three cruisers as escort. Both ships anchored in Lillesjona on the morning of the 16th, where the Hallamshire battalion on *Chrobry* and half the Lincolns on *Empress of Australia* began transferring in a very hurried fashion to five Tribal class destroyers, until interrupted by a heavy bombing attack in which the *Empress* was near-missed by a mere 50 yards. The destroyers then made a thrilling dash of 142 miles southwards at top speed through narrow twisting fjords, between innumerable islands and across the outer fjords of the Inner Leads to the Namsenfjord, where the troops were landed at Namsos about dusk. The remaining Lincolns and the Yorkshire battalion on the *Empress* were transferred by destroyers to *Chrobry*; the former ship now being considered too conspicuous and vulnerable to air attack to remain in the fjords. To speed up the transfer two chutes were provided from the *Empress* to the destroyers "down which everything cascaded, including kit bags, ammunition and food, some of which went straight into the sea, some was left on the *Empress* (which sailed for the Clyde) and some more was left on a destroyer".[6] *Chrobry* stood offshore during daylight hours of the 17th to escape air attack, and berthed that evening and the next following alongside the wooden jetty at Namsos to offload the remaining troops and stores. She returned to the Clyde with a large quantity of rifles, Bren guns and ammunition still on board due to lack of space on the quays at Namsos. The town was bombed to destruction from the 20th to 28th when two Sea Transport officers lost their lives. French reinforcements arrived during the night of the 19th/20th but the entire force of 5,400 engaged at Namsos was evacuated on 2nd May.

On the 16th April it was decided not to expose the liner *Orion* to the risk of air attack in the Norwegian fjords and so the troops of 148 Brigade who had embarked at Rosyth, were transferred to the cruisers *Galatea* and *Arethusa*, taken across to land at and subsequently be evacuated from Aandalsnes. During this latter operation, *Batory*, *Sobieski*, *Lancastria*, *Orion*, *Duchess of Atholl* and *Reina del Pacifico* were sent from the Clyde to Scapa Flow ready to receive the troops being hurriedly evacuated across the North Sea in warships, (from both Namsos and Aandalsnes). At Scapa the troops were transferred to the liners and taken to the Clyde.

The main sphere of operations in Norway took place at the small port of Harstad, where the troops of 24th (Guards)Brigade landed from *Monarch of Bermuda*, *Reina del Pacifico* and *Batory* on 15th April, to secure the port and begin the build up of a shore base for a subsequent assault on Narvik. The first reinforcements arrived aboard *Franconia* on the 20th, including 904 men of a Dock battalion to act as stevedores but who were sent home immediately on the same ship to reduce congestion in the town.[7] Units of the Royal Artillery with French and Polish troops, reached Harstad on 5th May aboard *Monarch of Bermuda*, *Empress of Australia* (on their second trips) and four French liners, while other French troops had disembarked from another four French liners during the previous week. Five liners were now released from the Norwegian operations: *Reina del Pacifico*, *Orion* and *Empress of Australia* being sent to West Africa (*see below*) (although the latter was diverted to Halifax), while *Franconia* and *Lancastria* carried 147 Brigade to Iceland for the establishment of bases on that island. *Chrobry* fell victim to German air attack on 15th May, when transporting 24 Brigade HQ and 1st Irish Guards from Harstad to Bodo, almost all of whom were rescued by the destroyer *Wolverine*. This incident was virtually repeated two days later aboard the cruiser *Effingham* when she ran hard aground carrying the same Guards HQ and 2nd South Wales Borderers to Bodo. This time, the rescue was effected by an escorting AA cruiser.

The decision to evacuate Allied forces from northern Norway was taken on 25th May even prior to the actual assault against Narvik. Six liners comprising Group One (*Franconia*, *Lancastria*, *Georgic*, *Batory*, *Sobieski* and *Monarch of Bermuda*) proceeded from the Clyde and embarked at isolated anchorages in the Andfjord, two at a time, during the three successive nights between 3rd and 5th June. A total of 14,682 troops were landed on the Clyde by this group on the 10th, while *Oronsay*, *Orama*, *Ormonde*, *Arandora Star*, *Vandyck* and *Duchess of York* comprising Group Two continued embarkation in the Andfjord until the morning of the 8th when they sailed for home with the remaining 10,000. *Orama* had been sent home empty and unfortunately met and was sunk by the *Admiral Hipper* on the 8th; *Vandyck* mistakenly entered Harstad where she was promptly bombed, disabled and abandoned as a total loss.

The beginning of the evacuation from Norway coincided with the ending of that from Dunkirk when 365,000 men were safely carried across the Dover Strait in cross-channel ships, destroyers and all manner of other smaller craft. Two British divisions remained south of the Somme, two others were still being sent to France, while about 150,000 British troops remained on lines of communication and other duties. By 13th June 11,059 had been evacuated from Le Havre, mainly by cross-channel ships; by the 18th a further 30,630 from Cherbourg; by the 16th 21,474 from St. Malo, and others from Brest where the ocean-going liners began to take over after being fortuitously released from the Norwegian campaign. *Batory*, *Sobieski*, *Georgic* and *Duchess of York* sailed from the Clyde on the 13th carrying 10,000 French and Polish troops for Brest, and were thereafter sent to St. Nazaire and embarked there over 16,000 for landing at Plymouth and Liverpool. More liners were required and by the 15th *Ormonde*, *Oronsay*, *Ettrick*, *Otranto*, *Arandora Star*, *Lancastria*, *Franconia* and *Strathaird* were available in southern ports awaiting orders. The latter ship (Captain Dene) had been refitting in Liverpool and having her trooping capacity increased, and left that port with almost everything adrift, primitive catering, lavatories unserviceable and one boiler shut down but while "at Brest, for eleven hours on 17th June, troops poured aboard her. There was no question of berthing them. They simply spread themselves around the ship, and when there was no more deck space on which they could sit or lie, *Strathaird's* moorings were cast off and she sailed for Plymouth: her only armament the Bren guns and rifles brought aboard by the troops. She carried away 6,000 troops and in addition, civilians, children - 200 of them in the saloon - cadets from the military school at Brest, gold from British banks in Paris, dogs, de Gaullists and fur coats".[8] During the overnight passage to Plymouth, "the Chief Steward and his staff turned-to and served out doorsteps of bread and cold meat, slop pails and buckets of tea, and on 18th June the troops were safely disembarked at Plymouth".[8]

During the evening of the 15th, *Franconia* (Captain Bissett) and *Lancastria* (Captain Sharp) left Plymouth for Brest and on arrival found the place "covered by a pall of black smoke from oil tanks which had been set alight".[7] Both liners were sent south to await further orders in Quiberon Bay and "steamed in company along the coast in fine weather and sunshine on that peaceful Sunday afternoon".[7] Four other transports were observed at the anchorage and when approaching the boom entrance a German dive-bomber suddenly appeared and released a stick of bombs which fell under the stern of *Franconia*, exploded on the seabed and lifted her stern clean out of the water. Some plates were sprung aft but, more seriously, one engine was thrown out of alignment: temporary repairs were made and at midnight *Franconia* was ordered to Brest where she arrived at dawn on the 17th to find the thick pall of smoke still evident. This was the day in which *Strathaird* was alongside embarking, but no instructions arrived until the afternoon when a W/T signal was received: "Do not enter French ports".[7] *Franconia* remained offshore until the evening, when again ordered to Brest and on approaching that entrance at midnight was instructed by a naval tug "Do not enter Brest".[7] The tugmaster confirmed the Germans were already in Brest. *Franconia* put back to sea and next day in the absence of further instructions shaped a course for Liverpool, where she arrived as an empty ship on the 19th for drydocking and repairs that lasted six weeks.

Lancastria was not so lucky and from Quiberon Bay was ordered to St. Nazaire with some cargo ships and arrived there on the morning of the 17th, where the Sea Pilot advised Captain Sharp the port had been bombed all night and was therefore unsafe, but *Lancastria* anchored nevertheless at 0600 near the outer end of the Charpentier Channel, 5 miles from shore and 9 miles from the port itself. Very soon the Naval Control Officer arrived on board and told Captain Sharp to expect embarkation from tenders almost immediately and "to embark without regard to the limits of International Law" [9] (having previously given his ship's capacity as about 3,000). "By lunchtime the decks were packed with soldiers sweating in their thick khaki; wherever I went I stumbled against kitbags and tin hats."[9] By 1415 hours *Lancastria* had 5,200 troops and refugees aboard and with 320 crew the grand total was 5,500. Captain Sharp would accept no more and being already overloaded sent the next destroyer/tender to *Oronsay* that had anchored nearby. As no escorts were available Captain Sharp decided to await the completion of *Oronsay* when both liners would proceed in company. It was while these fateful decisions were being made that an air attack developed. *Oronsay* was several times straddled and suffered a direct hit on the bridge so got under way to avoid the bombs but found her steering gear damaged and re-anchored for repairs. Frantic efforts were made to clear the shattered bridge and after a lull lasting nearly an hour, the next raid developed on *Lancastria* which received four direct hits causing furious fires and a settlement by the head. The boats were cleared away and lowered as a starboard list developed, then a port list and within 23 minutes of being hit, the bridge of *Lancastria* was under water. Captain Sharp and Chief Officer Grattidge stepped into the sea and began swimming, where with hundreds of others they kept themselves afloat amongst wreckage in the oil soaked sea for up to several hours until gradually everyone left alive was picked up by various small craft. The stern of *Lancastria* disappeared at 1630, the Chief Officer eventually landed on *Oronsay* and there reported to her Master, Captain Nicholls. From the total embarked on *Lancastria* over 1,500 lost their lives including 63 crew members. The wreck of the ship remains to this day, marked by a buoy 8 miles south of the holiday resort of La Baule.

Those rescued from *Lancastria* were embarked on many ships, not least being *Oronsay* that finally left the scene at 1830 hours with over 7,000 personnel aboard. Although the wheelhouse, chartroom and wireless room had been wrecked and all navigational instruments and charts destroyed, Captain Nicholls succeeded in bringing *Oronsay* safely to Plymouth with the aid of nothing more than a stained French motoring map and a penny ruler. His resource and coolness in action was rewarded by an O.B.E. *Oronsay* then proceeded to Liverpool and spent the next six weeks under repair.

The final evacuations from south Biscay ports were made by *Ormonde*, *Ettrick*, *Arandora Star*, *Batory* and *Sobieski*: the last two embarking 9,000 Polish and Czech troops at St. Jean de Luz. *Ettrick* picked up 2,000 of all nationalities from the same port, *Arandora Star* 4,000, while *Ormonde* was directed first to Brest, then La Pallice and finally Le Verdon but numbers embarked are not known. An estimated 32,584 troops and refugees were rescued from Brest, 57,235 from St. Nazaire, 16,000 from La Pallice, 12,000 Le Verdon and over 19,000 from Bayonne and St. Jean de Luz, making a grand total of 130,000 from the Biscay ports. The entire European coastline from the North Cape of Norway to the Spanish border now lay in German hands.

Meanwhile in far distant New Zealand, embarkation of the 5th Brigade troops took place as planned aboard *Andes* at Lyttelton on 1st May and aboard *Aquitania*, *Empress of Britain* and *Empress of Japan* at Wellington early next morning. The total comprised the Headquarters staff and four battalions numbering 6,638 all ranks. The cruiser

Canberra escorted *Andes* to join the other liners in Cook Strait where this first section of convoy US 3 formed up at midday on the 2nd, with *Leander* and *Australia* strengthening the escort while the Commodore on *Empress of Britain*, Captain J.W.A. Waller, RAN, settled into position leading the port wing column on what proved to be an uneventful crossing of the Tasman Sea. Although out of sight of the Australian coast on the morning of the 5th, *Canberra* and *Leander* detached into Sydney for fuel and sailed again five hours later behind *Queen Mary* and *Mauretania* setting out on their first of many trooping voyages and carrying respectively 4,381 and 2,300 troops including one third of the Australian Corps troops and the three battalions of 18th Brigade. Next afternoon *Empress of Canada* joined from Melbourne having embarked Divisional and Corps troops, the total Third Echelon of the Australian Imperial Force totaling 7,981 all ranks. Whilst settling down the convoy on passage to Fremantle, the Commodore expressed his concern on smoke, "when increasing speed and once a day when blowing boiler tubes all ships were liable to make heavy smoke".[10] *Empress of Japan* had been out of drydock for 16 months and with a foul bottom "was unable to maintain 20 knots in fair weather".[10] US 3 was however a very fast convoy.

The convoy reached Fremantle in the early afternoon of 10th May, concurrently with receiving news of the German offensive in Europe and foreshadowed an alteration of the convoy's future movements. Only *Queen Mary* because of her length and draft was unable to berth in Fremantle, being fuelled and watered in Gage Roads, while the other six liners with their troops and crews were able to enjoy two nights in town and at Perth. The same three cruisers continued with US 3 towards the next refuelling port of Colombo, until just after midnight on the 15th when instructions were received to divert towards the Cape of Good Hope. The course was altered 135° to port while *Leander* detached for Colombo and the Mediterranean, leaving *Canberra* and *Australia* to continue towards the Cape. Reports were then received of enemy mines on the Agulhas Bank, off the southern tip of the Cape and later of a disguised raider being in the South Indian Ocean. This later proved to be the German *Atlantis* which had laid 92 mines in the area extending 20 miles to seaward of Cape Agulhas, on the very day that US 3 reached Fremantle.

The cruiser *Shropshire* met the convoy to the SE of Mauritius on the 20th in relief of *Canberra* as SOE, which then detached for Australia after steaming "through the lines in a rainsquall and cheered by the troops."[10] The possible need for *Shropshire* had been foreseen by the Admiralty as early as the 10th when she was ordered from Freetown to the Cape in anticipation of the convoy's diversion. After passing well south of the Agulhas Bank, US 3 arrived off Capetown on the 26th where all ships berthed in the docks, except *Queen Mary* and *Aquitania* which because of their size had to anchor in Table Bay. Here the problems foreseen by the D of ST in handling such large vessels in ports unable to berth them alongside became manifest. "The difficulties of storing and provisioning them is aggravated by having to manhandle everything through loading ports, which in any swell was impossible. It was because of the swell, invariably present in Table Bay, that both ships had to be sent round to False Bay and anchor off Simonstown for fuel and water". [10]

However, these were far from being the only problems that beset US 3 in Capetown. It was the first of many troop convoys to call at the Cape in the next three years and left a vivid impression on the volunteers of the South African Women's Auxiliary Service (SAWAS), set up to provide facilities for the armed forces passing through the Cape. Their renowned efforts included the setting up of canteens, arranging dances and having buses and cars ready to take the men sightseeing. Their Provincial Commandant, Lucy Bean, recalled the Anzac force as being "indisciplined, who made a nonsense of the city but gave us lots of fun".[11] Their exploits were legendary, as when a group of Aussies took the horses from a wagon carrying crated beer and rode them bareback up the main street, while their pals helped themselves to the beer, even handing it round to eager bystanders; or the enterprising lad who cut the braces of a traffic officer from behind leaving him a single arm for the traffic while the other held his trousers. "It was all good fun and we were sorry when the Aussies departed".[11] The Convoy Commodore adopted a rather different view and said "the behaviour of the Australian troops in Capetown and their leave-breaking left very much to be desired".[10] There was trouble on *Queen Mary* whose troops and crew had been unable to land ashore from the anchorage at Fremantle and now faced a similar situation in Table Bay and then off Simonstown, where the discipline of the troops caused anxiety to their officers had leave not been granted. There had also been an outbreak of insubordination amongst the crew when 100 refused duty for the same reason. "The culminating act of indiscipline was for troops on *Empress of Canada* to break into the beer store and help themselves just before sailing".[10] And this was not all, the Chinese crews on *Empress of Canada* and *Empress of Japan* now declined to proceed any further towards the war zone. The Commodore arranged to retain the former ship, whose Chinese transferred to *Empress of Japan*, whilst troops from the latter were distributed amongst the other ships of the convoy; some being simply bedded down with mattresses on the Promenade Deck and Lounges. A draft of naval ratings taking passage on *Empress of Japan* replaced the crew losses on *Empress of Canada*, while the former ship now left the convoy and sailed for Hong Kong where the recalcitrant Chinese were duly discharged.

After five vivid days at the Cape, the convoy resumed its voyage on 31st May in exceptionally fine weather escorted by the cruisers *Shropshire* and *Cumberland*. On the first day out, the inexperienced crew on *Empress of Canada* allowed the boiler tubes to soot up, while *Aquitania* earned a reprimand from the SOE for voluminous smoke. The Commodore again commented on the "untrained state of the troops, and was reflected by numerous cases of scuttles and deadlights being opened after dark despite strict orders and frequent rounds".[10] The convoy and escort arrived at Freetown on 7th June to water and fuel amidst many lesser ships assembling for the next homeward convoy. The troops found the anchorage steaming hot and were glad enough to depart next day with the escort strengthened for the next three days by the carrier *Hermes*.

German forces were now in control of Western Europe and the Admiralty made special arrangements to ensure the safe onward passage of the Anzac convoy to the UK. The battleship *Resolution* and cruiser *Aurora* were readied at Gibraltar to provide additional cover. *Dorsetshire* accompanied the convoy between the Canary Islands and vicinity of Finisterre, where the mighty *Hood*, carrier *Argus* and six destroyers joined to remain with the convoy until it reached the SW Approaches on 15th June. The passage up the Irish Sea was made with Sunderland air escorts and by next afternoon all ships were safely anchored in the Clyde, on the eve of the French capitulation. After being on board for up to 49 days, the troops landed by tenders over the next three days and entrained to Aldershot and training areas on Salisbury Plain to prepare for an expected invasion. "The reception given to Australian and New Zealand forces was genuinely warm, even pathetic in its expression of gratitude".[12] It was the opinion of General Freyberg, who had not wanted them diverted, "that (their) arrival in such circumstances had been most opportune and steadied the nation considerably".[13] As for the liners engaged in this movement, their future employment was decided as early as 18th May when the UK diversion was confirmed. The US convoy series continued until the end of 1941.

The safe passage of the Anzac troops around the Cape to the UK was now matched by West African troops moving in the opposite direction and by British troops being sent home from India; both movements using three of the pre-war trooping fleet, two requisitioned liners and six from the B.I. company in a remarkable transhipment operation at Durban which soon became the norm.

In the spring of 1940, Italian and Native troops then in possession of Ethiopia, Eritrea and Italian Somaliland were thought to seriously outnumber and threaten the security of the Sudan, Kenya and British Somaliland, where British forces were very thinly spread. East Africa was considered a theatre of war quite distinct from the Middle East, and had to be protected as an alternative supply route to that area in the event of the Red Sea being closed to shipping. Reinforcements had been steadily moving into the area through the port of Mombasa from India, Rhodesia and South Africa, and on 29th April the War Cabinet approved the move of two brigade groups of the Royal West African Frontier Force to Kenya, but either that force was not then ready to move or shipping was not immediately available. My mid May however, six liners had been released from involvement in the Norwegian campaign including *Orion* and *Reina del Pacifico* which sailed for West Africa on the 15th of that month. A few days later the reduction of moves within the Mediterranean allowed *Dilwara*, *Devonshire* and *Lancashire* also to be sent there. All five ships called at Dakar for fresh water and Freetown for fuel and thereafter the three slower ships proceeded to Lagos escorted by AMC *Pretoria Castle* and there embarked 3rd Nigeria Brigade, while *Orion* and *Reina del Pacifico*, escorted by the cruiser *Cornwall*, embarked 4th Gold Coast Brigade at Takoradi. Both groups were back at sea on 1st June formed up as the CM convoy (Cape/Mombasa), under escort of *Cornwall* and having left the coast in the extremely wet, hot and humid conditions of the rainy season, were glad to be at sea and steering south towards the Cape. This passage was uneventful, until a full NW gale at Capetown prevented berthing the convoy there on 13th June. Alternative arrangements were made to refuel at Simonstown and thereafter the convoy continued to Durban where all ships were berthed within that harbour during the 18th.

Meanwhile, another troop movement was proceeding towards Durban from Bombay, where the B.I. liners *Karanja*, *Kenya*, *Aska*, *Rohna*, *Rajula* and *Talamba* had assembled under trooping requisition since the third week of May. On the 18th of that month, Allied forces were still engaged with the enemy in northern Norway, the BEF was about to begin its momentous withdrawal towards Dunkirk and the US 3 Anzac convoy had been diverted towards the UK. Churchill was advocating the replacement of eight regular battalions of British infantry in Palestine by eight units from India and the sending out of eight territorial battalions to India; the latter to be accomplished by using the US 3 liners due in the UK early June. Two weeks later as the successful evacuation of the BEF was being enacted, Churchill expanded his directive to include ten Territorial battalions and two days later was advised that eight regular battalions were leaving Bombay for the UK that same day.[14]

However, the eight chosen battalions were widely scattered in India with two at Nowshera and Rawalpindi on the NW frontier, and from where each required two days of rail travel and several changes to reach Bombay. The Battalions were at first given three days notice of the move but later delayed for two weeks to await the required shipping (the last two ships reached Bombay on 28th May to prepare for the voyage).

The troops were only aware of leaving for unknown overseas destinations and had to leave wives and families in India. Train journeys began on 3rd June, embarkation at Bombay was spread over the next three days and during the afternoon of the 6th, the six B.I. liners sailed out of the harbour, and formed up in three columns as convoy BC (Bombay/Cape) under the Commodore, (Captain E.S. Graham, RN), on *Karanja*; escort was provided by the cruiser *Kent*.[15]

The passage to Durban occupied thirteen days at an average speed of only 12 knots though possibly affected by steaming initially into the SW monsoon. Four days after leaving Bombay the weather improved and that night a serious fire broke out amongst military baggage stowed in No. 4 hold of *Karanja*, (Captain Bell) which enveloped the ship in smoke from a then following wind, but was extinguished three hours later by flooding the hold. The cause was later considered to have been an incendiary device but was not investigated further. The convoy berthed in Durban harbour on the morning of the 19th, some ships having their regimental bands and bugles playing on the upper decks. Eleven transports from two convoys were now in the harbour for fuelling, watering, storing and some transhipment, as the comparatively slow, 14 knots speed of *Rhona*, *Rajula* and *Talamba* necessitated their retention in the Indian Ocean area. Thus the 1st Royal Scots Fusiliers, 2nd Ox & Bucks, 2nd South Lancs and 2nd South Staffs battalions aboard these ships transferred and exchanged berths with the West African troops of the Gold Coast Brigade on *Orion* and *Reina del Pacifico*. Meanwhile the other battalions, 1st Royal Norfolk, 1st Royal Ulster Rifles, 2nd Royal Welsh Fusiliers and 2nd East Lancs from *Karanja*, *Kenya* and *Aska* went ashore on the morning of the 20th for a route march through Durban and were met by enthusiastic crowds who had not seen British troops since the 1914-18 war.

Whilst in Durban, responsibility for escort of the two convoys was exchanged between *Kent* and *Cornwall*. The former then sailed with the CM convoy at daylight on the 22nd, comprising *Dilwara*, *Devonshire*, *Lancashire* and the three B.I. ships for Mombasa. Speed was restricted to the 12.5 knots maximum of *Dilwara*, although this was reduced to 10 knots over the next two days by heavy easterly weather. The convoy passed up the Mozambique Channel and reached Mombasa at 0600 on the 30th, where the West Africa Brigades immediately disembarked and *Kent* left for Suez to join the Mediterranean Fleet.

For some reason the BC convoy was split in Durban into a Fast and Slow section, with the latter planned to comprise the three B.I. ships departing on the day of their arrival. However, the slow means of coaling *Aska* through side-loading ports prevented this and postponed their sailing by 24 hours and even then, the storing of ships was incomplete and had to be made up in Capetown. The SOE on *Cornwall* believed "the resources of Durban were overstrained by the two troop convoys".[16]   The BCS convoy comprising *Karanja*, *Kenya* and *Aska* with *Cornwall* as escort made the passage to Capetown without incident and berthed within the docks there on the 23rd, met by crowds of onlookers inviting the troops ashore, although some were to find a rather cool reception from a population barely recovered from the rumbustious Anzacs of US 3. After barely 24 hours in Capetown, BCS left again at 0700 on the 24th and joined *Cornwall*, which had refuelled at Simonstown, for the passage to the next replenishment port of Freetown and settled down to a speed of 16.5 knots; the maximum of *Karanja* and *Kenya*. Fine weather was enjoyed and when about the halfway mark, the CinC SA diverted the convoy to Takoradi for fresh water due to the lack of facilities at Freetown. However, the delivery rates were very slow at Takoradi but with great effort enough was shipped for the ships to reach the UK; the troops were able to enjoy bathing on the beach and some of their officers borrowed yachts to go sailing. *Cornwall* patrolled offshore while the liners were in Takoradi; the voyage was resumed at dusk on 2nd July and after a fast coastal passage, mostly at 17 knots, the convoy anchored in Freetown during the morning of the 5th, where the Fast Section already awaited them.

Convoy BCF comprising *Orion* and *Reina del Pacifico*, escorted by the light cruiser *Dragon*, sailed from Durban on 22nd June and proceeded at 15 knots to Capetown, where they arrived at 0900 on the 25th. After completing with water and fuel they sailed again that evening with the addition of *Stratheden*, homebound from Australia on a commercial voyage but also carrying a detachment of Australian troops for the Middle East. *Stratheden* had been diverted to the Cape route after leaving Colombo for Freetown, appropriately now escorted by *Australia*, and reached that port two days ahead of the slower portion at 0800 on 3rd July, and whence *Australia* went off to join the fleet in operations against Dakar in French Senegal.

The combined six ship convoy refuelled in Freetown where *Aska* again had problems in coaling and with barely sufficient to reach the UK, was given a shorter route to pass inside the Cape Verde islands. Whilst in Freetown the Commodore and his signaling staff transferred from *Karanja* to *Reina del Pacifico* (and losing out on their curry lunches). The convoy sailed from the very hot and sticky conditions of Freetown in the afternoon of the 6th, still escorted by *Cornwall* but without *Aska* which was then proceeding independently. While passing to the west of the Cape Verdes during the evening of the 9th, a Vichy-French submarine attacked but missed a British ship 50 miles NE of the convoy and proved a timely warning as U-Boats began operating in the area the very next week.

The cruiser *Australia* joined the convoy just after midday on the 11th, and two hours later *Aska* joined to complete the three columns of two ships apiece. No incidents occurred during the next three days until the early hours of the 15th when the visibility closed down and remained indifferent for the rest of the voyage; it cleared sufficiently for the local destroyer escort to make contact in the western approaches where *Cornwall* detached ahead to Liverpool followed by *Australia* to the Clyde. Very thick weather was experienced in the North Channel and Irish Sea but pilots boarded at the Bar Light Vessel on the morning of the 17th and very soon all ships were berthed in Liverpool. The country was in a mood of anticipated German invasion, the Australians from *Stratheden* disembarked to join their own formations at Aldershot, the eight British battalions to form two Independent Brigade Groups but having been abroad for some years and accustomed to India standards were ill-equipped for modern, motorized warfare. It took time to re-train, but they were at least home and able to take their place amongst the anti-invasion forces being formed on the south coast.

Chapter 4

The Early WS Convoys

WS 1 - Sailed UK 29 June 1940

We have seen that Churchill's directive of 18th May effectively mobilized eight regular infantry battalions in India for shipment to the UK, to be immediately replaced by eight or more territorial battalions from home, sent out in the liners of US 3 as soon as they had landed their Anzac troops in the UK.[1] By the end of May, however, the Chiefs of Staff were voicing concern over the difficulty of reinforcing the Middle East, in the event of Italy entering the war and preventing use of the direct route through the Mediterranean.[2] This may have caused the territorials' destination to be changed, although no infantry units territorial or otherwise were sent to either India or the Middle East at this time, all being needed at home to resist an expected invasion. Nevertheless Churchill emphasized his directive with another on 6th June, "the Australians are coming in the big ships...whenever they arrive (they) should be immediately filled with Territorials - the more the better - and sent off to India at full speed".[3] Italy declared war on the Allies four days later when the regulars from India were only crossing the Indian Ocean but the Anzac troops on the six liners of US3 were then nearing the U.K. and reached the Clyde six days later.

The 'big ships' referred to by Mr. Churchill may have been specifically *Queen Mary*, *Mauretania* and *Aquitania*, despite the latter carrying not Australian but New Zealand troops. At any rate these were the ships selected to rush the 'Territorials' to India and were given little time to prepare. Disembarkation was not completed until 21st June, when *Aquitania* (still in peacetime colours) and *Mauretania* were sent to Liverpool where they could berth within the docks, while *Queen Mary*, denied the use of Southampton as now unsafe, had to use the Clyde Anchorage as the only other port in the UK which could accommodate her size, albeit with all the difficulties of handling stores and provisions, repairmen, cleaning gangs, the fuelling and watering of such a large liner, the changing of crews and troop embarkations, all from tenders and other small craft. Nevertheless all was achieved by 28th June when 6,350 troops had embarked at Liverpool and 5,150 on *Queen Mary* on the Clyde.

The two liners from Liverpool cleared the Mersey on the morning of the 29th, escorted by the 8-inch cruiser *Cumberland*, two H and two V and W class destroyers. Passage up the Irish Sea was in line ahead at a speed of 22 knots to a rendezvous point midway between Ailsa Craig and the Mull of Kintyre, where *Queen Mary* was met and joined that afternoon. Line ahead formation continued until clear of the North Channel when the liners took up their cruising order of 11 *Aquitania*, 21 *Queen Mary* and 31 *Mauretania*.[4] The SOE was the Commanding Officer of *Cumberland*, who was disposed ahead of the center column while the destroyers provided an anti-submarine screen. By 1900 that evening the battleship *Nelson*, on an offensive sweep from the Clyde, was passed and during the early hours of the next morning the two older destroyers were detached as being unable to maintain even 18 knots in the heavy swell and high wind then prevalent; by early afternoon the H class were similarly detached and that evening the convoy settled on to a southerly heading at a speed of 22 knots to pass 60 miles east of the Azores, en route to their first refueling stop at Freetown.

The troops embarked on this first 'Winston Special' convoy are believed to have been territorial units for base and lines of communication duties in the Middle East, now required to relieve the garrison troops for front line duties in the desert. Although unaccustomed to the swell and motion of the ships as they exited the North Channel, this was early summer, the ships not overcrowded and with such a high speed of advance the weather soon improved and any discomfort quickly forgotten. Frequent exercise at PT, boat drills, training sessions, lazing in the sun or simply gazing at the adjacent liner all helped to pass the time between eating and sleeping.

From the Admiralty viewpoint all troop convoys whether on the Atlantic or Indian Oceans had to be escorted throughout their entire passage. On the long route around the Cape to the Middle East or India, the greatest danger was from U-Boats in the Western Approaches, which in June 1940 tended to concentrate on such focal areas and were countered by providing destroyer escorts as far as their endurance allowed. German pocket-battleships and battlecruisers made three separate forays into the North and South Atlantic in 1939, sinking twelve ships, and another during the evacuation of Norway when they sank the liner *Orama*, the carrier *Glorious* and four other ships. None were known to have been at sea when WS 1 left the UK but at least two disguised merchant raiders had been detected (*Atlantis* laid the mines off Agulhas in May and *Orion* a similar operation off Auckland in June). It was unlikely that such raiders would approach far less attack a fast escorted convoy, but heavy German units were designed for that very purpose and required a cruiser such as *Cumberland* to meet that possibility. Mines were a danger in all port approaches or adjacent headlands and required a constant sweeping to maintain a safe passage throughout the relevant channels. The danger of air attack in the northwest approaches was minimal until the German occupation of France allowed long-range aircraft to roam over this area and as far west as Iceland, bombing independent ships and unprotected convoys at will. They accounted for the loss of 95 ships in the second half of 1940 and more than double that number in the following six months before countermeasures became effective. The final danger facing the WS convoys was from Italian naval forces based in the Red Sea, which never actually hindered their passage and were removed by the seizure of Assab in June 1941.

The weather improved for the convoy with the sea and swell greatly reduced in the afternoon of 1st July, allowing *Cumberland* to have at least one of her Walrus aircraft on patrol during daylight hours until the day before arrival at Freetown when heavy rain squalls prevented flying. The squalls continued throughout that night causing poor visibility at times as the convoy approached the port in single line ahead; all three liners and *Cumberland* being anchored inside the Freetown boom on the morning of the 8th and immediately began to water and fuel from the tankers and barges released by the departure of a large homeward convoy. After less than 24 hours in port, the convoy continued with the same formation and escort towards the Cape, passing 60 miles west of St. Helena and then to a position west of Table Bay where line ahead was formed for the approach and arrival at Capetown on the morning of the 16th; *Cumberland* and *Mauretania* berthed in the Duncan Dock while the other two liners anchored in Table Bay one mile from the breakwater. Bomber aircraft of the South African Air Force kept up a seaward patrol with some A/S vessels to protect the liners at anchor.

Some of the troops and nursing staff embarked on *Mauretania* were entertained ashore during the first night in Capetown; those on *Aquitania* and *Queen Mary* could not be landed due to the swell which also prevented the tankers from lying alongside. Next day when *Cumberland* completed replenishment both liners were escorted round to a more sheltered anchorage off Simonstown naval base where they fuelled from two BTC tankers. Early on the 18th, *Cumberland* returned to Capetown, met *Mauretania* leaving the Duncan Dock and escorted her to the anchorage off Simonstown. Fuelling, watering and storing the two largest liners continued throughout that day and overnight. The convoy left Simonstown line ahead, in the early afternoon of the 19th, with *Cumberland* continuing as escort and heading into a very heavy SW swell with frequent rainstorms and poor visibility but maintaining the speed of 22 knots. When reaching a pre-arranged position some 300 miles south of Durban on the morning of the 21st, the cruiser *Kent* was met and relieved *Cumberland* which passed down the line cheering ships and being cheered by the troops in return. A very pleasant signal was sent by the Commodore (being the Master of *Queen Mary*, Commodore R.B. Irving) to *Cumberland*, which had escorted the three liners over a distance of 15,874 miles before returning to Simonstown.

No incidents occurred during the passage across the Indian Ocean with the convoy continuing in single line ahead under escort of *Kent*. Although intended for India, the Chiefs of Staff must have agreed to divert the troops of WS 1 to the Middle East as soon as the convoy reached Freetown, and to tranship into smaller ships in Ceylon for on-carriage to Suez, rather than risk such large liners in the Red Sea where Italian bases predominated. By mid July eleven of the 'Indian Ocean type' of liners were earmarked for this service and arrived in Ceylon concurrently with the three Cunarders on the 29th, having been taken up from trade or already trooping; significantly only two were not owned by the B.I. Company. *Queen Mary* proceeded up the east coast of Ceylon to anchor in Trincomalee, while *Kent* with the other two liners berthed inside the harbour of Colombo on the west coast.

This was the season of the SW monsoon when ships in Colombo harbour moored head and stern between buoys, heading west with their port anchors down. In normal circumstances the port accepted ships up to 800 ft. in length and 35 ft. draft, which included *Mauretania* but not *Aquitania* of 902 ft. and 36 ft. draft. There was a disturbed swell over the main entrance during the monsoon, ships had to negotiate this while rolling beam-on to the SW swell which considerably increased their draft and reduced bottom clearance. There is no record of protest from Captain Gibbons of *Aquitania* on that occasion but the matter was subsequently raised at great length with the C. in C. East Indies, and whilst *Aquitania* made three further calls at Colombo, none of these visits were made during the period of the SW monsoon.

In the splendid picturesque harbour of Trincomalee, *Queen Mary* transhipped all of her troops by accepting alongside in turn *Lancashire*, *Egra*, *Erinpura*, *Karagola* and *Rizwani* (Mogul Line), and after refuelling sailed on 1st August independently to Singapore for drydocking and annual overhaul. The five smaller ships then moved round to Colombo, where *Aquitania* and *Mauretania* transhipped to *Ekma*, *Ethiopia*, *Varela*, *Amra*, *Takliwa* and *Talamba*. The new convoy of 11 ships, still designated WS 1 and escorted by the AMC *Antenor*, sailed from Colombo on 1st August and reached Bombay five days later and where further transhipment took place. *Aquitania* and *Mauretania* then sailed independently from Colombo to Sydney to embark for convoy US 4.

On arrival at Bombay, all of the 6,500 troops on *Ekma*, *Ethiopia*, *Varela*, *Amra*, *Karagola*, *Erinpura* and *Rizwani* were disembarked and re-embarked on *Dilwara*, *Devonshire*, *Rohna* and *Rajula*, all recently arrived from Mombasa, and on the ex Egyptian *Khedive Ismail* now on charter to the Ministry of Shipping and managed by B.I. To these five ships and the original four were now added *Ethiopia* and *Khandalla* carrying reinforcement Indian troops for Aden. The convoy thus transformed and redesignated BN 3 left Bombay on 10th August carrying 9,820 troops for Suez and 1,453 for Aden. Escort was at first provided by the AMCs *Antenor* and *Ranchi* and later replaced by the New Zealand cruiser *Leander* with two K class destroyers and four sloops. On detaching the two ships for Aden, eight others joined from that port to make a 17 ship convoy which rounded Perim and entered the Red Sea during the evening of the 17th. Air and surface attacks were now expected from Italian forces based at Massawa but none developed and the 18th passed peacefully as the southern islands were gradually left astern. Next day an aircraft from *Leander* maintained an A/S patrol for several hours but had to force-land in the evening beside one of the destroyers, which picked up the crew. *Khedive Ismail* then detached ahead to Port Sudan for water and next day several other ships also detached for bunkers. On the morning of the 21st escorts were exchanged with the southbound convoy BS 3; the convoy continued to Suez and arrived there without further incident on 23rd August.

To accelerate disembarkation, *Talamba*, *Takliwa*, *Rhona* and *Rajula* passed through the canal and landed their troops at Port Said, a welcome and long awaited arrival for the troops after 55 days at sea. A Sister of the Territorial Army Nursing Service, who had travelled out on the *Queen Mary* summed it up thus: "A long train journey brought us at last to Palestine. All we wanted was a bath, a cup of tea and bed".[5] All ships returned independently to Bombay.

RS 5 - *sailed UK 24.7.40*

Even as the three liners of WS 1 were arriving in Ceylon, preparations had begun to mount the next, WS 2 convoy, but in addition, an extra sailing was arranged to carry urgently needed reinforcements and equipment direct to the Middle East around the Cape without transhipment in Ceylon. This was probably the result of a Chiefs of Staff meeting "at the beginning of July on general policy for the Middle East, which included the need for strengthening our forces there at the earliest possible moment".[6] Guns, tanks, vehicles, stores and ammunition were loaded on the *Clan Ferguson* (which thereafter sailed on more Malta convoy operations than any other merchant ship) at Glasgow and Birkenhead, while an accompanying 2,000 troops embarked on *Reina del Pacifico* at Liverpool on 23rd July, soon after arriving from Durban with the 'regulars'. Both ships left the Mersey next afternoon as convoy RS 5 for Suez and next morning to the SE of Orsay Light met the ocean escort comprising the AMC *Maloja*, carrier *Argus* and several destroyers, which had sailed from the Clyde. When clear of the Western Approaches and about to turn south on the morning of the 26th, *Argus* and the destroyers parted company for the Mediterranean to fly off Hurricane fighters for Malta.

The passage to Freetown was without incident, except that during the last three days, *Clan Ferguson* changed from oil to coal firing which reduced her speed (and that of the convoy) from 15.5 knots to 13.5 knots. *Maloja* was relieved at Freetown by the AMC *Carthage* which continued as ocean escort until Aden, the convoy calling en route at Capetown on 15th-16th August and Durban from 19th to 21st. Aden was reached on the 31st where all ships again bunkered. For the final stage of the voyage, escort was provided by *Hobart* and destroyer *Kandahar*; Perim was rounded at midnight on the 31st and next morning the *OBV Chakdina* joined on being overtaken and remained until detached to Port Sudan that evening when speed was increased to 15 knots. *Reina del* was detached ahead at 1800 on the 2nd and reached Suez at daylight on the 4th. Eight days were spent at the anchorage to disembark her troops and stores. She then returned home independently via Capetown, Freetown and Gibraltar, leaving the latter with refugees for the UK and ordered initially to Lough Foyle but later diverted to Liverpool where she arrived on 25th October. *Clan Ferguson* discharged her military cargo at Alexandria and thereafter undertook the first three of many famous convoy trips to Malta.

WS 2 - *sailed UK 5.8.40*

WS 2 was the first of the larger troop convoys around the Cape and established a pattern of including a number of fast cargo liners loaded with the military hardware required by the troops, in this case 24,000 destined for the Middle East, India and Malaya and for which arrangements were put in hand as soon as it was known that WS1 had safely reached Ceylon. At the beginning of July the Chiefs of Staff had reiterated the "need for strengthening our forces (in the Middle East) at the earliest possible moment".[6] This was soon after the departure of WS 1 and may well have influenced some of the arrangements for WS 2. The organization of a large military convoy to cover the 13,000 miles from the UK to Suez via the Cape was however a very complex matter involving three separate bodies, the War Office who largely decided the number of personnel to be moved, the Sea Transport Department who requisitioned or allocated the necessary shipping from whatever was available, and the Admiralty whose task was the general organization of the convoy; its composition, speed, defence, ports of replenishment along the route and the escorts which had to be drawn from four or five separate commands.

"The Admiralty had at first demanded that, with a few exceptions, all ships in military convoys on the North and South Atlantic should be capable of maintaining a speed of 15 knots"[7], but never actually enforced this until September 1941 as not enough ships could be found to meet that criteria. The exigencies of war had already denuded the passenger carrying fleet by almost half, to 88 liners, while the number of fast cargo liners (MT ships) never exceeded 70 even in 1939, and half of these were of the valuable refrigerated type which could be ill spared from their primary task of maintaining food supplies to the U.K. Another 70 fast cargo liners were built during the war years to help meet the need but only one liner was then completed as a troopship, whose complexity of construction equalled that of a warship of equal size. In time troopships came to be recognized as irreplaceable, indeed "instruments of war as essential as guns or tanks or naval vessels (but) unlike other instruments of war could not be increased by new construction, although their number could be, and was, diminished as a result of enemy attack or for other reasons".[7]

Once the shipping for the planned convoy became available, suitable berths were allocated for the loading of cargoes and embarkation of troops. By the summer of 1940 both the English Channel and east coast ports from the Thames to the Humber became untenable due to enemy bombing and mining, cargoes had then to be distributed to and loaded in Glasgow, Liverpool, Manchester and the Bristol Channel ports, while troop embarkation was confined to the first two named and the Clyde Anchorage, although Avonmouth came into use, to a very limited extent, from December 1940. Most of the troops embarked on the ships of WS 2 were from the vital base and communication units evacuated from the Biscay ports in June, but now re-organised and re-equipped on a tropical basis for service with the Army of the Nile in Egypt. The convoy was also to include a large contingent of evacuee children for Australia, together with Army and Air Force personnel for the defence and development of bases in West Africa, particularly Freetown in Sierra Leone, and the establishment of an aircraft delivery route across Africa from Takoradi to the Middle East.

Twelve troopships and five military storeships (MT) were earmarked for WS 2 with all embarkations planned for Liverpool where the liners had been assembling since their previous tasks: *Strathaird*, *Franconia* and *Otranto* from the Biscay evacuations in June, *Empress of Britain* and *Canada* also in June after disembarkation of the Anzacs in US 3, while in July came *Orion*, *Aska* and *Stratheden* in the BC convoy from India. The convoy was to complete with *Andes* and *Ormonde* which had recently taken reinforcements to Iceland, and finally *Monarch of Bermuda* and *Batory* after crossing from Halifax to the Clyde with Canadian troops in convoy TC 6 and then berthed in Liverpool with barely 72 hours for storing, fuelling, taking fresh water and completing embarkation before departing in WS 2. Because of acute congestion in Liverpool it was found necessary to send *Andes*, *Franconia* and *Empress of Canada* to the Clyde for embarkation, yet still left 28 large liners and altogether almost 200 overseas ships in the port with many berths double-banked. The situation at the Clyde Anchorages was little better with so many inward and outward ships for London and east coast ports awaiting northabout coastal convoys or outward ocean convoys from the U.K. *Andes* and *Empress of Canada* were embarked in Glasgow. At a small conference held for the Clyde portion, Captain Bissett of *Franconia* met Captain Kinley of *Empess of Canada*: their first encounter since sailing round Cape Horn 36 years earlier.[8]

This second WS convoy embarked over 17,000 for the Middle East, 3,000 for West

Africa, 1,850 for India, 1,230 for Singapore and 1,570 civilians including child evacuees for Australia.[9] The Liverpool section began leaving the Mersey at ten minute intervals from 2215 hours on 5th August, comprising the nine (above) troopships and MT
ships *Clan Macaulay* and *Waiwera*. Escort was provided by the cruiser *Cornwall* and
eight destroyers, and after proceeding up the Irish Sea, junction was made at noon next
day off the Mull of Kintyre with the three troopships and MT ships *Lanarkshire*, *Suffolk*
and *Memnon* of the Clyde section, escorted by the cruisers *Emerald* and *Shropshire*,
which had left the Clyde Anchorage at daybreak that morning.

The combined convoy was formed into a cruising order of six columns[10] by 1245 and
proceeded out of the North Channel, and when to the SW of Islay that afternoon, *Orion*
suffered a blown-out main steam pipe and returned to the Clyde for repairs but was subsequently able to resume her voyage and rejoin the convoy at Capetown.[11] Commodore
ML Goldsmith, DSO RNR was embarked on *Stratheden* and the Vice-Commodore,
Commodore Graham, RN on *Empress of Canada*. The completed convoy now of 16
ships proceeded westward throughout the 6th and 7th with two or three ships flying kites
as a deterrent to enemy aircraft which had suddenly appeared in the area by sinking a
ship near Stornoway three days earlier. In the forenoon of the 7th, *Emerald* went off to
investigate a Norwegian tanker reported by the Sunderland air escort that was found to
be an innocent straggler from an outward convoy. That same evening a rather indistinct
SOS was heard from the troopship *Mohamed Ali el Kebir*, which had been torpedoed
200 miles astern of the convoy. This was a chartered ex Egyptian liner carrying nearly
700 troops from Avonmouth to Gibraltar with a single destroyer escort. Two of the V
and W destroyers were detached from the convoy to assist the casualty that sank with
the loss of 60 lives. The U-Boat responsible was one of three that had been searching
for a homeward convoy from Halifax and from which WS 2 may thus have had a lucky
escape. Just before midnight on the 7th, *Emerald* and the remaining destroyers parted
company from WS 2 and at this point in longitude 20°W, the convoy altered course to
the SW.

Next morning course was altered to SSW and the convoy split into two sections
according to plan. The seven faster ships provisionally capable of 20 knots, i.e. *Andes*,
Strathaird, *Stratheden*, *Empress of Britain*, *Empress of Canada*, *Monarch of Bermuda*
and *Batory* were sent ahead under escort of *Cornwall* as WS 2F. Unfortunately
Strathaird and *Monarch of Bermuda* had foul bottoms and *Batory* could only just
exceed 18 knots and so these three steered a straight course while the remainder zigzagged across their front as it was necessary to reach Freetown 24 hours ahead of the
others, presumably to spread the load on the port replenishment services. When east of
the Azores on the morning of the 10th, *Cornwall* launched a Walrus aircraft to search an
area 100 miles ahead of the convoy but found nothing and that same evening the
Commodore had to warn *Strathaird* of the dangers in making exceptionally heavy
smoke. The passage was otherwise without incident in fine weather with little wind and
Freetown was reached at noon on the 15th when fuelling and watering began immediately. The slow portion of four transports and five MT ships had continued after the split
at a speed of 14 knots under escort of *Shropshire* until dawn on the 16th, when a faster
portion was sent ahead and berthed in Freetown at 1000 hours - 22 hours behind WS
2F. As *Franconia* came to anchor, near a British cruiser, troops lining the rails were
making humorous and sarcastic comments about the Navy. A naval rating, who was
wearing white shorts and a black beard, stood it for a while, and then sang out "where
are you evacuating from now?"[8] The slower ships and *Shropshire* arrived at Freetown

by sunset.

Monarch of Bermuda was carrying 2,000 Army and Naval personnel for Freetown and Takoradi; those for the latter were now transhipped to *Aska* which had RAF personnel for the aircraft delivery base at Takoradi and others for Lagos. After coaling at Freetown *Aska* sailed on the 19th for the two coast ports where she disembarked, loaded 600 tons of cocoa, embarked 350 French troops at Takoradi for service with de Gaulle, and finally left Bathurst for Liverpool as a fast independent sailing on 7th September. All went well until the morning of the 15th when a periscope was sighted as the ship approached the Irish coast. Four ships of an inward convoy had been sunk earlier that morning close north of *Aska* but no attack developed and an air escort was present for most of the remaining daylight hours. However, at 0230 next morning when 5 miles SW of the Mull of Kintyre in bright conditions with a full moon, an aircraft (probably a Heinkel) overflew the ship and dropped two bombs which passed through the engineers' quarters on the boat deck and exploded over the engine-room. Almost at once flames burst from the accommodation and boat deck, the aircraft circled and dropped another bomb which struck the fo'csle and set it ablaze. With no lights or power the ship was abandoned; 440 survivors later being picked up and landed at Greenock:[12] 11 crew and 19 troops were lost. By 0945 the burning wreck of *Aska* had carried 11 miles NW on the strong ebb tide and despite the Admiralty sending out the tug *Salvonia* to attempt salvage, the *Aska* drifted ashore on Cara Island just before noon on the 17th and became a Constructive Total Loss (CTL).

The loss of *Aska* in such circumstances was a startling revelation of the danger prevailing even in British territorial waters. Long range German bombers (Focke-Wulf Condors) began operating from a base at Bordeaux soon after the fall of France and at the beginning of September directed their attention to shipping in the NW Approaches, particularly independent sailings which were then very poorly armed with virtually no anti-aircraft defence whatever. The Condor attacks became an increasing menace for the next few years and were rightly described by Churchill as the "Scourge of the Atlantic".[13]

Back in Freetown, the 773 officers and men of 1/4 Territorial Battalion The Essex Regiment, who had arrived in the *Monarch of Bermuda*, had perforce to remain aboard for sixteen days while their accommodation ashore in Wilberforce Barracks was made ready. They were the leading unit of 161 Infantry Brigade sent out for the protection of convoy bases, for various guard duties and the training of West African troops in the area. The *Monarch* remained as an accommodation ship until the battalion finally disembarked on 31st August, when she sailed for home and reached Liverpool ten days later.

While anchored in Freetown, the ships of WS 2 began to experience the chronic difficulties of obtaining sufficient fresh water supplies in that port. Most of the requirements could not be adequately met and this problem intensified as the war progressed even although the size and frequency of troop convoys did not significantly change. Almost all ships whether in convoy or sailing independently, both outward and homeward bound, now called at Freetown for fuel and water or to join homeward convoys. Freetown had a large natural harbour and with a similar capacity to the Clyde Anchorage could accommodate 150 ships at a time, but unlike the former, had no large reservoirs and in the dry season from January to April could barely provide for the local population now swollen by large numbers of shore-based troops. Through time distilling ships were based at Freetown but the greatest supplies were met by sending out valuable tankers with fresh water from the U.K. In the meantime, those ships that could not obtain sufficient to last out the next leg of the voyage had to start rationing at considerable inconvenience to crews and troops alike.

Freetown was a port that served the Crown Colony of Sierra Leone, its greatest asset being the vast and safe anchorage enclosed by the anti-submarine boom. It had been a fleet base and convoy assembly port in the First World War and assumed a similar role from September 1939 without any great difficulty. It lay conveniently close to the Cape trade route and just over halfway from the U.K. to Durban, but had no pre-war requirements for deepwater berths and none existed. Bunker coal and oil fuels had to be brought into the port and stored afloat until used, although fortuitously few troopships were coal burners as the bunkering process in undeveloped places like Freetown, Aden or Port Said involved the time consuming and laborious business of shipment by native labour using canvas bags.

The climate of Freetown, which lies close to the Equator, is anything but healthy, the temperature varying from 70 to 90° and combined with a high humidity of 80 to 90%, produced sultry and oppressive conditions making life uncomfortable for all and not least those berthed in troop decks on liners designed for the cooler climes of the North Atlantic. Shore leave was never allowed at Freetown, neither tenders nor shoreside facilities existed for large numbers of visiting troops, there was additionally the risk of disease; malaria was endemic while dysentery, elephantiasis and skin diseases were common throughout all of Sierra Leone. The bum boats did a brisk trade with the troopships and provided almost the only link with the shore.

Having left *Monarch of Bermuda* behind, the fast portion now of six liners but still escorted by *Cornwall*, left Freetown at 1430 on 16th August and by 1700 had formed into three columns bound for the Cape. It soon became apparent that 17.5 knots was all that could be managed from *Strathaird* and *Batory* and therefore governed the convoy speed. On the 19th *Cornwall* carried out small calibre practice firing and next day an 8 inch full calibre firing using *Stratheden* as target. On the 21st the convoy ran into the strong head winds of the SE trades, force 5, with a moderate to rough sea, which gradually reduced the speed of *Batory* and thus the convoy to 17 then 16 knots and prevented arrival at Capetown before darkness on the 24th as planned. Speed was further reduced to allow arrival next morning, all ships being berthed within the harbour by midday to fuel, water, store and provide the troops with a welcome break ashore, while *Cornwall* proceeded to Simonstown.

During the passage south a number of signals were exchanged between the Admiralty, the Director of Sea Transport and the NOIC Simonstown concerning the reorganization of the convoy at Capetown into two sections, WS 2A for Suez and WS 2B for Bombay, Singapore and Australia. It appeared that *Strathaird* was required for a US convoy from Australia, which would have meant exchanging all of the personnel between that ship and *Batory*, with the balance of those for the Middle East on *Strathaird* being divided amongst the remaining ships. In the event the proposed transfer did not materialize but probably highlighted the need for such a body as the Movement Control Staff who were later established in South Africa. The slow portion of the convoy, less *Aska*, left Freetown two days behind the others, *Shropshire* continuing as escort, and reached Capetown on the 27th, and where, because of congestion, *Franconia* was next day sent on to Durban escorted by the cruiser *Dragon* and reached there on 1st September. The troops on *Franconia* had one night ashore in Capetown but a morning route march and afternoon leave only in Durban.

An additional ship that joined the convoy at Capetown was the Orient liner *Orion*, which had sailed with the original convoy and put back for repairs that were carried out at the Clyde Anchorage. The troops remained on board and *Orion* sailed again five days later in the ZA (Paddy) convoy of six liners bound for Halifax. One of the escorts was the AMC *Asturias*, which detached from the convoy with *Orion* on reaching 20°W longitude[11]; both ships then continued to Freetown and refuelled there on the 21st. *Orion* then continued, at first with the Dutch cruiser *Sumatra* until relieved by *Dorsetshire* on the latitude of Ascension. Both reached Capetown in the afternoon of 30th August with sufficient time to fuel and water before sailing with the reorganized convoy next day.

Further signals were exchanged between the Admiralty and CinC SA just before the convoy reached Capetown, concerning the onward escort of the two portions from Capetown. Because of the increasing urgency of reinforcing the Middle East and the probability of sailing another convoy from the U.K. early in September,[14] either *Shropshire* or *Cornwall* was required to return and meet that convoy at Freetown. The AMC *Kanimbla* was to be utilized for the Bombay portion i.e. WS 2B, and although previously allocated as escort for *Llangibby Castle* carrying 1,200 troops of 2nd South African AA Brigade to Mombasa, embarkation of these troops was accelerated to allow both *Llangibby Castle* and *Franconia*, with *Kanimbla* as escort, to sail from Durban in the late evening of 1st September, to meet and join the main body of the convoy.

From Capetown, the Suez portion comprising *Andes*, *Strathaird*, *Otranto* and the two *Empress* liners, with the five MT ships, cleared the port as WS 2A during the evening of 30th August and were soon joined by *Shropshire* from Simonstown. (*Cornwall* was selected to return to Freetown.) In the early evening of 2nd September the two liners and *Kanimbla* joined from Durban in a position 120 miles SE of that port, and where the AMC detached to keep another rendezvous with WS 2B. The Suez portion passed up the Mozambique Channel and when north of the Comoro Islands at midday on the 7th, rendezvous was made with the cruiser *Ceres* which then detached with *Llangibby Castle* for Mombasa. The remainder of the convoy continued up the East African coast, assisted by a 3 knot favourable current and force 5 SW'ly monsoon wind and passed through the Guardafui Strait during the night of the 11th.

With the Italians in control of Eritrea and having recently bombed several British convoys in that vicinity, the escort was strengthened as the convoy passed through the Gulf of Aden and formed into three columns for the 10 mile wide Straits of Perim. *Shropshire*, *Hobart*, the AA cruiser *Coventry*, two AA sloops and three modern K class destroyers surrounded the convoy but no attacks developed. Perim was passed in the early hours of the 13th and thereafter *Andes* and the two *Empress* liners went on ahead at maximum speed with *Hobart*, *Coventry* and two of the destroyers to reach Suez before dark on the 15th. The remaining ships were dispersed in the early evening of the 14th and arrived at Suez on the morning of the 16th after a passage of exactly six weeks from the U.K. The pattern of WS troop convoys had now been established and was to severely tax Britain's maritime strength and strategy over the next three years.

With no suitable berths alongside for such large vessels, the six troopships of WS 2A were dealt with at the anchorage in Suez Bay, by the laborious and time consuming means of disembarking all of the troops and stores into dumb lighters towed by ancient steam tugs. When this had been completed, empty cargo spaces were loaded with whatever homeward cargoes were offered, mostly baled cotton which again was a lengthy business causing inordinate delay to such large expensive liners. Most of the ships also embarked small numbers of women and children being evacuated from Egypt and

Palestine to South Africa. The five MT ships which had been in WS 2A passed through the Suez Canal to discharge their military cargoes at Port Said and Alexandria: all but *Suffolk* were then retained in the Mediterranean for a number of fast supply convoys to Malta. Even as the liners lay at Suez, the next fast convoy from the U.K., numbered AP 1 and comprising *Duchess of Bedford* and two MT ships, arrived and passed into the canal to land troops and supplies at Port Said[14].

Meanwhile the Bombay section of the convoy, designated WS 2B and comprising *Orion, Ormonde, Batory* and *Stratheden*, left Capetown one day behind the others, the last ship clearing the berth in the afternoon of 31st August. *Cornwall* joined the convoy that evening some 30 miles WNW of the Cape of Good Hope where a cruising order of four columns was formed and speed set at 17 knots. Next day it blew hard from the NW which served to upset the pre-arranged rendezvous with *Kanimbla* some 350 miles SE of Durban; *Cornwall* had to break wireless silence to make contact and junction was made at noon on the 3rd and by which time there was fog with poor visibility. *Cornwall* then parted company and transmitted a signal to Simonstown stating the speed of *Kanimbla* was actually 2 knots less than the slowest ship and would prevent the convoy reaching Bombay until the morning of the 15th. Course was then set to pass 220 miles SE of the southern tip of Madagascar and thence up the east side of and midway between that island and Reunion.

The passage to Bombay was made in fine weather with very light winds. *Kanimbla* sighted a suspicious vessel on the morning of the 5th that proved to be Harrison's *Adviser* bound Durban from Mauritius. At dusk on the 8th another suspicious vessel was sighted 9 miles ahead on the same course as the convoy, which latter then turned 60° to starboard and held this for 10 miles until course was resumed to pass east of the Seychelles and direct for Bombay. The SE trades were then encountered and next day, the 9th, and to the south of the Seychelles, a W/T report was received from the tanker *Athelking* being attacked by a raider, 1,000 miles to the SE. Next day a W/T message from *Benarty* reported being bombed by aircraft from the raider in a position not far from that of *Athelking*. It was later established that the German raider *Atlantis* had sunk both these ships. No further incidents occurred, the patrol vessel guarding the Bombay searched channel was sighted at 0600 on the 15th and all ships were anchored in the harbour by 1030.

The arrival date of WS 2B at Bombay coincided with that of US 4 from the Antipodes, comprising *Aquitania, Mauretania, Empress of Japan* and *Orcades*. A complicated transhipment followed the arrival of these eight liners and caused many problems to the port and military authorities. From WS 2B *Batory* and *Stratheden* were continuing to Singapore and Australia, while *Orcades* from US 4 was returning to the U.K. Most of the Anzac troops on US 4 ships were on-carried to the Middle East by *Empress of Japan, Orion* and *Ormonde* as a new convoy BN 5.5. *Batory, Stratheden* and *Orcades* left Bombay as convoy BM 1 on 21st September carrying 2,800 troops and children for Singapore and Australia, together with families of the regular battalions and returning service personnel bound for the U.K. on *Orcades*. This convoy was escorted by the Australian AMC *Westralia* and reached Colombo on the 24th, where *Orcades* was detached to proceed independently to the U.K., bunkering en route at Capetown and Freetown, and thereafter escorted by the new cruiser *Kenya* and in company with *Strathaird*. *Orcades* secured to a buoy in the Clyde Emergency Port for discharge of Australian cargo within the Holy Loch on 5th November; *Strathaird* discharged South African cargo in Glasgow. Both were now allocated for WS 4B.

From Colombo, *Batory* and *Stratheden* were escorted to Singapore by the cruiser *Capetown*, being joined en route by the B.I. *Ellenga* carrying 845 officers and men of 5/7 Rajput Regiment from Madras to Hong Kong. After disembarking in Singapore, *Batory* and *Stratheden* continued to Fremantle escorted by the Australian AMC *Manoora* and reached that port to refuel on 9th October. *Batory* then proceeded to land part of her child evacuees, totalling 391, at Melbourne and Sydney, where she arrived on the 16th after a voyage of six weeks from the U.K. *Stratheden* disembarked 1,179 passengers, including those from *Orion*, at Adelaide, Melbourne and Sydney; both liners were retained in Australia for convoy US 7 to the Middle East.

In Suez Bay it took eight days to turn round the six transports of WS 2A which sailed together as the unescorted convoy SW 1 with two empty MT ships, *California Star* and *Suffolk* in the afternoon of 24th September. When clear of the Gulf of Suez next morning, three columns were formed with the Commodore on *Empress of Britain* leading the centre column. The northbound AP 2 convoy of two ships was then passed and four hours later *Hobart* caught up as escort, having been delayed fuelling at Suez. Next morning a K class destroyer joined and 24 hours later the northbound convoy BN 5.5 from Bombay was passed and from which two other K class destroyers with an A/A sloop transferred to SW 1. A speed of 13 knots was maintained, the convoy exited the Perim Straits at 1500 hours on the 27th without having seen enemy forces and two hours later the AMC *Kanimbla* relieved *Hobart* as ocean escort, while the destroyers and A/A sloop were retained until daybreak on the 29th at the eastern end of the Gulf of Aden. That evening *Suffolk* detached for Colombo and Australia and immediately after, the convoy turned SE into the Guardafui Straits and continued down the East African coast without incident, until noon on 3rd October when *Otranto* was detached into Mombasa to load a consignment of sisal and coffee for the U.K. The remaining six ships of SW 1 passed through the Mozambique Channel at an average speed of 15 knots, strong head winds and a heavy sea being encountered for the last twelve hours before reaching Durban in the early afternoon of 8th October. Here all of the five liners berthed alongside to refuel and load various quantities of cargo, mostly small consignments of sugar, maize, bonemeal, wattle extract and canned fruit; *Franconia* shipped a total of 2,550 tons. Most of their passengers were landed and replaced by similar numbers of service families and drafts for the U.K.; *Empress of Britain* having 220 aboard and *Franconia* 190.

Being almost devoid of passengers the liners were now directed to proceed unescorted and independently from Durban via Capetown to the U.K. *Andes* and the two *Empress* liners left Durban virtually together on the 9th with the former ship enjoying a friendly coastwise race with *Empress of Britain* which she won by two hours. Both liners left Capetown together on the 12th, fully bunkered and bound direct for Liverpool. Although proceeding independently, the two ships were never far apart and despite having to zigzag for long stretches of that voyage of 7,000 miles, would have reached Liverpool together on the same tide of 27th October, had fate not intervened. This was the period of increasing activity from Focke-Wulf Condor bombers in the Western Approaches and large unescorted liners, then very poorly armed for AA defence, were particularly vulnerable and very conspicuous targets. The tragic loss of the 42,348 tons *Empress of Britain* by this means highlighted the Condor as an extremely dangerous aircraft and against which the Admiralty had as yet no effective deterrent, other than adequate A/A armament which was not to become available in appreciable quantities until early 1942.

The Master of *Andes*, Captain T.J.C. Buret, described the loss of *Empress of Britain* in a poignant statement in the Royal Mail Company's war history, "On the last day of our voyage a painful impression was caused on board by the news that the *Empress of Britain* was lost. For the last seven months (convoys US 3 and WS 2) we have been in almost daily company with this magnificent vessel. At 0823 hours Captain Sapsworth sent his first message. At 0833 he asked for help. At 0843 he abandoned ship. He was only 60 miles astern of *Andes* and but for the circumstances I would have returned for the survivors. The weather was perfect and those who were in the boats would undoubtedly be rescued."[15]

When first attacked at 0820 on 26th October, the *Empress* was making 22 knots towards a position north of Tory Island, then distant 90 miles and from where in four hours time she would have turned east for Inishtrahull and the North Channel. Captain Sapsworth planned to reach the Bar Light Vessel and there pick up the Liverpool pilot just before midnight , and by 0800 next morning both the *Empress* and *Andes* would have been safely in the Gladstone Dock. Captain Sapsworth and the officers on the bridge of the *Empress* first saw an unidentified aircraft away to port and flying in the opposite direction, but then turned towards the ship from astern and as it dived, opened fire with a cannon simultaneously with the ship's 3-inch AA gun sited aft. The aircraft was a Condor and flew straight over the ship from stern to bow at a height of about 500 feet and released a bomb that struck the port side abreast the centre funnel, penetrated to the Mayfair Lounge where it exploded and started fires which spread rapidly on the mass of gilded woodwork. The midships upperworks were soon fiercely ablaze and giving off clouds of choking black smoke. The Condor made two more attacks dropping three bombs: one of which missed, the second hit the stern without exploding and rolled overboard while the third hit the after steering position, wrecked the 3-inch gun and started a fire which set off the 6-inch ammunition.

Within a short while the fire service main was wrecked, lighting and communications destroyed and ammunition exploding. The bridge had been machine-gunned wounding the Chief and 1st Officers but Captain Sapsworth directed defence tactics until the bridge itself collapsed and he ordered 'abandon ship' amidst the dense smoke which required the crew to wear gas masks to reach the boats. Within half an hour of the first attack 598 survivors of the total 643 persons on board got away in boats in a calm sea and by 1600 had all been picked up. The fires were now apparently abating and a decision was made to try and tow the hull to port. By noon the next day the Admiralty had two tugs connected to the now gutted and still burning ship and towed her 40 miles nearer to Tory Island. Two destroyers arrived to provide A/S escort but failed to prevent *U 32*, one of three directed to the scene, putting in a successful attack at 0200 on the 28th which sank the ship ten minutes later in a position 56 miles west of Tory Island, just within the 100 fathom line.

The official history summed it up thus, "the loss of this splendid ship - the only one of our 'giant liners' to fall victim to the enemy - was a tragedy. It underlined the effect to Britain of the lack of air and naval bases in western Ireland, from which all shipping passing close off those shores could have been so much better and more easily protected".[16] *U 32* was herself sunk two days later but a poor consolation for the loss of such a grand and valuable ship with a potential to carry 7,500 troops by the standards reached in 1943.

The remaining liners of SW 1 reached home without incident, *Empress of Canada* also steamed non-stop from Capetown to the Clyde where she arrived on the 29th and where her Master, Captain W.T. Kinley, retired to his home on the Isle of Man after a long career at sea which had begun 46 years earlier in sail. Coincidentally he had been Mate of the barque *County of Cardigan* in 1904 when the 2nd Mate was James Bissett and now Master of *Franconia*. *Strathaird*, *Otranto* and *Franconia* each called at Freetown to refuel and reached the Clyde by 8th November and berthed in Glasgow to discharge. All of the SW 1 liners, except *Franconia* which then carried reinforcements to Gibraltar, were next employed in convoy WS 4B to Suez.

AP 1 and 2 - sailed UK 22.8.40.

From the time of sailing WS 2 from the U.K. on 5th August until the next WS depar- ture in October, three additional small convoys were sent around the Cape with urgent- ly needed reinforcements requested by General Wavell, the C.-in-C.Middle East. On 10th August the C.I.G.S gave the Prime Minister a note of the units and equipment he was preparing to despatch whenever shipping and escorts were available[17], i.e. 3rd The King's Own Hussars, 2nd and 7th Royal Tank Regiment together with their respective tanks, field guns, anti-tank guns, Bofors AA guns, Bren guns, anti-tank rifles and a quan- tity of respective ammunition. The provision of shipping was simply met by choosing those most suitable and readily available from a then plentiful supply: in this instance the *Duchess of Bedford* inward bound on a commercial voyage from Montreal to Liverpool, whose accommodation was increased from 1,570 to provide space for over 2,000 personnel. The tanks, guns, motor transport and ammunition were to be carried on the fast cargo liners, *Waiotira* (17.5 knots), *Denbighshire* (18 knots), and *Sydney Star* (16.5 knots) all then conveniently berthed in Liverpool discharging inward cargoes. The cruiser tanks of 2nd RTR were to be loaded on the former ship, the light tanks of the Hussars on the latter and the heavy, 25 ton Matildas of the 7th RTR on *Denbighshire* that had the most suitable lifting gear. All of the personnel would embark on the 18 knot *Duchess of Bedford*.

Complications then arose when the Chiefs of Staff began to consider including the fast MT ships in a plan to pass naval reinforcements to the Eastern Mediterranean in conjunction with the delivery of stores to Malta from Alexandria, the whole operation codenamed 'Hats'. The departure of the naval units from the U.K. was set for 20th August; but only two of the MT ships could be ready by that time and so the Matilda tanks on *Denbighshire* would have to go around the Cape. The Prime Minister was nat- urally loath to part with these precious tanks from the U.K. at such a critical time and felt they should be passed through the Mediterranean and thus get into action at the ear- liest possible moment. The C.-in-C.Mediterranean Fleet, Admiral Cunningham, did not agree and signalled his views to Whitehall on the 11th, that the convoy of four 16 knot merchant ships (being the speed of the slowest), "might pass unscathed, or it might become a total loss"[17]. Next day General Wavell gave his considered opinion "that the risk of losing on passage through the Mediterranean a quantity of valuable equipment, much of which would take several months to replace, would not justify the gain in time"[17]. It was finally "agreed to defer the final decision on the route to be followed by the two fast ships (unnamed - but presumably *Denbighshire* and *Waiotira*) until the 26th, when the whole expedition would be at a point to the west of Gibraltar, where it could be divided, if necessary, into two portions"[17].

Although it was confirmed on three separate dates up to the 17th that *Duchess of Bedford* would sail with 'Group One', by then codenamed AP 1, she embarked and sailed alone on the 19th, only to be recalled to the Mersey next day to await completion of loading on the three MT ships. Also sailing with AP 1 from Liverpool was the battle-ship *Valiant* (for the Mediterranean), carrier *Argus* with aircraft for Takoradi, cruiser *Ajax*, seven destroyers and Burns Laird Irish Channel vessel *Royal Scotsman* carrying troops to Gibraltar. *Ajax* was to escort the single ship AP 2 portion all the way around the Cape to Suez, at a speed of 1 knot less than AP 1 and showed there was then, no shortage of cruisers.

All ships were ready to leave the Mersey on 20th August but departure was delayed by the weather, which prevented *Valiant* leaving Gladstone Dock. The five merchant ships and three fleet units finally sailed during the afternoon of the 22nd while on the same date other units for the Mediterranean Fleet left from Scapa. The two convoys AP 1 and 2 proceeded as one out of the North Channel until next afternoon and about 110 miles west of Tory Island, when the cruiser *York* joined from Scapa. The convoys then turned south and split into the pre-arranged portions, i.e. *York* escorting AP 1 comprising *Duchess of Bedford* (whose Master, Captain W.G. Busk-Wood, was appointed Commodore) with *Denbighshire* and *Waiotira*. AP 2 consisted of *Sydney Star* and *Royal Scotsman* escorted by *Ajax*.

By the 23rd General Wavell had returned to the Middle East, where the three C.inC.s reported they did not believe the Italians could be ready for an offensive into Egypt for several weeks. This had been the prime reason for the haste in obtaining reinforcements and acting on these opinions, the War Cabinet decided on the 26th, when AP 1 was approaching the latitude of Gibraltar, "that the army convoy should go round the Cape and might be expected to reach Suez about 24th September"[17]. *Valiant* and other naval reinforcements for the Mediterranean were detached as planned and AP 1 continued to Freetown without further incident, where *York* and *Duchess of Bedford* were fuelled and watered in the space of eight hours on 1st September, the MT ships having no requirements. The passage to Capetown was made in uniformly fine weather without incident, and where *York* left AP 1 at the end of the searched channel in the afternoon of the 9th and proceeded to Simonstown to refuel. The voyage was resumed next afternoon and after passing through the Guardafui Straits in daylight, due to the urgency of early arrival, the convoy was off Aden in the afternoon of the 20th, where *York* was relieved by *Hobart*. Two destroyers and the AA cruiser *Coventry* strengthened the escort in the Gulf of Aden, paravanes were streamed by the two cruisers approaching mineable waters off Perim and not recovered until north of Jabal Tair on the forenoon of the 21st. That afternoon the northbound convoy BN 5 was overtaken and soon after *Coventry* detached, followed by the destroyers next morning. The Gulf of Suez was entered at midday on the 23rd, when both MT ships streamed paravanes. The convoy reached Suez at 2230 hours that night, 32.5 days since leaving Liverpool and was a record passage never subsequently surpassed. All three ships of AP 1 passed through the canal next day, *Duchess of Bedford* taking four days to disembark and discharge military stores at Port Said before returning to Suez to rejoin the southbound SW 2. The troops and armoured units which she landed soon joined 3 and 4 Armoured Brigades in the Western Desert, and served with distinction ten weeks later in the December battles at Sidi Barrani and advance to El Agheila. The MT ships partly discharged in Port Said, Haifa and Alexandria and were then released to load homewards on their owners' berths.

Meanwhile convoy AP 2 had detached *Royal Scotsman* and *Argus* towards Gibraltar on 26th August and continued south to reach Freetown 24 hours behind AP 1 (and which had left again the previous evening). *Ajax* and *Sydney Star* refuelled and left Freetown on 3rd September for Durban; they left that port on the 13th and had an uneventful passage to the Gulf of Aden, where *Ajax* was relieved by *York* which came out of Aden with the B.I. *Amra* carrying motor transport loaded there for Port Said. Two destroyers then joined and as with AP 1, the AA cruiser *Coventry* also joined for the passage between Perim and the islands at the southern end of the Red Sea. Despite passing Perim in daylight the convoy was not attacked and reached Suez safely in the evening of 25th September to make an overnight transit to Port Said where *Sydney Star* berthed a mere 18 hours behind AP 1. *York* became a war loss at Suda Bay, Crete, six months later.

The second in the series of southbound convoys from Suez comprised *Empress of Japan*, *Orion* and *Ormonde* from BN 5.5 , *Duchess of Bedford* and *Waiotira* from AP 1 and *Amra* with *Sydney Star* from AP 2. All seven ships left Suez at 0600 on 8th October and had an unhindered passage down the Red Sea, being joined on the 10th by two BI. liners from Port Sudan, another of the same next morning while escort through the southern islands was provided by *Hobart*, the AA cruiser *Carlisle*, one destroyer and a sloop. When passing Aden on the 12th, *Sydney Star* detached with *Hobart* on being relieved by *Shropshire*, and nearing Guardafui next morning *Waiotira* and the four B.I. ships detached for Bombay. The four liners continued in convoy towards Durban, *Shropshire* was relieved by the AMC *Carthage* at midday on the 15th and next afternoon *Ormonde* detached for Mombasa to begin loading homeward cargo. *Carthage* and the other three liners continued to Durban arriving on the 22nd to refuel and disembark refugee women and children from Palestine and Egypt; *Empress of Japan* landing 138 and 222 respectively of these passengers.

Orion was now ordered direct to Sydney for employment in US 7 and left Durban on the 24th while *Duchess of Bedford* and *Ormonde* sailed on the same date as independent sailings for the U.K., the *Duchess* loading both at Durban and Capetown, fuelled at Freetown and reached Liverpool on 15th November to spend six weeks drydocking and fitting out for further trooping service. *Ormonde* also loaded in Durban and Capetown and on reaching Freetown on 8th November, was held there for ten days and sent on a coastwise trooping voyage to Takoradi, Accra and Lagos, before finally clearing Freetown for the Clyde and reached there on 10th December.

Empress of Japan also left Durban on the 24th, carrying a mere 90 passengers, and having a suitable speed and endurance was directed non-stop to the U.K., a distance by zigzag and evasive routing in excess of 8,000 miles and proved an uneventful passage until the morning of 9th November when attacked by a Focke-Wulf Condor in a position 230 miles SW of Tory Island. This was now the most dangerous part of all voyages in and out of the British Isles, exacerbated by the denial of bases in Southern Ireland as Churchill aptly noted - "All (shipping) had to come in around Northern Ireland, where, by the Grace of God, Ulster stood a faithful sentinel"[18].

The Condor which attacked *Empress of Japan* raked the ship with machine-gun fire and dropped a total of eight bombs, three very close to the port quarter with one glancing off a lifeboat and another striking the after rail before going overside. The resulting underwater explosions lifted the stern of the ship clean out of the water, sheared off part of the rudder, started valves and stern glands leaking and smashed the port tailshaft bearings which necessitated stopping that engine altogether. The starboard engine was kept going by posting gangs of men in the shaft tunnel to keep the bearings supplied from buckets of oil. Captain J.W. Thomas, a sail trained Newfoundlander who had served in the ship as 2nd Officer to command since 1935, ordered off a W/T report which was received by F.O.I.C. Clyde at 0945. Three tugs were soon despatched to assist while RAF Coastal Command directed Whitley aircraft to provide air cover but failed to locate the ship until late afternoon, and were at first fired upon until a Verey light satisfied the gun crew of their identity. By steaming on one engine the *Empress* maintained a speed of 15 knots and passed through the North Channel to anchor safely off Gourock at 1420 on the 10th. For his skill in bringing the ship safely to port, Captain Thomas was rightly awarded the CBE. He remained in command of the ship until retiring to his home in Vancouver at the end of her last trooping voyage in 1948.

Empress of Japan, however, could hardly have reached the U.K. at a worse time and was long overdue for boiler cleaning and drydocking that had last been carried out in Hong Kong 22 months previously. There were now major machinery repairs to be attended, tailshafts to be drawn and the rudder to be repaired which necessitated drydocking but none of those on the Clyde were large enough and none were vacant at Liverpool or Belfast. There were no vacant repair berths in Glasgow and the ship was too large for Greenock, nor was it desirable to shut down boilers and machinery in the congested Clyde Anchorage. The problem was solved by simply placing the ship over sandbanks adjacent to the Tail of the Bank anchorage and close to the Greenock shore, where the *Empress* was anchored barely afloat at high water but safely fast on the bottom for the rest of each successive tide. While in this berth for the next three weeks, gangs of Fairfield's men were ferried out daily by motor launch from Princes Pier to work on essential repairs, for boiler cleaning and increasing the trooping capacity. On 1st December the *Empress* was drydocked at Belfast for underwater repairs, survey and bottom painting that was completed in time to sail with WS 5B.

A further reinforcement convoy for the Middle East was to follow the departure of AP 1 and 2 on 22nd August. Six days earlier the War Office issued instructions to investigate the provision of fast ships to carry personnel and certain equipment including anti-tank guns to the Middle East as rapidly as possible. On 23rd August it was confirmed the convoy would consist of four MT and three personnel ships sailing as AP 3.

AP 3 - sailed UK 10.9.40.

This urgent matter of additional reinforcements had been raised at Cabinet level and Mr. Eden, Secretary of State for War, wrote personally to H.V. Alexander, First Lord of the Admiralty on 23rd August explaining the reasons and urgency for the convoy which was to sail on 6th September. AP 3 "was considered outside the normal convoy programmeí and Eden asked for special escort arrangements despite "the additional burden upon the Royal Navy". Next day the Admiralty signalled the C.inC.SA asking for *Cornwall* or *Shropshire* then with WS 2 to return to Freetown and meet AP 3, from which *Cornwall* was selected There was also difficulty in finding cruiser escort for AP 3 from the U.K. to Freetown because of commitments to the impending Operation Menace at Dakar. Consideration was given to using one or two AMCs but on the 28th the Admiralty approved the cruiser *Newcastle* to escort the convoy as far as the Azores, from where *Sheffield* of the Mediterranean Force H would take over but in the event both cruisers remained on their respective stations leaving the convoy with AMCs.

The four MT ships *Brisbane Star, Imperial Star, Clans Campbell* and *Macarthur* were selected for the convoy and all were on their loading berths in Liverpool by 1st September and completed to capacity by the sailing date which was eventually fixed for the 10th. This was achieved in spite of air raids and rail delays which accounted for an average loss of two hours work per day on seven out of the ten loading days. The personnel ships embarked on the 7th and 8th and also loaded 370 tons of stores and equipment. The liners were requisitioned on 24th August, *Britannic, Dominion Monarch* and

Athlone Castle all then in Liverpool, the latter fitting-out as a troopship, while the first two were discharging from New York and Australia/New Zealand respectively. Also being included was *Durban Castle* still then employed on the South African mail service and discharging in Glasgow but sent to Liverpool to prepare for embarkation. A late and unusual inclusion was the Irish Channel ship *Ulster Prince* bound for the Middle East for use there on short sea personnel service. A further last minute addition was the Blue Funnel steamer *Glaucus* bound for the Far East[19].

The convoy cleared the Bar Light Vessel at 1800 on 10th September, escorted by five destroyers with the Commodore, Rear Admiral (Rtd) R.A. Creighton, embarked on *Britannic* while Captain Alderson of *Athlone Castle* acted as Vice Commodore. A speed of 14 knots was kept up through the Irish Sea and North Channel to Inishtrahull, where next forenoon *Ulster Prince* and the AMC *Cilicia* joined from the Clyde. The convoy proceeded out to the westward until next evening when some 400 miles west of Tory Island, where the destroyers detached back to base and the convoy turned south towards Freetown. (20)

At 1000 on the 13th the AMC *Wolfe* (ex CPS *Montcalm*) joined the convoy direct from the Clyde, having been delayed repairing and in substitution for *Canton*. Both *Cilicia* and *Wolfe* had been employed on the North Atlantic and were now being re-deployed to the Freetown area; *Cilicia* took station 2 miles on the port bow of the convoy and *Wolfe* a similar distance to starboard. Despite the moderate convoy speed of 14 knots, *Clan Campbell* (assumed to be burning coal) could not maintain that speed and broke down prior to *Wolfe* joining and did not regain the convoy until arrival in Freetown.[19]

There were no untoward incidents on the passage to Freetown; Rear Admiral Creighton recorded some impressions in his memoirs - "our passage proceeded smoothly...as we approached the tropics our blue uniforms gave way to whites while vests and pullovers disappeared into the bottom of our chests of drawers. For the soldiers, most of whom had never left England before, it was a pleasant change to be lazing in the fierce heat of the sun and there was keen competition to see who could get the best tan. Despite lurid warnings from officers and NCOs to take care if they wanted to sunbathe, and to do so only for short periods until they were acclimatized, there were numerous young men wandering around with bright pink blistered bodies feeling very sore and sorry for themselves. But by the time they reached Suez most had achieved their aims and were a healthy brown colour."[21]

During the night of the 22nd *Athlone Castle* dropped astern due to engine trouble and at daybreak next morning, a flying-boat air escort met the convoy at the outer end of Freetown searched channel and where also *Cilicia* was sent back to escort the lame *Athlone Castle*, while *Glaucus* parted company to proceed independently to Capetown. All ships were anchored in Freetown harbour by mid forenoon on the 23rd, the last being *Cilicia* and *Athlone Castle*. *Clan Campbell* did not arrive until 24 hours later and was instructed to continue independently to Durban.

The difficulties of obtaining sufficient fresh water at Freetown has already been mentioned, but was yet unknown on *Britannic* designed to sustain 1,500 passengers for five days across the North Atlantic and now carrying 2,600 trooops on a 15 day passage to Freetown. The troops "revelled in being able to have as much water as they liked and there was no means of rationing them."[21] *Britannic* "arrived at Freetown with tanks almost dry." With the stability of his ship and the needs of troops and crew in mind, Captain Brown rightly insisted on having his fresh water tanks filled, "and refused to sail further...until his requirements were fully met". Using the small local water boats would have taken days, in the end the Navy solved the problem "by using a RFA tanker which had just discharged fuel oil at Freetown. This ship was filled with fresh water and pumped into the Cunarder, apparently without first steam-cleaning the tanks; in any event *Britannic* received her water heavily tainted with the residue of the fuel oil. The convoy left for Capetown on time but many of the young soldiers who had recovered from the first normal bout of seasickness, now found themselves violently upset by oil-gripe from the water they had to drink...luckily no one had any permanent ill effects."[21] The Commodore also drew attention to another problem which beset North Atlantic liners on tropical voyages - their lack of fans or forced draught ventilation in the passenger accommodation. "As such, the living quarters on *Britannic* were designed to be snug and warm in high latitudes, but in the tropics were like ovens."[21]

Convoy AP 3 left Freetown on the morning of 25th September escorted by the AMC *Carnarvon Castle*, who reported that *Clan Campbell* left harbour with the convoy but did not form up and was lost sight of astern that afternoon. On the first night out, *Ulster Prince* dropped astern, was sighted again next morning but fell out of sight that afternoon and did not rejoin until reaching Capetown. The AMC *Canton* joined as SOE during the afternoon of the 27th, having been delayed repairing at the Tail of the Bank until the 13th, when she steamed at full speed to Freetown to catch up the convoy and now took station on the starboard bow with *Carnarvon Castle* on the port bow. On the morning of 1st October, *Clan Macarthur* fell behind but remained in sight until the following afternoon and did not rejoin until Capetown. The searched channel to that port was reached on the morning of the 4th where *Canton* detached for Simonstown while *Carnarvon Castle* remained to berth with the convoy inside the docks that afternoon. The average speed made good from Freetown to the Cape was 15 knots.[20]

At Capetown it was decided to split the convoy by forming the two wayward *Clans* and *Ulster Prince*, which could not maintain 15 knots, into convoy AP 3.5; in the event only *Clan Macarthur* proceeded by this means as the other two were delayed by boiler and engine trouble respectively but all three had reached Suez by 2nd November. *Durban Castle* left the convoy by disembarking at Capetown and transhipped all her 468 troops to the remaining three liners before continuing as a mail ship to Port Elizabeth and Durban, where she was again requisitioned to carry South African troops to Mombasa. The balance of this convoy AP 3 now of three liners and two Blue Star MT ships left Capetown on 6th October for Suez, escorted initially by the AMCs *Canton* and *Carthage*.

Admiral Creighton fondly recalled the passage up the east coast of Africa in his memoirs, "by now the convoy was well clear of the area where there was any likelihood of being attacked by submarines and the risk of meeting a surface raider was slight....the normal wartime risks seemed far away. And in the glorious tropical weather, with warm sun and cool breezes made by the ship, Captain Brown and I could thoroughly enjoy our forenoon drink when the sun was over the foreyard."[21]

In the vicinity of Durban the AMC *Canton* was relieved by the light cruiser *Ceres*, which remained until the 8-inch cruiser *Shropshire* took over on 15th October on the latitude of Mogadishu and where also *Carthage* was detached. The convoy passed through the Guardafui Strait during the night of the 16/17th, and in the Gulf of Aden the escort was strengthened by the AA cruiser *Carlisle* and three destroyers. The Straits of Perim were negotiated at 2100 on the 18th and at 0900 next day in the vicinity of Centre Peak island, an Italian aircraft dropped three bombs on the convoy from a very great height - quite out of range for *Shropshire* and *Carlisle* which did not bother to open fire. The bombs fell and exploded near *Carlisle* but no damage resulted. The explosion "brought the troops crowding to the rails of the ships to see what was happening. After a few minutes, as there was no firing and the plane had gone, they drifted away to get on with their drills and lectures on desert warfare."[21]

An Italian submarine was falsely reported at the entrance to the Gulf of Suez but the convoy passed through at 2000 on the 21st unhindered. The ships were anchored in Suez Bay by 0800 on 22nd October 42 days after leaving Liverpool. The troops had arrived in excellent health and began to disembark at once in the usual fashion by tugs, lighters and pontoons. The two MT ships first discharged some stores in Suez Bay then transited the canal to complete discharge of their military cargoes at Port Said and Alexandria.

Having disembarked and discharged at Suez in the leisurely space of six days, the three liners of AP 3 now joined with the Dutch liners *Christiaan Huygens, Indrapoera, Nieuw Holland* and *Slamat* which had arrived with Australian troops in convoy US 5, to form the southbound convoy SW 2A which sailed at 1500 on the 28th with Rear Admiral Creighton now aboard *Athlone Castle* as Commodore. *Britannic* was delayed awaiting her laundry, considered essential as she was now embarked with 1,400 women and children passengers. The cruiser *Kent*, having been damaged in the Mediterranean by an Italian torpedo-bomber, left Suez with the convoy as ocean escort en route to Simonstown and the U.K. for repairs. All ships were in ballast except *Dominion Monarch* which carried some outward general cargo consigned to Australian ports.

The convoy passed down the Gulf of Suez swept channel at a speed of 15 knots and cleared the Straits of Gubal at 0430 next morning when a cruising order of three columns was formed. *Britannic* caught up and took station at noon on the 30th, by which time the convoy was almost abeam of Port Sudan and where the northbound US 5A was passed and from which *Shropshire, Carlisle* and the sloop *Flamingo* transferred to stiffen the defence in the southern half of the Red Sea. No attacks developed, air escort was provided in the afternoon of the 31st and by 0500 on 1st November the convoy had cleared the Straits of Perim and turned into the Gulf of Aden without interference. *Britannic* was detached into Aden for bunkers that morning and by noon the convoy was 50 miles south of Aden, from where it was to proceed to the NE of Socotra and disperse. However, with no enemy activity evident the convoy was dispersed at sunset that evening, the four Dutch liners bound for Bombay where they were to embark Australian troops of US 6 for the Middle East. Admiral Creighton noted that "the signals observed in parting company show the good spirit obtaining between the British and Dutch ships."[21]

Dominion Monarch refuelled in Colombo before proceeding to discharge in Australian ports and was then requisitioned for service in US 8. *Athlone Castle* now alone, proceeded first to Mombasa for a paltry 250 tons of bagged coffee and was there released from requisition but taken up again while on passage to Durban. She then loaded in the Natal port, at Port Elizabeth and Capetown, leaving the latter on 23rd November direct for Liverpool. No incidents occurred on this passage but Rear Admiral Creighton concluded his narrative of the voyage with thoughts on reaching the North West approaches, "for Captain Alderson...the worst part of the voyage was *Athlone Castle's* dash through the danger zone at night with the ship darkened and showing no lights. This he found a great strain with always in the forefront of his mind the possibility of collision with another darkened vessel. But fortune favoured us and we arrived safely in the Mersey on 10th December, in good time for some to proceed on Christmas leave."[21] *Britannic* had a similar homeward voyage loading at Mombasa, Durban and Capetown, leaving the latter two days behind *Athlone Castle* but taking two days longer for the direct passage to Liverpool. Both liners were next employed in WS 5B back to Suez.

Chapter 5

Departures in October & November 1940
WS 3S & F, WS 4A & B

2 Armoured Division and 18 Australian Brigade move to the Middle East

WS 3S - sailed UK 3.10.40 and WS 3F - sailed 5.10.40.
The next Middle East convoy, WS 3, left the U.K. in two sections at the beginning of October 1940 after the Battle of Britain had become the general Blitz which rained on the country for a further seven months. Clydeside was bombed in September, Liverpool in October and in that same month the U-Boats caused the highest rate of shipping losses up until that time.

WS 3 was split into a slow section of 14 knots and another of 18 knots separated by a mere four days when leaving the U.K. and did not form into a combined convoy until reaching the Mozambique Channel four weeks later. Twice the number of escorts was thus required to protect both sections of the convoy at a time when cruisers were critically short - in November especially no escorts could be found for three portions of homeward convoys from Freetown. Bad weather, poor communications, enemy action, and a lack of information all contributed to one troopship of this convoy proceeding virtually all the way to Freetown without escort, and three others being similarly "on their own" for the first four days after leaving the North Channel. A total of 7,650 troops were carried aboard these four liners whose passage occurred at a time when the U-Boats first began to operate as a pack in the Western Approaches and although none mercifully located these liners, more than twenty other lesser ships were then torpedoed and sunk. With the whole country and the armed forces having been geared up for defence against the planned German invasion, all resources were allocated accordingly leaving many records of this period incomplete, some records are missing or perhaps never existed which includes some sections of the early WS convoys.

The slow portion of WS 3 was to comprise four MT ships and two personnel ships, the PSNC *Oropesa* of 14 knots and Royal Mail *Highland Brigade* of 15.5 knots. Both liners were requisitioned and fitted for trooping while discharging in Liverpool during the second half of September; the former to accommodate 1,936 troops and *Highland Brigade* 1,150. Of the MT ships, three loaded in Liverpool while *Clan Cameron* was handled in Newport and sailed north to join the remaining ships at the Bar Light Vessel outside Liverpool at 1300 on 2nd October. *Highland Brigade* was delayed storing and being unable to leave until that evening, was at first advised that a destroyer would join at the Bar and provide onward escort to join the others, but this was later cancelled by verbal instructions that the entire convoy sailing had been delayed 12 hours due to engine trouble on *Clan Cameron*. The sailing time was re-arranged for 0100 on the 3rd to include all six ships.[1]

Highland Brigade duly anchored at the Bar late evening on the 2nd and made unsuccessful attempts to communicate with the Commodore (of unknown identity) on *Oropesa* and the SOE. However, the convoy appears to have sailed as intended at 0100 on the 3rd, including *Highland Brigade* which proceeded at maximum speed on the first course given in the convoy instructions but failed to locate or join the other ships or escort, and having regard to the number of troops on board, Captain Cocks put the ship about at 0230 and returned to an anchorage at the Bar as he had insufficient information on the organization of the convoy to have allowed proceeding further in darkness[1]. It may also be assumed that neither the Commodore nor the SOE were aware of the intended later inclusion of *Highland Brigade*. Arthur Cocks had twenty years experience as Master with Royal Mail Lines and was no stranger to naval procedures in holding the rank of Captain RNR. After reaching retiral age in 1942, he served for the rest of the war as Commodore of convoys.

When daylight came Captain Cocks requested instructions from the examination vessel and at 1500 a destroyer returned from the convoy to provide escort. *Highland Brigade* then got under way and proceeded at maximum speed to catch up the convoy. When abreast of Inishtrahull at 0400 on the 4th, a second destroyer joined and for the next two days bad weather was encountered with no observations possible although the courses given in the convoy instructions were followed as closely as possible. By noon on the 5th *Highland Brigade* was south of the Rockall Bank where one of the destroyers parted company and at 1600 the remaining destroyer signalled that the convoy was approximately 80 miles ahead and at 0800 next day that destroyer also departed at the limit of her endurance, leaving the troopship alone and unescorted in a position some 400 miles west of the Shannon Estuary. Daybreak revealed no sign of the convoy but at 1600 and by then on the latitude of the Scillies, the masthead lookout reported a warship and several smudges of smoke. Captain Cocks sent an officer aloft who confirmed the warship, apparently a small vessel, but did not see the smoke smudges (which may well have been clouds). The small warship was lost sight of before dark, but at 1800 a periscope was seen two points abaft the starboard beam, distant 8 cables.[2] The report was made by two reliable men stationed at the 6-inch gun and although the sighting was not further confirmed, W/T silence was immediately broken with an SSS (submarine report) and a zigzag commenced. *Highland Brigade* was clearly in a dangerous area to be without escort, the tanker *British General* was torpedoed and sunk about the same time in a position 130 miles further north and close to where *Highland Patriot* had met the same fate five days earlier.

By good fortune no attack developed on *Highland Brigade* that for the next 36 hours continued to the southward adhering to the route instructions and slowly catching up the daily rendezvous positions but failing to sight the convoy. At 0400 on the 8th, stellar observations confirmed the ship to be 300 miles north of the Azores and on the course line but ahead of the convoy. Captain Cocks put the ship about and retraced the course for about two hours without sighting the convoy before resuming the original course. That same afternoon when about 100 miles north of Flores, the most westerly of the Azores group, *Highland Brigade* was missed by the track of a torpedo that passed close astern. The track was clearly seen by the starboard lookouts, by men on the gun decks aft and by several officers both ship's, military and naval. A swirl was seen about two points abaft the starboard beam, distant 8 cables[2], from which the torpedo was reckoned to emanate. Italian submarines were known then to have operated in that area although no sinkings were made that day. *Highland Brigade* reached Freetown without further incident on the 16th a few hours ahead of the convoy.

The convoy itself had sailed as previously noted from the Bar Light Vessel at 0100 on 3rd October, escorted by four H and two V and W class destroyers and with the Commodore on *Oropesa*, while the Master of the MT ship *Perthshire* acted as Vice Commodore. The MT ships *Clan Cameron*, *Dorset* and *Port Chalmers* completed the five ship formation whose cruising order is unknown. Somewhere in the Western Approaches the cruiser *Sheffield* joined as ocean escort, accompanied by the destroyer depot ship *Woolwich* then on passage to Capetown and the Mediterranean. During a gale on the night of the 4th, the destroyer escorts parted company, and when about 200 miles south of the Azores at 1700 on the 9th, *Sheffield* was relieved by the heavy cruiser *Cumberland* (latterly involved in the Dakar expedition) which continued with the convoy until reaching the Indian Ocean. Freetown was reached on the 16th where *Highland Brigade* finally joined up. After fuelling and watering to requirements the now complete WS 3(S) sailed from Freetown next day, 17th October, and reached Capetown ten days later, being delayed somewhat on the 24th by defective boilers on *Woolwich*. The average speed from Liverpool to Freetown had been 12.74 knots and from the latter to Capetown 13.79 knots.

We must now revert to the fast section of the convoy, known as WS 3F, comprising seven liners of which three were requisitioned for the first time on 14th September; *Capetown Castle* and *Winchester Castle* both from the South African mail service, the former making her second call at Liverpool and the latter about to make her second visit to Glasgow. Neither was converted for trooping but carried only their peacetime complement of service personnel as far as Capetown for on-carriage there by other vessels, also *Orontes* of the Orient Line, partly fitted for trooping while discharging from Australia in Liverpool. To relieve congestion in that port, *Capetown Castle* left the Mersey on 28th September to embark at the Clyde Anchorage, where also *Georgic* had been sent, while *Oronsay* moved up from Liverpool on 1st October to embark in Glasgow astern of *Winchester Castle* in KGV Dock. The remaining liners to complete the convoy were *Monarch of Bermuda* and *Duchess of York* which both embarked in Liverpool. An estimated 13,000 personnel were embarked on these liners whose speeds ranged from 18 to 20 knots and was therefore to be a fast convoy. No MT ships were included.[3]

The ships from Liverpool left the Mersey at 1230 on 7th October and formed up off the Bar Light Vessel at 1600 with the Commodore, Vice-Admiral F A Somerville on *Orontes* (Captain G.G. Thorne) and escorted by the destroyers *Douglas* and *St. Laurent*. A fine passage was enjoyed until the early hours of the next morning when bad weather was encountered in the North Channel, with a strong westerly wind that increased as the morning progressed, reducing the convoy speed and causing *St. Laurent* to fall out and return to harbour when holed by the steady pounding in the head seas and swell. This destroyer was soon followed by *Douglas*, leaving the three liners bereft of A/S cover while eagerly expecting to meet and join with the Clyde section. A flotilla of east-bound ex-American destroyers was met during the morning that mistakenly reported when signalled that they had not seen the other section of the convoy. The Commodore therefore turned astern of them until informed that that section was actually ahead and to the westward (and was then undoubtedly correct).

While these vulnerable unescorted liners were searching the Western Approaches for their consorts, the Clyde portion was also having problems of which bad weather proved of least importance. The Canadian destroyer *Ottawa* led the Clyde portion out of the Clyde boom gate at 1900 on the 7th, with *Oronsay*, (whose Master, Captain AE Nicholls, was to act as Vice Commodore of the convoy) ahead of *Capetown Castle*, *Georgic*, and *Winchester Castle*. Pilots were landed off Ascog where the destroyer *Active* joined and the convoy proceeded out of the Clyde searched channel in single line ahead at 17 knots with one destroyer close-to on each bow of *Oronsay*. It appears that the Clyde section passed out of the North Channel one or two hours ahead of the Liverpool portion with the distance apart increasing as the day progressed.

Ottawa was designated SOE of the Clyde portion and much of the following is taken from the report of her Commanding Officer. Daybreak on the 8th found this group about 25 miles NW of Inishtrahull with the Commodore on *Oronsay* far ahead of the others and ordered to reduce to 10 knots to allow them to catch up. There was no sign of the Liverpool section that *Ottawa* presumed should then have joined, but three additional destroyers joined at 0700; one being *Arrow* that took over the duties of SOE from *Ottawa*. The increased escort took up screening positions around the four ship convoy which was then formed in single line abreast. By 0800 the westerly wind had reached force 6 and by 0900 *Ottawa* reported that *Oronsay* had begun to drop astern. It later transpired that *Oronsay* had asked permission (from an unidentified source) to reduce speed for her surgeon to attend a badly injured seaman. Strangely there is no record of a destroyer being detached to stand by her.

Just over an hour later, at 1015 according to *Ottawa's* report and by which time the convoy was 70 miles NW of Tory Island and now clear of the land, a large four-engined bomber (presumably a Focke-Wulf Condor) approached *Capetown Castle*, the starboard wing ship, from astern and flying low dropped one bomb which missed about 50 yards astern and then turned back to the eastward. *Ottawa* closed *Capetown Castle* but no damage was reported or assistance requested. It may be reasonably assumed that *Oronsay* had then fallen so far astern as to have been virtually out of sight, but in any event, at the same reported time of 1015, *Oronsay* transmitted a W/T report of having been bombed and "requiring immediate assistance". This report was received by the Admiralty who immediately ordered out three tugs and, within half an hour, also directed the destroyers *Verity* and *Sabre* and inbound AMC *Cheshire* to the scene. At 1120 the Admiralty confirmed that three ocean-going rescue tugs had sailed from Greenock while another was under orders to follow.

For some unexplained reason no action was taken by the convoy escort to assist *Oronsay* until 1050, when the SOE on *Arrow* ordered *Ottawa* "to take *Active* under orders and close *Oronsay* in need of immediate assistance."[4] *Ottawa* in turn ordered *Active*, who misread the signal and remained with the convoy, while *Ottawa* proceeded alone towards *Oronsay* at 20 knots and found her less than half an hour later about 10 miles to the eastward. In respect of visual signalling in these conditions, it should be appreciated the destroyers were pitching heavily in head seas and swell, their open bridges frequently smothered in spray, and made both the transmission and receipt of messages by lamp extremely difficult. Even aboard the liners with bridges high above sea level, howling and screeching head winds may well have prevented audible detection of the Condor bomber until almost overhead, while ships stationed two or three columns distant may not even have seen or heard the aircraft.

The situation of *Oronsay* lying stopped in the Western Approaches, wallowing in a high westerly sea and swell with 2,500 troops aboard was perilous indeed. At 1108 she reported "her engines disabled but hoped to get going on one in about an hour."[4] *Ottawa* began an A/S sweep around the liner but felt the greatest danger in the prevailing bad weather was from further air attack. No details are given of the damage suffered by *Oronsay* but may have been similar to the near-miss bombs that had previously caused misalignment of shafting and machinery on *Empress of Japan* and *Franconia*. *Oronsay* later reported having a few casualties although the hull was intact. At 1152 *Ottawa* reported that *Active* had joined her but was later identified as the SOE on *Arrow* and confirms the difficulty of identification in the conditions then prevailing.

The Admiralty meanwhile took further steps for the protection of *Oronsay* and at 1615 confirmed the AA cruiser *Cairo* had left Belfast and was due to reach the disabled ship at 0730 next day. At about 1400 the AMCs *Cheshire* and *Salopian* (ex-*Shropshire*) reached *Oronsay*; the former was ordered to remain with her, while *Salopian*, outbound for the Northern Patrol, was "to join an outward convoy of three ships proceeding westward at 10 knots and to escort them until further notice."[4] The rendezvous position given to *Salopian* was 36 miles WSW of *Oronsay* and corresponds to the estimated position of the three ship unescorted Liverpool section of WS 3F. There is no record of *Salopian* actually locating those liners that must have continued unescorted for the next few days.

After lying disabled for almost five hours, *Oronsay* was able to get under way at 1440 and proceed at 9 knots towards the Clyde with *Cheshire* and the destroyers as escort. Soon after, *Ottawa* reported sighting the Liverpool portion of the convoy with the destroyer "*Douglas* well astern"[4] and being unable to keep up joined the screen around *Oronsay*. *Ottawa* then sped off to a plane seen to crash into the sea about a mile northwards but found neither wreckage nor survivors. At 1900 the destroyers *Verity* and *Sabre* relieved *Ottawa* and *Arrow* and together with *Cheshire* continued with *Oronsay* to the Clyde Anchorage where she arrived safely just after midday on the 9th. First her casualties and then all of the troops were disembarked, *Oronsay* was then surveyed for damage repairs but was unable to obtain a berth in Glasgow until the end of the month and with a further wait for drydocking was out of service for the next eight months. After more than two years in command of *Oronsay*, and having survived this and the previous bombing at St. Nazaire and successfully making port safely on both occasions, Captain Nicholls now proceeded on leave and was thereafter appointed to *Orontes*.

The reader must now return to the remaining three liners of the Clyde portion that had continued westward after *Oronsay* fell out, and by noon on that day was 120 miles WNW Tory Island, still escorted by *Active*, *Achates* and *Whitehall* and known to be well ahead of the three ship Liverpool section. The pre-arranged rendezvous for the combined convoy was at 0900 next day in a position 470 miles west of Inishtrahull[5], where the cruiser *Kenya* was to take over as ocean escort for the passage to Freetown. *Kenya* was a new ship, the second Colony class cruiser to come into service and had been working up at Scapa which she had left in the evening of the 7th and battled through a SW'ly gale outside Lewis and Rockall to keep the rendezvous; her port whaler being stove in by heavy seas en route. *Kenya* made the rendezvous position on time but found nothing, and after patrolling the immediate area the Clyde section was sighted at noon, having been delayed by the bad weather which now reached a full gale and continued throughout that day. Course was now set to the SW and at 1400 the two remaining destroyers (one being *Active*) were detached with the comment that they "had done very well to remain with the convoy so long in the heavy seas."[6] Speed had then to be reduced to 14 knots as *Georgic* became unmanageable on certain legs of the zizag. Sometime later *Active* reported by W/T to *Kenya* that she had passed the Liverpool portion 37 miles astern.

By noon next day, the 10th, *Kenya* and the three liners were 600 miles west of Ireland and altered course to the SSW for the most westerly of the Azores group. The gale gradually moderated allowing the speed to be increased accordingly to 17.5 knots, the maximum of *Georgic*. During the afternoon *Kenya* searched unsuccessfully to the eastward for the Liverpool portion. Visibility was only moderate and although she carried a Walrus aircraft, the bad weather precluded its operation and subsequent recovery by crane from the water. Strong southerly winds prevailed next morning and with the visibility under 10 miles another search for the Liverpool portion also proved fruitless. Fine weather was finally met on the morning of the 12th when north of the Azores; course was reversed at 0900 and fifty minutes later the Liverpool section was sighted ahead. The convoy was now amalgamated into three columns each of two liners by midday and at 1900, when 40 miles west of Flores, course was altered to SSE to pass west of the Cape Verde islands. Moderate SW winds with a slight sea prevailed for the next two days. *Kenya* catapulted a Walrus for reconnaissance on the 13th but the wings of this aircraft were damaged during recovery and rendered it unserviceable. The convoy changed formation to two columns for a time but was found to cause excessive straggling.

The morning of the 15th brought very fine weather with maximum visibility and allowed the troops out on deck for exercise in the warm sunshine and a welcome change from the bad weather and discomfort in the troopdecks that had prevailed until then. By noon on the 17th the convoy had averaged almost 17.5 knots during the past three days, the Cape Verdes were passed at a distance of 60 miles next morning when course was altered for the last leg of the voyage to Freetown. The weather then became overcast with rain squalls and moderate winds. At 1100 on the 18th with the approach to soundings the convoy formed into two columns and by 1230 the high mountainous land to the north of Freetown was sighted over 60 miles distant in extreme visibility, while passing a homeward SL convoy of eleven ships. The convoy entered the searched channel at 1430 and by 1600 was passing through the boom to anchor in Freetown harbour for water and fuel. The slow portion of WS 3 had sailed on the previous day for the Cape. While the six liners completed replenishment, *Kenya* was relieved of the escort by the heavy cruiser *Dorsetshire* and returned to the U.K. to join the Home Fleet. The convoy was underway again on the morning of the 20th to pass out of the boom at 0800 and formed into a two column cruising order two hours later.[7] Course was held to the westward to gain the maximum offing before settling onto a SE'ly heading at 1500 for the Cape. There were no incidents during this leg of the voyage, darkened ships were met and illuminated for identification on two occasions, three others were identified in daylight hours and the battleship *Royal Sovereign* was passed bound north on the 27th. After a very fine passage the convoy arrived in Capetown on the forenoon of 28th October having averaged just over 17 knots from Freetown; *Dorsetshire* proceeding to Simonstown.

At Capetown the four MT ships and two troopships of WS 3(Slow) were already in port, and here also *Capetown* and *Winchester Castles* left the convoy to return home, being fully requisitioned for trooping en route. Their troops were transferred to the B.I. *Erinpura* and an ex-Egyptian (though B.I. managed) *Khedive Ismail* for on-carriage to Mombasa, which showed the need for the transhipment organization later set up at the Cape for this very purpose. As the troops and crews enjoyed a welcome break ashore on South African soil, the remaining four liners of WS 3F, now strangely re-styled WS 3B, were watered, fuelled and provisioned, and sailed from Capetown at midday on the 30th to meet *Dorsetshire* off Cape Point an hour later when speed was increased to 16.5 knots. A wide berth was given to Cape Agulhas and a distance of 60 miles maintained off the Cape coast until north of East London, when the route became NE towards the Madagascar side of the Mozambique Channel and where, at 0800 on 3rd November, junction was finally made with the eight ships of the slow portion WS 3A.[8]

WS 3A had left Capetown on the morning of 29th October comprising *Oropesa*, *Highland Brigade*, *Erinpura*, *Khedive Ismail* and the three MT ships (*Clan Cameron* having been delayed for boiler repairs). Escort was still provided by the cruiser *Cumberland* which remained with the convoy until relieved by the AMC *Carthage* to the south of Durban late on the 31st. The inclusion of *Erinpura* with a maximum speed of 13.3 knots caused a delay to the convoy, but when junction was made with the fast section (above - WS 3B), *Erinpura* and *Khedive Ismail* dropped astern with the AMC *Carthage* to follow in the wake of the main convoy and proceed direct to Mombasa, where they arrived to disembark their troops on the morning of the 7th. The former was then released from requisition and returned independently to Bombay, while *Khedive Ismail* continued to Suez with South African troops from Mombasa.

After amalgamation of the convoys and detachment of the Mombasa bound ships on 3rd November, the nine ships of WS 3 proceeded at 14 knots towards the Mozambique Channel with *Dorsetshire* as escort. During that afternoon *Georgic* and *Duchess of York* moved ahead of the convoy with *Dorsetshire*, which catapulted an aircraft to act as A/S escort while the two liners stopped and nurses were transferred by the cruiser's cutter from *Georgic* to the CPS ship, to assist a Nursing Matron reported suffering from an haemorrhage. At dawn next morning the convoy was halfway through that Channel when *Oropesa* began to make continuous dense smoke despite making her utmost speed and being astern of station. The convoy speed was reduced accordingly to 13.5 knots that proved critical for the Doxford engines of *Port Chalmers* that had to make bursts of 14 and 9.5 knots to avoid vibration. That evening *Dorsetshire* illuminated a sight from the past in way of the Finnish four masted barque *Pamir* under sail for Auckland.

During the afternoon of the 5th a man fell overboard from *Monarch of Bermuda* but was successfully picked up, and that evening after clearing the Comoro Channel course was shaped to pass NE of Socotra but altered on the morning of the 10th when the Guardafui Straits were transited in the last hours of darkness. The lighthouse there being in Italian Somaliland was an excellent reporting point for their forces stationed at Massawa in the Red Sea; the maximum distance off was maintained when passing Cape Guardafui and full daylight passages generally avoided. The light cruiser *Caledon* was met off Guardafui which took *Georgic* and *Duchess of York* under escort and proceeded at their maximum speed for Aden, where they were to disembark some personnel and rejoin the convoy later.

The escort was strengthened on the 12th in the Gulf of Aden; two sloops joining early that morning, *Carlisle* with an Ellerman ship from Aden just before noon, *Caledon* with the two liners from Aden early afternoon and later still the destroyer *Kimberley*. The convoy rounded Perim at 2100 hours that day and by 1300 next day was clear of the islands and passing up the Red Sea. At 0800 on the 14th on the latitude of Port Sudan, the cruisers *Dorsetshire* and *Carlisle* parted company; the former returning around the Cape to Freetown. Later that day the four fast liners, *Orontes*, *Monarch of Bermuda*, *Georgic* and *Duchess of York* detached ahead at 17 knots with *Kimberley* as escort and anchored in Suez Bay at 1000 on the 16th. The slow portion of *Oropesa*, *Highland Monarch* and four MT ships (including *City of Lille*) with *Caledon* as escort arrived at Suez that same evening.

A reported 13,786 troops disembarked from the six liners during the course of the next week. On the 20th *Oropesa* began repairs to a paravane towing arm which took six days to complete and excluded her from the next southbound convoy. In his report of the voyage, Vice-Admiral Sommerville asked that Commodores be given definite information as to whether other sections of the convoy were ahead or astern of him. "A very difficult situation arose in this convoy due to the fact that I did not know whether the Clyde section was ahead or astern of the Liverpool section."[9] The reader will recall that *Active*, soon after being detached and inbound from the Clyde section then under escort of *Kenya* reported by W/T to that cruiser that she had passed the Liverpool section 37 miles to the eastward. As the Commodore was then far astern with the Liverpool section, and doubtless unaware of this information, only the SOE on *Kenya* was in a position to take appropriate measures for effecting an immediate junction of the two sections, rather than that which occurred four days later.

A return convoy known as SW 3 left Suez at 0900 on 23rd November comprising the five liners from WS 3 (except *Oropesa* and with British civilian evacuees from Malta and Egypt for South Africa on *Duchess of York* and *Orontes*) with two empty cargo liners, *Brisbane Star* and *City of Capetown* that had arrived in convoys AP 3 and US 5A. The Commodore was Rear Admiral Plowden, (who may have come out on *Oropesa*) and embarked on *Monarch of Bermuda* while Vice Admiral Sommerville remained on *Orontes* to act as Vice Commodore. Escort from Suez was provided by *Caledon* and strengthened when abreast of Port Sudan by *Kimberley* and two sloops. Air escort was also provided at the southern end of the Red Sea but no attacks: surface, air or otherwise were recorded. *Highland Brigade* was detached into Aden on the 27th and thereafter loaded a total of 6,690 tons of general and refrigerated cargo at Mombasa, Lourenco Marques, Durban and Capetown before making a non-stop passage for Avonmouth but diverted en route to discharge at the Clyde Anchorage Emergency Port where she arrived on 16th January 1941. Repairs and overhaul of her main machinery was carried out during discharge; she then towed to Glasgow for completion of repairs and long overdue drydocking.

The cruiser *Shropshire* joined the escort in relief of all others to the south of Aden on 27th November, and after detaching the empty cargo liners off the Somaliland coast next afternoon, convoy SW 3 passed through the Guardafui Straits that night and had a fast passage down the East African coast, detaching *Orontes* into Mombasa on 1st December while the three remaining liners reached Durban on the 5th, concurrent with the departure of WS 4A from that port for Suez. *Shropshire* accompanied the liners throughout as two auxiliary raiders were known to be operating in the Indian Ocean and could have been joined by a pocket-battleship of the *Admiral Scheer* class at any time. So long as cruiser escorts were available, the Admiralty could not afford to pass large personnel ships through the area undefended.

General cargo was loaded on all three liners at both Durban and Capetown; *Monarch of Bermuda* then proceeded via Freetown to discharge at Avonmouth, *Duchess of York* also via Freetown and *Georgic* non-stop both to the Clyde Anchorage port where they arrived within a few hours of each other on 4th January. *Orontes* was originally to have proceeded from Suez to Australia, but loaded homewards from Mombasa and the two Cape ports, refuelled at Freetown and reached the Clyde on 8th January before moving upriver to discharge in Glasgow. The last three named were then employed in TC 9 with Canadian troops from Halifax, *Monarch of Bermuda* next sailed in WS 5B and *Highland Brigade* in WS 6.

The last liner to make the homeward passage from WS 3B was the PSNC *Oropesa*, which left Suez independently on 30th November and loaded 8,285 tons of general cargo, including copper bars and maize, at Mombasa, Beira and Capetown, leaving the latter on Christmas Day for Liverpool direct and due there on 16th January but tragically never arrived. *Oropesa* was torpedoed by *U-96* early that same morning in brilliant moonlight, in a position 140 miles west of Barra Head. After remaining afloat for another two hours, two further torpedoes finally sent her to the bottom. Captain Croft and 96 members of the crew, nearly all from Liverpool, lost their lives, while the Chief Engineer and two others died of exposure in the boats before being picked up. There were five deaths among the 39 passengers and another died aboard the Canadian destroyer *Restigouche*. The survivors numbering 106 were landed at Campbeltown from the destroyer *Tenacity* - eight days after the ship had sunk. At least three other destroyers had also been engaged in searching for them.

WS 4A - Sailed UK 31.10.40.

Soon after the departure of WS 3F from the U.K. on 7th October, the Secretary of State for War, Mr Anthony Eden, was despatched to the Middle East to confer with the Chiefs of Staff on the forces they had available there to repel an expected Italian offensive, and to take stock of their likely requirements for the future. The result of these discussions was immediately actioned by the Prime Minister in a telegram of 13th October for the Chiefs of Staff - "Should October pass without invasion we should begin the reinforcement of the Middle East by the Cape route to the utmost extent our shipping permits, sending, as arranged, the armoured units, the Australians, and New Zealanders in November, another British division before Christmas and at least four more during January, February and March. All this would be in addition to the necessary drafts. Let me know how your present programme of sailings conforms to this."[10] Clearly the rate of reinforcing the Middle East was to be rapidly increased.

WS 4A therefore left the home shores carrying the leading elements of 2 Armoured Division, intended as a relief for 7 Armoured Division (later to become famous as the 'Desert Rats') who were already in the Middle East and about to join battle with Italian forces in the western desert.

The convoy comprised only four troopships, but eight MT ships and four other liners bound for other destinations and simply included for their general protection. The troopships were Royal Mail's *Almanzora*, lately employed for five months as Naval Accommodation at Scapa Flow and from 19th October fitting in KGV Dock, Glasgow for 2,055 personnel, also *Highland Monarch* then discharging in Glasgow from Buenos Aires and partly fitted with berths for 500, *Scythia* in Liverpool having arrived on her owners' berth from New York, and *Stirling Castle* also in Liverpool discharging on the South African mail service. Apart from *Scythia* that had taken part in the GC convoy in September 1939, none of these liners had previously been engaged in trooping. *Scythia* had insufficient time for fitting but had pre-war accommodation for 1,349, *Stirling Castle* was fitted in Liverpool for 1,100 troops and then required to embark 429 over that number and had to be hurriedly provided with additional berths. A total of 5,500 were embarked on these liners.[11]

The MT ships of the convoy were requisitioned during the first week of October and began loading in the middle of the month, *Clans Chattan* and *Lamont* in Glasgow, *Dunedin Star*, *City of Manchester* and Brocklebank's *Malancha* in Liverpool, while *Port Wyndham*, *Martand*, and *Delius* of Lamport & Holt loaded in Newport. The four liners remaining on trade but included in the convoy were *Duchess of Richmond* en route from Liverpool to Quebec and Montreal, Shaw Savill's *Akaroa* from Liverpool via Panama to Brisbane, Elder Dempster's *Abosso* for West Africa and *Warwick Castle* from Glasgow on her owners' mail service to South Africa.

Warwick Castle moved downriver from Glasgow to the Clyde Anchorage on 31st October and was followed next day by the embarked *Almanzora* and *Highland Monarch* and the two Clan ships, all being anchored ready for sea by 1800. Sailing time was arranged for 2300 that night when the Clyde portion proceeded down the searched channel in single line ahead, escorted by six destroyers of which the Canadian *Ottawa* suffered slight damage when in collision with the gate buoy at the boom.

The other troopships of the convoy, *Stirling Castle* carrying the Commodore Sir H R Crooke KBE CB RNR, and *Scythia*, embarked and sailed from Liverpool at 1100 hours on 1st November, accompanied by *Abosso*, *Akaroa*, and two MT ships *Dunedin Star* and *City of Manchester*. Captain Finlow of *Scythia* acted as Vice Commodore and after landing Pilots around 1300 at the Bar Light Vessel, the convoy proceeded at 10 knots along the swept channel towards the Chicken Rock at the SW tip of the Isle of Man, escorted by the AMC *Salopian*.

At 1430 the convoy formed two columns and at 1600 was joined by the MT ships from Newport, i.e. *Martand*, *Port Wyndham* and *Delius* escorted by two destroyers which then joined the screen. The nine ship formation increased to 13.5 knots at 1700 and proceeded up the Irish Sea and through the North Channel to the SW of Orsay[12], where at 0800 next morning, *Malancha* caught up and joined, having been delayed in leaving Liverpool. Two hours later when 26 miles WNW of Orsay, the five ship Clyde portion joined with the AA cruiser *Cairo* and six destroyers, (three British and three Canadian). Also about this time *Cornwall* joined as the appointed ocean escort, also

Duchess of Richmond (Captain W B Coyle) which had left Liverpool one tide later than the convoy but came on at maximum speed to join it. Cruising order was formed of five columns[13] and at noon the AMC *Salopian* detached on patrol.

The AA cruiser *Cairo* left the convoy at sunset and that same evening three ships were torpedoed in close proximity to one another in a position 190 miles SE of the convoy, i.e. the Fyffes liner *Casanare* at 2055, AMC *Laurentic* twenty minutes later and another AMC *Patroclus* at 2300. The Admiralty instructed *Cornwall* to detach a destroyer to assist *Casanare* and *Hurricane* was despatched accordingly. The Admiralty then asked *Cornwall* to send another destroyer to assist *Laurentic*, when *Hesperus* was detached at 2325 and shortly after the Admiralty ordered two other destroyers, *Active* and *Achates* to proceed to the scene. Two tugs were also despatched from Greenock but *Casanare* apparently sank soon after being hit, *Laurentic* sank from additional torpedoes at 0400 and *Patroclus* by another five torpedoes half an hour later. *Active* and *Achates* were first to reach the scene at 0430 and picked up 263 officers and ratings from *Patroclus*; by 0700 *Hesperus* had recovered 368 officers and men from *Laurentic* and all these survivors were landed at Greenock on 6th November. Despite an intense search the U-Boat was not located and subsequently proved to be the ace Commander Kretschmer in *U99*.

There were no untoward incidents for the next 24 hours, other than *Abosso* exchanging stations with *Delius*, until just before noon on the 3rd when *Garland* was detached to assist the inward bound *Windsor Castle* being bombed in a position 150 miles SE of the convoy. Almost immediately thereafter *Cornwall* detached another two destroyers for the same purpose, but then recalled one of them. On this second day at sea it was found that *Delius* was unable to maintain more than 13 knots in smooth water, which dictated the onward speed of the convoy as about 11.5 knots over the ground.

At dawn on the 3rd *Saguenay* turned back to screen stragglers and the convoy then altered to a SW heading. Next morning three destroyers left to meet an inward Halifax convoy and that evening the last two destroyers detached to meet a further Halifax convoy.

During the afternoon of the 4th, the Officer in Charge of Troops (OC Troops) on *Almanzora* was asked by Brigadier Rimmington aboard *Stirling Castle* to give details of the troops embarked. *Almanzora* signalled that her complement comprised 517 Officers, 237 Warrant Officers and 1,094 Other Ranks totalling 1,848, made up of numerous small drafts that included 17AA squad attached to the ship. Next morning further signals revealed that *Stirling Castle* carried the Headquarters of 3 Armoured Brigade, with 3 and 4 Battalions The Royal Tank Regiment (whose cruiser tanks were aboard the two Clan Ships), together with Signals, Field Park and Recovery Sections of 3 Armoured Brigade. *Scythia* signalled her complement as 2 Regiment Royal Horse Artillery from 1 Support Group, together with advance parties from Royal Artillery units, the King's Dragoon Guards and 1 Battalion Tower Hamlets Rifles, all of 1 Armoured Brigade and 2 Armoured Division HQ, which were to follow in WS 4B, plus 210 Australian officers and men as advance parties from units which also were to follow in WS 4B. No details were given of the personnel embarked on *Highland Monarch*, who may have been RAF.[14]

The Regimental historian of the King's Dragoon Guards summed up the experience on their advance party aboard *Scythia*:

"Life on a troopship necessarily entails many monotonous hours, but once the first few days were over (which had to be spent on such matters as boat drill and re-arrangement of accommodation) the Regimental Advance Party settled down to daily training, in small classes, with games in the afternoons. In this way time passed fairly quickly, and a fortnight after leaving Liverpool the convoy arrived at Freetown."[15]

But much was to happen before the convoy reached the safety of Sierra Leone. In the early evening of the 4th, *Almanzora* reported her steering gear defective but kept up with the convoy and effected repairs by 0930 next day. At 0310 on the 5th, when the convoy was about 600 miles west of the Shannon estuary, *Duchess of Richmond* detached to proceed independently to Quebec. Later that day the German pocket-battleship *Admiral Scheer*, on her foray into the Atlantic, attacked and sank the Fyffes banana steamer *Mopan* in a position not far north of the *Duchess*. Unfortunately the *Mopan* failed to transmit a raider alarm, which might have warned the approaching Halifax convoy, HX 84, comprising 37 ships escorted by the AMC *Jervis Bay*. *Admiral Scheer* sighted this convoy at 1545 and was identified at 1700 by *Jervis Bay*, who ordered the convoy to scatter while she herself turned towards the enemy and engaged her for over half an hour before being sunk. The CPS cargo liner *Beaverford* then took up the unequal fight but was not herself sunk (tragically with all hands) until after a tremendous explosion at 2245. Although four other ships were sunk by the *Scheer*, the remaining 32 ships of the convoy escaped unscathed into the darkness.

The *Duchess of Richmond* (Captain WB Coyle) indeed had a lucky escape. At 1700 she received the SOS transmitted by *Beaverford*, giving a position only 20 miles north of her. Star shells and flashes of gunfire could be seen from the bridge and so the *Duchess* turned away at maximum speed and disappeared into the gathering dusk. Meanwhile convoy WS 4A was safely about 250 miles SE of the action but nevertheless, on receiving the W/T alarms took evasive action by altering course to SSE to pass east rather than west of the Azores. This diversion would have brought the convoy nearer the protection of Force H from Gibraltar, were it deemed necessary, but in the event *Admiral Scheer* took a diverging course SW, away from WS 4A and did not further approach it.

Next morning, the 6th, *Highland Monarch* dropped astern while changing a fuel valve but regained station by 1100 hours. At 1330 *Delius* had to stop for engine defects and did not regain station until nearly 2200 hours. At 0430 on the 8th the convoy passed 90 miles east of San Miguel in the Azores, and at 1000 *Port Wyndham* fell behind when changing a piston on one engine and did not regain station until 1600. At 0630 on the 9th, when about 300 miles west of Madeira, *Akaroa* was detached to proceed independently to Trinidad and Panama with ultimate destination New Zealand.

There were no incidents for the next two days until 0855 on the 11th, when the AMC *Pretoria Castle* came up with the convoy, which was then about 400 miles NE of the Cape Verdes and steering to pass east of these islands. *Pretoria Castle* had left the Clyde on patrol four days ahead of the convoy; as soon as she joined the convoy was split into two, *Cornwall* going ahead with the eight faster ships while *Pretoria Castle* remained as escort for the six slow ships known as WS 4C.[16]

On the morning of the 13th, the day before arrival at Freetown, each ship signalled their requirements for fuel and water by visual lamp to *Cornwall*. Radio silence was not usually broken to pass such information, but it was always available for immediate visual transmission as soon as the Cape Sierra Leone signal station could be raised by the ocean escort. In this case, *Stirling Castle* required 1,950 tons of fuel, *Scythia* 1,200 tons and the two Clans 560 and 660 tons, a total of 4,370 which proved minimal compared to some later convoys. For stability reasons *Scythia* required the oiler immediately on arrival before she could transfer water from a deep tank, and estimated this to take 30 hours. *Cornwall* however, suggested that direct water shipment would be quicker and so 1,400 tons was requested. *Stirling Castle* required 700 tons of water, the two Clans 300 and 100 tons, *Port Wyndham* asked for only 70 tons and the remaining ships none. That evening *Cornwall* signalled the order of entering harbour with *Stirling Castle* leading and *Scythia* last.

An air escort met the convoy at the outer end of Freetown searched channel at 1500 on the 14th. At 1642 *Stirling Castle* passed inside the boom and by 1704 was safely anchored in berth S 8. Replenishment of ships with water and fuel began immediately. The slow portion escorted by *Pretoria Castle* arrived 24 hours later but the whole convoy was not replenished and ready for sea until 48 hours later.

The historian of The King's Dragoon Guards wrote a vivid impression of the short stay in Freetown:

"No one was allowed ashore at Freetown, but it was a welcome change to find no blackout restrictions and to see every ship a blaze of lights at night. The sight of land was a change after a fortnight at sea, and the vivid green of the tropical vegetation was a novelty for those who had not seen it before. By day the native boys diving for pennies were a source of endless amusement and everyone admired the tenacity of purpose of the R.H.A Major who organized a race around the ship for the natives in their canoes. Although the convoy only remained in port for three days, contact was made with the *Cornwall* and *Resolution* (lying damaged in port), and the officers of both ships were invited to the *Scythia*, the compliment being duly returned. (Could it have been due to this that the *Cornwall* was obliged to ship several cases of gin from the *Scythia* at Durban?)...

"The oppressive heat at Freetown, accompanied by periods of torrential rain and bright sunshine, was overpowering and nobody was sorry when the convoy sailed once more. By this time arrangements were in full swing for sports meetings and other entertainments, the best of which was a boxing tournament organized by 2 RHA...

"The advance part of the KDG organized a concert (or sing-song with a few turns and a band) and with the aid of the ship's Staff Captain a lounge was converted into a Theatre in which performances were given on twelve successive nights in order that as many as possible of those on board could attend; the only stipulation being that the officers present should provide unlimited beer for the performers."[15]

It was intended to detach *Abosso* at Freetown to proceed independently to Takoradi and other ports on the West African coast, but she initially sailed with the convoy on the afternoon of the 17th, *Stirling Castle* passing out through the boom at 1635 hours and forming the convoy into three columns at 1800 when nearing the outer end of the searched channel. A westerly course was maintained for another hour and a half when the heading was altered to SW and speed increased from 9 to 11 knots. *Cornwall* and *Pretoria Castle* continued as escort and when clear of soundings at 0030 the convoy altered to a SE'ly course for the long leg towards the Cape and speed increased to 12 knots, the maximum that could be maintained by *Delius*. The Commodore noted, however, that "from past experience of *Delius* in a head sea the speed made good was not expected to exceed 11 knots."[14] In fact the speed to Durban averaged only 10.93 knots, a lamentable waste of the 18 knot *Stirling Castle*. Further comments were made on the poor speed of *Delius* before the voyage was concluded.

No untoward incidents occurred during the passage to the Cape, other than the replenishment port being changed from Capetown to Durban (probably to avoid the convoy being in Table Bay while the liner *Queen Elizabeth* was being fuelled there, en route from New York to Singapore). The additional distance to Durban, when allied to the lateness of the convoy due to strong SE trade head winds and sea, necessitated *Scythia* calling at Capetown for water and fuel. She was detached with the mail ship *Warwick Castle* at 0800 on the 26th, escorted by the AMC *Pretoria Castle* to Capetown, where they arrived in the late afternoon of the 28th. None of the troops were allowed ashore; *Scythia* and *Pretoria Castle* left again next morning and rejoined the convoy just before 1300 to the west of Table Bay. *Warwick Castle* continued her normal mail voyage around the Cape coast to Port Elizabeth and East London, before reaching Durban a few hours ahead of the fast section of the convoy on 3rd December. On her return to the Clyde on the 29th, she berthed at Merklands Wharf on the last day of the year to discharge South African fruit, general cargo and mails. She was then requisitioned for a voyage to Halifax carrying Prisoners of War.

When near the end of Simonstown swept channel on the afternoon of 28th November, *Cornwall* passed the convoy requirements at Durban to a naval trawler, for onward transmission to that port. WS 4A continued around the Cape coast at a speed of about 10 knots, giving Cape Agulhas a wide berth, and at 1500 on 2nd December when east of East London, *Cornwall* went on ahead with the faster ships while *Pretoria Castle* remained to follow with the slow portion. The former group arrived off Durban at 0630 next morning and within an hour *Stirling Castle* was secured alongside in B Shed berth at the Point. The slow portion arrived that afternoon. Both *Scythia* and *Almanzora* were now to leave the convoy, all of the 1,323 troops on the former and about 700 of those on *Almanzora* were transferred to *Dunera*, which had been waiting at Durban for eleven days since completing her previous trooping voyage from Bombay to Penang. The remaining troops from *Almanzora* were presumably distributed between *Highland Monarch* and *Stirling Castle*.

After discharging in Durban, *Scythia* loaded 7,000 tons of general cargo in eight days and sailed for the UK via Capetown and Freetown, arriving at Liverpool on 8th January; her next voyage being in WS 6. *Almanzora* is believed to have drydocked at Durban and then loaded 2,200 tons of fruit and general for Glasgow, sailing on 20th December and after a brief call at Freetown, reached the Clyde on 16th January going straight upriver to discharge at Merklands Wharf. Like *Scythia* her next voyage was in WS 6. While the convoy was fuelling, watering and transhipping troops at Durban, Commodore Crooke cabled a lengthy report to the Admiralty on the frequent break-downs and poor speed of *Delius*, which he rightly considered "unsuitable for inclusion in fast convoys."[14] The Admiralty in turn complained to the Ministry of Shipping, naming not only *Delius* but also *Northern Prince* that was only then leaving the UK in the Excess Section of WS 5A bound for Piraeus. On 6th January 1941 the Ministry of Shipping replied, in respect of *Delius*, that her selection for WS 4A was based on assurances from the owners that the ship "could maintain 14 knots fully loaded or 14.5 knots in ballast. Subsequent enquiries of the Master elicited the information that she could not maintain more than 13 knots."[14] The Ministry reported this to the Admiralty but could not find any other suitable ship. No explanation was given of the further reduction to 11 or 12 knots. The Ministry however gave an assurance that ships for military convoys would be selected with "the greatest possible care,"[14] and in no instance would they report on speed "which has not been guaranteed by the Master"[14] which they hoped would avoid any repetition of the *Delius* complaint.

The King's Dragoon Guards again provide an interesting account of the call at Durban, where *Scythia* was berthed adjacent to *Dunera*, "so that little time was wasted in making the transfer of men and equipment. In fact fatigue parties had never been known to work so fast before, as they knew they would be allowed shore leave a soon as their task was finished. Our stay in Durban only lasted two days, but followed the same pattern as the stay of many other convoys that were to visit the port as the war proceeded. From the very moment of our arrival the people of Durban did everything in their power to entertain officers and other ranks alike, and to make their shore leave enjoyable. It is a beautiful city, and almost every English serviceman who visited it during the war has retained pleasant memories of his time there. It was of course very hot in early December, but the surf-bathing was a new experience for most of us and occupied many hours. By the end of the second day many friends had been made and plans worked out for the third day (everyone had to return to the ship for the night - or what was left of it) but there was to be no third day"...[15]

Convoy WS 4A sailed from Durban with *Dunera* (Captain E. Caffyn acting as Vice Commodore) in lieu of *Scythia* and *Almanzora* at 1030 hours on 5th December, still escorted by *Cornwall* but with the AMC *Kanimbla* replacing *Pretoria Castle*. *Delius* broke down immediately after leaving harbour but regained station at 1500. The cruising order was revised into four columns.[17] On the day following departure the Admiralty sent out a raider report of the action between *Thor* and *Carnarvon Castle* south of Rio de Janeiro. At least one raider was known to be in the Indian Ocean while the whereabouts of *Admiral Scheer* was unknown, and may have been the reason for the two escorts that accompanied WS 4A.

On 8th December in the Mozambique Channel, the Commodore informed *Cornwall* that the drivers of twenty lorries shipped on *Port Wyndham* for Port Sudan, were embarked on *Dunera* that was bound for Suez. At 1600 that day the drivers were transferred by boat from *Dunera* to *Port Wyndham*. "This proved the first of several occasions when ships had to stop. *Delius* required one hour to change fuel valves on the 10th and *Dunedin Star* stopped four times in connection with an outbreak of typhoid fever. The presence of *Kanimbla* was invaluable as she could act as sheepdog on these occasions and the remaining ships of the convoy were not delayed."[18]

Nothing else of interest occurred until the convoy reached the Gulf of Aden on the 18th. Shortly after 0900 that day the AMC *Kanimbla* detached to Aden where she was required as escort for two Dutch liners carrying refugees to Mauritius. *Kanimbla* was followed by *Cornwall* that fuelled at Aden before returning to Simonstown. These escorts were immediately replaced by the Australian cruiser *Perth*, recently arrived from her home country en route to relieve her sister, *Sydney* in the Mediterranean, and by the AA cruiser *Carlisle* and two sloops. When to the south of Aden just before midday, the convoy was joined by *City of Agra* and *Melbourne Star* escorted by the destroyer *Kingston*. At 1800 the convoy overtook the northbound BN 11 off Perim and entered the Red Sea. There were no incidents during the passage of the Red Sea and the convoy reached Suez at 1500 on 22nd December, 51 days after leaving the UK and only six days ahead of the main body of 2 Armoured Division in WS 4B.

The arrival at Suez was recorded in customary style by the KDG historian:

"As we were due to land on Christmas Eve the (*Dunera*) provided a Christmas Dinner on the previous Sunday, and an excellent party was enjoyed by all; there being plenty of drink on board - troopships were not 'dry' at that time - an issue of beer and rum was made on peacetime lines. The majority of the regimental advance party were regular soldiers and had spent more than one Christmas in India, but to those who had not done this, it seemed very peculiar to eat turkey and plum pudding on a really hot day.

"The convoy reached Port Tewfik (Suez) on 23rd December, and some of the ships were detached to disembark their passengers there, but the *Dunera* was to go through the Canal to Port Said. The first part of the Canal was negotiated that afternoon, and after anchoring for the night in one of the Great Bitter Lakes we arrived at Port Said the following morning...the *Dunera*, in common with others, was tied up alongside a pontoon jetty. After the usual waiting about the regimental advance party disembarked into a waiting train, which moved off at dusk and travelled through the night. At 0600 on Christmas morning the train stopped at a small station called El Qassassin, and weary men scrambled out, whence they were taken by lorry to a camp named Tahaq, (then only a small tented area but destined to become a very large base camp and about to receive 2 Armoured Division). During the ensuing week parties were despatched to Suez where the scout cars and transport vehicles had arrived."[15]

The ten MT ships of the convoy were variously discharged at Suez, Port Said or Alexandria and thereafter mostly returned to their owners' liner services, although *City of Manchester* first made two military trips to Sollum and one to Malta before returning south to load in New Zealand for the UK. Of the three troopships, *Dunera* was retained in the area to make three consecutive trips from Suez to Port Sudan with units of 4 Indian Division which, following the successful attack of Sidi Barrani, was being moved to the Sudan to counter the growing aggression of Italian forces in Abyssinia. *Highland Monarch* transited the canal on 23rd December and disembarked at Port Said while *Stirling Castle* was handled at Suez anchorage. Both these ships left Suez with the Blue Funnel *Memnon* and Egyptian steamer *Zamzam* at 1400 on 1st January 1941, as convoy SW 4A. Commodore Sir Ralph Crooke remained as Commodore on *Stirling Castle* while Captain Clayton of *Highland Monarch* became Vice Commodore. The convoy proceeded down the Red Sea without incident, escorted for most of the passage by the AA cruiser *Caledon*, destroyer *Kandahar* and two sloops, formed in line abreast. *Stirling Castle* was bound for Durban to drydock while *Highland Monarch* was to load for the UK at Capetown, but was diverted instead to Mombasa and loaded there in five days, completing at Capetown and then delayed there for seven days due to paravane repairs. She then proceeded direct to the Clyde, arriving on 25th February at the Emergency discharging port in the Holy Loch and where she was expeditiously handled before sailing outwards again in WS 7. *Stirling Castle* was drydocked to programme at Durban and then loaded at that port and Capetown, leaving the latter on 26th January and also proceeding direct to the Clyde, arriving on 15th February, but soon after embarking a pilot off Ascog, ran into thick fog and grounded on the mud north of Toward Point. She was refloated with tug assistance later the same day, anchored inside the boom and proceeded upriver next afternoon to discharge at KGV Dock. She remained in this berth for 31 days discharging, repairing and fitting, until sailing again in WS 7.

WS 4B - Sailed UK 17.11.40.
The departure of WS 4A on 1st November carrying the leading brigade and all of the tanks and vehicles of 2 Armoured Division, was followed by WS 4B carrying the remaining personnel of this formation, together with 18 Australian Infantry Brigade which was to be the nucleus of 9 Australian Division in the Middle East.

WS 4B was to comprise *Andes* and *Empress of Canada* recently returned from the US 4 convoy, and the P & O liners *Strathallan* and *Strathnaver* taken up on completing WS 2, *Reina del Pacifico* similarly back home from RS 5, *Orcades* from Bombay after an

Australian Mail voyage at Liverpool during October. Additional demands for berths required four other liners to be included, i.e. *Strathaird* and *Otranto* which reached the Clyde on 5th and 11th November on return from WS 2, the CPS *Duchess of Atholl* which docked in Liverpool on 11th November on a commercial voyage from Montreal and Quebec with barely six days to change over for a long trooping voyage, and finally the French liner *Pasteur* under Cunard management which anchored in the Clyde from a short Gibraltar trip on 14th November. These ten liners brought the total capacity of the convoy up to 23,800 personnel.

Embarkation of 18 Australian Brigade was divided amongst *Empress of Canada* and *Pasteur* at the Clyde Anchorage, and on *Strathaird* at KGV Dock in Glasgow, although these ships were also embarked with miscellaneous British Units, while *Otranto* also embarked in Glasgow wholly with British units. The HQ of 2 Armoured Division and 1 Armoured Brigade and 2 Support Group, together with 1 Bn The Rangers, 1 Bn Tower Hamlet Rifles, 4 Hussars and the Kings Dragoon Guards were spread amongst the remaining six ships which embarked at Liverpool.

When the advance party of 2/10 Australian Battalion embarked on *Pasteur* at the Clyde Anchorage it was found that suspected sabotage had damaged her generators, and that a fire on board the previous day caused damage to the degaussing gear, necessitating the ship being withdrawn from the convoy. The Australians returned ashore by tender and it was at first thought that this battalion would have to be left behind, as all the other ships were full. However, it's Commanding Officer, Lt. Col. A D Verrier, represented to Brigadier Morshead who went to Scottish Command, who in turn contacted the War Office. As a result one British unit was disembarked from *Strathaird* in Glasgow and 2/10 Australians embarked in lieu, on the morning of 17th November, *Strathaird* left her berth at 1230 and moved downriver to anchor close to *Pasteur*, whence 2/10 Battalion stores and baggage were transferred by barges.

Otranto came downriver fully embarked a day ahead of *Strathaird*, and these two ships with *Empress of Canada* and *Pasteur* at the anchorage, were to complete the Clyde portion of the convoy until the latter ship had to be withdrawn. As it happened, the P & O liner *Viceroy of India* had arrived at the Clyde Anchorage on the 13th on her last voyage on the China Mail Service; she had been requisitioned for trooping while homeward bound and was to be fitted accordingly. By a major effort at the anchorage in the short space of five days she was discharged, fitted out, stored and embarked with 1,050 troops in time to take the place of *Pasteur*.

The physical problem of finding sufficient materials, labour and time to convert large liners for trooping service have already been mentioned. However, the P & O war history[19] provides a graphic description of the hurried nature of conversion work in transforming *Strathnaver* into a troopship for WS 4B, which is quoted in full below:

"The cabin furniture of *Strathnaver* was uprooted, her bulkheads were taken down and her lower decks, converted into open spaces, were fitted with hammock billets and mess tables. Superimposed bunks were put in the upper-deck cabins over the existing bedsteads, and the dining saloons fore and aft were turned into sleeping accommodation and messing quarters. In a matter of weeks a quiet reading room became a pantry, the forward lounge an officers' dining room and the verandah cafe a warrant-officers' mess.

"These were early troop carrying days, days of sudden improvisation and rushed work. The ship was due to sail at noon on the Sunday (17th November), and the Officer Commanding Troops was already aboard. But although embarkation arrangements were well advanced, there were still squads of workmen about the ship and the noise of hammering was incessant. And on the Saturday the inspecting General arrived with his staff to give his approval of the ship. The conducted tour began with the officers' dining room on B deck.

"The dining room was inspected and the party then crossed to view the pantry. Here they found coffee-boilers, still in their casings, standing in position ready for connecting up, piping lying around for the attention of plumbers and electric wiring hanging in ends and bights at every point. Workmen looked up for a moment from their jobs and then resumed their banging. The inspection continued. Many of the promised extra boats had not yet arrived, and those already in position were without chocks or means of securing. In the cabins on C, D and E decks the finishing stages of the work were nowhere in sight. The canteen had been completed only that morning, so that what should have been a stream of supplies and stores was still no more than a trickle. Moreover, the congestion on the railways inland had held up delivery of beer for the troops - *Strathnaver* was dry as a bone.

"But in all this haste some of the pipeline connections had gone adrift. Tradition and experience combine to teach the troops to expect the worst, so that when the worst happens they shall not be at a loss for a suitable word or phrase. It is easy, therefore, to imagine the flow of language on *Strathnaver* that very first morning out, when their tea was served to them brewed in salt water.

"Such misadventures were frequent in the early days of trooping......."[19]
Strathnaver was embarked with the balance of the King's Dragoon Guards, 40 strong, and 1,500 RAF plus several other Army units. The 4 Husssars, also of 1 Armoured Brigade, were aboard *Orcades* where "all ranks were given accommodation in first class cabins, unchanged from peacetime layout except for the addition of extra bunks. At the end of the six weeks voyage the only damage was one mirror cracked by a door swinging loose in a storm."[20]

The six ship Liverpool portion of the convoy began passing the Rock Light at intervals from 1100 on 17th November. After disembarking pilots at the Bar, they formed into three columns at 1545, proceeding out of Liverpool Bay along the swept channel at a speed of 12 knots. Commodore E G Robinson, VC,OBE,RNR was embarked on *Duchess of Atholl* (Captain D Pert) and after passing 8 miles west of the Chicken Rock at 2200, by 0200 on the 18th was 4 miles off Killantringan Light on the Wigtownshire coast, where three of the old ex American destroyers joined as escorts.[21]

Meanwhile, pilots were boarded on the four ship Clyde portion at midnight on the 17th, and by 0100 these liners were passing out through the boom, escorted by the cruiser *Edinburgh* and one H class and four Canadian destroyers as A/S screen. The acting Commodore was the Master of *Empress of Canada*, Captain H A Moore, and the convoy proceeded in line ahead down the Firth of Clyde until clear of the minefield in a position 8 miles SSE of Sanda Light.[22]

The Clyde portion passed the Mull of Kintyre astern of the Liverpool ships at 0500 on the 18th, and by 0800 both sections had joined in a position 6 miles west of Orsay, where a cruising order of five columns was formed for the ocean passage to Freetown.[23] The cruiser *Norfolk*, which had left Scapa at 1730 the previous evening, also joined at this point to share the duties of ocean escort with *Edinburgh*, which latter cruiser was appointed S.O.E. After forming up the AA cruiser *Cairo* joined and remained with the convoy until it cleared the Western Approaches at 1800 that evening.

The historian of 2/10 South Australian Battalion noted that this first morning at sea 'was bleak and cold with rain and a very choppy sea.'[24] The Battalion found *Strathaird* to be overcrowded with miscellaneous British units, including 100 nurses and 500 RAF ground staff, in addition to 18 Australian Brigade HQ, 2/9 Queensland Bn and 2/10 Bn. This Brigade had travelled to the UK six months earlier in the comparative luxury of the *Queen Mary* and *Mauretania*. They had since spent four months training on Salisbury Plain and from mid October were stationed at Colchester for the defence of that city.

The Australian historian recorded that unlike their previous transports, the men on *Strathaird* were "mostly allotted to uncomfortable quarters below decks in cramped and stuffy holds with their equipment, rifles and kitbags. Hammocks were provided for sleeping, but many preferred the hard floors."[24] The comment on food was that "rations were on the British Army scale and meals accordingly. Four meals a day - Breakfast at 0730 was porridge and light meats. Lunch at noon, mostly stews and sometimes a roast or boil, with vegetables and a light sweet. Tea at 1530 of cake or a bun with an apple. Finally supper at 1730 of cold meat and pickles, perhaps soup. There was bread and jam at all meals and butter for two meals. Coffee could be had at breakfast. There were two messrooms, one on each side of the galley or kitchen, which although large were never intended to cater for such a large number. Each mess held approximately 1,000 troops."[24]

"During the first few days at sea orderly room staffs were busy rostering guards, fatigues and other duties including AA defence personnel. On board *Strathaird*, which had not been cleaned since her previous complement of troops disembarked,[25] "kitbags and rifles were placed in store-rooms to make more room for sleeping. Special cleaning-up gangs were organized and generally the troops were made more comfortable... Training periods and areas were allotted".....most of it being "carried out on the sundeck, and the work revolved around physical and recreational training. During the week an adjustment was made with the meals", and four meals were reduced to three by combining tea and supper.[24]

The KDG historian on *Strathnaver* noted that "squadrons and troops settled down to training and games, once they had mastered the intricacies of boat-drill and mess deck inspection, and classes were started to give instruction in the sun compass and desert navigation, while the medical officer endeavoured to renew everyone's knowledge of first aid."[26]

From the forming-up position off Orsay the convoy initially set a course slightly north of west, but the S.O.E. amended this to WNW. On reaching the first alter-course position at 1800 that day, some 80 miles WSW of Barra Head, the convoy altered to due west and at this point the AA cruiser *Cairo* departed the escort. By noon next day the convoy had reached a position 100 miles SW of the Rockall Bank. A submarine had been reported 70 miles ahead on the convoy track and so course was altered at 1240 to SSW to avoid it. At 1800 that day the three ex American destroyers left the escort, followed by *Highlander* at 0900 next morning, the 20th, and finally the four Canadian destroyers that left at 1800 that same day.

There were no incidents for the next two days, other than *Norfolk* complaining of "*Otranto* being invariably astern of her station, of continually making black smoke and being adrift in the zigzag turns."[27] As so often happens in such circumstances, Captain Hawker was making his first voyage in command which had nothing to do with the performance of *Otranto*. The trouble was caused by leaky rivets allowing water access to fuel tanks, with consequent contaminated fuel causing heavy smoke and reduction of steaming power. The ship was drydocked at Durban on her homeward voyage to effect this and other overdue repairs.

At 1800 on the 22nd the convoy reached a position 50 miles NW of Flores, the most westerly of the Azores, where it altered to SSE for the Cape Verde Islands. At 1530 next afternoon *Norfolk* was relieved by her sister *Devonshire* and during the night of 26/27th the convoy passed 50 miles west of the Cape Verdes and then turned SE towards Freetown. Two cruisers continued to be standard escort for WS convoys whilst uncertainty remained on the whereabouts of the *Admiral Scheer*, which it may be recalled, had narrowly missed the previous convoy WS 4A. Nothing was then heard of the *Scheer* until the *Port Hobart* made a raider alarm southeast of Bermuda on the 24th, but unfortunately did not say whether her assailant was a warship or a disguised raider. The uncertainty of the *Scheer's* whereabouts remained.

During the afternoon of the 28th the Commodore ascertained the fuel and water requirements for each ship at Freetown, which totalled 18,900 tons of fuel oil, 706 tons diesel and 6,950 tons of fresh water.[28] This information was passed visually to *Edinburgh* as S.O.E. for communication to the signal station when this was raised next afternoon.

The convoy entered Freetown searched channel during the late afternoon of the 29th led by the Commodore and with the two escorting cruisers to the rear. Pilots boarded each transport 3 miles west of the Fairway Buoy and by 1800 the ships were anchored inside the boom.

WS 4B had steamed a distance of 4,100 miles from Liverpool to Freetown at an average speed of 14.5 knots, a disappointing result considering the slowest ship was declared as 17 knots. The Admiralty, through a Chiefs of Staff report, had recently advised the Prime Minister that "a normal 16 knot convoy takes 38 days from the UK to Suez,"[29] which theoretically was correct but not in practice. The average passage to date was nearer 43 days and only one convoy had reached Suez in less than 42 days. There had been much discussion during November on a means of reducing the passage time to Suez, mainly by using the "very large (monster) liners"[29] for all or part of the route, of which more will be said later, but in the meantime the Admiralty and Chiefs of Staff advised against this because of poor facilities at Freetown, the small amount of time saved by transhipping at the Cape and most of all because of the risks involved in passing such large vessels through the Red Sea. On 27th November the Admiralty noted that the speed of ships in WS convoys was steadily decreasing from 16/17 knots to 14 knots, due to the need to produce the necessary number of ships to meet the ever-increasing requirements for accommodation. This proved to be the beginning of the crisis for personnel shipping and of the vital WS convoy route in particular.

WS 4B remained at Freetown for two days and nights fuelling and watering. A convoy conference for Masters was held aboard the Admiralty accommodation ship *Edinburgh Castle* on the morning of Sunday, 1st December, and *Duchess of Atholl* passed the boom outwards at 1650 that day, followed at five minute intervals by the other nine liners, escorted by the cruisers *Devonshire* and *Cumberland*, the latter having replaced *Edinburgh* which was returning to the Home Fleet. At 2030 the convoy formed into three columns outside the searched channel and set off on a SW'ly course to clear St. Ann's Shoals. At 0100 the convoy cleared soundings and three hours later altered course to the SE for the Cape. Five columns were formed at 0600 with the ships re-arranged from experience on the previous passage. [30]

The Australian historian of 2/10 Bn noted after Freetown that "the weather became cooler with rain which lasted for several days, again becoming fine, the ship's sport

1. *Ettrick* maiden voyage, leaving Southampton 13 January 1939 with
2 Bn King's Own Shropshire Light Infantry for Jamaica and Bermuda. (*IWM H971*)

2. Troop Messdeck, *Ettrick*. (*IWMH970*)

3. Families' Deckspace, *Ettrick*. (*IWM 19/33*)

4. Families' Lounge, *Ettrick*. (*IWM 19/21*)

5. Warrant Officers on foredeck, *Ettrick*. (*IWM 19/24*)

6. The Norwegian Campaign, late April 1940. *Sobieski* embarked and awaiting orders at the Clyde Anchorage. (*IWM N 19*)

7. Troops at Boat Drill aboard *Oronsay* at the Clyde Anchorage, 20 April 1940.
Destroyer *Fury* arriving with *President Doumer* (behind *Fury*) carrying French troops
from Brest. (*IWM N 42*)

8. Troops returning from Norway to the Clyde, June 1940. At Boat Drill aboard
Lancastria with *Georgic* behind. (*IWM N 355*)

9. *Ettrick* arrives Qantara in the Suez Canal with part of 16 Australian Brigade from Melbourne to join 6 Australian Division in Palestine, 17 May 1940. (*IWM E 46*)

10. Port Said, 26 August 1940, showing L. to R., *Takliwa*, unknown v/1, *Rohna*, *Talamba*. *Rajula* arrived to disembark troops from UK who travelled in WS 1 and transhipped in India. (*IWM E 488*)

11. British troops disembarking from *Takliwa* at Port Said, 26 August 1940. *(IWM E 474)*

12. *Lancashire* disembarking British troops at Suez 23 August 1940, having first travelled from the U.K. on *Queen Mary* in WS 1 and transhipped at Trincomalee. (*IWM E 472*)

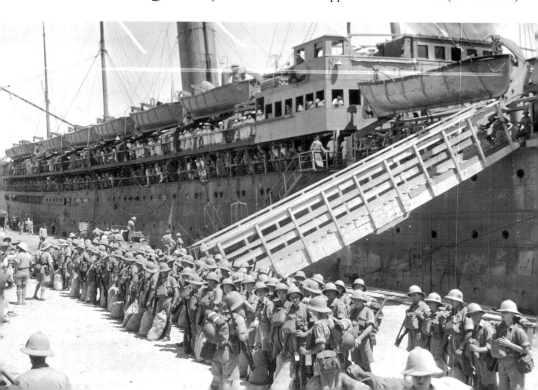

13. *Dilwara* preparing to disembark Suez, 26 August 1940. (*IWM E 471*)

14. *Strathaird* and *Empress of Canada* of WS 2 preparing to anchor outside Suez Bay, 15 September 1940. (*IWM E 626*)

15. *Franconia* of WS 2 disembarking Suez Bay, September 1940. (*IWM E 628*)

16. The officers disembark Suez, September 1940. (*Franconia* and *Empress of Britain* in background). (*IWM E 627*)

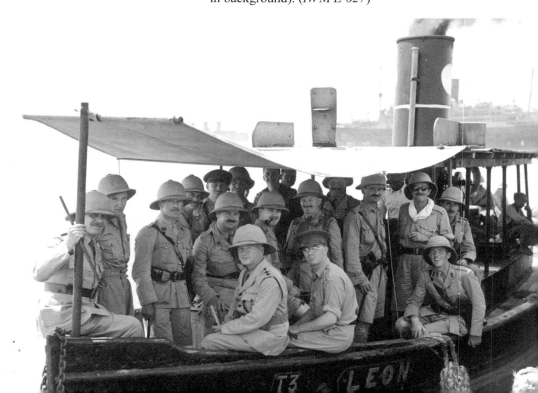

championships were commenced, and the events were followed with considerable enthusiasm. Interest in the other ships of the convoy was always maintained."[24]

The convoy now proceeded SE at a speed of 15 knots and crossed the Equator at 1700 on the 3rd. At 1030 next morning the cruiser *Hawkins* joined and relieved *Cumberland* which then moved across to the South American coast to search for the raider *Thor*. The convoy speed was then increased to 17 knots, the maximum speed of *Duchess of Atholl*. There were no incidents for the next four days until 0800 on the 8th, when the convoy was between Walvis and Luderitz Bay, where the cruiser *Hawkins* detached to proceed ahead at 22 knots to refuel at Simonstown. This opportunity of communicating with the shore was maximized by giving *Hawkins* details of the fuel and water required by the ten transports at Durban, which amounted to 19,020 tons of oil fuel and 20,200 tons of water. The S.O.E. on *Devonshire* also suggested to the Commodore that berthing in Durban would be expedited if the five faster ships were sent on ahead at daylight on 12 December to arrive two hours ahead of the remainder.

At 1900 on the 9th the convoy was approaching the Cape Coast at a distance of 60 miles off Cape Columbine, and just after midnight was abeam of the Cape of Good Hope, distant 20 miles. The cruiser *Hawkins* rejoined at 0600 next morning when the convoy was to the SW of Cape Agulhas.

It had been intended to pass WS 4B across the Agulhas Bank some 85 miles south of the Cape, but due to continued uncertainty that all the mines laid in May had yet been swept, a decision was made to pass 130 miles south of Cape Agulhas and clear of the bank altogether. This position was reached just before midday on the 10th, whence the convoy steered due east for five hours before turning ENE into the full strength of the Agulhas Current.

At 1500 next afternoon, the 11th, the convoy reached a position 70 miles south of East London, where it altered course to NE to maintain a course parallel to the coast. One hour later the Vice Commodore on *Empress of Canada* went on ahead with *Strathallan*, *Orcades* and *Reina del Pacifico* to proceed independently, and when 60 miles south of Durban at 0520 next morning, 12th, *Viceroy of India* also detached to berth ahead of the remaining five liners. All ships were berthed in Durban Harbour by 1000 hours that morning.

The convoy remained in Durban for four days that proved a welcome break for the troops, and again the Australian historian of 2/10 Bn provides a vivid impression of the city and its surroundings. "Durban is a fine city with wide streets, splendid buildings and lovely parks, with, of course, its poorer quarters too and problems of the coloured race. The recreational park covers acres of ground and caters for all tastes in amusement. Lawns, trees and flowers with winding paths that lead to entertainment of all kinds: refreshments, fun park, music and dancing. All night it was an entrancing place. The Durban people were awaiting the troops, and it was a common sight for a motor car to pull up alongside Diggers who would be asked if they would like to be taken for a look around. Many were welcomed in this manner and entertained in private homes".... "The gaily festooned Zulus and their rickshaws created much interest, and they were well patronized by the boys who delighted in racing around the streets behind these fine specimens of manhood"..... As with most other units, the Australians carried out route marches in Durban, each battalion giving the salute to the mayor and the brigade commander at the Town Hall. "It was extremely hot, and the troops felt the heat as they wore service dress and carried equipment and rifles".... "The Old Diggers tried to contact the well known Durban personality, Miss Ethel Campbell who, during the First

World War, welcomed and farewelled troopships by semaphore flags from a prominent point at the harbour entrance."[24]   She was not in Durban at the time but managed to appear and wish the troops "God speed and good luck" when they sailed out of the harbour .[24]

"The conduct of the troops on leave was excellent...and...there were not many who overstayed their leave."[24] Many of the British troops and all the nurses disembarked from *Strathaird* at Durban, and so the remainder had a little more space to move about. The 4 Hussars aboard *Orcades* commented on Durban that "Troops went ashore for morning route marches and afternoons and evenings of delightful hospitality. The South Africans were most kind. They took the troops to their homes, entertained them like prodigal sons, and took them sight-seeing, bathing, picknicking, riding and shooting."[24] Similarly the KDG on *Strathnaver* noted that "friendships were formed with South Africans (particularly of the fair sex) which lasted on postal terms for many years - and doubtless some still kept up."[26]

Among these who disembarked from the convoy at Durban were six officers and sixteen other ranks of Imperial Movement Control, sent out by the War Office to set up and operate the complicated military transhipment programme then being planned for South Africa as one means of saving on shipping, and of which details are given in a subsequent chapter.

WS 4B sailed from Durban on the morning of 16 December. The escorting cruisers were now *Devonshire* and *Shropshire*, the latter replacing *Hawkins* and these warships left the harbour at 0600 to be followed by the liners "in the order best suited to the arrangements of the port",[21] it was 0845 before all ships were clear of the breakwater. An hour later the convoy was formed up at the end of the 7 mile searched channel into the same five columns as on the previous leg from Freetown. The convoy route lay 200 miles ENE to clear the Natal coast, then NE towards the Madagascar shore and thereafter north through the centre of the Mozambique Channel to a point midway between the Comoro Islands and Cape Delgado, whence the course became NE towards Socotra. At 1000 hours on the 18th in the southern approaches to the Mozambique Channel, the cruiser *Southampton* from the Mediterranean met the convoy and relieved *Devonshire*, which returned to Simonstown and the South Atlantic.

During the voyage northwards from Durban the weather at first continued hot and on *Strathaird* at least, "the maximum number were sleeping on deck at nights. They were practically body to body, and the ship's orderly officer with his staff had great difficulty in making his way about the decks to check sentries, etc. Drill, games and lectures were carried out to the fullest extent but space was a handicap. The practice of wearing boots for an hour daily was being continued. On 21 December the boxing finals were completed..."[24]

The convoy passed between the Comoro Islands and the coast of Mozambique in the early hours of the 20th and thereafter adopted a NE'ly course in following the Somali coastline. In the late forenoon of the 20th *Strathnaver* had to reduce to 15 knots owing to boiler trouble but reported repairs completed by 1700 hours.

There were no incidents on the passage up the East African coast and by 1500 on the 23rd the convoy reached a position 180 miles SE of Guardafui, where course was altered to pass through the Straits that night. The Cape was passed about 40 miles distant soon after midnight and at 0300 the convoy turned west into the Gulf of Aden, and at this point the cruiser *Southampton* detached to proceed ahead to refuel at Aden. The Australians on *Strathaird* noted that Christmas Eve was a "delightfully mild evening in the Gulf of Aden, a concert was held on deck and carols were sung and the band played until late in the night."[24]   At noon on Christmas Day the convoy was 50 miles south of Aden where the escort was strengthened by the AA cruiser *Carlisle*, *Southampton* returned from Aden, and destroyer *Kimberley* whose sister *Kandahar* also joined that morning. As soon as these escorts were on station *Shropshire* was detached.

The Australians recorded that "Christmas Day was celebrated in traditional manner. A special Church parade was held in the morning. Dinner was really good with soup, poultry, pork, vegetables and the good old Christmas pudding. An extremely happy spirit pervaded the messes at the meal. Everyone was happy. Bottled beer was issued and tongues wagged freely. In the midst of it all, the Brigadier, Commanding Officers of units and the O.C. Troops visited them to wish them all a happy Christmas. The men reciprocated with cheers and happy greetings. The remainder of the day was spent on recreation."[24]

By 1800 on Christmas Day the convoy entered the Red Sea off Perim, and at midnight was passing east of Abu Ail, where the route was westward for five hours then NNW to Jebel Teir, which was passed at 0600 and where the convoy resumed the normal Red Sea route. At 0700 on the 27th, WS 4B was about 140 miles NE of Port Sudan and sighted the southbound convoy BS 11.25, comprising *Strathmore*, *Stratheden*, *Orion* and *Batory*, to which *Carlisle* and *Kimberley* transferred. The convoy route then passed 30 miles eastward of Daedalus Reef and The Brothers, and when about midway between these two outlying reefs at midnight on the 27th, the Vice Commodore on *Empress of Canada* detached with *Orcades*, *Strathaird* and *Andes* to proceed ahead at maximum speed and these ships reached Suez soon after midday on the 28th, followed by the remainder of the convoy which anchored at 1600 hours.

The arrival of this convoy in the Middle East marked the successful completion of the first six months of fast WS convoys, in which 33 liners in 8 convoys had safely landed an estimated 77,256 personnel.[31]

Next morning eight of the transports entered the canal for the daylight transit to Port Said, leaving *Strathnaver* and *Reina del Pacifico* to disembark at Suez anchorage. The following afternoon, the 30th, *Strathaird* and *Empress of Canada* continued on the overnight coastal passage from Port Said to Alexandria, where the Australians of 18 Infantry Brigade disembarked on the last day of the year and entrained to a tented camp 20 miles along the coast. This Brigade had left Australia in May 1940 to join 6 Australian Division in Palestine; it was now to form the nucleus of a new, 9 Australian Division, but this order was also cancelled and the brigade joined 7 Australian Division which was being sent to Greece. Even before this move occurred it was cancelled, and although remained officially part of 7 Division, it was detached in April and sent to Tobruk as part of the garrison that stoutly defended that town for the next five months, until they were relieved and returned to the Delta in August 1941.

The other six liners disembarked the main body of 2 Armoured Division at Port Said during the course of the next ten days, while *Orcades* also landed Australians at Kantara. 2 Armoured Division had assembled at Tahaq Camp by 1st January 1941, but the career of this formation in the desert was to be shortlived. Divisional Headquarters was captured at Tmini in April and the whole division disbanded four weeks later, along with 2 Support Group. The 1 Armoured Brigade had gone to Greece in March and after severe losses there and in Crete never subsequently re-formed and was disbanded in 1942. 3 Armoured Brigade, which had come out in WS 4A, formed part of the Tobruk garrison from April to December 1941, when it too was disbanded.

The arrival of WS 4B in the Middle East coincided with the movement of 4 Indian Division from the Western Desert to the Sudan, and of Italian prisoners of war to India. Whilst the transfer of the Indian Division is not covered here, it should be noted that *Reina del Pacifico* carried the second (11 Indian Infantry) brigade and 4 Indian Division Headquarters, leaving Suez on 4th January and reaching Port Sudan two days later. After disembarking the Indian forces she left Port Sudan on the 7th for Durban, and loading there for the UK then bunkering at Capetown on the 26th, she proceeded direct to the Clyde Anchorage arriving on 14th February. After discharging at the anchorage and undertaking repairs in Glasgow *Reina del Pacifico* proceeded to Avonmouth to embark for WS 7.

After completing disembarkation in the Middle East, the remaining nine liners were prepared for sailing south as a complete convoy. *Orcades* and *Strathaird* were embarked at Port Said with Italian prisoners of war for Bombay, while *Empress of Canada*, *Otranto* and *Strathallan* embarked families being evacuated to Durban. *Andes* was also to have carried POW to Bombay but instead was returning empty. All these ships were at Suez anchorage between the 5th and 10th and were there joined by the MT ship *Dunedin Star* from WS 4A, and finally by *Strathnaver* which was delayed at Suez loading military stores for Mombasa.

The southbound convoy, codenamed SW 4B, left Suez without *Strathnaver* at 0800 on the 12th, and two hours later formed into three columns and proceeded down the Gulf of Suez at a speed of 15 kts. The convoy consisted of nine ships as above with the Commodore still embarked on *Duchess of Atholl*. When approaching the Red Sea rendezvous close north of Port Sudan, at 0500 on the 14th, the destroyer *Kandahar* joined as escort and two hours later her sister *Kimberley* with the Australian cruiser *Sydney* and AA *Carlisle*. Two hours later the convoy was caught up by *Strathnaver* that had been delayed at Suez until 1330, five and a half hours after the convoy left, and had only rejoined by steaming at maximum speed on a direct route from Shadwan Island. At 1700 that day *Empress of Canada* detached with the cruiser *Sydney* as escort, to proceed ahead at her best speed of 17.5 knots, to reach Aden at dawn on the 16th for embarkation of personnel and in time to rejoin the convoy in the Gulf of Aden.

At daybreak next day, the 15th, when passing the Zubair Islands, the convoy reduced to 13 knots to allow time for *Empress of Canada* to keep the pre-arranged rendezvous next day. At 0800 that morning *Carlisle* fired on and sank a floating mine, and at 0930 the convoy was joined by an air escort prior to passing Abu Ail at 1130 and Perim at 1730 hours. The convoy then steered to a position 50 miles south of Aden, which was reached at 0200 on the 16th, and there turned east towards Socotra. *Kandahar* detached to Aden after daybreak. *Empress of Canada* left Aden with *Sydney* at 0800 and overtook the convoy at 1800 in a position 160 miles to the eastward. When *Sydney* resumed station as ocean escort, *Kimberley* and *Carlisle* were detached.

By maintaining the prescribed course and speed the convoy would have passed through the Guardafui Strait in daylight. The Admiralty approved this subject to ships not being within 40 miles of the Cape in daylight without permission, which the route easily allowed. As soon as *Sydney* rejoined, these instructions were confirmed to the Commodore on *Duchess of Atholl*, who mistakenly understood them to mean that permission had to be obtained to make a daylight passage of the Strait, and tried to obtain this from *Sydney* as an alternative to going around Socotra or reducing speed to waste time. The S.O.E. replied "am adverse to breaking W/T silence. Consider route should be through Guardafui Strait giving the Cape a clearance of 40 miles."[21]   No further signals or action was taken on the matter that day.

At 0600 next day, however, when the convoy reached a position 60 miles NW of Guardafui, the Commodore proposed to *Sydney* that the convoy alter course to NE for six hours, (presumably to mark time) before turning into the Strait about midday and thus secure a passage in darkness. The S.O.E. on *Sydney*, however, considered the daylight passage should be maintained "giving Cape maximum clearance unless you have contrary orders, otherwise we shall be very late at rendezvous with *Ceres*."[21] Unfortunately the Commodore knew nothing of the planned rendezvous with *Ceres*, a not uncommon occurrence at this time, but agreed to the daylight passage of the Strait. At 1045 therefore when 60 miles north of the Cape, *Orcades*, *Strathaird* and *Dunedin Star* were detached and dispersed to proceed independently to their destinations, the two former carrying POW for Bombay and *Dunedin Star* to Colombo en route to Australia and New Zealand. As soon as these ships were clear, the convoy turned SE into the Guardafui Strait and at 2100 that evening altered course for the Mozambique Channel four days distant.

During the afternoon of the 17th, Sydney received W/T instructions from the C. in C. East Indies, to detach *Andes* on reaching latitude 2° South, and direct her "to Mombasa to load cargo in accordance with Ministry of Shipping Instructions."[21]   Although *Strathnaver* was also bound for Mombasa, no mention was made of whether the two ships should proceed in company or independently. After much signalled discussion on the subject on the morning of the 19th, between the Commodore and the SOE, the latter suggested detaching *Strathnaver* forthwith to proceed Mombasa on a direct course, and this was effected at 1100 in a position 540 miles NE of that port. *Andes* was duly detached at 1800 prior to reaching 2° South, and at 1000 next morning the light cruiser *Ceres* relieved *Sydney* when the convoy was 300 miles east of Mombasa. *Sydney* then turned NW to cover the passage of both *Andes* and *Strathnaver* into Mombasa, where they arrived that afternoon. In addition to the stores discharged by *Strathnaver*, both liners loaded commercial cargo at Mombasa and left within three days, proceeding independently to Capetown.

The remaining five liners, escorted by *Ceres* continued southward through the Mozambique Channel. On the 21st *Ceres* advised the Commodore of a signal from the C.inC. East Indies, dated 11 January, to the effect that only the three ships evacuating families (i.e. *Empress of Canada*, *Otranto* and *Strathallan*) should go to Durban, others should bunker at Capetown subject to "information of bunkering, docking or homeward loading"[32] which was not known. The Commodore appeared to have no knowledge of this signal but the situation was clarified next morning, 22nd, when the C.inC. signalled *Ceres* to effect "If *Viceroy of India* can await arrival in UK for docking and repair and if she and *Duchess of Atholl* have sufficient endurance both ships are to be detached on arrival in latitude 29° South, and are to proceed independently at best speed to Capetown."[32]   Both ships were able to comply with this signal and were accordingly detached in 29° South, in a position 150 miles NE of Durban, at 2100 on the 24th.

The three liners carrying families, still escorted by *Ceres*, continued overnight to Durban, where they arrived at 0500 on the 25th and where SW 4B was officially dispersed. Next day the harbour became heavily congested when the 20 ships of WS 5A arrived and no doubt contributed to delaying *Empress of Canada* in port until the 30th, *Strathallan* to the 31st and *Otranto* to 1st February, the latter partly caused by drydocking for repairs to her rudder and leaky rivets.

All of the ten liners which had come out from the UK in WS 4B were bunkered at Capetown on their independent homeward voyages, *Reina del Pacifico* being first away on 26 January direct for the Clyde, while the last of the South African loaders *Strathallan* and *Empress of Canada*, left on 5th February. Of the two that proceeded to Bombay with POW, where they arrived on 19th January, *Strathaird* sailed again five days later for Capetown, and had the distinction of being sighted by the raider *Atlantis* on the 27th. *Atlantis* wrongly identified her as the *Queen Mary* and turned sharply away in accordance with orders.

Orcades was the last of the ten liners to leave the Cape, departing Capetown on 14th February for Freetown and the Clyde, where she arrived on 7th March. All proceeded to the Clyde except *Duchess of Atholl* and *Viceroy of India* which were sent to Liverpool, the latter being drydocked and fitted for 2,500 troops. *Reina del Pacifico*, *Otranto*, *Empress of Canada*, *Strathaird* and *Strathnaver* were all discharged, stored, watered and bunkered in Glasgow, the two sister Straths going upriver 15 minutes apart on 6th March. *Strathallan* discharged at the Clyde anchorage and then proceeded to Liverpool for drydocking, *Andes* was similarly handled at the Clyde anchorage, dry-docked at Belfast and then moved to Liverpool for embarkation. *Orcades* turned round entirely at the Clyde anchorage, where she arrived on 7th March. The round voyage of the ten liners had lasted from 90 to 111 days. All were next employed in WS 7.

Chapter 6

WS 5A & 5B

25 Australian and 5 New Zealand Brigades move to the Middle East

WS 5A - sailed UK 18.12.40

During the course of November 1940 the Ministry of Shipping requisitioned six more liners for sea transport trooping service. These were the Booth Line *Anselm* from their River Amazon service, the PSNC *Orbita* that arrived from the West Coast of South America, Shaw Savill's *Tamaroa* from Australia via the Cape, *City of London* and *City of Canterbury* from Ellerman's Calcutta service and the New Zealand Shipping Company's *Rangitiki*. The first four named were taken up at Liverpool in mid November, *City of Canterbury* was in Glasgow and *Rangitiki* discharging in Avonmouth after escaping from the *Jervis Bay* convoy. *Anselm* and *Rangitiki* were to be drydocked; all required extensive tween deck fitting to provide troop accommodation.

Also being fitted for trooping in Liverpool were two liners displaced by the German occupation of Europe, the Dutch *Costa Rica* from KNSM's service to the West Indies and the Belgian *Elisabethville* from the Antwerp/Congo route, which had recently been drydocked and surveyed at Barry. Also in Liverpool at the beginning of November was the ex German Hamburg-Sud liner *Cap Norte*, now renamed *Empire Trooper* and under British India management. The *Cap Norte* was intercepted by the cruiser *Belfast* in October 1939 when homeward bound from Pernambuco. After spending some months as an Accommodation Ship at Scapa Flow, the *Cap Norte* was sent to the Tyne in June 1940 and there converted into a Government owned troopship. The work was completed at the end of September when the ship proceeded to Liverpool to await suitable employment, and left the Mersey in November for the Clyde where she was to be fully bunkered and await embarkation orders.

These nine ships with the addition of the permanent trooper *Neuralia* due in the Clyde from Kingston (Jamaica) on 5th December were to comprise the personnel section of the next slow Middle East convoy, WS 5A, which was due to sail on 18th December. On 27th November the Admiralty indicated that twelve MT ships would accompany the ten transports carrying 15,000 personnel. The speed of the convoy would be 11 knots.

Embarkation of WS 5A began on 15th December, on which date Costa Rica left Liverpool to embark at the Clyde Anchorage with *Empire Trooper*. *City of Canterbury* and *Neuralia* were embarking at KGV Dock, Glasgow, *Rangitiki* at Avonmouth and the other five at Liverpool - *Tamaroa* in Brunswick Dock, *Elisabethville* and *Orbita* in Canada Dock and *Anselm* with *City of London* at Prince's Landing Stage.[1]

Amongst the personnel embarked on *Orbita* were 1,158 RAF and 301 New Zealand Signals staff, *City of London* carried 4 Bn Royal Tank Regiment and 5 Bn New Zealand Field Regiment, *Elisabethville* 25 Light AA Regiment and New Zealand advance parties, *City of Canterbury* 89 Heavy AA Regiment, *Empire Trooper* 14 Light AA Regiment and 1,271 RN personnel, *Costa Rica* 65 Anti-Tank Regiment and 474 RAF, *Rangitiki* 7 New Zealand Anti-Tank Regiment while *Tamaroa* and *Anselm* carried two Batteries each of 27 Searchlight Regiment. Almost all the troops on *Neuralia* were bound for West Africa, comprising a General Hospital, the Headquarters of 161 Infantry Brigade and 2/5 Bn The Essex Regiment. This and a sister battalion of that regiment sent to Freetown in WS 2 were specially sanctioned by the Prime Minister at the end of October, pending their relief by the West Africa Brigade from Kenya.[2]

When first planning the convoy the ten transports allocated were estimated to have a capacity of 15,200 when fitted out. A total of 15,027 personnel from over one hundred multifarious units, including New Zealand advance parties, were then allotted berths and issued with embarkation instructions. However the convoy sailed short - embarked with 1,389 berths or 9% of its available capacity unoccupied, (equivalent to a completely empty ship) which brought sharp comments, and complaints from the Department of Sea Transport and the Ministry of Shipping who were at this time under intense pressure to provide trooping capacity beyond their available means. It was found that no less than 506 berths were empty on *Orbita*, 219 on *City of London* and 210 on *Neuralia* while at the other end of the scale *City of Canterbury* was embarked with 109 over her stated capacity.

When replying to criticism of the short embarkation the War Office said that the New Zealand military authorities had complained of overcrowding on *City of London*, and that fitting out was not complete when embarkation began. The War Office supported the New Zealand view of overcrowding and unfinished fitting, and pointed out that soldiers had to be embarked in units or sub-units and could not be "poked in here and there as if they were bales of cotton."[3] However, the Ministry of Shipping did not agree that

City of London "would have been overcrowded on emergency standards had she embarked the full number for which we provided messing space, or that the short embarkations in the other cases were justified by the fact that the work on the ships had not been completed." The Ministry went on to point out that "it is not unusual in passenger ships to have workmen on board completing jobs up to the time of sailing, and in the case of these ships, I am assured that all work was completed before sailing time." To solve the problem the Ministry would in future arrange to embark naval ratings in lieu of army personnel where exact numbers could not be fitted into the accommodation available, but the War Office relented on 14 January 1941 by agreeing to "have some waiting personnel to fill up any unforeseen holes on embarkation."[3]

The departure of WS 5A began on 17th December when *Rangitiki* sailed from Avonmouth to join with the Liverpool portion in the Irish Sea next day. Also on that date, *City of Canterbury* moved downriver to the Clyde Anchorage from KGV Dock on the afternoon tide, and next morning adjusted compasses and carried out degaussing tests. That afternoon Convoy Conferences were held at Gourock and Liverpool with the Master of *City of Canterbury* (Captain H Percival) appointed Commodore of the Clyde section until its junction with the Liverpool portion; this latter portion sailed from the Mersey at 1600 hours that day comprising *Tamaroa* carrying the Convoy Commodore, Rear Admiral C N Reyne, with *Orbita*, *City of London*, *Elisabethville*, *Anselm* and six MT ships, *City of Derby*, Blue Funnel's *Stentor* and *Menelaus*, Hain's *Bhutan* and Harrison's *Settler*, in addition to the ex Blue Funnel HM ship *Atreus* now fitted out as a Mine Carrier and proceeding to join the East Indies fleet.

The Clyde portion sailed promptly at 2100 hours that same evening, 18th December, comprising *City of Canterbury*, *Neuralia* (which only completed embarkation in Glasgow that afternoon and sailed short of fuel and stores), *Costa Rica* and the Belgian *Leopoldville*: the latter bound for Halifax with RAF trainees but included in the convoy for protection through the Western Approaches. The *Empire Trooper* was delayed for a time in the Clyde, but sailed later and eventually caught up and joined the convoy just before dark on the 20th. MT ships from the Clyde were *Benrinnes*, *Ernebank*, *Arabistan* (F C Strick), the ex German *Empire Ability* now under Elder Dempster management, and the Harrison liners *Adviser* and *Barrister*.

Destroyer escorts and four corvettes for Freetown sailed with both the Liverpool and Clyde sections of the convoy while the cruiser *Bonaventure* sailed from the latter port in the early hours of the 19th, joining soon after the two sections had merged that morning. Cruising order was formed and the convoy proceeded out to the westward. An unidentified aircraft overflew the convoy just after midnight, in poor visibility with very low cloud, and another that proved to be friendly, just after *Empire Trooper* joined up at 1700 on the 20th.

During the forenoon of the 21st *Ernebank* broke down for a short time but rejoined later. She again broke down at 1600 and was left behind with the destroyers *Witch* and *St. Mary's* standing by. The remaining destroyer escorts were detached at 2300 hours. During the course of that night an easterly gale and two turns caused the convoy to be much drawn out by dawn on the 22nd, but at 1040 all ships had been accounted for except *Delane*, that did not subsequently catch up until the forenoon of the 24th. The sloop *Wellington* was detached at daybreak 22nd to stand by *Ernebank*, which ultimately put back to the UK with defective steering gear; with the destroyers detached *Bonaventure* and four corvettes remained as escort. The convoy was now on a southerly heading towards the Azores.

At 1000 hours on the 23rd the convoy reached the latitude of the Scillies and was some 700 miles west of these islands. At this point a fast section joined up, having sailed from the Clyde and Mersey 24 hours behind the main convoy, comprising *Northern Prince*, whose Master, Captain Buckley, was acting as Commodore, *Essex*, *Empire Song*, *Clan Cumming* and *Clan Macdonald*, which were to be passed through the Mediterranean to Malta and Piraeus with urgent military supplies as 'Operation Excess'. They were escorted by the cruiser *Naiad*, and accompanied by two aircraft carriers *Argus* and *Furious* ferrying aircraft to Gibraltar and Takoradi respectively. The combined convoy now comprised 28 ships proceeding south at a lowly 11 knots, escorted by two cruisers, four corvettes and two ferry-carriers. Despite the relatively high total of 12 coal burners in this WS convoy, including four of the troopships, no mention was made of errant smoke makers, although *Clan Cumming* had been a defaulter prior to junction with the main convoy.

The report of the Commodore for this leg of the voyage is somewhat brief and confines itself to details of vessels that joined and left, but the report from *Argus* notes that the fast section Commodore on *Northern Prince* "appeared to be unaware that the two convoys were to amalgamate, and when this eventually occurred he did not know who was the Commodore of the combined convoy."[4] *Argus* discovered later that the Commodore of the slow convoy was in similar doubt. Difficulty was also caused by the two convoys keeping different time, but this was adjusted during the day. *Naiad* reported similarly that the fast portion Commodore "had no instructions to join the slow convoy" and that the Commodore of the slow portion, Rear Admiral C N Reyne was of the opinion that "the fast convoy has nothing to do with me."[5] *Naiad* however was in no doubt that the two portions were to "act as one under the orders of Rear Admiral Reyne, until such time as the fast section parted company to proceed to Gibraltar."[5]

The combined convoy and escort spent the afternoon of the 23rd in expectation of an attack by six Focke-Wulf Condor aircraft, which the Admiralty reported as having left "Bordeaux at 1100 hours, probably to attack the convoy."[5] The Admiralty had previously informed *Naiad* that WS 5A "might have been reported by a U-Boat,"[5] and presumably concluded that a sighting report had been sent to the Condor base at Bordeaux-Merignac. *Furious* flew off a fighter patrol of six Skuas in expectation of this attack, but it never materialised.

During the night of 23/24 December the two portions of the convoy became separated, "probably because *Northern Prince* appeared to be steering 2° from the correct course and 1.5 knots below the ordered speed."[4] *Argus* informed *Northern Prince* of these facts but no corrective measures were adopted. As a result the fast section escorted by *Naiad* was 10 miles astern by dawn, but regained station during the day as did *Delane* which had been delayed by engine trouble. *Argus* reported that "the two sections of the convoy joined up in a most unsatisfactory manner as for some time different plan zigzags were in use by each."[4] The fast section was formed in two columns to port of the slow section comprising four columns.

At 0900 on the 24th the cruisers *Berwick* and *Dunedin* joined the convoy to act as ocean escort in relief of *Naiad*, but as the formation was then rather scattered and in process of reforming, *Naiad* remained until the manoeuvre was complete and detached at 1130 hours to return to Scapa. *Argus* flew off a Swordfish on anti-submarine patrol during the forenoon but had to recover this aircraft by midday when the weather became unsuitable for flying. The cruiser *Dunedin* had come from Portsmouth and was on passage to join the South Atlantic station; *Berwick* with her tail up was fresh from the Battle of Spartivento in the Mediterranean.

There is little doubt that the shortage of dockyard labour and materials, coupled with the necessarily hurried nature of trooping conversions at this stage of the war, left many ships, and especially those of the cargo liner type, with many problems to overcome from their own resources, once at sea with several hundred troops on board. In WS 5A, *City of Canterbury* was carrying more than a hundred troops above her stated capacity and there were major problems with her cooking and messing facilities. Captain Percival reported that "no Mercantile cooks were available at Glasgow and the Regimental cooks had taken over the cooking for the troops. The cooking facilities were considered poor for the number of troops embarked and it was realized that only perfect organization could offset the poor cooking facilities and inaccessibililty of the troop kitchen."[6]

The troop kitchen on *City of Canterbury* had in fact been fitted under the long foc'sle and Captain Percival's report continued - "the heat in the troop kitchen was appalling during the blackout and the fore welldeck was often awash during rough weather, and the Mess Orderlies experienced great difficulty in carrying the food to the Aft Mess Decks which contained some 800 troops."[6]

Another problem common to virtually all transports was the limited fresh water capacity relative to the large numbers embarked. On *City of Canterbury* "we have five gallons of water per man per day, with a maximum expenditure of 43 tons per day, but it was soon realized that with the excellent control which we had, we did not exceed 30 tons per day and at no time during the long voyage was there any stint of water as it was available to all hands for at least three hours per day and sometimes for eight hours per day."[6]

When the combined WS 5A finally re-formed and *Naiad* departed for home at 1130 on the 24th, the convoy had reached a position some 450 miles north of the Azores and was steering a SSE'ly course to pass east of these islands. The previous evening Captain Percival had "informed the Officer Commanding Troops" (OC Troops) on *City of Canterbury* that the rule for troops to sleep fully dressed "might be relaxed as I considered the ship to be out of the immediate danger area."[6] Unfortunately this proved premature as next evening "a heavy explosion was felt in the ship and flashes were seen off the starboard bow. It was dirty SE weather with drizzle and a high wind (on the port bow)."[6] Nothing further occurred and although dismissed as thunder Captain Percival remained uneasy, as well he might.

Quite unknown to the convoy and its escort, the German cruiser *Admiral Hipper* had gained touch with it that very evening and continued shadowing overnight. The *Hipper* had left Brunsbuttel on 30th November and passed through the Denmark Strait undetected with intent to attack Halifax and Sierra Leone convoys, but had no success until sighting WS 5A on Christmas Eve.

The first indication of danger seems to have been at 0740 on Christmas morning. Captain Percival then reported "exactly the same kind of explosion occurred and it was seen that an enemy ship was engaging our escort; all of them replied. In the mist and drizzle we sighted the enemy ship for a few minutes about four points off our starboard bow. The fall of shot from the enemy was at first slightly ahead of us and then shifted close astern, and *Empire Trooper* received two eight inch shell hits and *Arabistan* one. The action lasted only a few minutes on account of visibility and at 0750 the Commodore signalled two, four point turns to port (a total of 90°) and at 0820 scattered the convoy at full speed."[6]

A similar account was given by Captain Longstaff on *City of London* who concluded his report thus - "The visibility was too bad to enable us to make out the type of ship which was attacking us and many of the troops, in real contact with warfare for the first time, thought that a violent thunderstorm was in progress while others imagined that two escorting naval ships were carrying out battle practice...For three days I continued on my course alone and finally made a rendezvous where the convoy re-formed and continued on the voyage to Sierra Leone."[7]

Captain J D Matthews of the *Clan Cumming* briefly described the action with..."shells fell between the aircraft-carrier *Argus* and the *Clan Cumming*. Visibility was poor and those in the *Clan Cumming* could only see the orange flashes that accompanied the rumble of heavy guns. Two ships received direct hits".. [8]

A more detailed account was provided by Captain Almond of the *Rangitiki*."At 0730 one of the escort ships *Clematis* (corvette) reported that she was engaging an unknown enemy raider...The cruisers *Berwick* and *Bonaventure* went off at full speed in pursuit of the enemy while the convoy scattered. About a quarter of an hour later *Berwick* reported that she had sighted the enemy ship 12 miles to the westward, steaming hard on a westerly course. *Berwick* and *Bonaventure* engaged the *Hipper*, but lost sight of her a few minutes before 0900 owing to bad visibility and the chase was abandoned half an hour later. The *Berwick*, which was slightly damaged in the engagement, reported that she had made one hit on the *Hipper* abaft the funnel, and posssibly other hits."[9]

The official history makes only a brief reference to this action.."The *Hipper* approached to attack in the first dawn of Christmas Day. The strength of the escort took her by surprise..In a short engagement with the *Berwick* hits were scored on either side, and the enemy was driven off, but not before one transport had been damaged and the convoy prematurely obliged to scatter. The *Hipper* received only slight damage, but this, combined with her machinery defects, made her return to port and she entered Brest on the 27th."[10] The Admiralty ordered the heavy warships of Force H to sea from Gibraltar to round up the scattered convoy and give them extra protection, and in the ensuing bad weather *Renown* suffered damage which made it necessary for her to go into dock at Gibraltar. 'Operation Excess' in consequence had to be postponed to 6th January.

When the alarm rattlers sounded on *Argus* at 0740 on Christmas morning it broke up an early Communion Service and sent officers and men scuttling to action stations. The report of this ship is detailed and shows that *Argus* and *Furious* increased speed at the outset of the action and turned to the eastward to retire under a smokescreen, being unfit for offensive action with their flight decks cluttered with aircraft being ferried. *Argus* in particular was embarked with 12 Swordfish and 3 Fulmars in addition to her own two Operational Swordfish for anti-submarine patrols. Notwithstanding the problems, *Argus* decided to launch her two Swordfish, already armed with depth-charges, to try and locate and attack the enemy. Before this could happen, however, *Furious* asked *Argus* for two Swordfish which she intended arming with torpedoes. *Argus* replied that it would take 1.5 hours to fuel these aircraft and that she was meantime sending her own two Swordfish to attack with depth-charges. *Furious* then ordered *Argus* to reserve her Swordfish "for his (*Furious*) torpedoes and at 0920 said he would be ready in 20 minutes to receive them".

At 0815 it had been learnt from *Berwick* that the enemy was an 8-inch cruiser and at 0832 *Furious* and *Argus* turned to the westward in pursuit. It was not until 1123, however, that *Furious* flew off three Skuas and reported her flight deck ready to receive the two Swordfish from *Argus*. These were flown off at 1130 and landed safely on *Furious*, despite the rising sea and poor visibility that only just made flying possible (wind SE 6-7, visibility 2-5 cables and patchy). In the next half hour the weather deteriorated further, with very poor visibility, whereby *Argus* "considered that all chance of successful offensive action had passed, while there was a real chance of losing our own aircraft and quite possibly our own ships."[4] It was suggested to *Furious* that both carriers should rejoin the convoy but *Furious* said she was continuing the hunt alone and that *Argus* should proceed to Gibraltar independently. Shortly afterwards an Admiralty signal settled the matter by ordering both carriers to rejoin the convoy, which had been directed towards Gibraltar. The Skuas were landed on *Furious* at 1240 and both ships proceeded in company, but did not sight any other ships until the 27th when they met *Berwick*, *Sheffield* and nine destroyers escorting *Northern Prince*, *Empire Song* and *Clan Macdonald*. *Argus* joined the three merchant ships and the destroyers continued as A/S screen; *Furious* proceeded ahead for Gibraltar while *Berwick* and *Sheffield* went off to the westward in search of *Empire Trooper*. All the Gibraltar bound ships reached that port on the 29th: there, to await the readiness of *Renown* in pursuit of their passage through the Mediterranean. On 1 January, however, *Northern Prince* was driven ashore in a gale and sustained damage which rendered her unfit to proceed. Her 400 troops were transferred to *Bonaventure* and destroyers. The Excess convoy sailed from Gibraltar on 6 January, and despite frequent heavy attacks by Italian aircraft and the Luftwaffe, succeeded in reaching their destinations although the aircraft-carrier *Illustrious* was so badly damaged that she had to be sent to the United States for major repairs.

A rough sketch provided by *Berwick* showed the fast section of the convoy in the port columns 1 and 2, *Dunedin* ahead of the former with two corvettes on the port wing, the slow section of 21 ships being columns 3 to 6 with *Berwick* ahead of column 4, *Bonaventure* leading two corvettes on the starboard wing. When *Berwick* and *Bonaventure* at once turned towards the enemy and opened fire at 0812, *Dunedin* is believed to have followed *Berwick* but could not catch up and possibly did not open fire. At least one corvette similarly turned and opened fire. *Bonaventure* reported that the target was always indistinct partly due to the mist and partly to the spray flung up at high speeds, and this ship ceased fire at 0836 to avoid unnecessary expenditure of ammunition, but nevertheless expended 438 rounds from her three forward turrets in the space of 24 minutes. As the visibility got worse the enemy was lost sight of at 0926 and both cruisers turned back to rejoin the convoy.

Meanwhile the convoy had been scattered from a position some 300 miles NE of the Azores and 1,000 miles NW of Gibraltar. Those ships still in visual touch were reformed by the Commodore at noon and set a SE"ly course towards the next stated rendezvous due west of Gibraltar. The damaged *Empire Trooper* had fallen behind after receiving three hits during the action including one on the waterline that flooded No. 1 hold, putting her down by the head and causing steering difficulties. Nevertheless she continued on a SE"ly course towards the next rendezvous at 5 knots.

At 1900 on the 25th *Bonaventure* was detached from *Berwick* to search for *Empire Trooper*, and next morning came across the German supply ship *Baden*, which she proceeded to intercept but the crew set her ablaze and abandoned ship. After picking up the crew, *Bonaventure* was instructed by Force H to sink *Baden* which she did by gunfire and torpedo, and then proceeded at 20 knots for Gibraltar without having located *Empire Trooper*. Just after midnight that night *Bonaventure* ran straight into the northbound convoy SL 59 escorted by *Cathay*, apparently 100 miles ahead of its expected position. Only the vigilance of the lookouts and prompt action by the Officer of the Watch saved *Bonaventure* from a disastrous collision. The cruiser was turned on to a parallel and opposite course to the convoy and passed harmlessly through, between the 3rd and 4th columns. At 1100 on the 27th *Bonaventure* broke W/T silence to report the position of SL 59 to the Admiralty. At 1730 she was ordered to locate *Empire Trooper* and turned accordingly but an hour later had to report her low fuel position and at 2330 was again ordered to Gibraltar where she arrived at 1730 on the 29th.

By the evening of the 27th *Empire Trooper* reported her position to the Admiralty as 250 miles NE of the Azores and steering SE at 5 knots towards the convoy rendezvous at noon next day. It was readily apparent that *Empire Trooper* had no hope of making this rendezvous and so *Berwick* and *Dunedin* were directed to her assistance. The former cruiser escorted the trooper into Ponta Delgada in the Azores on the 29th, thereafter proceeding to Gibraltar to land her wounded before departing for the UK to repair and refit.

At Ponta Delgada, temporary repairs were carried out on *Empire Trooper*, sufficient to make her seaworthy. She left the Azores under escort and proceeded slowly to Gibraltar, arriving there safely on 5th January. The troops on board were re-embarked two weeks later on *Capetown Castle* and *Monarch of Bermuda* of WS 5B. *Empire Trooper* remained at Gibraltar under repair for the next four months; trials were carried out on 7 March but the ship was found to be unsatisfactory above 9 knots and was returned to the dockyard. She finally left Gibraltar for the Cape on 28 April, and after calling at West African ports reached Capetown on 2nd June and Durban on the 25th June. Further repairs at Durban were estimated to take eight weeks, but in fact occupied the next ten months; *Empire Trooper* was out of service for a total of 16 months until 14 April 1942.

In returning to the progress of WS 5A, the main body of ships had reached a position 500 miles west of Gibraltar at noon on the 28th. Here the convoy was re-formed in accordance with an Admiralty signal of 26 December, less *Costa Rica*, *Menelaus*, *Empire Ability*, *Adviser*, *Barrister*, *Benrinnes*; all of whose whereabouts were unknown, and of course *Empire Trooper* which had gone to the Azores. The Belgian *Leopoldville* had detached prior to the action with *Hipper* and reached Halifax independently on the 27th.

Because of the wide diversion and delay in re-forming there was a need to conserve fuel and therefore shorten the remaining route to Freetown; the convoy passed west of Madeira and the Canaries and then turned south to pass between the Cape Verde islands and the African coast. At 0900 on the 31st, when 200 miles south of the Canaries, *Menelaus* and the Dutch *Costa Rica* rejoined the convoy, leaving four MT ships still missing. WS 5A reached Freetown without further incident on the morning of 5th January, where *Empire Ability*, *Adviser*, *Barrister* and *Benrinnes* rejoined.

Whilst in Freetown, the troops of 161 Brigade HQ and 2/5 Bn The Essex Regiment on *Neuralia*, were disembarked to join their sister battalion landed by *Monarch of Bermuda* four months earlier. *Neuralia* embarked in lieu two French battalions proceeding to the Sudan for possible moves against Djibouti. After three days bunkering and watering to requirements, the convoy sailed from Freetown at noon on the 8th comprising nine transports, 11 MT ships and *Atreus*, escorted by the cruiser *Hawkins*, sloops *Milford* and *Bridgewater*, and corvettes *Asphodel* and *Calendula*.

The official history states that WS 5A was being searched for by the *Admiral Scheer* during this passage." On 8th January the *Scheer* moved from the rendezvous in the South Atlantic where she had fuelled and refitted and, acting on information from Germany, first of all searched for the troop convoy (WS 5A) which the *Hipper* had unsuccessfully attacked on Christmas Day. She failed, however, to locate it. Nor did her Captain desire to become engaged with so powerful an escort as was believed to accompany that convoy."[11]

On the available evidence it seems the latter was certainly true. On 11th January the cruiser *Devonshire* joined the escort and remained for the rest of the passage to the Cape. On the 9th the *Scheer* moved off slowly from her South Atlantic rendezvous in a NE'ly direction, towards the Freetown-Cape route, which could have brought her into contact with WS 5A roughly midway between St. Helena and the African coast on the 16th. On the 10th, however, *Scheer* altered course to a Northerly heading, away from the point of intersection, and never subsequently made any attempt to close the convoy route until the 15th, by which date WS 5A was already 750 miles ESE of her and rapidly approaching the relative safety of South African waters.

The convoy reached a position 60 miles SW of Cape Agulhas by the evening of 21st where *Devonshire* was relieved by *Shropshire*, and at 0100 on the 23rd *Orbita* was detached into Port Elizabeth. The remaining twenty ships continued to Durban where they arrived at 0700 on the 25th. Four days were spent in Durban watering, refuelling and storing, while the coal burners were bunkered at the Bluff. The troops were sent ashore on route marches and enjoyed the usual South African hospitality in the evenings. *Orbita* arrived from Port Elizabeth to rejoin the convoy while two additions were the B.I. *Talamba* and Dutch *Nieuw Holland*, the former recently arrived from Bombay and Mauritius while the Dutch liner had been engaged on the Durban-Mombasa route with South Arican troops for the past two voyages.

Approximately 1,000 of the personnel on *Orbita* now transhipped to *Talamba*, while the balance of 700 who could not be accommodated on the remaining ships of the convoy, were sent by train to Clairwood Transit Camp, newly established by Imperial Movement Control (later abbreviated to Impcon), in the southern suburbs of the city. The staff of this unit, originally 19 officers and men, had landed from WS 4B on 12th December and quickly set up an organization to deal with the many thousands of transhipment personnel of all categories now being contemplated. *Nieuw Holland* and *Orbita* were now embarked with South African reinforcements for Mombasa.

WS 5A sailed from Durban at 1000 hours on 29th January escorted by the cruisers *Ceres* and *Shropshire*, and formed into a cruising order of six columns.[12] *Empire Ability* had to be left behind at Durban awaiting a supply of CO_2 gas. At 0645 next morning, the cruiser *Enterprise* joined from Durban and relieved *Shropshire* which then returned to that port. The escort was disposed 30° and 5 miles on either bow of the Commodore, on *Tamaroa*, with *Ceres* to port and *Enterprise* to starboard. The speed of the convoy that should have been 11.5 knots, was then only 9 knots due to *Benrinnes* and *Anselm* having dropped astern during the night, due to bad coal. They both regained station at 1130 when speed was increased to 10.5 knots and at 1500 to 11.5 knots, but this had to be reduced again to 9 knots at 1815 when *Delane* suffered engine trouble, which turned out to be a broken piston. The weather was SE 4/5 on the starboard bow with very good visibility. *Ceres* investigated and identified two ships during the day. At 2015 the cruisers went to night cruising order with *Ceres* astern and *Enterprise* ahead each 2 miles distant from the convoy.

The convoy worked into the Mozambique Channel on a NE'ly course during the night

30/31 January and at 0735 managed to increase to 10 knots that was the maximum that could now be maintained by *Delane*. At 0920 when on the latitude of Lourenco Marques the Commodore suggested to the SOE on *Enterprise* that *Delane* should return to Durban whereupon the convoy speed was increased to 11.5 knots, but this had to be reduced to 11 knots at 1600 as *Anselm* was unable to keep up. The weather continued SE 4/5.

At daylight on 1st February *Ceres* reported *Anselm* to be 7 miles astern of the convoy and speed was reduced to 9 knots to allow her to catch up. At 1000 hours *Ceres* was ordered back to close *Anselm*, that was now out of sight, and subsequently reported that "she was going slow to repair defects and that the AMC *Kanimbla*, which had passed southbound an hour earlier, was standing by her."[13] At 1410 hours *Anselm* rejoined the convoy and speed was increased to 11 knots and later to 11.5, but had again to be reduced to 11 knots at 2130 when *Anselm* again experienced difficulties. At 1600 *Enterprise* went off to the eastward at 20 knots to investigate a vessel on similar course, which turned out to be the neutral Swedish *Hammaren* bound from Capetown to Aden. *Enterprise* rejoined at 2000 hours when both cruisers moved into night order.

The SE'ly wind of force 4/5 that this convoy experienced in the Mozambique Channel increased during the night of 1st/2nd February to force 6 and brought with it a short, steep sea. At 0900 *Enterprise* had one of her motor boats stove in by a heavy sea which broke on board. The wind and sea continued throughout the forenoon but moderated thereafter. Three southbound ships were sighted and investigated on the 3rd in the vicinity of the Comoro Islands - the *Clan Macarthur* from Colombo to Durban by *Ceres*, while a Norwegian tanker and Hogarth's *Baron Belhaven* were identified by *Enterprise* in the evening. When nearing the latitude of Zanzibar, at 1000 on the 4th, *Ceres* detached with *Orbita* and *Nieuw Holland* for Mombasa, and reached that port next morning. Both these transports were quickly disembarked and returned independently to Durban in time to meet the on-carriage requirements of the next following convoy, WS 5B.

At 1400 next day, the 5th, in a position 360 miles east of Mombasa, the AMC *Hector* joined the escort and took up station one mile on the port beam of *Enterprise*. A message was then received from East Indies Command which indicated that an enemy raider might be encountered, and that the cruiser *Capetown* was to join the convoy at noon next day. Records indeed show that *Atlantis* had been active in an area 200 miles from the convoy route three days earlier, and that she captured there Andrew Weir's *Speybank* and the Norwegian tanker *Ketty Brovig*; both surprised at night and unable to transmit a report. In between these captures, however, *Atlantis* sighted the Blue Funnel *Troilus* which turned sharply away and promptly signalled a 'suspicious vessel report', with her position, repeating this nine times which undoubtedly frightened *Atlantis* off and similarly alerted East Indies Command. Some dispositions were made to intercept but *Atlantis* moved away east from the convoy route and on this occasion got away. Light N'ly winds, with moderate to good visibility, were experienced for the next two days.

The cruiser *Capetown* was met at dawn on the 6th and *Enterprise* catapulted her aircraft to search astern of her to a distance of 45 miles, but nothing was seen. During the afternoon *Enterprise* sent the convoy information to *Capetown* in a seaboat, whereupon the latter ship assumed command of the escort while *Enterprise* took station 2 miles astern. This only lasted until 0430 on the 7th when *Capetown* detached and proceeded to support the land forces advance on Mogadishu, leaving *Enterprise* again in command. That same morning speed was reduced to 9 knots for a couple of hours to allow *Anselm* to regain station, being again affected by engine trouble. The wind veered to NNE and freshened to force 5, with a short moderate sea, unsuitable for flying.

During the night of the 7th/8th *Anselm* dropped 10 miles astern due to boiler defects. *Hector*, being in night station astern of the convoy, was despatched to investigate and found *Anselm* capable of only 7-8 knots and carrying out repairs estimated to take 24 hours to complete. *Hector* reported this to *Enterprise* who instructed the former to remain with *Anselm* while *Enterprise* continued ahead with the convoy. If the convoy had reduced to the speed of *Anselm* it would have been necessary to postpone the passage of Guardafui for 24 hours in order to maintain darkness, and in addition, the Commodore had already stated his anxiety about the fresh water supply in the convoy. At 0745 that day, the 8th, *Atreus* recovered some absentees by boat from *City of London*, who had missed the ship on sailing and who had been put on board the latter ship. These two ships rejoined the convoy at 1055 when speed was increased to 11.5 knots. At daylight next morning *Hector* and *Anselm* were surprisingly sighted astern of the convoy, which proved the latter had quickly made good her defects and found an extra knot or two to regain the convoy.

The convoy rounded Cape Guardafui during the night of the 9/10th in good visibility with the moon in its first quarter. When proceeding west in the Gulf of Aden, *Enterprise* left the convoy at 1730 and proceeded ahead for Aden to refuel. At midday on the 11th, WS 5A passed to the south of Aden where the AMC *Hector* was relieved of the escort by *Caledon* and two sloops. Perim was rounded at 2000 and *Enterprise* rejoined astern of the convoy at 2130.

At 0455 on the 12th the convoy passed east of Abu Ail and cleared the last of the islands at 1400 that day. At 0640 next morning *Caledon* reported *Stentor* had stopped during the night with engine trouble but was then 8 miles astern and catching up at 14 knots; she regained station at 0910. At 1830 that evening *Neuralia* detached under escort of *Grimsby* for Port Sudan, where she disembarked the French troops embarked at Freetown, and then continued to Suez. One of the sloops simultaneously detached to return to Aden.

The convoy experienced fine weather with good visibility during the Red Sea passage. The only incident occurred at 0320 on the 14th when a ship on the starboard wing column indicated she had sighted a submarine. The Commodore ordered an emergency turn, 40° to port, but at 0400 with nothing further reported the convoy resumed the mean course of advance. *Enterprise* left at the same time to meet and join the southbound convoy BSF 1.5.

The remaining 17 ships of WS 5A continued to Suez escorted by *Caledon*, and arrived there between 0700 and 0900 on the 16th after a passage of 61 days from the UK; the longest WS voyage to date but soon to be eclipsed by WS 6A. Despite the protracted nature of the voyage, Commodore Reyne merely remarked that the average speed from Liverpool to Suez had been 11.5 knots, and that the convoy speed was well maintained. "A few short stoppages occurred among the motor vesels for minor adjustments. *Anselm* had experienced some trouble with her watertube boilers and mechanical stoking system after bunkering with South African coal at Durban",[14] and had been astern of station on several occasions. Otherwise station keeping was very good.

The troops were certainly none the worse for the extended voyage in cramped conditions. The report of Captain Percival on *City of Canterbury* noted the ship "had arrived Suez almost nine weeks after sailing from Gourock; the troops in first class condition and I have no hesitation in saying that it was a most successful voyage; the incidence of sickness was practically nil and the troops left the ship looking smart, cheerful and well nourished."[6]

WS 5A arrived Suez just as the British advance in Cyrenaica was halted by the need to send forces to aid Greece. The Suez Canal had been closed for a fortnight while German mines were cleared and only re-opened on 13th February, but had to be closed again two days after WS 5A arrived, and remained so for the next three weeks. There was heavy congestion in Suez Bay with several liners from the US 8 convoy embarking Italian prisoners of war; these ships sailed in a large convoy for Bombay on the 17th, the second batch of POW out of a total 130,000 that had accumulated in the two month desert campaign.

Neuralia arrived from Port Sudan two days behind the main convoy, and after completing disembarkation at Suez, all nine transports waited in an air of mounting uncertainty about their future employment. *Talamba* was the first away, on the 27th, carrying Italian POW to Bombay after first proceeding to Port Sudan for fresh water. *Neuralia* followed next day, also with POW for Bombay and both these ships were retained on Indian Ocean routes. *Rangitiki* had reached Suez with engine trouble and was repairing until the 25th; she then embarked POW and also sailed with them for Bombay, thereafter going on via Fremantle to load on her owners' homeward berth at Auckland and Wellington. She returned via Panama to Avonmouth on 21st June and made her next trooping voyage in WS 10. *Tamaroa* was held at Suez awaiting orders until despatched on 4th March to proceed via Colombo to Auckland and Wellington, to load on the Shaw Savill berth, returning via Panama to Glasgow on 29th May. Her next outward voyage was in WS 9B.

On 21st February the other five transports were ordered "to remain at Suez on Special Service",[15] which presumably meant the movement of troops to Greece once the canal had been re-opened. The *City of Canterbury* had many different orders during her stay at Suez: the first to take 1,600 Italian POW plus 7% guard to Durban, sailing 22nd February, and the ship was watered and stored for this purpose. On the 20th the STO replaced these orders with "400 RAF for the UK sailing 27th February."[6] On the 24th these orders were again cancelled. The ship was placed on "six hours notice for steam to proceed through the canal as soon as it was cleared, for special duty in the Mediterranean."[6] These orders were maintained only until 4th March when *City of Canterbury* was instructed to take 1,550 prisoners plus 7% guard to Durban, sailing 7th March. In the meantime all five ships had moved to an anchorage outside Newport Rock, to make room for the sixteen large liners of WS 5B that arrived at Suez on 3rd March.

On 6th March, *City of Canterbury's* order for prisoners was confirmed and the ship was to be berthed alongside Port Tewfik at 0800 next morning for embarkation, and to sail for Durban that same evening. *City of Canterbury* accordingly entered Suez Bay at 0800 7th as instructed, but the following twelve hours were not as expected, as Captain Percival subsequently explained.. "As there was no Pilot as promised to take the ship to dock, I came to anchor in the Bay, which was very congested. At 1030 the Assistant STO boarded and informed me that there was no berth available for embarking prisoners and that they might be cancelled on that account, and he would confirm after 1500 hours."[6]

At 1500 Captain Percival was duly infomed by the STO "that the Prisoners of War were cancelled and that the ship would sail on 10th March at 1600 for the south as a light ship."⁶ The ship had been watered and stored for three weeks and the perishable stores such as potatoes, etc., were going bad. The situation was so fluid, however, with almost anything expected to happen next, that permission was now asked to blow down two boilers for cleaning, and this was granted. Two hours later, at 1700, the Assistant Naval Control Officer boarded and ordered Captain Percival to raise steam for sea at once, and that orders would be sent off shortly. At 1745 Captain Percival received his orders to proceed at once to Port Sudan. "It was dark by this time, there were no lights in the bay either on ships or beacons and we had steam for slow speed only. However, we were weighed and clear of Suez Bay shortly after 1900 hours."⁶ The reason given for the hurried departure was that a heavy air raid was expected. The Ship's Register had to be left ashore at Suez as there had been no time or opportunity to recover it from Agents.

City of Canterbury, *City of London*, *Costa Rica*, *Anselm* and *Elisabethville* all proceeded from Suez to Port Sudan as convoy BF 18.5, arriving at dawn on 10th March and berthing in the harbour shortly after. Neither the ships nor the Harbour Authority knew why they had been sent there, but the Authority was instructed to supply them the maximum amount of water. They sailed again at dawn on the 12th, proceeding again as a convoy as far as Aden, where *City of Canterbury* and *Costa Rica* parted company to continue independently and unescorted to Durban, arriving there on 28th and 29th respectively. They were now to be used for the on-carriage of troops in WS 6.

Elisabethville, *City of London* and *Anselm* all bunkered with coal at Aden on the 15th, then also sailed independently for Durban, arriving on 26, 27 and 29th March respectively. The first ship had been due to load homewards on both the Ellerman berth in Durban and her owners' berth at Matadi in the Belgian Congo, but this was cancelled and she too, with *City of London*, were to join WS 6 at Durban. *Anselm* loaded a full cargo on the Clan Line berth at Durban and sailed on 14th April for the UK, and waited nine days at Freetown to join the homeward convoy SL 74, which brought her to Liverpool on 4th June. Her next voyage, which proved to be her last, was in WS 9B.

Of the ten transports that left the UK in WS 5A, one was under repair for damage inflicted by the *Hipper*, another had been retained for the on-carriage of WS 5B, four more for WS 6 and one was sent to India: this meant that only three returned to the UK for inclusion in further WS convoys and as it happened, the Admiralty were now beginning to ask for a minimum of 14 - 15 knot ships for WS convoys. As there were only a limited number of liners that could maintain that speed, the balance was soon relegated to the slower and less dangerous routes on the Indian Ocean.

WS 5B - sailed UK 15.1.41.

Throughout the preparation period of procuring and allocating shipping for WS 5B, it became evident that the limited supply of fast passenger liners suitable for trooping service was virtually exhausted, and that liners for subsequent WS convoys could only be those that returned to the UK from previous convoys. Britain had begun the war with 152 such liners including five from the Southern Dominions and the six 'monsters' although the *Queen Elizabeth* was not then complete. Since then, nine had been lost when still on commercial service, another six as troopships and a further ten when serving as AMCs. Of those remaining, roughly one-third still continued as AMCs, another third was variously employed on liner services, or as Hospital Ships, fitting out for trooping, on special operations, two were repairing and six trooping on the US route between Australia and India/Middle East. Only 46 were actually employed on the WS route which alone could not sustain the present monthly flow of reinforcements beyond the sailing of WS 5B; more help was now required from the liners which had escaped from occupied Europe.

The commitment of Poland to the Allies was demonstrated at the outset when their six passenger liners were placed on charter to the Ministry of Shipping for British trooping service. Two had been lost by April 1940 while the others continued to give invaluable service under Lamport & Holt management for the next six years, retaining their Polish crews and flag.[16] Similarly in June 1940 the small Belgian merchant fleet, which included five passenger liners was placed at Britain's disposal. Unfortunately the most modern two were almost immediately lost by enemy action before reaching the UK while the other three converted for British trooping and also continued under Belgian crews and flag, although two were only suitable for Indian Ocean Service.[17] Of the three Norwegian passenger liners extant in 1939, one was laid up and seized during the German occupation, the others were chartered for British trooping but the newest was mined and sunk outside the Tyne before conversion work could begin.[18]

The Dutch position following occupation in May 1940 was complicated by the majority of their passenger liners being engaged in trading to their overseas possessions in the Dutch East Indies, which contrived to continue up until the time of Pearl Harbour. However, some Dutch owners had moved to the UK and chartered their ships to Britain while others had gone to the U.S. and managed their ships from there. There were 27 Dutch liners over 10,000 grt (including the 'monster' class *Nieuw Amsterdam*) of which 20 subsequently served as British troopships under the Dutch flag and crews; all of them eminently suitable for WS service. Seven became war losses including three during the evacuation from Greece, three more off the North African coast and the last when mined off Westkapelle on the Dutch coast eleven days after VJ Day. Two others were retained as Hospital Ships.

By far the largest fleet of passenger liners that might have assisted British trooping from 1940 onwards was that owned in France with 34 liners over 10,000 grt including such giants as the *Normandie*, *Ile de France*, *Champlain* and the newly completed *Pasteur*. Relations with France were greatly soured following their armistice with Germany and the British bombardment of the French fleet in Oran, which led to the ending of diplomatic relations with Britain. France as a whole was divided with the Vichy government clearly in the enemy camp. On 20th July Britain said that French ships then in British ports would be requisitioned, which led to *Ile de France* being taken over in Singapore, *Pasteur* in Halifax and some months later three others at Aden and Port Sudan. Three more were taken over in 1941 and another four captured at sea. Most of these ships retained a small number of French officers and crews (on the *Ile de France* only 41 out of a crew of 313) but the ships were transferred to the British flag and management for the duration of hostilities. Three further French liners found in North African ports during the Torch landings also came under British trooping requisition but retained their own crews and nationality although managed in Britain. Apart from the *Ile de France* and *Pasteur* that between them carried a quarter of a million Allied troops, mostly across the North Atlantic, the contribution of the French passenger fleet to the British trooping effort was abyssmally small.

The original plan for WS 5B was confirmed by an Admiralty note of 27th November 1940, and showed the convoy was to comprise 24 transports with accommodation for 45,000 personnel, a departure on 4th January 1941 and having a speed in advance of 15 knots. In the final analysis 21 ships were provided with a personnel capacity of 45,964 and was easily the largest troop convoy to that date.

Ten of the liners were taken up direct from their trade routes as they reached the UK during November and early December; *Durban Castle* and *Arundel Castle* in Glasgow where they were fitted out, also in that port the Anchor Line's *Cameronia* and former *Tuscania* but now Greek owned *Nea Hellas*, which had been offered to the British government and chartered by the Ministry of Shipping under British registry. This once pristine North Atlantic liner was found to have deteriorated in the short period since leaving her original owners and required much work to prepare her for the voyage ahead. Captain David Bone, her first Master in 1922, had almost reached retiral age in 1940 and was happily re-appointed to command his old ship. Fitting in Liverpool went ahead on the CPS *Duchess of Richmond*, Cunard *Samaria*, the U-C *Windsor* and *Winchester Castles* while *Highland Chieftain* was taken over whilst in the midst of extensive repairs in drydock. *Highland Princess* was fitted out in Avonmouth. Both *Samaria* and *Durban Castle* also required drydocking.

Those liners already on trooping service were taken in hand for voyage repairs and, where possible, alterations to increase their capacities. *Empress of Australia*, *Duchess of Bedford*, *Athlone Castle*, *Capetown Castle* and *Britannic* were handled in Liverpool, while *Empress of Japan* and the Dutch *Pennland* moved from the Clyde Anchorage to drydock in Belfast. *Franconia* and *Pasteur* were also made ready at the Clyde Anchorage while *Ormonde* was fitted in Glasgow and *Monarch of Bermuda* prepared in seven days between voyages in Avonmouth. With nine ships being fitted simultaneously for trooping, the pressure on repair yards was immense and absorbed large numbers of all outfitting trades, especially joiners, carpenters, plumbers, painters and electricians. On the two nights of 20th and 22nd December, Merseyside suffered from heavy air raids delivered by 200 aircraft and bomb damage inflicted on nineteen ships including *Samaria*, *Highland Chieftain*, *Windsor Castle* and the cruiser *Australia* due to sail as ocean escort to the convoy. It was at first reported to the War Office that these ships would have to be withdrawn from the convoy but all were repaired and ready to sail on time.

During the last week of 1940 and first few days of the new year, a number of positioning movements were made to allow eight of the liners reach their appointed embarkation points, *Durban Castle* and *Arundel Castle* from Glasgow to the Clyde Anchorage, *Capetown Castle* upriver to Glagow and from Liverpool, *Highland Chieftain* to the Clyde Anchorage, *Duchess of Bedford* to Newport and *Winchester Castle* to Avonmouth; from Belfast *Empress of Japan* to Glasgow and finally *Pennland* which only reached the Clyde Anchorage on the morning of 5th January. Six liners in Liverpool embarked 13,191, another six at the Clyde Anchorage 11,159, five in Glasgow 10,884, two in Avonmouth 2,090 (plus an empty ship) and one in Newport 2,783, altogether 40,107 personnel of which 31,734 were for the Middle East and the balance of 8,373 for India and Malaya.[19]

All of the accommodation on *Monarch of Bermuda* (2,200) together with 468 berths intentionally left empty on *Capetown Castle* was to be used for the on-carriage of troops on the damaged *Empire Trooper*, which had put into Gibraltar from the previous convoy. Quite apart from this and despite the intervening discussions and correspondence to prevent the serious short embarkation that occurred on WS 5A (*q.v.*), no less than 3,189 berths were empty on the ships of WS 5B that again equalled the capacity of an entire ship. These berths were additional to those provided for the troops on *Empire Trooper* and came to light when the convoy was preparing to sail after a week of unforeseen delays. Three liners were even carrying more than their accommodation offered but all the others were short embarked with *Pennland* and *Franconia* in particular having 570 and 538 empty berths. It later transpired that the Embarkation Medical Officer recommended short embarkation on *Franconia* due to a case of scarlet fever, also on *Empress of Japan* for a case of meningitis and on *Duchess of Bedford* for the shortage of cooking facilities. There was an epidemic of 300 cases of 'flu on *Franconia*, which included Captain Bissett and may have influenced the Embarkation Staff, but the Ministry of Shipping questioned the logic of reducing embarkation due to the isolated cases diagnosed on the first named liners. A further and major loss of berths occurred when *Pasteur* was unable to sail with the convoy.

To meet the original sailing date of 4th January, embarkation was well advanced at all five ports prior to that date. The Commodore, Vice Admiral Sir Richard Hill, KBE CB was aboard *Athlone Castle*, which anchored in the Mersey with *Windsor Castle* on the 4th, both fully embarked. They were followed on the 6th by *Samaria* and *Duchess of Richmond*, and when *Britannic* and *Empress of Australia* completed next afteroon, all six liners were led out of the river by the newly refitted cruiser *Australia*, which cleared the Bar Light Vessel at 1730 and set off to the westward along the swept channel with all ships in single line ahead. On reaching open water two hours later the convoy formed two columns and being joined by three destroyers as A/S escort set course for a position south of the Chicken Rock. Soon afterwards a signal was received that the Glasgow portion had been delayed by fog and a diversion was ordered to Moelfre Bay, close south of Point Lynas on the Anglesey coast, where they anchored at 2130 to await further orders. This was an exposed area and although two destroyers provided an A/S screen to seaward, the Admiralty was mindful of the recent air attacks on Liverpool and ordered the cruiser *Naiad* from the Clyde that night to increase the AA protection of the liners. Meanwhile the four liners of the Bristol Channel portion had sailed early on the 7th with two destroyer escorts to join the Liverpool portion in the Irish Sea, but were diverted into an anchorage at Bangor Bay on Belfast Lough to await the final sailing of the Clyde and Glasgow portions.

During the afternoon of the 8th, the two destroyers at Moelfre Bay were refuelled from *Australia*, which had over sixty cases of 'flu amongst her ship's company, including her Commanding Officer. Next afternoon the Liverpool ships were instructed to depart but this was postponed for 24 hours although two A/S Yachts relieved the destroyers that sailed for Belfast to fuel. That night there was another air attack in bright moonlight on the Mersey, during which enemy aircraft approached to within 7 to 10 miles of the Moelfre anchorage although the transports were not detected. Next day the Admiralty advised a further 24 hours postponement to the 11th and fearing a further air attack the Rear Admiral 15th Cruiser Squadron on *Naiad* proposed moving the ships to another anchorage which the Admiralty immediatly approved.

The air attack on Merseyside developed as expected during the evening of the 10th, when the six Liverpool ships sailed from Moelfre for Belfast Lough. There was considerable air activity during the Irish Sea passage but the liners reached the outer end of the searched channel into Belfast Lough at 0900 on the 11th, where there was some delay and confusion as the liners picked their way into the anchorage in Bangor Bay amongst the four that had previously arrived from the Bristol Channel. The continuing delay to the convoy meant that some ships would be short of fresh water before reaching Freetown, and while at Moelfre the transports were instructed to exercise the strictest economy and to reduce the daily allowance to 6 gallons per head. Even so,

Samaria had sufficient for only thirteen days and with barely enough to reach Freetown was topped up at Bangor anchorage while some hospital cases were landed and the escorts completed with fuel.

The delay of four days that prevented the Clyde portion from sailing was due to fog that descended on that whole area on the 7th, and enveloped the river and Glasgow in a dense pea soup for six days until the 10th and stopped all but the movement of very small vessels. To alleviate conditions on the Glasgow transports, the troops were sent ashore on route marches although probably not through the fogbound city. Movements resumed as the weather cleared at 0400 on the 11th when innumerable coasting vessels made the river passage, and by 0930 as the tide allowed, the first overseas vessels began moving. Priority was given to clearing the five transports, the last one being *Capetown Castle* that reached the anchorage ready for sea at 1300. After so many delays the convoy sailing had been set for 1400 but again had to be postponed when *Pasteur's* generators broke down at 1100 and required her withdrawal. The Ministry of Shipping immediately asked the War Office to make arrangements for the personnel on *Pasteur* to be transferred to other liners already at the anchorage or on passage downriver,[20] and also asked the Admiralty to delay the convoy sailing which was rearranged for late that same evening. Despite great efforts by the PSTO in pressing every available craft into the job of transferring personnel in the time available, only 495 of the 3,335 embarked on *Pasteur* were found alternative berths and mostly on *Capetown Castle*. The Ministry complained to the War Office that "the local military found insuperable difficulties in finding units of the right size to occupy the vacant spaces or that their baggage could not be got out for transfer,"[21] which was virtually a repeat of the vacant berths on WS 5A. The War Office subsequently maintained that units or sub-units could not always be made to fit into any or every vacant space.

The ten ship Clyde portion finally began leaving the anchorage at 2330 on the 11th, escorted by the battleship *Ramillies*, cruiser *Phoebe* and five destroyers. Pilots were disembarked off Ascog and the ships re-anchored for a few hours and where *Duchess of York* joined the convoy. This liner had only returned to the Clyde from Suez a week earlier but was discharged, watered, refuelled and embarked with German POW for Halifax, sailing on the 10th but ordered back to Rothesay Bay to join the delayed sailing of WS 5B.[22] The convoy got under way again at 0430, as had the ten liners from Bangor Bay to join up in the North Channel at daybreak, 0830. The four Bristol Channel ships with two from the Clyde then became the two port columns, the Liverpool ships columns 3 and 4 and those from the Clyde formed the starboard columns 5, 6 and 7.[23]

By 1130 the convoy was formed up off Orsay into seven columns with three ships in each and set a NW'ly course to clear the Western Approaches.[24] Australia led the starboard wing column while *Naiad*, *Ramillies* and *Phoebe* took station astern of the port, centre and starboard wing columns respectively, while an A/S screen was provided by eleven destroyers with the SO A/S escort on the ex-American *Lincoln*. This magnificent formation of 21 liners representing eight major passenger lines totalled 418,312 grt, and was never again surpassed by a WS convoy although once or twice by numbers of transports and several times in the number of personnel embarked.

After being aboard the transports for ten cold and tedious days, the troops were glad to get to sea, buoyed up by news of the spectacular British and Australian advance into Cyrenaica. *Athlone Castle* and *Duchess of Bedford* were embarked entirely with the troops of 5 New Zealand Infantry Brigade and virtually cleared the backlog of NZ forces awaiting transport from the UK to the Middle East. In a similar manner the last of the Australian troops from the UK, their 25 Infantry Brigade, were aboard *Franconia* and *Nea Hellas*, with the latter ship also carrying miscellaneous units of 18 Australian Brigade left over from WS 5A, plus 5 and 6 British General Hospitals. *Pennland* was mainly embarked with British units including two General Hospitals, 150 Nurses, 250 reinforcement officers and 250 RN, but also carried an Australian Machine Gun Company to assist with air defence (*sic*). The Anzacs it may be recalled had arrived in the UK at the crisis in June 1940 when invasion was imminent and were now anxious to join their own formations in the desert.

The convoy continued on a NW'ly heading until the first evening at sea when course was altered to west. Air escorts were provided throughout that day and overnight until 1020 on the 13th, and at noon that day course was altered to SW by Admiralty instruction to avoid a U-Boat reported ahead. At 1900 that evening the destroyer, *Churchill*, which had yet to join the escort, blatantly reported herself by W/T as being 30 miles astern and having to return to base. This unnecessary breach of wireless silence was immediately compounded by acknowledgement from the SO of the A/S escort on *Lincoln*, which destroyer was closed by *Naiad* and admonished for having given away the position of the convoy. At midnight the French destroyer *Leopard* had to turn back owing to shortage of fuel, a mere 45 hours since leaving the Clyde.

On the forenoon of the 14th the convoy received an air alert and the cruisers *Naiad* and *Phoebe* moved out to their air defence stations on each beam of the convoy, while some of the transports flew kites but no attack materialized. Immediately afterwards an Admiralty message indicated that U-Boats had twice reported the convoy during the morning watch[25] and ordered the convoy to alter course at once to 180°, which was quickly accomplished. The convoy was then 400 miles west of the Shannon Estuary and at 1400 the destroyer *Witherington* detached to return home with condenser trouble. The Admiralty concurrently ordered the convoy to revert to its original SW course to pass west of the Azores. *Naiad* was also instructed to retain the destroyers to the limit of their endurance and after passing these orders *Naiad* further instructed them to search astern on parting company and not to break W/T silence, except in emergency, until at least 150 miles distant from the convoy. Four destroyers left the screen at 0200 on the 15th and two others four hours later, at which point the cruisers moved out to positions on the bow and beam of the convoy as cover against the possibility of meeting a surface raider. Just before noon the cruiser *Emerald* joined the escort by which time the convoy was on the latitude of Ushant and 550 miles NNE of the Azores. Here also *Phoebe* and two destroyers detached with *Monarch of Bermuda* and *Capetown Castle* for Gibraltar, while *Naiad* left to return to Scapa leaving *Ramillies* to become SOE.

The Commander of 15 Cruiser Squadron on *Naiad* subsequently reported the convoy "to be visible for up to 20 miles and the smoke at a rather greater distance, *Pennland* was noted as making several mistakes in zigzagging and was put at the rear of her column, while 14 knots had been her maximum speed and not the 16 knots as stated."[26] The Commodore informed *Naiad* that 14 knots on the original route would leave *Ormonde* only the barest margin of fuel, while *Naiad* concluded his report by stating that *Nea Hellas* was the only offender in the matter of making smoke."[26] Captain Bone vividly recalled this in his "*Merchantmen Re-armed*", - "The important routine work of clearing the boiler tubes, complicated as they were in *Nea Hellas* by superheat, had either been neglected or indifferently performed, and if she did not quite display a pillar of fire by night she could certainly emit dense and sightly volumes of smoke by day - the major of all crimes in wartime convoy. The engine counters too, by which the propeller revolutions were adjusted, were out of register and could not handily be corrected whilst under way. It was well we had asked for sea room at the tail of the convoy."[27]

By 0400 on the 16th the convoy was about 360 miles north of the Azores where the two remaining destroyers parted company to return to Londonderry, and at 0600 next day when 60 miles north of the Azores, *Ramillies* detached with *Duchess of York* for Halifax and her next employment with Canadian troops in TC 6 back to the Clyde. WS 5B then continued south under escort of *Australia* and *Emerald*, reaching warm weather that day as it passed to the west of Fayal where course was adjusted to a position west of the Cape Verde islands, which were in turn passed during the evening of the 21st. Two corvettes had joined as A/S escorts earlier that day, the destroyer *Velox* next afternoon and two further A/S escorts at 0030 on the 24th. The convoy reached Freetown without further incident on the morning of the 25th, having averaged 13.2 knots from Liverpool, and where *Monarch of Bermuda* and *Capetown Castle* rejoined, having embarked to capacity at Gibraltar with the personnel from *Empire Trooper*.

Captain Bissett of *Franconia* recalled this particular call at Freetown, "the arrival of 20 liners and two cruisers, requiring fuel and fresh water, would be a sensational event in any port in the world; but at that remote port and small town the NCO had everything well organized. In four days all the ships were refuelled and watered." He also noted that *Nea Hellas* ran out of beer in the sweltering heat of Freetown, causing the troops to rename her "Near Hell as Possible",[28] but the accomplished author and Master of *Nea Hellas* viewed the beer story in a rather different light.. "The urgency of reinforcement had overcrowded the ships to a degree that rendered the extremes of cold and heat to be endured on the Cape passage an ever-present burden. Nor were we in *Nea Hellas* favourably embarked to meet complaint. Our troops were Australian and "Diggers" are not the men to be complaisant under stress...a curious distaste for cured fish in the dietary seemed productive of an abnormal appetite for beer, and if that could not be satisfied by canteen rationing, there were always mobsmen able and willing to augment supplies." Captain Bone also recalled his other anxieties within the depths of the machinery spaces while in Freetown .. "darkness had fallen as I tramped to and fro on the boat deck and thought of logistics to be solved... My old ship was not now the sea queen I had known .. so many years before...What wonder that she had infirmities..But voices I could hear (stout Clydeside echoes, rough, rude, but stimulating) as I passed and re-passed the stokehold ventilators gave me assurance that at least one of her ills was under treatment and my shoes crunched upon the mounting layers of boiler tube sediment that was being blown upward through the tall funnel from her hardening arteries". Nor were all the Diggers thinking of beer that evening, many massed on the foredeck singing *Waltzing Matilda* although this brought a rebuke signal from the shore that "lights (presumably matches) should not be shown on deck as the port is possibly under air observation by Vichy French from Dakar."[27]

WS 5B completed and sailed from Freetown on 29th January still escorted by *Australia* and *Emerald* and with two destroyers, two corvettes and a sloop as A/S escort. The cruising order was completely rearranged although seven columns were retained with two ships only in the port wing column. The ships were stationed three cables apart and the columns five cables apart. During the night of the 30th, a merchant ship on opposite course passed between the lines and had a slight collision with *Ormonde*. This was a moonless period when several northbound merchant ships were known to be near the route, and with a convoy frontage of at least three miles the night screen was re-disposed to give early warning of any other approaching ships.

The local escort vessels left the convoy to return to Freetown at 1800 on 1st February as the convoy crossed the Equator, by which time Captain Bone was happy to note his improved circumstances on *Nea Hellas* with the absence of complaints from the Commodore for being ahead or astern of station. "The ship's engineers had skillfully corrected the faulty counters, nor was there more ado concerning the emission of flagitious volumes of black smoke."[27] As the convoy neared the Cape, nine of the liners were directed to fuel and water at Capetown, with *Emerald* as escort, i.e. all the Union Castle liners except *Windsor Castle*, with *Duchess of Bedford*, *Empress of Japan*, *Empress of Australia* and *Monarch of Bermuda*, while the remaining eleven liners continued to Durban with *Australia* as escort, and were all berthed within that harbour during the forenoon of 11th February.

In stark contrast to the lack of facilities at Freetown, the ports of Durban and Capetown were most efficiently operated by the South African Railways administration in a highly developed and well equipped manner with each able to meet the needs of up to fifteen troopships at a time. All ships were berthed alongside with adequate cranage, fresh water and bunkers available on the quayside. Shore gangways, fenders, even coir springs were provided to counter the scend experienced in certain conditions. Powerful tugs were on hand to assist berthing operations that could be accomplished at almost fifteen minute intervals so that an entire convoy was safely alongside within the space of four hours. Adequate stores and fresh provisions were available, repairs could be undertaken and Durban provided a drydock for ships up to 1,000 ft in length. More importantly for the troops who had been confined to cramped conditions for over five weeks, both cities provided them with a release for relaxation and entertainment amongst the populations who so willingly accommodated them. Only the *Queens* and *Aquitania* were unable to berth in these two harbours although all three were able to use Capetown from 1942 onwards.

Eight of the liners at Durban, together with *Orbita* that had arrived simultaneously from Mombasa, were at seven adjacent berths at the Point with *Samaria* and *Franconia* double banked alongside *Orbita* and *Cameronia* respectively. *Nea Hellas* and *Pennland* were at Maydon Wharf, which also accepted the cruiser *Australia* after refuelling at Island View, and *Britannic* was at Q berth beyond the T Jetty. The troops on *Windsor Castle* and *Highland Princess* for the Middle East were transferred by marching the length of one berth along the quay to *Orbita*, and to the Dutch *Nieuw Holland* that arrived from Mombasa on the 12th. Also the troops on *Highland Chieftain* for India were transferred to *Windsor Castle* whose destination therefore changed to Bombay. This transhipment released both *Highland* ships that immediately left independently for Buenos Aires to load chilled and frozen meat for the UK, where they arrived in the first days of April and were next included in WS 8. A number of harbour shifts followed the departure of *Highland Chieftain* from Durban: *Franconia* occupying that vacated berth while *Samaria* had as many as three shifts before taking up *Windsor Castle's* berth. Additional troops embarked at Durban were the 700 left at Clairwood Camp from *Orbita* in WS 5A, whilst at Capetown there embarked the Capetown Highlanders, an unattached infantry battalion going to Suez for the express purpose of providing onboard guard for batches of Italian prisoners being sent to the Union.

The transhipment movements from one ship to another or between ship and camp were planned in great detail by the Impcon staff at Durban, acting on information from London once the convoy had left the UK. Ships for transhipment or complete disembarkation were directed solely to Durban, until a second transit camp was opened near Capetown in April 1942. In Durban the Impcon transport unit consisted of twenty women drivers, supplemented by Army drivers in transit, with nearly forty troop-carrier lorries, cars and motor-cycles. As soon as the ships berthed in the harbour, Embarkation Staff Officers (ESOs) boarded with movement orders, which started a few hours after arrival of the convoy and continued night and day until completed; not only personnel but their sea kitbags had to accompany them to other ships or to camp, while universal kitbags were stored elsewhere if the camp stay was short.[29]

At the convoy conference prior to departing Durban, Captain Bone of *Nea Hellas* remarked on the "unusual display of concord. No longer were defects, faults and malpractices the main issues for discussion."[27] The convoy had now been on passage for five weeks with personnel accustomed to an established routine, faults were mostly eradicated and the longest and most dangerous part of the voyage was now behind. Perhaps more than any other factor was the morale booster given to visiting personnel by the extreme hospitality of the South African people, which rightly became legendary.

While the troops and crews were thus refreshed in mind, body and spirit, the liners were fuelled and watered for the final leg of the voyage and left Durban during the afternoon of 15th February, still of eleven ships escorted by *Australia*, and next morning made rendezvous with the nine from Capetown escorted by *Emerald*, when the Commodore on *Athlone Castle* formed seven columns and set off northwards into the Mozambique Channel. No incidents occurred until midday on the 21st when the latitude of Mombasa was reached and where *Emerald* detached with *Ormonde*, *Windsor Castle* and the two *Empress* liners for Bombay as WS 5BX. At the same time the cruiser *Hawkins* joined *Australia* in escorting the main convoy now of sixteen transports towards Socotra and Suez. At 1600 that afternoon an RRR (Raider) alarm was received from the British steamer *Canadian Cruiser* in a position 300 miles SE of the convoy, which then added "Battle-cruiser chasing."[30] Both messages were also received by the C in C East Indies who ordered the cruiser *Glasgow*, then on patrol midway between the raider and the convoy, to intercept, and at 1934 directed WS 5BX "to Mombasa with all despatch,"[30] where it arrived safely next morning. In the evening of the 12th, the cruiser *Enterprise* relieved *Australia* to escort WS 5B which allowed the latter to join the hunt for the raider, as did *Emerald* from Mombasa.

The raider proved to be the pocket-battleship *Admiral Scheer*, which had "disappeared" into the South Atlantic after her attack on the *Jervis Bay* convoy in November, then made a feint towards WS 5A (*q.v.*) on the Freetown-Cape route before rounding the Cape to rendezvous with *Atlantis* and supply ships. On 20th February she captured a British tanker and sank a Greek tramp without being reported but the successful transmissions of *Canadian Cruiser* next day sent her hurrying eastward before turning south to round the Cape on her way back to Germany. The *Scheer* was actually sighted by a Walrus from *Glasgow* on the 22nd, which gave her position as 90 miles ahead, and although reported and pursued by *Glasgow*, the *Scheer* was not again sighted. A wide search ultimately involved five cruisers and the carrier *Hermes* and was not called off until the 24th.

The main convoy comprising six columns escorted by *Hawkins* had an otherwise uneventful passage as far as the Gulf of Aden, where the light cruiser *Caledon* and the Red Sea escorts took over from *Hawkins*. When south of Aden during the afternoon of the 27th, two B.I. troopers, the French *President Doumer* and a Shaw Savill MT ship joined the convoy from Bombay; the first three carrying Indian troops and from this point an additional column was formed. No incidents occurred in the southern Red Sea, *President Doumer* detached to Port Sudan on the morning of 1st March to land her reinforcements for the two Indian Divisions then engaged against the Italians in Eritrea. The remainder of the convoy continued to Suez where they arrived in the evening of 3rd March to find a very congested anchorage. *Nea Hellas* crept in a day later with the last of her fuel drawn from a reserve tank contaminated by salt water.

The situation at Suez and the Middle East generally was now somewhat tense. Rommel had arrived in North Africa some weeks previously, German aircraft had been raiding the area with frequent attacks on shipping and aerial mining, which closed the canal to through traffic from 18th February. The anchorage at Suez was heavily congested with six of the transports and some of the MT ships from WS 5A not yet cleared although the transports left for the south next evening. There was insufficient space in the normal anchorage above Newport Rock that left many ships in the unprotected area to the south. Ships were being held awaiting orders to assist in the expected movement of troops and stores to the Aegean, which began on the 5th from Alexandria and Port Said and increased as the canal was cleared and reopened on the 10th. Not all of the transports could be disembarked at once due to the shortage of attendant craft but priority was given to *Britannic* and *Winchester Castle,* which were emptied, re-embarked with Italian POW and sailed four days later for Bombay after first calling at Port Sudan for water. At Bombay, *Winchester Castle* first loaded on the Anchor Line berth then completed to capacity on her owners' berth at the Cape, sailing thence direct to the Clyde, discharging in Glasgow and thereafter taken up for "Operational Service", originally intended to mount an expedition against the Atlantic islands, but gradually extended into service as an HQ ship for assault landings which prevented further inclusion on the WS route. *Britannic* was drydocked in Bombay for bottom cleaning and then loaded homewards on the Clan Line berth, proceeding via Capetown and Freetown to berth in the Holy Loch for discharge on 5th May; she was next employed on a round voyage to Halifax before assembling with WS 10 in August.

As so often happens in critical defensive situations, there was much confusion at Suez and ships were given orders and counter orders almost daily. On the 9th, *Capetown Castle* was to embark 300 families for Durban but this was cancelled and replaced by POW for Bombay. There were frequent air raid warnings which brought disembarkation and the unloading of stores to a halt, ships had then to get underway and proceed down the Gulf of Suez until the 'All Clear' was given. On the 15th five more troopships arrived with 4,800 Anzacs but these were passed through the canal to land at Port Said. The New Zealand troops from WS 5B were first sent to Helwan Camp but soon embroiled in the campaign in Greece and Crete, and otherwise remained in the Mediterranean theatre until the end of the war in Europe. The troops of 25 Australian Brigade first joined the Matruh garrison then took part in the Syrian campaign until returning to Australia in February 1942. Whilst at Suez the troops and crews of the WS 5B liners witnessed the passage into the canal on the 10th of the fleet-carrier *Formidable*, going to relieve her badly damaged sister, *Illustrious*, which in turn passed out ten days later en route to Durban and the U.S. for major repairs.

Most of the disembarkation at Suez from WS 5B occupied fifteen days, *Capetown Castle, Athlone Castle, Arundel Castle, Monarch of Bermuda,* the two CPS *Duchess* liners, *Franconia* and *Samaria* with *Nieuw Holland* and the B.I. *Varsova* attached, sailed south at midday on the 18th as convoy SU 2 with the same Commodore remaining on *Athlone Castle*. The eight large liners were embarked with Italian POW, numbering almost 15,000, which began to clear some of the 130,000 captured at Bardia, Sidi Barrani, Tobruk and Beda Fomm. The usual POW embarkation was to 80% of the ship's troop capacity, plus 7 - 10% guard; those for South Africa being provided by the Capetown Highlanders who had been the first Union troops to reach Egypt.

The convoy proceeded south in five columns without escort until near Port Sudan on the 20th, when a destroyer and sloop joined and remained until the vicinity of Aden on the afternoon of the 22nd, when relieved by the cruiser *Glasgow*. Prior to entering Aden, *Capetown Castle* parted company and proceeded to Bombay while *Nieuw Holland* and *Varsova* also left the convoy at Aden. The remaining seven liners fuelled and watered to requirements and sailed from that port on the forenoon of the 25th, escorted by *Glasgow* and after forming up by *Illustrious* en route from Alexandria to Durban. The convoy passed through the Guardafui Strait during the night of the 26/27th and thereafter without incident towards Durban but limited to 14.5 knots due to boiler trouble on *Samaria*. On the afternoon of the 29th, *Hawkins* joined as relief for *Glasgow* which then left the convoy with *Arundel Castle* for Mombasa. The remaining liners continued to Durban and arrived there on 6th April to disembark the Italian POW who entrained for up-country camps in the Transvaal. *Monarch of Bermuda* was cleared and re-embarked with civilian and government personnel and families for the UK, sailing again under escort of *Dorsetshire* in the late evening of the 15th to rendezvous with *Empress of Japan* from Bombay. The homeward passage of these two liners is referred to later. Of the others, *Duchess of Bedford* loaded and sailed from Durban on the 13th for Freetown and Liverpool, arriving there on 7th May but then diverted to the Clyde and Glasgow. *Duchess of Richmond* loaded in Durban and Capetown, sailing on the 17th for Freetown and Liverpool but also diverted to the Clyde arriving there on 9th May. *Samaria* loaded in the same ports and proceeded via Freetown to reach Liverpool on the 10th. *Franconia*, *Arundel Castle* and *Athlone Castle* were all drydocked in Durban and loaded in coast ports; the first two calling at Freetown and reaching Glasgow and Avonmouth on 21st May and 1st June respectively: *Arundel Castle* having additionally called at Gibraltar to embark civilians. *Athlone Castle* also loaded on the Cape Coast and proceeded non-stop to Liverpool where she arrived on 7th June. The homeward passage of *Capetown Castle* from Bombay involved a call of eight days for repairs at her name port at the Cape from where she sailed direct to the Clyde and Glasgow, arriving on 11th May.

Two of the liners were held at Suez for "Special Operations", thus on 18th March *Cameronia* and *Pennland* were earmarked for Operation Lustre, the movement of troops and stores from Egypt to Greece. They entered the canal next day to proceed to Alexandria for embarkation; each made three successive trips to Piraeus and while *Pennland* did not survive these operations, *Cameronia* subsequently returned to Suez on 26th April to join the southbound convoy SW 6 with liners returning home from WS 6 (*q.v.*). She was the last of the WS 5B ships to reach the UK.

The last three ships to be disembarked at Suez were *Durban Castle*, *Orbita* and *Nea Hellas*. All three sailed independently on 25th March, the first for Bombay to load on the Ellerman berth, completing at Capetown and proceeding thence via Freetown to the Clyde, where she arrived on 16th May and berthed in Glasgow five days later. *Orbita* loaded in Durban and Capetown and after fuelling at Freetown reached the Clyde Anchorage on 22nd May. *Nea Hellas* was still suffering from choked boiler tubes and contaminated fuel, having been unable to make good either due to the necessity of maintaining steam at Suez for immediate movement during air alerts. She struggled south to

Mombasa at not much more than 10 knots with only a few troop details and convalescents on board. Homeward cargo was loaded at Mombasa, Zanzibar, Durban and Capetown; at each major port, Captain Bone requested "dockyard assistance for refitment and repairs but always there were prior claims on the machines and engineering facilities. At Durban in particular, every shipwright and engine-fitter was employed in repair of the gallant *Illustrious* to make her seaworthy for the long voyage to a dockyard in the United States."[27] There had been no great cause for concern about the poor speed in the Indian Ocean, but with reports of increased U-Boat activity off Freetown there was a vital need for improvement before sailing from Capetown. However, the STO there had no knowledge of urgent repairs for *Nea Hellas*, only that she was to "load to capacity on the Ellerman berth for UK urge utmost despatch."[27] Captain Bone was not so easily disuaded in having his ship returned to some of her former glory, and after arranging for a deep tank containing water ballast to be emptied and cleaned and ready to stow a further 1,000 tons of cargo, the STO cabled London and obtained agreement. By these means *Nea Hellas* spent fourteen days in Capetown, loading and completing urgent boiler repairs and cleaning of tubes.

Nea Hellas left Capetown on 6th May and immediately proved the wisdom of her recent repairs; the absence of smoke and gaseous fumes was the result of having cleared the choked superheater tubes, and being loaded to her marks with a full cargo was soon creaming her way northwards at a comfortable 16 knots in the following SE trade winds. After fuelling at Freetown and embarking there a number of MN and civilian survivors from torpedoed ships, she was ordered to Gibraltar and there embarked about 1,000 Gibraltarians for passage to the UK. She was accompanied homewards by the carriers *Argus* and *Victorious* for part of a day, and reached the Clyde on 13th June to begin discharge in Glasgow next day. Captain Bone was relieved there and sent to the U.S. to take command of the old *George Washington* being transferred to British registry.

We must now revert to the Bombay section of the outward convoy, WS 5BX, which sailed from Mombasa on the forenoon of 24th February escorted by *Enterprise* and formed into two columns with *Ormonde* and *Empress of Australia* to port while *Empress of Japan* and *Windsor Castle* were to starboard. The appointed Commodore was Captain Norman Savage, the Master of *Ormonde*. A NE'ly course was set, more or less direct for Bombay, and a speed of 16 knots maintained throughout in which light NE winds with good visibility prevailed. The cruiser *Capetown* joined the escort on the 27th and the four liners arrived at Bombay on 3rd March to join *Aquitania*, recently arrived in US 9, at anchor in the stream.

It appears there were troops on all four ships of WS 5BX destined for Singapore that transferred at the Bombay anchorage to *Aquitania* and *Empress of Japan*; both liners then continued as WS 5BX on the afternoon of the 5th with *Enterprise* as escort. A speed of 21 knots was maintained on a southerly course to gain a distance of 100 miles off the Indian coast. On the first evening at sea *Enterprise* closed and identified a fully illuminated Japanese steamer on passage from Madras to Bombay, during which time the convoy took evasive action. Other ships which all proved to be British were sighted and identified during the voyage. The convoy passed 40 miles south of Ceylon during the evening of the 7th and thereafter avoided the direct route to the Malacca Strait by steering to pass through the Ten Degree Channel between the Nicobar and Andaman islands. When 300 miles east of Ceylon on the forenoon of the 8th, the cruiser *Durban* joined the escort and next morning as the convoy entered the Ten Degree Channel,

Enterprise detached to return to Colombo and subsequently reported that Aquitania produced great volumes of smoke at 21 knots although her Master, Captain Battle, had explained at the convoy conference that this was unavoidable (the smoke had been sighted by Durban at a distance of 30 miles). No other incidents occurred and both liners reached Singapore at daylight on the 11th. These were the first of many reinforcements from the UK to reach Singapore by the WS route, and after disembarkation *Aquitania* was drydocked for repairs and a long overdue overhaul that lasted seven weeks. *Empress of Japan* was embarked with a number of service and civilian passengers, some for South Africa but mostly for the UK, together with a small tonnage of cargo, and sailed on the 23rd to load and embark further similar consignments at Colombo and Bombay, whence she proceeded under escort of the AMC *Hector* for the Cape but initially crossing the Indian Ocean towards Mogadishu.

When 150 miles east of Mogadishu at midday on 10th April, the single ship convoy and escort was sighted and challenged by an aircraft from the cruiser *Cornwall*, and soon after, the northbound convoy WS 6 was seen to the SW, under escort of *Cornwall* and *Glasgow*. A Swedish ship was sighted and identified that evening and the AMC *Corfu* on patrol two days later. Otherwise, the *Empress* and *Hector* had an uneventful passage down through the Mozambique Channel to a position 100 miles ENE of Durban, which was reached at 0230 on the 16th, where *Hector* was relieved by *Dorsetshire* which had come out from Durban with *Monarch of Bermuda*, also embarked with civilian personnel and families for the UK. Both liners continued in convoy to Capetown where they arrived on the 18th to allow *Empress of Japan* to disembark some of her passengers and embark others in lieu. Both ships sailed again on the 23rd as convoy CF 1 for Freetown, and from Freetown were ordered to Gibraltar where more civilians were embarked for the UK. For the final leg of the voyage the two liners left Gibraltar on 8th May escorted by the battlecruiser *Repulse* and ferry-carrier *Argus*, which latter provided air escort as and when the weather allowed. Convoy CF 1 was due to meet the AA cruiser *Cairo* with an A/S destroyer screen on the morning of the 13th when in position 500 miles west of the Shannon estuary, but fog prevented this rendezvous until that afternoon. The convoy was then routed to a position 250 miles SW of Rockall Bank and thence to 150 miles west of Barra Head before turning SE into the North Channel. *Empress of Japan* was directed to the Clyde Anchorage and *Monarch of Bermuda* to Liverpool, both were disembarking on the 15th and were next employed on WS 9A and 9B respectively.

Meanwhile at Bombay and following the departure of *Empress of Japan* for Singapore, *Ormonde* moved into the Alexandra Drydock for bottom cleaning before loading pig iron and general cargo for the UK. She then proceeded to Mombasa, loading again there and at Capetown, before sailing for the UK via Freetown for fuel and was the first of the main body of WS 5B ships to reach home waters by anchoring in the Clyde on 26 April. *Ormonde* berthed in Glasgow two days later to begin discharge and was then taken over to join *Winchester Castle* on 'Operational Service'.

Windsor Castle and *Empress of Australia* were required at Bombay to assist in completing the on-carriage of Anzac troops to the Middle East from the liners of US 9. Abut 1,100 were embarked on the former and 1,500 on the *Empress*, while the Dutch liners *Indrapoera*, *Johan de Witt* and *Nieuw Zeeland* each carried almost 1,000 to make a total of 5,600 Anzacs who had been languishing in British Army camps beyond Bombay for the past two weeks. The five liners sailed from Bombay as convoy US 9.5 during the afternoon of 12th March with the cruiser *Capetown* as escort. The Commodore,

Captain Wakeman-Colville RN was aboard *Empress of Australia* while Captain J C Brown, the Master of *Windsor Castle*, acted as Vice Commodore. A speed of 13 knots was maintained and few incidents were reported. *Capetown* remained as escort until south of Aden when she proceeded to that port to land a cot case from *Johan de Witt*. The onward escort was then provided by *Caledon*, one destroyer and a sloop that joined with three other ships to the south of Aden and remained until halfway up the Red Sea. The convoy reached Suez on 23rd March by which date most of the WS 5B ships had already departed. The serious congestion prevailed, however, and twelve days passed in disembarking *Windsor Castle* and *Empress of Australia* and re-embarking them with Italian POW for Mombasa, where the former began loading, completed at Durban and Capetown and proceded via Freetown to Glasgow where she arrived to begin disharge on 17th May. The *Empress* was held at Durban for the on-carriage of troops to Suez from WS 7, and did not return home until August.

WS 5B may rightly be viewed as one of the largest of the WS series comprising twenty of the largest liners used on the route with a passage time of fifty days to both Suez and Bombay. From the date of embarkation, however, until the first of these liners returned to the UK was a period of almost four months, or seven months when the last came home. By adding turnround time in the UK it became apparent that few, if any liners on the WS route could complete more than two round trips per annum and would be hopelessly inadequate if the present rate of Middle East reinforcement was to be maintained. The measures adopted to solve this problem evolved as the year 1941 progressed.

Chapter 7

WS 6 and the Beginning of the Troopship Shortage

WS 6 - sailed UK 6 - 8 February 1941

Prior to the autumn of 1940 there was little if any forward planning or agreement on the provision or allocation of shipping for personnel transport and other military purposes. The "War Office merely stated their military requirements and the Ministry of Shipping found ways and means of meeting them as far as possible."[1] The system could only last as long as the supply of suitable ships, which by the end of 1940 with WS 5B committed to embarkation was almost exhausted. Even more importantly, however, the continual withdrawal of ships from trade to meet military requirements began to seriously affect the UK import programme.

In October 1940 the Directorate of Movements at the War Office "foresaw that military movements to the Middle East in the next few months must be limited to the shipping available."[1] Discussions then began between the Trade Division and the Director of Sea Transport "with a view to making the best use of the shipping available, e.g. by grouping the faster ships and by transhipment from Union Castle liners at the Cape" - the latter system then being tried in WS 3F and WS 4A.

The object of these discussions was to prepare an appreciation for the Chiefs of Staff so that their commitments to the Middle East and India might be kept within the practicable. The discussions were cut short by a request for a six months forecast of military requirements which finally evolved in a paper dated 27 November, showing a need for 289,000 Army and RAF personnel for the Middle East and India during the first six months of 1941. When RN requirements were added the forecast was for 60,000 to sail in January, 50,000 in February and 55,000 in March: a total of 165,000 during the first three months of the year. The War Office planned on this basis and arranged the mobilization and equipment programme accordingly.

However, on 20 December the Ministry of Shipping sent a warning letter to the War Office, pointing out that trooping and other demands to the Middle East "are likely to curtail the already curtailed food and supply programme in the near future to such a substantial extent that the Ministry of Shipping hesitates to make the necessary arrangements until the other Ministers concerned have been warned of their effect."[2] The Ministry further stated that "eight ships are still being held after a lapse of three or four months against the contingency of special moves having to be undertaken at short notice.[2] This referred to ships kept at four days notice for a probable expedition to seize the Atlantic Islands, and in addition to cargo liners, referred to *Sobieski* and *Kenya* still at Freetown and "probably now so foul that they would be unable to...sail in convoy."[2] There was also *Ettrick*, *Karanja* and *Pulaski* in the Clyde at similar notice and the Ministry urged their release and also asked the War Office to consider if some fast personnel and MT ships, or even homeward loaded ships could use the Mediterranean route and so reduce the turnround time of Middle East voyages. The War Office placed these points before the Chiefs of Staff for consideration.

The Admiralty viewpoint on WS convoys began to emerge on 30 December when they stated that the escort situation would only allow one Middle East convoy per month, and that the maximum number of ships per convoy should be 35, both from the safety point of view and the limited facilities at Freetown.[3] The Admiralty said that "the monthly convoy should proceed in two parts sailing within a few miles of each other, personnel ships being protected by two cruisers and the MT ships by one AMC".[3] They also thought "not more than 25 troopers (should be) in any one convoy but should as far as possible be equally distributed between the two convoys."[3] On this basis WS 6 could proceed as planned in two parts, a slow portion of 10 knots at the end of January comprising about 21 troopers and 14 MT ships, while the fast portion of 15 knots would sail at the end of February containing as many troopers as could be got ready plus a few fast MT ships.

On the same date the Ministry of Shipping advised the War Office of deficiencies on the Middle East trooping programme, i.e. the short embarkation of 1,300 on the slow December convoy WS 5A, a shortage of 2,000 berths on the fast December convoy WS 5B, sailing 7 January, due to two ships having been damaged and no others being available,[4] and to a shortage of 7,000 out of 63,000 planned for WS 6 in January and February, but increased to 10,300 by the shortages already referred to in WS 5A and B.

On 1 January 1941 the Ministry told the War Office that WS 6A could sail on 27 January comprising 22 personnel ships carrying 33,000 plus 14 MT ships, but thought the convoy unsatisfactory as several ships of 15 knots and one of 16 knots would then be in a convoy limited by ships of not more than 12 knots giving a speed of advance of only 10 knots.[5] WS 6B (which ultimately became WS 7) could sail at the end of February containing 19 personnel ships with a capacity of 33,000 and speed of advance of 15 knots (ships of 17 knots) but only two fast MT ships would be available. This convoy would reach the Middle East about ten days after WS 6A. The Ministry of Shipping asked for urgent approval of these two convoys as four of the ships for WS 6A would have to be taken over next day to start fitting, while some of the fast liners of WS 6B had first to make a voyage to Canada sailing from the UK about 9 January.

Next day the Chiefs of Staff produced a lengthy memorandum on the subject of Middle East convoys, which noted the constraints imposed by the Admiralty and implied that instead of the 165,000 personnel provided for in the first three months of 1941, the Ministry of Shipping could now only produce shipping for an absolute maximum of 86,000 and even this would further curtail the food and supply import programme.

The Chiefs of Staff deliberated two possibilities of making the best possible use of the maximum 42 liners and 16 MT ships which could be provided before the end of March, i.e. either

Case A   WS 6 to sail 28 January of 23 liners and 14 MT ships with a speed of 12 knots and capacity for 34,400 personnel, plus
WS 7 to sail 1 March of 19 liners and 2 MT ships with a speed of 17 knots and capacity of 51,600. Total 86,000 personnel
or

Case B   WS 6A to sail as above with capacity for 34,400 personnel, plus
WS 6B to sail 14 February of 9 liners and 2 MT ships, speed 17 knots and capacity 23,800,
and
WS 7 to sail 1 March of 10 liners speed 17 knots and capacity 27,800. Total 86,000 personnel

After a long and detailed analysis it was finally agreed to adopt case A as this met the Admiralty's wishes and also permitted four liners to complete an intermediate North Atlantic voyage prior to WS 7, which in turn would clear all January commitments in respect of RN, RAF, MN crews, War Missions and Prisoners of War bound to Canada.[7]

The Ministry of Shipping again warned that it would still be necessary to curtail in the near future the already curtailed food and supply programme. The Chiefs of Staff therefore asked for a further review of Middle East requirements to ascertain if some not vital personnel might be excluded from the January/February convoys, and thus minimize any further curtailment of the food and import programme. This resulted in a reduction of WS 6 from 34,400 to 28,000 by releasing four mainly cargo ships not yet converted but already allotted, i.e. the Blue Funnel *Bellerophon*, B.I. *Mulbera*, Ellerman's *City of Marseilles* and Royal Mail *Highland Brigade* whose large and invaluable refrigerated capacity outweighed her small trooping capacity even if fully converted. The Ellerman ship had been used for trooping during the First and between the two World Wars, but agreement was reached "on 5 January to exclude all four ships which are least suitable for troops and most valuable for cargo";[8] their total cargo deadweight capacity was 41,000 tons.

In a similar manner WS 7 was to be reduced from 51,000 to 48,000 by releasing

Georgic to remain on North Atlantic service and provide for the monthly programme of RAF personnel training in Canada, in addition to having a cargo deadweight of 16,000 tons including deck space for up to 20 aircraft.

The reduction of numbers in WS 6 was to be met by cutting out 2,000 RAF, one Searchlight Battery of 400 and 3,600 Reinforcements giving a total of 6,000. The whole revised programme was approved on 5 January and only slightly amended a week later when the sailing date of WS 7 was put back from 1 to 8 March. This still did not resolve the personnel ship problem, for on 8 January the War Office deferred the move of an entire Division to the Middle East, but "now felt the situation had been reached where good cargo ships were to be converted to indifferent troop carriers and good liners withdrawn to carry cargo."[1] They urged "joint planning to obtain the best approach to the right solution of the combined strategic and shipping problem,"[1] and similarly wrote the Ministry of Shipping seeking closer co-operation between the Department of Sea Transport and War Office "to secure the most intelligent and economic use of shipping to meet military requirements."[1] Even before WS 6 sailed, however, the Vice Chief of the Naval Staff had to complain about the low speed of some of the ships being included in the convoy. Although the Ministry of Shipping had stated on 3 January that the slowest ship would be 12 knots, subsequent meetings revealed that 11.5 knots would be the slowest ship. Nevertheless, all parties had agreed to this lower speed, but on 17 January the Ministry asked Admiralty approval for an 11 knot ship to be included, which was refused. On 1 February the D of S T produced a list of the ships that were to form WS 6, which showed that five were below the minimum approved speed of 11.5 knots. Although the Admiralty appreciated that nothing could then be done to find suitable substitutes and therefore had to accept the slower ships, they nevertheless complained that "The D of S T by neglecting to inform the Admiralty in sufficient time of their inability to produce ships of the required speed, have failed to co-operate with other departments concerned in this most important troop movement."[9]

By the end of December 1940, 16 of the 24 transports selected for WS 6 were in UK ports either discharging inward cargoes or being fitted out for trooping. They comprised the Shaw Savill *Mataroa*, which had landed her New Zealand cargo at Glasgow, then moved to Liverpool on 22 December for fitting; the Blue Funnel *Ascanius* which berthed at Liverpool from the Far East on 3 December, the New Zealand Shipping Company's *Ruahine*, discharged and fitted at Avonmouth, *Rangitata* and *Federal Northumberland* similarly handled at Liverpool. Three Henderson ships were taken up from the Rangoon service of which *Burma* and *Yoma* were fitting at Liverpool, while *Salween* was handled by Barclay Curle in Glasgow. Also included were Furness Lines *Nova Scotia* which berthed at Liverpool from Halifax on the last day of the year, Norwegian America Line *Bergensfjord* which arrived at Liverpool from Halifax on 17 December, and *Llangibby Castle* which came into the same port from South and East Africa one week earlier, after temporary trooping employment between Durban and Mombasa.

On 8 January 1941 *Scythia* reached Liverpool with 7,000 tons of general cargo to discharge from Durban, after her voyage in WS 4A; she was drydocked, overhauled and fitted for 3,000 troops and was thus by far the largest carrier in WS 6. *Almanzora* reached Glasgow on 16 January with 2,200 tons of cargo, also from Durban and WS 4A, while *Highland Brigade* moored in the Holy Loch section of the Clyde Emergency Port next day, having 6,690 tons to discharge, also from Cape ports on completion of her WS 3 voyage to Suez. The PSNC *Oropesa* should also have reached Liverpool that same day, with 3,000 tons of South African general cargo after a similar WS 3 voyage, but was torpedoed and sunk in the Western Approaches. Two other liners allocated to the convoy were the Union Castle intermediate liner *Llandaff Castle* that berthed in Liverpool with 5,223 tons of general from South and East Africa on 13th January, and *Llanstephan Castle* with 6,368 tons from the same ports, which berthed in Glagow on 26 January. Finally two Belgian Lloyd liners became available: the elderly coal burner *Thysville*, a sister of *Elisabethville* which sailed in WS 5A, and the more recent motor ship *Leopoldville*, which berthed at Liverpool from Halifax on 15 January for discharge and fitting. *Thysville* similarly reached Liverpool from Halifax with 3,868 tons of cargo on 11 January. By the end of that month 19 ships were being fitted and prepared for embarkation, planned for the first week of February, but *Northumberland* and *Llanstephan Castle* were not completed in time, and left the UK ten days behind the main convoy.

The positioning of ships for the complicated business of embarkation began on 30 January when *Llangibby Castle* left Liverpool for the Clyde, reaching there next day and moving upriver at 1600 on 2 February, close astern of *Highland Brigade* from the Holy Loch. On 1st February *Mataroa* left Liverpool for the Clyde Anchorage, and was followed next day by *Scythia*, *Leopoldville*, *Rangitata* and *Bergensfjord*; the latter going upriver to KGV River Wall on 3 February, passing *Salween* moving down to the anchorage. Embarkations were carried out approximately as in[10] with an estimated 22,875 being embarked on the sixteen transports, all but 800 for the Middle East.

After completing embarkation at KGV Dock, the four transports from Glasgow moved downriver to join those at the Clyde Anchorage and were all ready for sea by midday on 7 February. *Ruahine* locked out of Avonmouth 24 hours earlier and joined the Liverpool portion in the northern half of the Irish Sea during the evening of the 8th February, while the Clyde portion simultaneously left that anchorage; the whole convoy of 17 transports and 12 MT ships forming up in the North Channel at 1230 next day. Ocean escort was provided by the cruisers *Birmingham*, *Phoebe* and AMC *Cathay* while the A/S escort was made up of 13 destroyers with the S.O. in *Ottawa*. The Commodore, Vice Admiral F A Martin, was embarked with his staff on *Llangibby Castle* (Captain J Lecky).

The convoy had barely settled into cruising order, when the SOE in *Birmingham* received an Admiralty signal to the effect that an enemy pocket-battleship had been sighted by *Ramillies*, then escorting a homeward Halifax convoy, in a position 900 miles west of Ireland. Home Fleet units were at once sailed to the westward to take up intercepting positions, and although the *Admiral Hipper* was in fact in the North Atlantic at this time, the sighting by *Ramillies* had actually been the battlecruisers *Scharnhorst* and *Gneisenau*.

WS 6 meanwhile remained on its course, minus *Burma* and *Yoma* which left the convoy to return to the Clyde and Liverpool with engine trouble. During the evening of the first day at sea, 9 February, several destroyers fired off starshells in response to flares, the origin of which was unknown, but which were mistakenly interpreted as signals that an attack was in being. The Canadian destroyer, *Ottawa*, reported that a derelict tanker was passed at 2300 that evening. It seems likely that outlying escorts fired off illuminating flares to warn the approaching convoy of such a danger to navigation. The Commodore reported a speed of 9.5 knots during the first day at sea, but thereafter until past the Azores on 17 February, the speed varied between only 7.5 and 8.5 knots.

At daylight on the 10th, *Cape Horn* and *Opawa* were badly astern of the convoy. The destroyer *Napier* was sent to cover them against air or submarine attack, while the convoy speed was reduced to 7 knots to allow them to catch up. In the early hours of the 11th, *Ottawa* obtained a doubtful Asdic contact and dropped a depth charge, without any apparent result. The position given was south of the Rockall Bank and very close to the sunken position of *Athenia*. During that same day *Cape Horn* was hove-to for an hour to make good a defect; the destroyer *Restigouche* provided cover until she rejoined, but at daylight, 12th, she was again badly astern and was ordered to steer a straight course (i.e. without zigzagging) until she caught up.

Also during the 11th when WS 6 was northwest of Ireland, the *Hipper* attacked and was reported by an unescorted SL convoy from Sierra Leone, in a position 600 miles west of Gibraltar. Heavy fleet units of Force H at once prepared to sail from the latter port to intercept, and although none of the German warships made contact with WS 6, Force H joined the escort from the 15th onwards.

At midday on 12 February, in a position 430 miles west of Bloody Foreland, the destroyer escort detached from WS 6 to return to their bases, two going to Scapa, three to Londonderry and eight to Greenock. The ocean escsort now disposed itself with *Cathay* zigzagging ahead, *Birmingham* and *Phoebe* astern to port and starboard respectively.

There were no incidents for the next two and a half days, until 0200 on the 15th, when *Thysville* and *Cape Horn* were found to be badly astern of the convoy. As it was necessary to alter course to the northwestward, to rendezvous with the battleship *Rodney* at daylight, *Birmingham* dropped astern to pass instructions to both ships "to steer to starboard and catch up on the turn." When *Rodney* subsequently joined WS 6 with two E class destroyers, she took station three miles ahead of the port column, while *Birmingham* took up a similar station on the starboard column. *Cathay* moved astern and *Phoebe* detached for Gibraltar to refuel, but rejoined ten days later.

Lame ducks among the MT ships continued as the convoy slowly steamed south. On the 16th *Manchester Citizen* had to stop for half an hour at daylight to effect repairs, and was covered by *Cathay* while astern of the convoy. The SOE on *Birmingham* subsequently remarked that *Thysville* and *Cape Horn* were very often badly astern of station, but never in danger of losing touch with the convoy.

On 17 February in the vicinity of the Azores, the great battlecruiser *Renown* and aircraft carrier *Ark Royal*, both of the famous Force H, joined the convoy escort, while the battleship *Malaya* also joined and relieved *Rodney* which left the convoy in pursuit of other orders. The weather conditions now improved and speed was increased to a steady 9.5 to 10.5 knots.

WS 6 passed the Cape Verde islands on 25 February, where *Mulbera* detached into St. Vincent to refuel, while *Renown* and *Ark Royal* left and returned to Gibraltar just as *Phoebe* rejoined. *Malaya* remained with the convoy until the day prior to arrival at Freetown on 1st March. A whole week was spent in this port awaiting the arrival and replenishment of the smaller, following convoy WS 6B.

It will be recalled that the two Henderson transports *Burma* and *Yoma* returned to the Clyde and Liverpool respectively from WS 6, and were later incorporated in WS 6B. Added to these were *Llanstephan Castle* and *Northumberland* which had been unable to complete fitting in time to sail with WS 6. The former moved downriver from Yorkhill Basin to embark at the Clyde Anchorage on 15 February, and was followed by *Northumberland* two days later, and that same evening all four ships sailed from their respective ports, with the addition of Elder Dempster's *Adda*, still on West African commercial service but included in the convoy for protection purposes.[11] All four transports and *Adda* were formed up as WS 6B on the morning of 18th February. Two destroyers accompanied the two ships from Liverpool while three others with the cruiser *Mauritius* and AMC *Cilicia* sailed with the Clyde portion.[12] The Commodore was embarked on *Llanstephan Castle* while the Master of *Burma*, Captain F E Jones, acted as Vice Commodore. Shortly after forming up, *Burma* developed a machinery defect and had to return to the Clyde. Her troops were disembarked and she returned to Glasgow for repairs and was then returned to the Liner Division, but later provided local trooping service on the East African coast.[13]

The remaining four transports continued towards Freetown. When south of the Cape Verde islands on 2 March, the AMC *Cilicia* detached from the escort to join the homeward convoy SL 67. On the 5th *Mauritius* arrived in Freetown with WS 6B to water and fuel, and to join with the main body of WS 6.

Highland Brigade was partly disembarked at Freetown and left that port on the 8th to land her remaining personnel at Takoradi and Lagos. She departed the latter port on the 14th for Buenos Aires to load refrigerated produce for home, reaching Liverpool on 11 May and sailed outward again in WS 9A.

The combined sections of WS 6 sailed from Freetown as one convoy on the forenoon of 8 March, comprising 16 transports with accompanying MT ships, escorted by *Birmingham*, *Phoebe*, *Cathay* and a local anti-submarine escort. On that same date, in a position 900 miles northwards, a patrolling aircraft from the battleship *Malaya*, then escorting the homeward convoy SL 67 sighted the German battlecruisers *Scharnhorst* and *Gneisenau*. Due to the presence of *Malaya* they did not attack SL 67 and their subsequent direction of movement was unknown, but their appearance was sufficient to alert the Admiralty who sent the cruiser *Cornwall* to strengthen the escort of WS 6. This cruiser joined in a position 50 miles north of the equator at midday on the 11th. *Cathay* was then released to proceed ahead independently to Capetown. Unknown to the Admiralty, the pocket battleship *Admiral Scheer* and raider *Kormoran* were in the Southwest Atlantic at this time, but neither approached the Cape - Freetown route until some time after WS 6 had passed clear.

When *Cornwall* was in process of joining WS 6, the Commodore on *Llangibby Castle* had dropped astern due to a breakdown of the ship's main engines, and the destroyer *Vidette* had been sent back to stand by her. After consulting by signal, *Cornwall* ordered the Commodore to transfer to *Scythia* by means of a boat provided by *Phoebe*. *Llangibby Castle* eventually got under way and was escorted back to Freetown by *Vidette*, where they arrived on the 15th. She remained at Freetown, most likely with the troops still on board, until these could be transferred to the next outward convoy WS 7. *Llangibby Castle* then left Freetown with convoy SL 71 on 8 April, reached the Clyde on 3 May and moved upriver to spend four weeks undergoing machinery repairs.

WS 6 enjoyed air cover from the cruisers *Birmingham* or *Cornwall* from 11 to 13 March, when a heavy swell put a stop to flying. On the 12th *Cornwall* had one machine damaged on landing, and as that ship was short on aircraft spares it was taxied over to and hoisted aboard *Birmingham*. This left each cruiser with one operational aircraft. Also on the 12th *Cornwall* transferred medical supplies to *Salween*, who reported a case of cerebro-spinal meningitis and had insufficient medicines to deal with any spread of the outbreak. At midnight that night, in accordance with a signal from the C in C South Atlantic, course was altered to east, presumably to distance the convoy from the normal Cape - Freetown trade route.

There were no incidents for the next week as the convoy steadily steamed SE towards the Cape, experiencing fine weather throughout. The cruisers carried out range and inclination exercises and occasional practice firings. On the 19th *Mulbera* dropped astern reporting trouble with the main engine lubrication system. As she still dropped astern with the convoy reduced to 8 knots, she was ordered to proceed direct and independently to Capetown for repair and obtain further orders and did not rejoin the convoy.

The slow and lengthy voyage from Freetown to the Cape now began to reveal shortages of fresh water on five of the transports. Arrangements were therefore made to water these ships at Capetown, even though they were actually designated part of the Durban portion of the convoy. At 0800 on 20th March, *Birmingham* accordingly detached ahead with *Scythia*, *Almanzora*, *Bergensfjord*, *Llanstephan Castle* and *Ruahine*. They reached Capetown late next afternoon and berthed alongside to water as requisite, sailing again the following morning to catch up and rejoin the convoy.

Birmingham left the convoy at Capetown and subsequently sent an interesting report to the Admiralty, which commented that the Freetown - Cape leg of the passage was so slow and long that fuel would not allow the cruisers to zigzag at a higher speed, independently of the convoy. *Cornwall* additionally remarked on the "small fuel capacity of *Phoebe* which had to be nursed as much as possible between Freetown and the Cape."[14] *Birmingham* also remarked that "the difference in maximum speed between the largest and smallest (ships) was almost too great for them to be included in the same convoy,"[15] which echoed a similar line of thought from the Ministry of Shipping as early as 1 January (*q.v.*).

Some correspondence resulted from the arrival of WS 6 at the Cape. It appears that a subsequent Commodore's report, (not seen amongst the official records) complained about "the lack of forward information on the re-arrangement of the convoy at the Cape, resulting in decisions which had to be made by the Commodore on the 18th." The D of S T replied by stating that the delay in providing the information "arose from the necessity to release the four refrigerated ships in South Africa. The difficulty of providing (onward) transport for the personnel etc. on these ships was very great and the final signal giving the arrangements could not be got out until the 10th."[16] The reader is referred back to the arrival of WS 5A at Suez, where, after much confusion and change of orders, four ships were eventually despatched to Durban for the on-carriage of personnel in WS 6. These ships arrived at Port Sudan for water on the same date as the signal was transmitted to WS 6. However, the D of S T further stated that the signal of the 10th "was passed to the C in C South Atlantic and to ships of the escort, and that the C in C made consequential arrangements on the 12th." Clearly there was some breakdown in forwarding the plan of arrangements for WS 6 at the Cape. It is possible that signals were misplaced in the haste of transferring the Commodore from *Llangibby Castle* to *Scythia* on 11 March.

The convoy continued on its way and at 1800 on the 21st, the Capetown portion was detached with *Phoebe*, comprising *Llandaff Castle*, *Nova Scotia*, *Ascanius*, *Leopoldville*, *Consuelo*, *Opawa*, *City of Athens*, *Burdwan*, *Kina II*, *Cape Horn* and *City of Marseilles*. At 2300 that same evening *Port Alma* was also detached to Capetown in response to a signal from N.O.I.C. Simonstown. The Capetown portion berthed in the harbour next morning to water and fuel, and to allow the troops to exercise ashore. The four transports, with an unknown number of MT ships, sailed again five days later and rejoined the Durban portion outside that port on 1st April.

Cornwall remained with the Durban portion which passed around Cape Agulhas during the night of 22/23 March. At 1527 on the afternoon of the 24th, some distance to the SE of Port Elizabeth, *Cornwall* sighted *Phoebe* with the five transports that had diverted to Capetown for water, plus *Consuelo*, and ordered them to rejoin the Durban portion two hours after daybreak next morning. It is presumed there was insufficient daylight left to allow them to rejoin on the 24th without unduly slowing down the convoy, which proved a wise decision as they did not finally take up their stations until 1500 on the 25th. The convoy was then approaching Port St. Johns, and at dusk *Phoebe* was sent on ahead with six of the faster ships, to arrive at Durban at 0800 next day. *Cornwall* arrived with the remainder of the convoy at 1030 hours that same day.

Of the 11 transports that reached Durban on 26 March, *Almanzora*, *Rangitata*, *Ruahine*, *Northumberland* and *Mataroa* were completely disembarked and detached from the convoy. All of the 7,700 troops from these five ships were transhipped at Durban to *Dilwara*, that arrived empty from Bombay on 17th March, and on *Elizabethville*, *Costa Rica*, *City of London* and *City of Canterbury* sent down from Suez after completing their outward voyage in WS 5A, which all arrived independently between the 26th and 29th, but could not be accommodated in the harbour until the latter date. *City of Canterbury* berthed initially at the Bluff to bunker with 2,300 tons of coal, and to store for the coming voyage, before shifting berth to begin embarkation in a very crowded harbour. There was some mixing of the troops after transhipment, although the 1,500 on *Northumberland* were fully accommodated on *City of Canterbury*. Miscellaneous units for East Africa on various ships were transhipped to *Llandaff Castle* at Capetown, as this vessel was to terminate at Mombasa. The entire transhipment programme was planned and carried out by the Impcon staff in conjunction with orders from the War Office. The large transhipment camp at Clairwood had a capacity of 10,000, mainly under canvas, and was gradually increased to a maximum of 30,000. Special trains ran between the Camp and Durban docks, the troops retaining only their 'Seakit' bags while the 'Universal' bags remained in store at the docks.

Of the liners detached from WS 6 at Durban, *Almanzora* left on 29th March to load a general cargo at Lourenco Marques, East London and Capetown. After fuelling at Freetown, she reached the Clyde on 8 May to find the river closed due to enemy mining and had to wait five days before proceeding to Glasgow to discharge and prepare for her next voyage in WS 8B. The other four liners that were left at Durban were refrigerated carriers directed to the River Plate to load meat for home. *Ruahine* and *Mataroa* left on 29 March, *Rangitata* next day and *Northumberland* on the 31st. *Rangitata* carried passengers on her homeward voyage from Buenos Aires, including a number of Polish and other volunteers for the services; she reached Liverpool on 24 May and next sailed in WS 9B. *Mataroa* similarly reached Avonmouth on 1 June and also sailed in WS 9B, *Northumberland* berthed at Liverpool on 2 June and then made a round trip to Halifax and New York, and finally the elderly *Ruahine* that loaded her homeward meat cargo at La Plata and reached Liverpool on 13 June. She also made her next voyage with RAF recruits to Halifax then proceeded to the Plate for a further homebound meat cargo.

WS 6 continued on its voyage from Durban on 1 April after six hectic days of troop transhipment and route marches, of bunkering, fuelling, watering and storing. The convoy comprised 11 transports, i.e. six from the UK and five that joined in Durban, and outside the port joined the four transports and MT ships from Capetown escorted by *Dorsetshire*. The total number of MT ships is not known, but the re-formed convoy set off for Suez with the cruisers *Cornwall*, *Dorsetshire* and *Phoebe* as escorts. *Dorsetshire* detached on the 7th and when nearing the latitude of Mombasa on the 9th, *Llandaff Castle* was detached into that port where she disembarked, cleaned and replenished to await an impending troop movement to Berbera. She was thereafter used exclusively on the CM route until her loss in 1942. Soon after the detachment of *Llandaff Castle*, the convoy was joined by the three-funnelled B.I. *Talamba* that had embarked native troops at Mauritius and the Seychelles for service in the Middle East. *Phoebe* detached next day while *Cornwall* continued with the convoy until it dispersed in the Red Sea.

No incidents occurred during the passage northwards until the convoy was passing through the Straits of Perim at 2000 hours on 16 April, when the Master of *City of Canterbury*, Captain Percival, reported "a very sudden and complete breakdown of the main engine air pump and we narrowly missed collision with *City of London*, the next ship astern."[17] Captain Percival noted that "with the help of the troops embarked, temporary repairs were effected to the air pump by noon next day, 17 April, and we then proceeded alone to Suez, arriving at 1500 21 April."[17] where he requested time for permanent repairs. Captain Percival also remarked that there had been some dissatisfaction about the food on the passage from Durban; "the flour was not quite as good as it should have been and biscuits were served in lieu occasionally."[17] The fault undoubtedly was due to storing problems at Durban where "the large number of ships...and the very short time in port" (only three days), had made it "difficult to obtain the necessary stores for the voyage, particularly flour, ice, beer, biscuits and potatoes, and we were short of all these commodities before reaching Suez."[17]

The independent arrival of the ships of WS 6 at Suez on 20 April coincided with the desperate need for personnel ships to evacuate Allied forces from Greece, and seven liners were immediately allocated for this purpose even before they had disembarked. On the 21st, *Dilwara*, *Salween*, *Ascanius*, *City of London* and *Costa Rica* passed up the canal to disembark that night in Port Said, followed next day by *City of Canterbury* and finally *Yoma* on the 23rd. Charts of Grecian waters were placed aboard each ship, they were ordered to be ready for sea at short notice, and sailed at various times during the afternoon and evening of the 23rd for Alexandria. A full account of their subsequent operations to Greece and Crete is outwith the scope of this volume, however, *Yoma* and *Ascanius* were not required and after cruising around outside Alexandria on the 24th, returned next day with *Cameronia* to Port Said and through the canal to Suez, where they anchored on the 26th to await further orders and were thereafter retained on the East Africa/Middle East route, as were *Thysville* and *Elizabethville* retained for the Durban/Middle East service.

Five liners that were handled at Suez as a matter of urgency were *Scythia*, *Leopoldville*, *Bergensfjord*, *Nova Scotia* and *Talamba*. As soon as all were disembarked the first three named re-embarked with Italian prisoners of war for South Africa. Added to this group was *Cameronia* (previously of WS 5B) which had been ferrying troops from Alexandria to Piraeus, and was now to load homewards on the Union Castle berth from Mombasa and Cape ports. These six liners sailed from Suez as convoy SW 6 at 0800 on 1st May, with the Commodore, Vice Admiral F A Martin, remaining on *Scythia* for the voyage home.[18]

The cruiser *Ceres* joined the convoy as ocean escort in the Red Sea and continued to Aden which was reached on 5 May and where *Nova Scotia*, a coal burner of only 13 knots speed, was detached to proceed independently to Durban, where she arrived a day behind the others and thereafter continued on the CM route between South and East

Africa and the Middle East.

After fuelling and watering at Aden, convoy SW 6 sailed again at 0830 on 6 May for Durban. An average speed of 14 knots was now maintained and *Ceres* continued as escort, being stationed three miles ahead of the Commodore on *Scythia*. Next morning *Talamba* was detached to proceed independently to Bombay, where she arrived on 11 May to begin conversion to a Hospital Ship for service on the newly developing route between India and the Persian Gulf. SW 6 passed through the Guardafui Strait during the night of 7/8 May and thereafter, unlike previous convoys, kept close to the East African coast.

When in a position 150 miles ENE of Mombasa, at 0730 on 11 May, *Ceres* was relieved as ocean escort by the AMC *Hector*, and left the convoy with *Cameronia* for Mombasa where they arrived that same day. *Cameronia* then began loading homeward cargo, embarked 1,800 Italian prisoners for South Africa and sailed on the 16th for Durban. Further loading was carried out there and at East London and Capetown before departing for Freetown, and at this latter port she was held for fourteen days awaiting escort, necessitated by increased U-Boat activity in the area between West Africa and Gibraltar. *Cameronia* was sent from Freetown to Gibraltar, where she caught up with *Scythia* (see below) and embarked refugees for the UK. The Commodore of SW 6 had cause to report on "the very heavy smoke made by *Cameronia* during the whole passage from Suez to Mombasa, apparently caused by dirty boiler tubes and defective burners", and noted that "these defects should be rectified before she is next included in convoy, which caused her to be a menace."[18]

After detaching *Cameronia* near Mombasa, SW 6 now of three liners continued due south for Durban. Three independent ships were sighted and identified during the next 24 hours, including *Thysville* that had left Suez five days ahead of the convoy, and which was overhauled at 0500 on the 12th. Just before noon that day, the convoy had to reduce speed to 13 knots on account of boiler trouble on *Scythia*, which continued for the next 24 hours and thereafter at various times, apparently due to water in the fuel system. At 0730 next day, 13th, when about 70 miles east of the port of Mozambique, *Hector* was relieved by the AMC *Ranchi*, which continued with the convoy to Durban and where they arrived on the 16th.

All three liners disembarked their Italian prisoner-passengers at Durban. *Scythia* then loaded a full general cargo of 5,299 tons including maize and copper, in ten days and sailed for home, fuelling at Capetown on 31 May and reaching Freetown on 9 June, where she was held for six days due to U-Boat activity before being sent to Gibraltar to embark refugees for the UK and await the arrival of *Cameronia*, which liner had loaded 3,366 tons in Durban also including maize, copper, sugar, meat and sisal. Both ships left under escort on 4 July bound for Glasgow carrying 2,202 and 1,607 personnel respectively including those from the Services, Merchant Seamen and refugees, and reached the Clyde on the 12th to pass upriver that same afternoon. Both liners berthed at the Anchor Line Yorkhill Quay terminal. *Scythia* spent four weeks in Glasgow discharging and repairing before moving to Liverpool to embark for WS 11, *Cameronia* sailed again two weeks later in WS 10: the Anchor Line having agreed to postpone drydocking to meet that sailing date.

After disembarking in Durban, the Norwegian *Bergensfjord* left that port as an empty ship on 27 May, proceeding direct to Victoria in the British Cameroons, where she embarked a full complement of native troops under British officers and sailed for Freetown, arriving there on 13 June to join WS 9A for Suez. *Leopoldville* spent three weeks undergoing engine repairs in Durban before loading there and at East London and Capetown. She left the latter port carrying 2,282 tons of homeward cargo on 18 June, bound not for Freetown but Trinidad, where independent shipping was being diverted to avoid the U-Boat concentration off the West African/Canaries route. She refuelled at Trinidad and Bermuda and arrived at the Holy Loch discharging port on 21 July. Her next service was to be three round trips to Iceland.

The last homeward ship of WS 6, *Llanstephan Castle*, left Suez independently on 5 May going direct to Durban where she arrived on the 20th to load there and at Capetown, before calling at St. Helena and Ascension as on an Intermediate Union-Castle voyage, then fuelled at Freetown and reached the Holy Loch on 22 July, where 5,000 tons of cargo was discharged in nine days. She then proceeded to Liverpool to prepare for an operational voyage to North Russia, and was not again used on the WS route.

Six of the 18 transports that had left the UK in February 1941 were thus retained for service on the Indian Ocean. With *Burma* withdrawn from Trooping as unsuitable, *Llanstephan Castle* allocated to Operations, *Ruahine* and *Northumberland* placed on Halifax voyages and *Leopoldville* to Iceland, only six liners returned to the UK for early inclusion in subsequent WS convoys.

Chapter 8

WS 7 - the Largest of the Series
in Gross Tonnage

WS 7 - Sailed UK 24.3.41

It was originally planned to sail this convoy at the end of February 1941 as the fast portion of WS 6, i.e. WS 6B, but the widely dissimilar speeds of the ships in the slow portion of the convoy, i.e. WS 6A, meant that even that portion had to be split into a slow and fast portion, and so the original WS 6B became WS 7, with a suitably delayed sailing date, which actually suited the War Office who required three of the liners to first make a round voyage to Halifax.

On 12 January the War Office gave their personnel requirements for WS 7 as 48,000, with a sailing date of 8 March. This was to be met by 18 liners with anticipated capacity of 48,466 when all were fitted-out, and having speeds between 17.5 and 21 knots. Only two MT ships were to be included, as no others were available with the required minimum speed of 17.5 knots. Although the sailing date was yet two months distant, shipping was already allocated and comprised one liner from WS 4A - *Stirling Castle,* the entire ten liners of WS 4B, the four liners of US 7 - *Strathmore, Stratheden, Orion, Batory*, and three from TC 9 - *Duchess of York, Orontes* and *Warwick Castle*.

Four additional liners mentioned as "might be available for WS 7" were *Pasteur*, which had failed to sail in WS 5B and was unsuitable because of her speed for WS 6. *Pasteur* actually remained at the Clyde Anchorage for three months from Christmas Day undergoing repairs to her generators and degaussing gear. Another liner suggested for WS 7 was the French Line's *Cuba*, which had been stopped and seized by a British warship at the end of October and sent into Freetown. Here she was requisitioned by the Ministry of Shipping and began trooping around the West African coast under Elder Dempster management, but was never made available for WS 7 and left Freetown in June 1941 for a full trooping conversion in the United States. It was hoped that the Dutch liners, *Dempo* (Rotterdam Lloyd) and *Johan van Oldenbarnevelt* (Nederland Line), would be included in WS 7, both having been idle at New York since the end of December. On 13 January they were chartered by the Ministry of Shipping and loaded with cargoes for the U.K. Two weeks later they sailed for Halifax where they were armed, degaussed and embarked with Canadian troops to their normal peacetime passenger capacity. After crossing the Atlantic with the three British transports in TC 9, they were fitted for trooping at Liverpool, but only half the work was completed on *Oldenbarnevelt* before sailing in WS 7, and unfortunately the speed of this ship reduced the convoy speed to 16 knots. The Polish *Batory* was not included as intended in WS 7, having been sent on a voyage to Halifax, but her place was taken by *Highland Monarch* from WS 4A, which brought the total estimated capacity of the convoy up to 53,446. The two MT ships allocated were the Glen/Shire Line's *Glenorchy*, which loaded at 2-3 KGV Dock in Glasgow, and her sister *Denbighshire*, which loaded in Liverpool.

Of the 21 liners allocated to WS 7, ten were already fitted for trooping but the remainder had very little troop fittings or none at all. The shiprepair yards therefore came under intense pressure during the months of February and March to prepare these ships for embarkation. The three liners from US 7 reached the UK between 2 and 4 February, *Strathmore* and *Orion* going to Liverpool and *Stratheden*, after discharging at the Clyde Anchorage moved to 8 KGV Dock in Glasgow for fitting. The ten liners of WS 4B arrived home between 14 and 27 February, except *Orcades* which had taken POW to Bombay and did not reach the Clyde and Glasgow until 7 March. Of these arrivals *Viceroy of India* and *Duchess of Atholl* were directed to Liverpool, also *Strathallan* for drydocking there after first discharging at the Clyde Anchorage. The others all discharged in Glasgow or the Clyde Anchorage whence *Andes* moved to Belfast for drydocking before embarking at Liverpool. *Stirling Castle* reached the Clyde on 15 February and was discharged, fitted and embarked at No. 1 KGV Dock over a period of 31 days. *Highland Monarch* was similarly handled entirely at the Clyde Anchorage over a period of 27 days from 25 February. The five liners of TC 9 anchored in the Clyde to disembark their Canadian troops on 28 February; *Duchess of York* and the two Dutch liners then moved to Liverpool, *Orontes* to Avonmouth and *Warwick Castle* to Yorkhill Quay in Glasgow. One further liner which joined the convoy for outward protection was the Cunard *Georgic*, then employed on Halifax round voyages from Liverpool, carrying RAF trainees outward and homeward in addition to full homeward cargoes which included aircraft on deck.

The War Office had originally planned to send 50 Northumbrian Division to the Middle East in WS 7, but Wavell did not agree this and wanted the convoy to comprise only drafts and non-divisional units. Wavell pointed out that "his fighting formations were well below strength...and that experience had shown the absolute necessity for a strong administrative backing of base and transportation troops."[1]

Beginning with WS 5B in the first week of January, just over half the total embarkation on WS convoys was carried out on the Clyde, divided between Glasgow and the Clyde Anchorage. Two ships of WS 7 embarked at Avonmouth and the remaining eight lifted nearly 20,000 personnel from Liverpool. By including *Georgic* carrying 3,000 for Halifax, an estimated 55,740 were embarked on this convoy which left the UK on 24 March.[2]

A few days prior to the commencement of embarkation, the Clydebank area of Clydeside was subjected to intense air raids on the two successive nights of 12/13 and 13/14 March. Damage to civilian property was severe while several oil storage tanks at Dalnottar and Old Kilpatrick were set alight. On the morning of 15 March a Norwegian tanker caught fire at an Oil Wharf, and had to be towed clear to an upriver berth at KGV Dock; during this passage one of the tugs exploded a mine and sank in the river near Renfrew Ferry. The river was closed for several days while minesweeping operations were carried out. Fortunately the enemy raids found no hits on John Brown's shipyard where the battleship *Duke of York* and monitor *Roberts* were fitting out in the basin, with the cruiser *Bermuda* in an advanced stage of construction on the stocks. Even better targets could have been found in the Glasgow docks which included 12 large liners and the battleship *Howe* in Fairfield''s Basin. All of these ships escaped damage and by 17 March shipping movements in the river had returned to normal and *Strathaird* that afternoon moved down to the anchorage fully embarked. Two days later *Empress of Canada* and *Stirling Castle* followed suit with *Orcades* in light condition, also *Warwick Castle* similarly light on 20 March. Next afternoon *Strathnaver* and *Otranto* had embarked and moved to the anchorage with an empty *Stratheden*.

A convoy conference was held at Gourock on 22 March and departure arranged for that evening, but the German battlecruisers *Scharnhorst* and *Gneisenau* had been sighted by aircraft from *Ark Royal* in the late afternoon of 20 March, some 600 miles WNW of Cape Finisterre, and the convoy sailing was delayed for 48 hours. The Admiralty disposed forces to intercept the enemy ships, which were sighted again by a Hudson of Coastal Command on the evening of 21 March within 200 miles of the French coast. Although it was believed they had gone into Brest, they were not definitely identified there until six days later, but the Admiralty allowed normal movements of Atlantic shipping to be resumed and for WS 7 to sail on 24 March with a heavy escort, which included the battleship *Nelson* then engaged in the search for the German ships.

At 2145 on 24 March the A/S escort comprising five Tribal and one of the ex American destroyers passed out through the Clyde boom gate, followed at 2200 by *Empress of Canada*, carrying Commodore R Elliott, OBE RNR, and at four minute intervals thereafter in the order *Warwick Castle*, *Stratheden*, *Strathnaver*, *Pasteur*, *Strathmore*, *Stirling Castle* (carrying the Vice Commodore E. Manner, RNR), *Glenorchy*, *Strathaird*, *Otranto* and *Orcades* at 2240. At midnight these ships were followed out by part of the ocean escort comprising *Edinburgh* of 18 Cruiser Squadron, which was to act as S.O.E., the battleship *Revenge* and two accompanying destroyers. The Clyde ships dropped their pilots off Toward Point where *Orontes* from Avonmouth joined up and all continued at 13 knots down the swept channel in single line ahead, spaced three cables apart and preceded by the destroyers of the A/S escort. It was an extremely dark night, heavily overcast with driving misty rain and poor visibility, in which it must have been difficult to maintain station with nothing other than the customary blue sternlights being shown.

All went well until "in the vicinity of Ailsa Craig the A/S escort was overtaken by *Empress of Canada* and another ship, presumed to be *Warwick Castle*, the second ship in the line. The destroyers increased speed to get ahead again and signalled *Empress of Canada* to reduce speed. Avoiding action was necessary by the destroyers to avert a collision."[3]   Unfortunately this near miss and another between *Stirling Castle* and *Strathnaver* was quickly followed by a serious collision between *Stirling Castle* and *Strathaird*.

The Clyde Searched Channel was maintained to a width of four miles divided centrally into an inward and outward lane by certain lighted buoys, one of which was positioned 7 miles NE of Ailsa Craig Light at a point where the channel changed direction by 45° degrees. It was shortly after this turn of four points to starboard that *Strathaird* ran into the port quarter of *Stirling Castle*, causing considerable damage to both ships. Captain Spradbrow of the latter ship subsequently reported that shortly after the turn, at 0150 hours, he "sighted a large ship very close on the starboard bow and heading across my bow to port, with no lights showing except a dim blue sternlight. The helm was immediately put hard a-starboard and the engines to full astern."[4] Two minutes later this ship, which was believed to have been *Strathmore*, the next ahead, miraculously cleared *Stirling Castle* by about 15 feet. At 0156 Captain Spradbrow steadied *Stirling Castle* "back on her course...at dead slow ahead to allow *Strathmore* to regain her correct station ahead."[4]   Unfortunately the short delay in being stopped was not observed or allowed for by the ships following astern, and at 0202 *Strathaird* caught up and struck the port quarter of *Stirling Castle*. Alarm gongs were rung on the latter and everyone sent to boat stations, but were later dismissed. After examination of the damage Captain Spradbrow decided "to proceed until daylight then make a further examination,"[4] and "at 0232 speed was increased and course set for the rendezvous" off Orsay which was reached at 0800. A daylight examination revealed the damage to be well above the waterline and Captain Spradbrow therefore decided to proceed on the voyage. *Stirling Castle* had been struck on the stern about 15 ft. to port of the centerline causing 11 frames to be badly twisted between C and D decks and spread over three strakes of plating. Most fittings remained intact although the Thermotank ventilation system and some wiring required replacement.

The damage to the bows of *Strathaird* was, however, sufficiently serious to prevent her continuing the voyage and she returned to the Clyde Anchorage where the troops were disembarked by tender to Gourock. On 30 March *Strathaird* returned upriver and berthed in Yorkhill Basin for repairs, which were completed in just over three weeks in time to sail with WS 8A. Captain Harry Williams, who had just taken over *Strathaird* following the retiral of Captain Dene, remained in command of the ship until his own retiral at the end of 1945.

Meanwhile the nine ship Liverpool portion, plus *Georgic*, left that port on the afternoon of 24 March with destroyer escort, and at 0800 next morning made rendezvous with the Clyde portion six miles west of Orsay Light. The two liners from Avonmouth, i.e. *Orontes* and *Reina del Pacifico*, were to have joined the Liverpool portion 20 miles NW of the Bar Light Vessel, but with the convoy sailing delayed by 48 hours these two liners were sent on to the Clyde to sail with that portion, by which time *Reina del Pacifico* had struck a submerged object and was unable to sail. Her troops were disembarked and she proceeded to Liverpool on 27 March for drydocking to effect bottom damage repairs and the fitting of a new starboard tailshaft; this work was completed in time to allow her to sail with WS 8A.

In misty weather to the west of Orsay the twenty liners and two MT ships were formed into six columns, while *Edinburgh, Nelson, Revenge* and the AA cruiser *Cairo* comprised an additional column in the centre of the convoy. *Nelson* and *Cairo* had joined from Scapa with three destroyers, which latter then detached to Londonderry for fuel while three others joined in lieu.[5]

In terms of gross tonnage of the troopships, totalling 412,580 tons, WS 7 was the largest WS convoy to date and was never subsequently surpassed, although the numbers embarked was four times exceeded in 1942. An interesting colour movie of this convoy came to light in 1988, taken by an officer on *Nelson*, which clearly shows the different paint schemes used on merchant ships at this stage of the war, before uniform grey became standard. *Pasteur, Empress of Canada* and *Stirling Castle* were certainly grey or differing shades of grey, but *Andes, Orcades, Orontes, Strathmore* and the two *Duchess* liners showed black hulls, grey upperworks and either black or grey funnels; *Strathallan* and *Strathnaver* had black hulls and black funnels with stone coloured upperworks. Most retained red coloured boot-topping and some even had their original name letters in white paint clearly visible on bows and sterns. Some shots of the liners arriving and departing Freetown reveal the characteristic troopship profile with hundreds of men crowded on deck and some in the rigging to gain a better vantage point. The unsuitablility of the North Atlantic liners in tropical climes is clearly demonstrated by scenes of one *Duchess* liner with a makeshift awning rigged on the foredeck and double shell doors open on the maindeck to assist ventilation into stifling and crowded accommodation.

Once formed up off Orsay, the convoy proceeded WNW until midday, when 30 miles NW of Tory Island, where course was altered to almost due west for a position 300 miles distant to the SW of Rockall Bank. At 1330 two destroyers joined from Londonderry and another three from that port at 1830, making 15 A/S escorts forming a screen around the convoy. At 0800 on 26 March course was altered to SW to pass midway between the islands of Fayal and Flores in the Azores group. At 2130 that evening six destroyers left to return home, by which time the convoy was 400 miles due west of Eagle Island on the Irish Coast. At 2300 the AA cruiser *Cairo* was also detached. Two destroyers of the ex-American type, *St. Clare* and *Broadwater*, were detached at 0830 on 27 March; these ships were to have left at 2130 the previous evening but the signal instructing them was not passed on owing to a mistake on *Eclipse*.

By noon on 28 March the convoy was only 500 miles north of the Azores group, at which time the four Tribal class destroyers which had sailed with the Clyde portion were detached to proceed to Scapa. This may have left the three destroyers which had originally joined wth *Nelson* from Scapa, but no record appears of their subsequent detachment. At 1230 that day *Georgic* detached with *Revenge* for Halifax, where they both arrived on 1 April. *Georgic* returned to the Clyde with Canadian troops in TC 10A and was then employed in WS 8B to Suez.

During the evening of 29 March the convoy passed between the westerly islands of the Azores group and at 2200 the cruiser *Edinburgh* handed over the duties of S.O.E. to the battleship *Nelson* and detached for Gibraltar. From this area most previous WS convoys had passed west of the Cape Verde islands, but WS 7 was routed SE to pass between these islands and the Senegal headland of Cape Verde.

At 1000 on 1 April the convoy was 400 miles north of the Cape Verde islands and here two destroyers, *Duncan* and *Foxhound* joined from Freetown to provide A/S escort. At 1300 next day when 100 miles east of the Cape Verdes, two more destroyers, *Wishart* and *Vidette* joined but "*Wishart's* Asdic was only effective ahead and *Vidette's* maximum speed was about 17 knots. Two enemy submarines were reported to be in the Cape Verde islands/Dakar area which we were now passing."[6]

At 0300 on 3 April the convoy reached a position F, some 160 miles SW of Bathurst, where it was directed to steer 112° direct to Freetown and distant 390 miles. Commodore Elliot did not agree this route, which was a typographical error and should have read 120°, a serious enough mistake, but even more importantly the real course of 120° "led the convoy through some 200 miles of mineable waters. The risk was not taken as I was not prepared to slow the convoy down twice in a submarine area to get paravanes out and in, especially after receiving warning that two submarines were working in the Dakar/Verde area."[7] The Commodore therefore shaped a course to keep the convoy outside soundings, until 134 miles west of Cape Sierra Leone when the final approach would be made to the end of the searched channel.

The Admiralty, however, subsequently did not agree the Commodore's action and considered "that the route of the convoy from position F should not have been altered. There were submarines in the area as stated and the route given by the Admiralty was the best calculated to clear the area in which these have generally operated. The alteration was not known or expected and might have required further instructions to be given. A ship was sunk 15 miles south of the course actually steered on the night after the convoy passed."[8] (This was the Kaye steamer *Marlene* torpedoed and sunk by *U105*.)

Nelson led the convoy safely into Freetown at 1230 on 4 April and simply commented that "the passage had been completely uneventful, no aircraft or submarines being sighted, and only two merchant ships, which were examined by *Edinburgh*. Except for the first two or three days when speed had to be reduced occasionally on account of the destroyer screen, the passage was made at 16 knots in perfect weather conditions."[6]

It was learnt on arrival in Freetown that fuelling and watering the 19 liners and 2 MT ships would take three days. *Nelson* therefore blew down two boilers for cleaning and landed about 600 libertymen each day as a break to shipboard routine. *Nelson* then reported that "there were no leave breakers and only eight cases of drunkenness which, considering the temperature was 92° Fahrenheit in the shade (33° Celsius), and extreme youth of the majority of the men landed is very creditable. Tropical kit was issued whilst at Freetown"....[6]

The convoy began leaving Freetown at 1315 on 7 April and *Nelson* followed the last ship out at 1530; once the convoy formed up she took up her original station between columns 3 and 4. *Highland Monarch* was left behind at Freetown, having troops for that port and for Takoradi and Lagos, whence she proceeded light ship to the River Plate to load on her owner's berth at Buenos Aires and La Plata. After bunkering at Montevideo and Trinidad, she reached Glasgow for discharge on 17 June, moving thence to drydock in Liverpool before sailing again in WS 10.

The A/S escort from Freetown was again provided by the same four destroyers of the Freetown Escort Force, and while an enemy submarine was known to have sunk a ship that morning about 60 miles west of the searched channel, nothing was seen of her. At 2130 that evening a boat with a light on it passed between the columns of the convoy. *Nelson* detached *Foxhound* to investigate, who rescued three natives who had been torpedoed in the Bullard King steamer *Umona*, eight days previously in a position 90 miles SW of Freetown. Shortly after rejoining the convoy at daylight next morning, *Foxhound* developed 'condenseritis' and was ordered by *Nelson* to return to Freetown. *Nelson* reported the temperature that day reached 101° Fahrenheit (38° Celsius) and that there had been one or two cases of heat exhaustion in the engine room.

The report of *Nelson* on WS 7 shows that the convoy crossed the Equator at 1250 on 9 April, "and in spite of not being able to stop the ship, Father Neptune and his retinue managed to get aboard and kindly held two courts, to allow men closed up at defence stations to obey his summons."[6] No less than "1,137 initiates were enrolled as his subjects with the usual rites and acclamations."[6] (The total war complement of *Nelson* was given as 1,314.) These scenes are shown in graphic detail on the movie film referred to above. At 1800 that evening the remaining three destroyers were detached to return to Freetown, and shortly after this *Johan van Oldenbarnevelt* reported her speed reduced to 9 knots for two hours by engine trouble. The convoy speed was reduced to 10 knots, zigzagging continuously, until *Oldenbarnevelt* rejoined and speed increased again by 2244. Next morning *Nelson* being the sole ocean escort took station 1.5 miles ahead of the convoy.

At 1600 on 13 April *Nelson* sighted and identified two ships, both Ellerman owned and at approximately the same time, i.e. *City of Florence* to port and *Kioto* to starboard. These were the only ships sighted on this long leg of the voyage between Freetown and the Cape.

At 1430 on 15 April the cruiser *Newcastle* joined and took over escort duties from *Nelson*. The convoy was then only 270 miles NW of Capetown so *Nelson* detached and proceeded ahead at 20 knots for that port, where she berthed next day at A berth in the Duncan Dock. The Capetown portion of the convoy also arrived that forenoon consisting of *Empress of Canada* (Commodore ship), *Andes, Pasteur, Orcades, Orion, Strathallan, Stratheden. Strathmore, Dempo, Duchess of Atholl* and *Duchess of York*. Also in Capetown at this time were *Duchess of Richmond* and *Capetown Castle* loading homewards from WS 5B, and the AMC *Carnarvon Castle* undergoing repairs after her action with *Thor* four months earlier. A fine panoramic photograph was taken of the harbour at this time, copies of which appear in the Harbour Master's office and in the P&O archives. These photographs and another of the convoy in the Indian Ocean,[9] again clearly show the differing colour schemes in vogue at this time ranging from the all grey of *Capetown Castle, Empresses of Canada* and *Australia, Andes* (possibly repainted in Capetown) and *Pasteur*, through dark grey hulls and light grey upperworks of *Warwick Castle, Strathallan* and *Strathmore* (also probably repainted) to the others still showing black hulls with grey or stone coloured uppers. All paint schemes other than overall and uniform grey were gradually being phased out, although it was late 1941 or early 1942 before this was standardised.

The splitting of the convoy had taken place 30 miles west of Capetown, at 0900 on 16th April when the Vice Commodore on *Stirling Castle* continued ahead with *Otranto, Orontes, Warwick Castle, Viceroy of India, Strathnaver, Johan van Oldenbarnevelt, Denbighshire* and *Glenorchy* as the Durban portion escorted by *Newcastle*, and arrived at that port at daybreak on 19 April. Both *Nelson* and *Newcastle* now left WS 7, the former ship concluding her report that the convoy "was a most inspiring sight to see and....their station keeping on the whole was very *good...Nelson* although presumably designed for tropical climates proved to be a very hot ship. A temperature of 140°F was reached in the engine room and the mess decks were surprisingly warm. This may be caused by wartime restrictions and lack of awnings and ventilation. Special arrangements had to be made to protect ready-use ammo lockers, etc."[6]

The nine ships which had gone to Durban found the port already crowded with five transports from WS 5B virtually being cleared out to provide berths for WS 7, i.e. *Arundel* and *Winchester Castle*, *Orbita*, *Franconia* and *Nea Hellas*.

The Dutch *Dempo* had also been due to bunker at Durban, but was first diverted into Capetown to embark 33 Army, 20 European and 42 Chinese and Javanese survivors, making a total of 1576 on board when she reached Durban on 20 April. *Dempo* had a cracked liner on the starboard engine which was temporarily repaired in Durban. All of the troops on *Dempo* and *Stirling Castle* were disembarked at Durban and transhipped to *Empress of Australia* and the remaining ships of the convoy. The *Empress* had only reached Durban a day ahead of the convoy, from Mombasa, and was really a homebound ship. *Stirling Castle* left the convoy at Durban where collision damage repairs were put in hand; she was then to load refrigerated produce in South America, but when repairs were completed on 26 April she sailed for Melbourne arriving there 14 days later and loaded a full refrigerated and general cargo for the UK in nine days. Her homeward voyage was via Panama and Halifax, embarking Canadian troops at the latter port and sailing in TC 11 for the Clyde; she arrived there on 30 June in time to disembark, discharge and complete repairs ready for sailing outward in WS 10.

In addition to engine repairs in Durban, *Dempo* also completed her DG equipment and embarked 1,512 South African troops, the advance parties of 2 South African Division going to Egypt, together with their military vehicles and equipment. The eight transports and two MT ships left Durban and assembled off the port at 1530 on 23 April. With the AMC *Carthage* as escort, the convoy set off eastwards at 11 knots to make a rendezvous with the Capetown portion, which had left that port on 20 April and came round the coast escorted by the cruiser *Hawkins*.

The two portions of WS 7 joined up in a position 150 miles ENE of Durban at 0500 on 25 April. *Carthage* then left the convoy in charge of *Hawkins* and proceeded on patrol. There were no incidents on the passage northwards, and when reaching latitude 5° North on 1 May, *Strathmore*, *Warwick Castle*, *Duchess of York* and *J V Oldenbarnevelt* detached as WS 7X under escort of the cruiser *Colombo* for Bombay, where they arrived on 5 May. *Duchess of York* left two days later for Colombo and Singapore, reaching the latter on 14 May. *Strathmore* spent four days in Bombay disembarking and re-embarking Indian reinforcements for Suez. She sailed in convoy BR 3, which also comprised four B.I. troopships bound for Basra. Escort was at first provided by the AMC *Antenor*, then *Kanimbla*, and *Strathmore* detached on 12 May to proceed independently to Suez where she arrived on the 19th. Both *Warwick Castle* and *J V Oldenbarnevelt* disembarked at Bombay, the latter then loaded commercial cargo for Singapore where she berthed on 20 May to discharge and to have extra accommodation fitted; she remained in Singapore for six weeks then proceeded to Sydney for service on the US route between Australia and the Middle East. *Warwick Castle* left Bombay on 15 May, loaded at Durban and Capetown and was the first ship to reach home, berthing at Liverpool on 24 June. Her next voyage was in WS 10.

After detachment of the Bombay section on 1 May, the transports and two MT ships continued northwards under escort of the cruiser *Glasgow*, without incident and were dispersed north of Perim late on 3 May. All 16 ships reached the Suez area on 6 May, to find that four ships of CM 8 had arrived five days earlier with South African troops, but more importantly the two monster liners *Queen Mary* and *Queen Elizabeth* were in the bay disembarking Australian troops, having arrived a day ahead of WS 7 on their first visit to Suez. The authorities therefore had to arrange the disembarkation and dispersal of 50,000 troops of three nationalities from twenty large transports. To add to the difficulties the canal was closed due to mining on 8 May for a period of fifteen days. The risk of having so many crowded transports within range of the Luftwaffe was indeed appalling, but the stakes were then extremely high; German forces were preparing to attack Crete while Rommel had driven the remnants of the Army of the Nile back to the Egyptian frontier and besieged British and Australian forces in Tobruk. On the credit side the Italians were being defeated in Eritrea, which now allowed unescorted shipping to use the Red Sea route without hindrance.

Disembarkation and discharge of the WS 7 ships at Suez was carried out on a phased basis so that only two or three ships were handled in the bay at any one time, thus reducing to a minimum the concentration of troops and ships in case of air attack. The remaining ships were kept at distant anchorages further down the Gulf of Suez.

The arrival of WS 7 coincided with that of a prominent shipowner sent out to Alexandria by the Ministry of Shipping to report on the increasing difficulties in the Middle East. He found that "arrangements had been plunged into a chaos...and the most appalling muddle,"[10] with the military authorities discharging whatever they needed most at any one time at the total expense of everything else, causing an impossible disorder and accumulation of quayside cargo for which there was no transport to clear. Obviously those troops and stores needed most were quickly handled, but the ships then emptied had to wait for southbound cargo or homeward personnel, and this took much longer and clearly was unacceptable; *Otranto* was at Suez for 25 days, *Orion* and *Empress of Australia* 23 days.

The handling of troopship personnel was further complicated in May by the despatch of Hospital Ships with wounded from the desert battles and Greece, *Vita*, *Tairea* and *Karapara* were there being despatched to Bombay, *Dorsetshire* to Durban and *Manunda* to Australia, the latter having arrived at Suez from Fremantle on 18 May on the first of many visits to pick up Australian wounded. Also on 21 May *Llandovery Castle* arrived from the UK via the Cape to commence a shuttle service to Durban. On 13 May three other monster liners, *Aquitania*, *Mauretania* and *Ile de France* arrived with Australian and New Zealand troops in US 10A.

The first ships to be disembarked and despatched from Suez were naturally the two *Queens*, thereafter *Andes* and *Pasteur* which left Suez on 11 May direct for Capetown, where they were bunkered and departed on 24 May not for Freetown but for Trinidad in the West Indies. Increased U-Boat activity off the West African coast necessitated the substitution of Trinidad for Freetown as a homeward bunkering port, adding 3,000 miles to the voyage or 8.5 days extra time at 15 knots. From Trinidad the liners were either sent direct to the UK or via Halifax where Canadian troops were embarked for the last leg of the voyage. All of the WS 7 ships except two were routed home via Trinidad. *Andes* and *Pasteur* formed part of, and joined *Stirling Castle* in TC 11 from Halifax (embarking 2744, 3570 and 1500 respectively), although they had to wait twelve days for embarkation to commence, which was utilized by loading cargo in Canadian ports: *Pasteur* at St. John's NB and *Andes* at Halifax.

Stratheden left Suez on the same date as *Warwick Castle* left Bombay, and whilst the latter had a relatively quick passage home, *Stratheden* called at Port Sudan, Aden and Mombasa, before drydocking at Durban for two weeks survey and overhaul. She then loaded at Capetown before crossing to Trinidad for fuel, being thereafter directed to the

Clyde and berthing in Glasgow on 19 July to discharge, some 25 days later than *Warwick Castle*. The Dutch liner *Dempo* left Suez on 17 May for Bombay and was retained on the India/Middle East route. *Strathallan* was next away from Suez on 18 May carrying 1,007 Italian POW and 155 British Army including guards all for the UK; she fuelled at Aden and loaded cargo at Mombasa and Capetown, bunkering again at Trinidad and sailing then direct to Glasgow where she berthed at KGV Dock on 11 July. The next departures from Suez were *Empress of Canada*, *Orcades* and *Viceroy of India* which cleared away on 22 May; the first carrying 800 Merchant Seamen for the UK, *Orcades* and the *Viceroy* with 1,000 POW each. The *Empress* bunkered at Aden and loaded at Durban, where the 800 Merchant Seamen were landed to follow in *Empress of Australia*. More cargo was loaded in Capetown before the *Empress* proceeded to Halifax via Trinidad to embark Canadian troops for the Clyde. *Orcades* loaded in Durban and Capetown and thereafter direct to Liverpool via Trinidad. *Viceroy of India* went to Aden to await convoy, as did *Duchess of Atholl*, which left Suez with 300 civilian personnel on 24 May, also *Strathnaver* and *Strathmore* with service personnel from Mombasa on 26 May and *Orontes* with 300 civlians a day later. On 29 May *Orion* left Suez empty and proceeded home via Mombasa, Durban, Capetown, Trinidad and Halifax. *Empress of Australia* also left on 29 May with 800 RAF and some Turkish Navy personnel for Aden, and finally *Otranto* was the last ship away on 31 May carrying POW to join the southbound convoy for Mombasa.

Having loaded homeward cargo at Singapore, *Duchess of York* left that port on 24 May and called again at Colombo before crossing the Indian Ocean to join six other liners at Mombasa. The two MT ships of WS 7 were discharged at Suez, Port Said, Haifa and in the Great Bitter Lake between 6 and 29 May. *Glenorchy* then loaded homewards from East and South Africa while *Denbighshire* loaded home from Singapore and Penang. The entire convoy had been at Suez from five to 25 days, the latter being unacceptably high for such large and valuable ships.

The six liners which gathered at Aden between 26 May and 21 June, were *Viceroy of India*, *Duchess of Atholl*, *Strathmore*, *Strathnaver*, *Orontes* and *Empress of Australia*. Commodore Elliot had transferred from *Empress of Canada* to *Strathnaver* for the homeward voyage, and reported that "while the convoy was collecting at Aden the heat was very trying, especially for ships at the outer anchorage where blackout was in force. *Duchess of Atholl* and *Strathnaver* each had two deaths on board before sailing, and the former ship obtained permission to proceed to sea p.m. the day before sailing on account of sickness on board; she joined the convoy at the outer end of the swept channel on the following morning. *Strathnaver* and *Viceroy of India* each had one death on the day of sailing."[11]

The southbound convoy was appropriately designated SW 7 and sailed from Aden at 0600 on 2 June escorted by the cruiser *Ceres*.[12] The Commodore noted that "the full force of the SW monsoon was met after clearing Cape Guardafui and speed was reduced to 14 knots before altering course to the SWestward at 1940 on 3 June. By 0630 on 4 June speed was reduced to 10 knots on request from the escort and remained at that until 0130 5 June when the wind and sea began to go down. A speed of 16 knots was gradually attained by 0715 on 5 June when force 6 - 7 with rough sea and moderate swell was experienced for about 24 hours."[11] The convoy maintained a distance of about 100 miles off the African coast until 0825 on 7 June, when the cruiser *Colombo* was met in a position 150 miles ENE of Mombasa. This cruiser then took *Duchess of Atholl* and *Empress of Australia* under escort and detached with them for Durban, where they arrived on 12 June. The other four liners with *Ceres* were berthed inside Mombasa harbour by 1900 on 7 June.

Whilst at Mombasa all ships loaded homeward cargo while the two *Straths* landed the personnel bound for that port. On 9 June they were joined by *Otranto* from Suez and *Duchess of York* from Singapore and Colombo. These six liners sailed from Mombasa as convoy SW 7A between 1500 and 1700 on 9 June bound for Durban, and by 1920 had formed up and proceeded south at 16 knots, but at 2100 *Viceroy of India* signalled she could not keep up and speed was reduced to 15.75 knots. The *Viceroy* had apparently damaged a propeller when entering Mombasa two days earlier.[13]

Commodore Elliott remained on *Strathnaver* and Captain Sapsworth of *Duchess of York* was appointed Vice Commodore. Escort was again provided by *Ceres*, which at 2320 on the evening of departure asked for a reduction of speed to 14 knots, presumably due to the SW monsoon weather, but by next morning the wind and sea had moderated and speed was again increased to 15.5 knots. On 12 June the sea was calm and speed was increased to 16 knots at 0835, but that morning the *Viceroy* had to blow down one boiler for cleaning and could not maintain 16 knots. Next morning the wind was NNW 4 - 5, but by 1100 hours had backed to SSW 6 - 7 with a moderate sea and speed had again to be reduced to enable *Viceroy* to keep up, finally by 2230 speed was down to 15 knots. The convoy arrived at the outer end of the Durban swept channel at 1030 14 June, when *Otranto* and *Duchess of York* entered harbour while the other four ships anchored in the roads to await a berth.

Also in Durban at this time were *Empress of Canada*, *Orion* and *Stratheden*, and with a brief call *Otranto* and *Duchess of York* left again the same day with the two latter ships: *Otranto* loading thereafter at East London and Capetown before proceeding to Liverpool via Trinidad. *Duchess of York* and *Otranto* both completed with cargo at Capetown and sailed for Halifax via Trinidad before reaching the UK in TC 12 with Canadian troops. *Viceroy of India* and *Strathmore* left Durban on 15 June, the former routed via Capetown and Trinidad to Liverpool, the latter to Port Elizabeth, Capetown, Trinidad and Halifax for the TC 12 convoy to the UK. *Empress of Australia* left Durban on 17 June, completed cargo at Capetown on 28 June but put back three days later for repairs, which lasted until 11 July. She finally left Capetown escorted by the AMC *Canton* for Freetown, thence to Liverpool where she arrived on 8 August, the last of the 19 liners of WS 7 to reach the UK.

Strathnaver had left Capetown on 27 June, *Duchess of Atholl* on 1 July and *Orontes* 6 July. The first ship was directed to Trinidad and Halifax for inclusion in TC 12, the other two liners bunkered at Trinidad and thereafter sailed direct to the Clyde, where they arrived on 26 July and 1 August respectively.

The homeward voyages of the WS 7 liners had therefore been rather protracted; *Andes* and *Pasteur* had loaded only in Canada but nevertheless took 37 days to reach the UK. Of the other five which returned via Halifax, their homeward voyages lasted from 62 to 67 days, while those which proceeded direct from the Cape, Freetown or Trinidad took 40 to 71 days. Undoubtedly they carried full cargoes of much needed commodities including foodstuffs, but their next outward voyages in WS 10 and 11 must have been delayed in consequence. The fastest round voyage out and home had been 80 days and the longest nearly four months.

Chapter 9

Departures in April and May 1941
WS8A, 8B, 8C, 8X and the HP Convoy

50 (Northumbrian) Division to the Middle East

WS 8A - sailed UK 26.4.41

The Ministry of Shipping first formulated plans for convoy WS 8A on 17 January 1941, which provided for 19 liners with a combined capacity of 39,000 personnel, to be sailed from the UK about the end of the first week in April. This capacity was 11,000 short of the War Office requirement for 50,000 personnel, but to make matters worse the Ministry of Shipping proposed cutting out the three slowest ships: *Dunera, Orbita* and *Orduna*, each of 14 knots speed. It was further noted that five or six MT ships could be available with a speed of 15 knots or over, but if more than eight were included the convoy speed would reduce to 12 knots.

It was eventually agreed to split the convoy into a fast group WS 8A of 15 knots leaving the UK 24 April, followed by a slow group WS 8B of 13.5 knots sailing approximately 2 May, later amended to 22 May. The combined convoys would carry not the required 50,000 but only 30,500 personnel. In the final analysis only eight liners were provided for WS 8A of which the CPS three-funnelled coal burning sisters *Empress of Asia* and *Empress of Russia* were the first to become available. Both were requisitioned from the North Pacific route between Canada and the Far East in December 1940. *Empress of Russia* was drydocked in Victoria BC and her sister at Vancouver; the former left Vancouver on 6 February for the UK, followed by the *Asia* a week later. Both proceeded via Panama, Kingston (Jamaica) and Bermuda to the Clyde, where the *Russia* arrived on 9 March and the *Asia* nine days later. On 23 March both proceeded to Liverpool for fitting out and embarked at that port.

Mention has already been made of the pressure exerted by the Ministry of Shipping on the War Office to release some of the five liners still being held at four days notice for Special Operations.[1] By late February 1941 these ships were all on the Clyde and with a combined personnel capacity of 8,892 were a serious loss to the trooping programme. From January onwards *Ettrick* was permanently engaged in training troops to embark from landing craft at the Combined Operations Centre on Loch Fyne. *Karanja*, *Kenya* and *Sobieski* were released in April but the BI pair were immediately taken over for conversion to Landing Ships and became permanently attached to that service. *Pulaski* was released on 3 May but was suitable only for Indian Ocean service. *Sobieski* alone of this group was available for sailing with WS 8A. The net gain of one ship out of five being available for trooping was quickly lost on 26 April, the final sailing date of WS 8A, when *Winchester Castle*, *Ormonde*, *Batory* and *Narkunda* with a combined capacity of 7,775 were also taken up for Special Service on Combined Operations . The holding of ships for such purposes continued to be a bone of contention for the Ministry of Shipping, which on 1 May 1941 became the Ministry of War Transport, for some time to come.

The other five liners for WS 8A came from diverse sources: *Strathaird* and *Reina del Pacifico* which had both put back from WS 7 for repairs; *Dominion Monarch* reached Liverpool to discharge South African produce on 18 March, after the US 8 voyage from Australia to the Middle East, and had her capacity increased in the interval by over 200 berths, while *Highland Chieftain* reached Liverpool from Buenos Aires on 1 April. On 25 March the newly completed BI steamer *Aronda* anchored in the Clyde after delivery on the Tyne; the last of a coal-burning trio built for the Company's Calcutta to Rangoon mail service, which had been launched too late to join the service as intended in May 1940.

Embarkation was carried out on five of the liners at Liverpool, two in Glasgow and *Aronda* at the Clyde Anchorage; the total amounting to 17,000 all for the Middle East. Six MT ships of minimum 15 knots were loaded to sail with the convoy, four in Glasgow and two in Liverpool, while *Imperial Star* bound for Cape ports and Australia was included for her general protection.

On 20 April, just as the troopships were about to begin embarkation, Churchill received a telegram from Wavell, then C in C Middle East, which indicated the arrival of a German armoured division at Tripoli, against which the Desert Army was desperately short of tanks, though not of trained personnel to fight and crew them. Amongst the troops due to embark on WS 8A was the entire personnel and vehicles of 1st Army Tank Brigade, whose 295 tanks were loaded on five of the MT ships along with 53 Hurricane fighter aircraft. The convoy was not due to reach the Middle East until the second week of June, but Churchill immediately understood that the fate of the war in the Middle East might well turn on a few hundred armoured vehicles. He therefore resolved to detach the five MT ships carrying the tanks and vehicles from the convoy off Gibraltar, and pass them directly through the Mediterranean to Alexandria, thus saving 40 days. This was known as the 'Tiger Convoy', secrecy was to be of the highest importance and "everyone aboard the convoy must think they are going round the Cape."[2] A sixth ship, *Abbekerk*, was prepared to carry a further 67 tanks, but could not be loaded in time and sailed without tanks in the main convoy around the Cape.

Strathaird embarked her troops as she completed repairs in Glasgow's Yorkhill Basin and left that berth at midday on 23 April to sail downriver to the Clyde Anchorage. She was followed next day by *Sobieski* from KGV Dock. On 25 April the MT ships *Clan Campbell* and *Empire Song* (the latter also Clan Line managed) also moved downriver and finally *Abbekerk* and *Clan Lamont* on 26 April which, with *Aronda* already embarked at the Clyde Anchorage, completed the Clyde section of the convoy.

Amongst the troops embarked on the Liverpool section was 150 Infantry Brigade, the leading formation of 50 (Northumbrian) Division which had spent the early months of 1940 in France and Belgium, and became embroiled in the battles around the Ypres-Comines Canal prior to evacuation at Dunkirk. The three battalions of this brigade were embarked on the two *Empress* liners; *Empress of Russia* carried 50 Division HQ, 150 Brigade HQ, 4 Bn East Yorks Regiment, 4 Bn The Green Howards and 232 Field Regiment RA, while the *Asia* embarked 5 Bn The Green Howards, 72 Field Regiment RA and 150 Field Ambulance. Whilst in Liverpool discharging from South Africa and loading outward general cargo for New Zealand, *Dominion Monarch* had her trooping capacity increased from 1,500 to 1,712. She was to have sailed for New Zealand via Panama, but a few days before departure was embarked with RAF personnel and priority civilian passengers and included in the convoy as far as the Cape.[3]

The five transports in Liverpool were embarked on 23 and 24 April and within the next two days sailed up to the Clyde Anchorage where their Masters were able to join in the convoy conference prior to departure. All eight transports and four MT ships weighed anchor and cleared the Clyde boom by 2000 hours on 26 April, preceeded by the battlecruiser *Repulse* as ocean escort, the light cruiser *Naiad*, AMC *Pretoria Castle* and nine destroyers of which three were Canadian and two Polish. The convoy Commodore, Vice Admiral The Hon. A C Strutt, RN, was embarked on *Strathaird*. Two further MT ships, *Clan Chattan* and *New Zealand Star* (plus *Imperial Star* bound for Australia), sailed from the Mersey at midday 26 April and joined with the Clyde portion in a position six miles SW of Orsay Light at 0600 next morning. A record of the original convoy formation showing five columns but omitting *Clan Chattan* and *Imperial Star* survives only amongst Admiralty archives, perhaps due to the secrecy maintained for the Tiger section for Mediterranean passage,[4] but the artist John Nicolson subsequently recorded his impressions of the voyage whilst embarked as an Army signaller on *Empress of Asia*.[5]

"We soon settled into a shipboard routine, usually PT followed by lectures each morning with most afternoons free. Most of my colleagues were soon fed up and bored with shipboard life but I must admit I enjoyed it and found it a pleasant change from normal Army routine despite the crowded conditions in the mess decks. After the evening meal we had to clear the tables and sling our hammocks, which I found far more comfortable than some of the Army billets I had had ashore. I enjoyed the large amount of free time, most of which I spent leaning on the rail watching the other ships. Even on a cruise one does not have so many ships in sight all the time!...The next few days were uneventful with a moderate swell most of the time. The course was WNW, then westerly for a couple of days before turning south, zigzagging about every 20 minutes....The *Repulse* was constantly signalling by morse lamp to other ships in the convoy..these messages were often directed at our ship, and at very slow speed, but even so we could often read them before the officers on the bridge just above and we must have caused much annoyance by shouting each letter up to them...The ship also had a permanent list to starboard due to unskilled trimming - apparently many of the trimmers and stokers had joined the Merchant Navy to avoid being conscripted and had never been to sea before."[5]

Despite the uneventful days at the outset of the passage of WS 8A, there was much in the surrounding area to occupy ships of the escort. At 1019 on 29 April, when 600 miles west of Eagle Island, the destroyers *Beagle* and *Eridge* were detached to investigate an unknown merchant ship, prior to joining the inward convoy SL 71 from Freetown. This ship proved to be *Rochester Castle* outward bound for Freetown; the escorts reported that she "did not appear to know the challenge and also said she thought she had seen a periscope one hour before."[6] (This could have been *U-75* which sank the *City of Nagpur* to the SW of the convoy that morning.)

At the instant when *Beagle* and *Eridge* were detached, *Naiad* received a signal from the C in C Western Approaches that lifeboats had been reported by a Catalina of Coastal Command in a position given as 80 miles to the SW of the convoy. At 1107 the destroyer *Hurricane* was detached to search for the boats and the following story is largely culled from the subsequent report made by the Commanding Officer on his return to the Clyde.

Hurricane left the convoy on a course of SSW and steamed at 31 knots until she reached the reported position of the boats at 1349. "Visibility was excellent and the sea was calm but there was no sign of any boats or wreckage and I thereupon commenced an expanding rectangular search. To avoid any possibility of missing the boats each leg was five miles outside the preceding leg on each course. Throughout *Hurricane* proceeded at 27 knots with doublebank masthead men."[7]

"At 2030 when a diameter of 45 miles had been covered without success, and in view of the perimeter now being 124 miles I reported to the C in C that lifeboats had not been found, but at 2200 with the last of the daylight the lifeboats were seen right ahead. I reduced to sweeping speed and carried out an all round search before picking up survivors who were all in boats....At 2300 all survivors were on board,"[7] being the officers, native crew and passengers from Ellerman's *City of Nagpur* which had been torpedoed at 0200 the previous day. Only 16 were lost from the 478 passengers and crew of this ship.

After reporting her success *Hurricane* was directed to search for another lifeboat reported 280 miles ENE on her way home. This boat was found at 1430 next day and when the occupants had been recovered, *Hurricane* then had 465 survivors on board and proceeded at 27 knots for the North Channel. But this was not all. At 0100 on 1 May when 96 miles west of Tory Island, *Hurricane* was directed to search for more lifeboats in a position 66 miles NNE and on reaching this position searched with a Whitley aircraft which dropped parachute flares. At 0700 on 2 May *Hurricane* was joined by the destroyer *Veteran* which found the boats an hour later. *Hurricane* then proceeded to the Clyde and berthed at Gourock pier at 1700 that same day to land her survivors.

The Commanding Officer of *Hurricane* also reported on the exceptional care rendered to the passengers and crew of the *City of Nagpur*. "The officers and ship's company gave up all their accommodation and high tribute should be paid to the Cooks and

Caterers of all messes as this large number managed to be provided with the normal needs, even including Indian dishes for the Lascars. The ingenuity shown by the Seamen and Engine-Room Ratings in making boots and shoes out of canvas and felt and babies creches out of cork and bunting deserves at least a mention.."[7] Happily the Admiralty replied "that they have read with pleasure of the skilful and determined search made by *Hurricane* for the lifeboats of the *City of Nagpur* and of the admirable care of the survivors shown by the ship's company."[8]

Meanwhile the convoy continued on a course of SSE towards the eastern side of the Azores, and reached the cut off point for the Tiger ships at 1430 on 2 May in a position 900 miles WNW of Gibraltar and 150 miles NNE of San Miguel, the most easterly of the Azores group. Here the cruiser *Naiad* detached with the three *Clan* ships, the *New Zealand Star* and *Empire Song* for Gibraltar, where they were met and fought through the Mediteranean by Force H to Alexandria. *Empire Song* was lost due to mining in the Sicilian Narrows, but the other four ships reached Alexandria safely on 12 May (while WS 8A was at Freetown) and discharged 238 tanks and 43 Hurricane aircraft. *Repulse* is believed to have detached from WS 8A at the same time as *Naiad*, when the latter cruiser was relieved by *Mauritius*. The next ocean escort found the convoy formed in four columns and zigzagging at 15 knots with the AMC *Pretoria Castle* also in company.

John Nicholson continued his narrative of the voyage: "After a week at sea the course was SSE, still zigzagging; occasionally a flying-boat would appear and circle round the convoy (possibly the aircraft of *Mauritius*) and sometimes the routine was broken with an 'Abandon Ship' drill or an evening concert put on by the Green Howards. This was staged in what had been the First Class dining saloon, a superb room still with its tastefull peacetime decor and with surprisingly good ventilation for the days before air-conditioning."[5]

The convoy passed to the east of the Azores during the night of 2-3 May, and during the afternoon of 4 May passed an unoccupied merchant ship's raft which bore no name or other marking; the convoy was then 400 miles west of the Canary Islands. At 1645 on 5 May, in a position 400 miles north of the Cape Verde Islands, the destroyers *Duncan* and *Wishart* joined from Freetown as A/S escorts and a further two destroyers, *Highlander* and *Boreas* at 1430 next day.

The anti-submarine screen was reformed when the last two destroyers joined. The convoy was then only 160 miles NE of the nearest of the Cape Verde islands and was within sight of the Spanish steamer *Arraiz* bound NE from the latter islands to the Canaries. *Mauritius* reported that "she was closed and scrutinized but not boarded. A W/T transmission on an unknown frequency was later detected by RDF and in view of the possibility that this emanated from the *Arraiz*, *Boreas* was sent back to board. This was effected at 1810, the ship being released on completion."[9]

In attempting to rejoin the convoy during the night, *Boreas* failed to locate it and having in the process passed ahead of it, rejoined from the southard at 1600 on 7 May. One hour later the convoy reversed course for an hour and a quarter to avoid an undue reduction in speed in maintaining the ETA at Freetown. At 0600 next morning, 8 May, *Highland Chieftain* and *Dominion Monarch* were involved in what *Mauritius* termed a "minor collision..and fell out of convoy. The damage sustained appeared to be almost entirely above water and both ships rejoined the convoy at normal speed after daybreak. It being undesirable to break W/T silence, *Mauritius'* aircraft was flown off to Freetown at 1740 with advance information as to repairs etc. required."[9] The collision occurred in the area between Bathurst and Freetown.

The convoy arrived at Freetown searched channel buoy at 0700 on 9 May. Single line ahead was formed and the ten ships proceeded into harbour preceded by *Mauritius* and *Pretoria Castle*. John Nicolson aptly described the scene at Freetown anchorage.. "before long the ship was surrounded by canoes and boats full of fruit to sell, the canoes being slender and long, hewn out of solid tree trunks. Then coal barges came alongside swarming with men who soon began coaling the ship...On the other side a large collier came alongside and her large complement soon formed a human chain by means of which sacks of coal were passed up and emptied into the shutes on D deck. They seemed to do the work easily enough in spite of the heat while we perspired profusely just watching them!"[5]

"There was no blackout in Freetown so we were able to enjoy the luxury of having the lights on and the portholes wide open. After the blackout of Britain it was grand to see all the lights on shore and on the other ships, especially *Empress of Russia* which looked just like the pre-war posters of cruising liners in tropical ports, with her lights reflected on the water."[5] (The lack of blackout was in contrast to that experienced by the ships of WS 5B four months earlier.)

"The heat below decks was really oppressive so most of us slept anywhere that we could find on deck. The convoy was in Freetown for five days, coaling and taking on water and we were not sorry to leave...[5] Similarly the 50th Division history described Freetown as the place "where the ships coaled (the two *Empress* liners and *Aronda* were coal burners) and were surrounded by bumboats whose clamorous occupants dived for pennies and tried to persuade the troops lining the decks to exchange their boots, shirts or trousers for bananas and oranges."[10]

The time in Freetown was also spent in making temporary repairs to *Highland Chieftain* and *Dominion Monarch*, but the work on the former was not complete when the convoy sailed again at 1010 hours on 14 May. *Highland Chieftain* left Freetown a day behind the convoy but was unable to catch up before arrival at the Cape.

When clear of Freetown searched channel, the convoy formed in four columns[11] with *Mauritius* as ocean escort and the same four destroyers, *Highlander*, *Wishart*, *Duncan* and *Boreas* providing A/S escort, but *Boreas* and *Wishart* had to part company at 0710 and 1700 respectively next day, to return to Freetown with engine defects. The other two destroyers detached for Freetown at 0715 on 16 May with orders to search for a U-Boat reported that morning 300 miles northward and close to the Liberian coast.

"It was pleasant to be at sea again and get the ship cleaned up after all the coal dust and when we crossed the equator on Friday, May 16, the traditional ceremony was duly performed on the officers and a few volunteer soldiers. Surprisingly, the weather did not seem too hot that day and became quite cool in the evening. Next day there was a glorious sunset followed by several hours of continuous lightning but no rain. The next few days were uneventful and sunbathing on deck every afternoon one could almost imagine one was aboard a Union-Castle liner bound for the Cape, but the illusion was always shattered on returning to the crowded mess deck for meals."[5]

The report by *Mauritius* on the convoy showed there were no incidents on the passage to the Cape, which was made in good weather with the convoy zigzagging by day and in moonlight until reaching latitude 20° south. Fog patches were experienced on 23 May as the convoy approached the Cape coast. *Strathaird* was detached at 1830 that day to proceed into Capetown, where she berthed at 0900 next day to disembark the

High Commissioner, Lord Harlech. After a short stay of only two hours alongside, *Strathaird* sailed again in a freshening westerly wind for Durban. At dawn next morning she was experiencing a full westerly gale and by 0900 had to heave to, but was able to proceed at 16 knots from 1400. She arrived at Durban at 1100 on 27 May, just ahead of the convoy.

The morning of 24 May found the convoy 100 miles west of Capetown with a westerly gale and heavy rain developing. *Imperial Star* was detached at 0530 for Capetown and other coast ports to discharge, before proceeding to Australia; she was lost on her next voyage in a Malta convoy. At 1305 on 24 May when 80 miles SW of the Cape of Good Hope, *Hawkins* took over the duties of ocean escort from *Mauritius*, which then parted company for Simonstown. The report of *Mauritius* on the convoy noted that "individually most of the ships were markedly less proficient in convoy than many cargo vessels. Station-keeping was not good and mistakes in zigzagging occurred. The darkening of the ships left a good deal to be desired, also the disposal of all floating rubbish".. "the striking of matches and use of electric torches on deck after dark was noticeable."[9] It seems likely these remarks were appropriate to *Aronda* and the two *Empress* liners, which were all coal burners and making their first voyages in convoy.

The convoy continued to experience the westerly gale as it passed south of Cape Agulhas on the morning of 25 May, and at 0820 *Empress of Asia* was found to be well astern of station. The convoy reduced speed to 12 knots but she was still unable to rejoin and with the sea increasing, speed was increased at 1410 to 13 knots. The gale moderated as the convoy passed along the South African coast on 26 May. *Empress of Asia* remained out of sight so speed was increased to 14.5 knots and at 1200 next day, 27 May, the convoy arrived at Durban.

Empress of Asia had in fact put about for Capetown, as John Nicolson recalled in '*Sea Breezes*' 47 years later. "On Saturday 24 May we ran into heavy seas which made the ship pitch and roll violently but both ourselves and *Empress of Russia* seemed to ride the storm better than some of the other larger ships. Next morning the storm was even worse and no one was allowed out on the open deck; there were no other ships in sight, and the horizon could not be seen for waves and spray. The wind was now on the port beam and from time to time the ship rolled alarmingly; no sun was visible and so we could not ascertain our course but rumour spread that we had left the convoy and were heading for Capetown for repairs - all the alleyways around the galley and messdecks were flooded. This rumour proved to be true, much to everyone's delight, and at about 2.30 p.m. the next day we were relieved to see Table Mountain looming out of the cloud and rain. Shortly after this two pilot cutters approached from the shore, one minute only their mastheads could be seen above the waves, the next they were poised on top of the crest. The pilot could not get aboard, however, so shouted orders for us to follow him into the bay. By this time most of the troops were looking forward to an evening ashore after a month at sea and had gone below for a meal and to change into their best uniforms, but I was more interested in watching the docking procedure and decided to forego the meal. Once we got past the breakwater it was quite calm but the pilot said we could not berth but should anchor, so the port anchor was let go. When it apparently did not hold the chain was hauled in again, but no anchor came with it - a link had snapped and the anchor was lost! Much shouting and arguing ensued between the foc'sle and bridge as a result of which it was decided not to risk losing the starboard anchor and so the ship steamed out to sea again. Next morning dawned bright and sunny, the sea was calm and the ship berthed with no difficulty....Beyond the docks the city looked clean and inviting in the morning sunlight....There followed a week of holiday while our ship was repaired, coaled and re-stored. Soon it was all over and we bade farewell as the ship steamed out of Table Bay on a flat calm sea under a cloudless blue sky, in stark contrast with our arrival the previous week."[5]

The storm encountered by the convoy off the Cape also features in the 50 Division history, reportedly as the worst in that area for 60 years. "It certainly looked impressive to 3,000 odd landlubbers cooped up in rolling vessels. During the storm *Empress of Asia* proved a lame duck and had to put in at Capetown."[10] In fact the *Asia* had to return to Capetown for coal as she had insufficient to reach Durban. She did not leave Capetown until 2 June by which time many of her stokers had deserted; she reached Durban on the afternoon of 5 June to find WS 8A long since gone and continued northward in convoy CM 11. With the arrival of the main WS 8A convoy in Durban, the Divisional history noted that "as the ships moored up, the men saw the first evidence of the generous hospitality that awaited them after being confined in stuffy uncomfortable quarters through tropical waters, as cars drew up at the dockside, ready to take them to see the sights of the city."[10]

The convoy remained in Durban for four days to replenish fuel and water and provide leave for the troops ashore. The 4,200 troops on *Reina del Pacifico* and *Dominion Monarch* disembarked at Durban to be on-carried in a later convoy, as were the 1,200 troops landed from *Highland Chieftain* at Capetown, where she arrived on 25 May and spent four weeks carrying out further temporary repairs to her collision damage. *Highland Chieftain* then proceeded to Durban, where permanent repairs were undertaken, lasting seven months, of which seven weeks were spent awaiting drydock: she finally left Durban on 17 January 1942 for the River Plate and loaded at Buenos Aires for Avonmouth, arriving there on 12 March from a voyage which had lasted eleven months.

The arrival in Durban of WS 8A was the start of a very busy fortnight for the Impcon staff (Imperial Movement Control). In addition to the disembarkation and transhipment from the ships of the convoy, the 1200 troops from *Highland Chieftain* had to be entrained from Capetown to Durban and to complicate matters, the entire 19,500 men of 2 South African Infantry Division were now being moved from Durban to the Middle East although their embarkation was handled separately by Union Movement Control. To provide for all these movements, seven Indian Ocean type troopships with a total capacity of 10,000 were sent to Durban from Suez and Mombasa of which all but one was already in port when WS 8A arrived, and in addition, three of the 'Monster' liners which had been employed between Australasia and India and the Middle East, were to be used on a shuttle service carrying South African troops from Durban to Suez. *Nieuw Amsterdam* berthed in the port the day after WS 8A while *Mauretania* and *Ile de France* arrived soon after the convoy left.

After disembarking at Durban, *Dominion Monarch* spent 19 days in drydock for repairs to her collision damage, then sailed for Wellington and Auckland where the outward general cargo was discharged and a full cargo of refrigerated produce loaded for the UK. In Auckland she embarked 1,230 officers and men, mostly of the Royal Australian Air Force, including 440 trainees going to Canada. The *Dominion Monarch* sailed from Auckland on 27 July and after being escorted to the eastward by the AMCs *Monowai* and *Prince Robert*, proceeded independently via Panama and Curacao to Halifax, where the trainee airmen were landed and RCAF personnel embarked in lieu.

She arrived at Liverpool on 1 September in convoy TC 12B and next sailed outward in WS 12 for Singapore.

Reina del Pacifico spent eleven days in Durban disembarking and loading general cargo there and at Port Elizabeth and Capetown, all for the UK, and proceeding direct from the latter port reached Liverpool on 7 July. Her next voyage was in WS 10 back to Durban.

WS 8A was now reduced to four transports and a single MT ship, and sailed from Durban at 1630 on 31 May with *Hawkins* remaining as ocean escort. A speed of 14.75 knots was set for the passage northwards through the Mozambique Channel.[12] The cruiser *Hawkins* reported that fine weather was experienced and there were no events to record. At noon on 9 June, in a position 100 miles ESE of Aden, *Empress of Russia* left the convoy and proceeded at full speed to make that port in daylight, for the purpose of landing a military officer critically ill.

The Straits of Perim were entered at 0300 on 10 June and at 0530 that morning the convoy dispersed in a position 34 miles NNW of Perim and about halfway towards the Hanish Islands. During the passage from the Cape, *Hawkins* had been disposed by day at maximum signalling distance ahead of the convoy, and by night at maximum visibility distance on the bow. The speed maintained from Durban to Perim was 15 knots.

After dispersal, *Strathaird* proceeded first to Port Sudan and reached Suez on 14 June one day behind the other three transports and MT ship. Suez Bay was in a very different state from when the previous convoy arrived. Most of the congestion had been cleared and few ships were in the bay although the Hospital Ships *Somersetshire* and *Atlantis* were prominent. The recommendations made by the visiting representative of the Ministry of War Transport, which body now encompassed the duties of the former Ministry of Shipping, had clearly been acted upon. Unlike the long delays suffered by the previous convoy WS 7, the ships of WS 8A were rapidly cleared; *Aronda* in three days on a return voyage to Durban for continued service on the CM and Indian Ocean routes.

The troops of 1 Army Tank Brigade comprising 8, 42 and 44 Royal Tank Regiments proceeded to Alexandria to collect their tanks and prepare for warfare in the desert. They subsequently distinguished themselves in the Battle of Tobruk in November, and later at Gazala and Alamein, before returning to the UK to retrain and re-equip for the Normandy invasion. The Yorkshire troops of 150 Brigade landed with Brigadier C W Haydon and were quickly whisked away for duty with the Western Desert Force, but later moved with the rest of 50 Division to Cyprus, thence to Iraq and Syria before returning to the desert and engagement in the Gazala battle in June 1942. It was here that the Brigadier lost his life when the entire Brigade was overrun and captured by the Germans. It never re-formed.

The three principal transports of WS 8A were disembarked and cleared at Suez within the space of five days, and were then required for the movement of Italian POW from Massawa. The Principal Sea Transport Officer in Egypt sent a confirmatory signal to the C in C East Indies, stating that *Strathaird*, *Sobieski* and *Empress of Russia* would be used for this movement, but was not actually approved. The port of Massawa in Eritrea had been captured by units of 5 Indian Division on 8 April, but much damage had been done to the harbour; ships scuttled and a great deal of equipment and supplies dumped in the sea. Supply ships began using the port on 1 May and Indian Ocean type transports soon afterwards, but there was as yet no provision for such valuable ships as *Strathaird*, which would have to anchor outside the harbour.

The three liners were therefore directed to Port Sudan, where they embarked 1,000 POW each and sailed independently for the south. *Sobieski* loaded in Mombasa, Durban and Capetown, where she arrived on 6 July with a broken liner on her port tail-shaft. After spending 16 days in Capetown, where the POW were landed, she returned to Durban to drydock where both tailshafts were drawn for survey and a new port shaft fitted in the space of 25 days. *Sobieski* then embarked West African troops and joined convoy CF 2 bound for Lagos (dealt with under the homeward voyage of WS 8X *q.v.*).

Strathaird left Port Sudan on 21 June, bunkered at Aden two days later and loaded a small amount of cargo at Durban, completing to capacity at Capetown where she too was drydocked for two days bottom cleaning and painting. She departed Capetown on 18 July for Trinidad and Belize, where it is believed Italian POW were landed on 5 August. She then returned to Trinidad for bunkers and proceeded thence direct to the Clyde, arriving 22 August and moving upriver to discharge at Yorkhill Quay next day, which was almost the berth she had vacated four months earlier. Her next voyage was in WS 12 back to Suez.

Empress of Russia sailed from Port Sudan on 22 June, bunkered with coal at Aden between 24 and 26 June, then proceeded to Durban where she remained for 17 days loading and carrying out repairs. She bunkered again at Capetown and left that port on 27 July, proceeding homewards via St. Thomas, San Juan (Puerto Rico), Hampton Roads and Halifax. The Canadian Pacific history states that "by the time the *Empress* reached Puerto Rico, the Chinese crew had been confined to the ship (many countries would not allow Chinese crews ashore) for considerably longer than a normal voyage and their desire to stretch their legs was understandable. Not surprisingly some failed to report back on time. The *Empress* had to sail short of firemen. The Officer Commanding Troops on board called for volunteers to act as trimmers from Puerto Rico to Newport News; among them was the young naval officer, Prince Philip of Greece, who duly received a CPS trimmer's certificate."[13] The *Russia* left Halifax on 25 August in convoy TC 12B, and anchored in the Clyde on 1 September where she remained until next sailing out in WS 12 for Suez.

The reader may recall that *Empress of Asia* was due to continue from Durban in convoy CM 11; in fact she was not then ready to sail but followed a day later escorted by the AMC *Carthage*. It may have been intended to catch up and join CM 11, but this had not happened when *Carthage* detached from the *Empress* to the SW of Aden on 20 June. Convoy CM 11 was itself dispersed at the southern end of the Red Sea next morning, when the *Asia* was still 130 miles astern of that position. The average speed from Durban was just 13.5 knots and *Carthage* commented that "the darkening of *Empress of Asia* was not up to the required standard, frequent signals were made to her on this matter."[14]

Undoubtedly the desertion of many stokers at Capetown and possibly poor steaming coal contributed to the poor speed of *Empress of Asia*. The 50 Division history noted that troops had to be sent below and "stoke the ship through the fiery heat of the Red Sea. This they manfully did under the direction of 5th Green Howards."[10]

Empress of Asia reached Suez on 23 June and after five days disembarking and discharging military stores sailed again on the return voyage. Amongst a few service passengers was Prince Philip of Greece, who was bound for the UK and travelled as far as Durban, where he transferred to *Empress of Russia* (see above). The *Asia* called at Port Sudan for Italian POW, bunkered at Aden and loaded at Durban and Capetown. The homeward voyage was made via Trinidad to New York, where she was drydocked and repaired over an eight day period at the beginning of September. She then proceeded to Halifax and continued to Liverpool in convoy HX 150: a twelve day passage which ended on 28 September. Her next voyage in WS 12Z proved to be her last.

The "HP Convoy" - sailed UK 9.5.41

On 17 January 1941, *Highlands Chieftain*, *Monarch* and *Princess* were included in the allocation of transports for WS 8, but the *Monarch* was turned round in time to sail with WS 7, the *Chieftain* sailed as intended in WS 8A on 26 April, but *Highland Princess* was delayed in completing repairs at Liverpool until 3 May, having been 25 days undergoing repairs and spending 31 days in that port which was severely congested.

Highland Princess was embarked at Liverpool to her capacity of 1,200, with troops whose presence in the Middle East presumably could not be deferred until the next sailing two weeks later. *Highland Princess* left the Mersey in the late afternoon of 9 May under the command of Captain F R Miles. She was accompanied by the Union-Castle cargo ship *Roslin Castle* and escorted by the AA cruiser *Cairo* and two destroyers, *Wanderer* and *Ripley*, the latter being one of the four funnelled ex-American type.

At 0625 on 10 May, in a position six miles SW of Orsay, the convoy, known as HP and likely an abbreviation for *Highland Princess*, was met and joined by the cargo liners *Benalbanach* and *Bayano* from the Clyde, the former bound for Freetown and the latter for Montreal, and escorted by the Canadian destroyers *Ottawa* and *Restigouche*.

After forming up the convoy set off on a WNW course at a speed of 12.5 knots with an air escort initially of two aircraft, and as all four ships were equipped with kites, these were hoisted and flown as a deterrent against low flying aircraft, but only *Highland Princess* appears to have kept hers up, until recovered on 12 May due to lack of wind. At 1125 that morning *Ottawa* dropped depth charges on a contact at the southern edge of the Stanton Banks, and again at 2200 that evening when both *Ottawa* and *Wanderer* depth charged a contact. At this latter time *Cairo* informed the convoy that the AMCs *Arawa* and *Moreton Bay*, which had left the Clyde at 1030 that morning with two Canadian destroyers as escort, were due to catch up and join the convoy as ocean escort at 0600 on 12 May. *Moreton Bay* had just completed a five month refit on the Tyne while *Arawa* had been under repair for the past two weeks in KGV Dock, Glasgow.

At 0723 next morning, 11 May, when to the SW of Rockall Bank, Commodore E O'Corran embarked on *Benalbanach* signalled the convoy that an air attack was expected and to have all guns manned and cleared away for instant action. Two minutes later *Cairo* reported a Focke Wulf aircraft in sight but no attack developed. An air escort arrived at 1345 and at 1836 *Wanderer* again depth charged a contact in the vicinity of the convoy.

At 0530 on 12 May the convoy was joined by the AMCs *Arawa* and *Moreton Bay* of the ocean escort, accompanied by the destroyers *Saguenay* and *Beagle*. The convoy was then 500 miles west of Inishtrahull and steering SW. The cruiser *Cairo* and all six destroyers parted company from the convoy at 2200 that evening and one hour later *Roslin Castle* parted company for Trinidad and the River Plate. The convoy then turned to a SSW course to pass west of the Azores. The Ellerman Wilson *Bayano* detached next day bound for Montreal leaving the two ship convoy of *Highland Princess* and *Benalbanach* escorted by the AMCs *Arawa* and *Moreton Bay*.

There were no incidents for the next three days and the convoy passed 60 miles west of Flores, the most westerly of the Azores group, shortly after midday on 15 May and that evening passed a Portuguese schooner steering a WNW course, and being well to the SW of the island group appeared suspicious but no action was taken. The convoy then steered south then SE to pass inside the Cape Verde islands, and when 120 miles east of the most easterly of that group, at noon on 22 May, the corvette *Clematis* joined from Freetown as local escort. Two other corvettes, *Asphodel* and *Calendula* were to have joined the convoy next day from Bathurst, but the convoy was then making 14 knots and was 33 miles south of the estimated noon position given to the corvettes as a rendezvous that day, i.e. 120 miles SW of Bathurst, and they did not appear to have made contact or joined up. The two ship convoy with *Arawa, Moreton Bay* and *Clematis* arrived safely at Freetown during the afternoon of 24 May.[15]

The subsequent movements of *Benalbanach* are unknown. *Moreton Bay* left Freetown on 30 May as ocean escort to the homeward convoy SL 76, while *Arawa* followed with SL 77 on 8 June and was released on arrival in the UK for conversion to trooping service. After fuelling and watering at Freetown, *Highland Princess* sailed on 26 May and proceeding by way of Takoradi and Lagos to Durban, arrived there on 13 June and disembarked 1,042 personnel for on-carriage to Suez by *Nieuw Zeeland* in WS 8B due in the port a week later.

Highland Princess sailed from Durban for Buenos Aires on 19 June, and there loaded frozen and chilled meat in the space of 11 days, completing in another three at La Plata. She bunkered at Montevideo and Trinidad on the homeward voyage and berthed at Liverpool on 18 August. She remained in the Mersey for six weeks and made her next voyage to Halifax and New York in convoy CT 3.

WS 8B - sailed UK 22.5.41

WS 8B was notable in being the one troopship convoy to be at sea in the North Atlantic during the battles that culminated in the sinking of the *Bismarck* on 26 May 1941. The convoy assembled and embarked entirely on the Clyde, due to the loss of facilities at Liverpool following the heavy air raids on that city during the first week of May.

This convoy was to embark the divisional troops and two remaining brigades of 50 Northumbrian Division, i.e. 151 (Durham) Brigade comprising 6, 8 and 9 Bns. Durham Light Infantry and 69 Brigade with 5 Bn East Yorks and 6 and 9 Bns. The Green Howards. The Division also included 2 (Machine Gun) Bn the Cheshire Regiment, 50 Bn. Recce Regt. RAC, 72, 74 and 124 Field Regiments RA. The Cheshires were embarked on *Georgic* under their commanding officer Lt. Col. C Gentry-Birch; the ships that embarked the Durham battalions have not been identified. The whole of 69 Brigade was to embark on *Mooltan*, but this liner could not be made ready in time and these troops therefore followed in the next convoy WS 9A. The convoy was to comprise nine transports and three MT ships, but only six liners and one MT ship were ready to sail on the appointed date of 22 May.

The Cunard liner *Georgic* had been berthed at the Clyde Anchorage from 19 April, when she arrived in convoy TC 10 with Canadian troops from Halifax. After carrying out minor repairs and having her armament increased, she lay idle for nearly four weeks until embarkation began for WS 8B. *Georgic* had been largely employed on Halifax voyages carrying RAF trainees westbound and Canadian troops and aircraft eastbound, but was now to exchange roles with her near-sister *Britannic*, which arrived in the Clyde on 5 May from Bombay and Capetown after an outward voyage in WS 5B. *Britannic* discharged her Clan Line Bombay cargo at the Emergency Port in the anchorage; then carried out repairs and DEMS work until 18 May, when she embarked for Halifax and sailed on the same date but some hours ahead of the convoy, independently routed and escorted by the battleship *Rodney* en route to the United States for refit.

The PSNC liner *Orduna* was requisitioned for trooping service at Liverpool on 14 March, after completing discharge from the West Coast of South America, her fifth commercial round voyage since the outbreak of war. *Orduna* was fitted for 2,163 troops and left Liverpool for the Clyde on 3 May after the fearful explosion and destruction caused when the Brocklebank steamer *Malakand* exploded in Huskisson Dock on the night of 2 May. The *Malakand* was loading bombs and shells for the Middle East and was set on fire in the midst of a raid and blew up, causing a trail of devastation over acres of dock space, with vast damage to buildings even in the centre of the city. Tonnages of cargo handled in the port were reduced to a quarter of their normal level, but up to 1,300 men and 162 tipper lorries were employed clearing the debris and the port was almost back to normal working by the middle of June.

Almanzora arrived in the Clyde on 8 May from Cape ports, after the WS 6 voyage to Durban. She was to discharge in Glasgow but there had been two heavy air raids on the Greenock area during the nights of 5/6 and 6/7 May, when considerable damage was done to shipyards and property. There were also mining activities which closed the river for four days and allowed only restricted movements for the next three days; normal movements then resumed after the river had been checked each morning by a fleet of minesweepers. *Almanzora* moved upriver to the Riverside berth at KGV on 13 May, where her cargo was discharged and repairs effected, until it was time to embark for WS 8B.

Duchess of Richmond reached the Clyde a day behind *Almanzora* with general cargo loaded on the Ellerman berth at Durban and Capetown. The *Duchess* was completely discharged in the Holy Loch within six days of arrival and moved to the anchorage to complete minor repairs and to store, water and fuel in preparation for embarkation.

Duchess of Bedford was also to be included in WS 8B and like her sister (above) was returning from the WS 5B Suez voyage with general cargo loaded on the Harrison berth at Durban. After bunkering at Freetown the *Bedford* was directed to Liverpool and reached there on 7 May to find the port in a state of chaos after the recent air raids and catastrophic explosion. She was therefore re-directed to the Clyde and moored in the Holy Loch close to the *Richmond* to begin discharge, but after a day shifted to the anchorage to await a berth in Glagow. She moved upriver to complete discharge of hides and other cargo at KGV Dock on 17 May, and remained there until embarkation began four days later.

The Dutch liner *Christiaan Huygens* also sailed in WS 8B, having reached Liverpool on 23 April after trooping service in the Indian Ocean and drydocking at Durban. She remained at Liverpool four weeks having her troop capacity and armament increased, then moved to the Clyde where she anchored to begin embarkation on 21 May.

Of the three liners unable to sail with the convoy, the most important was P&O's *Mooltan* which had been employed as an AMC since September 1939, mostly on the Freetown convoy route and was now the first of these liners to be released for trooping; largely the result of persistent lobbying by the Ministry of Shipping in an effort to alleviate the growing shortage of troopships. *Mooltan* spent 15 days repairing at Belfast in November and began a further spell on the Tyne in December, which lasted four weeks during which time the Admiralty decided to release her. She arrived at Tilbury to begin conversion on 24 January 1941, was paid off as a commissioned ship on 1 February and handed over to the Ministry of Shipping three days later. The conversion lasted four months and *Mooltan* only reached the Clyde on 25 May, three days after WS 8B had sailed.

The Furness Withy liner *Eastern Prince* was another liner then in the midst of conversion that was doubtless delayed by the lack of men and materials which was then prevalent. *Eastern Prince* had been employed on the North Atlantic since the outbreak of war, first between London and New York, and later using Liverpool as the UK terminal when the Thames was closed due to bombing and mining. She completed seven such round trips carrying valuable cargoes until requisitioned for trooping at Liverpool on 9 December. She was damaged in an air raid on the night of 20/21 December and subsequent repairs delayed the work of conversion; drydocking was carried out in April but she was not completed in time to meet the embarkation date of WS 8B.

After being utilized for the on-carriage of WS 5B troops from Durban to Mombasa, *Orbita* was also planned for inclusion in WS 8B, but only reached the Clyde on 22 May as the convoy was about to sail. With 8,800 tons of South African cargo on board, she only managed to complete discharge in the Holy Loch on 3 June, giving barely sufficient time to embark and sail in WS 9A.

The embarkation of *Orduna*, *Christiaan Huygens*, *Georgic* and *Duchess of Richmond* took place at the Clyde Anchorage on 21 and 22 May 1941, while *Almanzora* and *Duchess of Bedford* embarked at their berths in Glasgow. Since the Greenock raids of 5 - 7 May, the constant threat of mining and possible blockage of the river was a very real danger. The import and export programme was then almost entirely dependent on the West coast ports of Liverpool, the Clyde and Bristol Channel, and with Liverpool working on reduced capacity, it was imperative to keep the other two areas clear at all times.

After the usual morning safety sweeps of the channel, *Almanzora* left her berth at 1030 on 22 May and proceeded downriver with two tugs ahead to assist steering and act as exploders in case of undetected mines. Three cargo ships followed, then *Duchess of Bedford* left the KGV Dock at midday, by which time it was virtually high water. This meant proceeding downriver on the ebb tide and although not the best practice with such a large ship was one that often had to be accepted as part of the exigencies of war. The *Duchess* passed Bowling at 1306 with two Clyde Shipping tugs steering from ahead, and very soon after, ran into fog which considerably slowed her and caused a most anxious passage to reach clear water at Greenock. Unfortunately, when almost clear of the channelway, she grounded at 1529 on the edge of the bank abreast the Albert Harbour and stuck fast. Other tugs were soon on the scene and Canadian Pacific officials boarded by Munro's motor launch to assist and muster whatever additional assistance was necessary, but the *Duchess* had grounded on the edge of a sandbank at half ebb and could not therefore be refloated until about half flood. Although fully bunkered, watered, stored and embarked to capacity, the ship was not in any immediate danger. She was refloated with the assistance of twelve tugs at 2141 hours and could then have caught the convoy, which was then disembarking pilots off Ascog, but the *Bedford* proceeded to the anchorage for inspection and survey and was therefore unable to sail. On 24 May she was instructed to sail in a subsequent convoy WS 8X departing 27 May (*q.v.*) [16]

Two other ships included in the convoy were Elder Dempster's *Abosso* and the Brocklebank MT ship *Martand*. The former liner was the company's flagship, a motorship of 14.5 knots built in 1935 and still retained on their mail service between Liverpool and West Africa. *Abosso* was commanded by Captain C W Tate, and left

Liverpool on 18 May with instructions to join WS 8B in the Clyde. The Brocklebank *Martand* was a 14 knot coal burner which had loaded military transport, guns, ammunition, stores and two aircraft at Liverpool, destined originally for Greece. She left the Mersey on 6 May but returned next day and was then sent to the Clyde to join WS 8B; the evacuatioin of Allied forces from Greece caused her military cargo to be re-directed to the Middle East. Also included in the convoy was the light carrier *Argus* then in use as a ferry carrier and loaded with aircraft destined for *Furious* at Gibraltar.

The convoy sailed from the Clyde Anchorage at 2130 on 22 May 1941, comprising five transports, one passenger ship, one MT ship and *Argus*, escorted by the cruiser *Exeter* as ocean escort, the AA cruiser *Cairo* for the passage through the Western Approaches, and eight destroyers of the 4th Flotilla, i.e. *Cossack* and three other Tribals, one Polish, two Canadian and the Hunt class *Eridge*. The Captain of the 4th Flotilla on *Cossack* was appointed SOE, Commodore Burke RNR was aboard *Georgic* and Captain Moore of *Duchess of Richmond* acted as Vice Commodore. Cruising order was formed on the morning of 23 May when 6 miles SW of Orsay Light.[17]

Two alternative cruising orders had been prepared at the last minute according to whether *Duchess of Bedford* would make the sailing or not; her appointed station at the head of column four was taken by *Argus*. At about 0900 on 23 May, soon after forming up, a report was received that Commodore Burke was seriously ill and unfit for duty; the SOE therefore appointed *Exeter* to act as Commodore. The convoy speed was 13.5 knots.

At 0828 on 24 May, when 300 miles west of Orsay, an aircraft was observed approaching the convoy from the port quarter. This proved to be a Focke-Wulf Condor, which flew very low over the length of the convoy between the first and second columns, and was engaged first by *Cairo* acting as AA escort and stationed in a centre column astern of *Exeter*. The aircraft passed directly over *Abosso* which opened fire from several machine guns, but two bombs were dropped, both of which fortunately missed but exploded close to the port side causing the ship to be violently shaken. The Condor disappeared ahead out of sight.

The bomb explosions caused both engines of *Abosso* to stop and she fell rapidly astern of the convoy, which in turn reduced speed. Shortly afterwards the starboard engine was re-started at half speed and by 0930 had worked up to full speed. The port engine was re-started at 1134 and by 1158 both engines were at full speed and *Abosso* was able to rejoin the convoy. Captain Tate paid tribute to the engineers who "worked extremely hard under what might easily have been dangerous conditions, and that we were able to continue the voyage was due largely to their efforts."[18] He also reported that "during this action the discipline of the passengers and crew was excellent, and there were no casualties."[18]

Exeter reported that the Condor was "engaged by all ships of the convoy and escort that could do so without endangering other ships...no hits can be claimed with any certainty but what appeared to be two red glows were seen on the starboard side of the fuselage. These might have been hits."[19] *Exeter* also noted that "the tactics adopted by the aircraft of flying at masthead height, made AA fire extremely difficult for fear of hitting other ships of the convoy and escort."[19]

Since the enemy had now located the convoy, further attacks were expected but never materialized. In fact the Condor may have been searching for and observing possible targets for the *Bismarck*, which at 0600 that very morning had engaged and sunk the *Hood* southwest of Iceland. The Admiralty was then directing all its resources towards the location and destruction of the *Bismarck*, which had successfully entered the North Atlantic and might at any time locate and destroy any one of the numerous convoys then at sea. Units of the Home Fleet and of Force H from Gibraltar were steaming at high speed to intercept, while WS 8B turned SW on its previously appointed course and retained its escort intact. In a position 200 miles further west and bound for Halifax, the battleship *Rodney* and three destroyers detached from escorting *Britannic* to join the hunt, leaving the Cunarder with the destroyer *Eskimo*, herself bound to Boston for refit. Both reached their destinations safely and without incident.

The convoy continued to the southwest during 24 and 25 May without further incident, while shadowing cruisers pursued the *Bismarck* across the North Atlantic in a SE'ly direction towards Brest. At midnight on 24 May *Bismarck* was attacked by aircraft from the *Victorious* and three hours later the cruisers lost touch with her. Throughout 25 May ships and aircraft searched for the enemy battleship which might at any time have been closing on WS 8B; Captain Vian as SOE on *Cossack* stationed *Cairo*, which was equipped with Radar, or RDF as it was then known, 30 miles from the convoy to give advance warning of *Bismarck's* approach.

The enemy, however, remained undetected as 25 May drew to a close and at 0030 26 May *Cairo* detached with *Eridge* and the two Canadian destroyers *Ottawa* and *Restigouche*, presumably to meet an inward convoy or return to base. WS 8B was then 660 miles due west of the Scillies under escort of *Exeter* and the 4th Destroyer Flotilla. At 0330 the Admiralty ordered these destroyers to detach from the convoy; *Cossack*, *Sikh* and *Zulu* to join the battleship *King George V*, while *Maori* and *Piorun* were directed to the *Rodney*; both heavy ships were NE of the convoy and in pursuit of the *Bismarck*, which subsequent records indicate had crossed 60 miles astern of the convoy at 0345, just as the destroyers detached.

The *Bismarck* continued on a SE'ly course towards Brest, and was sighted and reported by a Catalina of Coastal Command at 1030 on 26 May. She was attacked by Swordfish aircraft from *Ark Royal* that evening, which damaged her propellers and jammed the rudders. The five destroyers of the 4th Flotilla attacked with torpedoes during the early hours of 27 May, and likely scored two hits. *Bismarck* was finally sunk by the big guns of the battle squadron at 1036 that same day; a total of 110 survivors were rescued.

Unknown to the Admiralty or indeed anyone until the facts were later assembled, WS 8B and possibly *Britannic* had narrowly escaped a disaster. The news of the sinking of the *Bismarck* must have been received with heartfelt relief by all ships on the North Atlantic that day, and not least by everyone concerned with the liners of WS 8B embarked with almost 12,000 troops for the Middle East.

Four hours after receiving the news of the sinking of the *Bismarck*, the ferry carrier *Argus* detached from the convoy at 1500 bound for Gibraltar, and was met next morning by two destroyers which escorted her safely to that port. When *Argus* left the convoy, *Exeter* directed Captain Greig, the Master of *Georgic*, to assume the full duties of Commodore "since the Commodore's Yeoman and Staff were embarked on that ship."[19] *Exeter* later reported that Captain Greig "carried out this function for the remainder of the passage to Freetown with marked success."[19] In fact Captain Greig was exceedingly well qualified to hold the post of Commodore, having obtained his Master's Certificate in 1906 and later gained his Extra Master's Certificate. He was an Aberdeen man who had held the rank of Captain RNR since 1929 and was therefore well versed in naval procedures; *Georgic* was to be the last of his ten commands in Cunard service before retiral in 1944.

After the sinking of *Bismarck*, the convoy is believed to have passed east of the Azores and no further incidents occurred for the next four days until at 0500 on 31 May when *Orduna* developed a steering gear defect under port helm and collided heavily with the starboard side amidships of *Almanzora*. *Exeter* proceeded to the rear of the convoy to ascertain the extent of the damage, and found from both stopped ships that the collision had been a glancing one and that damage to both was above the waterline and not serious. The convoy was delayed and had to turn back to allow these ships to regain their station, and at *Exeter's* suggestion *Orduna* was ordered to form astern of the centre column. The collision took place at night, all ships steaming without lights, about halfway betwen the Canary and Cape Verde Islands.

At 0700 on 2 June the convoy was 120 miles WSW of Cap Vert and the Vichy French port of Dakar, where the destroyers *Duncan* and *Boreas* joined as A/S escorts. At 1300 that day a Sunderland from Freetown met the convoy to provide air escort and was joined by another from time to time later in the afternoon. At 1905 *Exeter* sighted a warship to the southeast causing her to go "to action stations and steam ordered for full ahead."[19] but the ship proved to be a Vichy French escort vessel proceeding in the direction of Dakar.

It had originally been hoped to reach Freetown within the last of the daylight on 3 June, but the various delays necessitated abandoning the attempt and speed was adjusted to arrive at the outer end of the searched channel at daylight on 4 June. The corvette *Marguerite* joined the convoy as additional A/S escort at 0600 3 June and at 0800 that day *Exeter* catapulted her aircraft to carry out a three hour A/S search ahead of the convoy.

The convoy anchored in Freetown on the morning of 4 June. *Exeter* noted that the speed had averaged approximately 13 knots which was varied slightly as a result of varying winds and weather. At one time the convoy "had proceeded at 14.5 knots, which was the maximum that could be maintained by *Orduna*, the slowest ship of the convoy."[19] It is interesting to note the comparative daily fuel consumption of the ships in WS 8B, given as *Almanzora* 109 tons, *Orduna* 101, *Duchess of Richmond* 66 and *Martand* 40 tons all Furnace Oil, while the two motorships *Georgic* and *Chr. Huygens* consumed only 45 and 32 tons Diesel respectively.

Of the seven ships of WS 8B which watered and fuelled at Freetown, only five were ready to proceed with the convoy on 6 June. The Elder Dempster *Abosso* was sent on to Port Harcourt in Nigeria where she embarked and returned to Freetown on 22 June with the troops of 4 Bn The Nigeria Regiment; she then resumed the usual coastal trip with calls at Accra, Lagos and Takoradi before leaving Freetown for Liverpool on 16 July and was requisitioned for trooping service at the end of that voyage. Whilst at anchor in "Freetown the Dutch *Christiaan Huygens* was run into by the 1912 built warship *Centurion* mocked up as a dummy battleship of the *King George V* class and then en route to the East Indies. *Christiaan Huygens* suffered considerable damage and was delayed for an estimated 10 to 14 days to complete repairs and inclusion in the next following convoy WS 9A.

The remaining five ships sailed from Freetown at 1330 on 6 June, still escorted by *Exeter* and with the destroyers *Boreas*, *Duncan* and *Highlander* acting as A/S screen. *Exeter* remained in the centre column astern of *Georgic* while the destroyers were present. A revised cruising order was adopted from Freetown, where also Commodore

Cochrane had joined *Georgic* in lieu of Commodore Burke. Captain Moore of *Duchess of Richmond* continued to act as Vice Commodore.[20]

During the first three days out from Freetown, in an area where enemy submarines were prevalent, *Exeter* catapulted her aircraft at 0800 and 1630 daily for A/S patrol ahead of the convoy. The destroyers parted company at 1730 on 8 June, whereupon *Exeter* took station ahead of the convoy and zigzagged broadly across its front. The convoy averaged only 13.5 knots until 15 June when head winds and the consequent inability of *Orduna* to maintain that speed reduced the average to approximately 13 knots, which made it necessary to abandon the attempt to reach Durban before darkness on 19 June. *Orduna* dropped well astern on the morning of 17 June, when the convoy was to the west of the Cape of Good Hope. Cape Agulhas was rounded that night and next morning the convoy passed the B.I. steamer *Waroonga* bound in the opposite direction for Capetown. The convoy reached Durban on the morning of 20 June and berthed in the harbour, where the Commodore noted that the station-keeping had been good except for "*Orduna* who was steaming at approximately her maximum speed and at times had difficulty in keeping up."[19]

The ships of WS 8B spent three days in Durban fuelling, watering, storing and exercising the troops ashore. Also in port were the last four homebound liners of WS 7, all loading general cargoes including *Orontes* which had been drydocked for cleaning and painting. Whilst in Durban the convoy was joined by the Dutch liner *Nieuw Zeeland*, which had reached Durban light ship from Suez ahead of the convoy, and was one of the last two merchant ships to leave Crete before the German landings on that island. *Nieuw Zeeland* spent the time in Durban undergoing minor repairs, then embarked 1,042 troops which had been landed from *Highland Princess* on 13 June. The 742 troops on *Duchess of Richmond* for Singapore were landed ashore to the transit camp to await on-carriage.

All six ships sailed from Durban between 1300 and 1600 on 23 June, with *Exeter* retained as ocean escort and stationed ahead of the centre column, and being now clear of the submarine danger did not zigzag. The speed maintained to the Gulf of Aden was 13.5 knots and the same cruising order was adopted as on the previous passage with *Nieuw Zeeland* taking station 22 astern of *Georgic*.

During 24 June *Nieuw Zeeland* dropped astern in spite of the convoy reducing to 13.3 knots and at daylight next day was out of sight astern. The convoy then reduced to 10 knots for five hours to allow her to regain station and continued "for the rest of that day at 13 knots which appeared to be the maximum that *Nieuw Zeeland* could maintain."[19] *Exeter's* aircraft was catapulted that afternoon to exercise all ships' A/A armament.

The convoy passed uneventfully through the Mozambique Channel and by midday 27 June was 70 miles eastward of Porto Mozambique. At 1530 that day the Anchor Line's *Elysia* was passed, bound south to Durban, and soon after this *Exeter* launched her aircraft. At 1715 hours, when carrying out a low level bombing exercise on her own ship, the aircraft crash dived into the sea, killing all its crew. A funeral service was held aboard *Exeter* next morning with full military honours accorded those who had lost their lives; the one body that had been recovered being then buried at sea. The Newcastle steamer *Hoperange* was passed that afternoon, bound from Aden to Lourenco Marques.

No incidents occurred on the remainder of the passage to Guardafui, the only other ship sighted being the Houston *Harmonides* on the morning of 29 June bound from Colombo to Durban. The convoy passed through the Guardafui Straits during the night of 2-3 July and next morning altered course for Aden. A Norwegian ship was passed that morning and the Strick Line *Baharistan* at 1250 bound from Aden to Capetown. The destroyer *Janus* joined and exchanged duties with *Exeter* at 2023 that evening and the convoy reached Aden outer anchorage at noon next day, where *Exeter* detached and officially dispersed the convoy.

It is not known why WS 8B put into Aden.   The Gulf of Aden and Red Sea were devoid of the enemy and Suez Bay relatively quiet, indeed the desert front was at a stalemate following the British failure in *Operation Battleaxe* to relieve Tobruk in June. All six ships left Aden between 4 and 6 July and proceeded independently at their best speeds to Suez, where *Georgic* and *Duchess of Richmond* were first to arrive on 8 July. These two ships and *Almanzora*, disembarked first and the *Duchess* sailed again on 12 July, loading for the UK at Mombasa, Durban and Capetown. Her homeward voyage was via Trinidad and she reached Liverpool on 5 September, being next employed in WS 12 which sailed 25 days later.

Also in Suez at this time were the Hospital Ships *Atlantis*, *Somersetshire* and *Tairea*, while the Indian Ocean troopships *Salween*, *Ascanius* and *Dempo* arrived on 9 July, the two former from Mombasa and *Dempo* from Massawa, whence also *Westernland* arrived two days later. The smaller *Cap St. Jacques* was also in Suez repairing, and sailed for Mombasa on 11 July.

On 12 July the Australian cruiser *Hobart* reached Suez from Sydney, and entered the canal next evening with intent to join the Mediterranean Fleet in relief of her sister ship *Perth*. Unfortunately the enemy had just renewed their mining attacks on the waterway and the possibility of encountering unswept mines caused *Hobart* to return down the canal stern first to Suez Bay. Shortly after midnight heavy air raids developed on Suez port area and at 0300 groups of dive bombers began to attack shipping at the anchorage. *Almanzora*, *Georgic* and the Blue Funnel *Euryades* were singled out for particular attention.

The first stick of bombs "found no target, a second aircraft straddled *Almanzora* but missed on both sides and inflicted no more than blast damage."[21] Despite an accurate and determined AA fire the enemy was not deterred from making a third attack at 0313 in which one bomb glanced off *Georgic's* side, "exploded in the water and did considerable damage to the hull in No. 4 hold, causing heavy flooding. A second struck the after end of the boat deck, penetrated five decks and exploded in an elevator shaft. Heavy damage was caused in No. 5 hold and fire broke out in the after accommodation. Oil fuel from ruptured double bottom tanks ignited....the fire reached the ship's 6-inch gun ammunition which exploded and the whole after end of the ship was soon a mass of flames."[22]

The ship nearest to *Georgic* appears to have been HMS *Glenearn* lying completely immobilized from damage sustained in the evacuation from Greece. In response to a request from *Georgic* for boats to assist in taking off her passengers, which included a number of women and children being evacuated from the Middle East to South Africa, *Glenearn* promptly manned and sent off a whaler, but this boat soon had to fend for itself and spent the rest of the night alongside the Greek cruiser *Averett*.

Meanwhile *Georgic* developed a port list, was heavily down by the stern and surrounded by an immense pall of smoke. At 0330 Captain Greig decided to get his ship under way and attempt to beach in shallow water. Despite the acute trim and list, her engineers with great gallantry remained below to operate the massive 10 cylinder B & W engines. The fire spread forward to the bridge and cut all communications as the ship began to move ahead. *Georgic* sheared to port and collided at an acute angle with the starboard side amidships of *Glenearn*. Still driving ahead, *Georgic's* stern grated along the plating of *Glenearn* and finally caught across her buoy cable to take both ships and the buoy further up the bay. The two ships came alongside one another, boat davits interlocked and the mass of flames from *Georgic* set fire to *Glenearn*, to add to the general holocaust. *Georgic* finally grounded and almost struck the West Shoal Beacon, but *Glenearn* being lighter in the water continued ahead for a short distance until she too brought up on the same shoal 300 feet from *Georgic*.

While the two ships had been locked together, *Georgic's* Third Officer had been cut off by the fire and landed aboard *Glenearn* with the alarming news that No. 8 hold was full of ammunition and with the fire raging in the adjacent No. 7 hold, was liable to explode at any moment. In fact the ammunition was "300 cases of condemned 4.7 inch" being returned to the UK, which subsequently "exploded with a grand barrage effect throught the forenoon",[23] but without harm.

Intermittent bombing continued until the break of dawn at 0350 and when the 'All Clear' sounded at 0438, *Georgic* was still burning furiously from the bridge all the way aft to the stern. By 0500 she was abandoned by all hands, although most of the passengers and crew had been taken off during the night by a combination of her own boats, those from *Hobart* and by the motor lifeboat and others from *Almanzora*, also small tugs and other port craft.

During the afternoon *Hobart* towed *Glenearn* clear of the shoal and tugs thereafter towed her to a berth alongside at Port Tewfik. *Georgic* remained fast aground and burned fiercely throughout the day. At 1830 she suddenly took a greater list, settling finally at 17 degrees, and sat down lower in the water by the stern, with her after deck nearly awash and the engine-room flooded to above the tops of the main engines.

Having witnessed the tragedy which befell *Georgic*, Captain Bridges of *Almanzora* determined "not to remain another night in so exposed and unprotected an anchorage. The authorities agreed, and *Almanzora* sailed soon after midday 14 July"[21] for Mombasa, but was diverted to Durban to load at that port and Capetown, leaving the latter on 17 August, Freetown 27 August and reaching the Clyde and Glasgow on 9 September, to berth at Yorkhill Quay that afternoon. Her next voyage was in WS 12 back to Suez.

At first light on 15 July, a party of Royal Engineers boarded the foredeck of *Georgic* and with the help of a floating crane operated by protesting local labour, successfully lifted off a prized German Mark IV tank which was being taken to the UK for examination. *Hobart* proceeded into the canal that morning and reached Alexandria without further incident.

The fire on *Georgic* burnt itself out after two days, leaving the entire superstructure a blackened and twisted shambles. On 18 July *Georgic* was officially declared a total loss and would in peacetime almost certainly have been scrapped, but these were dark days for Britain that could not afford her ninth largest troopship to be so lightly disposed of. On 14 September an attempt was made to begin salvage and eight days later this work was proceeding satisfactorily. By 26 October the ship was safely afloat and anchored, with work beginning to pump out and drain all compartments. It was estimated that a further four to six weeks preparatory work was required before the hull could be made sufficiently seaworthy to allow towage to a safe port where repairs could be put in hand. On 27 November a fire occurred in the cold storage flat but was extinguished and did not affect the work of making the ship ready for sea. The long subsequent saga of returning the ship to service is now given in some detail, being most appropriate to this chapter.

After nearly six months at Suez, the burnt out shell of the *Georgic* was towed out of the bay on 29 December 1941 bound for Bombay. Tugs were not available and the tow was undertaken by the cargo liner *Clan Campbell*, requisitioned for the job while on a ballast voyage from Alexandria to Calcutta, with Ellerman's *City of Sydney* made fast astern to assist with steering. The tow was reported to make about 6 knots, but strong winds were encountered and with the rudder jammed for good measure, the abandoned hulk of the *Georgic* sheered about wildly and to such an extent that on 3 January both after wires connected to *City of Sydney* carried away. The hulk was still leaking and began to develop a list. A party of volunteers boarded and got the temporary pump going, there being no one else aboard and no power, light or accommodation available. The list was reduced to five degrees but it was decided to take the tow into Port Sudan to reduce the leaks.

On 10 January the *City of Sydney* again made fast astern, and assisted by a port tug, the *Clan Campbell* brought the unwieldly hulk of the *Georgic* into the Port Sudan anchorage, having averaged 2.5 knots for the 700 mile passage from Suez. The *Georgic* remained in Port Sudan for nearly eight weeks during which time pumping was almost continuous, cement boxes were rebuilt and strengthened and the jammed rudder cleared.

For the next leg of the tow, the Harrison liner *Recorder* was engaged in lieu of *Clan Campbell* which had been sent back to Alexandria on 25 January, only to be sunk two months later and almost within sight of Malta. The hulk of *Georgic* left Port Sudan under tow of the *Recorder*, assisted by the tug *Sampson*, on 5 March 1942 bound for Karachi. The tug proved too small for the job so *Recorder* continued alone until 8 March when the B.I. steamer *Haresfield* took over the steering position and later the tug *Pauline Moller* assisted. The tow passed Aden on 15 March and reached Karachi safely on the last day of the month. It was estimated that four months work was required to get the main machinery operational, after which the *Georgic* would hopefully proceed to the USA or UK under her own power.

During the 8.5 months that *Georgic* lay at Karachi, quite exceptional work was carried out by the ship's engineers. Everything in the engine room had been covered in oil and had to be cleaned and restored to working order. Once the first generator was started, power and light returned which greatly speeded up the remainder of the work. Even the stem, which had been twisted by the collision with *Glenearn*, was strengthened by a combination of heat, purchases, levers and heavy hammers. Some accommodation was built up, an Indian crew signed on and on 11 December, *Georgic* left Karachi under her own power, and proceeded at a speed of 11 knots to Bombay, where she arrived two days later and docked in the Hughes Drydock within the Alexandra Dock.

Whilst at Bombay the hull damage was repaired and the machinery overhaul completed. The *Georgic* loaded 5,000 tons of pig iron on the Anchor Line berth and left Bombay on 21 January 1943 for the UK, proceeding at a speed of 16 knots. So ended an eighteen month struggle to make the ship seaworthy and able to make the homeward voyage. Minor repairs and fuelling were carried out in Capetown between 5 and 8 February, from where the *Georgic* proceeded direct to Liverpool, arriving on 1 March. After completing discharge the *Georgic* proceeded to Belfast to be taken in hand for a complete rebuild by Harland & Wolff. She was out of service for almost four years, and finally returned to trooping service in March 1945.

Meanwhile the Dutch liner *Nieuw Zeeland* had also been at Suez during the burning of *Georgic*, and thereafter embarked 804 Italian POW for Durban, with 120 troops of the Sikh Regiment as escort, and 100 crew from *Georgic* being repatriated to the UK. The *Nieuw Zeeland* called at Mombasa en route, and reached Durban on 5 August, where all her personnel were disembarked. In lieu she embarked 184 RAF for the UK and 877 Nigerian troops for Lagos, and left Durban in convoy CF 2 on 21 August.

The last liner of WS 8B to reach Suez was *Orduna* which had been held outside Suez and did not begin disembarkation until 15 July, and was then held up awaiting orders until despatched on the 29th to Port Sudan for fresh water, thence to Berbera where she embarked the balance of 877 troops of 23 Nigerian Brigade being returned to West Africa. *Orduna* proceeded in convoy to Mombasa, arriving 13 August and reached Durban six days later, where the Nigerians transhipped to *Nieuw Zeeland* (see above) and *Sobieski*. Homeward loading was completed at Capetown on 2 September, from where *Orduna* proceeded via Trinidad and Halifax, leaving the latter in convoy HX 152 for Liverpool, and arrived on 12 October. Her outward voyage lasted 54 days and the homeward leg 77 days. Two weeks were spent at Suez and 31 days at Liverpool repairing her collision damage and preparing for her next voyage in WS 12Z back to Suez. The round voyage in WS 8B had therefore occupied almost six months.

The sole MT ship of WS 8B, Brocklebank's *Martand* proceeded through the canal on reaching Suez on 9 July, to discharge at Alexandria. She had carried a valuable cargo of MT, vehicles, guns, ammunition, stores, one Sea Gladiator and one Fulmar aircraft. She was then released from requsition and proceeded to Calcutta to load on her owners' berth for the UK, reaching the Clyde via the Cape, Trinidad and Halifax.

The troops of 50 Division, including 151 (Durham) Brigade who landed at Suez from this convoy, were initially sent to Quassassin Camp for two weeks before moving to Cyprus. The Brigade then moved to Iraq and in January 1942 to the Western Desert, where one of its battalions was destroyed at Matruh in June of that year. The Brigade later took part in operations in Sicily and Normandy, and was disbanded in November 1944.

WS 8X - sailed UK 31.5.41

This was a single transport convoy which left the UK a mere nine days behind WS 8B, presumably dictated by the necessity of completing the numbers and military stores originally intended for that convoy. Although the short interval increased the escort programme and exactly that which the Admiralty were at pains to avoid, the sailing date was postponed for four days to coincide with the departure of the carrier *Victorious* carrying 50 Hurricanes to be flown off to Malta.

The 3,100 troops embarked on *Duchess of Bedford* had remained aboard at the Clyde Anchorage after her grounding on 22 May, and with Captain W G Busk-Wood back in command after the luxury of a voyage off, this liner sailed at 2230 on 31 May, escorted by *Victorious* acting as SOE, the cruisers *Norfolk* and *Neptune* and AMC *Esperance Bay* (the cruisers having only just arrived in the Clyde after taking part in the destruction of the *Bismarck*). At 0700 next morning when 10 miles west of Orsay, two 16 knot MT ships joined from Liverpool (Shaw Savill's *Waiwera* and Port Line *Port Wyndham*) whilst the A/S escort consisting of *Legion*, Polish *Piorun*, Canadian *Saguenay*, three V and W and three similar vintage ex American destroyers provided the protective screen.[24]

The speed of the convoy was initially dictated by the 14.5 knots of *Esperance Bay*. Once the cruising order was formed, *Victorious, Norfolk* and *Neptune* took station in line abreast half a mile astern of the convoy, which steered to the westward until the early hours of 2 June when to the south of Rockall Bank, course was altered to the SW and the general direction of the Azores. At 1445 that day *Piorun* obtained an Asdic contact and attacked, but rejoined an hour later without conclusive results. Unusually this small convoy was routed to pass only 200 miles west of the County Mayo coast, perhaps because of the carrier escort and at 0600 on the 3rd, when 500 miles west of the Scillies, the three V & W destroyers were detached for Gibraltar and two hours later two of the ex-American type left to return to base. At noon *Esperance Bay* detached on patrol en route to Freetown while *Legion* left at 1400 to meet the OBV *Malvernian*. That evening the remaining destroyers also parted company. By the afternoon of the 4th the convoy was 600 miles west of Finisterre and at 1830 some 260 miles NE of the Azores, where *Neptune* detached to intercept an enemy merchant ship reported by *Esperance Bay* and stopped by an aircraft from *Victorious* after detection by radar operators., At 2100 *Victorious* left the convoy to join this operation leaving *Norfolk* as the sole ocean escort. *Neptune* found the German *Gonzenheim*, which proved to be one of *Bismarck's* supply ships, which scuttled herself while *Neptune* sank her with a torpedo and picked up 63 survivors.

At 1400 on the 5th the convoy passed 45 miles east of San Miguel, the most easterly of the Azores and was rejoined by *Victorious* and *Neptune* that evening. By midnight on the 6th the convoy was 300 miles west of the Canaries where *Victorious* and *Neptune* parted company to proceed NE for Gibraltar. Until this time aircraft from *Victorious* had flown daily A/S patrols ahead of the convoy and this task was now taken up by the Walrus from *Norfolk*. The convoy was routed to pass between Cape Verde and the islands of that name during the forenoon of the 9th, with a rendezvous arranged with the destroyer *Velox* at noon, and having deduced the convoy would be six hours early, *Norfolk* detached at 1250 the previous day to a position 40 miles distant where she transmitted that information to the CinC SA by High Frequency W/T, rejoining at 1800.

At midday on 9 June the convoy passed through the Cape Verde gap, *Velox* joined at 1245 and course was altered SE towards Freetown. The corvette *Aster* was expected to join the escort at 0800 next day when the convoy reached a position 120 miles SW of Bathurst, where she was to refuel, and despite a three hour search by the Walrus from *Norfolk*, *Aster* was not located and reckoned to have been late arriving in Bathurst. The AMC *Arawa* was passed and spoken at 1130 that day at a distance of 10 miles, escorting the homeward convoy SL 77 of 15 ships. *Norfolk* then shut down two boilers to allow cleaning to begin on arrival at Freetown, where all the ships and escorts arrived and anchored at 0715 on 11 June. Also in harbour were the cruiser *London*, AMC *Queen of Bermuda* and four destroyers. *Norfolk* left the convoy at Freetown, embarked 28 naval and mercantile officers and 182 German POW from intercepted and scuttled supply ships and sailed late on the 12th to overtake *Arawa* and the northbound convoy. *Norfolk* reported that WS 8X kept good station with a single regrettable incident when *Waiwera* nearly collided with *Duchess of Bedford* at night due to a wrong alteration during zigzag. The report also stated that the Commodore, not named but may have been the Master of the liner, was not in possession of the Mercantile Convoy Instructions.[25]

After completing replenishment the three ships of WS 8X left Freetown on 15 June, escorted by *Neptune* which had arrived from Gibraltar, and proceeded on an uneventful passage to the Cape. As the convoy neared Capetown, eight homeward liners of WS 7 were being priority loaded and fuelled in the port so WS 8X was diverted to Simonstown where it arrived on the 24th, and thereafter continued to Mombasa where a brief call was made on 6 July before reaching Aden on the 11th where dispersal took place. *Duchess of Bedford* was the first ship to reach Suez on 15 July and there witness the smouldering wreck of *Georgic* aground on the West Shoal. The two MT ships passed through the canal to discharge at Port Said and thereafter proceeded to Australia and New Zealand to load homewards.

Despite the bombing attacks that had recently taken place and the obvious need to handle large liners with the utmost despatch, *Duchess of Bedford* spent nine days at Suez, being delayed latterly by the lack of lighters and attendant craft when *Mauretania* and *Nieuw Amsterdam* arrived from Durban on the 21st. The *Duchess* only cleared the area before *Queen Mary* arrived from Sydney on the 25th. From Suez, *Duchess of Bedford* was directed to the small anchorage port of Berbera, on the then British Somaliland shores of the Gulf of Aden, almost due south of Aden. She arrived there on 31 July just as *Cap St. Jacques* departed with Italian POW for Mombasa, and began to embark the troops of 23 Nigerian Brigade over a period lasting nearly four days. Embarkation was interrupted on 2 August when *President Doumer* arrived and shipped out more Italians, and as the *Duchess* departed on the 4th, *Orduna* arrived to embark the balance of the Nigerians.

Duchess of Bedford and *Orduna* left Aden together on 6 August under escort for Mombasa, where a small amount of homeward cargo was loaded on the 13th and 14th, and both ships reached Durban on the 19th. Here all of the troops on *Orduna* were transhipped to *Nieuw Zeeland* and *Sobieski*, 877 going to the former ship and the balance, about 1300 to the Polish liner which had just come out of drydock. *Orduna* continued to the UK,[26] while the *Duchess* joined at Durban with *Nieuw Zeeland*, *Sobieski* and *Durban Castle* to form convoy CF 2 (Cape - Freetown). The latter liner was homeward from Bombay, having gone out in WS 9A, and was fully embarked with women and children for the UK. Some officers and men were transferred to *Sobieski* in Durban to make room for more passengers at Capetown. The West African troops of 23 Nigerian Brigade had originally journeyed around the Cape to Mombasa in June 1940 as 1st West Africa Brigade, and having successfully concluded the campaign against Italian forces in East Africa were now required to reinforce Freetown which was in danger of being threatened by the Vichy French in retaliation for events in Syria.

The four liners of convoy CF 2 sailed from Durban at 1815 on 21 August with Commander B W Barrow embarked on *Durban Castle* as Commodore. The four liners were escorted by the AMC *Queen of Bermuda*, with an average speed of 16.16 knots being maintained on the coastal passage to Capetown, which was reached at 1400 on the 24th. Homeward cargo was loaded in Capetown on *Duchess of Bedford*, *Durban Castle* and *Sobieski*. A further 61 passengers were embarked on *Durban Castle*, including HM The King of the Hellenes, eleven others of the Greek Royal Family and members of the Greek government now in exile.[27]

After two days in port, the convoy left Capetown at 1400 on the 26th, still escorted by *Queen of Bermuda*, bound northwest in the direction of St. Helena. On the third day out from Capetown, the escort was strengthened when the AMC *Cilicia* joined, and next day *Durban Castle* hoisted the Dutch ensign in honour of Queen Wilhelmina's birthday.[28]

At 0715 on 31 August St. Helena was sighted at a distance of 40 miles to the SW, and at this point *Cilicia* detached with *Duchess of Bedford*, *Sobieski* and *Nieuw Zeeland* all for Lagos, while *Durban Castle* continued on a NW course with *Queen of Bermuda* for Trinidad, where most homeward ships were being diverted to escape the U-Boat activity off Freetown. The cruiser *Newcastle* joined the escort of *Durban Castle* on the morning of 2 September and took station ahead. Commander Barrow commented on the difficulty of approaching Trinidad without a D/F station, but an excellent landfall was made on the evening of the 8th and *Durban Castle* with escorts were anchored in Port of Spain at 0930 on the 9th. Whilst fuel and water were being shipped, the Commander and an Admiral Leatham went ashore and paid their respects to the Governor, who in turn boarded *Durban Castle* to call upon the King of Greece. The Royal Party then landed and was entertained at the Governor's House, while the cruiser *Diomede* arrived in the afternoon with the CinC North Atlantic and West Indies on a routine visit. In the light of events elsewhere in the world, the social occasions at Trinidad were surely bizarre.

All three ships departed Port of Spain at 2100 on the 10th and gave Martinique a wide berth to eastward before shaping a course to meet the next escort in a position 700 miles west of the Azores, where at 1400 on the 15th the Canadian AMC *Prince David* relieved *Newcastle*. On the 17th with a N'ly wind increasing to force 6/7, *Prince David* had to reduce speed and finally heave-to before *Queen of Bermuda* instructed her to proceed to Halifax where she ultimately spent ten weeks refitting. The weather moderated on the 18th and two destroyers were met next morning to the west of Ireland where *Queen of Bermuda* detached for Newport News also for a ten week refit. A Catalina air escort arrived over *Durban Castle* on the morning of the 20th and remained until dusk. Low visibility accompanied the passage through the North Channel and Irish Sea but *Durban Castle* berthed on the Liverpool Princes Landing Stage that evening where HRH The Duke of Gloucester boarded to welcome the Greek Royal family. In his report of the 'convoy', Commander Barrow commented that the voyage had been a "happy and comfortable one, that the navigation of *Durban Castle* was excellent due to the skill and care of Mr. Lorraine, 2nd Officer, and that Captain Harris, her Master, was not in the best of health."[27] (Although he remained in command of the ship until his retiral at the age of 63 in June 1942.) *Durban Castle* was next employed in convoy CT 5 to Halifax.

Meanwhile the three ships carrying the Nigerians arrived at Lagos on 4 September and disembarked all 5,200 troops during the course of the next four days. This 23 Nigerian Brigade now reverted to its original title of 1 West Africa Brigade and remained in West Africa for the next three years until moving to Burma with 82 West African Division. All three liners may have embarked other Nigerian troops at Lagos and landed them at Freetown on 13 September to increase the defences of Sierra Leone. Their arrival at Freetown anchorage coincided with that of WS 11 being replenished and a homeward convoy being prepared for departure, all of which claimed priority. *Nieuw Zeeland* joined WS 11 for return to the Indian Ocean, while *Duchess of Bedford* and *Sobieski* had had to wait until the 25th before their requirements were fully met. Both liners were now embarked with service personnel for the UK, 846 mainly military and RAF being on the *Duchess* and 562 mainly RN and DBS on *Sobieski*; they were escorted northwards by the AMC *Cheshire* until the latitude of 49° North was reached when they were joined by a local destroyer escort. *Duchess of Bedford* was directed to Liverpool where she arrived on 11 October and was next employed in WS 12Z to Singapore. *Sobieski* reached the Clyde on the same date, disembarking and discharging at the anchorage port before moving upriver to Glasgow for repairs, and was next engaged in CT 5 to Halifax. Despite the delay and homeward diversion to West Africa, *Duchess of Bedford* had accomplished a round voyage to Suez in four and a half months, a heartening improvement on the ships of WS 7. The MT ship *Waiwera* which had accompanied the *Duchess to Suez*, reached Liverpool five days behind her with a refrigerated cargo from New Zealand.

WS 8C- sailed Clyde 9.8.41 for Scapa

This convoy designation was in use from May 1941 to cover the movements of seven liners assigned to 'Operational Service' for the training of ships, troops and landing-craft crews in amphibious operations. These were conducted within the confines of the Firth of Clyde, principally Loch Fyne, until a final major exercise was arranged at Scapa to add realism to the event with a convoy passage to the scene of the landings.

WS 8C proper comprised *Karanja, Narkunda, Winchester Castle, Batory* and *Ormonde* with six MT ships and smaller Landing Ships on an operational exercise which sailed from the Clyde on 9 August 1941 for Scapa Flow, and returned eight days later. These five ships, however, with *Ettrick* and *Kenya* (later renamed *Hydra* and then *Keren*) continued to be held on the Clyde with 5,000 troops for a possible expedition to sieze the Canary Islands and so ensure the protection of our lifeline to the Middle East and Australasia. Frequent representations were made to the War Office to release some or all of them for WS trooping. *Narkunda* and *Ormonde* were therefore released at the end of August and *Batory* in mid September while the remainder were retained; *Karanja* and her sister transferring to the White Ensign in July, *Ettrick* continuing to develop as a Training Landing Ship and *Winchester Castle* as a Headquarters Ship for landings, both based at Inveraray near the head of Loch Fyne.

Chapter 10

WS 9A and WS 9B

The completion of 50 (Northumbrian) Division in the Middle East,
161 Brigade leaves Sierra Leone and more reinforcements for Singapore

WS 9A - sailed UK 3.6.41

The British and Allied position in the Mediterranean and Middle East as convoys WS 9A and B were being assembled and despatched in the late spring and early summer of 1941 was growing increasingly grave. The evacuation and loss of Greece to Axis forces at the end of April was followed by a similar loss of Crete a month later, by which time Tobruk was invested and being supplied by sea from Alexandria. At the same time Rommel began to concentrate his forces on the Egyptian border which threatened the whole Nile Delta and might well have had disastrous consequences. On the credit side good progress was made in ejecting the Italians from East Africa, while British and Indian troops gained control of Iraq in early June and prepared to enter Syria, where the Nazis had stirred up the Vichy-French against the Allied cause. The pressing need to reinforce the Middle East by every possible means continued to dominate War Office strategy for more than a year ahead.

WS 9A was planned with 11 transports ranging in size from 6,300 to 27,000 tons, with speeds between 13.5 and 20 knots, and having a total capacity for 21,900 personnel. It was not the most compatible mix of ships for convoying over such a vast distance, but quite simply that which was then available to accommodate the numbers called-for by the War Office for embarkation. Five MT ships were to be included having speeds of 14.5 to 17 knots of which four were American owned C2 and C3 types loaned to Britain for inclusion in fast military convoys.

Six of the transports had previously sailed in WS 5B and returned to UK ports in the middle of May, i.e. *Franconia*, *Durban* and *Capetown Castles*, *Empress of Japan*, *Orbita* and *Samaria*. They were expeditiously discharged and embarked for WS 9A at these same ports, the first three named in Glasgow, *Orbita* and the *Empress* at the Clyde Anchorage and *Samaria* at Liverpool, having arrived there in the midst of clearance operations after the recent explosion in that port. Two other transports, *Highland Brigade* and *Llangibby Castle* had returned from WS 6, the former to discharge Argentine meat in Liverpool and *Llangibby Castle* for machinery repairs at Queens Dock in Glasgow.

The remaining transports to complete the convoy were *Eastern Prince* which had been unable to sail in WS 8B, the small Polish coal burner *Pulaski*, a recent addition to the trooping fleet but having just completed two round trips to Iceland, and finally the P&O *Mooltan*, newly converted for trooping at Tilbury by a lengthy process lasting almost four months due to the shortage of men and materials, and only just missed inclusion in the previous convoy WS 8B. By providing berths for 3,200 personnel, *Mooltan* quickly demonstrated the value of those liners to the overall capacity of the trooping fleet. Unfortunately of the 55 originally taken up for service as AMCs, 15 had since been lost by enemy action.

Embarkation was carried out in Glasgow during the first two days of June, on *Llangibby Castle*, *Capetown Castle* and *Franconia* in KGV Dock and on *Durban Castle* at Yorkhill Quay. Two of the berths normally used for troop embarkation in KGV Dock were occupied by ex-American MT ships *Empires Widgeon* and *Egret* (operated by Royal Mail Lines), while the similar *Empires Condor* and *Curlew*, managed by the Donaldson Line, loaded at riverside berths nearer the city.[1] All eight ships were at the Clyde Anchorage ready for sea by 0900 on the 3rd, where also *Empress of Japan*, *Orbita* and *Mooltan* had embarked from tenders with the latter ship carrying the entire personnel of 69 Infantry Brigade comprising 6 and 7 Bns. The Green Howards and 4 Bn East Yorks Regiment.[2] 69 Brigade was a second line territorial formation which served in France with 23 (Northumbrian) Division for five weeks in the spring of 1940, originally for labouring duties but latterly called into the line for the ten day retreat to Dunkirk. The Brigade was now commanded by Brigadier GWE Erskine, who later went on to command the famous 7 Armoured Division in North Africa and Italy.

At Liverpool, *Samaria*, *Eastern Prince* and *Highland Brigade* were embarked on the last day of May and 1st June, and together with the four-masted maeirform bow and 17 knot Dutch MT ship *Aagtekerk*, left the Mersey at 1400 on the 3rd under destroyer escort (two ex-American - *Ramsey* and *Richmond*) to meet and join with the Clyde portion next morning.

One additional ship allocated to the convoy was the ex-French *Mendoza* of the Vapeur Company, captured from Vichy control and now under the Red Ensign and Blue Funnel management. After major repairs in Glasgow her trooping conversion was delayed pending completion of a voyage to New York. One troopship which did not sail was

Pulaski and probably excluded by reason of her stated speed of 13.5 knots, although she later sailed in WS 9B after making a third trip to Iceland.

Commodore AW Barrow DSC was embarked with his signals staff on *Empress of Japan*, while Captain Bissett of *Franconia* was detailed as Vice Commodore. The 11 ship Clyde portion sailed from the anchorage off Gourock at 2100 on 3rd June, escorted by the AA cruiser *Cairo* and four Tribal class fleet destroyers of the 4th Flotilla, *Cossack* (SOE), *Maori*, *Sikh* and *Zulu*, together with the AMC *Dunnottar Castle*. They were followed two hours later by the cruiser *Birmingham*, AMC *Ausonia* and two Canadian destroyers which overhauled and joined the convoy in the forming up position off Orsay at 0600 on the 4th, where also the Liverpool section of four ships joined with their escort when WS 9A became five columns of three in addition to the escort of two cruisers, two AMCs and eight destroyers.[3]

Captain Vian of the 4th Destroyer Flotilla on *Cossack*, passed a number of air alarms as the convoy progressed through the Western Approaches and during one of these, between 0600 and 0925 on the 5th, ships on the port wing column fired a number of rounds at a plane, which was not seen by the Commodore. The convoy speed was limited by that of *Orbita* to 13.5 knots, and when speed was increased to 14 knots, *Orbita* started to straggle and the convoy had to reduce to allow her to regain station. At 0400 on the 6th Captain D4 detached with his four destroyers, plus *Cairo*, by which time the convoy had reached a position 700 miles due west of the Scillies and was then steering a southerly course for the eastern side of the Azores. *Ausonia* detached soon after this to the westward to meet and escort convoy SC 35 from Halifax.

At 0700 on the 6th the two Canadian destroyers *Ottawa* and *Restigouche* detached to search for survivors from the Dutch steamer *Eibergen*, torpedoed and sunk in a position 80 miles SSW three days earlier. The destroyers searched an arc of 60 degrees to the east of this position without success, and at 1315 were advised by the Admiralty that *Eibergen's* boats were drifting in an area which encompassed 12,000 square miles, the nearest point of which lay 60 miles NE of *Ottawa*, where she now proceeded. At 1355 however, *Cossack* signalled that transmissions from the boats gave a D/F bearing of 140° and so *Cairo* and *Zulu* were detached to search accordingly. As this position placed the boats 210 miles from *Ottawa*, that destroyer and *Restigouche* then abandoned the search and set course for St. John's, Newfoundland. Happily, at 1830 *Cairo* signalled *Ottawa* that *Eibergen's* 33 survivors had been picked up.

The Commodore reported that the station keeping of *Mooltan* was unsatisfactory for some days but improved later, probably the result of her having been under repair and conversion for an extended period of six months. The weather on the passage to Freetown was noted as average but on the 9th the convoy ran into a heavy sea for some hours, when both *Empires Egret* and *Widgeon* dropped astern to secure deck cargoes, while *Birmingham* maintained touch until they rejoined. The Commodore later questioned *Empire Widgeon* on the cargo that had shifted, and was advised that 6 and 9 ton cased trucks stowed athwartships on Nos. 2, 3, 5 and 7 hatches had shifted and carried away lashings when the vessel began to roll heavily. "The trucks had been loaded in Glasgow by Sea Transport staff using Army labour, by means of a heavy lift crane which had insufficient reach across the ship to stow the cases fore and aft on deck. The decision to stow athwartships on top of the hatches was a combined one made by Sea Transport, War Office and Ministry of Shipping representatives. A gang of labourers spent two days lashing this cargo after which the ship's crew took additional precautions."[4]

The remainder of the passage to Freetown was without incident. The local escort destroyers *Boreas* and *Velox* joined at 1410 on the 14th in a position 100 miles NW of Cape Verde, which indicates the route unusually lay closer to that headland and the Senegal coast than to the Cape Verde islands, and may have been due to anticipated U-Boat dispositions. It was also then known that U-Boats were storing from German ships anchored in the Canary Islands, but this was stopped in July by diplomatic action on the Spanish government.[5] The convoy anchored in Freetown harbour just after midday on the 16th.

The regimental histories of the troops in this convoy make no mention of the time spent in Freetown, other than confirming that no one was allowed ashore. *Dunnottar Castle* detached from the escort and sailed with the homeward convoy SL 79 on the 27th. Two additional transports joined in this port, *Christiaan Huygens* having affected temporary repairs after the collision with *Centurion* while in WS 8B (*q.v.*), and with her troops still embarked, also the Norwegian *Bergensfjord* which had gone to Suez with WS 6 and recently returned to Freetown with 11 Bn The Nigeria Regiment. The Norwegian liner was re-embarked with Brigadier JWLS Hobart and HQ staff of 161 Infantry Brigade, together with 1/4 and 2/5 Bns The Essex Regiment which had been stationed at Freetown for ten and five months respectively, and were now relieved by 6 West Africa Brigade comprising two battalions each from Nigeria and Sierra Leone. The longest serving 1/4 Bn in Freetown had as many as 300 cases of malaria passed through the hospital, but nevertheless happily boarded *Bergensfjord* with a full military strength of 38 officers and 837 other ranks. The strength of 2/5 Bn was 32 officers and 725 O.Rs with everyone in buoyant spirits on leaving West Africa.[6]

The convoy now comprised five storeships and twelve transports carrying almost 24,000 personnel, and sailed from Freetown in the late afternoon of 20th June with *Birmingham* retained as ocean escort and two destroyers providing an A/S screen for the first two days. There were few incidents on the passage to the Cape; the Essex Regiment records that "the line was crossed with traditional ceremony on 23rd June, when the many novices attended Court."[6] Actually the Equator was crossed on the previous evening but it proved convenient to hold the customary ceremonies next day as the local escort detached at 0600 that morning when the convoy was reckoned to have cleared the submarine zone.

On 24th June "the convoy speed was reduced to enable *Empire Widgeon* to repair steering gear, and again for four hours on the 26th to allow *Llangibby Castle* to make good defects on one engine. This ship's speed is now 13.5 and not 15 knots as very strong SE Trades were experienced from the Equator until the day before Capetown."[7]

Birmingham reported that the whole convoy was reduced to 12 knots for two days from the 27th due to strong head tradewinds. Commodore Barrow commented most favourably on the voyage to date on *Empress of Japan*, "Captain Thomas was a pleasant companion who commands a well found and efficient ship. He saw his officers were at all times trustworthy and most helpful. The ship was navigated with accuracy."[7]

When abreast of Capetown on 1st July, *Empress of Japan*, *Llangibby Castle*, *Capetown Castle*, *Durban Castle*, *Eastern Prince* and *Empire Widgeon* were detached to proceed into that port for fuel, water and stores and to exercise the troops ashore, while the remainder of the convoy proceeded with *Birmingham* for Durban. The distance steamed from the Clyde to Capetown was 7,298 miles at an average speed of 12.9 knots. All ships were berthed within Capetown docks on arrival, where the population, as always, were ready to entertain the troops as they landed ashore.

Birmingham was relieved off Cape Point by *Hawkins* and proceeded into Simonstown, while the 11 ship portion continued to Durban and arrived there on the 4th to find a massive transhipment programme arranged for all seven transports. Already in port were two of the smaller 'Indian Ocean type' troopers and two of the 'Monsters', *Mauretania* and *Ile de France*, while *Nieuw Amsterdam* was expected on the 7th; all three having completed their first round trip on the Durban-Suez shuttle service with South African troops. They were now to be cleaned, watered, fuelled and provisioned before embarking all but 2,500 of the 16,200 troops that arrived at Durban in WS 9A and so relieve these seven transports for direct return to the UK for inclusion in WS 11 and 12.

The 70 troops on *Christiaan Huygens* bound for Singapore now joined 742 landed from *Duchess of Richmond* in WS 8B and boarded the Dutch liner *Sibajak* which sailed that same day, arriving Singapore on the 19th. The remaining 1,522 RAF and troops on *Christiaan Huygens* were transhipped to the B.I. *Aronda*, which had returned to Durban after completing her maiden voyage to Suez in WS 8A, together with 950 from other ships to the Belgian *Thysville*, recently drydocked for engine and boiler repairs at Capetown. The remaining troops from *Bergensfjord*, *Highland Brigade*, *Franconia*, *Samaria*, *Mooltan* and *Orbita*, numbering almost 14,000 were sent by rail to Clairwood Camp, six miles outside the city, and neighbouring bivouac areas at the race course, drill hall, schools, woolsheds, etc., while the three 'Monster' liners were being prepared to accept them. This was the largest transhipment programme handled by the Impcon staff to date but soon became the norm.

With disembarkation at Durban complete the transports were soon dispersed, *Highland Brigade* sailed after hardly a day in port to load at Buenos Aires and other South American ports for the UK, and returned via Trinidad to Avonmouth on 3 September, after landing a number of passengers at Holyhead. The remaining six liners were under urgent consideration by telegrams during the first five days of July by the War Office, who wanted them brought home immediately and without cargo to take part in the August WS 11 convoy, while the Ministry of War Transport protested this would mean leaving behind 23,000 tons of much needed import cargo. The Ministry view prevailed and over 19,000 tons was shipped on the four British liners and *Bergensfjord*, but only *Mooltan* whose capacity was less than 1,000 tons was able to make the WS 11 sailing and did so even after calling at Trinidad for fuel, Curacao for a day of engine repairs and Bermuda for passengers. She reached the Clyde on 21 August and was discharged, bunkered, stored, carried out voyage repairs and fully embarked in Glasgow within the space of eight days. The other British liners were despatched from Capetown between 20 and 24 July, all proceeding via Trinidad from where *Franconia* was directed to the Clyde but diverted to Liverpool where she arrived on 17 August. *Samaria* called additionally at Halifax and reached Liverpool a week later, both next sailing in the September, WS 12 convoy. *Orbita* also called at Halifax and being of slower speed docked in Liverpool mid September and was thereafter engaged in Operational Service on the Clyde. The Norwegian *Bergensfjord*, in addition to shipping bagged ore, oranges and crayfish at Durban, Capetown and Walvis Bay, also carried 500 women and children from Durban to the UK, making the homeward voyage via Trinidad, a four day stop at St. John (NB) for drydocking and final embarkation at Halifax (also to change the Master) before berthing in Glasgow on 23 August. Her next employment was to be four consecutive round trips from the Clyde to Iceland. *Christiaan Huygens* was detained at Durban for almost three months repairing the collision damage sustained earlier at Freetown, and also drydocked at St. John NB on the homeward voyage which ended by arrival Liverpool on 22 November in time for the next outward sailing in WS 15.

From Durban, the now reconstituted convoy of two transports, *Aronda* and *Thysville*, together with the four MT ships, sailed from Durban as WS 9AX early on 8 July escorted by *Hawkins*, and made rendezvous with the Capetown portion which had left that port at 1400 on the 5th, comprising *Empress of Japan, Llangibby Castle, Durban Castle, Capetown Castle, Eastern Prince* and single MT ship escorted by *Birmingham*, which cruiser detached as soon as the complete formation was in place. The Commodore on *Empress of Japan* soon found that the speed of *Thysville* was 10.5 rather than 12.5 knots as stated but when stationed outside the convoy her speed increased to 11.5 knots; her Master pleaded poor coal and sick firemen. Otherwise there were no incidents on the passage northwards; the AMC *Hector* met the convoy in a position 75 miles SSE of Ras Hafun at 1245 on 18 July, which must have been difficult in the SW monsoon with poor visibility although not specifically mentioned. *Hector* immediately detached with the *Empress*, *Capetown Castle* and *Durban Castle* for Bombay and after an uneventful passage all ships were anchored in that harbour by 1330 on 22 July. The monsoon on passage had been moderate to fresh, no ships had been seen and the Commodore praised "Captain Thomas and his officers for their most helpful contribution to the success of the convoy with excellent navigation, lookouts and handling of his ship. The Chief Engineer and his staff maintained a steady speed for 13,430 miles all the way from the Clyde to Bombay".

Durban Castle disembarked completely in Bombay, embarked some service personnel and families for the UK, together with Commodore Barrow transferred from *Empress of Japan*, and departed on the afternoon of 27 July with that ship and *Capetown Castle*, escorted by the AMC *Antenor* and arrived at Colombo three days later. *Durban Castle* there embarked further civilian passengers and left next day for Mombasa on the first leg of her homeward voyage (see WS 8X). The remaining two liners of WS 9AX continued from Colombo on 1 August, escorted first by *Mauritius*, later relieved by *Durban*, and arrived at Singapore on 5 August to land some 4,500 reinforcements in strengthening the garrison of a colony on which the Japanese were to launch an offensive four months later.

After an interval of 15 months, *Capetown Castle* was drydocked in Singapore for bottom cleaning and painting and after embarking a small number of service personnel and civilians for Sydney, sailed on 12 August to reach the Australian port ten days later, and then proceeded to Auckland to load a full cargo of refrigerated and other produce for the UK. Loading was completed in ten days, *Capetown Castle* sailed on 5 September also carrying 152 servicemen and 100 merchant seamen passengers, and was escorted for the first three days by the New Zealand AMC *Monowai*, as the German raiders *Komet* and *Atlantis* were then believed to be cruising in the Pacific. *Capetown Castle* reached Balboa at the Panama entrance on the 21st, called at Bermuda on the 27th and reached Halifax two days later where Canadian troops were embarked for passage in convoy TC 14 to Liverpool where they disembarked on 17 October. The complete round the world voyage of this liner had lasted 4.5 months with her next sailing scheduled for WS 12Z back to Bombay.

From Singapore, *Empress of Japan* crossed the Pacific to her home port of Vancouver for four weeks of repairs, boiler cleaning and drydocking at Esquimalt, where also Captain Thomas enjoyed his last home leave before retiring at the end of the last trooping voyage of that liner seven years later. *Empress of Japan* sailed for Panama on 30 September, calling at Los Angeles en route. Leaving Cristobal on the Atlantic side of the canal on 12 October, the *Empress* proceeded direct to the Clyde Anchorage where she arrived on 21 October and began to prepare for her next voyage in WS 12Z also back to Bombay and Singapore.

Meanwhile the Suez portion of WS 9A, comprising *Aronda, Thysville, Llangibby Castle, Eastern Prince* and five MT ships rounded Guardafui on the night of 18 July after detaching that day from the Bombay section. These ships were sent into Aden on the 21st and held there for nine days to await the clearance of other ships at Suez, in particular the three 'Monster' liners on the Durban-Suez shuttle which had overhauled WS 9A and reached Suez on the 21st carrying the troops previously landed at Durban, and additionally *Aquitania* and the two *Queens* with Australians from Sydney. Because of the danger of bombing attacks at Suez, PSTO had adopted the principle of having only one of these large liners in the anchorage at any one time. The remote Ashrafi Roadstead just inside the Gulf of Suez proved a convenient holding area only six hours steaming from Suez. During the twelve day period from 21 July, Suez handled six of these giants landing 26,000 troops and embarked 5,000 Italian POW for South Africa. The four transports of WS 9A finally reached Suez on 3 August and were fairly quickly despatched, *Llangibby Castle*, the only one returning to the UK, had a fire in her No. 5 hold on the 6th but was extinguished four hours later. The *Llangibby* left Suez for Port Sudan on the 10th, loaded at Durban, Port Elizabeth and Capetown, then proceeded by way of Trinidad to Halifax and there joined convoy HX 154 for the Clyde where she arrived on 22 October and berthed at Merklands Wharf in Glasgow to discharge South African fruit and general cargo. Her next employment was in convoy CT 6 to Halifax and New York. The three remaining transports of WS 9A were retained in the Indian Ocean for service on the CM route between Durban, Mombasa and Suez, some of the traffic being the on-carriage of troops from WS ships.

The two Essex battalions from Freetown, which landed at Suez from their Durban voyage on *Ile de France*, proceeded first to El Tahaq camp but within a few days were in the Bagush Box west of Alamein and joined 4 Indian Division. The 1/4 Battalion remained with that Division for the rest of the war and was all but destroyed in the Cassino battles of March 1944; 2/5 Bn moved to 8 Indian Division and was captured in July 1942 and never reformed. The three battalions of 69 Brigade which landed from *Mauretania* went first to Quassassin Camp then to Cyprus and remained with 50 Northumbrian Division to feature in many desert battles, in the Sicily landings and later in Normandy.

WS 9B - sailed UK 27.6.41

This convoy left the UK just three weeks behind WS 9A and in the aftermath of the failed Battleaxe offensive to relieve Tobruk and the massive, surprise German invasion of Russia, which inadvertently gave the British Empire their first fighting ally after nearly two years of war. The convoy was of similar size and personnel capacity as the previous one and similarly contained three of the refrigerated liners for disembarkation at Durban and so allow their subsequent early return to the UK with chilled and frozen meat from the Argentine. The primary purpose of these ships as produce carriers, prevented any simple conversion of their insulated 'tween deck spaces into troopdecks and restricted their capacity in relation to non-refrigerated liners of comparable size, although the NZS pair were able to accommodate 2,600 troops by January 1942.

Two of the liners allocated for the convoy had previously been to Suez in WS 5A: *Tamaroa* then returning from New Zealand with a refrigerated cargo to Glasgow on 30 May, and the Booth Line *Anselm* which docked in Liverpool with a general cargo from South Africa on 4 June. Three of the larger liners had returned from WS 5B voyages to Suez: *Monarch of Bermuda* and *Athlone Castle* to Liverpool on 15 May and 7 June respectively and *Arundel Castle* to Avonmouth on 1 June. The other two refrigerated liners being included had previously gone to Durban in WS 6, both returning from the Plate: *Rangitata* to Liverpool on 24 May and *Mataroa* to Avonmouth on 1 June. The two remaining transports for the convoy were the small Polish coal burning *Pulaski*, previously rejected from WS 9A but now required for Indian Ocean Service, and the Orient liner *Oronsay* having completed eight months extensive repairs in Glasgow after being bomb damaged in WS 3. *Oronsay* was drydocked in Liverpool during the first two weeks of June and moved to the Clyde Anchorage on 17 June to await embarkation. The nine transports were being accompanied by three MT ships, of which *Clan Forbes* and the relatively new Royal Mail motorship *Pampas* loaded in Glasgow, while the Norwegian *Elisabeth Bakke* loaded in Liverpool. Also being included in the convoy for protection as far as the Cape was the four-masted Shaw Savill *Ceramic* carrying 346 passengers on a commercial voyage to Australia. The embarkation of personnel began on the transports on 25 June which allowed them to begin leaving their respective berths next day in prepartion for sailing.[8]

Clearance operations within the Liverpool docks following the massive explosion on 2 May now allowed a resumption of embarkations from that port, which in turn helped to ease pressure at the Clyde Anchorages where the emergency discharging port was now operating at peak capacity by handling over 70,000 tons of cargo per month. *Arundel Castle* and *Mataroa* locked out of Newport and Avonmouth respectively on 26 June and proceeded up the Irish Sea to join the Liverpool portion comprising *Athlone Castle*, *Anselm*, *Rangitata*, *Monarch of Bermuda*, *Ceramic* and *Elisabeth Bakke* which left the Mersey during the afternoon of the 28th escorted by the destroyers *Reading* and *Piorun* (Polish). The Clyde portion left that anchorage at 2200 the same day comprising *Oronsay*, carrying Commodore G H Knowles DSO RNR and his staff, with *Tamaroa*, *Pulaski*, *Clan Forbes* and *Pampas*. Escort from the Clyde consisted of the AMCs *Cathay*, *Chitral* and *Moreton Bay*, the Ocean Boarding Vessel *Corinthian* and destroyers *St Francis*, *Wolverine* and *Garland* (Polish), while the ocean escort was provided by the cruisers *Edinburgh* and *Galatea* which left four hours behind the convoy; *Galatea* was continuing with the convoy to Suez.

The convoy formed up at 0900 on 29 June in the usual rendezvous position 6 miles west of Orsay. *Anselm* had been unable to maintain the 12 knot speed of advance after leaving Liverpool and was in consequence ordered by *Piorun* into the Clyde. As with *Pulaski*, *Anselm* was a coal burner which had experienced steaming difficulties on her previous voyage in WS 5A (*q.v.*) and was now (with *Pulaski*) being sent to the Indian Ocean station though destined never to reach it. The cruisers *Edinburgh* (bearing the flag of Rear Admiral Syfret of 18 Cruiser Squadron) and *Galatea*, ran into fog off the Holy Isle when steaming out of the Firth of Clyde, which reduced their speed and made them late at the Orsay rendezvous The fog persisted until just after 1300 but the convoy was sighted 10 miles distant an hour later; *Edinburgh* joining at 1430 and *Galatea* shortly afterwards by which time a five column formation was in place.[9] The convoy was then screened by only three destroyers (*St Francis*, *Wolverine* and *Piorun*), but within the next two hours *Vanquisher*, *Winchelsea*, *Maori* and the AA cruiser *Cairo* joined from Londonderry and destroyers *Castleton* and *Wells* from Kyle of Lochalsh. The German onslaught on Russia had diverted the attention of the Luftwaffe from shipping in the Western Approaches but had not affected U-Boat attacks or losses from that cause.

The route lay out to the westward and on the morning of 30 June the convoy was exercised in emergency turns and speed increased to 12.5 knots but at 1015 *Corinthian* fell far astern whereupon *Edinburgh* as SOE ordered her to proceed independently. The speed of 12.5 knots was then found to be too much for other ships of the convoy and had to be reduced to 12 knots. An air escort had been present for most of the time since leaving the North Channel but parted that evening. At daylight next morning, 1 July, *Corinthian* had rejoined by cutting corners on the route and by improved steaming. Most of the escorting destroyers parted company on 2 July to return to their bases, the last being the ex-American *St Francis* which detached at 0400 on the 3rd and by which time the convoy had reached a position 950 miles west of Ushant and steering a southerly course towards the western side of the Azores.

At midnight on 3 July when the convoy was 300 miles north of the Azores, *Edinburgh* detached to return to the Clyde and prepare for Operation Substance, a convoy for Malta scheduled to sail on 11 July. At 0630 on 4 July with the convoy now 200 miles from the Azores, the AMC *Cathay* detached ahead on patrol, continuing until about 100 miles from the islands when she would reverse course and steer north until meeting *Anselm* and her escorts following astern of the convoy. During the early hours of the following morning the convoy passed between Flores and Fayal of the Azores group and at this time a U-Boat torpedoed *Anselm* some 300 miles astern of the convoy.

Having been ordered back from the original convoy, *Anselm* anchored in the Clyde at 1430 on 29 June and was immediately given a warning order for the 990 RAF and 419 troops on board to prepare for disembarkation and return to their bases. This order was very soon rescinded, however, and *Anselm* sailed again at 0130 next day, 30 June, escorted by HM Survey Ship *Challenger* and three corvettes, *Lavender*, *Petunia* and *Starwort* which were being sent to Bathurst and Freetown for local escort duties.

The route given to *Anselm* and her escorts was similar to WS 9B for three days until reaching a point 350 miles west of Eagle Island on the coast of County Mayo. From this point *Anselm* and her escorts were to pass through positions taking them 500 miles west of the Spanish and Portuguese coasts until passing east of the Azores, thence west of the Canaries and thereafter more or less direct to Freetown by passing inside the Cape Verde islands. Three days after leaving the Clyde, however, the Admiralty radically altered the route by signal at 1230 on 2 July, probably by estimating the disposition of U-Boats. From the position west of Eagle Island, *Anselm* was directed southwest to the longitude of 25° on the latitude of the Scillies, and from that position SSW to a point 380 miles north of Fayal, thence to pass between Terceira and San Miguel (the most easterly island of the group), and upon which island was the port of Ponta Delgada, where permission was being sought from the Portuguese Ambassador for *Challenger* and the corvettes to refuel.

The outward voyage of *Anselm* and her escort was without incident until the evening of 5 July. *Anselm* was stationed 4 cables astern of *Challenger* with a corvette on either wing and another astern. A speed of 11 knots was being maintained and the visibility, which had been bad at times, improved after 0215 when course was altered from 212° to 162° for passage through the Azores group. Light winds and a slight swell were being experienced and at 0500 as daylight approached, the formation began zigzagging.

According to a later report by *Cathay*, the previous night's U-Boat dispositions indicated a submarine close to the position of *Anselm* and which, despite the three corvette anti-submarine screen, allowed *U 96* to put in a successful attack at 0537 when a torpedo struck the port side reserve bunkers of *Anselm*. The stokehold and engine-room were soon flooded and with the engines stopped, the ship lost way and within eight minutes, Captain Elliott "reported that *Anselm* was badly down by the head."[10] While the crew were preparing and lowering the lifeboats which were filled with personnel as they calmly filed up from the troopdecks, *Challenger* approached and skilfully placed her bow under the port quarter of *Anselm*. "Many men jumped on board before the two ships became separated.[12] By 0547 all remaining boats were being rapidly filled by the use of side ladders and side decks while the remaining personnel jumped into the sea to grasp the lifelines of boats and rafts. At 0555 all the boats but one had cleared the ship, by which time "the foredeck was completely submerged and the water almost up to the level of the promenade deck. There were still some men on the after deck, but could not see if they had jumped clear before the ship sank. I myself slid into the water shortly before the ship took up a vertical position stern up and then disappeared completely at 0559."[10] This was 22 minutes after first being torpedoed.

Captain Elliott concluded that *Anselm* was abandoned without "panic or unnecessary confusion. The men went to their boats in an orderly and quiet manner. Many were singing songs while the boats were being lowered. All were willing and did their best to help abandon ship quickly in the short time available."[10]

The survivors in the water and boats were picked up by *Starwort* and *Challenger*: approximately 230 on the former and 820 on the latter, but owing to the intense overcrowding an accurate count was not possible. By 0820 both escorts were proceeding at 6 knots towing *Anselm's* empty boats, but as speed increased to 13 knots these gradually broke away and were lost.

A total of 254 officers and men lost their lives in the sinking of *Anselm*, of which 176 were RAF, 70 from other services and 4 crew. Most of the casualties were considered to have been killed by the explosion and subsequent flooding in No. 3 hold. The troopdecks in this compartment contained many RAF and RAOC and "the number of casualties was probably increased by the wooden ladders...being smashed by the explosion."[10] *Anselm* was indeed unfortunate to have been sighted and torpedoed whilst within the supposed protection of an anti-submarine screen by an isolated homeward bound U-Boat. Conversely, it was fortunate that fair weather allowed the rescue of 80 per cent of the total on board.

Meanwhile the AMC *Cathay* had carried out her patrol on a southerly course at 10 knots to the latitude of 41°N which she reached at 2100 on the 4th. She then reversed course to the northward until 0515, when mist began to form and course was again reversed to 180° to regain clear weather. At 0600 course was altered to 090° towards *Anselm's* route and at 0745 *Cathay* intercepted a "Most Immediate" signal from *Challenger* giving *Anselm's* position followed by a corrupt group which was not understood but assumed to be reporting a U-Boat sighting. In fact it was *Challenger* reporting the loss of *Anselm*.

Cathay continued eastward through indifferent visibility varying from a half to one mile, and at 1200 when reckoned to be on *Anselm's* route, turned on to her known course of 162° and reduced speed of advance to 9 knots to allow *Anselm* and her escorts to catch up. As visibility improved a fix was obtained at 1415 and course reversed to 350° with "speed adjusted to arrive at the original rendezvous as expressed in a signal at 1159 on the 5th, which I did not receive until 1330."[11] From 1530 onwards *Cathay* "experienced declining visibility with heavy patches of fog and mist followed later by rain squalls."[11] At 1700 three signals were received from *Challenger* which had first been transmitted at 0603, 0930 and 1700, "which made the position clear."[11] (Presumably that *Anselm* had been sunk.) When *Cathay* reached the appointed rendezvous position at 2000, visibility again varied "from a half to one mile with occasional small clear patches of up to 3 or 4 miles."[11] *Challenger* was not seen, and *Cathay* remained in the area until 2251 when D/F bearings indicated that *Challenger* had passed ahead and so *Cathay* altered course to follow. "Visibility during the night remained variable from nil to 2 miles."[11]

At 0610 on 6 July *Cathay* finally made contact with *Challenger* which had been following 4 miles astern. The sea was calm with a slight westerly swell, the wind SSW force 3. *Cathay* turned to WNW, reduced speed to 5 - 6 knots and at 0715 *Challenger* came alongside her starboard side, transferred the *Anselm* survivors and left again at 0820. The corvette *Starwort* was similarly alongside from 0830 to 0925 transferring survivors and injured, the latter being hoisted in an ammunition tray using the motor boat derrick. Three of the survivors were dangerously ill and 30 seriously injured. "Most of the survivors had minor injuries but all appeared in good spirits, though tired. During transfer the remaining ships carried out a continuous screen around *Cathay*."[11]

The Commanding Officer of *Challenger* reported that "it is a source of great personal satisfaction that Captain A Elliott, Master of *Anselm*, was among those rescued by *Challenger*. This fine officer was swept from his bridge as the ship plunged under but arrived on the bridge of *Challenger* after his rescue completely unshaken and physically fit despite his years (then aged 59). He was most anxious to be of any assistance possible and his cheerful bearing was a great asset. Surgeon Lieut. WAB Cooper RNVR of *Challenger* laboured unceasingly for 24 hours both in getting on board the injured and with the assistance of Sqdn. Leader Munro, RAF MC and his orderlies in their care thereafter until transferred to *Cathay*. All officers and men of the ship's company worked with the greatest energy and good sense in the rescue and subsequent care of the survivors and provided matting and bedding from their personal effects with unstinting generosity."[12&13]

After completing the transfer *Cathay*, *Challenger* and the three corvettes got under way again at 0930 and proceeded SSE at 12 knots towards the Azores. *Lavender* was detached ahead at her best speed to Ponta Delgada on the south coast of San Miguel to refuel. *Cathay* and the three escorts passed through the Azores group between Terceira and San Miguel during the forenoon of 7 July and at 1730 that day *Lavender* rejoined in a position 75 miles SW of Ponta Delgada, and at which point the other three escorts detached to return to that port for fuel, and from where *Petunia* was ordered homeward with a Gibraltar convoy, while *Challenger* and *Starwort* were to proceed independently to Bathurst and Freetown respectively.

Meanwhile the convoy, after passing west of Fayal in the Azores, continued on a southerly course until 0100 on the 6th, when the AMC *Chitral* and OBV *Corinthian* were detached, the former for Halifax and latter on a routine patrol. The cruiser *Galatea* and AMC *Moreton Bay* continued as ocean escorts and course was altered to SE for the passage between Cape Verde and the island group of that name. At 1700 that same day a boat containing the Master and some of the crew of the London tramp steamer *St. Anselm* was picked up by *Moreton Bay*. This ship had been one of eight torpedoed in the space of three days in the homeward convoy SL 78 escorted by the AMC *Esperance*

Bay but without A/S escorts. However, the 'happy days' for the U-Boats in this area were about to end as an increasing number of escort vessels began to reach Freetown.

The *St. Anselm* had been sunk six days earlier during which time the Master's boat made good 130 miles in a NW'ly direction and hoping to make the Azores, but from the course made good it is likely this boat would have missed the islands. Another boat from the same ship, in charge of the Chief Officer, had set off ENE towards Madeira, distant 450 miles up wind and against the current; it is believed this boat was never picked up.

The convoy had an uneventful passage for the next four days until 1115 on the 10th when 150 miles NE of the Cape Verde islands. At this point the Freetown local escort destroyers, *Brilliant*, *Wild Swan*, *Wivern* and corvette *Asphodel* joined, although an hour late and in bad visibility. An air escort also appeared at 1800 that same day and continued at intervals until the convoy arrived at Freetown at 0300 on 13 July.

At Freetown the Commodore on *Oronsay* reported that *Pulaski* and *Ceramic* made a great deal of smoke, while *Elisabeth Bakke* was a careless station keeper to begin with, but improved as the result of many signals. The Commodore also noted that *Pulaski*, while able to maintain the convoy speed of 12 knots, was unable to make her declared speed of 13.3 knots. *Galatea* similarly reported on *Pulaski* although noting she "had evaporator trouble at first and sometimes lost ground when discharging ashes, but in spite of her age and assistance of RN personnel on board, she did well."[14]

The ships remained in Freetown fuelling, water and bunkering with coal for three days. The AMC *Moreton Bay* detached from the convoy and returned to the UK escorting SL 81 and thereafter decommissioned and converted for trooping; one of nine AMCs being similarly released. The AMC *Cathay* arrived in port on 14 July with the survivors from *Anselm* but there is no record of their ultimate movements from there.

WS 9B sailed from Freetown at 1200 on 16 July comprising eight transports, three MT ships and the passenger liner *Ceramic*, with an unchanged formation of four columns and local escort of the destroyers *Boreas*, *Brilliant*, *Vansittart*, *Velox*, while *Galatea* continued as ocean escort. The destroyers parted company at 1800 on the 18th, when the convoy was 40 miles north of the equator. The passage from Freetown to the Cape was accomplished without incident in the space of 11 days.[15] At 0715 on 27 July *Galatea* left the convoy and proceeded ahead to refuel at Simonstown, where she arrived at 1335 that day and left four hours later to rejoin. Meanwhile, when abreast of Capetown that morning, *Ceramic*, *Pulaski*, *Rangitata* and the three MT ships detached and proceeded into that port for replenishment. The average speed of the convoy from the Clyde to the Cape had been 12.7 knots.

With six of the slower ships detached, the convoy speed was increased to 14 knots and *Galatea*, which had considered it advisable to remain astern in the dark hours and regain contact in daylight, did not rejoin till 1100 on the 28th. No record appears to exist of an escort during the absence of *Galatea*, but this may have been the AMC *Queen of Bermuda* which later escorted the Capetown portion onwards to Durban.

From a position northwest of the Cape of Good Hope, the liners for Durban ran into a whole gale from the NW, later backing to west and finally WSW, which was accompanied by a very heavy swell and following sea. Commodore Knowles noted that "the swell was of considerable height and very vertical, the ships became almost unmanageable and steering had to be assisted by engines. This was mostly due to the reduction of speed to 12.5 knots to enable *Mataroa* and *Tamaroa* to keep up, and was unsuitable for the large ships like *Oronsay*, *Athlone* and *Arundel Castles* which were rolling and pitching heavily with minimal amounts of military equipment in their holds and no ballast in the latter two.[16]

Commodore Knowles also reported that "in routing and loading ships, especially heavily laden storeships, some with deck cargoes, due consideration should be given to the weather conditions likely to be met."[16] He went on to describe the deck cargoes of locomotives, lorries, crated aircraft, etc., carried on *Clan Forbes* and *Pampas*, and how the Master of the former would never have allowed his ship to have been so loaded had he known of the intended voyage and furthermore that the best weather from the Cape to Durban was to be found close to the coast and not offshore. However, this was wartime, ships might not always have been loaded as they would in peacetime, but the need to keep offshore at Cape Agulhas, the most southerly point of the African continent, was to avoid mines which German raiders had laid fourteen months earlier and had not all been successfully swept up. Shipping had therefore to keep outside the mineable waters of the Agulhas Bank.

Once past the Agulhas Bank, the convoy route followed "the 100 fathom line along which the Agulhas current generally attains its greatest rate (i.e. in a westerly direction against the wind setting up a very nasty steep sea)."[14] *Galatea* recommended that an inshore route would be more practicable to avoid the heavy seas and strong current peculiar to that locality. The six transports and *Galatea* arrived in Durban at 1000 hours on 30th July.

From Capetown, *Rangitata* sailed on 29th July and proceeded independently to Durban where she arrived three days later. *Ceramic* left the convoy at Capetown and also proceeded independently to Durban and thence to Fremantle and other Australian ports on a commercial voyage. The remaining four ships left Capetown at 1700 on the 30th, escorted by *Queen of Bermuda* and with the Master of *Clan Forbes*, Captain H Cater, acting as Commodore.[17&18] A speed of 12.5 knots was ordered and *Pulaski* soon became a straggler, partly due to the quality of coal supplied at Capetown, but was able to maintain 12 knots comfortably. She subsequently detached ahead of the convoy to disembark 16 sick and 300 ratings at Durban, where she berthed on 2nd August.

Whilst in Durban, *Mataroa*, *Tamaroa* and *Rangitata* disembarked all their personnel to the transit camp to await on-carriage in convoy CM 15 twelve days later. Priority in Durban was given to the four large transports which were continuing the voyage northwards, and these ships with *Pulaski* and *Galatea* left the port on the morning of 3 August, to rendezvous at the outer end of the swept channel at 0900 local time with the three ships from Capetown, and from where the escorting AMC *Queen of Bermuda* detached.

With the departure of the main convoy from Durban, the three disembarked refrigerated ships were replenished and sailed empty for the River Plate: *Tamaroa* and *Mataroa* on 6 August and *Rangitata* two days later. The Principal Sea Transport Officer at Simonstown filed a report that *Tamaroa* required drydocking for extensive examination and repairs to main engines, boilers and auxiliary machinery and refrigeration plant. So great was the need of these ships for carrying personnel outwards and refrigerated produce homeward, however that the drydocking was deferred for six months. After loading full cargoes of meat and other products these three ships fuelled at Montevideo and proceeded by Trinidad and Halifax where they joined homeward convoys for the North Atlantic passage to the UK. *Tamaroa* crossed in HX 151 and reached Avonmouth on 9 October, *Mataroa* in HX 152 to dock in Liverpool on the 14th of that month and *Rangitata* in HX 153 also to Liverpool on the 20th. Their next outward voyages were in CT 6 to Halifax, WS 12Z to Durban and WS 12 to West Africa respectively.

As noted above, WS 9B now comprising five transports and three MT ships left Durban on 3rd August with *Galatea* continuing as ocean escort. No incidents were reported during the ten day passage up the coast of East Africa. At noon on 13 August when about 100 miles north of Socotra, the convoy was met by the AMC *Hector*, which took *Athlone Castle* and *Elisabeth Bakke* under escort and detached eastwards for Bombay as convoy WS 9BX. The three day passage was covered at an average speed of 16 knots with a 0.5 knot favourable current in the fresh to strong SW monsoon then prevailing. All three ships were anchored in Bombay harbour by 1600 on 16 August.

The further movements of *Elisabeth Bakke* are not known, but *Athlone Castle* spent only two days in Bombay, another in Colombo and reached Singapore on 25 August, where the last of her troops were disembarked. She left Singapore next day and proceeded through the Java Sea and round the north of Australia to Sydney, thence on to the New Zealand South island port of Lyttelton, where she began loading a refrigerated cargo, completed at Wellington and left that port on 24 September for the UK via Panama. Escort was provided for the first few days until eastward of the Chatham Islands by the AMC *Monowai*. Two German raiders were known to be active in the Pacific at this time[19] but escorts, even for high value refrigerated personnel ships, could only be provided on a local basis. From Panama, *Athlone Castle* proceeded direct to the Clyde, arriving there on 25 October and going upriver next day to discharge at No. 6 KGV Dock. She was to spend 44 days in Glasgow discharging, and carrying out engine and voyage repairs, and again set out for Singapore on her next voyage in WS 14.

The remaining four transports and the two MT ships of WS 9B arrived at Aden with *Galatea* during the night of 14/15 August, where the convoy was formally dispersed although the transports were held there until the three 'Monster' liners of CM 15 from Durban, (*Mauretania*, *Nieuw Amsterdam* and *Ile de France*) were handled at Suez with first priority. The cruiser *Galatea* left Aden on the 16th and proceeded at high speed up the Red Sea to Suez, passed through the canal and reached Alexandria on the 20th, where she joined the Mediterranean Fleet. Sadly she was torpedoed and sunk four months later when about to enter the searched channel into Alexandria; over 500 of her ship's company lost their lives when she went down in five minutes.

The MT ships were not held at Aden but also left that port on the 16th and proceeded through the canal to discharge at Alexandria. The *Clan Forbes* then embarked 400 Royal Marines and with HMS *Glenroy* proceeded south to the Maldive Islands where a fleet base, known as Port T, was to be established at Addu Atoll. The *Clan Forbes* was subsequently retained in the Indian Ocean serving Addu Atoll and Diego Garcia as a stores and supply ship for the next twelve months. The later movements of *Pampas* are not known but this ship was destroyed by bombing at Malta in March 1942. Her name was later allocated to a sister ship launched in 1944, which became the HQ Landing Ship Infantry HMS *Persimmon* although ultimately renamed *Pampas*.

The 'Monster' liners of CM 15 from Durban passed Aden on 19 August, and so *Oronsay*, *Arundel Castle* and *Pulaski* left there independently a day earlier. *Oronsay* and *Arundel Castle* reached Suez anchorage on the 22nd along with *Mauretania* and *Ile de France* (*Nieuw Amsterdam* being held meantime at a Red Sea anchorage to help reduce congestion at Suez). *Pulaski* reached Suez on the 24th, was turned round in two days and returned to Durban for retention on Indian Ocean trooping. *Monarch of Bermuda* left Aden on the 21st and reached Suez on the 25th as *Oronsay* and *Nieuw Amsterdam* departed (the latter having arrived the day before).

17. *Duchess of Bedford*, southbound on Suez Canal, 8 October 1940, after landing three Armoured Regiments at Port Said from convoy AP 1/2. *(IWM E 697)*

18. Convoy WS 5B in the South Atlantic, February 1941, *Highland Princess*, (note black hull, grey uppers). *(Ambrose Greenway)*

19. WS 5B in the Red Sea, March 1941; *Takliwa* (note awnings spread fore and aft).
(*Ambrose Greenway*)

20. WS 5B in the Red Sea, March 1941. *Nieuw Holland* and *Samaria*.
(*Ambrose Greenway*)

21. WS 5B in the Red Sea, March 1941. L. to R: *Orbita*, *Nea Hellas*, *President Doumer* (with *Monarch of Bermuda* behind). Note windsails into troopdecks to increase ventilation. (*Ambrose Greenway*)

22. *Athlone Castle* anchored at Suez in WS 5B, March 1941. Note paintwork on hull, 14 months out of drydock. (*Ambrose Greenway*)

23. *Empress of Canada* at Inverary 9 August 1941 preparing for Spitzbergen raid.
(*IWM E 13749*)

24. *Empire Pride* the only troopship to be built in Britain during WW2, running machinery
trials at mouth of Loch Long, Firth of Clyde, 4 September 1941.
(*TRK 4/4/84/2*) (*Glasgow City Libraries and Archives*)

25. *Stirling Castle* berthing at Singapore 30 September 1941 having arrived in WS 10. (Note lack of defensive armament) (*IWM FE 96*)

26. *Westernland* berthing at Singapore 25 September 1941 with Indian reinforcements from Bombay. (*IWM FE 75*)

27. Above - WS 17 on passage between UK and Freetown and prior to 31 March 1942, showing 14 ships of columns 1 to 4, from L to R: 43. *Dominion Monarch*; 42. *Duchess of Atholl*; 34. *Arundel Castle*; 41. *Tamaroa*; 33. *Oronsay* with 24. *City of Lincoln* (hidden); 32. *Empress of Russia*; 23. *JV Oldenbarnevelt*; 14. *Dunedin Star*; 31. *Abosso* (C); 13. *Kina II*; 22. *Samaria*; 12. *Port Wyndham*; 21. *Leopoldville*; 11. *Glaucus*. (Photo probably taken from cruiser *Shropshire*). (*Ambrose Greenway*)

28. Below - WS 17 concurrent picture looking westward over columns 6 to 8, from L. to R: 81. *Largs Bay*; 71. *Mataroa*; 82. *Bhutan*; 72. *Sobieski*; 61. *Almanzora*; 73. *HMS Adamant*; 83. *Rembrandt* (hidden;) *HMS Illustrious* 62. *Cameronia*; 84. *City of Edinburgh*; 63. *HMS Karanja*. (*Ambrose Greenway*)

These remarkable pictures show 24 of the 31 ships comprising WS 17.

29. *Largs Bay* (left) and *Nieuw Zeeland* berthing Singapore 6 November 1941 having
arrived in WS 11. (*IWM FE 307*)

30. *Duchess of Atholl* berthing in Belfast 2 March 1942 in convoy AT 12 with first US
troops to land in the UK. (*IWM H 17557*)

The quick turnround of *Oronsay* at Suez was matched by her homeward despatch. She was loaded at Durban and Capetown and left there on 21 September direct to Freetown, rather than Trinidad as U-Boat activity in that area had now greatly reduced, and departed the Sierra Leone port on 3 October to reach the Bristol Channel 14 days later for discharge at Avonmouth, escorted most of the way by the AMC *Cilicia*. She next sailed in CT 5 with British troops for Halifax and on-carriage to the Middle East in American ships as convoy WS 12X.

Monarch of Bermuda returned to the UK on the same date as *Oronsay*, and having been turned around at Suez in two days, returned to Durban via Port Sudan. She was loaded at Durban in six days (but had relatively little cargo capacity), fuelled at Capetown and left there on 17 September for Halifax via Trinidad, arriving on 6 October. Here American troops were embarked for Iceland, sailing on the 9th for Reykjavik and thence to Liverpool. Her next voyage was in WS 12Z to Bombay.

Arundel Castle was longest at Suez, being delayed until 30 August. She was then eleven days loading in Durban, another two at Port Elizabeth and completed at Capetown on 28 September, proceeding thence via Trinidad to the Clyde where she anchored on 24 October. Her passage upriver to discharge in KGV Dock in Glasgow two days later, was coincidentally made 20 minutes astern of *Athlone Castle* which had arrived from New Zealand via Panama. Both liners were berthed and discharged on opposite sides of the dock. The next voyage of *Arundel Castle* was in WS 12Z to the Middle East.

Although in many respects it seemed that the fortunes of the British Commonwealth and its Allies were then at a very low ebb, with the vast Axis war machine ranged against them from the North Cape of Norway to Odessa in the Ukraine, much had been achieved; not least being the successful completion of the first twelve months of operating WS troop convoys around the Cape. Twenty of these convoys had then made that passage comprising 76 store-ships and 149 transports carrying almost 291,000 personnel. *Anselm* was the only ship to have been lost although not really attached to the convoy when attacked. Three liners of the WS class had been lost while on independent homeward voyages, all in the Western Approaches, two others were lost during the evacuation from Greece and three more including *Georgic* severely damaged. Another five had been damaged by collision whilst in convoy as the inevitable result and risk of large high speed ships steaming in close company, which necessarily kept them out of service for months at a time while undergoing repairs, and was to be a recurring problem throughout the war years. The WS 9 convoys were the last of the series to be sailed in separate sections.

Chapter 11

WS 10 and WS 10X
The Critical Shortage of Trooping Tonnage

Troops for Iraq and 22 Armoured Brigade for the desert.

WS 10 - sailed UK 2.8.41

From the records concerning the compilation of convoys WS 10 and 11, it is clear that a crisis was fast approaching on the shortage of personnel ships to meet the steadily increasing demands of the War Office in sending troops to the Middle East. After the failure of Operation Battleaxe to relieve Tobruk, the desert war entered a quiet phase with the two opponents facing one another a short distance east of the Egyptian/Cyrenaican frontier. The British intention, however, was to build up forces and equipment for a planned 'Crusader' offensive in the month of November. In Europe, Britain's unexpected and erstwhile Russian allies found themselves pushed back halfway to Moscow by the first week of July.

The previous Middle East convoy WS 9B had hardly cleared the Western Approaches on 1 July when a statement was issued that WS 10, with a speed of 13 knots and capacity of 28,000 personnel, would sail on 26 July. On the same date, however, a War Office statement gave the combined services requirement for WS 10 and 11 as 114,000 personnel, which was 51,000 above and beyond the capacity of the ships planned for both convoys.

On 1 July 1941, the Director of Movements in the Ministry of Shipping (which technically had then become the Ministry of War Transport), detailed the varying demands and shortages of personnel tonnage, stating that the Director of Combined Operations had asked for three more transports and two MT ships in addition to those already held for special operations, (*Narkunda*, *Winchester Castle*, *Ettrick*, *Ormonde* and *Batory* having a total capacity of 10,000), in addition to *Karanja* and *Hydra* (ex *Kenya*), which were soon to be commissioned as HM ships. The Naval Staff had simultaneously put forward a proposal for three troopships to be continuously employed on transatlantic movements. There were also small requirements such as *Pasteur* being sent to Gibraltar instead of sailing in WS 10, and a WS ship to assist in the relief of the Iceland garrison. The shortage of 51,000 berths for WS 10 and 11 was a serious enough matter, but here in addition were demands for at least six other troopships that could only be met at the expense of WS movements. The Director rightly stated "that all these requirements cannot be met with the available shipping,"[1] and asked the Chiefs of Staff to give an order of priority.

The Director of Movements went on to give details of the present shortage of shipping which would provide WS 10, 11 and 12 with a total capacity of 93,500 and therefore a long way short of the services' total requirements. The removal of *Pasteur* from WS 10 meant the loss of 3,500 berths, a WS ship for the relief of Iceland a further 2-3,000 and the allocation of *Orcades*, *Strathallan* and *Stratheden* for transatlantic movements another 8,600 berths. (This presumably meant a reduction of WS 10 and 11 from 63,000 to 47,900, but this is not entirely clear from the surviving correspondence.) The Director accompanied his statement with a suggested re-allocation of shipping to increase WS 10 by including *Strathallan* or *Orcades*, combined capacity 5,200, from the transatlantic movement and at its expense, also by allocating no other ships to Combined Operations and by using *Ulster Monarch* or similar sized vessel for the Iceland relief. However, the plan was recognized as inadequate and two or three ships would have to be detached from WS 10 and 11 to provide for transatlantic movements and the relief of Iceland. The only hope of obtaining additional ships in time was to represent for the release of some liners from Combined Operations. The situation was summed up on the 1 July statement: "We have constantly drawn attention to the shortage of personnel shipping,...the Ministry of Shipping cannot disgorge more personnel ships than are in service for they do not exist. The Americans have so far been unable to supply any assistance in this class of shipping. Furthermore the turnround of such shipping as does exist has been delayed by (a) congestion at Suez, (b) routing all homeward ships via Trinidad and (c) delays in discharging and fitting at home ports due to bombing."[1] The Director gave the present forecast for WS 10 as 27,600 and WS 11 as 34,200 and suggested the means by which the latter could be increased, but none for WS 10. He concluded his summary by stating "the Ministry of Shipping are however preparing a full appreciation which would be available within a day or two, before WS 10 and 11 are discussed by the Chiefs of Staff."[1]

Two days later the Ministry of Shipping presented their appreciation of the situation as it then appeared, i.e.

The service requirements for WS 10 and 11 totalled 114,000 personnel.

When originally planned in late April it was thought that WS 10 would provide 50,000 berths, but when shipping allocation was reviewed a short while ago it was proposed that WS 10 would sail on 26 July having a capacity of 31,000 (WS 11 was to be 33,000 and WS 12 - 37,000; all three totalling 101,000).

The position had then to be amended because the Admiralty would not agree to splitting WS 10 into a fast and slow portion, so that slow personnel ships had to be omitted. One ship was brought forward to WS 9B[2] and another taken for WS 9C (i.e. *Pasteur*). The situation then became WS 10 - 27,600 and WS 11 - 34,200.

The reasons for the reduction of WS 10 from 51,000 to 27,600 were that almost 30,000 of the original capacity was made up of 12 liners returning from WS 7. These ships had been delayed up to three weeks by congestion at Suez,[3] by loading delays in South Africa and a further week by the homeward diversion via Trinidad and Halifax. Only seven had reached the UK by 11 July; the remaining five arrived on various dates between 19 and 30 July too late for inclusion in WS 10.

The suggested means of increasing WS 10 was to include two ships (*Orcades* and *Strathallan*) capacity 5,200 from transatlantic movements at the expense of RAF and Merchant Seamen, although this would only make good the loss of two ships held at Gibraltar awaiting escort (*Scythia* and *Cameronia* - see WS 6) or to include some of the seven ships held for Special Operations or use two of them for WS 9C to Gibraltar in lieu of *Pasteur*, which would provide 3,500 extra berths.

At this date WS 10 was seen to comprise the following ships, of which four had not yet reached the UK; the figures against each being estimated capacities: *Stirling Castle* 1,474, *Andes* 2,744, *Britannic* 2,725, *Windsor Castle* 1,168, *Indrapoera* 1,011 (all arrived Clyde 30 June in TC 11 from Halifax), *Highland Monarch* 1,200, *Nea Hellas* 2,268, *Rangitiki* 1,747, *Warwick Castle* 1,382, *Reina del Pacifico* 2,500, *Scythia* 3,117, *Cameronia* 3,215, *Volendam* 2,350 (the last four due UK between 7 and 15 July). The total capacity of the convoy was therefore 26,901 plus 600 berths still to fit on *Andes*, *Nea Hellas* and *Indrapoera* which were ignored as being uncertain. *Scythia* and *Cameronia* being held at Gibraltar awaiting escort were then deleted with a proposal to substitute *Strathallan* and *Orcades* making a revised total of 25,903. It was thought unlikely the Admiralty would release any of the ships being held for Special Operations, other than to replace *Pasteur* in WS 9C to Gibraltar, but even this was not agreed. One significant change in Admiralty policy, however, was that nine of the liners then in use as AMCs were to be released for trooping, but the first only paid off from HM service in June, and only one completed conversion in time to sail with a WS convoy before the end of 1941. In the final analysis 12 of the 13 ships listed were able to sail with the convoy. *Scythia* had to be excluded when she arrived in Glasgow with a machinery breakdown requiring four weeks repairs, but *Strathallan* and *Orcades* were included to make a total of 14 ships with an estimated capacity of 28,984.

The foregoing lengthy appreciation of 3 July by the Ministry of Shipping was followed next day by another which gave the capacity of WS 10 as 26,500 (presumably excluding *Scythia* and *Cameronia* but including *Stathallan* and *Orcades*), and would also have allowed for an estimated 600 extra berths still to be fitted. The sailing date was retained as 26 July and speed was to be 13 knots. The Ministry appreciation continued "It has for some time been clear that our limited resources in personnel shipping must restrict overseas troop movement...the only possible sources of additional shipping are:-

• United States vessels that are being investigated but this is such a long term possibility that it could have no effect on WS 10 or 11.

• The Admiralty release of nine AMCs but which cannot possibly be made available and fitted out in time for WS 10 or 11.

• Fitting cargo ships - a lengthy process and again not for WS 10 or 11. In any event the number of suitable vessels is very small and experience has shown such conversions to be a most uneconomic process.

• Special Operations commitments that presently claim ships with a capacity of 10,000 and which may shortly be increased to 16,000."[4]

This paper was drawn up jointly by the War Ofice and the Ministry of Shipping and was sent to the Chiefs of Staff with the following conclusion,

"No additional personnel shipping can be provided by mid August for it does not exist....Even allowing for drastic measures like those suggested above, our personnel shipping will not provide an efficient flow of more than 35,000 per month from the UK, at least until October. Our coat must be cut according to its cloth."[4]

So far as the U.S. vessels referred to above were concerned, Britain "had been appealing to the United States for fast troopships since the autumn of 1940. The British Ambassador in Washington, the British Supply Council in North America, the British Merchant Shipping Mission after it was set up in March 1941, had all sponsored appeals in turn. At first they appealed for help in the future, and asked the Americans to enlarge their building programme; then they appealed for ships at once.... "In response the Americans increased their building programme and made provision in it for more fast ships; they handed over several to the Admiralty at once (five cargo liners); but in the summer of 1941 this appeared, for the time being to represent the limit of their generosity. In the immediate present there seemed no hope of supplementing the trooping fleet with American ships."[5]

The Americans at this time actually had less to offer than was generally understood. In January 1941 they employed just seven liners on trooping service with a capacity of 22,251 personnel and therefore comparable to the British pre-war trooping fleet. Six months later their trooping fleet had increased to 22 liners with a capacity of 58,308 personnel (the UK fleet was then 158 ships of 283,205 capacity), and with the advent of Pearl Harbor the U.S. trooping fleet had doubled to 44 liners with capacity of 91,910, i.e. by the end of December 1941. The subsequent increase in the U.S. trooping fleet during the remaining war years was quite remarkable, although their numbers and capacity did not begin to exceed the British fleet until the second half of 1944. The final count in December 1945 was of 391 ships with a capacity for 817,021 personnel, almost double the size of the British fleet with 186 ships having a capacity of 410,934 personnel. Even in July 1941 the U.S. authorities recognized that a state of war would exert a very heavy demand for troopships and accordingly began designing and ordering purpose built ships for the task, which could not be contemplated in Britain where shipbuilding capacity was taxed to the limit producing cargo ships and warships to combat the very real threat to existence from the U-boats. The United States owned many elderly passenger liners, some even laid up in the summer of 1941, of which three coal burners built between 1908 and 1915 were offered to Britain in June. Officers and crews were sent over to prepare these ships for sea under British registry. The *H F Alexander* of 1915 was still in the U.S. when that country entered the war, and then reverted to U.S. registry. The *George Washington* of 1908, under Anchor Line management, was actually embarked with 4,110 troops and ready to sail from Halifax in January 1942 when her boilers failed and she too returned to U.S. ownership. Only one, the *Emma Alexander* built in 1913 actually got to sea under the Red Ensign and continued so as the *Empire Woodlark* under CPS management for the duration of hostilities.

Whilst all these high level discussions were being enacted in the first week of July, only nine of the 13 ships allocated for WS 10, due to sail on 26 July, had reached the UK. The remainder arrived between 7 and 15 July leaving barely two weeks for discharge of inward cargo and to arrange the multifarious tasks required to prepare them for their next voyage. Leave and crew reliefs had to be arranged, voyage repairs of all kinds put in hand, troop fittings increased, deck, engine-room and saloon stores had to be shipped, including fresh and dry provisions sufficient to feed 3 or 4,000 men on a six to eight week voyage to the Middle East, together with bunker fuel and fresh water at least to reach Freetown plus a comfortable reserve for the unknown. Security needs and the restriction of wireless traffic precluded these liners giving notice of their arrival or even being given advance warning of their next voyage. Owners were, however, apprised of their vessels' impending arrival in the Clyde or Mersey or Bristol Channel and could give warning to port authorities, repair firms, chandlery and provision merchants but the final requirements were not known until the ships reached port. There was then the desperate need to make them ready for the next available WS convoy, and for those vessels that had of necessity to be handled at the Clyde Anchorage there were all the additional difficulties that working in the stream entailed. It was indeed remarkable that so much was achieved in the very limited time allowed. Strenuous efforts were made to complete these liners for their military requirements in what were undoubtedly very difficult and trying circumstances where less experienced owners and operators might well have failed the cause.

On the Clyde it appears that most of the embarkations were carried out in Glasgow, which then had 14 large liners in the port in addition to several large warships under repair or fitting-out. *Strathallan* moved downriver from 1 KGV Dock on the afternoon of 25 July, followed next afternoon by *Nea Hellas* from Yorkhill Basin, *Windsor Castle* from 2-3 KGV Dock on the morning tide of 29 July and *Cameronia* from the Riverside KGV that same afternoon; finally *Indrapoera* on the afternoon of 1 August. These five liners joined *Britannic* and *Volendam* at the Clyde Anchorage which had embarked on varying dates up to the sailing date of 2 August.

Two newcomers to the WS route were the Dutch liners *Volendam* and *Indrapoera*. The former, Holland-America liner, had continued on her owners' transatlantic service till the end of July 1940 when she arrived at Liverpool from New York and Halifax. She was then chartered for a westbound voyage with Child Evacuees and left the Mersey on 27 August, only to be torpedoed three days later in a position 75 miles NW of Tory Island. The *Volendam* did not sink and was towed into the Clyde on 2 September and beached in Kames Bay, where in the space of nearly four months some outward cargo was discharged and some patching was effected to the hole made by the torpedo. She was then refloated and lay idle in Rothesay Bay for a further seven weeks before being towed upriver to drydock on 30 January 1941. After three days on the blocks she was towed back downriver and beached off Craigendoran where she remained a further nine weeks before being towed to Liverpool, arriving there on 4 April for drydocking to effect permanent repairs and to fit-out for trooping. The conversion and repairs lasted nearly three months and her first trooping voyage was from the Clyde to Iceland, from where she returned to the Clyde Anchorage on 15 July to prepare for embarkation in WS 10.

The other Dutch liner *Indrapoera* was of the Rotterdam Lloyd company, employed on the route between Holland and the Dutch East Indies until May 1940 when she was sent to Australia, chartered by the Ministry of Shipping and allocated for trooping service, being fitted at Sydney in August of that same year. She was then employed on a US trip to Suez and three others from Bombay to Suez before proceeding via the Cape to New York, where she was drydocked and loaded 3,040 tons of homeward cargo, thence to Halifax for inclusion in TC 11 with Canadian troops for the Clyde. She berthed at Meadowside Quay to discharge on 2 July and spent four weeks in Glasgow before proceeding to the Clyde Anchorage to begin embarkation for WS 10.

Embarkation on the six liners at Liverpool totalled 13,207, on *Rangitiki* at Avonmouth 1,779, on the five from Glasgow 12,095, on two from the Clyde Anchorage 4,919, to make the sum of 32,000 of which 18,654 were bound for the Middle East, 4,780 for Iraq, 4,001 for India, 1,650 for Malaya, 2,658 for South Africa, 182 for West Africa and 75 for East Africa and Aden.[6] The total was 3,301 over the originally stated capacity and was doubtless due to extra berths having been fitted on more than one ship. Capacities were frequently being increased as labour and fittings allowed; it had become the practice to remove cabin partitions to increase space for berths and public rooms were also being fitted with bunks as the situation allowed. Despite the high number embarked, this convoy also suffered from the short embarkation problem highlighted in WS 5A and B, with 285 empty berths of which 178 were on *Volendam*.

The sailing telegram for this convoy also showed that 539 tons of guns and vehicles were shipped on *Stirling Castle*, 107 tons on *Warwick Castle*, 24 tons on *Orcades*, 21 tons on *Reina del Pacifico*, 91 tons on *Rangitiki*, 68 tons *Windsor Castle*, 71 tons *Britannic*, and 62 tons *Strathallan*, while 2,145 tons of stores were aboard *Warwick Castle*, 2,000 tons on *Windsor Castle*, 102 tons on *Britannic* and 64 tons on *Strathallan*. Twelve reconnaissance planes were also shipped on the transports. These tonnages should be taken into account when assessing the time spent in the ports of destination. Although embarked for the Middle East, *Rangitiki* and *Highland Monarch* were to tranship/disembark at Durban and thereafter proceed to the River Plate while *Stirling Castle* was to similarly load meat in Australia after completing disembarkation in Singapore. Of the MT ships in the convoy, the Dutch *Nigerstroom* was bound for Egypt while *Manchester Port*, *Indian Prince* and the Blue Funnel *Phemius* were originally loaded for Egypt but later directed to Basra. *Diomed* was loaded at the outset for Basra.

Convoy WS 10 began passing out through the Clyde boom at 1925 BST on 2 August, the ships spaced five minutes apart with the last one clearing at 2055. The Commodore, Vice Admiral F M Austin and his staff were aboard *Orcades* and Captain Biggs of *Strathallan* was appointed Vice Commodore. The local destroyer escort with the Senior Officer on *Beagle* joined the Commodore's ship off Toward Point, before pilots were landed, and warned that fog was expected in the North Channel, which proved a timely warning of conditions that were experienced later in the Western Approaches.

No incidents were however reported as the convoy proceeded out of the Clyde and North Channel, probably in single line ahead through the swept channel to the forming up position 6 miles west of Orsay, where at 0800 on 3 August, the 19 ship convoy set off on a westerly course at 13 knots, with the cruiser *London* and AMC *Worcestershire* as ocean escort and which with the AA cruiser *Cairo* formed a separate column in the centre of the convoy. Ten destroyers formed the anti-submarine screen, the SOE being the CO of 9th Escort Group on *Gurkha*, with *Legion*, *Lance*, *Piorun* and Dutch *Isaac Sweers*, all of which had sailed with the convoy from the Clyde. The local escort was relieved off Orsay by the destroyers, *Whitehall*, *Witch*, *Winchelsea*, *Jupiter* and

Broadway. Kites were hoisted by the convoy and flown until 7 August. A cruising order of six columns was formed in addition to that of the ocean escort.[7]

At 1115 on this first morning, when 30 miles NW of Tory Island, a distant explosion was heard and considered to have been a mine. At 1530 *Legion* was detached to search for an aircraft alleged to have crashed into the sea, having been reported by a lookout on *Cairo*, but nothing was found. At 1615 the convoy altered course to Northwest on receipt of an Admiralty message giving a new route designed to avoid the northward movement of U-Boats.

Shortly after 1830 hours *Gurkha* obtained two HF/DF[8] intercepts thought to have originated from a shadowing U-Boat to the South'ard. The SOE informed *London* and at 2050 detached *Legion*, *Piorun* and *Broadway* to search on the port quarter of the convoy and to return before dark, which they duly did by 2300 having discovered no enemy. During the first night *London* zigzagged 3 to 5 miles ahead of the convoy at 18 knots, keeping in touch by Type 284 Radar, and followed this procedure on all occasions except when the visibility or bad weather precluded high speed.

At 0635 on 4 August *Windsor Castle's* kite fouled her aerial and triatic stay, and having tried unsuccessfully to raise the Commodore for permission to haul out of convoy, found she had to do so to rectify matters which became urgent. The air escort arrived over the convoy at 0820 and at 1000 all ships exercised their AA armament at balloons released by *London*. At noon the convoy was west of the Rockall Bank and altered course to a WSW heading. The weather deteriorated during the day and by evening was blowing force 6. At 1905 *Rangitiki* had to slow down to 6 knots for repairs that lasted four hours. *Legion* stood by until she rejoined shortly after midnight.

The report of *Gurkha* on this convoy noted that kites were flown during 5 August when in 24°W and possibly when later in fog, as far as 27°W. *Gurkha* considered "that these kites were of sufficient size to give a mark for shadowing U-Boats and should not be flown when so far out,"[9] which no doubt was acted upon for subsequent convoys.

During 5 August the wind decreased and simultaneously the visibility gradually decreased until by 1830 the convoy ran into fog that lasted nearly three hours until it cleared temporarily at 2115. At 2140 in an estimated position 650 miles west of Barra Head, the AA cruiser *Cairo* with local escort destroyers *Whitehall*, *Witch* and *Winchelsea* parted company and the A/S screen was redisposed. The convoy at this point altered course to the SSW on a heading to pass west of the Azores. At 2200 the visibility decreased to 5 miles and very shortly afterwards to thick fog that persisted with occasional clear patches for about 40 hours until the evening of 7 August; a fog belt extending for 400 miles.

At 0845 on 6 August, while the convoy was still in dense fog, an aircraft was detected by radar at a distance of 20 miles, which closed the convoy and passed overhead at 0925 without being seen. No information about friendly aircraft had been received and it was therefore noted as unidentified. The weather cleared somewhat at intervals during the day but at 1935 again set in thick, when fog buoys were veered to at least 180 fathoms (1.8 cables), and by 2000 the fog became dense. At 2100 in accordance with previous orders, *Worcestershire* and *Broadway* detached for Halifax and St John's NF respectively, while the 4th Flotilla destroyers *Gurkha*, *Legion*, *Lance*, *Piorun* and *Isaac Sweers* were also detached to return home, leaving *London* and *Jupiter* as escort for the remainder of the passage to Freetown. Due to the poor visibility, however, none of the destroyers was able to locate their leader which set off from the port side of the convoy on a course of ENE at a speed of 14 knots.

As may be imagined, the task of disengaging these warships from a convoy steaming at 13 knots in dense fog was not an easy one and resulted in a collision which, although serious and damaging, mercifully did not cause the loss of ships or lives.

The collision occurred on the starboard wing column at about 2108 hours, by which time the convoy had been in dense fog for over an hour. The wind was SW force 3 with a slight sea and swell, the visibility ranging from 50 to 200 yards. The starboard (6th) column was led by *Windsor Castle* which was sounding numeral 6 on her whistle and attempting to keep on the correct bearing from the next leader to port, ie. *Reina del Pacifico* and distant 5 cables. Course was 186° and speed 12.5 knots. The next ship astern, distant 3 cables, was *Warwick Castle* whose later evidence stated she last saw *Windsor Castle* at 2003 but heard her whistle signal every 10 minutes.

At 2100 *Windsor Castle* observed a white light fine on her port bow. Two minutes later the light became brighter and had opened out further on the bow: it was thought to be a destroyer dropping astern but considered too close for safety so the helm was put to starboard and when the ship began swinging, the destroyer loomed up about 90 feet distant with her bow in line with that of *Windsor Castle*. The helm was now ordered hard a-starboard, one short blast given and the starboard engine rung full astern to assist the swing. One minute later the port engine was also ordered full astern. A collision seemed inevitable but at the last minute the destroyer's bridge swept past to starboard but only just cleared the bow of *Windsor Castle*. The liner's engines were then stopped and ordered full ahead with a double ring for emergency and the helm put hard a-port, as *Warwick Castle* was suddenly reported on the starboard side, having closed up as *Windsor Castle* reduced her speed. There was however, insufficient time to gain headway and a minute later the bows of *Warwick Castle* crashed into the starboard side of *Windsor Castle* about 40 feet abaft her bridge, between her funnels at an angle of about 120°.

At 2115 *Windsor Castle* reported the collision to the Commodore and eight minutes later that she was "stopped and listing and preparing to abandon ship". On *Warwick Castle* the boats were lowered to embarkation positions and the rafts cleared away; troops were mustered at boat and raft stations. On receipt of these reports, which were made by Radio Telephone on Medium Frequency, *London* ordered *Gurkha* and her destroyers to proceed to the assistance of *Windsor Castle* and for *Jupiter* following astern of the convoy, to assist either of the damaged ships. In the darkness and poor visibility however, it would have been extremely difficult for any of the destroyers, once detached from their stations, to find and locate the damaged ships.

Fortunately at 2143 *Windsor Castle* reported that her damage was not as serious as first indicated and at 2200 *Warwick Castle* reported in a similar vein. *London* asked whether they could proceed to their destinations and at what speed, and at the same time ordered *Worcestershire* and *Broadway* to remain in the vicinity in case either of the *Castles* had to be sent to Halifax, 1550 miles distant but deemed the nearest repair port, other than returning them through the U-Boat zone; the Clyde being only 850 miles distant by comparison.

At 2209 *Gurkha* heard a ship in the fog sounding "an occasional long blast and when about 40 yards distant made attempts by sound and light signals to communicate, but contact was lost owing to having to alter course to avoid collision with this or another ship. At 2339 *Gurkha* suggested to *London* that both damaged liners be sent to Halifax for repairs, under escort of *Worcestershire* and *Broadway*. *Gurkha* regained contact "with the large ship steaming slowly south'ard at about 0030, and by closing to 80 yards communication was established by light. As this ship was assumed to be *Windsor Castle* a little while elapsed before she was established as *Warwick Castle*. She had no knowledge of the position of *Windsor Castle* and finally signalled 'am altering course to starboard' which necessitated a drastic manoeuvre to prevent *Gurkha* being run down. Contact was in consequence lost at 0110."

Gurkha then searched unsuccessfully for *Windsor Castle* and at 0145 tried to contact the remaining destroyers, which was also unsuccessful. She then tried to rejoin *Warwick Castle*, but at 0615 (7 August) gave this up and resumed her eastward course for home and passed out of the scene.

At about 2200 on the 6th, the Master of *Windsor Castle*, Captain J C Brown, reported to the SOE on *London* that her No. 2 Oil Fuel tank was flooded, her other damage was above the waterline and the ship could proceed at 13 knots provided weather conditions permitted. She was therefore ordered to rejoin the convoy at best speed and at 0245 reported her speed as 14.2 knots. Meanwhile Captain Shaw of *Warwick Castle* reported her bows to be turned, her anchors out of commission, her forepeak leaking and speed reduced to 10 knots. At 0021 *London* ordered *Warwick Castle* to proceed to Halifax and that she would be escorted by *Worcestershire*. At 0116 *London* transmitted this information by W/T to the Admiralty, while the same instructions were relayed via the destroyer *Whitehall* to *Worcestershire*, which latter vessel could not be raised on 500 kc/s. The persistent fog prevented *Worcestershire* from sighting *Warwick Castle* and by 0600 *Gurkha* and her destroyers of the 4th Flotilla, which had also failed to locate her, had to leave the area due to lack of fuel. Not until 2226 that day did *London* receive a signal from *Worcestershire*, timed 1715 hours, that she had at last contacted *Warwick Castle* and was proceeding with her to Halifax.

Although *Warwick Castle* now passed out of the convoy, it will be convenient at this point to record the remainder of her voyage and that of her troop passengers to their ultimate destination in the Middle East. *Warwick Castle* and her AMC escort safely arrived at Halifax on 13 August, where temporary repairs were effected and her troops disembarked, presumably to a transit camp. She then proceeded to New York where collision damage repairs were put in hand, and expected to take five weeks to complete. On 19 August arrangements were made for a replacement troopship from WS 11 to uplift the waiting personnel at Halifax and rejoin the main convoy at the Cape. *Duchess of Atholl* was selected and this liner with a capacity of 3,056 was embarked with 1500 troops in Glasgow and left the River Wall at KGV Dock on 26 August, to proceed downriver and sail for Halifax via Iceland as a single ship transatlantic movement. This arrangement however was cancelled at the last moment and *Duchess of Atholl* was held at the Clyde Anchorage for a further ten days, and may well have embarked a further 1500 RAF trainees for Canada in the interval. WS 11 left the Clyde on 30 August while *Duchess of Atholl* and *Pasteur* sailed on 5 September as convoy CT 2 for Halifax. During the first night at sea, *Duchess of Atholl* developed engine trouble and both ships returned to the Clyde Anchorage, where it was found on examination that major repairs were required. *Pasteur* sailed alone on 8 September and next day *Duchess of Atholl* returned upriver to 9 KGV Dock where engine repairs took four weeks to complete. *Stratheden* was then selected as a replacement, having arrived at the KGV Dock from Halifax a week previously in TC 12B, and was due to sail with WS 12 at the end of September. The 1500 troops or possibly all of those embarked on *Duchess of Atholl* were now marched along the quay from 9 to 6 Berth KGV Dock and re-embarked on *Stratheden*, which left Glasgow and the Clyde on the morning of 16 September and reached Halifax safely as a single ship movement eight days later. Here the troops from *Warwick Castle* were finally embarked after spending an unexpected 7.5 weeks in Canada.

Stratheden left Halifax on 27 September and proceeded via Trinidad to Capetown, arriving on 23 October and at Durban five days later. Her arrival at the Cape was almost midway between the passage of WS 11 and 12, but a special convoy CM 18X was organized to move the troops to the Middle East without causing further delay. This convoy comprising *Stratheden* and the BI *Aronda* left Durban on the forenoon of 29 October escorted by the battleship *Revenge*. When the latitude of Mombasa was reached on 3 November, *Revenge* was relieved by the cruiser *Ceres* that continued with the two ship convoy at a speed of 15 knots as far as Aden, which was reached on 8 November. Both liners left that port two days later and reached Suez on 14 November, by which time the troops who had originally left the UK on *Warwick Castle*, had been 15 weeks on passage but nevertheless arrived safely. The homeward voyage of *Stratheden* began from Suez two days later and was made via Port Sudan, Durban, Capetown, Trinidad and Halifax, where the first U.S. troops for the UK were embarked on that ship and on *Bergensfjord*. Both transports left Halifax as convoy NA 1 on 10 January 1942 and reached the Clyde nine days later. Escort was provided by two of the ex-American destroyers *Beverley* and *Rockingham*. The next voyage of *Stratheden* was in WS 16 to Bombay. As a final note on *Warwick Castle*, this ship returned to Halifax after completing repairs at New York. Canadian troops were there embarked and she sailed homeward in convoy TC 14 on 9 October, proceeding via Iceland and reaching Liverpool on 17 October. Her next voyage was back to Halifax in convoy CT 5.

The foregoing paragraphs serve to illustrate the logistical problems and knock-on effect, in this case lasting several months, of arranging replacement tonnage for vessels delayed in convoy by collision damage or other major repairs. The danger and risk of collision was a very real one and always prevalent when ships of moderately high speed were steaming in close formation in convoy. The accident between the two Castle liners in WS 10 was the fifth collision in the WS series and was far from being the last. It was a risk however that had to be seen as part of the exigencies of war.

We must now return to WS 10 and take up the story following the collision and detachment of *Warwick Castle* to Halifax. *London* had remained with the convoy overnight in station between columns 3 and 4. At 0200 with *Strathallan* leading column 4 far ahead of station and on a converging course, *London* went ahead at high speed and directed *Strathallan* to regain his correct station. *Strathallan* was again admonished at 0555 for having his fogbuoy on too short a line, and was asked by the Commodore to lengthen it, but *Strathallan* replied 20 minutes later that he had been using paint drums which tended to sink in use and having already lost two was making up others.[10] The fog however cleared somewhat within the hour, i.e. by 0700 on 7 August.

As soon as the visibility improved that morning, *London* detached *Jupiter* to find and escort *Windsor Castle* back to the convoy, but the search was unsuccessful. When the fog cleared completely that afternoon *Jupiter* was stationed to zigzag 2 miles ahead of the convoy by day and astern by night. *Windsor Castle* was still not in sight, even with the visibility increased to 10-15 miles, so *London* at 1537 hours catapulted an aircraft to search astern which also proved unsuccessful. That same evening the Admiralty advised *London* of a U-Boat reported to be 140 miles west of the convoy's next noon position, and with the approach to the Azores and five or six U-Boats reported to the SW and West, *London* expected to be diverted from the route laid down.

On the morning of 8 August *London* ordered a slight course alteration to the eastward to bring the supposed U-Boat 160 miles off the convoy's track, but was hampered from doing more until contact had been made with *Windsor Castle* following astern and unaware of the convoy's movements. The aircraft flight that morning fortunately located the *Castle* liner at 0907, being 26 miles astern and slightly to the westward of the convoy track. The aircraft observer passed to her the position, course and speed of the convoy. At 1240 hours, when in the midst of a wheel, undertaken to enable *Windsor Castle* to catch up, *London* received the expected Admiralty signal altering the route. The wheel was stopped and course altered to the Southeastward, to pass through the eastern gap of the Azores. On completion of the movement at 1345 hours the convoy speed was reduced by 2 knots while *London* steamed to the Northward to locate *Windsor Castle*, leaving *Jupiter* as convoy escort. *Windsor Castle* was soon sighted, closed with and escorted back into the convoy and was observed to be capable of 16 knots, although not apparently able to follow a zigzag diagram without each course being signalled to her, and failed to take action when an emergency turn was ordered to avoid an asdic contact. The CO of *London* subsequently stated in his report that "the general impression was that she (*Windsor Castle*) was badly handled." Captain Brown was, however an officer of the RNR who had held the rank of Commodore since 1930. Aged 56, he had been Master since 1937, including the command of two other mail ships before taking over *Windsor Castle* in September 1940. He was subsequently commended for war services and awarded the CBE in 1945.

Upon rejoining the convoy after an absence of almost three days, *Windsor Castle* signalled a report of the collision to the SOE on *London*. *Jupiter* attacked a submarine contact at 1400 and *London* dropped depth charges on another contact at 1545 but both were probably shoals of fish. *Jupiter* then detached to proceed ahead to Ponta Delgada in the Azores to refuel and rejoin at daylight on the morning of 10 August.

On the morning of 9 August while approaching the Azores group, *Windsor Castle* signalled details of the damage suffered in the collision with *Warwick Castle*, which included Nos 1 and 2 oil fuel tanks holed and full of water, three lifeboats lost and three others out of commission, a 7 ft square hole in the orlop deck which had been patched with wooden hatches, and the upperworks on B deck pushed in about 10 ft over a length of 30 feet. Captain Brown said his maximum speed was presumed to be 15 knots, but for a very special emergency would risk 19 knots. Subject to divers' examination of tank damage and strengthening of the 7 ft patch on B deck, Captain Brown considered his ship could proceed with safety. Extra raft accommodation was required for 350 persons. On referring again to the collision, Captain Brown said that no signal was heard from the destroyer and that *Windsor Castle* had sounded one short blast ('*I am directing my course to starboard*') three times. The fogbuoy was streamed and a large cargo cluster was burning over the stern to assist the vessel next astern.

Most of the previous WS convoys had passed clear to the west or east of the Azores group, a few had recently passed through the 120 mile wide western passage between Flores and Fayal, while only the *Challenger* group with *Anselm* survivors (WS 9B) had used the 75 mile wide eastern passage between Terceira and Sao Miguel where the latter island contained the principal port and city of the group, Ponta Delgada, on its southern coast. As previously stated, however, U-Boats were believed disposed to the south and west of the Azores group, thus WS 10 was directed SSE towards the eastern passage. At 0930 on 9 August the mountainous land of Terceira was visible in conditions of extreme visibility at a distance of 55 miles. The convoy was abeam of the island by 1100 at a distance of 45 miles and continued steering SSE towards the NW'ly point of

Sao Miguel. To avoid possible U-Boats *London* ordered the Commodore at 1014 to continue steering that course until 23 miles north of Sao Miguel, which point was reached at 1430. The CO of *London* judged that any U-Boat watching the 75 mile wide passage would likely be in the centre, and therefore held the convoy over to the eastern side of the passage. At 1430 course was altered to the SW and at 1600 the convoy was passing only 15 miles off the lighthouse at Ponta da Ferraria - the western tip of Sao Miguel, where the keeper's dwelling at 289 feet above sea level would have provided a clear view to a sea horizon at least 4 miles beyond the convoy. Between the alter course position at 1430 and the passing of Pta da Ferraria at 1600 one or two aircraft were detected by *London's* radar at a distance of 20 miles, approaching from the northward, but were not sighted. During this entire daylight passage *London* kept one or other of her Walrus aircraft constantly in the air, either to keep any U-Boat down or prevent it getting into an attacking position. Course was held to the SW until dusk at 2000 hours, when a 30° alteration was made to the southard for the next position on the route. *Jupiter* rejoined from Ponta Delgada next morning and informed *London* "that the convoy had been duly reported to the Portuguese authorities as passing to the westward and proceeding to the westward with the cruiser steaming south at high speed" - the latter doubtless due to *London* operating aircraft at the time.

At 0430 on 10 August *London* observed a bright light showing on the starboard side of *Windsor Castle* below the forward funnel. *London* was then 5 miles distant and estimated the light could have been seen for another 5 miles. At 0830 London signalled the Commodore and asked him to report the details to *Windsor Castle*, who replied at 0845 that the light was caused by DG coils fusing and bursting into flames at the point of the recent collision, which rendered the DG out of action but with hopes of it being repaired.[11]

At 0934 *London* left the convoy to meet the relief cruiser *Edinburgh*, flagship of the Rear Admiral commanding 18 Cruiser Squadron, then 50 miles to the southeast. *Edinburgh* was sighted at 1040 and by 1200 *London* had turned over the convoy and departed for the north to intercept a raider breaking out from the Bay of Biscay area. The subsequent report of *London* showed the speed maintained to have been 13 knots and the handling of the convoy by the Commodore as very good, with excellent signalling. *Andes* and *Phemius* were noted to have been handled "outstandingly", keeping perfect station and making no mistakes. *Britannic* was similarly praised after a settling down period and "her station-keeping in the fog most praiseworthy" (her station being directly behind the Commodore in column 3). *Reina del Pacifico* was noted as "good" but *Strathallan* "only mediocre."[12]

Soon after taking over the convoy at 1230 on 10 August, *Edinburgh* instructed the Commodore to reduce speed for three quarters of an hour to allow *Indian Prince* to catch up, when 13 knots was resumed. The convoy was now steering SSE to pass between the Cape Verde islands and Cap Vert on the African mainland. Once *Edinburgh* settled down to the escort she generally took station between the leading ships of Nos 3 and 4 columns or zigzagged independently astern by night. The destroyer *Jupiter* zigzagged independently across the front of the convoy. *Edinburgh* had only one of her Walrus aircraft serviceable.

The convoy had an uneventful four day passage from the Azores to the Cape Verde gap where the Freetown local escort was to be met. There were a few minor incidents on 11 August; in the early hours *Rangitiki* dropped out with one engine stopped and *Edinburgh* remained with her until relieved by *Jupiter* at 0200 next day. The convoy speed was reduced to 9 knots from 0320 until both *Rangitiki* and *Jupiter* caught up at 0505. At 0619 Edinburgh complained to *Cameronia* and *Manchester Port* about making smoke and pumping bilge water, and at 1102 the Commodore had again to enquire from *Manchester Port* about heavy smoke that was apparently due to a change in the quality of her coal. At 1845 that same day the Blue Funnel *Diomed* reported boiler trouble but endeavoured to maintain the convoy speed. At 1944 *Edinburgh* advised the Commodore that Admiralty intelligence reported one U-Boat in the Cape Verde area or north of it and ten or eleven at sea unaccounted for. Finally on 11 August *Jupiter* reported to *Edinburgh* that she would reach Freetown with only 20 tons of fuel remaining, or 50 tons if she reduced her zigzag and maintained only the convoy speed. Next day *Edinburgh* solved the problem by transferring 90 tons of fuel to *Jupiter* by the 'hose towed astern' method and also transferred mails.

By the morning of 14 August WS 10 was 180 miles NE of the Cape Verde islands. At 0730 *Edinburgh* launched an aircraft to search for the local escort that was located 42 miles directly ahead of the convoy at 0830. This escort, comprising the corvette *Pergamot* and destroyers *Velox*, *Vansittart* and *Wrestler*, was sighted at 1000 hours and five minutes later was joined by an air escort. During this day *Nea Hellas* advised the Commodore she would require to carry out condenser repairs at Freetown, *Manchester Port* stated her bunker coal replenishment must not exceed 4-inch cubes to cope with her mechanical stokers and *Andes* asked for 150 bags of flour.

As the convoy was now only three days distant from Freetown, *Edinburgh* through the Commodore ascertained the fuel and water requirements of each vessel so that this information could be taken by aircraft in advance. In examining this list it is interesting to consider the physical implications of supplying such requirements at Freetown to eighteen ships within the space of a few days. A total of 11,060 tons of fresh water was required for sixteen ships: the most for *Cameronia* being 1,500 tons, 17,225 tons of fuel oil for eight ships, 6,990 tons diesel for eight ships and 706 tons of coal of which all but 6 tons was for *Manchester Port*.

At 0520 on 15 August the destroyer *Wrestler* parted company to refuel at Bathurst and rejoin 24 hours later. *Edinburgh* received a signal from the CinC SA that the convoy should plan to arrive Freetown as early as possible on 17 August; arrangements were made for the order of entry into harbour and for the composition of two columns for proceeding up the swept channel to the Fairway Buoy, where Pilots would be picked up. The corvette *Cyclamen* joined the escort at 1730 that day. An air escort had been with the convoy for most of the daylight hours and so *Edinburgh* did not use her Walrus. The convoy's ETA was passed by lamp to the Sunderland escort before they departed for base on the evening of 14/15 August.

The convoy was completely reorganized on 16 August with ships changing columns and also stations in column to suit the order of entry into harbour next day. These manoeuvres began at 0900 and the daily air escort arrived an hour later. The destroyer *Wrestler* rejoined at 1515 hours from Bathurst. It was arranged during this day that the requirements for flour on *Andes* would be met from the stores of *Orcades* and *Highland Monarch*. At 1400 the Walrus from *Edinburgh* was sent off to Freetown with information on the expected ETA and the various convoy requirements when in harbour. At 1419 *Edinburgh* ordered *Velox* and *Vansittart* to leave the convoy at 0100 and proceed ahead to locate and mark the entrance to the swept channel by searchlight vertical beam, and at 1552 *Edinburgh* advised the Commodore that a trawler would also be in position to mark the swept channel from 0400 on 17 August.

Thick weather was experienced in the approaches to Freetown; the destroyer *Velox* went ahead at 0100 on the day of arrival to locate and mark the swept channel entrance as ordered. At 0450 with the convoy steering 087°, the searchlight beam (presumably from *Velox*) was sighted bearing 137°, and the convoy made an emergency turn of 45° to starboard at 0504 to bring the beam almost ahead. At 0530 however the searchlight beam of *Velox* was identified bearing 115° and the convoy resumed its course of 087° towards No. 2 Searched Channel Buoy. The first buoy was passed at 0600 and the convoy began entering Freetown Harbour at 0730 in the order: *Edinburgh, Indian Prince, Indrapoera, Highland Monarch, Volendam, Cameronia, Rangitiki, Orcades, Nigerstroom, Phemius, Stirling Castle, Britannic, Andes, Windsor Castle, Manchester Port, Diomed, Strathallan, Reina del Pacifico,* until the local escort vessels followed the last ship *Nea Hellas* through the boom at 0900 on 17 August. The passage to Freetown from the Clyde had taken 14.5 days at an average speed of 12.6 knots. Fuelling and watering began immediately and a convoy conference was ordered for 1100 hours on 19 August aboard the Commodore's ship *Orcades*. Whilst in Freetown the convoy received details of the transhipment programme arranged at Cape ports.

In fact it took four days to complete the replenishment of WS 10, which sailed again from Freetown on 21 August led by *Orcades* which passed the Base Hospital Ship *Oxfordshire* at 1430, and was followed by the remaining ships of the convoy at four minute intervals, escorted by *Jupiter* and the local escort of four corvettes. The cruiser *Edinburgh* continued as ocean escort and left Freetown at 1645 and increased speed to overtake the convoy, which initially steered to the Southwest and South before altering to an ESE heading at 0700 next day. Whilst in Freetown the entire convoy had been re-organised: *Britannic* and *Stirling Castle* became column leaders in lieu of *Phemius* and *Strathallan*, which latter vessel also lost her status of Vice Commodore to *Britannic*, while every other ship except the two Anchor liners *Cameronia* and *Nea Hellas* changed stations. [13]

At daybreak on the first morning out *Manchester Port* was found to be 10 miles astern and stated she would not be able to steam at more than 11 knots, but actually caught up later in the day. An air escort was with the convoy from 1040 until 1730 that day. At 1320 *Edinburgh* instructed the Commodore to alter course from 109° to 220°, an alteration "of 111° which was accomplished in 37 minutes which reflects great credit on the Commodore and Masters of all ships."[14] This alteration resulted from a signal sent by the CinC SA to avoid a U-Boat known to be in the vicinity. At 1606 the Commodore advised *Edinburgh* that the convoy speed was to be reduced for *Manchester Port* who reported a breakdown in her mechanical stoking equipment. *Edinburgh* retorted that unless *Manchester Port* was able to improve her speed by next morning she would be instructed to proceed independently. At 1900 speed was reduced to 11 knots to allow *Manchester Port* to catch up and at 2200 course was altered to 180° and later that night to a SE'ly heading for the Cape. On 23 August *Manchester Port* continued to experience trouble with her mechanical stokers. At 1030 an aircraft from *Edinburgh* sighted HM ships (un-named) escorting the BI liner *Dumana*, then an RAF accommodation ship and bound to Bathurst where she was to become base ship for flying-boat squadrons.

The convoy crossed the equator in the Middle Watch of Sunday 24 August and at 0700 the corvettes parted company to return to Freetown. In being clear of the submarine zone, the destroyer *Jupiter* left half an hour later to proceed ahead at best speed for Suez, in pursuit of previous orders. WS 10 was the first of the series to have a

destroyer escort all the way from the UK to the equator; *Jupiter* subsequently joined
Force Z at Colombo in November 1941 and took part in the Battle of the Java Sea three
months later, where she was lost by mine or torpedo.

WS 10 experienced very strong SE tradewinds with high seas and head swell from 31
August, and this type of weather continued until the day before arrival at Durban. Two
ships were censured for showing unauthorized lights from portholes during this passage.
At 1700 on 31 August *Edinburgh* ordered the small *Nigerstroom* to proceed independ-
ently for Capetown, being hove-to while securing deck cargo. At 1400 next day
Edinburgh catapulted her Walrus aircraft when 200 miles NW of Capetown to proceed
to that port with hand messages and correspondence for the FOIC Simonstown. At daylight next day, 2 September, the Capetown portion comprising *Reina del Pacifico*,
Windsor Castle, *Volendam*, *Indrapoera*, *Stirling Castle*, *Britannic*, *Strathallan* and
Phemius were detached and proceeded to the port arriving later that morning. The
remaining ships continued for Durban and at 1046 hours the relieving cruiser *Hawkins*
was sighted: the convoy then being abreast the Cape of Good Hope. *Edinburgh* was
relieved of the duties of ocean escort and detached at midday for Simonstown. When
south of the Cape of Good Hope at 1400 hours the Blue Funnel 'goalposter' *Diomed*
had to heave-to while securing deck cargo and was not in sight at dusk; she subsequently
reached Durban a day behind the convoy.

The cruiser *Hawkins* continued around the Cape Coast with *Andes*, *Orcades*,
Cameronia, *Nea Hellas*, *Rangitiki*, *Highland Monarch*, *Manchester Port* and *Indian
Prince*. At 1500 on 2 September, *Cameronia* had to reduce to 6 knots to repair a pump
but regained the convoy in the evening. At 0711 next day a signal was received from
the NOIC Simonstown that transhipment was to be effected at Durban from all six transports, and that *Rangitiki* might now continue to Suez. By 1600 that same day the convoy was about 30 miles south of Cape St Francis and due to reach Durban at 0800 on 5
September.

At 0640 on 4 September the destroyer *Jupiter*, which presumably had been to
Simonstown, came up from astern to rejoin the convoy, and at 1229 NOIC Durban signalled the order of entry into that port. *Manchester Port* notified the Commodore she
would require repairs to her mechanical stokers in Durban and at 1425 *Hawkins* proceeded ahead with *Cameronia* at maximum speed. At 0600, being daybreak on 5
September, the convoy formed single line ahead and entered the swept channel; commencing at 0900 the convoy began entering Durban Harbour in the order: *Andes*, *Nea
Hellas*, *Orcades*, *Rangitiki*, *Manchester Port* and *Indian Prince*, while *Highland
Monarch* remained meanwhile in the outer anchorage.

The transhipment of troops and onward voyages of WS 10 ships from South Africa
was a rather complex matter. All of the 2,476 troops on *Reina del Pacifico* were destined for South Africa, being largely RAF trainees, and this ship would normally have
disembarked in Durban, but the South African authorities thought her personnel could
best be distributed from Capetown, and she was accordingly directed to that port, where
she disembarked entirely and sailed on 7 September direct to Halifax NS. She carried
out engine repairs there and sailed for the UK with Canadian troops in TC 14, reaching
Liverpool on 17 October to sail out next in WS 14 for Bombay.

Four of the five transports bound for India and Malaya had been sent into Capetown,
while *Cameronia* which was almost equally embarked for the Middle East and India,
was sent on with the Durban portion and berthed in that port at daylight on 5 September,
where her 1,615 troops for India were to be transhipped to the BI *Aronda*. Of the 7,481

troops disembarked from *Andes*, *Orcades* and *Highland Monarch*, plus 1,516 for the Middle East on *Cameronia*, all these plus some South African troops were now re-embarked on *Dunera* which was to join the convoy, and upon *Mauretania* and *Nieuw Amsterdam* which latter two ships sailed as convoy CM 18 for Suez on 10 September. The port of Durban at this time was much congested; in addition to the six transports and three MT ships of WS 10 that arrived on 5 September, there were already in port ten other transports and the cruisers *Exeter* and *Australia*. The transports included the four mentioned above plus *Nova Scotia*, *Eastern Prince*, *Thysville*, *Christian Huygens*, *Highland Chieftain* and *Empire Trooper*, the last four named undergoing long term repairs while the others had recently arrived from Suez. *Ile de France* and *Oronsay* entered Durban on 6 September and *Monarch of Bermuda* two days later making 19 transports and 3 cruisers in port that severely taxed the facilities of everyone concerned.

Andes remained only four days in Durban and left on 9 September to load in Port Elizabeth and Capetown, proceeding then via Trinidad to Halifax where she too joined TC 14 for Liverpool, and was next employed in CT 5 for Halifax. *Orcades* left Durban on 13 September and Capetown five days later, returning via Trinidad to Liverpool on 13 October, the first of the WS 10 ships to reach the UK, and was next employed in CT 5 for Halifax and thereafter WS 14. *Cameronia* also disembarked entirely in Durban and re-embarked with Italian POW and service personnel for the UK. She also loaded homeward cargo and was escorted to Capetown by the AMC *Carnarvon Castle*, where cargo loading was completed on 21 September. She then sailed for home via Freetown escorted by the cruiser *Edinburgh* which had completed boiler cleaning in Simonstown. *Cameronia* reached the Clyde on 17 October and berthed at 2 KGV Dock to disembark and discharge; after 35 days in her home port she sailed outward again in WS 14 for Suez. *Highland Monarch* did not berth in Durban until 8 September and left four days later for Buenos Aires, loading there and at La Plata and Montevideo with refrigerated meat for Avonmouth, proceeding via Trinidad. She reached the Bristol Channel port on 6 November and was also next employed in WS 14. Whilst the convoy was in Durban, the Commodore, Vice Admiral F M Austin, transferred from *Orcades* to *Aronda* for the onward passage to Bombay that was entitled WS 10B. He subsequently lodged a report with the Admiralty thus: "*Orcades* was the best organized and commanded ship in which I have travelled. Every convoy order and instruction was carried out with metic-ulous care and punctuality. The safety and comfort and wellbeing of the troops was the first thought of Captain Charles Fox and his officers. She was a very happy ship."[15]

The eight ships from Capetown appear to have left that port on 6 September escorted by the AMC *Carnarvon Castle* as WS 10B. At 1100 on 8 September *Britannic* left the convoy and proceeded ahead for Durban where she arrived next morning and where Captain Brown left to take command of *Mauretania*, whose Master then proceeded on home leave. Captain W C Battle, who had lately been relieved on the *Aquitania* at Suez, then took command of *Britannic*. That same morning, 9 September, the Commodore on *Aronda* came out of Durban Harbour with the cruiser *Hawkins* and anchored off to await the departure of *Britannic*. This latter ship sailed at 1300 and all three formed up at 1340 hours and proceeded Southeast at 16 knots to make rendezvous with the seven ships from Capetown, which was accomplished later that afternoon. *Carnarvon Castle* then detached with *Volendam*, *Indrapoera*, *Phemius* and *Nigerstroom* for Durban while the remainder formed up as the revised WS 10B for Bombay.[16]

By noon the next day the convoy was 260 miles NE of Durban and had settled down to a speed of 15.5 knots, the maximum speed that could safely be maintained by

Windsor Castle without causing undue stress to her already damaged shell. The convoy proceeded up the Mozambique Channel and by the morning of 12 September was north of Aldabra Island and on a direct course for Bombay. *Hawkins* exercised the convoy in scattering and turning under smokescreen, but excused *Windsor Castle* from these manoeuvres at the request of Captain Brown, who was concerned about pressure on the exposed bulkhead of the forward stokehold. At 1120 hours *Hawkins* ordered *Britannic* to haul out of line and stop, whereupon a rating and mails were transferred by boat. Next afternoon *Hawkins* was relieved as ocean escort by the cruiser *Emerald*, the convoy then being 700 miles east of Mombasa and 270 miles NW of the Seychelles.

There were no incidents on the seven day passage across the northern Indian Ocean to Bombay. On 16 September the Commodore enquired from the SOE on *Emerald* about the best time for berthing at Bombay Harbour relative to high water, as it seemed the convoy would be hard pressed to make the midday tide on 20 September. *Emerald* thought it was necessary to arrive before high water for berthing at Ballard Pier, but considered himself no authority on the port and rightly suggested consulting *Strathallan* as the most knowledgeable. This proved to be so and Captain Biggs advised that Pilots preferred arrival at their station three quarters of an hour before high water, so that large vessels approached Ballard Pier once the ebb had started.

WS 10 duly arrived at the Bombay cruising pilot station at 1000 hours on 20 September, and *Stirling Castle* berthed at Ballard Pier an hour later, while the remaining ships anchored in the stream amidst several Indian Ocean troopers, of which there were no less than 15 in the port at that time. The troops on *Stirling Castle* were bound for Malaya and were given shore leave in Bombay until the following morning when she hauled off to allow *Strathallan* and *Aronda* alongside. The 1,615 troops on *Aronda* and 907 of those on *Strathallan* were disembarked for destinations in India, while the remaining 2,346 on the latter ship were disembarked for onward transhipment to Iraq. Similarly these two ships hauled off on 22 September to allow *Britannic* alongside to disembark 653 for India and 2,062 for Iraq, and finally on 23 September *Windsor Castle* replaced her at the berth on 23 September to land 793 for India and 372 for Iraq.

It may be understood that secrecy precluded any of the troops or ship's staff knowing troop destinations in advance. Even two days before arrival at Bombay, *Strathallan* was unaware of the onward destination of most of the passengers. A clue was given by the Sea Transport Officer in Durban when he enquired the vessel's least possible draft if sent to Basra. Troops proceeding onwards by ship from Bombay were instructed prior to arrival, to disembark with sea kitbags only, all clothing and other gear not required during the onward voyage was to be packed in universal kitbags, prior to arrival Bombay for stowage in baggage rooms. All disembarking personnel except those for Malaya on *Stirling Castle* were to be provided with midday haversack rations.

Thus did the newcomers to India first sight the Bombay Floating Light and pass up the harbour to anchor off the Taj Mahal Hotel and Gateway to India, or berth at Ballard Pier outside the Alexandra Dock, where they were introduced to the mysteries of the east amongst the teeming millions of this overburdened city.

All of the 4,928 troops disembarked at Bombay for Iraq were immediately re-embarked on the Bibby Line's *Devonshire* and *Lancashire* and on the BI *Neuralia*. These three troopers left Bombay at 1000 hours on 25 September as convoy BP 15, with Captain C H Harris of *Devonshire* acting as Commodore. They reached Basra five days later where all the troops were disembarked, being the first British troops to reach Iraq direct from the UK and comprised a Line of Communications Signals Company,

Supplies and Transport units, Engineer units, Docks Operating and Maintenance Companies and the advance parties of Inland Water Transport units, Railway Construction and Workshop Companies. From the very onset of the German invasion of Russia in June 1941, Stalin appealed to Britain and the United States for supplies of all kinds to be shipped in through the Persian Gulf and brought overland 1,000 miles to the Russian border. Both the road and rail route were tenuous links across deserts, bogs and mountain ranges. Both had to be improved and expanded and these initial British units were landed in Iraq to progress this plan and handle the many shiploads of military vehicles and equipment that were to follow, the first being aboard *Diomed* in the other section of WS 10.

Stirling Castle was the first of the WS 10 ships to leave Bombay, sailing on 23 September and reaching Singapore seven days later where all her troops were disembarked. She left that port on 2 October and proceeded via Thursday Island and Sydney to Auckland, where she loaded meat and other refrigerated produce for the UK. Sailing from Auckland on 25 October and returning via Panama she reached Liverpool on 28 November. *Stirling Castle* was drydocked in Liverpool and carried out voyage repairs before her next sailing in WS 15 back to Bombay. *Aronda* left Bombay on 28 September and returned to Durban for further service on the CM route to Suez. *Strathallan* loaded on her owners' berth at Bombay and embarked 414 miscellaneous personnel for the UK, sailing on 30 September for Durban and Capetown where further cargo was loaded. Proceeding via Trinidad she reached the Clyde on 16 November and berthed at No. 1 KGV Dock in Glasgow next day, this being the same berth that she vacated at the start of her WS 10 voyage almost four months earlier. Her next voyage, after just 13 days in Glasgow, was in WS 14 back to Bombay.

Britannic spent over three weeks in Bombay where she was drydocked in the Hughes Dock to repair collision damage to her stern, the source of which is unknown. Shen then loaded at Bombay, Colombo and Capetown, proceeding thence via Trinidad to Liverpool arriving there on 29 November and one day behind *Stirling Castle*. She spent 39 days in Liverpool undergoing voyage repairs and having troopdeck fittings replaced before sailing again with *Stirling Castle* in WS 15 for Bombay.

Windsor Castle was also drydocked in Bombay to repair the damage sustained when run into by *Warwick Castle*. This work was expected to take at least two months but in fact lasted nearly four months. She finally loaded on the Ellerman berth and sailed on 7 January 1942, prceeding homewards via Capetown and Trinidad to the Clyde, arriving on 16 February to discharge at the anchorage before moving up to Glasgow KGV Dock to prepare for her next voyage in WS 17, also to Bombay.

We now return to the remaining WS 10 ships that we had left at Durban. Of the 7,544 personnel for the Middle East disembarked at Durban from *Andes*, *Orcades* and *Cameronia*, all were re-embarked on the 'Monster' liners *Mauretania* and *Nieuw Amsterdam*, which left the port on 8 September as convoy CM 18 escorted by the cruiser *Australia*. The speed of this two ship convoy was 20 knots and it arrived at Suez ten days later. The balance of the personnel and ships for the Middle East were re-organised in Durban to proceed onwards as the ten ship convoy CM 17, which sailed at 1300 on 11 September escorted by the cruiser *Exeter* and proceeded at 12.5 knots.[17]

The Commodore, not identified, was embarked on *Dunera* while Captain Barnett of *Rangitiki* acted as Vice Commodore. No unusual incidents occurred during the passage north through the Mozambique Channel. On 15 September, *Manchester Port* developed engine trouble when a boiler room fan and the mechanical stokers broke down;

Exeter ordered her into Mombasa for repairs. On 19 September *Rangitiki* developed engine trouble followed by *Indian Prince*, the latter due to a broken camshaft that necessitated reducing the convoy speed to 10 knots for 14 hours while repairs were effected. Fine weather was experienced and no monsoon. *Exeter* recommended to the Admiralty that northbound convoys should be routed closer to the Somaliland coast to take advantage of the current, and would then have been possible with that entire coastline now in Allied hands. At 1305 on 21 September *Diomed* was detached to proceed independently to Basra. The remainder of the convoy reached Aden on 23 September where it was dispersed.

On 24 September *Dunera*, *Nea Hellas*, *Volendam* and *Rangitiki* left Aden as independent sailings for Suez. *Rangitiki* diverted into Port Sudan and remained five days undergoing engine repairs, the other three liners were disembarked at Suez between 29 September and 2 October when they sailed again southbound. *Indrapoera* followed from Aden on 28 September and left Suez on 4 October while *Rangitiki* was at Suez from 4 to 8 October. The NZS liner then proceeded to Auckland to load refrigerated produce for the UK, going via Bombay, Colombo, Singapore and Adelaide. She left Auckland on 11 December for Panama, thence via Bermuda and Halifax before reaching Avonmouth on 12 February 1942. After a complete discharge she was drydocked and her machinery given an extensive overhaul before sailing outward in CT 12 to Halifax and then to the River Plate for a homeward meat cargo. From Suez, *Dunera* returned to Durban via Massawa, Aden and Mombasa and was retained on Indian Ocean service.

The two Dutch liners and *Nea Hellas* were utilised for the part homeward movement of 24 Gold Coast Brigade from Berbera to West Africa. *Volendam* embarked 1,296 West Africans at Berbera on 7 October, *Indrapoera* 772 between 8 and 9 October and *Nea Hellas* the balance of the Brigade between 11 and 12 October. All three ships on completion proceeded across the Gulf of Aden to await convoy at Aden and where they were joined by *Dunera* carrying homeward South African troops embarked at Massawa. The West Africa Brigade had been in East Africa for 16 months of which five months had been on active operations. The Brigade comprised 1, 2 and 3 Battalions The Gold Coast Regiment. All four liners sailed from Aden at 0730 on 13 October 1941 as convoy SW 10, the Commodore H D Wakeman-Colville RNR being embarked on *Dunera*, while Captain J M Brown of *Nea Hellas* acted as Vice Commodore. Escort was given by the AMC *Carthage*.

On 16 October between Guardafui and Mombasa the convoy passed the 22 ship formation of WS 11 bound in the opposite direction, escorted by the cruiser *Ceres*. The passage was made in calm, quiet weather with no monsoon and there were no incidents until 0200 on 19 October when *Nea Hellas* stopped with turbine condenser trouble. *Carthage* stood by until both ships regained the convoy. When just 100 miles NE of Mombasa on the morning of 20 October, *Nea Hellas* broke down again with a burst feed pipe. All ships reached Mombasa that day and while in harbour *Indrapoera* replaced a cracked cylinder cover, but the repairs to *Nea Hellas* could not be completed in time for her to continue with the convoy next day. The remaining three liners of SW 10 reached Durban safely on 27 October while *Nea Hellas* arrived three days later. The convoy was dispersed in Durban and only *Volendam* at that time continued to West Africa, sailing on 31 October direct to Lagos where she arrived 12 days later, disembarking there and at Takoradi before leaving Freetown in convoy SL 94 for the UK. She subsequently docked at Avonmouth on 21 December and her next voyage was in CT 9 to Halifax.

Repairs in Durban to *Nea Hellas* lasted three weeks, during which time she loaded homeward cargo, completed at Capetown and proceeded thence via Trinidad and Halifax, where she joined HX 167 and reached the Clyde on 10 January 1942 to berth in Glasgow at Yorkhill Quay five days later. Her next voyage was in WS 16 to Suez. Engine repairs to *Indrapoera* proved a very protracted affair involving an extensive refit of both main engines that was scheduled to last three weeks but actually occupied two months; her next employment was in WS 12Z from Durban to Bombay.

The Gold Coast troops on *Indrapoera* and *Nea Hellas* had remained aboard those ships in Durban until *Ormonde* reached the port in the outward convoy WS 12 and disembarked. She was then re-stored, fuelled and watered and re-embarked the West Africans from the former two ships and sailed on 14 November, completing homeward cargo at Capetown eight days later. *Ormonde* reached Takoradi on 1 December and left Freetown for home on 17 December. She reached the Clyde on 28 December and made her next voyage in WS 16, also to Durban.

Although some of the WS 10 ships had disembarked and been released in South Africa to return home on a round voyage time of ten weeks, those like *Rangitiki* which had continued all the way to Suez and thereafter proceeded to New Zealand for homeward produce, turned out a voyage time of over six months. Undoubtedly the system of turning some ships in South Africa for transhipment to Indian Ocean or 'Monster' liners meant that those ships could make more trips per annum and this, coupled with the steadily increasing number of berths being fitted, brought a sharp rise in the number of troops being shipped. In the second half of 1940 a total of 105,297 troops left the UK in WS convoys, in the first half of 1941 the figure had increased to 189,469 and was therefore a remarkable achievement by the Sea Transport authorities.

WS 10X - sailed UK 16.8.41

Despite the painstakingly intricate and lengthy correspondence between the War Office and MOWT in early July when attempting to resolve the shortage of personnel shipping for WS 10, 11 and 12, no mention was made of an additional sailing departing midway between the first two convoys in the middle of August. The decision to arrange this extra sailing was made by the Defence committee in London after an exchange of opinions with the new Middle East Army CinC, General Auchinleck, who arrived by air on 29 July. The stalemate in the Western Desert was the result of neither side having the preponderance necessary for a successful offensive. Mere numbers of men were not enough. It was recognized that only armoured divisions could deliver a major blow in desert warfare and Auchinleck required at least two but preferably three armoured divisions to retake the whole of Cyrenaica, but had then ony one, the 7th, as the 2nd Armoured Division which only reached Suez in WS 4B, seven months earlier, had now ceased to exist following the retreats from Greece and Benghazi. There was also a need to change tank types in the desert, and despite the home forces being at concert pitch from September onwards in expectation of invasion, "The Defence Committee decided to send out the 22nd Armoured Brigade (of the 1st Armoured Division) from the UK as soon as possible."[18] The Brigade had been trained in the anti-invasion role, would require time to re-train for desert navigation and have their cruiser tanks altered to suit local conditions. "It was hoped the Brigade would reach Egypt about the middle of September and be ready for action by the 1st November. In the event, the convoy did not arrive until 4th October."[18]

On 1st August the Admiralty declared the escort requirements for a special convoy

WS 10X and next day the MOWT and War Office issued a list of the planned personnel sailings for that month that revealed that troops and tanks for the Middle East were
to be carried in the extra convoy WS 10X departing on the 16th, comprising *Orion* with
a capacity of 3,100 and *Strathnaver* 3,150 sailing from Avonmouth on the 12th. Tanks,
trucks and other vehicles, as many as 1,000 wheeled units for the whole Brigade, were
to be carried on *Brisbane Star*, *Port Jackson* and the Royal Mail Lines *Palma*, which
had just completed her maiden voyage.[19] As finally arranged on 6 August the convoy
also included *Strathmore* of capacity 3,590. All three liners had returned from WS 7 by
inclusion in TC 12 from Halifax carrying, with *Duchess of York* and *Empress of
Canada*, the greater part of 3 Canadian Division. The disembarkation process in the UK
was spread over three ports, *Orion* being sent to Avonmouth, *Strathnaver* to Liverpool
and *Strathmore* to the Clyde Anchorage. All were disembarked by the last day of July
when voyage repairs and extra fitting work was put in hand, *Strathmore* berthing in
KGV Dock, Glasgow for six days prior to embarkation for loading military stores. The
guns, vehicles and 150 Crusader tanks of 22 Armoured Brigade were loaded on *Port
Jackson* at Newport and the other two MT ships in Liverpool. The speed of the six ship
convoy was declared as 15 knots. The armoured regiments of the Territorial 22 Brigade
were 3 and 4 Regiments The Sharpshooters, (County of London Yeomanry) and 2
Regiment Royal Gloucestershire Hussars. The Brigade was commanded by Brigadier
J Scott-Cockburn, had formed in September 1939 but not yet served outside the UK.
The ports or ships allotted to each regiment for embarkation is unknown but a total of
10,004 was declared with perhaps 102 personnel over-embarked. By sailing date the
combined capacity of the liners had risen to 9,902 due to extra fitting on *Orion* and
Strathnaver.[20]

Strathmore was the only ship leaving from the Clyde, and having embarked and
stored at 1 KGV Dock in Glasgow, moved downriver in the late afternoon of 16 August
and with a mere two hours waiting at the anchorage, sailed out of the Clyde boom at
2230 that same evening with Commodore LLB Willan RNR and his signals staff on
board. Escort was provided by the cruiser *Dorsetshire* and destroyers *Gurkha* (SOE),
Lance, *Piorun* and *Isaac Sweers*. Rendezvous was made with the Liverpool portion
comprising *Strathnaver*, *Palma* and *Brisbane Star* escorted by the destroyers *Whitehall*
and *Witch*, and with *Orion* and *Port Jackson* escorted by the Dutch AA cruiser
Heemskerk from the Bristol Channel, at 0800 next morning in the customary position 6
miles west of Orsay. Captain EJEH Starling, the Master of *Strathnaver* was appointed
Vice Commodore of the six ship convoy which formed into three columns and set off
to the westward at 14 knots.[21]

It had originally been intended to include the AMC *Dunnottar Castle* as part of the
ocean escort to Freetown, until it was noted she could not maintain 15 knots and was
therefore sailed as escort to the slow convoy OS 3 in lieu. The two destroyers which
had escorted the Liverpool portion, returned to Londonderry from the rendezvous point
to refuel and rejoined that afternoon. The Commodore was warned to expect two
inward convoys off the Mull of Kintyre and Orsay but did not record their passing.
Otherwise, no incidents occurred until the morning of the 19th when the two Liverpool
destroyers with *Heemskerk* parted company to return to base, followed by *Gurkha* and
Lance at midday and finally *Isaac Sweers* and *Piorun* at 1900 leaving *Dorsetshire* as the
sole ocean escort. Two hours later *Strathnaver* reported a submarine ahead when two
emergency turns were carried out but from subsequent enquiries by the Commodore the
accuracy of the report was considered doubtful. During the second of these turns in low

visibility *Brisbane Star* lost touch and did not rejoin the convoy until 0550 on the 22nd when 70 miles SW of Sao Miguel in the Azores. Fine weather was experienced from the Azores onwards which allowed *Dorsetshire* to catapult an aircraft on most days for reconnaissance which on the morning of the 25th sighted the AMC *Dunnottar Castle* (and presumed to be with convoy OS 3 of 36 ships). Next morning three destroyers joined as A/S escort in a position 100 miles west of Cap Vert, and at midday on the 27th, one of these was replaced by two corvettes, thus allowing four A/S escorts from that point onwards to Freetown. The searched channel was entered at 1300 on 28 August and all ships were anchored in the harbour by 1530. The average speed from the Clyde was 15.04 knots.

Despite the small size of the convoy, four days were spent in Freetown of which two were idle awaiting arrival of the battleship *Revenge* which was to provide the onward ocean escort in lieu of *Dorsetshire*. The convoy sailed at midday 1 September with *Revenge* and four corvettes as local A/S escort, which proved unsuitable in having a nominal speed of 14 knots but actually 13.5 which produced a hot bearing on one and required her return to Freetown next afternoon. The three remaining corvettes detached to Lagos at midday on the 3rd. However, while still in the submarine zone and making the most of the Guinea current to the west of Cape Palmas the previous evening, a serious collision occurred between *Revenge* and *Orion*, although both ships were able to continue on voyage. The convoy was disposed in two columns with *Revenge* in the centre and slightly astern of *Strathmore* leading *Orion* in the starboard column, steering a SE"ly course with a light to moderate SSW wind and sea, on a moonlit night of good visibility. *Revenge* developed a steering defect and swung "rapidly to starboard apparently out of control and passed through the line between *Strathmore* and *Orion*. *Orion* took avoiding action by turning away using full starboard helm..and then going full astern on both engines,"[22] but quite unavoidably *Orion* "struck the starboard side of *Revenge* just before her mainmast then scraped down her side."[22] *Port Jackson* and the corvette *Armeeria* were ordered to stand-by *Orion* while damage was assessed and convoy speed reduced to 12 knots but all ships rejoined and 13.5 knots resumed shortly after midnight. *Revenge* suffered superficial damage in two compartments but no leaks while the bow of *Orion* was crushed back 8 ft. and twisted to starboard over a depth of 24 ft. Temporary repairs and shoring was made to the store compartment above the forepeak flat and very soon Captain Owens of *Orion* reported his ship capable of steaming 15 knots in moderate weather, the subsequent repairs being referred to later. In respect of *Revenge*, it transpired her Officer of the Watch had chosen an inopportune moment to exercise a steering breakdown, for which he was subsequently court martialled and disciplined for having endangered both his own ship and *Orion*.

Once the corvettes left the convoy on 3 September a speed of 15 knots was resumed. Continuous zigzags were maintained until reaching latitude 10°S when reckoned to be clear of possible submarines and from which point the passage to Capetown was accomplished at an average speed of 14.6 knots without further incident. All ships including *Revenge* were berthed in Capetown on 11 September and left again at 1400 on the 14th to form two columns until clear of the coast.[23] The passage northwards was without incident, *Revenge* was relieved of the escort by the cruiser *Ceres* in the vicinity of Mombasa on the 22nd where she proceeded as the first unit of a planned build up of the Eastern Fleet. The convoy reached Aden at midday on 26 September nearly two days ahead of schedule where it was officially dispersed as escorts were not now required for the Red Sea passage. However, WS 10X had reached the area close on the heels of WS 10 with four of its liners only halfway up the Red Sea, their arrival at Suez having been delayed by the turnround of the two *Queens* disembarking Anzac troops and was only completed on the 26th concurrent with the arrival of WS 10X at Aden. *Strathmore* and *Orion* (the latter carrying most of 22 Armoured Brigade) were sailed from Aden on the 29th while *Strathnaver* was held there until 1 October.

All three liners of WS 10X had completed disembarkation of the troops of 22 Armoured Brigade at Suez by 7 October, with no more than a month to train and prepare themselves for engagement in the coming Crusader offensive. "It was then discovered that all its tanks required a special modification which trebled the time normally spent by new units in the base workshops; the task was not completed until 25 October....which led to a searching enquiry in Whitehall, for the Middle East had given warning of this particular weakness in the Crusader tank".[24] Equally worrying was that "the 22nd had still no training as a brigade in the totally unfamiliar desert conditions."[24] The offensive was several times delayed and finally began on 18 November; Tobruk was relieved on 10 December and British troops entered Benghazi on Christmas Day. The Brigade served in the battle for Tobruk and subsequently throughout the desert campaign to its conclusion at Tunis, thereafter in Italy and landed in France two days after D-Day to continue all the way to the Rhine. Their special fast voyage in WS 10X had been fully justified.

The dispersal of the three liners from Suez was first dictated by the need to move Italian POW from Port Sudan to Bombay. They arrived there independently between 14 and 15 October and where *Strathmore* was drydocked over a ten day period and then loaded homewards, completing at Durban, Port Elizabeth and Capetown, to proceed via Trinidad and reach the Clyde on 14 December for berthing in Glasgow next day. Her next voyage was in WS 15 to Bombay. *Strathnaver* loaded in the same ports, had repairs made to her refrigerated chamber in Durban, and also proceeded from Capetown via Trinidad to the Clyde, arriving on 6 December and berthed in Glasgow next day. She too was next employed in WS 15 to Bombay.

The return of *Orion* because of her damaged stem was a rather different matter. After thirteen days in Bombay she was included in WS 11X (*q.v.*) and proceeded via Colombo to Singapore where she arrived on 6 November for repairs to her collision damage, which included drydocking and where the port tailshaft was drawn for a scheduled inspection. Just over four weeks later the Japanese landed in northern Malaya and soon began to threaten Singapore, and may have expedited the completion of collision damage repairs. In any event *Orion* got away on the last day of 1941 with over 1,000 refugees for Australia, proceeding via Fremantle to Sydney, where within a week she loaded produce for home and after fuelling at Auckland, proceeded via Panama and Bermuda to Halifax. Here *Orion* embarked U.S. troops and sailed on 1 March with *Cameronia* in convoy NA 4 for the Clyde, arriving on the 8th and berthing in KGV Dock Glasgow next afternoon to disembark and discharge from an extended voyage of nearly seven months. Her next employment was in WS 17 for Bombay.

Chapter 12

WS 11, WS 12, 12X and 12Z
Troopship Shortages Continue

1st Armoured Division moves to the Middle East while
18th Infantry Division deploys to Singapore in U.S. transports

WS 11 - sailed UK 30.8.41

The wide disparity between War Office demands for personnel capacity on the WS route, and what the Ministry of War Transport was able to provide, has been referred to previously in some depth.[1] It was to continue throughout the summer of 1941 as the threat of invasion on the British Isles once again receded and allowed the War Office to focus attention on wider issues in the Middle and Far East. Not only were more fighting formations required to meet the growing Axis presence and threat to Egypt and the Suez Canal, the necessary complementary base and administration complex had to be greatly expanded in that Delta region. At the same time there was a demand for transport units in Iraq to maintain the new supply route to Russia, while Malaya was in dire need of every kind of reinforcement in case of a threat from Japan, even although the

Prime Minister as late as 8 August considered this unlikely until Germany had success-fully invaded Britain. The result of all this was a significant increase in the proportion of WS personnel being directed to Iraq, India and Malaya. Whereas until June 1941 no more than a quarter, and frequently less, the total number sailing on the WS route was landed at these destinations, the proportion increased with WS 10 to a third while more than half those sailing on WS 11 were sent there rather than the Middle East without any change in the overall numbers carried.

On 3 July 1941 the M.O.W.T. gave the proposed composition of WS 11 due to sail in mid August with a speed of 13.5 knots, as fifteen liners with a combined capacity of 42,291 personnel. This was 8,000 more than the Director of Movements had forecast two days earlier but a massive 30,000 short of War Office requirements and could not be bridged in the intervening six weeks before the convoy sailed. Nevertheless the Ministry made valiant efforts to reduce the gap by offering to include five slower ships, i.e. *Chantilly, Banfora, Kosciuszko, Northumberland,* and by bringing the NZS *Ruahine* home direct from North America without loading a much needed refrigerated meat cargo from the Plate. These five ships would have increased the convoy capacity to more than 50,000 but would necessitate splitting it into two sections. There would then be difficulties in finding escorts for both sections although it might avoid congestion in ports along the route and in the UK.

There was also a proposal to include six liners then only reaching Durban in WS 9A, by bringing them home direct without cargo and thus at the expense of 25,000 tons of valuable imports. *Mooltan* of this group returned with only 915 tons of cargo and was able to make WS 11, the remainder were loaded to capacity on the Cape coast and reached the UK too late for inclusion. On 4 July the Ministry once again pursued the by now thorny question of releasing ships being held for Special Operations, such as the plan to occupy the Atlantic Islands. Not only was this refused, but *Empress of Canada*, already allocated for WS 11, was additionally taken up for Special Operations when returning to Glasgow from WS 7. After barely a week in port this valuable liner was sent round to the Combined Operations Base at Inverary on Loch Fyne, where troops had a week's practice in the use of the ship's own lifeboats and some landing craft before sailing on 18 August for the Spitzbergen raid.

Every possible avenue of increasing the personnel capacity of WS 11 was explored by the M.O.W.T. On 5 July their Director of Sea Transport made enquiries in the Antipodes "to see whether there was any chance of getting either *Awatea* or *Aorangi* here in time for a late August sailing,"[2] which was unrealistic considering both liners were still employed by the Canadian Australian Line on their trans Pacific route. Enquiries revealed that *Awatea* was then preparing to leave Vancouver for Sydney while *Aorangi* was at Auckland and due to complete her westbound voyage at Sydney two days later. There she was requisitioned for trooping and conveniently fitted out whilst undergoing annual overhaul but did not leave Sydney until 5 September. Proceeding via Panama *Aorangi* crossed the Atlantic with Canadian troops from Halifax in TC 14 to reach Glasgow on 14 October in time to sail in WS 12Z.

Of the original fifteen liners planned for WS 11, three were sent off in the special con-voy WS 10X (*q.v.*), *Cameronia* was similarly advanced and sailed in WS 10, *Pasteur* was allocated a Gibraltar trip in WS 9C (actually a Malta convoy) and thereafter switched to the Halifax route, while *Llanstephan Castle* was taken up for 'Operational Service' which became the first Arctic convoy carrying 550 RAF personnel to Archangel and *Empress of Canada* became the troop component of Operation Gauntlet to Spitzbergen. As the month of July drew to a close it became clear that only one of the five slower ships already proposed could be included in the convoy. *Ruahine* had continued her voyage to the Plate and did not return to the UK until October. Of the two French liners, *Banfora* was a 14.5 knot unit of the Fabre Line's service between Marseilles and West Africa. She was intercepted and sent into Freetown in April 1941 and from there on to Liverpool, arriving on 4 July to be transferred to the British flag and Elder Dempster management. Allocation and conversion began to increase her capacity from 307 passengers to 2047 troops, but with the inevitable ancillary repairs, proved a protracted business which was not completed until October. In a similar manner the 13 knot Messageries Maritimes *Chantilly* was intercepted off Morocco on New Year's Day 1941 and sent into Gibraltar, leaving there on 25 March for Liverpool where she was allocated and began conversion under B.I. management, first as a Military Hospital Ship then almost immediately changed to trooping service and sent out to the Indian Ocean route. Also the 12.5 knot Polish *Kosciuszko* which had lain almost idle as a Depot Ship at Dartmouth since the outbreak of war, was now offered to the M.O.W.T. as a transport. Both completed conversions in late September and proceeded by slow convoys to Freetown and thereafter to Durban. The Federal *Northumberland* was therefore the only ship of the slow group to be included in WS 11.

Despite the deletion of personnel ships from the composition of WS 11, worse was to come. On 31 July the Executive Planners of the War Cabinet Joint Planning Staff, issued a directive that required five other liners being removed from the convoy to carry two extra brigades now considered essential by the force commanders for the expedition to the Atlantic Islands. Those selected were *Strathmore* and *Strathnaver*, *Duchess of Atholl*, *Scythia* and *Llanstephan Castle*. They were to be ready to sail to Scapa for exercises with the transports already held for Combined Operations, the whole force to be known as WS 11A while the original convoy WS 11 would be re-styled WS 11B. These five liners would have reduced the convoy capacity by 13,724 personnel, but were to be partly compensated by fitting four other liners for trooping, *Largs Bay*, *Abosso*, *City of Paris* and *Mendoza* with a total estimated capacity of 4,360 and therefore a poor substitute, which was further reduced when it was later found the latter two ships could not complete fitting until mid September. Of the five liners intended for the Scapa exercises, all were soon re-allocated back to the convoy as the plans to mount the expedition then receded. The liners were, however, allocated elsewhere, the two *Straths* to the Special WS 10X convoy (*q.v.*), *Llanstephan Castle* to Russia and *Duchess of Atholl* for an Iceland voyage from which she had to return to Glasgow for four weeks engine repairs. *Scythia* alone was included in WS 11 and during the first two weeks of August *Orontes* and *Empress of Australia*, recently returned to the Clyde and Liverpool from WS 7, were also allocated to the convoy. Two further allocations made on 1 August were *Empire Pride* and *Highland Princess* but neither were able to join the convoy: the former was a new ship, launched by Barclay Curle on 14 May and not due to complete until mid September. On her return voyage from the HP convoy, *Highland Princess* only reached Liverpool on 18 August and could not have been discharged and ready to sail twelve days later in WS 11.

As August progressed, the ten transports finally selected for the convoy were busy discharging, repairing, fitting out or otherwise planning for the voyage ahead, with *Viceroy of India*, *Otranto*, *Empress of Australia*, *Duchess of York*, *Abosso* and *Northumberland* in Liverpool and *Scythia*, *Orontes*, *Largs Bay* and *Mooltan* in Glasgow. The last named arrived from the Cape via Trinidad and Curacao with a bare eights days to discharge, undertake voyage repairs, ship fuel, stores and embark personnel in time to join the convoy. Eight MT ships were to be included, *City of Manchester* and *Manchester Progress* from Newport, P&O/Hain *Bhutan* and Harrison's *Barrister* from Swansea, *Glenorchy* and Holts *Glaucus* from Liverpool, *City of Edinburgh* and the ex Danish *Kina II* (under United-Baltic management) from Glasgow.

On 12 August *Scythia* had to vacate her Glasgow berth for one at the Clyde Anchorage and on the 20th proceeded to Liverpool to complete her previous lengthy repairs before returning to the Clyde on the 28th to embark, where also *Largs Bay* embarked on the 30th. Otherwise, all embarkations were made at the ports given above.[3] In the early evening of the 29th, the two MT ships together with *Orontes* and *Largs Bay* moved downriver from Glasgow, followed 24 hours later by *Mooltan* which completed the Clyde portion ready for sailing later that night.

Amongst the 24,430 personnel embarked on this convoy (which was 310 over the stated capacity), were the advance Headquarters and divisional troops of 1st Armourerd Division going out to establish themselves in XXX Corps of Eighth Army in the desert. Also embarked were three regiments of the RAC posted to India to form 50 Indian Tank Brigade and a further three Field Regiments of Royal Artillery posted to 8 and 10 Indian Divisions then in Iraq. The RAC regiments had been converted from infantry, having begun life as 9 Duke of Wellington's, 10 York & Lancaster and 7 Kings Own Yorkshire Light Infantry as part of sixty new battalions raised in June 1940 to meet invasion. They were reorganized at Cheltenham in June 1941 whence they moved to Liverpool for embarkation between 26 and 28 August on *Otranto*, *Viceroy of India* and *Duchess of York*. The Duke's history refers to "8.5 weeks at sea, the monotony of life relieved by lectures on tanks and tactical employment of vehicles."[4] while the York & Lancaster noted "the voyage around the Cape was uneventful, but included four days of overwhelming welcome and hospitality from the South African people at Durban."[5] The Royal Artillery Field Regiments were embarked on the same three liners for transhipment at Bombay.

On 18 August the Admiralty notified the passage plan whereby WS 11 would leave the UK on 30 August and split north of the Azores with the fast portion escorted by *Sheffield* moving ahead for Freetown, while the slow portion escorted by the AMC *Derbyshire* followed astern. However, the Admiralty had plans to create an Eastern Fleet based in Ceylon from the beginning of 1942, and by using the four R class battleships meantime, would deploy them there while escorting WS convoys to the Indian Ocean,[6] the first being *Revenge* which had joined the escort of WS 10X at Freetown. Churchill did not like these dispositions [6] and by the end of August the Admiralty agreed to send out the battleship *Prince of Wales* and the battlecruiser *Repulse* as the first instalment of the Far Eastern Fleet. Both ships were then at Scapa, the former not yet ready but on 28 August *Repulse* was ordered to escort WS 11 to the Indian Ocean and subsequently to reach Trincomalee on 7 October.

The Liverpool portion of WS 11 left that port with a local escort on the late afternoon tide of Saturday, 30 August, comprising six transports and two MT ships, to be joined by the four MT ships from the Bristol Channel somewhere in the Irish Sea. The Clyde portion of four transports and two MT ships, escorted by *Derbyshire*, passed out of the boom at 0200 on the 31st and at 1030 made junction with the other portions off Orsay where the complete convoy formed into five columns and set off to the westward.[7] *Repulse*, *Furious* and *Sheffield* joined at this point, together with *Cairo* and nine destroyers as A/A and A/S escorts, plus destroyers *Encounter* and *Nestor*, the new sloop *Sutlej* on passage to India and ex US Coastguard cutters *Totland* and *Sennen* all as ocean escorts to Freetown.

Commodore HH Rogers RNR and his staff were accommodated on *Orontes* while Captain ACG Hawker, the Master of *Otranto* was appointed Vice Commodore. The weather on passage to Freetown was reported as good except for fog encountered on the first three days. There were several aircraft alarms on 1st September when also *Furious* left the convoy but rejoined next morning when a Focke Wulf Condor was seen but no attack developed. The cruiser *Sheffield* left at 1730 that evening to rejoin her previous station with Force H at Gibraltar, having spent the past four weeks refitting at Rosyth. Two Polish destroyers of the escort left next day but movements of the others are not recorded.

At 1100 on 4 September *Furious* parted company for Gibraltar where she was to transfer aircraft for ferrying to Malta. Two hours later the convoy was split in a position 450 miles due north of Sao Miguel island of the Azores. *Repulse* then continued with the eight large transports plus *Glenorchy*, *Kina II*, *City of Edinburgh*, *Bhutan* and HMS *Guardian*, all minimum speed 16 knots, with the destroyers *Nestor* and *Encounter* as A/S escorts which probably refuelled at Ponta Delgada en route. The fast section continued without incident to Freetown, being joined in the approaches by two destroyers and the corvette *Starwort* as local escort and where all arrived safely at midday on the 13th. The slow section comprised the remaining four MT ships plus *Abosso* and *Northumberland* which continued at 12 knots escorted by *Derbyshire*, *Sutlej*, *Totland* and *Sennen*. At 1730 on the 8th this section was joined by the RFA *Rapidol* (which may have refuelled *Repulse*). From the 11th onwards *Sutlej*, *Totland* and *Sennen* each reported and attacked contacts with depth charges, none yielding results. In fact U-Boats had deserted the Cape Verde - Freetown area simply because every possible ship had been diverted elsewhere. Captain AE Lettington of *Northumberland* acted as Commodore of the slow section and Captain RW Tate of *Abosso* as Vice Commodore; all ships being anchored in Freetown two days behind the fast section at 1910 on the 15th. A homeward convoy of eleven ships had left the day previously, losing seven of its number to U-Boats in the area west of the Canaries.

The only comments made on the passage to Freetown was that by Commodore Rogers, who reported that *Manchester Progress* with an alleged speed of 13.5 knots could often do only 12.25, while *Largs Bay* which claimed 15.5 had an actual speed of 14 knots apparently due to low grade fuel shipped at Curacao on her previous homeward voyage.

Whilst at Freetown, the RFA *Rapidol* and HM ships *Guardian*, *Totland* and *Sennen* were detached from the convoy for other duties, while the transports *Northumberland* and *Abosso*, whose complements were almost wholly for West African ports, left a day or so behind the convoy to disembark independently along the coast between Bathurst and half a dozen other destinations as far east and south as Pointe Noire in the French Middle Congo, where an escort base was under consideration. *Northumberland* then proceeded to the Plate, loaded meat for the UK and returned home via Halifax and Avonmouth where she was released from trooping requisition and the troop fittings removed. *Abosso* loaded home on her owners' berth to Liverpool and next sailed out in WS 14.

Joining WS 11 at Freetown was the Dutch *Nieuw Zeeland*, previously trooping on Indian Ocean routes until she brought West African troops back to Lagos in convoy CF 2 (see WS 8X). She then moved to Freetown and embarked 91 civilians and DBS

(British Seamen who had lost their ships), 32 Army and 534 Asiatic crew survivors, almost all bound for India and Singapore.

The revised convoy, now comprising nine transports and eight MT ships, sailed from Freetown in the afternoon of 18 September, with *Repulse* and *Derbyshire* continuing as ocean escorts while the destroyers *Encounter*, *Velox* and *Wrestler*, with sloop *Sutlej* and corvette *Woodruff* provided local A/S protection until the 20th/21st. On the first morning at sea Harrison's *Barrister* was found unable to maintain 12 knots "owing to the sickness of three firemen and others being lazy."[8] Although a modern cargo liner reportedly capable of 14.5 knots, *Barrister* like all coal burners proved a severe handicap by inclusion in such fast convoys. On the morning of the 20th, *Empress of Australia* dropped astern for an hour due to engine trouble, otherwise the only incident of note on this passage was range and inclination exercises carried out between *Derbyshire* and *Repulse*, which latter ship detached on the evening of the 23rd but made contact again on the 25th.

Six days prior to arrival at the Cape, a signal was received giving revised proposals for a complicated programme of troop transhipment at Capetown and Durban, which had then become standard practice to allow some transports to return direct to the UK while those with refrigerated spaces were able to return home with meat cargoes from the Plate. Rapid turnround for inclusion in the next possible WS convoy was now a priority for all transports.

At 1300 on 29 September, *Derbyshire* detached with *Largs Bay*, *Duchess of York*, *Nieuw Zeeland*, *Orontes*, *Viceroy of India* and six MT ships for Capetown where they berthed within the harbour next morning. The remaining transports, *Empress of Australia*, *Otranto*, *Scythia*, *Mooltan* with *Barrister* and *Manchester Progress* continued under escort of *Repulse* to Durban, where they arrived on 3 October to find seven Indian Ocean type troopships already in port preparing for on-carriage of some of the troops on the liners of WS 11.

On arrival at Capetown, Commodore Rogers commented most highly on the navigation and efficiency of *Orontes* (Captain AE Nicholls) as a Commodore ship, but also referred to the waste of keeping ten ships capable of 16 knots for the whole passage to Capetown at a speed of less than 12.5 knots.[9] Clearly Commodore Rogers was unaware of the critical shortage of both transports and MT ships at this time.

The transhipment plan at Capetown simply meant landing 208 personnel for the Middle East aboard *Orontes*, *Nieuw Zeeland* and *Duchess of York*, whence they were moved overland for re-embarkation at Durban. Four liners (less *Nieuw Zeeland* see below) and five MT ships (less *Glaucus* delayed with a fouled propeller but rejoined later) sailed from Capetown at 1300 on the 3rd still escorted by *Derbyshire*, and proceeded around the Cape to a rendezvous outside Durban where a re-formed and enlarged portion was met at 1130 on the 8th, and where also *Repulse* relieved *Derbyshire* which returned to Capetown to rectify defects.

Whilst in Durban, all of the troops on *Scythia* and *Empress of Australia* were disembarked, 411 being for South Africa while 3866 for the Middle East amd 1322 for Singapore transhipped to other vessels. The *Empress* then left Durban on 9 October and proceeded via Capetown and Trinidad to reach the Holy Loch on 14 November and berth in Glasgow seven days later; her next voyage was in WS 14. *Scythia* however was delayed in Durban for engine repairs and having been aground while entering the port; she finally sailed on 16 October and was routed via Capetown and Freetown to reach Liverpool on 16 November, also making her next voyage in WS 14.

Also in Durban, a further 995 were embarked on *Otranto* and 880 on *Mooltan* to make up for those disembarked for South Africa and the Middle East as the destination of the former ship had been changed from Suez to Bombay. From Capetown, *Nieuw Zeeland* was brought round to Durban to increase the transhipment lifting and capacity for Union Defence Force troops moving to Suez (of which 2146 were classed as Non-European). A total of 8640 embarked at Durban on *Nieuw Zeeland, Dilwara, City of Canterbury, Pulaski, Eastern Prince, Llandaff Castle, Nieuw Holland* and *Johan de Witt*, while *Barrister* and *Manchester Progress* were bunkered with coal at the Bluff.

The reconstituted convoy of nine transports and two MT ships under escort of *Repulse* sailed from Durban in the afternoon of 7 October and joined with the four transports and six MT ships from Capetown next forenoon by forming into six columns: two of three ships and four with four ships per column.[10] *Johan de Witt*, which had been delayed at Durban, finally joined on the morning of the 11th. At 1500 on the 13th, in a position 180 miles SE of Mombasa, the cruiser *Ceres* took over the escort from *Repulse* which then proceeded to Mombasa for fuel, before continuing for Colombo to await the arrival of her erstwhile consort *Prince of Wales*.

WS 11 continued up the East African coast towards Cape Guardafui. An appendix case, transferred from *Johan de Witt* to *Viceroy of India* on the 14th, died aboard that ship the following day and was buried at sea. By the afternoon of the 17th, the convoy reached a position 140 miles SE of Guardafui, where the cruiser *Glasgow* was met and detached with the Bombay section now styled WS 11X and comprising *Duchess of York, Johan de Witt, Largs Bay, Nieuw Zeeland, Orontes, Otranto, Viceroy of India* and MT ships, *Barrister, City of Edinburgh, Glaucus, Glenorchy* and *Kina II*. The remaining ten ships of the three port columns continued around Guardafui and arrived at Aden outer anchorage on the 19th, where *Ceres* left and split the convoy to continue in four independent groups to Suez.

Enemy bombing and mining of the Suez Canal, which had caused many lengthy closures of that waterway in the early months of 1941, slackened off from July as the Luftwaffe lent more support to the ground forces of the Afrika Corps. Nevertheless the canal was closed for six days in early September and two days each in the first week of both October and November.[11] A concentration of shipping there was undesirable, consequently *Mooltan* (probably carrying 1st Armoured Division HQ) together with *Dilwara* and *Eastern Prince*, moved first from Aden to Suez where they were turned around within two days of their arrival on the 24th. These liners were replaced by *City of Canterbury* and *Pulaksi* and finally by *Nieuw Holland* and *Llandaff Castle* on the 28th, the latter having called at Port Sudan on route. All three MT ships passed through the canal to discharge at Port Said and Alexandria. From Suez all but *Mooltan* and *Dilwara* proceeded to Berbera and embarked Italian POW for Mombasa before continuing to Durban for further Indian Ocean service. *Dilwara* was also retained for Indian Ocean service on arrival at Durban, while *Mooltan* proceeded direct to Durban and loaded for the UK after spending two weeks cleaning boiler tubes. She was delayed a further five days for boiler defects at Capetown and with her speed reduced by these handicaps and in need of drydocking was directed not via Trinidad but to Freetown, where she suffered the ignominy of being included in the slow homeward convoy SL 96 taking 15 days to reach Liverpool on 10 January 1942. Her Master, Captain Roche, a native of Holyhead who had also been her Commander before the war, found his ship had lacked maintenance when serving as an AMC but resigned himself for a further voyage or two until his retiral came in September 1942. *Mooltan* next sailed out in WS 16.

Meanwhile the Bombay section of the convoy as WS 11X had detached SE of Guardafui and proceeded under escort of the cruiser *Glasgow* on the afternoon of 17 October on a direct route towards Bombay. On the 19th the fast MT ships *Glenorchy* and *City of Edinburgh* were detached independently for Basra and the slower *Barrister* two days later for that same destination, each presumably without escort although neither U-Boats nor commence raiders had been known to operate in that area. The remaining two MT ships and seven transports reached Bombay in fine weather on the morning of 22 October, where they anchored in the stream to await turns for disembarking at the Ballard Pier passenger terminal. The transports brought 6363 troops bound for Iraq and 2306 for Malaya in addition to 5010 for India, 50 for Burma, 13 for Hong Kong and 9 for Australia.

By reason of their dimensions and priority requirements for further WS service, none of the transports were considered suitable for a further extension of their voyage to the confines of the narrow Shatt el Arab river where the Iraqi port of Basra stands. The Indian divisions already in that country had been carried there by a series of smaller Indian Ocean transports (mostly B.I. or Bibby owned) operating from Bombay or Karachi, of which twelve were already berthed in the former port when WS 11 arrived. A partial re-enactment of the Cape transhipments now took place in Bombay, when the troops for Iraq transferred to *Devonshire, Lancashire, Nevasa, Takliwa, Ethiopia* and *Khedive Ismail* and together with Indian troops already embarked sailed for Basra in three small convoys between the 24th and 27th and reached their destination six days later.

Also disembarked at Bombay were the troops for Burma and India, including the three RAC regiments which proceeded to Poona and formed into 50 Indian Tank Brigade to complete their training and await delivery of tanks. One regiment was in action in the Arakan early in 1943, another was sent to Kohima in support of 2nd British Division in April 1944 while the third operated with 19 and 20 Indian Divisions during the advance through Burma in 1945. All were disbanded in India during the spring of 1946.

The four transports completely disembarked in Bombay were *Orontes, Otranto, Duchess of York* and *Viceroy of India*; all then part loaded in Bombay and Cape ports for the UK. The latter was despatched from Bombay on the last day of October, made a three day stop at Capetown and then proceeded via Trinidad to Glasgow and arrived on 12 December. *Duchess of York* left Bombay on 3rd November, *Otranto* two days later and *Orontes* on the 6th; all three being routed via Trinidad whence the *Duchess* was directed to the Clyde and berthed in KGV Dock on 22 December. The Orient ships were sent to Liverpool where they arrived on 20 and 26 December respectively and where both were drydocked before their next voyages with the *Viceroy* in WS 15. The *Duchess* spent seven weeks repairing and drydocking in Glasgow and was not further employed until WS 16.

Also in Bombay at this time were *Orion* and *Strathnaver* from WS 10X (q.v.) which had arrived during the previous week from Port Sudan. The former ship was conveniently bound for Singapore to repair bow damage, so the balance of troops destined for Malaya but landed at Bombay from *Otranto* and others, were now embarked on *Orion*. A revised convoy known as WS 11X sailed from Bombay at daybreak on 27 October comprising the transports *Orion, Largs Bay, Nieuw Zeeland* and *Johan de Witt*, with the remaining MT ships *Glaucus* and *Kina II*. Escort was provided by the AMC *Hector* while Commodore LLB Willan RNR, on his homeward voyage from WS 10X, was aboard *Orion*.[12] The passage down the west coast of India was without incident; off the southern tip of that continent *Kina II* was despatched to proceed independently around Ceylon to the naval base at Trincomalee. The convoy reached Colombo at midday on the 30th where all ships were berthed within the harbour. The convoy had averaged 12.5 knots in fine weather from Bombay.

The reason for the 24 hour stopover in Colombo is unknown; only two of the total number originally embarked having been bound for Ceylon. However, WS 11X sailed again at midday 31 October with the liner *Rangitiki* taking the place of *Kina II* and with the cruiser *Mauritius* now acting as escort for the final leg of the voyage to Singapore. Holt's *Glaucus* left Colombo behind the convoy and rejoined soon after dark. Next aftenoon the B.I. *Ellenga*, on a commercial trade voyage from Madras to the Straits, joined the convoy to the east of Ceylon. Two columns were maintained until reaching the Malacca Straits when ships were placed in single line ahead. The convoy arrived off the Sultan Shoal outside Singapore at 0930 on 6 November and proceeded into Keppel Harbour to disembark and discharge while *Mauritius* proceeded to the naval base. 80 Anti-tank Regiment R.A. were amongst the troops who now disembarked from the UK and were sent to join 11 Indian Division in northwest Malaya.

The onward voyages of *Rangitiki* to New Zealand and of *Orion* to the UK have already been referred to.[13] Of the remaining transports at Singapore, *Largs Bay* disembarked her contingent of 804 troops (including 13 for Hong Kong) but did not sail until 15 November when she continued with general cargo and some passengers for Sydney. Here she was drydocked and loaded, topped off at Auckland and returned home via Panama, Curacao (bunkers), Bermuda and finally Halifax, where she embarked to capacity for the UK and left on 30 January 1942 in the fast two ship convoy NA 2 with the Dutch liner *Volendam* carrying 1,699 newly trained RAF aircrew. The large ex-American liner *George Washington* on charter to the MOWT and under Anchor Line management with Captain Bone in command, was also to have sailed in this convoy but developed serious boiler defects and was returned to New York and U.S. control. Convoy NA 2 had a fast passage and reached the Clyde on the morning of 9 February where both liners were disembarked at the anchorage, *Largs Bay* then continuing to Glasgow that afternoon to discharge at Plantation Quay and was next employed in WS 17 to Durban. *Volendam* requested ten days for the repair of heavy weather damage but was turned around in seven days to sail in WS 16 for Suez.

Of the two Dutch liners that disembarked at Singapore, *Johan de Witt* loaded commercial cargo and 46 personnel, mainly RAF for Durban and was retained on Indian Ocean service for a further twelve months until the end of 1942. *Nieuw Zeeland* carried out boiler repairs at Singapore and left on 22 November bound for the UK with 195 service and civilian personnel and proceeded via Sourabaya and Batavia, then called at Singapore on 4 December to repair a defective aerial and where a further 55 personnel for the UK were embarked. *Nieuw Zeeland* continued via Durban, Port Elizabeth (for cargo and strengthening for guns), Capetown for cargo and embarkation of 404 mainly RN and RAF for the UK, Freetown for bunkers and thence to the Clyde where she arrived and disembarked on 15 March. Thereafter she proceeded to Liverpool for drydocking, troop fittings, DEMS equipment and sailed in WS 18 to Bombay.

Most of the liners of WS 11 were on their homeward voyages when Japanese aggression caused war to suddenly erupt in the Far East. It hardly affected the liners of WS

12 which had then reached their destinations, but caused widespread disruption to both the liners and their embarked personnel on the next four convoys.

WS 12 - sailed UK 30.9.41

Plans for the despatch of WS 12 to leave the UK in mid September 1941, began to evolve during the month of July. For the first time since the start of the WS series thirteen months earlier, there were indications that the chronic shortage of personnel ships might soon be partly relieved, although the War Office meantime continued to demand personnel capacity which could not be met.

From the end of May 1941 the Admiralty realized their plans to provide continuous escort throughout the entire passage of North Atlantic convoys, and from mid July also applied this to the protection of Sierra Leone convoys. This was achieved by the steady flow of newly constructed escorts and the transfer of others from the American flag. This in turn allowed the Admiralty to release nine AMCs from convoy escort work and begin their conversion to more effective employment as troopships.[14] The liners affected were *Arawa*, *Esperance Bay*, *Laconia*, *Letitia*, *Maloja*, *Moreton Bay*, *Wolfe* (ex *Montcalm*), *Antenor* and *Cathay*. Although nominally released in July, it was another month or two before conversion could actually begin and a further three to five months before these liners were able to take their place in the trooping fleet.

Three days after the despatch of WS 10X on 19 August, the MOWT sent a note to the War Office stating that "WS 12 due to sail at the end of September would have a capacity of 35,000 for all destinations."[15] The intended liners were not named, however, the note suggested that "capacity could be increased to 43,700 by allocating four liners making September trips to Iceland, Gibraltar and Halifax."[15] Coincidentally, Churchill had just returned from visiting Roosevelt in Washington, and with a notion that two more British divisions should be "moving eastward for something in hand for unknowable contingencies,"[16] wrote to the CIGS and MOWT on 22 August, asking for the shipping requirements for such a move and saying that he would ask the President for the loan of American shipping for this purpose. Churchill addressed his request to the President on 1st September and received an offer five days later, of U.S. naval transports to carry the necessary 20,000 men (of one division).[16] This movement subsequently became convoy WS 12X (see below).

The sheer scale of troop movements from the UK around the Cape at this period of time is illustrated in a late August paper from the War Office, which estimated the numbers to be transported overseas in the four months from September to December 1941 as 94,900 Army to the Middle East, 14,400 to India, 13,200 to Iraq, 6,500 to Malaya and 3,000 to West Africa. To this had to be added 32,000 RAF and 6,000 RN, making a grand total of 170,000 spread over four convoys.[15]

On 15 September the list of personnel ships made available for WS 12 to sail at the end of September, revealed thirteen liners with a speed of 15 knots or over (which the Admiralty considered necessary) and three slower ships of 14 knots. The convoy capacity would be 35,372 if all sixteen liners were included but 30,248 if the slower ships were not. Of eleven MT ships proposed, only five could attain 15 knots while the slowest ones of 13.5 knots were excluded at the outset. This convoy was to carry the bulk of 1st Armoured Division to the Middle East which demanded suitably fast MT ships able to handle tanks with their own cargo gear.

Of the sixteen cargo liners listed, *City of Paris* and *Mendoza* were new to trooping and had been fitting-out in Liverpool since the end of July. The Ellerman ship completed four commercial voyages on her owners' routes before coming under trooping requisition. *Mendoza* was a Vichy French liner of the Marseilles registered Vapeur Company that had been captured off Puerto Rico by the AMC *Asturias* on 18 January. Both liners were of 14 knots and destined for the Indian Ocean routes. The new liner *Empire Pride* carried out trials in the Clyde during the first week of September and returned upriver to Glasgow to complete fitting-out and was placed under Bibby Line management. *Samaria* and *Franconia* had been repairing in Liverpool and *Strathaird* in Glasgow since the third week of August from previous WS voyages. The remaining ten liners for WS 12 reached the UK ports during the first half of September of which three were then allocated elsewhere.

The reader is referred to the collision of *Warwick Castle* in WS 10 that caused *Duchess of Atholl* being ordered to Halifax as a replacement yet having to return to Glasgow for major engine repairs and re-allocation to WS 12. It soon became clear that the *Duchess* could not be ready for this convoy and was replaced by *Stratheden* that left Glasgow for Halifax on 16 September. The third removal from WS 12 was *Orbita* that reached Liverpool on 12 September at the end of her WS 9A voyage, and could yet have been included as voyage repairs were completed on the 24th in ample time for embarkation. However, *Orbita* was removed and retained for 'Operational Services' on the Clyde for the next six weeks, to be replaced by *Ormonde*, which had previously been on 'Operational Services' for five months before completing with an Iceland trip on the Clyde on 25 September. This allowed a mere five days to prepare at the anchorage for a Middle East voyage. Although the trooping capacities of *Orbita* and *Ormonde* were very similar, it must be assumed the authorities now realized that the 16.5 knots of *Ormonde* was better employed on the WS route than the 14 knots of *Orbita*.

The removal of these liners from the convoy reduced the total capacity by 7,066 personnel to 28,306. The inclusion of *Ormonde* increased this to 30,780 but remained 5,000 short of the numbers which by that date must have been en route to their nominated ports of embarkation. It would seem that a compromise was reached to reduce the shortfall. The MOWT had been frequently pressurising the War Office and Admiralty to release some of the valuable liners being held for the planned expedition to the Atlantic Islands as Operation Pilgrim. These forces had been assembled since April; at the end of July the operation was postponed until September and thereafter receded from the forefront of strategic thinking "as it became clearer that Spain would not allow German troops to pass through to attack Gibraltar"[17] the possible loss of which had first prompted the planning for Pilgrim. Thus the release of *Ormonde* from operational mode was followed by that of *Narkunda* for the voyage to Freetown only, where she could still be conveniently re-allocated should the need arise. *Narkunda* was a P&O liner which had remained on owners'' routes until April 1941, when taken up for Pilgrim which kept her much under-utilised for the next five months. Her stated capacity of 2,155 helped close the shortfall and may have been further reduced by personnel carried on two H.M. ships.

The principal units to embark on WS 12 and those most urgently needed in the Middle East were those of 1st Armoured Division, whose leading formation, 22 Armoured Brigade, had been rushed around the Cape in the special convoy WS 10X for the opening of the Crusader offensive in November. The divisional troops, which included 12 Royal Lancers who embarked at Avonmouth on *Highland Brigade*, together with the artillery units of 1st Support Group variously embarked, were accompanied by those of 2nd Armoured Brigade with The Queens Bays who embarked from Gourock to *Empire*

Pride at the Clyde Anchorage, 10 Royal Hussars on *City of Paris* at the same location, while 9 Royal Lancers and 1st Bn The Rifle Brigade boarded *Strathaird* at No. 1 KGV Dock, Glasgow. The remaining embarkations of Army, RAF and RN units were completed on *Almanzora* at 6 KGV, Glasgow, *Empress of Canada*, *Empress of Russia*, *Ormonde*, *Narkunda* and *Leopoldville* at the Clyde Anchorage, and on *Duchess of Richmond*, *Dominion Monarch*, *Samaria*, *Franconia* and *Mendoza* at Liverpool. A further inclusion in the convoy was *Highland Princess* carrying RAF trainees for Canada which was to be detached for Halifax on clearing the Western Approaches.[18]

The MT ships of the convoy were *Clan Lamont* and *Perthshire* which had loaded in Liverpool, and *Clan Campbell*, the Blue Funnel 'Goalposter' *Perseus* and *Empire Trust* which loaded in Glasgow; the latter being a cargo-only sister of *Empire Pride* under Brocklebank management. Also being included in the convoy as far as the Cape was the Blue Funnel *Sarpedon*, which had loaded general cargo in Liverpool for Australian ports. Two H.M. ships included from the Clyde to Freetown were *Royal Ulsterman* and *Prince Baudouin*, partly fitted as Landing Ships for Operation Pilgrim.

On completion of embarkation at Avonmouth, *Highland Brigade* sailed up to the Clyde Anchorage, where she arrived on the morning of 30 September just as the last of the Glasgow MT ships, *Clan Campbell*, cleared the river channel. *Strathaird* had come downriver in the evening of the 28th and *Almanzora* the following morning. The final embarkation list showed the five liners from Liverpool carried 12,302, the two from Glasgow 5,101, seven from the Clyde Anchorage 13,945 and the single ship from Avonmouth 1,225. Sixty-five percent of the total number was destined for the Middle East.

From Liverpool, the five transports, two MT ships and *Sarpedon* began leaving the Mersey at 1600 on 30 September under the appointed Vice Commodore, Captain Harry A Moore of *Duchess of Richmond*. Captain Moore was a Birkenhead man, an Extra Master and Commander RNR making his second WS voyage on the *Richmond* although he had previously served as her Master for almost five years up to 1939. Captain JG Bissett of *Franconia* beginning his fourth (and last) WS voyage on that ship, was the appointed Rear Commodore of the convoy.

The earliest departures from the Clyde were at 1930 on the 30th when three of the destroyer escort left for Londonderry to top up with fuel and join later. At 2040 that same evening the AMC *Cathay*, which the Admiralty had released from that service, left the Clyde in company with the carrier *Argus* ferrying aircraft to Gibraltar. Both were to accompany WS 12 for the first few days of its passage. The convoy itself began clearing the Clyde boom at 2100 hours, led by Commodore BS Thesiger RNR, who was embarked with his signals staff on *Strathaird* and whose Master was Captain Harold Williams.[19] Following behind the ten liners and three MT ships from the Clyde were the two Cross-Channel type HM ships *Royal Ulsterman* and *Prince Baudouin* bound for Freetown, the AA cruiser *Cairo*, minelayer *Agamemnon* (Ex Blue Funnel), and the 8-inch cruiser *Devonshire* acting as ocean escort. Although no German warship raiders were believed to be at sea during this period, the Admiralty maintained its policy of providing minimum cruiser escort throughout the entire passage of WS convoys.

When still in the Firth of Clyde in the early hours of next morning, *Cairo* was ordered to join and supplement the AA cover of the Liverpool section which was probably proceeding under escort of two local destroyers. By dawn, *Devonshire* noted the visibility as 3 to 4 miles, and at 0700 sighted the Liverpool section 6 miles south of the Mull of Kintyre and apparently late for the rendezvous off Orsay at 0900. *Devonshire* joined with this section, ostensibly to exchange signals with the Vice Commodore on *Duchess of Richmond*, and at 0730 two of the Clyde and ex US destroyers joined that section and relieved two of the V and W type which then proceeded to Derry for fuel. At this point the transport *Mendoza* began to drop astern and in danger of being ordered back but caught up later and able to maintain the steaming speed of 13 knots. The whole convoy was eventually formed up in six columns: each of four ships by noon that day, 1st October,[20] in a position 14 miles north of Inishtrahull Light off the Eire coastline. The HM ships *Cathay*, *Argus* and *Cairo* formed an additional column between columns 3 and 4. A westerly course and speed of 13 knots was set on the first leg of the voyage with an A/S escort of ten destroyers, (two Canadian, five ex American, two Hunts and one Tribal) with the SOE on *Sikh*. Just before 1800 hours three of the V and W destroyers joined and at this point an Admiralty signal diverted the convoy to a SW'ly course which was maintained for the next two days.

The visibility continued poor varying from 3 to 6 miles on this SW leg during which time several friendly aircraft were detected by radar on *Cairo* but not seen. An unconfimed asdic contact on the evening of the 2nd caused the convoy to make an emergency turn of 90° to port for half an hour, and at which point another of the ex American destroyers joined, making a total A/S escort of fourteen. The troops soon adjusted to life at sea, although the Hussars on *City of Paris* commented that "the congestion on board was considerable...with many difficulties regarding accommodation...nevertheless, after a few days of grumbles and complaints, it was amazing how those unaccustomed to cramped conditions on board gradually settle down and solve their troubles...very soon the inevitable games of House-Housey appeared...and comparative harmony reigned afloat."[21] The Queens Bays on *Empire Pride* acknowledged their ship as new but small with "not much room for exercise..but everyone made the best of it with various forms of training and recreation."[22]

The weather and visibility increased on the 3rd which allowed *Argus* to operate aircraft on A/S patrol, presumably Swordfish, but unable to deter a Focke-Wulf Condor which shadowed and reported the convoy that morning by flying low and out of range of *Cairo* which opened fire upon it just before the convoy disappeared into a patch of fog. Seven of the ex American destroyers were detached that evening to return to Derry when at the prudent limit of endurance. At midnight the convoy turned to a southerly heading towards the central Azores group, and one hour later two V and W destroyers were detached.

At 0930 on the 4th, *Highland Princess* and HM ships *Cathay* and *Agamemnon* were detached for Halifax as convoy CT 3 under escort of two Canadian destroyers. They made a safe arrival there on the 9th where the first named disembarked and proceeded to New York for a refrigerated cargo and return to the UK. *Cathay* was also sent to New York and there decommissioned and converted for trooping service at the Brooklyn Navy Yard. The AA cruiser *Cairo* was detached on the afternoon of the 4th to return to the UK with three of the V and W destroyers, while one of the Hunts and six of the ex American types had previously and similarly detached on the 3rd. *Sikh* and three other destroyers remained meanwhile as A/S escorts.

By the morning of 5 October, it was becoming appreciably warmer and WS 12 was 400 miles north of the Azores where another of the US destroyers detached for Londonderry. Also at this time *Perthshire* had to reduce speed to secure a tank which had broken adrift in one of her holds but caught up and rejoined at 1500. Soon after this the northbound convoy CF 2 comprising *Duchess of Bedford* and *Sobieski* escorted by the AMC *Cheshire*,[23] was met and passed. At 1700 the carrier *Argus* detached with *Sikh* for Gibraltar and at 2030 HM ships *Royal Ulsterman* and *Prince Baudouin* detached ahead at 15 knots for Ponta Delgada to refuel and rejoin later. The convoy was now four hours behind schedule owing to a strong head wind and that evening altered course to SSW to pass through the westerly Azores passage between Flores and Faial, a gap of 120 miles.

The speed through the Azores was reduced to 11 knots by the head wind and sea but was without incident; the light at Ponta Camprida being seen at a distance of 21 miles just before midnight on the 6th. A course of SSE was next morning altered to SE and at 1300 on the 7th the Dutch destroyer *Isaac Sweers* joined the escort which allowed the two remaining destroyers, *Stanley* and *Blankney* to detach north for Ponta Delgada to refuel. At 2330 on the 7th a southerly course was set towards the Cape Verde islands, 1000 miles ahead.

During the afternoon of the 8th the Spanish tanker *Campas* was sighted then stopped and boarded by *Isaac Sweers*. With the weather now suitable for recovering aircraft, the Walrus from *Devonshire* was launched on the morning of the 9th for an A/S search but sighted only an empty ship"s lifeboat. Also on that date the troops on *Strathaird* "discarded battledress for drill and shirt sleeves, and the swimming pool was filled. Permission for men to sleep out on deck at night brought instant relief to those on the overcrowded and unbearably hot troop decks."[24] From the 8th onwards, *Devonshire* made a practice of sweeping 15 miles astern of the convoy at sunset but without any sightings. A U-Boat report was received on the 10th which placed it 55 miles east of the convoy route and that afternoon radio transmissions were heard from a possible U-Boat to the SW, which caused an emergency turn to the eastward for half an hour but nothing materialized. *Royal Ulsterman* and *Prince Baudouin* rejoined at 1430 that day, following which the U-Boat situation report showed an unusually heavy concentration in the Cape Verde islands 300 miles ahead. *Devonshire* now flew off her Walrus on an A/S search that evening but damaged a wing tip during recovery which rendered it unserviceable for the next two days. *Clan Campbell* straggled overnight due to engine defects but regained station by dawn.

The approach to a danger zone was felt throughout the ships, as the 9th Royal Lancers recorded, "near the Cape Verde islands the sea became flat and oily-looking..and by evening a commotion was on. A pack of U-Boats lay ahead..so once more all ranks were ordered to sleep in their clothes (we had to do so on the first four nights of the voyage).[24] Two V and W destroyers from Freetown joined as A/S escorts during the afternoon of the 11th when the convoy was 70 miles NE of the nearest of the Cape Verde islands, and close to the U-Boat report of the previous day. The course of SSE was continued to pass to the east of these islands. At 0704 on the 12th, in a position 200 miles west of Cap Vert in Senegal, *Devonshire* was relieved as ocean escort by her sister *Dorsetshire* which then continued as escort to Freetown where the convoy anchored within the harbour shortly after midday on th 14th. The Commodore reported an average speed of 11.73 knots from Gourock and complained that *City of Paris, Empress of Russia, Sarpedon* and *Almanzora* made bad smoke throughout, sometimes visible up to 30 miles distant, and although said to be due to bad coal on two of these ships, was a real danger to the convoy.[25] The C.O. of *Devonshire* said that *Mendoza* and *City of Paris* should not be included in 14 knot convoys.

The 23 ships and ocean escort of WS 12 reached Freetown on the same date as the outward OS 7 convoy of 41 ships. When added to the 21 ships of SL 87 due to sail next day for the UK, more than 87 ships were in that harbour requiring fresh water and bunkers of coal, oil or diesel. Nevertheless, most of the requirements of the transports were met within the space of five days, during which time they shipped 18,079 tons of Furnace oil, 2,605 tons of diesel, 4,783 tons of coal and 9,000 tons of fresh water: a grand total of over 34,000 tons delivered throughout that vast anchorage and was a considerable administrative achievement.

The Royal Lancers perhaps echoed the memories of all who visited Freetown at that time, i.e. "No one was allowed ashore and there was a daily issue of quinine. It was very hot and damp, but a relief to be free from the vibrations of the ship's engines. Our main amusement was to throw pennies into the water and watch the native boys diving down after them. The practice of wrapping a half-penny in silver paper was much deplored by the natives, who seemed to have acquired a remarkable vocabulary of the simpler English adjectives. There was a brisk trade between ships and shore - bananas and coconuts coming up in baskets while payment went back in the same baskets."[24]

The convoy sailed from Freetown at 1430 on 19 October without *Narkunda*, which fully disembarked at Freetown and being urgently required for further troop service, left on the 20th for the Clyde, spent seven days in Glasgow and sailed again in WS 12Z. One addition at Freetown was HMS *Ulster Monarch* on the same service as the two other channel ships which had come out directly in WS 12. The post of Vice Commodore was now transferred from *Duchess of Richmond* to Captain George Goold of *Empress of Canada*. Captain Bissett of *Franconia* remained as Rear Commodore. The cruiser *Devonshire* continued as ocean escort, while two V and W destroyers and three corvettes gave A/S cover for the first three days. Soon after clearing the searched channel, course had to be altered and evasive night alterations made due to the reported presence of submarines. No attacks materialized although post-war records show that *U 126*, which sank a ship near the convoy route on the morning of the 10th, then moved south to the Freetown approaches and sank two more ships in that area, one shortly before the convoy left harbour and another close to the convoy route next morning.

At 1830 on 21 October and 120 miles north of the equator, *Ulster Monarch* and *Royal Ulsterman* detached for Takoradi and *Prince Baudouin* for St. Helena. The two destroyers also left on that date to return to Freetown, followed next day by the corvettes. The convoy then settled down to a fair weather passage to the Cape and adopted a series of variable daily courses laid down by the Admiralty rather than steering a direct route.

There were no incidents on this passage and on the morning of the 30th the convoy split when the Commodore on *Strathaird* detached with *Dominion Monarch*, *Empress of Canada*, *Empire Pride*, *Leopoldville*, *Mendoza*, two MT ships and *Sarpedon* all for Capetown where they were berthed by early evening. The remaining seven transports and three MT ships continued for Durban under escort of the AMC *Derbyshire* which came out from Capetown that evening, met *Prince Baudouin* from St. Helena and joined up next morning. The convoy passed 60 miles south of Cape Agulhas, met and passed the AMC *Alcantara* near East London during the afternoon of 1st November, and were joined by Ellerman's *City of Hong Kong* at 0800 next morning. At 0930 *Ormonde*, *Franconia*, *Empress of Russia* and *Samaria* detached ahead at their maximum speed for Durban but when arriving off the Bluff at 1540 were refused entry and steered off to the NE to await instructions. The entire portion of WS 12 was berthed in Durban harbour next morning, 3rd November.

Back in Capetown the troops enjoyed four days of South African hospitality best described by 9th Royal Lancers: "In the evening we were allowed ashore into a town brilliantly lit, a town which welcomed every single one of us with open arms. Never has such hospitality been shown before as that which greeted us in South Africa. It seemed that everyone who owned a car was there at the dock gates ready to take us into their homes, to show us the town and the surrounding countryside. The next three days were complete joy after so long at sea. After the Brigade, less 10th Hussars, had marched through Capetown and the GOC Capetown had taken the salute, we fell out, had a bath, and spent the afternoon at the races. Our stay in that hospitable place was all too short, but many men, left firm friends behind them and resolved to return to South Africa after the war".[24]

On 4th November the Capetown ships (less *Sarpedon* which had sailed for Durban and Australia) left that port under escort of the AMC *Dunnottar Castle* and proceeded around the coast to join up with the Durban section. The Commodore on *Strathaird* was ordered on ahead to pick up mails in Durban and entered that harbour on the 7th, only to be directed to the Inner Anchorage where shore leave could not be given. The harbour was a hive of activity with every berth taken, *Mauretania* was in the drydock which had recently been vacated by *Nieuw Amsterdam* now allocated for the on-carriage of WS personnel to the Middle East. Only *Nova Scotia* of the smaller Indian Ocean type ships, with a capacity of 1,100, was available at Durban to assist with this movement, almost all others being engaged in the movement of Indian troops to Iraq.

Full details of the WS 12 transhipments in South Africa are not known, however, *Ormonde* and *Highland Brigade* terminated at Durban; the latter sailing on 4 November for the River Plate where she loaded meat for home, proceeding via Trinidad direct to Avonmouth to arrive there on 1st December, and next sailed in CT 10 to Halifax and onwards to the Plate for a further refrigerated cargo. *Ormonde* required 12 days repairs in Durban before sailing via Capetown to Freetown and being there used for a coastal trip to Takoradi, before returning to the Clyde on 28 December and next voyage in WS 16. From these two ships in Durban, there landed 2,188 for the Middle East and 1,352 for India and Iraq. Other known movements were 805 landed from *Duchess of Richmond*, *Empress of Canada* and *Dominion Monarch* for the Middle East, 10 for East Africa and 56 for India and Iraq. The numbers embarked leaving Durban are not known, except that *Nieuw Amsterdam* carried 4,305 which was 5% over her stated capacity.

As may be imagined, the warm hospitality received by the troops in Capetown was matched by those who called at Durban, and recorded by the history of 10 Hussars, "here we must pay a grateful tribute to the South Africans, who were kindness personified to the troops in the British convoys on their way to the war "up north". Dozens of attractive and smartly dressed young ladies assembled on the quayside to seize the Englishmen and take them off to see the high-lights of their gay and attractive city".[21] But the gaiety soon ended.

WS 12 sailed from Durban on 8 November comprising *City of Paris*, *Nieuw Amsterdam*, *Franconia*, *Samaria*, *Almanzora*, *Empress of Russia*, *Duchess of Richmond*, *Strathaird* and *Nova Scotia* plus three MT ships. Beyond visible range of the port, junction was made with *Dominion Monarch*, *Empress of Canada*, *Empire Pride*, *Leopoldville*, *Mendoza* and two MT ships from Capetown under escort of *Dunnottar Castle*. The onward ocean escort of WS 12 was now taken over by *Repulse* which had previously escorted WS 11 from the UK to Mombasa. The convoy was formed into six columns with Commodore Thesiger remaining on *Strathaird*.

No incidents were reported on the northward passage through the Mozambique Channel. At 0700 on 14 November, *Ascanius* joined from Mombasa and *Repulse* was relieved of the escort by *Revenge* which had left Mombasa the previous morning. *Repulse* then proceeded to Colombo to await the arrival of her consort *Prince of Wales*; war with Japan and the loss of these ships was barely three weeks ahead. WS 12 continued on a NE'ly course until the morning of the 17th when the convoy split in a position 350 miles south of Guardafui and where *Glasgow* was met. This cruiser then detached with *Empress of Canada, Dominion Monarch* and *Perseus* for Colombo and *Duchess of Richmond* for Bombay as convoy WS 12J. The route was through the Nine Degree Channel where the *Duchess* detached northwards and the others with *Glasgow* to Colombo, all reaching their destinations on the 23rd.

At Bombay the troops for Iraq immediately transhipped to smaller B.I type troopers and departed for Basra. The *Duchess* then loaded in Bombay and Capetown and proceeded via Trinidad to reach Liverpool on 18 January to be next employed in WS 16 back to Bombay. The remaining three ships left Colombo as Convoy WS 12V shortly after midday on the 24th, still escorted by *Glasgow*, and with Captain Goold of *Empress of Canada* acting as Commodore. When 200 miles west of the entrance to the Malacca Straits on the 26th, the three ship convoy met the cruiser *Dragon* escorting *Awatea* on passage from Hong Kong and Singapore for the UK, where she arrived on 18 January and was first emplpyed in WS 16. The cruisers exchanged charges and *Dragon* reached Singapore with WS 12V on the 28th, the same date as the Chiefs of Staff were reminded that operations "to forestall a Japanese landing in southern Siam, had to be ordered in time."[26] Amongst the troops which landed from WS 12 at Singapore were 88 and 137 Field Regiments, Royal Artillery.

The Japanese landings on Malaya began at 0100 local time on 8th December, coincident with their attack on Pearl Harbour. By that date both transports had disembarked at Singapore where *Dominion Monarch* was drydocked for overhaul and survey and where much of her main machinery was stripped for inspection. The wisdom of undertaking this work at such a critical time might well be questioned, however, the instructions had been issued earlier by the DoST who had to ensure docking facilities were available at the appropriate intervals to maintain these valuable liners in class, and to prevent excessive fouling of their bottoms with consequent loss of speed.

The first air raids on Singapore coincided with the attack on Malaya and caused the dock labour force to be withdrawn from the ship. Without main engines the *Dominion Monarch* would have fallen into Japanese hands, so the "Chief Engineer and ship's crew did a magnificent job in face of the greatest difficulties, when most people regarded her case as hopeless and the ship already doomed, and contrived to get her engines running so that she was able to clear the port before the end came."[27] *Dominion Monarch* left Singapore on 10 December for Auckland, where she loaded a full refrigerated cargo and proceeded home via Panama and New York to Liverpool, arriving on 19 February and next sailed in WS 17.

Empress of Canada spent four days in Singapore and sailed for Vancouver to be drydocked and overhauled at her home port but was instead directed with evacuated personnel to Sydney and Wellington, and thereafter proceeded via Panama to drydock at Newport News. This overhaul lasted nearly seven weeks, the *Empress* crossed in convoy NA 5 with *Orbita* from Halifax on 14 March and reached the Clyde eight days later to be next employed in WS 18. Amongst the personnel who crossed from Halifax in *Empress of Canada* were 2 Bn King's Shropshire Light Infantry who had gone out to the peacetime station of Jamaica in January 1939, were moved by destroyers to Curacao in May 1940 and to New York by US destroyers in February 1942; the voyage had lasted almost six months, *Dominion Monarch* had returned with a refrigerated cargo in under five months, while the two liners turned round in Durban, including *Highland Brigade* with a refrigerated cargo from the Plate, turned out a voyage time under three months.

In returning to the main body of WS 12 to the south of Guardafui on 17 November, these eleven transports and four MT ships continued northwards under escort of the battleship *Revenge*. Next day *Nieuw Amsterdam* was sent on ahead at her maximum speed of 20 knots to arrive at Aden the following afternoon. The convoy transited the Guardafui Strait during the almost moonless night of 18/19 November, and because a Vichy submarine was believed to be in the area, zigzagging was continued in daylight hours through the Gulf of Aden. The convoy arrived at Aden and was there dispersed by *Revenge* at 0600 on 20 November.

On account of continued enemy air attacks on Suez, it had become necessary to restrict the number of ships being handled in Suez Bay at any one time and for transports this was limited to two. The troopships in all arriving convoys were now held at Aden and sent on to Suez as independent sailings to arrive there as others left.

Of all the troops embarked on WS 12 for the Middle East, those comprising the main body of 1st Armoured Division, including 2 Armoured Brigade, were those most urgently required, and as the Headquarters of that Brigade were on *Empire Pride*, that ship and *Leopoldville* were the first to leave Aden on 21 November, followed next day by *Nieuw Amsterdam*. The short delay in starting these movements was due to the two *Queens* being at Suez on the last of a series of trips from Sydney with Australian troops. They had preceded WS 12 into the Gulf of Aden; *Queen Mary* sailed from Suez on the 23rd and passed *Strathaird* at high speed in the lower end of the Red Sea, *Queen Elizabeth* followed south a day later. *Leopoldville* had first gone to Massawa, so *Empire Pride* and *Nieuw Amsterdam* were handled at Suez on the 25th and 26th, followed by the others in sequence until *Nova Scotia* sailed again on 8 December on a return voyage to Durban. *City of Paris*, *Mendoza* and *Ascanius* were also retained on the Indian Ocean routes.

The troops of 12 Royal Lancers were the Divisional troops of 1 Armoured Division and the earliest into action. After collecting their modified and re-painted vehicles, they set out for the desert on 6 December and by the 15th came under command on 7 Armoured Division in pursuit of a then beaten enemy. The troops of 2 Armoured Brigade had first to undergo a period of intensive desert training, but later distinguished themselves either in 1st and 7th Armoured Divisions in all the battles throughout North Africa and Italy up to Argenta Gap in April 1945. The four MT ships of WS 12 had brought to the Middle East and discharged at Alexandria 236 tanks of three types, locomotives, stores, ammunition, guns and all manner of military vehicles.

The clearance of the large WS 12 liners from Suez was spread out for ten days from 27 November, when *Nieuw Amsterdam* and *Empire Pride* sailed, the former returning to Durban for continued service, with *Mauretania* and *Ile de France*, on the ferry service from that port to either Bombay or Suez, which they maintained until the latter half of 1942. *Empire Pride* had been completed without cargo space and proceeded via Port Sudan, Durban, East London, Capetown and Trinidad to the Clyde arriving 22 January to be next employed in WS 16. *Strathaird* left Suez on the last day of November, embarked Italian POW at Port Sudan for Mombasa, thence sailed via Durban,

Capetown and Trinidad to New York. Here she embarked U.S. troops who had now joined the war, and crossed in convoy AT 10, probably as a single ship, to Belfast Lough where she arrived on 25 January and disembarked by cross-channel steamers into Belfast city centre. Although not the first U.S. troops into Northern Ireland, they were the first to land at Belfast. *Strathaird* then proceeded to Liverpool and sailed again in WS 16.

The Belgian *Leopoldville* left Suez on 2 December, also embarked POW at Port Sudan for Mombasa and thereafter loaded there and at Dar-es-Salaam, Durban (including three weeks repairs) and Capetown, returning via Freetown to Liverpool on 19 February for her next sailing in WS 17. On 4 December *Empress of Russia* and *Franconia* sailed from Suez, the former coaling at Aden by the laborious hand basket method and then proceeding to Bombay for drydocking and exchange of crew. The first task could not be accommodated at that port but was achieved at Durban, before returning home via Capetown and Freetown (more coal and DG repairs) to reach the Clyde on 26 February and next sailed in WS 17.

Samaria and *Franconia* were two other liners of this convoy in need of drydocking which the DoST had arranged in Durban. *Franconia* first proceeded to Aden, crossed to Berbera and embarked there 1,435 Italian POW and 95 guard provided by the Kings African Rifles for Mombasa, and thereafter sailed for Durban to await her turn for the drydock. She then loaded at that port and Capetown, a total of 3,542 tons general and 3,914 bags of mail, and with 460 passengers aboard, left the latter port on 15 January for Freetown and there was ordered to Trinidad, ostensibly to avoid a homeward passage near the Biscay area where air attacks on shipping had intensified. After fuelling and watering, *Franconia* was delayed for six days due to generator repairs and during this period Captain Bissett was visited by the Cunard agent with a cable from head office ordering him ashore with his gear to "await further orders."[28] The Staff Captain took *Franconia* home to the Clyde and Glasgow KGV Dock on 24 February and sailed again in WS 17. From Trinidad Captain Bissett was flown to Key West where he took command of the *Queen Mary* in relief of Captain Townley who had reached retiral age.

The last departures from Suez were *Almanzora* and *Samaria* on 6 and 7 December; the former embarking the balance of West African troops in Berbera for West Africa, the latter taking Italian POW from Berbera to Mombasa. Both thereafter loaded in Durban and Capetown. *Samaria* spent three weeks drydocking and repairing in Durban and returned via Freetown to Liverpool on 18 February. *Almanzora* landed the West Africans at Takoradi, bunkered in Freetown and berthed in Glasgow to discharge at Meadowside on 1st February. Both were next engaged in WS 17.

Although the general shortage of personnel shipping lessened as the year 1942 progressed, it was never entirely eradicated. However, after sailing WS convoys as military operations for a year and a half, there were clear signs that these liners were everywhere being used to their best advantage with many examples of interlocking movements across the Atlantic and Indian Ocean and with drydockings and repairs being undertaken abroad on homeward voyages to help ease the burden on overstretched facilities in the UK.

WS 12X - sailed UK 30.10.41
The cordial response of President Roosevelt on 6 September 1941 to make US naval transports available for Churchill's quest to move another British division eastwards,

and for which British shipping could not be found, was readily accepted (see WS 12). The Prime Minister's earlier intention and request was for the movement of two divisions and it was still hoped that U.S. ships could achieve this by carrying 20,000 men on each of two round voyages. With this in view, the PM emphasised to the Chiefs of Staff the need to accelerate these movements and of a fast turnround in the east. The U.S. offer also provided ten or twelve fast cargo liners to carry the military hardware of these divisions; four had actually been sailing under the British flag since May (see WS 9A) and three others crossed the Atlantic with them in a special convoy in October to begin loading in the UK and sail with the WS convoy scheduled for December.

The division selected for the unknown eastern destination was the 18th, a second line Territorial infantry division formed in September 1939 by duplicating the first line 54 East Anglian Division. The 18th had served from the outset in various home commands with only one of its battalions having served in France and that on line of communication duties. In September 1941 the division was ordered abroad when mobilization began to prepare for embarkation towards the end of October.

To ease the shortage of troopships the plan was for British liners to carry the division across the Atlantic where they would transfer to waiting US naval transports. The American Neutrality Act permitted these transports to enter any port,[29] however, it also proved expedient to use British liners on the first leg as part of another major troop movement from Canada. Even more fortuitously at this time, the U.S. Navy had begun to escort Halifax convoys, both eastward and westward, between a position south of Newfoundland to the Mid Ocean Meeting Point (MOMP) south of Iceland, which greatly relieved the R.N. escort situation by having then to provide only for the section between the MOMP position and the Western Approaches.

Eight liners with a total capacity of 19,640 personnel were selected for the North Atlantic movement of which seven had been listed for WS 13 (later re-numbered 12Z) sailing at the end of October. Six of these ships reached UK ports between 10 and 20 October from previous WS convoys[30], while *Durban Castle* had been in Liverpool since 22 September after completing her homeward voyage in CF 2.[31] The eighth liner allocated was *Duchess of Atholl* which had been undergoing engine repairs in Glasgow and had lain idle at the Clyde Anchorage since 9 October.

Embarkation was carried out in Avonmouth on 27 October when the Divisional troops including 5 Bn The Loyals, then serving as a Reconnaissance Regiment, embarked on *Oronsay* which left next day for the Clyde Anchorage. Between the 27th and 29th, tenders from Gourock served the four liners embarking at the Clyde Anchorage, where 53 Brigade Headquarters with 5 and 6 Bns The Norfolk Regiment boarded *Duchess of Atholl* while 2 Bn The Cambridgeshire Regiment were allotted the Polish *Sobieski*. The HQ of 55 Brigade with 1/5 Bn Sherwood Foresters and 1 Bn The Cambridgeshires were on *Orcades* and 5 Bn Beds & Herts on *Durban Castle*. At Liverpool the HQ of 54 Brigade with 4 Bns The Norfolk and Suffolk Regiments were on *Andes*, 5 Bn Suffolks on *Reina del Pacifico* while *Warwick Castle* carried the divisional machine-gun battalion (9 R. Northumberland Fusiliers), Field Regiments of Artillery, Field Companies of Engineers, Signals units, etc.(32)

The four liners of the Clyde portion of CT 5 sailed at midnight on 30 October with Captain WS Brown of *Duchess of Atholl*, the only ship of the convoy experienced on the North Atlantic, acting as Commodore and Captain Charles Fox of *Orcades* as Vice Commodore. Escort was provided by the AA cruiser *Cairo* and six Town class destroyers with the SOE on *Newark*. The Liverpool section left the Mersey five hours earlier and were sighted by *Cairo* at 0700 next morning and by 1030 hours the convoy formed into three columns to the west of Orsay and proceeded out to the westward.[33]

The route of this convoy began much like the WS series proceeding due west for the first day until the morning of 1st November when the fairly new Hunt class destroyer *Badsworth* joined and the convoy turned to a WSW heading. At 0840 next morning a U.S. carrier borne aircraft made contact, and one hour later the Cargo convoy of seven US loaned cargo liners complete with a US naval escort was sighted, bound to the UK. The escorts of both convoys were now exchanged and by 1030 that morning, 2nd November, CT 5 was being screened by the battleship *New Mexico*, aircraft-carrier *Yorktown* (lost at Midway seven months later), cruisers *Philadelphia*, *Savannah* and nine destroyers. This exchange occurred 480 miles west of Donegal; the convoy then turned to a SW'ly course and *Andes* moved to station 13 to allow *Yorktown* to operate her aircraft from the rear centre. The US had certainly joined the war at sea.

The large US escort undoubtedly provided the troops with a feeling of additional security yet believing they were destined for the Middle East could not have imagined their immediate landfall would be in Canada. Fine weather was enjoyed throughout this passage; another eight US destroyers joined when the original nine were understood to be low on fuel. The convoy arrived safely and berthed within the harbour at Halifax, NS, on the morning of the 8th to find six US naval transports already berthed alongside. The eight liners of CT 5 spent five days in Halifax during which time they transhipped all of their troops to the US transports, were then cleaned, stored, fuelled, watered and re-embarked with 20,000 troops being the greater part of 5th Canadian Armoured Division. Together with the Dutch *Christiaan Huygens* having been drydocked for collision repairs at St Johns NB, and now embarked with a mere 80 RAF, all nine liners left Halifax as convoy TC 15 in the afternoon of 13 November and returned across the Atlantic with the same US escort as CT 5, to reach the Clyde and Liverpool on the 21st and 22nd; seven were able to sail with WS 14 just over two weeks later.

Meanwhile in Halifax, the three regiments and 53 Brigade HQ from *Sobieski* and *Duchess of Atholl* transhipped to *Mount Vernon*, those of 54 Brigade from *Andes* and *Reina del* to *Wakefield* and 55 Brigade troops to *West Point*. The Loyals from *Oronsay* moved across to *Leonard Wood* and the remaining divisional units were spread amongst *Orizaba* and *Joseph T Dickman*. The first named US transport had a tonnage similar to *Andes* and began life as the *America*; *Wakefield* and *Mount Vernon* equalled *Orcades* and all three had operated as passenger liners of the United States Lines with speeds of 18 to 24 knots, *Orizaba* was the eldest and slowest at 16 knots which compared to *Sobieski* at 15.5 knots being the slowest of CT 5.(34)

Once settled aboard the American transports, the troops found conditions quite different from the British trooping system. Instead of hammocks they were berthed in standee metal bunks several tiers high. The Foresters on *West Point* commented that "amenities were not very good, the ship being crowded, canteen facilities poor and dry, and the officers and crew lacking that degree of friendliness which later became such a feature of Anglo-American relations."[35] Contrary views were recorded by the Suffolks on *Wakefield*, whose battalions noted "that ship was their home for more than two months..a magnificent transport fitted to carry 4,600 troops which included the whole of 54 Brigade, 18 Divisional HQ and 148 Field Regiment. Few will forget the friendliness, kindness and efficiency of her officers and crew, particularly her Commander WK Scammell."[36] Subsistence of the British troops was paid for out of lend-lease funds, but all other expenses were on the US Navy. The troops were required to conform to US naval regulations in respect of berthing, drills and the absence of liquor on board.[37]

As a US convoy, WS 12X sailed from Halifax on 10 November while the CT 5 liners were still in port preparing to embark the Canadians for the UK. Escort was provided by the carrier *Ranger*, cruisers *Quincy*, *Vincennes* and eight destroyers, the latter having refuelled at Casco Bay in Maine while the transports were in Halifax. The convoy proceeded south for Trinidad and entered the Caribbean through the Mona Passage between Puerto Rico and the Dominican Republic. Fuelling was carried out at Trinidad between 17 and 19 November when the convoy began the long passage of twenty days to Capetown. The destroyers had insufficient endurance for this leg and so the US naval tanker *Cimarron* joined at Trinidad and subsequently refuelled them at sea, twice en route to the Cape and again on the return leg. When more than halfway across the South Atlantic the carrier *Ranger* was detached homeward with two destroyers as escort. The *Leonard Wood* fell behind for two days with boiler trouble but rejoined through the ingenuity of her engineers.

Three days after leaving Trinidad, the Admiralty advised WS 12X that the cruiser *Devonshire* had intercepted and sunk the German commerce raider *Atlantis* in the South Atlantic, some 300 miles north of the convoy's course. This was followed nine days later by *Dorsetshire* sinking the supply ship *Python* some distance to the SW of the convoy route, leaving four U-Boats in that area without support and their absolute need to return home.

Two days before reaching the Cape the convoy ran into a SE gale and "had to slow down and alter course as the destroyers could not take the punishment; before the gale was over, Japan had attacked Pearl Harbour and Malaya and was at war with the United States and the British Empire."[37] The convoy berthed in Capetown on 9 December and on this same date the next following convoy WS 12Z was only four days behind, while the next again, WS 14, was leaving the UK; all three convoys and their embarked personnel were to be much affected by events in the Far East.

The arrival of American transports at Capetown, complete with their own escorts, virtually at the moment of Japanese aggression, must have been viewed as more than coincidence. The Impcon staff noted the movement in great secrecy but were not deterred from "studying the cafeteria method of feeding the troops"[38] on the US transports. Nor were the troops denied the customary hospitality extended to visiting forces and best summed up by the Suffolks on *Wakefield*, "the troops received an outstanding welcome from local residents. Mornings were spent route marching and the rest of the day to sightseeing. At midday there were lines of cars at the docksde to give both officers and men their best ever holidays. The South African Premier Smuts welcomed the Anglo-American convoy in a speech while Major-General Beckwith-Smith, commander of 18th Division, thanked the Lord Mayor of Capetown and the S.A.Women's Auxiliary Services for their great share in reception of the men. He was in turn informed that the Capetown people were much impressed by the uniformly good behavior of the troops."[36]

WS 12X resumed its voyage by sailing from Capetown at 1600 hours on 13 December, with everyone depressed by news of the loss of *Repulse* and *Prince of Wales* off Malaya and with no information on their destination, most believed this would be Suez, although the US history claims this was originally given as Basra.[37] At this point the Admiralty assumed responsiblity for the escort when *Dorsetshire* joined from Simonstown at the outer end of the Capetown swept channel at 1730 hours, where the convoy formed into two columns with an A/S screen of six US destroyers; these parted company 24 hours later to return to Capetown and rejoin their cruisers.

Whilst the convoy was in Capetown the Chiefs of Staff decided to place 18 Division at the disposal of the CinC India, and on its sailing from the Cape decreed it "should be disembarked at Bombay and its destination settled later."[39] By 16 December the reverses and heavy losses in Malaya caused the CinC Far East to ask for immediate reinforcements to stem the Japanese advance and was advised these would include 18 Division, whose 53 Brigade (in one ship, i.e *Mount Vernon*), should proceed direct to Malaya.[39] These far reaching decisions reached *Dorsetshire* next day, 17th, as the convoy was about to enter the Mozambique Channel, and the destination was altered from Aden to Bombay. At the same time the cruiser *Ceres* was instructed to meet the convoy to the east of Mombasa on the 21st and detach with *Orizaba* into that port for fuel. This all went to plan and *Orizaba* arrived at Mombasa that evening.

Although no instructions were given to divert *Mount Vernon*, urgent deliberations were taking place between the Chiefs of Staff in London and the CinC Malaya Command, Lieut-General Percival, whose need for reinforcements became the more pressing almost day by day. WS 12X would reach Bombay on 27 December with the stores and equipment of 18 Division following in WS 12Z a week or more later. "The troops had been cooped up on the transports for almost two months and would need at least a week at Bombay to stretch their legs before going on to Malaya."[39] The alternative for 53 Brigade was to send *Mount Vernon* to Mombasa for fuel and then join a convoy leaving Durban on the 24th direct for Singapore, which was actually part of WS 12Z. Even although this would allow 53 Brigade troops only two or three days ashore at Mombasa and land them in Malaya without their guns and equipment, they would nevertheless arrive two weeks earlier than going via Bombay. The Chiefs of Staff approved this plan early on the 23rd and at 1045 that day, by which time the convoy was almost halfway across the Indian Ocean, *Mount Vernon* was detached and turned back to proceed independently to Mombasa, where she arrived on Christmas morning and by which date American approval had been given of her continuing to Singapore. This last section of the voyage is covered by her later inclusion in convoy WS 12Z.

With the departure of *Mount Vernon* from the convoy, the duties of Commodore were assumed by *West Point* and all four transports with *Dorsetshire* as escort continued towards Bombay without further incident. The Suffolks' history takes care to mention Christmas Dinner on *Wakefield* consisting of Roast Turkey, Braised Virginia Ham with candied carrots, Christmas Cake and other goodies; four years were to pass before the survivors of 18 Division were to see another Festive Dinner. When some 200 miles SW of Bombay on the morning of the 27th, the faster ships *West Point* and *Wakefield* were sent on ahead at maximum speed and berthed in the harbour that afternoon; *Dorsetshire* continued with the "*Wood* and *Dickman* where they arrived by 1730 hours when the cruiser berthed on the Alexandra Dock wall". *Dorsetshire* commented most favourably on the US Commodore on *Mount Vernon*, Captain DB Beary, as having "handled the convoy in a most efficient manner and gave me every assistance and co-operation...these duties later being carried out in the same manner by Captain FH Kelley of *West Point*."[40] In fact the entire voyage from the UK lasting 58 days had proved an early and glowing example of Anglo-American co-operation.

On arrival in Bombay, all the troops were disembarked and entrained 200 miles east, to the hot and dusty cantonment of Ahmednagar in the Deccan for two weeks intensive training and preparation for a destination then unknown. *Leonard Wood* and the *Joseph*

Dickman were released and returned to the States but *West Point* and *Wakefield* remained at anchor in the stream to await the onward movement of the two Brigades. On 1st January 1942 the Chiefs of Staff ordered that the whole of 18 Division should move at once to Malaya, but in practical terms this had to await the arrival of WS 12Z transports due in Bombay within the next week, which were also carrying reinforcements and most importantly the balance of 18 Division stores and equipment. Their onward movement is related with that of convoy WS 12Z.

WS 12Z - sailed UK 12.11.41

This convoy originally scheduled to sail at the end of October 1941 was to be numbered WS 13 though sensibly changed to 12Z, and by mid September 21 transports were listed for inclusion with a total personnel capacity of 43,024. Within two weeks seven of these liners had departed in CT 5 with 18 Division for Halifax, while seven others were delayed for one reason or another and unable to make the sailing date despite this being postponed until 10 November. Two of the latter group had been required for a Halifax trip with RAF trainees from which *Tamaroa* continued to the Plate to load homewards and was not again available for WS service until March 1942. Similarly *Rangitata* went off on a trooping voyage to Gibraltar and West Africa and also went on to the Plate for a meat cargo. *Ruahine* was rejected due to her low speed of 12 knots while *Christiaan Huygens* from WS 8B did not reach the UK until late November, and *Awatea* from Hong Kong and Vancouver in January. *Cameronia* was brought home especially from WS 10 at Durban and was in Glasgow by 17 October but required five weeks voyage repairs.

Of the seven liners remaining from the original allocation, *Empress of Asia* was in Liverpool from 28 September for extensive voyage repairs, all the others arrived between 12 and 24 October: *Capetown Castle, Duchess of Bedford, Monarch of Bermuda* and *Mataroa* in Liverpool and *Aorangi* and *Arundel Castle* in Glasgow. Later allocations were *Orduna* which arrived in Liverpool on 12 October from WS 8B, *Empress of Japan* to the Clyde Anchorage from Vancouver on the 21st and a late arrival, *Narkunda*, returned from WS 12 at Freetown which berthed in Glasgow on 2 November. Although the latter ship was turned around within nine days and *Arundel Castle* in less than three weeks, most of these liners required four weeks in the UK, partly the result of blackout restrictions and the general shortage of labour, materials and shiprepair facilities.

One feature which had evaporated from the preparation of these liner convoys was the many acrimonious exchanges which had previously taken place between the War Office demands for personnel berths and the inability due to shipping shortages of the MOWT to meet them. There were indications in September 1941, however, that the problem remained and that it had reached the Prime Minister's hearing. On the 14th he sent a note to the Chiefs of Staff deprecating RAF demands for additional groundcrews being asked for the Middle East and reaffirming that only 20,000 "can be accommodated in the convoys up to the end of December", that the US ships of 12X were "for complete divisions only and cannot be used for details and drafts", that priority troops for India "should be Anti-Tank and Anti-Aircraft artillery" and that additional drafts for Eighth Army in the desert "should fit in as convenient."[41] Clearly the shortage of personnel shipping was still prevalent.

Embarkation of the ten liners was carried out between 10 and 12 November on those previously named in Liverpool, three in Glasgow and *Empress of Japan* at the Clyde

Anchorage. The total declared on the sailing telegram was 21,767[42] which included 85 Anti-Tank and 35 Light AA Regiments believed to be on *Narkunda* and 6 Heavy AA Regiment. The majority of those embarked must have been drafts and details for all three Services but mostly Army. Most significantly at this date 49% of the total number were destined for Iraq; evidence of the recent occupation of that country and neighbouring Iran by British and Soviet forces in forestalling Axis designs on the oilfields and in meeting a southerly thrust towards Suez.

One feature which persisted with embarkations was the almost inevitable numbers beyond stated capacities which had previously been highlighted with WS 5A and B. WS 12 had sailed with 385 empty berths while 12Z was 105 over, and seemed to be a problem which could not be entirely resolved, especially when the embarkation process was necessarily conducted in a relatively brief peiod with numerous units arriving from establishments throughout the UK.

Five MT ships were sailing with the convoy of which *Adrastus* (Blue Funnel), *Sussex* (Federal) and *Empire Star* loaded in Liverpool while *Deucalion* (Blue Funnel) and Dutch *Abbekerk* were handled in Glasgow. The NZS liner *Rimutaka* with passengers and general cargo for Australia and New Zealand, also loaded in Glasgow and was included in the convoy for protection purposes as far as South Africa.

The three transports from Glasgow came downriver fully embarked and followed by *Abbekerk* in the late afternoon of 11 November and joined *Empress of Japan*, *Deucalion* and *Rimutaka* at the Clyde Anchorage. The appointed Commodore was MC Goldsmith DSO, RNR aboard *Narkunda*, whose P&O Master, Commander Malcolm Draper RNR from Hastings, had served on the ship during her past five voyages and was now approaching retirement. The Vice Commodore was with the Liverpool section, Captain WG Busk-Wood on *Duchess of Bedford*, who led these ships out past the Bar Light Vessel at 1530 on the 12th to make rendezvous with the Clyde section which *Narkunda* led out of the boom just before midnight. The Liverpool section was escorted by two V and W destroyers and the Clyde section by the Tribal class *Maori* who also carried S.O. A/S escort. No AA escort was attached to the convoy as an indication of the much reduced enemy air activity in the Western Approaches, due to heavier commitments of the Luftwaffe on the Russian front. Ocean escort was being provided by the battleship *Royal Sovereign* in furtherance of a plan to station all four of that class in the Indian Ocean, recently confirmed in an Admiralty meeting with the Prime Minister on 20 October. On account of their low endurance, *Royal Sovereign* would first be fuelled at Milford Haven and join the convoy thereafter to the south and west of Ireland.

The convoy set off in cloudy though fine weather with a light NE'ly wind and no hint of adverse conditions later. Both portions passed the Mull of Kintyre at 0615 on the 13th where two columns were continued until reaching Orsay at 0900 and here the convoy began to form into a broad front of five columns.[43] This was completed by 1030 when a WNW'ly course was set at a speed of 14 knots. During the forming up process the three destroyers returned to Derry for fuelling on relief by *Vanquisher* and four of the Hunt class; the original three rejoined at 1600 and at 1730 when 10 miles clear of soundings, course was altered to the SW, much sooner than usual, which proved a further indicator that enemy air activity was almost extinct in that area.

The weather continued clear with a freshening southerly wind throughout the 14th which reached force 6 next day and by the 16th veered to become gale force 8 from the WNW with occasional squalls of rain and sleet. This was right on the beam with heavy seas and set all ships rolling heavily, causing miserable conditions throughout the overcrowded and frequently claustrophobic troopdecks. Few if any of the troops had ever crossed the English Channel let alone be exposed to the rigours of the North Atlantic. There were no portholes, and ventilation came from the open access hatches which had to be closed at night when the ships were darkened. "Arrangements for those who succumbed to seasickness consisted of 40 gallon drums which slid about the deck with unpleasant splashings. Sanitary arrangements were, as usual inadequate."[44]

One of the old V and W destroyers detached home at midday on the 15th with condenser trouble; two of the Hunts left next morning and the remaining two V and W at 1800 hours that evening, leaving the escort to *Maori* and two Hunts. However, an hour later, *Royal Sovereign* joined from Milford Haven as SO Ocean Escort with three F class destroyers as additional A/S screen. The convoy was now steering SSW towards the Azores, being 400 miles to the north of these islands and 600 miles west of Finisterre. The battleship took station between columns 3 and 4 while the wind backed southerly and continued at gale force overnight with heavy rain squalls during which time "the convoy became disorganised but reformed at daylight."[45] Speed had steadily reduced in the worsening weather until 10 knots proved to be the maximum possible.

A southerly course was maintained throughout the 17th while the gale from that direction continued until evening. A man was washed overboard from one of the Hunt class destroyers that afternoon and was not recovered. *Adrastus* had to heave-to during the forenoon to secure cargo which had broken adrift and was left to catch up as able but did not achieve this until three days later. By midday the convoy was 270 miles north of Sao Miguel; at 1600 *Maori* was detached to Gibraltar and at 1900 the two Hunts, *Southwold* and *Dulverton*, were sent on ahead to refuel at Ponta Delgada and rejoin later.

The convoy passed through the 75 mile wide eastern passage of the Azores between Terceira and Sao Miguel during the forenoon of the 18th without incident or sighting reports of any kind. Course was then altered to SSE to pass between Cap Vert and the Cape Verde Islands. The Hunt class destroyers rejoined next morning relieving the three F class fleet units which detached to oil at a rendezvous from the RFA *Dingledale*. This facility was provided also for *Royal Sovereign* but now confirmed her ability to reach Freetown without refuelling. The F class destroyers did not rejoin.

No incidents occurred on the four day leg to the Cape Verdes. Two of the V and W destroyers of the Freetown Local Escort Force joined at 1800 on the 21st and the corvette *Clover* next morning by which time the convoy was 120 miles east of the island group. Course was now altered to a point SW of Bathurst and thereafter by keeping that distance off the coast until west of Freetown. During the 22nd it became evident that arrival before dark on the 24th was marginal but when advised the latest acceptable time, the attempt had to be abandoned. Next day, the 23rd, a signal from the CinC instructed the convoy to be split into fast and slow sections. By this means *Narkunda*, both *Empress* liners, *Monarch of Bermuda*, the two *Castle* liners, *Duchess of Bedford*, *Empire Star*, *Sussex* and *Royal Sovereign* detached at 1500 with the two Hunts and *Velox* as escort and proceeded ahead at 16 knots. Overnight *Empress of Asia* dropped astern with *Velox* as escort; the remainder of the fast section led by the battleship entered Freetown at 1520 that day, followed by *Empress of Asia* three hours later. The slow section of five ships with *Clover* and *Vimy* had followed at 13 knots and arrived on the morning of the 25th.

Freetown was not then unusually busy, a homeward SL convoy had left five days earlier and the next outward one was not due until the 28th when WS 12Z would be leaving. The transports requirements were not exceptional, 17,500 tons of Furnace oil,

5,900 tons of diesel and 2,500 tons of coal for *Empress of Asia*. On account of the fresh water problems, all ships were instructed to ship only the minimum at Freetown, or would otherwise delay the convoy; only 2,100 tons was ordered of which half was for *Duchess of Bedford* and yet the Commodore found it necessary to comment that fresh water supplies were the main problem. The laborious business of coaling *Empress of Asia* was not completed as the convoy left harbour but she sailed two hours later and caught up as darkness fell.

WS 12Z was led out of the Freetown boom just before 1500 on 28 November by *Narkunda*, followed by *Royal Sovereign* and the two Hunt class destroyers with *Milford*, all continuing to the Cape. The previous cruising order of five columns was formed by 1710 when the convoy set a course of SSW and worked up to a speed of 12 knots.

It was evident that both this convoy and the US ships of WS 12X would be around the Cape at the same time, and as it may have been desirable, with America still neutral, to prevent their meeting, the British convoy was to be handled entirely in Durban rather than the original plan to split it between that port and Capetown where 12X was berthed. It was envisaged that neither *Royal Sovereign* nor the smaller escorts were capable of this passage without refuelling, and so arrangements were made for an oiler to be available for this purpose at Pointe Noire in French Equatorial Africa.

Rather than follow the more direct route to the Cape, WS 12Z had perforce to keep about 100 miles off the Liberian coastline until reaching Cape Palmas, and then set a course almost directly for Pointe Noire, five days distant. Speed was reduced to 9.6 knots to make a pre-arranged rendezvous on 6 December. *Royal Sovereign* left the convoy in the evening of the 2nd, proceeded ahead at 17 knots and anchored in the bay close north of Pointe Noire at 0745 on the 5th. The Anglo Saxon tanker *Bullmouth* berthed alongside "and considerable difficulty was experienced owing to the swell. If conditions had been only slightly worse oiling alongside would have been impracticable and a very awkward situation would have arisen as *Bullmouth* was not fitted for oiling at sea."[45] The Hunt class destroyers were simultaneously oiled from the other side of *Bullmouth* and all ships completed by 1900, when, again due to the swell, the tanker had some difficulty in getting away from *Royal Sovereign*, but the warship was underweigh and proceeded at 2030 to rejoin the convoy which was standing off 75 miles to the westward.

Royal Sovereign and the two Hunts relieved *Milford* and the two corvettes at 0640 on the 6th, which in turn were refuelled at Pointe Noire and rejoined 24 hours later in a position 85 miles SW of the port. A southerly course was then set towards the Cape. The difficulties experienced in oiling in the wide open bay at Pointe Noire, which provided a bottom clearance of only 10 ft. on account of the swell which forms heavy rollers, was not repeated.

By the 10th December as the convoy approached the latitude of Walvis Bay and 2,500 miles short of Durban, it became clear that the corvettes and Hunt class destroyers could not make the distance without refuelling at Simonstown, which required *Royal Sovereign* to break W/T silence to arrange the necessary relief escorts. By the 13th the convoy was 180 miles west of Cape Columbine, the peacetime landfall of shipping from Europe, and here the wind began to freshen from the west and by next day reached gale force which repeated the heavy rolling and misery in the troopdecks experienced on the first leg of the voyage.

The convoy maintained a distance of 130 miles from both the Cape of Good Hope and Agulhas during the nights of the 13th and 14th and at 1400 on the 15th the relief corvettes joined and allowed the Hunts and corvette pair to detach for Simonstown. The convoy was now 170 miles SE of Agulhas and maintained a similar distance off Cape St. Francis before shaping up towards the coast of Natal on the 16th. The gale continued from astern but moderated next morning and died away during the 17th. At midnight *Royal Sovereign* and *Milford* proceeded ahead and berthed in Durban harbour next morning. The convoy with the two corvettes began to arrive an hour later but a further deterioration of the weather during the day and congestion in the harbour caused 12 of the 16 ships having to anchor outside. The Commodore reported that *Narkunda*, *Orduna*, *Duchess of Bedford* and *Empress of Japan* were compelled to leave the outer anchorage that night and proceed to sea for an expected gale which never developed, even causing *Milford* to be sent out to protect them and leaving half her crew ashore. These liners spent a calm starlit night cruising up and down the coast but were all berthed alongside within the harbour next morning.[46] The distance steamed from Freetown to Durban was recorded as 5,215 miles over 19 days 12.5 hours at an average speed of 11.13 knots.

If previous WS convoys had reached Durban in momentous times it was nothing compared to WS 12Z on 18 December 1941. Both Britain and the U.S. were now at war with Japan, whose invading armies in Malaya had reached Penang and within six weeks would be at the causeway leading to Singapore Island. The diversion of some ships from both convoys and from WS 14 then nearing Freetown must have seemed inevitable. With ten transports in port, most with units for transhipment to as yet unknown destinations still being decided in London, the difficulties were considerable. *Nieuw Amsterdam* was nominated for on-carriage to Suez, also *Indrapoera*, *Aronda* and *Eastern Prince* of the Indian Ocean class for any destination to allow the planned turnround of *Mataroa*, *Aorangi* and *Arundel Castle*. It was probable that *Empess of Asia* would be retained in the Indian Ocean and proved to be a prophetic statement from the Director of Operations at the Admiralty.[47] The congestion was increased further on the 22nd when *Franconia* and *Leopoldville* from WS 12 arrived to await drydocking on their homeward voyages.

The embarkation arrangements of WS 12Z in the UK were first intended to allow *Mataroa* to turnround at Durban, *Arundel Castle*, *Empress of Asia* and *Orduna* to proceed to Suez, *Capetown Castle*, *Duchess of Bedford*, *Empress of Japan*, *Monarch of Bermuda* and *Narkunda* to Bombay and *Aorangi* to Singapore. With embarkation complete the destination of *Narkunda* was changed to Singapore, and on 18th November when the convoy was halfway to Freetown, four other changes were made to allow *Capetown Castle* to continue to Singapore, *Aorangi* and *Arundel Castle* to turnround at Durban while *Narkunda* was to revert to her original destination of Bombay. On completion at Singapore, *Capetown Castle* was then to proceed to New Zealand to load for the UK while *Mataroa* was similarly to load in the Plate. These arrangements with the transhipment and on-carriage plans from South Africa were made prior to the outbreak of hostilities in the Far East.

On the day prior to arrival in Durban, the D of ST in London signalled the Impcon staff in Durban with several changes in the arrangement for ships and personnel. For the ships it meant *Monarch of Bermuda* and *Empress of Asia* would turn at Durban (in addition to *Mataroa* and *Arundel Castle* above), *Duchess of Bedford* and *Empress of Japan* would terminate as planned at Bombay with three of the MT ships, as would *Capetown Castle* rather than continue to Singapore. *Narkunda* and *Aorangi* with the two remaining MT ships would proceed to Bombay with a possible diversion to

Singapore. In respect of personnel, however, vast changes now reflected the changing situation in Malaya with 5418 for that destination rather than 295 as first intended, 2374 for India instead of 1283, and 3169 for the Middle East rather than 8077 as at embarkation. The confusion continued when a further signal 18 hours later reduced the number for Malaya to 3838; this was received in the evening prior to arrival of the convoy. *Narkunda* and *Aorangi* were to carry all these personnel and proceed direct to Singapore with the two MT ships; *Indrapoera* and *Johan de Witt* would now be surplus for these movements and were to be used for personnel from South Arica to the Middle East. The details of transhipment for Middle East and India personnel, a not inconsiderable task, was left to the small Impcon staff in Durban, whose Lieut. Col. FL Carroll subsequently reported in October 1944, "Never had our Staff Officers known so many changes of destinations, of units on board. These changes continued to come in from London up to three hours before arrival of the convoy. We had then been working 48 hours without sleep planning the convoy and tearing up the plan and movement orders as changes took place. The last major alterations which arrived by immediate signal from London, was concluded by message from the Director of Movements to the effect that it was appreciated that these last minute alterations gave us an almost impossible task to achieve, but having regard to the gravity of the Far Eastern position, he knew we would do all in our power to get the convoys through as directed...It was an irony of fate that the hard work we put in to tranship so many men and stores to the Far East, should have resulted in tragedy, for all fell into Japanese hands."(*WS 14 q.v.*)[48]

In accordance with instructions, four ships were emptied in Durban but none was ready to leave until 23 December, on which date the revised convoy would also have sailed, had it not been prevented from doing so by a SW'ly gale which prevented movements after the first ten ships had sailed. Next day *Mataroa* sailed for the Plate and *Monarch of Bermuda* for Liverpool via Capetown and Trinidad, arriving in the Mersey on 21 January for a subsequent departure in WS 16; *Mataroa* returned via Trinidad and Bermuda to Glagow on 21 February, discharged at Plantation Quay and next sailed in WS 17. *Arundel Castle* was delayed in Durban for two weeks engine repairs and loaded home on her owners' berth at Port Elizabeth and Capetown, returning via Freetown to Liverpool on 18 February for next employment in WS 17. *Empress of Asia* as had been indicated was retained at Durban for Indian Ocean service and after a few days repairs was ready to sail with WS 14 (*q.v.*)

With transhipment and fuelling complete the revised convoy with *Nieuw Amsterdam*, *Indrapoera*, *Eastern Prince* and *Aronda* replacing the ships left behind, formed up by 1030 on Christmas Eve outside Durban with *Royal Sovereign* continuing as ocean escort. *Nieuw Amsterdam*, *Orduna*, *Aronda* and *Eastern Prince* comprised the port column bound for Suez; *Narkunda*, *Aorangi*, *Abbekerk* and *Sussex* the starboard column for Singapore with the remaining ships for Bombay in the two centre columns.[49] The Commodore, Vice Admiral Goldsmith, was now aboard *Capetown Castle*, the Vice Commodore now Captain JV Langford of *Orduna* and the Rear Commodore, Captain Draper of *Narkunda*.

The convoy set off to the eastward until 1600 when course was altered to NE towards the Mozambique Channel. The SOE reported there was some difficulty "making good the required speed of 12.5 knots owing to minor breakdowns in *Orduna*, *Aorangi* and *Eastern Prince*, and to the loss of a man overboard from *Duchess of Bedford*."[45] This was an RAF fitter which occurred in the early hours of Boxing Day when the convoy was abreast of Inhambane. *Empress of Japan* and *Empire Star* both fell astern and carried out an unsuccessful search while *Indrapoera* turned a complete circle on the impression that *Empire Star* had engine trouble. The convoy passed to the west of the Comoro Islands in the early evening of the 28th, and at 1000 on the 30th, when 370 miles due east of Mombasa, the cruiser *Emerald* joined with the US transport *Mount Vernon*, which had been waiting in that port since Christmas Day. The starboard column of four ships then detached with *Emerald* and *Mount Vernon* for Singapore as convoy DM 1 (Durban/Malaya), and this passage is taken up later.

The main convoy WS 12Z comprising four liners each for Suez and Bombay, plus the three MT ships, continued ahead with *Royal Sovereign*, until 0900 on the 31st when the cruisers *Cornwall* and *Colombo* were met with the US transport *Orizaba* (ex WS 12X) from Mombasa. At this point the Suez ships continued as WS 12ZA with *Colombo* as escort towards Guardafui, while *Royal Sovereign* and *Cornwall* detached with the eight ships for Bombay as WS 12ZB. Off Aden on 4th January the Suez ships were dispersed to proceed independently; all left that port next day and were handled at Suez between the 8th and 16th. *Orduna* embarked Italian POW at Berbera on the 19th, bunkered at Aden, landed the POW at Mombasa and Dar-es-Salaam and thereafter loaded in Durban and Capetown reaching the Clyde in SL 101 from Freetown on 8 March. Her next trip was to Iceland. The other three ships were retained on Indian Ocean service.

Four hours after detaching the Suez portion, *Royal Sovereign* detached from 12ZB to proceed to the Seychelles for fuel and was retained as the second of the R class battleships on the Indian Ocean. *Ramillies* was to follow with WS 14 and *Resolution* with WS 15. No incidents were reported by WS 12 ZB on the passage to Bombay which was accomplished in fine weather at an average speed of 13.4 knots. The Commodore on *Capetown Castle* led the eight ships into Bombay harbour at 1000 on 6th January to find the US transports *West Point* and *Wakefield* already at anchor; all ships now awaited orders while 12 smaller ships were embarked with 44 Indian Brigade plus the MT and stores for 18 Division now destined for Malaya. These smaller personnel and store ships sailed on the 8th and reached Singapore on the 25th, and before continuing the liner voyages from Bombay, it is necessary to revert to those of DM 1 which detached east of Mombasa on Christmas Day 1941.

Not a great deal is known about the passage of DM 1, other than it passed north of the Seychelles and proceeded on an easterly course to Port T, i.e. Addu Atoll at the southern tip of the Maldives Group where refuelling was carried out about 9-10th January, and where the escort was strengthened by the cruisers *Exeter* and *Durban*, the RIN sloop *Jumna*, and Dutch cruiser *De Ruyter*. From Addu Atoll there was an easterly passage of almost 2,000 miles to the Sunda Strait between Sumatra and Java, and whence through that Strait, then Banka, Berhala and Durian Straits, Singapore was approached from the south by that route over a distance of 572 miles by maintaining the maximum possible distance from Japanese aircraft now established in southern Malaya. The disadvantage of this route was that some of the channels were sufficiently narrow as to restrict manoeuvring in the event of an air attack, but clearly the alternative approach by the Malacca Strait, now overlooked by the Japanese, was not feasible.

In the approach to Sunda Strait, guarded by the giant crater of Krakatoa, two British and one Australian destroyer strengthened the escort and although air attacks were expected throughout the passage of the four straits leading to Singapore, none materialized until the convoy was split on 13 January in the port approaches where *Mount Vernon* and *Sussex* were directed to the naval base in Johore Strait. "A heavy rain squall fortunately blew up as the ships were dividing and spoiled the aim of a squadron of

Japanese bombers which came in to attack them. The bombs fell harmlessly between the two sections of the convoy."[50] *Mount Vernon* disembarked the troops of 53 Brigade, who were quickly thrown into the fighting in Johore without even the opportunity to unpack, while the ship sailed for Suez where she assisted in the movement of Australian troops via Colombo to Australia, before proceeding to San Francisco. The MT ship *Sussex* discharged 54 crated Hurricanes, the guns of an Anti-Tank and AA Regiment, ammunition and stores all by the ship's company as the native dock labour had disappeared, in the space of five days and nights and thereafter sailed for Australia. The remaining ships of DM 1 were handled in Keppel Harbour, from where *Aorangi* and *Narkunda* sailed on the 16th by way of the Straits route to Fremantle. *Aorangi* thereafter loaded in Sydney and returned by Panama and convoy NA 6 from Halifax to Glasgow on 28 March, being next employed in WS 18. Both ships had carried evacuees to Australia; *Narkunda* returned from Fremantle to Durban for drydocking and was then used for an on-carriage trip to Bombay and did not return to the UK until May.

There now remained the five transports and three MT ships which had arrived in Bombay on 6 January as WS 12ZB. The transports appear to have disembarked, following which *Indrapoera* (which had landed 1,388 destined for Basra) then re-embarked 1,192 and sailed with *Nevasa* and *City of London* on the 11th for that same port. A further series of sailings were made by other ships of the Indian Ocean class to clear all those bound for Iraq. *Capetown Castle* left Bombay on the 17th for Colombo, Fremantle and Sydney, loaded a full cargo in Auckland and returned home via Panama and convoy NA 6 from Halifax to reach Liverpool on 28 March for further service in WS 18. The US transport *Orizaba* returned to the eastern seaboard of the U.S. via the Cape.

Re-embarkation now began on *Duchess of Bedford* and *Empress of Japan* of the troops who had landed in Bombay for exercise and of other reinforcements for Malaya, in addition to those of 54 and 55 Brigades who returned from two weeks at Ahmednagar to *Wakefield* and *West Point* respectively. Together with *Empire Star* carrying a light tank squadron and AA Batteries (*Abbekerk* had gone to Basra) all five ships sailed from Bombay on 19 January as convoy BM 11. Escort was provided by the cruiser *Caledon* until the 24th, when relieved by *Glasgow*, *Durban* and *Dragon*. On the 27th when entering the Sunda Straits, *Glasgow* was relieved by *Exeter* and four destroyers.

BM 11 was essentially the final leg of the WS voyages of two British and two U.S. naval transports, estimated to be carrying 17,000 troops including the two brigades to complete 18 British Division in Malaya. As the convoy began its passage of the Straits on the 17th, the Japanese had reached Muar less than 90 miles from Singapore Island whose defence now gained the highest priority. The destination of the troops was made known whenever the ships left Bombay and pamphlets on jungle warfare distributed amongst them. Despite the depressing news from Malaya, spirits remained high and as the ships turned into the scenic confines of Banka Strait on the morning of the 28th, they were spotted by a single aircraft which dropped six bombs without result. The convoy had then formed into the single line of *Exeter*, leading *West Point*, *Electra*, *Wakefield*, *Encounter*, *Duchess of Bedford*, *Express*, *Empire Star*, *Danae*, *Empress of Japan* and *Durban* in the rear. That night the three fastest ships (*West Point*, *Wakefield* and the *Empress*) were sent on ahead and next day, 29 January, the convoy reached Singapore where the troops of 54 and 55 Brigades disembarked from *Wakefield* and *West Point* respectively to be taken by MT to tented camps; within a matter of days they were in positions holding the line from Changi to Seletar and were under a gruelling, though short lived baptism of fire two weeks later. *Duchess of Bedford* landed 4,000 Indian reinforcements and 40 Nurses then embarked 875 women and children for evacuation to Batavia; the *Empress* also embarked 1,200 evacuees. All but three of the escorts which brought the liners into Singapore, were lost in the Battle of the Java Sea one month later.

The liners were less than two days in Singapore, during which time there were frequent air raids when the British liners suffered slight damage above the waterline due to fragments and bullets. *Wakefield* was struck by a bomb which killed all in the sick bay, temporary repairs were first made whence that ship and *West Point* proceeded to Batavia from where they departed on 1st February; *Wakefield* returning to the U.S. via the Cape. The return of *West Point* was delayed, despite the crisis of Pearl Harbor and American needs in the Pacific, by a British request to assist with the urgent movement of Australian troops to that country from the Middle East.

Although both the CPS *Duchess* and *Empress* left Singapore on 31 January with evacuees, the former for Batavia (now Djakarta) and latter for Colombo, it is not known whether any were landed at these ports; others may have been embarked as both ships were reported congested with women and children when they reached Durban from Colombo. Both loaded on the Ellerman berth at Durban and Capetown, where the *Empress* transferred excess numbers to *Letitia* of WS 15 and sailed direct to Liverpool arriving on 18 March. The *Duchess* left Capetown eleven days later and proceeded via Freetown to reach Liverpool on 2 April. Both were next employed in WS 18.

Considering the Japanese mastery of the air space around Singapore and that their forces had virtually reached the Johore Strait as the four large transports sailed from the port, it was somewhat remarkable that none of these great liners suffered loss or major damage and contrasted severely with the fate awaiting the troops on shore.

Chapter 13

WS 14 and WS 15
Final Reinforcements for the Far East

WS 14 - sailed UK 8.12.41

In the four weeks since the previous convoy sailed on 13 November, there had been a significant improvement on the Allied fronts in the Western Desert and Russia. The 8th Army's Crusader offensive not only relieved Tobruk but set in motion the withdrawal of Rommel's Afrika Corps back to Tripolitania. In Russia the Panzer Armies were halted within 20 miles of Moscow on 27 November and a week later began to withdraw to winter positions; an immediate counter attack by the Red Army pushed them back 150 miles, and stabilised that front. The Caucasus front leading to Middle East oil remained a grave threat; the Russians appealed for twenty or more British divisions to help, to which Churchill and the Chiefs of Staff had considered sending the 50th (then moving into Iraq) and 18th due at the Cape on 9 December,[1] but later decided both might be needed to pursue the war in the desert. However, the good news from the desert and Russia was shattered during the later stages of embarkation on WS 14 by the simultaneous Japanese attacks on Pearl Harbour, Hong Kong, Siam and Malaya throughout the evening of 7 December, and later caused much diversion and transhipment of many units on this convoy.

As with the previous four convoys, planning for WS 14 began two months before the scheduled sailing date at the end of November, and once again less than half the ships listed were able to be included; five being late in reaching UK ports from previous WS convoys and four delayed in fitting-out for trooping.[2] Seven replacements were found from the eight liners of TC 15 which returned to the UK from Halifax on 21 November. Four others were found from *Cameronia* which had been unable to complete repairs in time to sail with WS 12Z, *Highland Princess* and *Highland Monarch* which both reached Avonmouth in the first week of November and the newly fitted ex AMC *Esperance Bay*, which, despite the blitz, had been converting in London since August and only arrived at the Clyde Anchorage on 3 December in sufficient time for embarkation. The sailing date was scheduled for 6 December with a convoy of 16 transports and 11 MT ships; seven of the transports were destined for Suez, five for Bombay, two for Singapore, one for Durban and *Abosso* as on previous voyages to West Africa.

Embarkation was carried out on the two *Highland* ships at Avonmouth on 4 December; both sailed next morning with the American loaned MT ship *Empire Widgeon* from Newport and proceeded to the Clyde Anchorage where all were berthed during the afternoon of the 6th. At the same time the transports *Abosso, Scythia, Reina del Pacifico* and *Orcades* arrived fully embarked from Liverpool with the MT ships *City of Pretoria, Empire Condor* and *Empire Curlew*; the latter two also being American loaned, and were joined at the anchorage by five other MT ships which had loaded in Glasgow, i.e. *Clan Cameron* and four other American loaned: *Empires Oriole, Pintail, Fulmar* and *Peregrine* making eight of these invaluable fast cargo liners generously made available to meet our greatest need.

Eight of the transports were embarking on the Clyde, all except *Esperance Bay* had completed their previous voyages or were undergoing repairs or fitting in Glasgow but could not be embarked there simultaneously. On the last day of November *Strathallan* moved downriver to embark at the Clyde Anchorage, allowing *Cameronia* to occupy and embark at No. 1 KGV Dock, which liner in turn moved to the anchorage on the 3rd and allowed *Athlone Castle* to embark at that berth and move to the anchorage during the afternoon of the 8th. *Durban Castle, Warwick Castle, Duchess of Atholl* and *Empress of Australia* all moved downriver on the first three days of December to embark at the anchorage although the *Duchess* was returned upriver to embark at the Riverside Wall on the 4th and completed on the 6th. The sailing date was postponed to 8 December by which date 14 transports and nine MT ships of the convoy were ready for sea at the Clyde Anchorage. Two other transports, *Andes* and *Oronsay* with Blue Funnel MT ships *Orestes* and *Troilus* left the Mersey on the ebb tide that afternoon to rendezvous with the Clyde section next morning.

Over 38,000 personnel were embarked on WS 14 with almost half in drafts and details destined for the Middle East, one third for Bombay or Iraq and just over 3,000 for Malaya which demonstrated the low priority then given to the reinforcement of that latter area.[3] Complete units known to be in this convoy were 10 Lancashire Fusiliers (embarked on *Athlone Castle*), 67 and 77 Heavy, 21 and 48 Light AA Regiments, RA; the first named for India and remaining three for destinations ultimately revealed as Java. Embarked on *Strathallan* was the 7th York & Lancaster Regiment also for India. Although unexpected, the Japanese attack on Malaya hardly changed the makeup of subsequent WS convoys other than eliminating a destination. In respect of departures from the UK, the WS convoys had now been in operation for eighteen months, almost half a million men had embarked on them with the load shared almost equally between the Mersey and the Clyde, with the latter being the most convenient assembly point and where the convoy conferences were usually held in a requisitioned mansion in Greenock.

As with the previous convoy, another R class battleship being positioned to the Indian Ocean was the appointed ocean escort. *Ramillies* carried the SOE, Rear Admiral SS Bonham-Carter, who first attended the convoy conference then left the Clyde with three V & W class destroyers as escort to Milford Haven, where they were to top up with fuel and join the convoy in a position 500 miles north of the Azores at midday on the 12th. There are missing records for this convoy, but it seems Commodore EK Boddam-Whetham DSO RNR on *Duchess of Atholl* led the Clyde section out of the boom at 2200 hours on the 8th, comprising 13 transports, 10 MT ships and the converted Clan liner HMS *Engadine* carrying 40 crated Hurricanes for the Middle East. Escort was provided by ten destroyers and the AA ship *Ulster Queen* (a converted Irish Channel vessel). The SO A/S escort was on the Australian destroyer *Nestor*. It was planned to make junction with the four ships from Liverpool at 1030 on the 9th in a position west of Orsay, where the convoy was to form into eight columns and proceed at a speed of 13 knots.[4] Also escorting the convoy to Freetown was the AMC *Cilicia* being sent to the South Atlantic for ocean patrolling.

An unusual aspect of this convoy was that four ships on the port wing columns, i.e. *Empress of Australia*, *Warwick Castle*, *Troilus* and *City of Pretoria* were to be known as WS 14D and "may be ordered to part company...and proceed to another destination as a separate unit."[5] Also, the SOE was warned that two ships had left the Clyde 46 hours earlier, i.e. Brocklebank's *Malancha* and the Dutch KPM passenger ship *Plancius*. They were escorted by two corvettes from Derry and formed "part of convoy WS 14D."[5] As both these ships were capable of 14 knots, and therefore able to maintain the convoy speed, the reason for sailing them separately is unknown. *Malancha* joined the main convoy at Capetown while *Plancius* appears to have proceeded independently to Bombay; all six vessels of WS 14D eventually arrived at Singapore or Batavia where they may originally have been destined.

There is no record of the first two days' passage of WS 14, other than it encountered strong SW'ly headwinds on the 10th and 11th, which veered W'ly on the 12th. *Nestor* and some of the other destroyers lost touch during this weather and were ordered to Gibraltar in being due to join the Mediterranean Fleet. On the 15th they sank a U-Boat to the SW of Cape St Vincent on its first patrol to the Mediterranean.

Ramillies was unable to make contact with the convoy, which was behind time at the rendezvous on the 12th due to the weather, but successfully joined up at 0940 next day in a position 150 miles north of the Azores. *Ramillies* was accompanied by the three V and W destroyers that had escorted her to Milford Haven; also joining on the 13th were the Hunt class destroyers *Badsworth* and *Beaufort*, which may have been trying to catch up since refuelling at Derry, the latter was proceeding around the Cape to Alexandria. At 1800 on the 13th when about 80 miles north of Sao Miguel, *Badsworth* and *Beaufort* detached ahead to refuel at Ponta Delgada on the south side of that Azores island, the former escort then proceeded to Gibraltar. After passing through the Azores group, one of the older destroyers detached back to refuel followed by the other two on the 15th when *Beaufort* rejoined.

On commenting on this leg of the voyage, the SOE noted that *Empire Oriole* reported being hove-to during the night of 11th/12th and that *Scythia* broke down with engine trouble at 0500 on the 13th and expected her speed for the next 24 hours to be 8 knots and thereafter 12 knots. This breakdown occurred about the time that *Ramillies* made radar contact with the convoy and might have allowed the SOE to detach one of his destroyers to stand-by *Scythia* although this is not recorded. *Scythia* certainly reached Freetown 24 hours behind the convoy and may well have sailed unescorted for the nine days prior to arrival and undoubtedly caused great anxiety to her Master, Captain JA Macdonald, a most experienced and highly qualified officer but unable to communicate his predicament due to wireless silence.

From the Azores the convoy made an almost direct course to Freetown, *Orestes* was reduced to 8 knots on the 17th with engine trouble and *Clan Cameron* fell back with 'condenseritis' that same day but regained station next morning. Two destroyers from Freetown joined on the 18th to the east of the Cape Verde islands and another two next day, on which morning a Sunderland flying-boat approached close to the convoy without prior warning, fired the wrong recognition signal and was in turn fired upon by one of the destroyers but luckily without damage. That same morning a British cableship with corvette escort was sighted ahead and at dawn next day another British ship on opposite course: both were investigated by destroyers and their identities confirmed but the SOE noted "the convoy had no previous knowledge of these ships."[6] The convoy reached Freetown without further incident, *Ramillies* passing inside the boom at 0700 on 21st December, and where the SOE left with his staff to join *Mooltan* due in Freetown next day on the homeward leg of her voyage in WS 11. (*q.v.*)

WS 14 reached Freetown a day behind the 45 ships in OS 13 from the UK, making 75 ships all requiring fuel and fresh water. The requirements of WS 14 were signalled by the DoST to the Freetown naval authorities seven days before arrival and were given as 35,500 tons of fuel in three grades and an astonishing 36,300 tons of fresh water, which excluded the requirements of the escort. It is not known if these quantities were actually supplied. A total of 791 military, RAF and RN personnel were landed at Freetown from the transports (including 30 from the AMC *Cilicia*) for onward conveyance to Bathurst, Lagos, Accra and Takoradi on the West African coast.[7]

WS 14 sailed from Freetown on Christmas afternoon without HMS *Engadine* for reasons unknown although this ship subsequently reached Suez some ten days behind the convoy. *Ramillies* and *Beaufort* continued as ocean escorts with the addition of another Hunt class destroyer, *Hurworth*, and sloop *Bridgewater*, while two of the local V & W destroyers acted as additional A/S escort. There was a complete change round of ships in each column except that of the Commodore's, column five, while the post of Vice Commodore continued as the master of *Orestes* and Captain HRL Shaw of *Warwick Castle* as Rear Commodore. The speed remained at 13 knots.

At 1800 on Boxing Day *Abosso* detached with one of the local destroyers for Takoradi and Accra with 469 personnel for these ports and thereafter loaded on her owners' berth for Liverpool, to arrive there on 16 February and was reallocated for full trooping service to sail in WS 17. On the morning of the 27th *Orestes* broke down with fuel pump trouble but later got under way at 14 knots to regain the convoy and at which point the remaining local destroyer was detached to return to Freetown. The only other incident mentioned on this leg by the SOE on *Ramillies* was that 700 of her ship's company (over 60% of the total) were initiated into King Neptune's domain when crossing the line on the 27th.

Throughout the passage of this convoy to the Cape, the Japanese forced the steady withdrawal of British and Indian forces down the Malayan peninsula and by 5 January were halfway to Singapore as WS 14 arrived in Capetown. Not surprisingly there is evidence of many signals between the DoST in London and Impcon Staff in Durban concerning transhipment and on-carriage of personnel and the changed destinations of liners in this convoy. On 31 December the DoST confirmed that the four ships previously listed for WS 14D plus *Malancha* were to proceed first to Durban, that 3301 personnel on *Highland Princess, Athlone Castle, Esperance Bay, Strathallan, Duchess of Atholl, Andes* and two of the MT ships were to be transhipped to other ships, (suggested as *Dunera* and *Dilwara*) to accompany WS 14D to Malaya. Cargo was also to be transhipped to WS 14D from *Athlone Castle* while 386 personnel for India and the Middle East on *Andes* and *Empress of Australia* were to be found alternative berths. All this proved to be an over-simplification of what actually occurred when the liners arrived in South Africa a week later.

Under command of Captain EA Bridges who had recently been appointed from *Almanzora*, and who later became Commodore of the Company, the Royal Mail liner *Andes* was detached ahead at 0100 on 3rd January, proceeding at her maximum speed of 21 knots to reach Capetown next morning and there land delegates of the South African Parliament. During the morning of the 4th the destination of some ships was changed from Durban to Capetown and at 0900 the convoy was rearranged accordingly. The AMC *Derbyshire* then joined from Simonstown and took station as escort between columns 6 and 7. At 1800 that same day *Ramillies* and the two Hunt class destroyers detached with *Orcades, Empress of Australia, Highland Monarch, Warwick Castle* and all the MT ships (less at least two which had become stragglers) for Capetown and berthed there next morning, except the Hunts which detached to Simonstown. The remaining ten transports continued for Durban with *Derbyshire* and *Bridgewater* and were joined by *Andes* from Capetown in the afternoon of the 5th, while the cruiser *Ceres* joined as additional escort next morning. No incidents occurred during the passage to Durban where the eleven transports arrived, split into three groups to prevent delays in berthing, on the morning of the 8th.

The continued progress of the Japanese in Malaya called for urgent reinforcements to defend Singapore and Java and required a further rearrangement of the troops on WS 14. There was additionally an instruction to turn around not one but five of the transports in Durban and replace them with seven of the Indian Ocean type. In the space of five days 24,350 personnel were transhipped at Durban, best described by Impcon as "some 8,500 troops were transhipped from every vessel for onward passage in Middle East ships, 5,600 for India bound ships, 3,250 to Far East ships and 7,000 disembarked from convoy to Clairwood Camp. Twenty-nine special trains full of troops were brought in from the Camp for embarkation and we had in addition to make arrangements for the daily running of ten special leave trains for use of personnel berthed on the southern side of the harbour."[8] And this was not all, as the liners with changed destinations had also to tranship military stores and cargo to other ships, which prompted the DSTO Simonstown to remonstrate with London that "transhipment of cargoes should only be necessary on exceptional cases."[9] The ports of Durban and Capetown were interdependent as WS delays in Durban also held up the Capetown section even after completing fuelling, until the sailing date of the Durban section was known. The DSTO said that "while WS 14 was at Durban all other traffic for that port was suspended. The port held 75 seagoing ships of which as many as 27 had to lie in the outer anchorage and Capetown held 70 of which half were in Table Bay."⁹ Included in the Durban numbers were two of the Monster liners, 17 of the WS type and 7 Indian Ocean troopers.

It is convenient here to record the homeward voyages of the five liners that disembarked and returned from Durban. *Highland Princess* sailed two days later for the Plate, loaded at Buenos Aires, La Plata, Santos and Rio, thence to Freetown and joined convoy SL 101 to reach Belfast Lough on 7 March where she was directed for discharge at Swansea and Avonmouth. After four weeks in the latter port she next sailed in WS 18. The next ship away was *Scythia*, on the 16th, loading on the Harrison berth also at Port Elizabeth and Capetown, thence to Freetown to join SL 101 with *Highland Princess* (above) and *Orduna* from WS 12Z. *Scythia* reached her home port on 9 March and spent nine weeks undergoing repairs before another voyage in WS 19. Five other liners still remained in Durban, but *Duchess of Atholl*, *Samaria* and *Leopoldville* (both ex WS 12 *q.v.*) sailed on the 20th, the first named having repaired the turbine defect that sent her back from WS 14. The *Duchess* was able to make 16 knots on passage via Trinidad and Bermuda to New York, where in the short space of four days she was drydocked and embarked with American troops for Northern Ireland. As the sole British transport in U.S. convoy AT 12, which called at Halifax on 21 February, the *Duchess* berthed in Belfast on 2nd March and thereafter proceeded to Liverpool where Captain HA Moore assumed command for the next voyage in WS 17.

Oronsay loaded at Durban and Capetown on the Union Castle berth but on leaving the latter port on the 28th had then to put back with engine defects, which took five days to rectify. Her homeward passage via Freetown to Liverpool was completed on 25 February where she was drydocked and next prepared to sail in WS 17. *Cameronia* was the last to clear Durban on 27 January and having loaded on the Ellerman berth at that port and Capetown proceeded via Trinidad and Bermuda to Halifax, being then the last of the troopships to use Trinidad. Five U-Boats began operating in the Caribbean on the day that *Cameronia* left Trinidad and one boldly entered the harbour three days later and sank two ships. The official history does not refer to a diversion of the liners away from that area, although Churchill does, "this latter incident (at Trinidad) forced us to divert the liners..which frequently refuelled there."¹⁰ In fact several of the liners returning by Trinidad "had been in difficulty in respect of distance between the Cape and Trinidad,"¹¹ which was 2,000 miles greater than that to Freetown, and prompted the MOWT to ask the Admiralty for a revised route and distance. At Halifax, *Cameronia* embarked Canadian troops and crossed in convoy NA 4 (with *Orion* from WS 10X) to the Clyde, where she disembarked on 8 March and next day moved upriver to her owners" berth at Yorkhill Quay: she too next sailed in WS 17.

The ships allocated for on-carriage from Durban virtually arrived within a day or so of WS 14, including *Mauretania* and *Ile de France* which embarked almost 8,000 for Suez; *Nova Scotia*, *Dunera*, *Dilwara*, *Thysville* and *City of Canterbury* which between them lifted another 8,000. Captain Percival of the last named ship arrived one day ahead of WS 14, "with 400 tons of heated coal. It was necessary to shift this from the lower bunkers to shelter decks and in addition to bunker with 2,300 tons of fresh coal. Those operations took from the 8th to 11th and immediately on completion we commenced to embark troops. There was some dissatisfaction with regard to the outward appearance of the ship and a number of the troops refused to embark."¹² The final embarkation on this ship was 1100 RAF and RAOC upon which Impcon reported rather more strongly: "Personnel walked off complaining of uncleanliness; (the ship had just disembarked

1,000 POW from Suez but had been thoroughly cleaned internally). Convoy departure was held up for some hours whilst we endeavoured to persuade the men to return. Delay was all the more serious as this ship, as well as several others, was proceeding to Singapore with urgently needed reinforcements. We managed to persuade all but 189 to return to the ship. Those left behind were placed under arrest and subsequently court martialled."[8]

Meanwhile the four remaining transports and nine MT ships (which now included *Malancha*) had been moving round the coast from Capetown, having left that port on the morning of the 9th escorted by *Ramillies* and two corvettes, which latter detached back next morning while *Troilus* and *Clan Cameron* joined, having been delayed leaving harbour. *Ramillies* left the convoy for a while on the morning of the 12th to carry out practice firings and *Empire Oriole* was sent ahead to land a sick seaman at Durban. At 1400 on the 13th rendezvous was made at the entrance to the Durban swept channel with the portion from that harbour and where also *Orestes*, delayed leaving Capetown, rejoined. One hour later the combined convoy of 21 ships went ahead in seven columns with *Ramillies* and the AMC *Corfu* as ocean escort, stationed between the 4th and 5th columns. The two port wing columns with *Highland Monarch* and *Thysville* were destined for Suez, the starboard wing columns with *Warwick Castle, Empress of Australia* and *City of Canterbury* for the Far East and centre columns with *Nova Scotia, Esperance Bay, Dunera* and *Dilwara* for Bombay,Basra or the Far East. We shall return to this convoy later.[13]

To add to all this activity outside Durban, which began with the first ships of WS 14 leaving harbour at midday, another faster convoy known as CM 25 began leaving the harbour an hour later comprising *Mauretania, Ile de France, Athlone Castle, Strathallan, Duchess of Atholl, Durban Castle* and *Reina del Pacifico*, with Commodore Hobart embarked on the first named liner. Rendezvous was made at 1400 at the outer end of the searched channel with the cruiser *Dorsetshire*, as ocean escort, and about an hour later *Orcades* joined from the Capetown portion of WS 14. Twenty minutes later *Duchess of Atholl* developed turbine trouble and had to return to Durban whereupon Captain JH Biggs of *Strathallan* assumed the duties of Vice Commodore. A man fell overboard from *Athlone Castle* at 1700 that same day but was recovered by that ship. This convoy continued without incident at 18 knots until the afternoon of the 20th when *Durban Castle* twice reduced speed due to engine trouble. The Guardafui Strait was passed that night and at 0500 on the 21st, when north of Ras Alula, on the Somaliland coast, *Dorsetshire* went on ahead at 25 knots to reach Aden at 1700, passing en route the Free French sloop *Commandant Domine* going to meet the convoy and detach with the Bombay portion (*Athlone Castle, Strathallan, Durban Castle* and *Reina del Pacifico*) for that port. *Dorsetshire* refuelled at Aden, sailed again at midnight and proceeded east at 23 knots to overtake the Bombay portion which was accomplished at 1500 when the French sloop returned to Aden. No incidents occurred on the fine weather passage to Bombay: *Dorsetshire* flew her Walrus on patrol on three afternoons without any sightings. Bombay was reached on the morning of the 26th January when *Dorsetshire* berthed on the Alexandra Dock Wall, the SOE commenting that similar splits of CM convoys should be made in the vicinity of Guardafui,to avoid a wasteful doubling back from the Gulf of Aden.

The troops of CM 25 (ex WS 14) were disembarked at Bombay either for destinations in India or on-carried in smaller ships to Basra, combined with others arriving in the main WS 14 convoy on the 28th. The 67 HAA Regiment moved first to Calcutta and by 1943 were at Imphal and ended the war in Rangoon. 7 Bn Yorks & Lancs were on-carried to Karachi, later served on the NW Frontier and finished the war in Burma. 10 Lancs Fusiliers went first to Quetta, then Comilla and in July 1942 moved to Chittagong and served in the Arakan until May 1943, when they returned to India. The four liners of CM 25 were now dispersed, *Athlone Castle* sailing on the 30th via Fremantle to load a full refrigerated cargo at Auckland in the space of twelve days, returning then by Panama direct to Liverpool where she arrived on 5 April. *Strathallan* and *Durban Castle* were now to be used in the Second Flight of moving two Australian Divisions from the Middle East, originally to the East Indies but finally to Australia. The P&O liner then loaded in Sydney and Auckland and returning via Panama reached the Clyde on 9th and Glasgow on 10th May to occupy the berth she had vacated exactly 23 weeks earlier. *Durban Castle* loaded in Lyttelton on the Shaw Savill berth and proceeded via Panama and Bermuda to Liverpool, arriving on 10th May. These liners were next employed in WS 19, 19P and 20 respectively. *Reina del Pacifico* was not required for the Australian movement and loaded in Bombay and Colombo on the B.I. berth, return-ing via Durban and Capetown direct to Liverpool on 14 March to be next engaged in WS 18.

The remaining three liners of CM 25 were refuelled at Aden between 21 and 23 January and disembarked at Suez on the last three days of the month. The two Monsters then carried troops on return trips to Bombay while *Orcades* was used for the First Flight of the Australians and left Suez on 1st February carrying 3,700 and called at Colombo to refuel on the 9th. Here she was ordered to Pandjang (Oosthaven) at the SE tip of Sumatra close to the entrance of the Sunda Strait where she arrived escorted by the destroyer *Encounter* on the 15th, the day of the surrender in Singapore. The troops were first transhipped by a small Dutch KPM steamer but were re-embarked on *Orcades* that night and next day Captain Charles Fox was ordered to Batavia with Henderson's *Yoma* where *Orcades* berthed that afternoon and disembarked 2,400 of the Australians. Chaos and confusion reigned in Batavia so Captain Fox took *Orcades* to an anchorage outside the port to await orders.

Incredibly this valuable liner remained at Batavia for the next five days while the Japanese landed and occupied the neighbouring islands of Sumatra and Bali. On 21 February an Admiralty signal ordered *Orcades* into Batavia to embark the maximum number of refugees and sail by 2200 to clear the Sunda Straits by daybreak next morn-ing. Those embarked included RN survivors from the *Repulse* and *Prince of Wales*, RAF, refugees and Dutch personnel: an estimated total of over 10,000. *Orcades* left Batavia at midnight and clearing the Sunda Straits by daybreak proceeded independ-ently to Colombo where all were safely landed on the 27th. Captain Fox who was from Hull, brought honour to that city and his officers and crew when awarded the CBE a year hence.

At Colombo, *Orcades* embarked Australian troops who had been brought forward from Suez; these were landed at Adelaide when the ship moved to Sydney for dry-docking, loading there and in Wellington and proceeding via Panama to Halifax, where 200 RAAF cadets were landed for training. Here also Canadian troops were embarked on four transports including *Orcades*, which reached Glasgow on 11 May in convoy AT 15 which had originated in New York with American transports carrying U.S. troops to Iceland and the UK.

In reverting to the remaining sections of WS 14 in the Indian Ocean, *Highland Monarch* was to be the sole remaining transport of the original convoy which proceeded to Suez, and having joined the Durban section outside that port in the afternoon of 13 January, this 21 ship convoy proceeded NE at a speed of 12 knots, with Commodore HW Wakeman-Colville RNR embarked on *Dilwara* while Vice Commodore Boddam-Whetham, who had brought the main convoy out from the UK, had transferred from *Duchess of Atholl* to *Dunera*.

Duchess of Atholl as related above had returned to Durban from CM 25 with engine trouble. As soon as Impcon learned of this a hurried consultation took place with the PSTO at Durban "and it was decided that when the ship returned to port, all troops and stores would be transhipped into *Andes*, which should have returned to the UK. We worked through the night arranging the re-berthing of troops and stores whereupon *Andes* sailed next afternoon, 14th, to catch up WS 14,"[8] which was accomplished at 0500 on the 16th in the Mozambique Channel. The Belgian *Thysville*, which had just completed four months of boiler repairs at Durban, dropped astern on the first night claiming bad coal as the reason but was later reported following at 10 knots and does not appear to have rejoined. *Clan Cameron* also complained of bad coal but changed over to oil fuel and was then able to maintain 14 knots.

At 0730 on the 19th when some 200 miles ESE of Dar-es-Salaam, the convoy was met by the battleship *Royal Sovereign* and cruiser *Ceres*, and where also the convoy was split into three sections. *Highland Monarch* and the four MT ships from the port wing columns detached as WS 14A with *Ceres* towards Guardafui and were dispersed off Aden, where the liner first called before continuing to Suez and arrived on 1 February after a passage of 55 days from the Clyde, almost nine weeks since her troops embarked at Avonmouth. The straggling *Thysville* bunkered with coal at Aden and reached Suez two days behind the Royal Mail liner and thereafter continued on Indian Ocean service. *Highland Monarch* spent eight days at Suez and carried POW to Mombasa and Durban, before proceeding to the Plate to load at La Plata and Buenos Aires. Her homeward voyage was made direct from Montevideo to Belfast Lough and was there directed to discharge at Avonmouth, arriving on 17 April and was next included in WS 19.

The middle section of WS 14 comprising three columns, less *Dunera* which transferred to the starboard columns, proceeded direct to Bombay as WS 14B under escort of the AMC *Corfu*. On the 25th on the latitude of Socotra, four of the MT ships, including *Clan Cameron* were detached independently for Basra in the Persian Gulf, while *Dilwara*, *Andes*, *Nova Scotia* and *Esperance Bay* continued with *Empire Condor* for Bombay and arrived there on the morning of the 28th, two days behind the other four liners from CM 25.

From Bombay there was a steady procession of Indian Ocean troopers operating to Basra, including *Khedive Ismail* which sailed on the 28th, *Lancashire* on the 30th, *Nevasa* 31st and *Dilwara* with *Nova Scotia* on 2nd February; all these ships were part of the large fleet retained on Indian Ocean service, many now being employed carrying reinforcements from India to Rangoon and Singapore, and from Suez to Colombo, Singapore and Australia. *Esperance Bay* as a WS ship disembarked at Bombay and Karachi before returning to Bombay to embark Australian troops for Batavia, sailing on 13 February and Colombo three days later by which time the Japanese had landed in Sumatra and Borneo and on the 16th occupied Bali to complete the isolation of Java. "On the 21st the Chiefs of Staff...agreed that no more reinforcements would be sent there".[14] *Esperance Bay* was therefore ordered back to Colombo, landed her troops and left on the 28th for Fremantle and Adelaide with refugees, before continuing to Auckland to load on the Shaw Savill berth. She returned via Panama and Belfast Lough to Avonmouth on 26 May for discharge and drydocking; the last of the WS 14 ships to complete a voyage that had begun almost six months earlier.

Andes was the other WS ship that arrived at Bombay with WS 14 and following disembarkation, took the place of *Duchess of Atholl* in moving the Second Flight of the Australian divisions from the Middle East. She left Bombay on 5 February, fuelled at Aden on the 8th and anchored at Suez four days later. Embarkation was protracted over six days but *Andes* sailed on the 18th for Colombo and was there sent on to Fremantle, Adelaide and Melbourne. From there she carried RAAF trainees via Panama to Halifax and then proceeded to Boston for nine days drydocking, thereafter embarking Canadian troops in Halifax to cross in convoy NA 8 with *Orcades* and other liners reaching Liverpool on 11 May. Both were next employed in WS 19P.

The two column section of WS 14 destined for Singapore and Batavia and known as DM 2, detached as above from the main section on 19 January and proceeded north of the Seychelles under escort of *Royal Sovereign* which had relieved her sister *Ramillies*. This section comprised *Dunera* carrying the (now) Commodore Boddam-Whetham, *Warwick Castle*, *Empress of Australia*, *City of Canterbury* and MT ships *Troilus*, *Malancha* and *City of Pretoria*. All were now destined for Batavia except *City of Canterbury* which was for Singapore.

From north of the Seychelles, DM2 proceeded on an easterly course to a position 30 miles south of the new fleet refuelling base at Addu Atoll, where at 0900 on the 26th *Royal Sovereign* detached for that port on relief by the AMC *Ranchi*. The convoy then proceeded ENE to a position 300 miles south of Ceylon, where at 1030 on the 28th, a prearranged junction was made with the four ship personnel convoy BM 12 from Bombay and bound to Singapore under escort of the cruiser *Emerald*, following which *Ranchi* detached in pursuit of previous orders. Course was now altered to the SE towards the Sunda Strait and distant 1400 miles.

Throughout the fine weather passage from the vicinity of the Seychelles, the Commodore on *Dunera* had been encouraging the active co-operation of Lieut Colonel Pearson, Commanding 48 Light AA Regiment embarked on that ship, to improve the AA defences of all ships in anticipation of Japanese air attacks on arrival at their destinations. The D.E.M.S. staff at Durban was initially enlisted to assist 48 Regiment mounting their own weapons on *Dunera* and with the assistance of the Master, Captain Fred Caffyn and his officers, this ship ultimately mounted and tested 12 Bofors, 17 Bren and 6 Lewis guns. The Commodore then requested the O.C. Troops on all other ships to do likewise. On reaching Addu Atoll, which all seven ships were first intended to enter, men from the AA Regiment were to be spread amongst all ships to man their Bofors, but only the *Empress* short of fuel actually entered the atoll. Not to be outdone and on explaining the situation to *Ranchi*, *Dunera* went ahead five miles with *Troilus* and the two Ellerman ships which then stopped while 150 officers and men were placed aboard to man the Bofors which had been got up to various positions; all ships were again underway an hour later. The seven ships eventually mounted and manned 46 Bofors, 85 Bren and 78 machine-guns in addition to ships' ordinary armament and proved the most commendable initiative of the Commodore and all concerned.

The four ship section of BM 12 comprised the Dutch *Plancius* which had left the UK in WS 14D, the Bibby trooper *Devonshire*, and Bibby managed Messageries Maritimes *Felix Roussel*, having been taken over by a Free-French crew in September 1940 and fitted for Indian Ocean trooping in Bombay. Among those embarked on the French liner were 9 Bn Royal Northumberland Fusiliers. Together with *Empress of Asia* from WS

12Z (*q.v.*), whose complement included 5 Bn Loyals, these ships, presumed embarked to capacity with 7,000 personnel, of which 3,800 were drafts for 9 and 11 Indian Divisions in Malaya, also carried other divisional troops for 18 British Division which had been delayed in India. Added to this Singapore group was *City of Canterbury* with 1100 RAF and RAOC from WS 14D, leaving *Warwick Castle*, *Dunera* (with the Commodore), *Empress of Australia* and the three MT ships carrying 6,000 for Batavia in Java and believed to comprise an HQ Wing and RAF Ground Staff, 77 Heavy, 21 and 48 Light AA Regiments of Royal Artillery.

Emerald continued with the 11 ships of DM 2/BM 12 towards the Sunda Strait, until 1430 on the 31st when relieved by the cruisers *Danae* and *Java* (Dutch). Anxiety on what lay ahead was heightened by reports of air attacks on the previous convoy (BM 11/WS 12X and Z) as it reached Singapore on the 29th. By 1400 on 1st February the convoy was 400 miles west of the entrance to the Strait where two sloops of the local escort joined i.e. RAN *Yarra* and RIN *Sutlej*; the latter having a good AA capability. The escort was further strengthened at 0730 next morning by the heavy cruiser *Exeter* and two hours later by the destroyers *Jupiter* and *Vampire*, all three with *Yarra* and *Java* soon to be lost in the coming Battle of the Java Sea.

By 0530 on the 3rd the 11 ships and seven escorts emerged from the Sunda Strait into the Java Sea and detached those for Batavia where they arrived just before midday and began to disembark and unload. *Warwick Castle* and the *Empress* sailed again on the 5th carrying refugees, the latter directed to Colombo then Durban where she was delayed 12 days for engine repairs. After loading small quantities of cargo at Durban and Capetown on the Union Castle berth, the *Empress* returned via Freetown to Liverpool on 12 April for drydocking and nine weeks of repairs before next sailing again in WS 20. *Warwick Castle* being a refrigerated carrier was conveniently sailed for Australia, escorted by the cruisers, *Dragon*, *Durban* and two destroyers. When 200 miles south of the Sunda Strait and in the vicinity of Christmas Island on the 6th, a northbound convoy of 11 ships escorted by the cruiser *Canberra* was met. The escorts of both changed over, *Canberra* continuing with *Warwick Castle* to Fremantle and from where the liner was directed to Melbourne, then loaded in Sydney and Lyttelton before proceeding via Panama to Halifax for Canadian troops to cross in convoy NA 7 to the Clyde and Glasgow, berthing to disembark at KGV Dock on 19 April and was next employed in WS 19P.

From Batavia, *Dunera* returned via Colombo to Bombay and was retained on the Indian Ocean, the Commodore having transferred and returned to Colombo on *Empress of Australia*. Of the MT ships, *City of Pretoria* did not survive the war, and after towing the stricken submarine *Rover* from Batavia via Trincomalee to Bombay, the Ellerman ship was engaged in the Vigorous convoy to Malta in June then returned around the Cape to New York and the UK, and tragically was lost with all hands on her next homeward voyage in March 1943.

Returning to the five transports for Singapore that continued from the Sunda Strait, escorted by *Danae*, *Yarra* and *Sutlej*. During the forenoon of the 4th this convoy was bombed in the Banka Strait but suffered only minor damage from near misses. This attack, as recorded by the CO of *Yarra*, "was not in my opinion pressed home with determination equal to that shown by German or even Italian aircraft, and bombs were jettisoned clear of any target."[15] It was to be a different story next day.

The R.A.N. history records that no convoy since Japan entered the war had entered Singapore in daylight hours until BM 12 arrived in two groups in the forenoon of 5

February and proved to be a costly change of policy dictated by an apparent and urgent need of reinforcements for Singapore island. All British and Commonwealth forces had withdrawn from Malaya to the island five days earlier, the Japanese then demanded their surrender and four days later made successful landings which a week later caused the catastrophic capitulation and "the greatest disaster in British military history"[16] - the surrender of Singapore.

There is evidence that *Empress of Asia* may have fallen astern after the air attack in the Banka Strait, but the convoy of five transports certainly reached Singapore in two groups during the forenoon of the 5th with *Devonshire* and the Dutch *Plancius* in the leading group. These ships reached the eastern end of Selat Sinki, a mere 3 miles from the entrance to Keppel Harbour, escorted by *Sutlej* without incident. However, the other three transports were then some 8 miles to the westward and approaching Sultan Shoal, where at 1115 they were attacked in a series of dive-bombing and machine-gunning attacks by 27 aircraft. All ships including *Danae* and *Yarra* put up a most spirited defence but the *Empress* being the largest ship was singled out and hit by several bombs, the first exploding in the officers' saloon and killing three. The attacks continued for about half an hour and left the ship a blazing inferno with the fires out of control. The ship was then in the swept channel between two minefields, and while still making headway, Captain JB Smith calmly swung the ship around and anchored half a mile SE of the Sultan Shoal Lighthouse. The bridge and ship had then to be abandoned due to the smoke and heat of the fires.[17]

Throughout the air attacks, the CO of the Loyals, Lt. Col. HA Fitt, "though badly burned, displayed great gallantry in directing operations against low-flying aircraft and inspired all ranks by his fine example and was later awarded the DSO."[18] It was fortunate that the sloop *Yarra* and several small craft were close at hand in fine weather to take off the troops and crew. Lieut. Comdr. Harrington laid Yarra's bow under the quarter of the *Empress* which allowed 1,334 to file quietly aboard, the troops having to leave all their arms and equipment behind. Those on the forward part of the *Empress* were cut off by the flames and slid down ropes to be picked up by small craft of which 470 were transferred to *Yarra*. Another 78, including Captain Smith and the Chief Engineer were rescued by Australian minesweepers; all were off the ship by 1300 hours and landed later at Singapore. A later check showed that 15 military personnel out of 2,235 on board were unaccounted for. All of the 416 officers and crew were rescued although one died later in hospital. On returning home, Captain Smith was awarded the OBE and went on to command *Empress of Russia*, while the 1st Officer was given an MBE and the Chief Officer mentioned in dispatches.[17]

The *Empress* sank in a depth of only 8 fathoms and with most of the superstructure, masts and funnels remaining above water, became a familiar sight to shipping for many years to come. Salvage work to recover material from the wreck began in 1952.

Felix Roussel and *City of Canterbury* also of the *Empress* group received superficial damage in the air attacks, the former being hit by two bombs killing 3 and wounding 14 of the Fusiliers, wrecking the radio, and fires broke out but were promptly extinguished. The Ellerman ship had her steering gear damaged by blast and had to be steered from aft but both ships berthed alongside in Keppel Harbour with *Devonshire* and *Plancius* to disembark. Captain Percival reported "the conditions at Singapore were chaotic. There was no labour and the 400 tons of military stores had to be discharged by the ship's crew and the embarked troops, which went on during the whole of our stay."[10]

On hurriedly completing disembarkation and discharge of stores, *Plancius* proceeded independently to Batavia and thereafter with refugees to Colombo. The remaining three transports embarked large numbers of both military personnel and civilian refugees at Singapore (well over 2,000 on *City of Canterbury*) and sailed at 2300 on the 6th as convoy EMU escorted by the same three escorts, *Danae*, *Sutlej* and *Yarra*. The Ellerman ship had been unable to repair her steering gear and had to manoeuvre out of Keppel Harbour and through the minefields in the dark by steering from aft. Next day the convoy was warned to expect an attack from 16 enemy aircraft which were scattered by two Hurricanes before this could take place; two being shot down close to Berhala Lighthouse in the strait of that name.

On 9 February *Devonshire* and *Felix Roussel* passed through the Sunda Strait and continued independently to Bombay while *City of Canterbury* was sent to Batavia and berthed there that same morning, where all the troops from Singapore were disembarked and 4-500 naval ratings embarked in lieu. The City liner sailed on the 12th as Commodore ship of a 20-ship convoy for Colombo (including *City of Pretoria* and *Malancha*, the latter towing the damaged destroyer *Isis*). In Bombay Captain Percival was relieved and returned home on the *Narkunda* for some well earned leave.

Thus two of the WS liners from WS 14 and one from 12Z contributed to the final and by then pointless reinforcement of Singapore a few short days before the capitulation. On that island and in Hong Kong and Java an estimated 152,132 Indian, British and Australian troops were then incarcerated for three and a half years of barbaric captivity under the Japanese, from which little more than half survived. Every one of those unfortunate servicemen had been taken to the Far East by British troopships of one kind or another. Of those liners that brought the released prisoners home in 1945, *Devonshire* and *City of Canterbury* were among the many troop and hospital ships to uplift Indians from Singapore, while *Empress of Australia* brought some of the British survivors home from Hong Kong and Singapore.

WS 14 had been an unusual convoy in requiring five separate sections to carry personnel to five destinations beyond Durban, and to have suffered not only serious air attacks at the end of a voyage of 14,000 miles, but to sustain the total loss of a valuable liner at this point as a clear demonstration, if ever that was needed, of their extreme vulnerability to air attack and was repeated fourfold at great cost within the next seventeen months.

Another aspect of WS 14 was that seven of the liners returned to the UK after having made round-the-world voyages lasting from four to nearly six months. In the process, two had carried three separate shipments of personnel across the same number of oceans and four had brought refrigerated cargoes of much needed foodstuffs from the Antipodes. Altogether the entire convoy was a classic example of Britain successfully pursuing her maritime strategy.

WS 15 - sailed UK 11.1.42

As the first of the series to set out in 1942, this convoy was very similar to the number of transports and overall capacity provided by WS 14, the last departure of 1941. However, at this stage of the war with every possible personnel ship long since requisitioned to increase the trooping fleet, WS 15 was unusual in that five of the liners (one third) had never previously been used on trooping service. Six months previously the Admiralty agreed to release nine AMCs from commissioned service for conversion into troopships, but this could not become effective immediately. The AMCs had first to complete their escort or patrol service and proceed to a suitable Admiralty dockyard for de-commissioning and stripping out their hardware, before conversion and outfitting for trooping could begin in a mercantile dockyard. In most instances this work was combined and usually required drydocking in addition to boiler or machinery overhauls which all added to the strain on men and resources in repair yards.

We have seen that *Esperance Bay* was the first of the released AMCs to sail on trooping service in WS 14, and while her sister ships *Moreton Bay* and Shaw Savill"'s *Arawa* (an ex Bay liner) were concurrently fitting out in Liverpool, *Moreton Bay* was unable to make that convoy and sailed on 23 December with RAF trainees in CT 8 for Halifax, thereafter proceeding to the Plate to load a refrigerated cargo for the UK and did not become available for the WS route until May.

In these months at Birkenhead, *Arawa* achieved only a partial conversion with berths for 1,100 until the intervention of the Sea Transport Department had this increased to 1,500 prior to embarkation, and with a further increase before her next voyage to 1,840. In addition to *Arawa*, two other released AMCs were able to join WS 15, i.e. the Cunard *Laconia* (planned to be fitted for 2,500 berths but increased to 3,000 before sailing) which had also been fitting out in Liverpool, and Donaldson"'s *Letitia* which was a sister ship to the ill-fated *Athenia*.

The United States had earlier agreed to assist with naval repair work and arranged to accept three of the AMCs in their naval dockyards, *Letitia* was handled at the Philadelphia Navy Yard and thereafter crossed in TC 16 with trained RAF personnel to the Clyde Anchorage where she arrived with *Pasteur*, also to form part of WS 15, two days before Christmas. On completion of disembarkation, *Letitia* then moved to Liverpool for embarkation. The remaining conversions were on the P&O *Maloja* and *Cathay* being handled in Southampton and New York respectively; the Blue Funnel *Antenor* converted in Calcutta but none of these ships completed until April and the last named only became a WS ship in July. The last of the nine released AMCs was HMS *Wolfe*, which on being de-commissioned at Portsmouth, reverted to CPS management and adopted her former name of *Montcalm*. Under the command of Captain Thomas Jones, *Montcalm* sailed from Milford Haven in the two ship CT 9 on 8 January, and after disembarking in Halifax, proceeded to Baltimore for trooping conversion which was never completed. By April the Admiralty purchased the ship outright for conversion to a submarine depot ship, the CPS crew was brought home and Captain Jones took command of *Duchess of Richmond*.

Two other newcomers to the WS route were Bibby's *Staffordshire*, and the MOWT owned *Empire Woodlark* (ex *Emma Alexander*) as one of three, aged, laid-up U.S. liners offered in June 1941 to augment the British trooping fleet and the only one to join that service. The same Captain Jones (above) was sent to the States with a CPS crew and joined the *Emma Alexander* then fitting-out in San Francisco, but did not complete and leave there until 24 October. The speed of this ship was first given to the MOWT as 16.5 knots but later amended to 16 then 14 knots, but on the passage from Los Angeles to Panama turned out as 13.5 and from Cristobal to Halifax was less than 13 knots. The *Alexander* reached Liverpool on 6 December in HX 161 where Captain Jones was relieved by Captain HH Davies and managed a few days leave before sailing on *Montcalm* back to Halifax and a further spell in the States. The *Alexander* was meanwhile prepared for WS 14 and on 7 January adopted the *Empire* nomenclature.

The Bibby motorship *Staffordshire* had continued as that company's sole representative on their Rangoon service from the outbreak of war until March 1941, when bombed

140 miles WNW of the Butt of Lewis outbound on her fifth such voyage. Three attacks were made by a Focke-Wulf Condor and despite a barrage from Bofors and other guns, the ship suffered serious damage with 28 passengers and crew killed. Largely due to the efforts of the Chief Officer and Chief Engineer, *Staffordshire* was brought into Loch Ewe and beached with a 15° list. Dock labour was sent up from Greenock and in very trying conditions 900 tons of cargo was discharged to lighten the ship for patching and allow safe passage to a repair port. After eight months in the Tyne where she was allocated and fitted for trooping, *Staffordshire* anchored in the Clyde on 29 December to await embarkation orders.

Eight of the principal liners to complete WS 15 had reached Liverpool or the Clyde from previous WS 8A, 10, 10X and 11 voyages during the four weeks up to 26 December, the last being *Orontes* having barely two weeks for turnround in Liverpool after a four month voyage, and for such a large liner with berths for over 3,000 troops was a considerable achievement in wartime Britain. The remaining two liners were *Pasteur* and *Llangibby Castle* which had returned to the Clyde from Halifax voyages in convoys TC 16 and HX 164 respectively; the latter berthing at Yorkhill Quay in Glasgow in the early evening of Christmas Eve.

Embarkation began in Liverpool on 6 January aboard *Laconia, Britannic, Stirling Castle* and the Dutch *Christiaan Huygens*, and these liners left the Mersey on the 7th, followed by the MT/Storeship *Dorset* on the 8th, all proceeding to the Clyde Anchorage to ease congestion in the Mersey and allow their Masters to attend the convoy conference being held in Gourock on the morning of the 10th. Attending this meeting was the Commodore, AT Tillard, DSO RNR, with the SOE, Vice Admiral WEC Tait CB MVO, commanding the embryo 3rd Battle Squadron of the Eastern Fleet from *Resolution*, and the SO A/S Escort from the destroyer *Vanquisher*.[1] Also moving to the Clyde Anchorage were the storeships *Port Chalmers* and *Pardo* (Royal Mail) from Newport and Dutch *Aagtekerk* and Blue Funnel *Autolycus* which loaded in Glasgow and moved downriver on the 7th and 8th.

Troops also began boarding *Strathmore* at 1 KGV Dock Glasgow on the 5th, this ship moving to the anchorage on the 6th, followed by *Strathnaver* on the 7th and *Viceroy of India* on the 8th, which left *Llangibby Castle* to complete at the berth vacated by *Strathmore. Pasteur* and *Staffordshire* embarked at the anchorage by tenders from the railway terminus at Gourock. The remaining five liners, *Arawa, Letitia, Empire Woodlark, Otranto* and *Orontes* completed embarkation at Liverpool by midday on the 10th and began leaving the Mersey that afternoon with the MT ships *Elisabeth Bakke* (Norwegian) and *Melbourne Star*.[2] The sailing telegram shows that 37,843 were embarked on the 15 transports of WS 15, with a further 913 spread amongst the seven MT/Storeships, i.e. 310 on *Melbourne Star*, 299 on *Autolycus*, 251 on *Port Chalmers* and 53 spread amongst the other four which clearly showed the extreme shortage of personnel capacity on this convoy. Just over half the total embarked were for the Middle East while the vast majority of all personnel were drafts and details, RAF, RN but mainly military and included 56 Anti-Tank Regt., RA, recently converted from 4 Bn The King's Own.

The Clyde portion of the convoy comprising ten liners and five MT ships was due to be led out of the Clyde boom by the Commodore on *Strathmore* at 2130 on the 10th, but *Llangibby Castle* was held up by fog in Glasgow and the sailing time had to be delayed for an hour and later put back 24 hours. The fog only cleared and allowed the Castle liner to leave KGV Dock on the morning of the 12th and passed out of the boom

12 hours behind the convoy. Captain RF Bayer was given two destroyers as escort and instructed to proceed at maximum speed (15.5 knots) to catch up and join the convoy on the 14th.

Meanwhile the seven ship Liverpool portion cleared the Bar at 1600 on the 10th with two destroyers as escorts and proceeded towards the anticipated rendezvous with the Clyde portion off Orsay next morning. At 2325 however, when coming abreast the entrance to Belfast Lough, the C.-in-C. WA advised the 24 hour delay to the Clyde portion and instructed the Liverpool ships to enter Belfast Lough and anchor to await further orders - but not to enter the Lough before 0800. It is presumed the intervening time was spent sailing up and down the Irish Sea. Air cover was arranged for daylight hours whilst the ships remained in Belfast Lough.

The escort plan for WS 15 was similar to that of the two previous convoys in that an R class battleship, in this case *Resolution*, was to act as ocean escort by joining about 500 miles north of the Azores, while the AMC *Cheshire* would act as SOE until that occurred. As soon as the convoy conference ended on the 10th, *Resolution* left the Clyde screened by two destroyers, reached Milford Haven next morning and completed with fuel but deferred departure until next day in emulating the delay to the convoy. *Resolution* sailed in the afternoon of the 12th, screened by the same two destroyers plus RAN *Norman* which was going round the Cape with the battleship to join the Eastern Fleet. This group proceeded out to the south of Ireland to make rendezvous with the convoy at midday on the 15th and quickly ran headlong into a full SW'ly gale.

The main A/S destroyer escort comprising *Vanquisher* and four others (including the brand new H class Turkish *Demirhisar*, temporarily commissioned RN for her delivery voyage) left the Clyde behind *Resolution* and proceeded to Moville to complete with fuel and join the convoy next morning but were held there pending orders of a revised convoy departure. Similarly two local escort destroyers for the Clyde portion were sent to wait in Rothesay Bay.[3]

After the false start on the 10th, the 14 ship Clyde portion sailed during the evening of the 11th, and proceeded at 10 knots to rendezvous with the seven Liverpool ships, which had left their anchorage in Belfast Lough at 0100. On emerging from the North Channel to the forming up position 16 miles west of Orsay, the convoy ran into the teeth of a W'ly gale which reduced the intended speed from 13 to 9 knots.[4]

In addition to the AMC *Cheshire*, which was continuing with the convoy to the Cape, the AMC *Ascania* was also included being en route for service with the RNZN, and the Dutch submarine depot ship *Colombia* and AA cruiser *Heemskerck* both on passage to the East Indies. With the convoy formed into seven columns during the forenoon of the 12th, the A/S screen was provided by the five destroyers of the *Vanquisher* group from Moville and by *Vanoc* and *Walker* which had been escorting the Liverpool section. All ships were now pitching heavily into the head swell and sea, making life very unpleasant in the crowded troopdecks with a sharp drop in numbers attending at mealtimes. The westerly course was maintained until 0200 on the 13th, when an alteration to WSW brought the weather on to the starboard bows with consequent heavy rolling and a further deterioration of conditions below decks. This weather continued for the next five days as the wind gradually backed to SW then South. The weather only improved as the temperature increased when south of the Azores.

From Milford Haven, *Resolution* and her three destroyers were experiencing the same SW'ly gale in proceeding towards the convoy rendezvous. On the day prior to this junction an Admiralty signal moved the rendezvous 180 miles ENE due to the suspected presence of U-Boats, which was then confirmed by D/F bearing of a U-Boat transmission received by *Anthony*, one of the battleship's destroyers. The Admiralty ordered *Resolution* to remain NE of the rendezvous position, and at 0430 on the 15th again altered the rendezvous 40 miles further north, which *Resolution* reached at the appointed hour of 1000 but found nothing, and continued on a S'ly course until dusk, when *Vanquisher* signalled that the convoy had been 4.5 hours late in passing through the rendezvous. Next forenoon, 16th, the Admiralty signalled that WS 15 was being reported by a U-Boat and *Resolution* decided to delay joining the convoy until next morning. Shortly after this *Llangibby Castle* of the convoy reported being bombed but was later amended by *Boreas* to the effect that the Castle liner had been both torpedoed and bombed, and was hardly believed on *Resolution*, which nevertheless detached *Garland* to investigate. That afternoon a further Admiralty signal indicated "an enemy aircraft was homing three U-Boats on the convoy which was ordered to proceed at utmost speed."[5] This aircraft was seen from *Resolution* but out of range; the battleship with *Anthony* and *Norman* finally joined the convoy at daylight on the 17th in a position 600 miles west of Finisterre and 360 miles NE of the Azores.

After being delayed for two days by fog, *Llangibby Castle* passed Gourock outwards at 1300 on the 12th to catch up the convoy. Escorted by the destroyer *Verity* from the Clyde and Hunt class *Lamerton* which joined from 'Derry, the *Castle* liner soon ran into the W'ly gale encountered by the convoy, but was given a shortened route and successfully joined up at 1330 on the 15th, by which time the convoy was 450 miles west of Land's End and making only 6 knots headway in the gale which was now WSW. This junction was 24 hours later than planned but Captain Bayer had found the convoy delayed by the weather and 90 miles astern of its intended position. Unfortunately his obvious relief on joining was to be short lived.

The two destroyer escort of *Llangibby Castle* detached back to base after joining the convoy and those from Liverpool that same evening with *Vanquisher*, *Witherington* and *Volunteer*. This left *Boreas* and *Demirhisar* as sole A/S escorts for the convoy in a known U-Boat area, although three more destroyers were with *Resolution* in close proximity. The simple fact was that Britain then had insufficient long-range escorts; those that detached having reached the limit of their endurance. Even aboard *Resolution*, the delays caused by bad weather now seriously affected her ability to reach Freetown without refuelling; provisional arrangements had been made earlier for an oiler to wait in the vicinity of Madeira should the need arise, and was now requested to be near the Cape Verde islands.

From the time of *Llangibby Castle* joining up, the convoy steered a S'ly course at 10 knots with a W'ly wind force 7 to 8, until 1700 that day when five ships hoisted 'Not under command' lights by reason of their inability to steer at such a low speed in the conditions prevailing. *Llangibby* dropped back to the rear of the convoy and thereafter maintained the course and speed using one engine only. Overnight the convoy course and speed was altered to 230° and 13 knots; at dawn *Llangibby* resumed full speed and regained her station. By 0800 the convoy reverted to the S'ly course and speed of 10 knots with the wind now SW gale force 8, heavily overcast and moderate visibility. At 0815 *Llangibby Castle* was struck by a torpedo on the waterline aft which exploded "upwards with a terrific bang, a brilliant flash and a huge column of water thrown up."[6]

Llangibby Castle was now in a dangerous predicament with her stern, including the rudder, steering gear and main armament blown clean away. The Bosun was injured, 8 service personnel killed, 18 missing and 5 injured. *Llangibby* displayed the appropriate signals and initially believing the ship might sink, Captain Bayer first endeavoured to keep up with the convoy by proceeding at full speed and using the twin engines for steering. The destroyer *Boreas* ranged alongside but was unable to remain and simply ordered *Llangibby* to the Azores, then distant 500 miles.

Three hours after being torpedoed, a low-flying Focke-Wulf Condor approached *Llangibby Castle* from the starboard bow with a Hudson apparently in pursuit and the convoy visible in the distance. The Condor flew directly over the ship, which opened fire with all the guns which could be brought to bear and may have detracted the aircraft's aim. Two bombs were dropped but fortunately fell 30 yards astern. The aircraft was so low that its crew was clearly seen and was thought to have been hit and losing height with a trail of smoke, before disappearing into a rain squall and did not return.

Immediately prior to the air attack the Dutch *Aagtekerk* approached *Llangibby* to offer assistance and Captain Bayer gladly replied "I want you to stand-by me to the Azores."[6] *Aagtekerk* confirmed this and the two ships remained in company but with an alteration of course overnight became separated and lost touch. That was the morning of the 17th, when *Resolution* joined the convoy and having earlier detached two of her destroyers was now left with *Norman*, *Boreas* and the Turkish H Class (with her Asdic inoperative) as A/S escorts towards the Azores and Freetown.

The subsequent passage of *Llangibby Castle* to the Azores, then Gibraltar and finally to the safety of a Southampton drydock became a twelve week saga of outstanding seamanship with few equals at that time. The ship was torpedoed and bombed on the 16th and finding himself alone and without escort next morning, Captain Bayer called a conference with his senior officers and those of the RN, RAF and Army units on board. The Admiralty had ordered the ship to the Azores and it was explained that service personnel would be unable to land without being interned. The SW gale continued and the *Llangibby* continued at about 9 knots steering by her engines towards Horta on the small island of Faial in the central Azores Group. Captain Bayer had received no communications from the Admiralty or otherwise since the verbal instructions two days earlier from *Boreas* ordering him to the Azores. When approaching these islands on the afternoon of the 18th, he therefore broke W/T silence to report to the Admiralty but received no reply, and when 90 miles distant asked the British Consulate in Horta for assistance. An immediate reply advised that a Portuguese destroyer then in the harbour would remain on call overnight ready to proceed and assist if needed, but was not required. The *Llangibby* arrived in the approaches to the port at 0830 on the 19th and safely anchored three hours later.

The Portuguese authorities allowed *Llangibby* to remain for 14 days and although little could be done to repair the major damages, it was a relief for all to see the lights of the town and have the portholes open for ventilation. The Portuguese destroyer *Douro* was berthed in the harbour and whilst the naval authorities in Lisbon had given permission for the troops to be exercised ashore under guard, in parties of 40, this was later refused by the military when the first group comprising Seaforth Highlanders tried to land by ship's boat.[7] The Portuguese threatened to open fire leaving the CO of the Seaforths no option but to order his men back on board. A later offer to allow the troops landing facilities on the neighbouring island of Pica was declined.[6]

As soon as *Llangibby* reached Horta, the Admiralty began to make arrangements for the 1,149 personnel on board to return to the UK and proposed to the Portuguese government that another transport should call at Horta for this purpose, (*Almanzora* homeward bound from WS 12 and about to leave Freetown on the 20th could arrive on the

27th), but this must have been refused. The Admiralty then made arrangements for a salvage tug and A/S escorts to accompany *Llangibby* to Gibraltar, a further ocean passage of 1,080 miles. The DoST asked the Admiralty to assist the movement of *Llangibby's* personnel from Gibraltar to West Africa on *Ulster Monarch* and *Royals Scotsman* and *Ulsterman*, all then still assigned to Operation Pilgrim, to which the Admiralty replied that the Polish *Batory* leaving Glasgow on the 29th with 293 mixed service personnel for Gibraltar, would thereafter convey the required personnel to West Africa.[3]

On 2nd February *Llangibby Castle* left Horta under tow of the Dutch tug *Thames* and with three destroyers as escort. Waiting outside were three U-Boats, two of which were those that encountered WS 15 on 16 January including *U 402* which had fired the successful torpedo. Their efforts now were unsuccessful and *U 581* was driven off and sunk by the destroyer *Westcott* which picked up all but five survivors. Once in the open sea the tug was cast off and *Llangibby* continued on her own until approaching the Straits when the *Thames* again assisted until reaching Cape Spartel. The liner again proceeded unaided and reached Gibraltar on the 8th having been successively escorted by no less than 19 destroyers and corvettes. The service personnel were disembarked next morning, transferred to the waiting *Batory* and sailed on the 12th for Freetown where they safely arrived six days later to be subsequently accommodated on WS 16 due from the UK in ten days time.

On concluding his report at Gibraltar, Captain Bayer paid tribute "to the great courage and exceptional devotion to duty of the Chief Engineer and Chief Officer whose leadership, dogged determination and encouragement to staff, regardless of danger to themselves...contributed in the very highest degree to the safe arrival at Gibraltar."[6]

Llangibby Castle remained eight weeks at Gibraltar and was drydocked, strengthened and strapped up but nothing could be done to replace the lost rudder. A further seven day passage was made with tug and A/S escort to Southampton where the ship arrived on 12 April to be repaired in time to begin training for the Torch Assault landings in November. Captain Bayer, who had been promoted from the cargo ship *Sandown Castle* to the *Llangibby* at the beginning of this remarkable voyage, became a CBE when still at Gibraltar and moved to the *Durban Castle* after a well earned leave. Several other officers and ratings were also decorated.

From the moment of joining WS 15 on the morning of 17 January, *Resolution* found that *Llangibby Castle*, *Aagetekerk* and *Pardo* were missing, the latter having had to heave-to, leaving 20 ships plus the two AMCs, *Heemskerck* and three destroyers. That afternoon with all reported U-Boats being well astern, *Boreas* and *Demirhisar* were detached ahead to Ponta Delgada for fuel. Next morning the S'ly wind reduced to force 6 and *Pardo* rejoined. That afternoon *Heemskerck* was detached for fuel and *Norman* after dark as the convoy passed south and west of Sao Miguel. *Boreas* rejoined on the 19th by which time the convoy was steering SSE towards the Cap Vert gap with the weather blissfully moderated for the first time since leaving the UK seven days earlier. *Norman* rejoined on the 20th followed by *Heemskerck* but the Turkish destroyer had damaged her stem in Ponta Delgada and was delayed having this repaired.

By the afternoon of the 21st the convoy was about 350 miles north of the Cape Verde islands, where the destroyer *Vansittart* joined from Freetown and after nightfall *Resolution* went ahead to keep a rendezvous with the RFA oiler *Rapidol* next morning. Two attempts were made to refuel but in the strong NE trade winds force 6 these proved unsuccessful. The fuel situation was now becoming serious and consideration given to an offshore anchorage at Bathurst as a last resort: there being insufficient fuel to reach Freetown without some replenishment.[5]   Meanwhile *Resolution* with *Rapidol* and escorting corvette *Jasmine* moved south to find a lee on the western side of Sal island, the most NE'ly of the Cape Verde group.   There at 0830 on the 23rd outside territorial waters the wind and sea were still too great for oiling, so at 0920 *Resolution* anchored within Mordeira Bay where *Rapidol* was able to come alongside and supply the vital fuel.   On completion at 1230 *Resolution* sailed unescorted at 18 knots for Freetown, leaving *Vansittart* to fuel and rejoin later, but was unable to do in having one engine out of commission, and was replaced by *Vimy* from Freetown at 0830 on the 25th. *Resolution* anchored in Freetown harbour at 1700 that day, the convoy having arrived six hours earlier.

There were only some thirty other ships in harbour when the convoy arrived, most of them clearing out with the next homeward convoy on the 27th, which then allowed the fuelling and watering of WS 15 to be accelerated and completed on the 29th. Freetown was always hot with the daily year-round temperature ranging from 21 to 33°, high humidity and very little breeze, if any. Military personnel were relieved to be in light khaki drill with topee headwear as protection from the blazing sun.   The troops were kept amused by throwing coins to the natives who recovered them by diving from the many canoes gathered around each ship.   The evenings were of course cooler when ships whose personnel included military bands gave performances on the upperdecks.

Few if any of the personnel knew their ultimate destination but could certainly guess. News from the active theatres was not good with Allied forces abandoning their last defensive position in Malaya while in the desert, 2nd Armoured Brigade had largely been destroyed in the German advance around Msus.   Nevertheless *Resolution* was cheered out of the harbour in the afternoon of the 29th with her Royal Marine band playing on the roof of a forward turret.   The same 22 ships formed up into the same formation as on arrival, with the escort provided by *Resolution*, AMC *Cheshire* and destroyers *Norman* and *Demirhisar*.   There was no local A/S escort.

No incidents occurred on the eleven day passage to the Cape, the Equator was crossed on 1st February and the SE tradewinds picked up on the 6th which blew strong for the next few days and set the ships pitching and rolling.   No one was allowed to get bored as each day passed with the customary drills and PT, lectures, talks, orderlies, practising abandon ship and action stations.   There were morning parades, kit inspections, even pay parades, while sport was taken care of with relay races and the occasional boxing tournament.   There was also study time for those specializing in all manner of subjects including the learning of Hindustani for those thought to be India-bound.   Queuing for food and washing up were two of the long remembered orderlies of troopship life as were 'porthole picquets' at night.   And for those who wished to get their first tan, sunbathing was available on deck.

On 9 February *Resolution*, *Cheshire* and *Demirhisar* detached with *Laconia*, *Orontes*, *Pasteur*, *Dorset*, *Elisabeth Bakke* and the Dutch *Colombia* for Capetown where they were berthed next morning.   *Resolution* left the convoy at Capetown and subsequently joined the other three R class battleships of the Eastern Fleet based at Mombasa.   The remaining 11 transports and five storeships continued around the Cape under the escort of the AMCs *Worcestershire*, *Dunnottar Castle* and sloop *Milford*.   *Norman* apparently fuelled in Simonstown.   The Durban ships arrived on 13 February where the usual transhipment programme was activated, and with the capitulation of Singapore taking place while the convoy was being re-arranged there was much changing of personnel between ships, exacerbated by a complete lack of Indian Ocean type troopers for on-carriage from Durban. Forty-seven of these ships were then in service plus the three 'Monsters' but the majority were then employed moving troops from the Middle East and India to Burma, Java and Australia. Only *Llandaff Castle* remained for the Durban-Suez route and was then northbound in the Red Sea.

Of the three liners sent into Capetown, *Orontes* and *Pasteur* originally turning round at Durban were now proceeding to Suez with *Laconia*. Of the Durban ships, *Arawa* and *Viceroy of India* were planned to turnaround there but the *Viceroy* was now to continue to Suez. *Britannic* and *Stirling Castle* were continuing as planned to Bombay as was *Otranto* for Suez. *Letitia* originally for Suez was now turning in Durban, while *Empire Woodlark* and *Christiaan Huygens* originally for Singapore then Java were liable for diversion to Bombay, and *Staffordshire* similarly to Colombo. The two Strath liners caused the Impcon staff the greatest problem; both were originally scheduled for Bombay, *Strathnaver* was then directed for Suez, changed again to Singapore, then Java and finally diverted to Bombay, while *Strathmore* was altered to Singapore/Java and also reverted to Bombay.

The three liners and *Dorset* left Capetown in the early evening of 13 February, leaving *Elisabeth Bakke* behind, and with *Cheshire* as escort, proceeded around the coast to meet with the Durban ships at the end of that searched channel in the afternoon of the 17th, where WS 15 reformed into five columns with *Worcestershire* stationed abreast the Commodore between columns 2 and 3, destroyer *Norman* as A/S screen 1 - 2 miles ahead of the AMC, and cruiser *Ceres*, 4 to 5 miles ahead of *Norman*.[8] The two port wing columns of seven ships were for Aden and Suez while *Britannic*, *Stirling Castle* and *Strathmore* were for Bombay. The remaining eight ships and *Colombia* were now destined for Batavia. Course was set towards the Mozambique Channel at a speed of 13 knots. In the early hours of the 19th a man was reported overboard from *Strathmore*; *Norman* was instructed to conduct a search but found nothing.

With all the Indian Ocean type troopships engaged elsewhere, and no enemy raiders or U-Boats then believed to be operating in the Indian Ocean, some or all of the 2,890 personnel disembarked in Durban from *Arawa* and *Letitia* were probably berthed amongst the nine remaining transports, causing them to be above their capacities and with most simply accommodated on promenade deck mattresses. It was the fine weather season of the NE monsoon and with little possibility of enemy interference the advantage of prompt arrival must have outweighed the inconvenience and risk to the transports.

The two emptied liners in Durban were soon dispersed, *Arawa* sailing on the 18th for the Plate, where she loaded on the Royal Mail berth at Buenos Aires, Santos and Rio, returning home independently via Freetown to reach Liverpool on 30 April for a next sailing in WS 19P. *Letitia* loaded on the Union-Castle berth at both Durban and Capetown, proceeding thence via Freetown to join the slow convoy SL 103 and docked in her owners' Princes Dock berth in Glasgow on 29 March. Her next four trips were on the familiar route of her officers and crew to Halifax.

The combined WS 15 convoy of 19 ships proceeded north without incident through the Mozambique Channel, and by the evening of 21 February was approaching the passage between the volcanic Comoro islands and the coastline of Portuguese East Africa. At this point a signal was received giving effect to Wavell's instruction that no further reinforcements were to be sent to Java and that portion of the convoy should now proceed to Colombo.

An early attempt at 'replenishment at sea while underway' was made on the morning of the 21st in N'ly winds force 4, when *Worcestershire* with some difficulty delivered 85 tons of fuel to *Norman*; the destroyer detached ahead next morning to refuel in the Seychelles. At 1300 on the 22nd when 90 miles east of Cape Delgado, the Colombo portion of nine ships detached with *Ramillies*, which had come south from Mombasa, to the NE towards Addu Atoll and Colombo. Commodore Tillard on *Strathnaver* retained control of this portion which also comprised *Staffordshire, Empire Woodlark, Christiaan Huygens*, the Dutch *Colombia* with *Aagtekerk, Pardo, Autolycus* and *Port Chalmers*, and was known as DM 3 (i.e. Durban/Malaya).[9] The remainder of WS 15 continued on a N'ly heading to a rendezvous east of Mombasa with the B.I. *Khandalla*.

The passage of DM 3 north of the Seychelles then east towards Addu Atoll was without incident for the first six days until 1300 on the 28th, by which time the convoy was 250 miles west of Addu Atoll and where the CinC EI ordered the convoy not to enter that lagoon, except *Ramillies* and *Norman* which both detached six hours later to refuel there. By 0800 next morning, 1st March, the convoy passed through the Equatorial Channel some 20 miles north of the atoll when the AMC *Corfu* joined as an additional escort. On that same date the Japanese landed on Java and four days later occupied Batavia; the Allied forces on the island surrendered on the 12th. *Ramillies* and *Norman* rejoined that evening by which time the convoy was steering NE towards Colombo. At midday on the 2nd the convoy was 300 miles distant when ordered by the CinC EI to split; *Corfu* detached immediately with *Strathnaver, Empire Woodlark, Christiaan Huygens, Port Chalmers* and *Aagtekerk* for Bombay, which was reached on the 6th under local escort of the sloop *Falmouth*, concurrently with *Mauretania* from Suez. The three liners of WS 15B had arrived two days earlier, all seven being disembarked in turn at Ballard Pier. On completion of the voyage, Commodore Tillard commented unfavourably on *Empire Woodlark* as a "source of constant anxiety having to go all out to make 13 knots, her speed dropped in the slightest head sea and when oil fuel was low her instability caused the Master great concern..(she made) almost incessant heavy smoke (and was) a most unsuitable ship for a troop convoy."[10] On receipt of this report the DoST advised that the vessel would be retained in the Indian Ocean if subsequent repairs did not materially improve that position. These repairs were carried out at Capetown in May, but the *Woodlark* remained on Indian Ocean service until returning to the UK in May 1945 and was then laid up. She was scuttled off the Hebrides with chemical ammunition in November 1946.

The remaining five ships of DM 3 continued to Colombo with *Ramillies* and *Norman*, entering the swept channel at 0700 on the 4th and berthing in the harbour an hour later. All of the personnel on *Staffordshire* were disembarked to form part of the island defences as were those of 16 British Brigade which arrived ten days later on the *Nieuw Amsterdam* from Suez. *Staffordshire* sailed again on the 16th, refuelled at Durban on the 29th and left Capetown six days later for Freetown to join SL 107 for the UK; she berthed in Avonmouth on 1st May to next prepare for WS 19P.

In reverting to the main portion of WS 15 which parted from DM 3 off Cape Delgado on 22 February, comprising five liners with two MT ships for Suez and three liners for Bombay, all under escort of *Worcestershire* and *Ceres*, and from which point the Vice Commodore, the Master of *Orontes*, Captain AE Nicholls, now assumed the duties of Commodore. Two days later rendezvous was made with the BI mail steamer *Khandalla*, on a commercial mail voyage from Mombasa to Bombay, and where also the cruiser *Colombo* relieved *Ceres* which then detached to Mombasa. It was noted that

Khandalla's best speed was 13 knots although all of that class of ship were listed as 15 knots.

WS 15 continued up the East African coast until on the latitude of Mogadishu on the morning of the 26th, when the three liners for Bombay, i.e. *Stirling Castle*, *Britannic* and *Strathmore* detached NE as WS 15B on a direct course for that port with *Worcestershire* as escort and with Captain WD Roach of *Stirling Castle* acting as Commodore. No incidents occurred on this passage, the four ships being met 10 miles west of the searched channel by a sloop and minesweeper of the RIN on the morning of 4 March, and undoubtedly gave some relief to Captain Roach, just promoted from the intermediate class *Llangibby* and having served most of his life with Union Castle, was less than familiar with a 'winter' morning approach to Bombay where a smoke haze frequently obscured everything from view.

The CO of *Worcestershire*, Captain EH Hopkinson RN, made several pertinent comments on this convoy, not least being "the outsize funnel of *Pasteur*", which he recommended "should be camouflaged."[11] He was concerned about the lack of security for inter-ship signalling between ships in convoy where ships' names, ports, ETAs, etc. were given in plain language easily read by Army signallers or civilian passengers and could be inadvertently passed around on arrival in harbour. Similarly he recommended that all convoy details from pre-sailing conferences be delivered on board to Shipmasters rather than "be carried by them through the streets to their ships."[11]

In Bombay the PSTO was under extreme pressure to expedite the dispatch of the six WS ships then in port; *Christiaan Huygens* sailed on 7 March, loaded on the Union Castle berth at Durban and Capetown and thereafter sailed direct to Liverpool arriving 2 May for a next voyage in WS 19P. *Stirling Castle* left a day behind the *Huygens* and was directed via Colombo to carry refugees to Melbourne, thence to Auckland to load a refrigerated carge on the Blue Star berth and returned via Panama to Liverpool on 17 May, the last of the WS 15 ships to return home and next sailed in WS 20. The remaining three liners at Bombay left that port between the 11th and 18th March and proceeded direct to Capetown and loaded there very small amounts of cargo; *Britannic* then sailing direct to the Clyde Anchorage arriving 23 April, *Strathmore* and *Strathnaver* both via Freetown to Liverpool and Glasgow respectively on 18 and 23 April, and where Captain Starling of the latter ship, which he had commanded almost continuously since 1935, now retired to his home in Cambridge. These three liners were next employed in WS 19P, 20 and 19.

Meanwhile WS 15A for Suez, comprising *Orontes* (with her master as Commodore), *Otranto*, *Viceroy of India*, *Pasteur*, *Laconia*, and storeships *Dorset* and *Melbourne Star*, which had detached from the Bombay portion on 26 February, proceeded at 15 knots towards the Guardafui Strait under escort of *Colombo* and arrived at Aden on the morning of 1st March where the convoy was dispersed.

The situation then in the western desert had stabilised in February with the front line 500 miles from Suez and no recent air attacks on the Suez Canal. Nevertheless the five liners of WS 15 moved north independently from Aden to arrive in Suez Bay a day apart from the 5th onwards and would have prevented congestion there had they been handled expeditiously, but the first to leave was *Pasteur* on the 9th just as *Laconia* arrived. Except *Pasteur* which had no cargo space, the liners of this convoy carried MT, stores, ammunition and tinplate with 1,450 tons of that commodity on *Otranto*. Their discharge at Suez anchorage was therefore delayed somewhat, four days for *Laconia* and five days for *Otranto*, but these cargoes may have been due to a lack of suitable storeships when loading in the UK. The two MT ships of WS 15A preceeded the transports up the Red Sea and passed directly through the canal where *Dorset* discharged in Port Said and *Melbourne Star* in Alexandria. Both returned home with refrigerated cargoes from Wellington and were later sunk in the August 'Pedestal' convoy to Malta.

The homeward passage of *Pasteur* began with 1,969 POW and guard from Suez to Durban, thence via Capetown and Freetown to the Clyde Anchorage where she arrived on 16 April as the first of the WS 15 liners that had proceeded beyond Durban. The voyage time was 4.2 months and was the minimum even for fast liners without cargo. The only means of reducing this was to turn more ships in South Africa by transhipping to the Indian Ocean ships less suitable for the Atlantic section of the voyage, which facts were already well known to both the Admiralty and DoST but could not always be implemented.

From Suez, *Laconia* first carried troops of 70 Division to Bombay while *Otranto* and *Orontes* similarly proceeded with divisional troops via Port Sudan and Aden to Colombo and were then to have continued to Australia to load on their owners' berth, but this was replaced by loading for Union Castle at Durban and Capetown. *Laconia* sailed direct from Bombay to Capetown, all three left that port between 14 and 19 April for Freetown and whence *Laconia* and *Orontes* were directed to Liverpool arriving on 9 May, while *Otranto* was sent to Glasgow arriving five days earlier. *Viceroy of India* left Suez on 11 March, bunkered at Aden, loaded small quantities of cargo at Durban and Capetown on the Union Castle berth and returned home via Freetown to Liverpool on 25 April.

Of the twelve liners of WS 15 that had continued beyond the Cape and returned home in the period between 16 April and 20 May, *Pasteur* and *Strathnaver* were next employed in WS 19, *Strathmore* and *Stirling Castle* in WS 20 and the remainder in WS 19P.

Chapter 14

WS 16, WS 17 and WS 18

Increased personnel capacity, the assault landings on Madagascar and
movement of 5 and 2 British Infantry Divisions to India

WS 16 - sailed UK 16.2.42
Although the threat of a German invasion of the British Isles continued to influence military planning throughout 1942, it was the Far East that now focused the attention of the
Chiefs of Staff in finding the means of preventing the Japanese incursion into Malaya
from spreading to Burma and Ceylon or even India. The present level of reinforcements
around the Cape would have to be substantially increased if these territories were to be
successfully defended. At the same time the CinC Middle East enquired "to what extent
he could be reinforced in the spring,"[1] to replace the many Army and Air Force units
being removed from his theatre to reinforce India and the Far East.

The Sea Transport Division of the MOWT produced a document entitled 'General
Trooping Appreciation 1942' immediately prior to the loss of Singapore. "The immediate object was to enable a decision to be taken as to whether a choice of risks must be
adopted as between the Middle East and the Far East, but this developed into a desire to

appreciate the limitations which shipping must impose on our whole strategic plan,"[1] and which Churchill came to regard as "the shipping stranglehold."[2]

It transpired that 185,000 personnel would be carried on the four WS convoys from February to May 1942, which included two divisions for India and one for the Middle East, but was 115,000 less than that which the War Office wished to send around the Cape at that time. This huge shortfall was simply a repeat of the problems which beset the authorities in January and August 1941.[3]

The MOWT document put forward six ways of increasing the personnel flow, which included increasing the frequency from the present monthly to three-weekly intervals and allowing the very fast liners to proceed unescorted from, say, South Africa to the Midde East or India. The Admiralty responded by agreeing the increased frequency "for the present emergency,"[1] and would consider outward transports being run unescorted from Durban to Suez or possibly Freetown to Suez "in relation to the raider and sub-marine situation then prevailing."[1] Another suggestion was to cut out homeward load-ing of WS ships giving a 20% increase in capacity but with the loss of three-quarters of a million tons of imports annually, which was never adopted. The fitting of cargo ships, both British and American, was remotely considered while the possibility of obtaining more Dutch passenger liners was being pursued and came to fruition when their base port Batavia was lost to the Japanese in March. Three splendid 16 knot KPM motor-ships were thereafter delivered to MOWT charter and began to join the British trooping fleet four months later.

This latest trooping appreciation proved lucrative in more ways than one. It showed that the capacity of the present WS fleet (then of 81 ships) was 190,000, and that "emer-gency measures are now in hand to increase the numbers carried in each ship. The work will take some months to complete but we hope for an ultimate increase in capacity of 20% and expect to reach a total of 240,000."[1] Specific details were not given, howev-er the Union Castle history refers to "bunks being rapidly fitted (wooden ones four high) in the public rooms, gymnasiums and swimming baths. Cabin partitions were ripped away to provide dormitory accommodation and nothing met the eye except tier upon tier of berths."[4] This feverish and salutary activity had the remarkable effect of increas-ing the capacity of seven liners being included in WS 16 by just over one-third and pro-vided 7,482 extra berths, which confirmed an early January estimate when four of the liners were examined for additional accommodation, probably the result of pressure from the PSTO Simonstown following a study of the American system found on WS 12X at Capetown some weeks earlier.

These figures were based on certain assumptions, which included the provision of Indian Ocean shipping for the on-carriage of 25,000 personnel per month from South Africa, of which 18,000 would originate in the UK. It also allowed "a good proportion of returning troopships loading cargo, in particular the refrigerated ships on the Plate and in New Zealand."[1] It was noted that the loss of the Far East repair facilities would increase pressure on those in the UK, that the performance of troopships would deteri-orate through continued hard running and that a loss of capacity through sinkings would not exceed 5%. In fact the fourteen WS liners lost by enemy action in the autumn months of 1942 exceeded 15% of the total capacity, and proved to be an even more seri-ous problem.

Another welcome result of the trooping enquiry was the Admiralty agreeing the release of four more AMCs, *California*, *Circassia*, *Derbyshire* and *Dunnottar Castle*, which took effect between February and June although the first conversion for trooping was not completed until July. Together with the promised Dutch liners these seven ships provided almost 19,000 additional berths for the WS fleet but served only to help offset the irreplaceable losses suffered in the autumn of that same year.

Fourteen liners and seven M/T storeships were scheduled for WS 16 due to sail on Sunday 15 February, most of the liners having returned from WS convoys 10,11, 12 and 12Z in the last week of December and throughout the month of January. Three others not previously utilized on the WS route were the French CGT liner *Cuba*, which had been seized by a British warship in October 1940 while on passage from Martinique to Casablanca and taken first to Takoradi and then Freetown. In June 1941 she was sent to Boston then Norfolk VA where conversion was carried out for trooping, completing in November. Placed under the British flag and Cunard management, *Cuba* crossed from Halifax to the Clyde with Canadian troops in TC 16 and thereafter docked in Liverpool on Christmas Day for outstanding repairs prior to embarkation. Also being included was the magnificent 21 knot Trans-Tasman liner *Awatea* of the Union Steamship Company of New Zealand, which had left Vancouver on 27 October with Canadian troops to help defend Hong Kong. Proceeding then via Manila, Singapore, Colombo, Capetown and Trinidad, *Awatea* reached Liverpool on 18 January with women and children evacuees from the East Indies. The Dutch Rotterdam-Lloyd *Sibajak* had been trooping since June 1941 on the Indian Ocean and the US route from Australia to Singapore and reached Liverpool on 24 January to join WS 16. Two other liners from earlier WS convoys were *Bergensfjord* which had lately been employed on Halifax and Iceland voyages, reaching the Clyde (with *Stratheden*) in NA 1 from Halifax on 19 January, and *Volendam* in NA 2, the last to reach the UK and the Clyde on 9 February, less than a week before the convoy was due to sail.

All of the liners were embarked in their ports of arrival in the UK, except *Duchess of York* and *Empire Pride* which moved downriver from Glasgow to the Clyde Anchorage on 10 February, followed next day by *Bergensfjord* just fitted with 600 additional berths whilst storing at the KGV Riverside berth. Embarkation in Glasgow was first completed on *Stratheden* which vacated 1 KGV on the morning of the 12th, followed by *Ormonde* from the adjacent No. 2 berth next morning and *Nea Hellas* which left 4 KGV at 1000 hours on the 14th. A single MT ship from Glasgow, *City of Edinburgh*, was loaded at 4 KGV and moved to the anchorage ready for sea on the 9th. Also at the anchorage were the MT ships *Brisbane Star* and *Potaro* (the latter Royal Mail owned) previously loaded at Newport and *Port Jackson* from Swansea, which had anchored in the Clyde on the 14th so that eleven Shipmasters were able to attend the convoy conference in the office of the NCSO, Gourock, at 1030 on the 15th.

Embarkations in Liverpool were completed on *Monarch of Bermuda* on the 11th, *Duchess of Richmond*, *Mooltan* and *Sibajak* on the 14th which all had then to anchor in the river or at the Bar, but were held up on *Awatea*, *Cuba* and *Strathaird* until the 16th due to fog, which then delayed the entire convoy departure by 24 hours.[5] *Strathaird* was then further delayed with a defective steam pipe and sailed a day later than the convoy with instructions to catch up and join on the 21st. From the Clyde the cruiser *Newcastle* and almost-new destroyer *Paladin*, which had also been delayed by defects, met with *Strathaird*, now fully embarked to an increased capacity of 4,202, and acted as escort until joining the convoy four days later. The total embarked on the fourteen transports was 45,340, with seven originally bound for Suez, four for the Far East and three for Bombay; the destinations of eight were changed during the course of the voyage. Drafts and details and all manner of transport and administation units were embarked on this convoy.

Escort for the first leg of the voyage to Freetown was the largest then assembled for a WS convoy. "When the *Scharnhorst* and *Gneisenau* began to show signs of activity in Brest, the Admiralty became anxious about a break-out into the Atlantic, and, in particular, for the safety of the big troop convoy WS 16...due to sail on the 15th of February."[6]   Force H then comprising the battleship *Malaya*, carrier *Eagle*, cruiser *Hermione* and attached destroyers was therefore brought from Gibraltar to the Clyde to accompany WS 16, but in the event the German warships made a spectacular dash through the English Channel on the 13th to their home ports without affecting WS 16. Admiral Sir James Somerville late of Force H and now appointed to command the Eastern Fleet, was taking passage in the carrier *Formidable* to Colombo and escorting the convoy as far as Freetown, while the cruiser *Newcastle* would act as ocean escort as far as Durban. The SO A/S escort was on the newly completed destroyer leader *Laforey*, Vice Admiral LE Crabbe as convoy commodore on *Stratheden* while Captain WS Charlton, the Master of *Monarch of Bermuda* acted as Vice Commodore.

With clear weather on the Mersey the Liverpool section of six transports and with storeships *Denbighshire*, *City of Lincoln* and Dutch *Delftdyk* began clearing the Bar at 1300 on the 16th and proceeded up the Irish Sea at 10 knots under escort of the V and W destroyers, *Walker*, *Verity* and *Witherington*. The Clyde section of seven transports and four storeships was led out of the boom by the Commodore at 2130 that same day, escorted by destroyers *Panther* and *Firedrake* and also proceeded at 10 knots towards the rendezvous 6 miles west of Orsay next morning.   Three hours behind the Commodore were *Formidable*, *Eagle*, *Hermione* and destroyers *Laforey*, *Lightning*, *Duncan*: all of Force H.

Both sections began to form into six columns each of three or four ships shortly after 0900 on the 17th, and where the Liverpool destroyers detached into 'Derry for fuel on relief by *Active*, *Anthony*, *Blankney* and *Croombe* from that port."[7] By 1130 the convoy was 10 miles north of Inishtrahull and set off on a course slightly south of west at the speed of the slowest ship, *Delftdyk*, stated to be 14 knots but had continual trouble with her main engine cooling system and was eventually reduced to 13 knots. The weather was cloudy with mist and very poor visibility, the wind S'ly force 4. At 1530 the convoy altered to a SW'ly course which was held for the next two days.

By next morning, 18th, the wind had backed to SE and increased to force 6 with a rough sea and short, heavy swell and poor visibility. During the afternoon the two Ellerman ships and *Potaro* had to heave-to with cargo shifted, a heavy tank having damaged the shell and hull frames on *City of Lincoln* and with similar cargo adrift on *City of Edinburgh* both returned to Liverpool and the Clyde respectively and subsequently sailed in the next convoy WS 17. On *Potaro* a 44 ton motor launch had shifted due to rolling but was again secured and this ship continued independently to Freetown and there rejoined the convoy. The Commodore duly noted these events in his report, but Admiral Somerville went further and considered "the bad stowage of cargo on these ships merit close investigation since the weather conditions were by no means severe."[8] Bad stowage or insufficient means of securing cargo had also occurred on WS 9A and were probably due to inexperienced labour when loading and securing cargo in each case. The strong winds with rough sea and heavy swell continued until the next afternoon when course was altered to due south to pass east of the Azores group and for the first time since departure, *Formidable* was able to fly off three aircraft in search of stragglers although these were not seen.

Moderate winds from the west prevailed until the 24th when the NE trades were picked up two days south of the Azores. *Formidable* flew daily A/S patrols with Albacores from the 19th all the way to Freetown during which time one of these aircraft failed to return, three of them and a Martlet crashed on landing, while *Eagle* similarly lost two Swordfish. Admiral Somerville commented that "the weather conditions were by no means severe (and) it was abundantly clear..the majority of pilots lacked the training and experience of deck landing to a regrettable degree."[8] Such were the exigencies of war.

On the morning of the 20th the destroyer *Anthony* dropped astern with condenser trouble and failed to rejoin. At 1800 that same day when in position 480 miles north of Sao Miguel of the Azores, *Panther* was detached to refuel at Ponta Delgada on that island. Next morning *Croombe* was detached to Gibraltar while Albacores searching astern for *Strathaird* and her escorts located them at 1130 and were joined up two hours later. At 1430 the three major units and five destroyers of Force H detached to Gibraltar and were soon flying air reinforcements to Malta. *Firedrake* detached back to the UK at 1800 leaving the three V and W destroyers as A/S screen.

By the forenoon of the 22nd the convoy was 10 miles east of Sao Miguel and continued a S'ly course towards the Cap Vert gap and at 1800 the three V and Ws detached to fuel at Ponta Delgada and thereafter proceed to Halifax. For the next 22 hours the convoy had no surface A/S escort although Albacores continued to provide this cover in daylight hours from *Formidable*. *Cuba* dropped astern with engine trouble for four hours on the 23rd and thereafter could only manage 13.5 knots. *Paladin* rejoined at 1600 and *Panther* at 2235 both from Ponta Delgada.

From the 24th until arrival at Freetown the warships and aircraft carried out daily firing exercises, dummy dive-bombing and torpedo attacks interspersed with deck landing training, which helped to relieve the boredom of the troops. On the 25th four Albacores carried out a search to a depth of 200 miles for the German supply tanker *Charlotte Schliemann* reported sailed from Las Palmas. Unfortunately nothing was seen of the *Schlieman* and Admiral Somerville was reluctant to detach *Newcastle* to search on account of her fuel status and convoy protection duties. The *Schliemann* was thereafter able to supply raiders on the Atlantic and Indian Oceans until caught up with, appropriately by *Newcastle* and destroyer *Relentless* in February 1944, and was then scuttled to prevent capture.

At 0900 on the 26th the destroyers *Boreas*, *Brilliant* and *Wild Swan* joined from Bathurst as local A/S escort, the convoy then being 140 miles NE of the Cape Verde islands, and that afternoon a Sunderland aircraft also from Bathurst joined as additional A/S escort and reported *Potaro* being 33 miles astern. Sunderland air patrols were continued in daylight hours until reaching Freetown. On the 27th *Potaro* was reported as 26 miles astern and at 0430 next day the convoy altered course to ESE direct for Freetown then 300 miles distant. At 1630 three columns were formed preparatory to arrival. The swept channel, marked by a trawler, was entered at 0600 on the 1st March when single line ahead was formed and at 0755 *Formidable* anchored in Freetown, the convoy and *Potaro* all being similarly berthed by 1030. The average speed from the Clyde was 12.68 knots.

Without waiting for the convoy, *Formidable* replenished and sailed for the Cape, probably retaining *Panther* and *Paladin* as escorts. She arrived at Capetown on the 10th, left two days later and moored in Colombo as part of the Eastern Fleet on the 24th.

Within two days of the convoy's arrival at Freetown there were 100 ships in the port but pressure on fuel and fresh water supplies was relieved on the 4th when 39 ships left in convoy SL 102 for the UK. A total of 9,633 tons of water was shipped on 15 ships of WS 16 and 24,645 tons of fuel amongst all ships of the convoy with more than 2,000 tons each on *Mooltan* and *Volendam*. A number of personnel were disembarked at Freetown and some transhipments made to allow *Bergensfjord* accommodate the 1,149 from *Llangibby Castle* of WS 15, which *Batory* had brought forward from Gibraltar. *Port Jackson* also embarked 16 personnel for South Africa, *Brisbane Star* 7 and *Nea Hellas* 11. While the convoy busied itself in Freetown, news came through of Japanese landings in Java, the occupation of Batavia and surrender of the Dutch East Indies which completely removed the Far East from the list of possible convoy destinations.

The convoy was led out of Freetown boom at 0830 on 6 March by the Commodore on *Stratheden*, but *Newcastle* had sailed two hours earlier for exercises, followed by the A/S escort comprising *Brilliant* and *Wild Swan*, sloop *Bridgewater* and corvettes *Jasmine* and *Nigella* which carried out an A/S sweep outside the harbour before returning to meet the convoy off the boom. Although U-Boats had not been reported in the Freetown area since their abortive attempt in October 1941, the Ben Line's *Benmohr* was torpedoed and sunk 150 miles south of the port the previous evening, while a Norwegian tanker was sunk (by the same U-Boat) 240 miles south of Freetown as the convoy was leaving the port next morning. A wide evasive route was therefore taken out to the westward for the first 24 hours, then a further leg to the south'ard before the convoy turned to the SE for the Cape at 0800 on the 8th.

WS 16 retained its six column formation after Freetown but only the Commodore (on *Stratheden*), *Monarch of Bermuda*, *Empire Pride* and *Port Jackson* maintained their previous stations. *Bridgewater* and the two corvettes were continuing to the Cape although *Nigella* had engine trouble from leaving Freetown and was ordered direct to St. Helena, to refuel there from RFA *Abbeydale* and continue to Simonstown. On the morning of the 8th *Newcastle* attempted to fuel *Bridgewater* but was unsuccessful owing to the swell. *Brilliant* and *Wild Swan* were then detached to return to Freetown. A further attempt was made to fuel *Bridgewater* on the 9th and met with some success but had to be interrupted to allow *Newcastle* to recover her Walrus which had been launched for an A/S patrol.

About midday on the 10th, WS 16 was 150 miles NE of Ascension and continued on the same course towards the Cape. On the afternoon of the 12th, *Newcastle* successfully fuelled *Bridgewater* and by darkness the convoy was 70 miles NE of St. Helena where *Jasmine* was detached to fuel from *Abbeydale*, and after fuelling *Nigella* the RFA was ordered to Freetown.

On this particular leg of the voyage the weather seldom changes from the constant SE trades which blow throughout the year from north of Ascension until a day or so before reaching Capetown, but are not recorded for the passage of WS 16. The convoy was given an opportunity to practise high angle firing at a kite towed by *Newcastle* on one occasion and apart from the cruiser's refrigeration plant giving repeated trouble, no other incidents occurred on this passage until the morning of the 16th when FOIC Simonstown signalled that the Dutch *Alcyone* had been mined about 3 miles NW of the outer end of the Capetown searched channel, which the convoy was due to reach in less than two days time. Six local minesweepers were sent to extend the searched channel, the port was closed and warnings issued of the suspected area and channel extension. Late on the 16th an exploded mine was reported to the westward and another next day.'⁹ These mines had been laid by the German *Doggerbank*¹⁰ in the Capetown approaches overnight on the 12th, and on the next night close to Cape Agulhas. Although these minelaying operations remained undetected for almost four days, *Doggerbank* had been sighted and passed by several ships off the Cape, not realizing she was other than the Bank Line's *Levernbank* as claimed by signal to an Anson patrolling aircraft, to the cruiser *Durban* and AMC *Cheshire* all between the 12th and 14th. There was then no means of verifying the authenticity of ships as later introduced in October 1942. Miraculously the *Queen Mary* passed through Capetown unscathed two days later carrying 8,000 US troops to Australia.

At 1800 on the 17th the convoy reached a rendezvous position 110 miles NW of Capetown, where *Newcastle* handed over the escort to the AMC *Dunnottar Castle* and sloop *Milford*, detached with *Nea Hellas*, *Bergensfjord*, *Sibajak* and the five MT ships for Capetown, and arrived there safely after the morning sweep had been made and berthed in the harbour at midday on the 18th to replenish stores, fuel, fresh water and allow the troops much needed exercise and recreation on shore. They had been onboard the transports for five weeks.

The remaining eleven ships of the convoy continued on voyage towards Durban and at 0600 on the 18th when 30 miles south of Cape Point (otherwise the Cape of Good Hope) were joined by the AMC *Cheshire* and two corvettes, and soon after the sloop *Bridgewater* detached to Simonstown followed by the corvettes that afternoon by which time the convoy was steering east from a position 75 miles SSW of Cape Agulhas. *Newcastle* meanwhile had discharged some tank spares at Capetown and moved round overnight to Simonstown where the 4-inch gun barrels were changed and where her refrigeration plant failed completely and arrangements were made for repairs to be carried out in Durban. *Newcastle* left Simonstown at noon on the 22nd and met the Capetown portion of WS 16, relieved the local escort *Bridgewater* and continued without incident to the rendezvous outside Durban where that portion was met, *Newcastle* then remaining in company with the combined convoy for seven hours until returning to berth in Durban harbour.

The main Durban section of the convoy had continued east from Cape Agulhas until the following morning when course was altered to pass 50 miles SE of East London on the 20th, and 24 hours later the convoy arrived at Durban. The Commodore made two recommendations: one being the addition of a stanchion on the funnel of some ships to carry a triatic stay for improved flag signalling, and was certainly adopted. The other concerned the low speed of the AMCs *Dunnottar Castle* and *Cheshire* at 12.5 knots, which made them unsuitable as escort in such convoys, especially when stationed in the protected centre with liners outside of them capable of 18 knots or more and carrying 4,000 troops.¹¹ The average speed from Freetown was recorded as 12.99 knots.

In Durban, none of the Indian Ocean class transports were yet available for on-carriage, mainly because a quarter were still engaged in returning the Australian divisions to their homeland. However the three "Monsters" had now completed troop movements to India from the Middle East and reached Durban between the 20th and 28th March to embark 16,000 personnel being landed from *Cuba*, *Mooltan*, *Strathaird*, *Ormonde* and *Monarch of Bermuda*, which were returning to the UK for inclusion in WS 19. The first four named were originally destined for Suez while *Monarch of Bermuda*, with *Awatea*,

Sibajak and *Empire Pride* had embarked for the Far East. The destination of the remaining liners of the convoy were unchanged with both of the CPS *Duchess* liners and *Stratheden* bound for Bombay and the three liners at Capetown proceeding to Suez.

As with all of the WS convoys handled at Durban, the authorities met the challenge of urgency and dispatched WS 16 in the space of four days, despite *Mauretania*, *Ile de France* and three of the homeward liners of WS 15 being in port at that time. War in the Far East had now reached Burma, the Japanese occupied Rangoon on 8 March and from where began the long withdrawal of British and Indian forces almost to the Indian frontier. In the desert both German and British armies faced each other between Gazala and Bir Hacheim, gathering strength for the next offensive in June.

Two of the liners returning from Durban were sailed within a day of their arrival, *Ormonde* and *Mooltan* then loading small quantities of cargo at Capetown whence they sailed on the 29th for Freetown and arrived there on 8 April to find the very large WS 17 convoy in the midst of replenishment. Because of this it took five days to refuel *Ormonde* and six for *Mooltan* but they reached Liverpool and Glasgow respectively on 24 and 26 April. *Monarch of Bermuda* left Durban on 24 March and Capetown on the same day as the other two but reached Freetown two days earlier and Liverpool on 23 April. *Strathaird* was a day behind the *Monarch* in leaving Durban, two days later from Capetown and by spending less time in Freetown reached the UK on the same date to berth in Glasgow. The last to leave Durban was *Cuba* on 29 March and was delayed for eleven days of repairs at Capetown and loaded there on the Bullard King berth. From Capetown *Cuba* was directed to Lagos then Takoradi, Freetown and Belfast before docking in Avonmouth on 18 May for next inclusion in WS 20.

The remaining six liners of WS 16 sailed from Durban at 1030 on 25 March led by Commodore Crabbe on *Stratheden*, with the cruiser *Glasgow* and AMC *Worcestershire* as escorts, proceeding then to a rendezvous 40 miles SE of the port where junction was made at 1330 with the three liners and five MT ships from Capetown under escort of *Newcastle*. Cruising order was formed of five columns, the port hand column being the three Capetown liners for Suez.[12] Course was set towards the Mozambique Channel at a speed of 13.5 knots and at midnight *Newcastle* parted company for Durban where she was to undertake refrigeration repairs.

The Vice Commodore of the combined convoy, who acted as Commodore of the Capetown section and later the Aden section, was Captain RW Smart of *Nea Hellas*. He had been Master of her near sister *California* virtually from 1928 until she became an AMC in 1939, then served on various Anchor Line ships until appointed for a single voyage of *Nea Hellas* while her regular master, Captain JM Brown continued in the less onerous role of Staff Captain.

No incidents occurred on the passage northwards, the aircraft from *Glasgow* provided an air patrol on the first three days whilst the convoy kept to the Portuguese rather than the more usual Madagascar half of the channel. By the morning of the 29th, WS 16 was abreast of Mozambique, altered to a N'ly course and that night passed 40 miles west of the Comoro islands. On the late forenoon of the 31st the convoy was 160 miles east of Mombasa where a NE'ly course was set towards Guardafui, and at 0600 next morning the cruiser *Colombo* and AMC *Alaunia* joined the escort, the latter having served on the North Atlantic station since October 1939 until joining the East Indies fleet in January. The increased escort may have been due to a possible threat from Japanese warships, raiders or submarines.

The splitting of WS 16 occurred in the evening of 2nd April by which time the convoy was almost midway between Mogadishu and Guardafui on the Somaliland coast. *Colombo* detached with the three liners for Suez and passed through the Guardafui Strait during the afternoon of the 4th and reached Aden to disperse on the morning of the 6th. Independent sailings were then made to Suez, *Bergensfjord* arriving on the 10th and the other two a day later, the *Nea Hellas* having been in collision with the American steamer *Susan V Luckenbach* on the previous day. *Mauretania* as an independent sailing from Durban left there two days ahead of WS 16 and cleared Suez on her return trip on the 4th.

The Bombay section of WS 16, comprising six liners and five MT ships under escort of *Glasgow* and the two AMCs, had an uneventful passage across the north Indian Ocean and arrived in the harbour on the morning of the 8th. The CO on *Alaunia*, Captain CA Kershaw RN, commented on the doubtful value of including two moderate speed AMCs in such a fast convoy.

Over 19,000 personnel were disembarked from the six liners at Bombay of which a small number may have been on-carried to Basra on *Lancashire* and *Rohna* later in the month, the balance being retained for service in India whose situation since the loss of Malaya and Rangoon "was in many ways similar to that of Great Britain after Dunkirk: well-trained troops were scarce and equipment scarcer still."[13]

The process of disembarking personnel, stores and equipment from six liners in turn at the Ballard Pier facility was drawn out over two weeks, and homeward cargo loading confined to Capetown rather than Bombay. Durban calls were avoided to prevent congestion with the ships of the next convoy WS 17. *Stratheden* was the first departure from Bombay on the 14th, followed at intervals by *Empire Pride, Sibajak, Duchess of Richmond, Duchess of York* and *Awatea* on 27 April. The storeships each required two weeks for discharge in Alexandra Dock and thereafter were widely dispersed to load homeward cargoes.

Stratheden reached Capetown just before WS 17 sailed and where loading on the Union Castle berth occupied eight days, thereafter a call was made at Freetown and Glasgow reached on 23 May. *Duchess of Richmond* was similarly dispatched three days behind the *Strath* liner and docked in Liverpool on the 26th, while *Duchess of York* another two days behind was directed from Freetown to Halifax and crossed with *Batory* in NA 10 to reach Liverpool on 11 June. *Awatea* sailed direct from Capetown to the Clyde, arriving on 28 May for boiler cleaning and repairs before joining her next sailing in WS 20. *Empire Pride* was delayed for two weeks engine repairs at Capetown and sailed direct to reach the Clyde on 6 June, also for sailing in WS 20 with *Stratheden* and *Duchess of Richmond*, whose sister ship was held for WS 21P. The lame duck proved to be *Sibajak*, delayed for 25 days at Capetown for overhaul of her main engines, troop fittings and drydocking and with a further delay of eight days at Freetown did not reach Liverpool until the last day of June to be included in WS 21 but then brought back for a later special sailing.

In Suez the three remaining liners of WS 16, having arrived with over 9,000 personnel on the 10th and 11th, were under instruction to disembark and thereafter receive POW: 400 German and 1100 Italian on *Bergensfjord* which was quickly dispatched on the 12th, while *Nea Hellas* was to sail on the 13th with 1,600 Germans and *Volendam* to embark 1,400 Italians from Port Sudan on the 16th. The PSTO Egypt then amended the arrangements, *Bergensfjord* sailed with 1,000 Germans and *Volendam* with 2,400 POW and 712 other personnel on the 13th. The uplift from Port Sudan was to be made by *Nea Hellas* which requested time at Durban to rectify long standing machinery defects, some of which had first to be made good at Suez anchorage, and during which time *Nieuw Amsterdam* arrived with 5,500 on-carried from WS 16 ships in Durban. This liner was then embarked with a further 1,955 POW plus other personnel destined for Durban and sailed on the 16th.

These POW arrangements were part of a plan to transfer all to *Queen Elizabeth* in Table Bay at Capetown. This liner was returning empty from Sydney to New York and due to refuel in Table Bay on 3rd May where she duly anchored. *Bergensfjord* arrived there on 28 April, *Nieuw Amsterdam* two days later and *Volendam* on 1st May, all having called at Durban en route to land non-POW personnel. Unfortunately the weather prevented transhipment in Table Bay so all four liners moved round to improved shelter in Simons Bay,[14] where tug tenders transferred 600 at a time to *Queen Elizabeth*, then under the command of Captain EM Fall. *Bergensfjord* then returned to Capetown, loaded oranges and tinned crayfish, embarked some civilians and sailed on 13 May for Freetown and the Clyde arriving on 7 June for inclusion in WS 20. *Volendam* also loaded in Capetown, carried out engine repairs, embarked 657 personnel for the UK and sailed on the 20th and due to her low speed of 13.5 knots was included in convoy SL 112 from Freetown to reach Liverpool on 23 June and next sailed in WS 21.

The last part of the POW transhipment from *Nieuw Amsterdam* to *Queen Elizabeth* was carried out under floodlights when several Germans took the opportunity to jump overboard and swim for the shore but were quickly rounded up, apart from one who drowned and another who hid behind a panel in the Dutch liner until the *Q.E.* sailed on the 7th for New York via refuelling at Rio.

Nea Hellas did not leave Suez until 19 April, embarked Italian POW and loaded on the Ellerman berth at Port Sudan, disembarked the POW at Durban, loaded there and spent three weeks completing much needed engine-room repairs. Further loading was made in Capetown where she departed on 4 June for Freetown and the Clyde arriving on the last day of June and was to make her next voyage in WS 22.

WS 16 had achieved a fast turnround in Durban for one-third of its liners allowing their return to the UK within nine weeks for a next WS voyage, and proved to be the key to increased capacity on the route although dependent on sufficient Indian Ocean tonnage then being available for on-carriage from Durban to Suez and Bombay.

WS 17 - sailed UK 23.3.42

At the beginning of February 1942 the War Office made known its intention of sending one division in each of the convoys around the Cape leaving in March, April and May and in adhering to this plan, 5th Infantry Division destined for India was selected for the first of these sailings.

By the second week of February nineteen liners were nominated for WS 17 having a total capacity of 39,000, later amended to 42,000 and then by increased fitting to 53,000 by the new emergency measures and this figure was met even after *Rangitiki* was withdrawn for a Halifax and Plate voyage in lieu.

Early in March, by which time all eighteen liners were in the UK preparing for WS 17, the Chiefs of Staff, backed by Churchill, decided to mount "Operation Ironclad - to seize and hold the Vichy French naval and air base of Diego Suarez at the northern tip of Madagascar and so forestall a possible Japanese landing on the island."[1] The date of the operation was to be early in May and conveniently allowed the necessary forces and shipping to leave the UK with WS 17 and which subsequently absorbed part of 5 Division.

There had been anxiety about the Vichy controlled island ever since the fall of France in June 1940, plans to seize control of it were discussed six months later but could not proceed due to lack of the necessary forces. Rumours of Japanese interest in occupying the island came to light in December 1941 but even then shipping could not be found. The fall of Singapore and consequent threat to the lines of communication on the Indian Ocean made it imperative to forestall a Japanese landing and by 14 March an outline plan was ready to seize Diego Suarez.

The assault landings were to be made by No. 5 Commando and 29 Independent Brigade Group which had both reached an advanced stage of training in amphibious operations on the Firth of Clyde and were to be carried on four additional ships hastily allocated on 14 March. The ships were berthed ready to begin embarkation three days later but only on the 18th was the decision taken to go ahead with the operation and only then were the military units, then in the Borders or afloat on exercises in the Clyde area, told they were to embark immediately for a secret destination.

29 Brigade Group was formed in July 1940 with four of the regular battalions then arrived from India and had first to be re-equipped and mechanized for modern warfare. The brigade were then stationed near the south coast for the anti-invasion counter-attack role until May 1941 when entrained to Greenock and there embarked on the liners of WS 8C for intensive training in amphibious warfare and some of the units were still exercising in these tasks when ordered to embark for what they believed to be just another exercise.

5 Infantry Division en route to India was a regular British Army formation (not to be confused with 5 Indian Division) comprising 13, 15 and 17 Brigades which had served in France and Belgium from the autumn of 1939 until their subsequent evacuation from Dunkirk, thereafter being occupied in defensive positions near the south coast until warned for overseas tropical service in January 1942. Mobilization was complete by the end of February and on 19 March the divisional units began entraining to their appointed embarkation ports and on which late date, the War Office earmarked 17 Brigade as a follow-up formation for the Madagascar landings but too late to amend their order of shipment. Much of the divisional vehicles and equipment had already sailed in a slow convoy on 13 March and none of the division had any experience or training in amphibious warfare.

Including these units and ships specifically assigned to the assault phase on Madagascar, the 22 liners of WS 17 embarked 59,230 personnel; the highest number then carried on these convoys and only once succeeded thereafter. Embarkations in Liverpool were carried out from 15 to 20 March on *Abosso*, *Samaria* (carrying 15 Brigade HQ and 1st Bn The Green Howards), *Leopoldville*, *Nieuw Holland* and *Johan van Oldenbarnevelt*; the last two having arrived from Indian Ocean service on 28 January and from the US Australia/Suez route on 23 February respectively. All other liners from Liverpool had recently returned from previous WS convoys and *Tamaroa* in the Bristol Channel from a Halifax and Plate voyage. Together with the MT ships *Glaucus* (Blue Funnel) and *City of Lincoln* (from WS 16 *q.v.*), these liners left the Mersey on 20th March and anchored in the Clyde next day. From Avonmouth *Tamaroa* embarked and sailed on the 20th with MT ships *Clan Macdonald* also from that port, *Kina II* from Newport and *Port Wyndham* and *Dunedin Star* from Swansea, all five anchoring in the Clyde to join those from the Mersey on the 21st, although the Port Line ship had then to dock in Greenock to load additional military stores.

The next embarkations in Liverpool were on *Arundel Castle, Empress of Russia* and *Duchess of Atholl*, the latter having cleared Gladstone Dock with part of 17 Brigade units, including 2 Bn Northamptons, to anchor with the others in the river on the 21st. The final Liverpool embarkations were on *Dominion Monarch* and *Oronsay* from Princes Landing Stage, the latter carrying nearly 5,000 personnel, including the Headquarters of 17 Brigade, together with their 2 Bn Royal Scots Fusiliers, 6 Bn Seaforths and a Heavy AA Regiment. All five liners left the river on the last of the flood tide that afternoon with the destroyers *Volunteer* and Hunt class *Aldenham* as escorts, to make rendezvous with the main section from the Clyde next morning.

All the liners on the Clyde, except those for the assault on Diego Suarez, had returned from prior WS convoys 10 to 14, the most recent arrival being *Cameronia* on 9 March. The first movements for the convoy began on the 14th when *Largs Bay* moved downriver from Glasgow to embark at the anchorage, only to return upriver two days later to ship stores and again reverted to the anchorage on the 22nd where embarkation was accomplished next day. *Windsor Castle* and *Mataroa* moved to the anchorage on the 16th and 17th, the former embarking some units of 15 Brigade including 1 Bn York & Lancaster Regiment.

The embarkation and loading of stores and equipment in Glasgow was completed on six liners in as many days by utilizing four berths in KGV and adjacent Riverside Wall, No. 1 being used for three liners in succession beginning with *Almanzora* which then moved downriver on the 18th. *Franconia* followed next day carrying 13 Brigade Headquarters complete with their 2 Bn Cameronians, 2 Bn Royal Iniskilling Fusiliers and 2 Bn Wiltshire Regiment. *Orion* followed downriver on the 20th and *Cameronia* on the 21st. Three MT ships from Glasgow were *City of Edinburgh*, which had been re-storing and securing cargo since returning from WS 16, Hain's *Bhutan* and the Dutch *Rembrandt* which had previously sailed in WS 12.

There now remained the embarkation and loading of units assigned to the Madagascar assault and for which four liners had been hastily allocated, principally *Winchester Castle*, engaged for the past ten months in the Firth of Clyde as a training ship for troops and landing-craft crews learning amphibious warfare, and now fitted out to serve as the Brigade HQ. Captain SF Newdigate had been Master of the ship throughout this period and later wrote that "details of the assault on the island were worked out and gone over by those in charge of the combined operations. In the former gymnasium a scale model of the complete island terrain was built, in sand."[2] The two HM transports *Keren* and *Karanja*, which had been held in the Clyde to the greatest chagrin of the MOWT since the failed Dakar expedition in September 1940, and now fitted like *Winchester Castle* to carry LCAs in place of most lifeboats, were also allotted, as was the Polish *Sobieski* with no such experience or fitments but having just arrived from Gibraltar, was quickly loaded and stored for the voyage. One further ship allocated to the assault was the former Glasgow/Belfast overnight liner *Royal Ulsterman*, by now an HM ship stationed at Freetown awaiting possible operations against the Atlantic islands. The *Ulsterman* was a most convenient ship for inshore work and was fitted with hand-hoist landing craft. She was dispatched empty from Freetown on 26 March, called at Simonstown to effect outstanding repairs and arrived at Durban one day ahead of WS 17 to join the assault force which was by now codenamed Force 121. Captain GA Garnon-Williams RN was appointed the Senior Naval Oficer for the landings and Maj-

General RG Sturges, Royal Marines, the military commander, both being carried on *Winchester Castle*.

Winchester Castle berthed at the Riverside Wall and *Sobieski* at 6 KGV to begin embarking on the 17th, the former accommodating Brigadier FW Festing and his staff together with two companies of 2 Bn East Lancs Regiment and No. 5 Commando, while the other two companies and all of 2 Bn South Lancs were on *Sobieski*. Both liners sailed downriver on the afternoon of the 23rd and were berthed in the anchorage by 1800 ready for sea.

Finally the HM Landing Ships *Keren* and *Karanja* which had been at the naval Tail of the Bank anchorage for most of the month, were conveniently brought alongside the Greenock railway terminus at Princes Pier, where 1 Bn Royal Scots Fusiliers embarked on *Keren* during the 17th and 18th, followed by 2 Bn Royal Welch Fusiliers on *Karanja* over the next two days, both ships then returning to their anchorage berths.[3] Also accompanying the convoy was the newly completed submarine depot ship *Adamant* proceeding to Colombo to join the Eastern Fleet.

The Clyde section of the convoy then comprised 15 merchant and 2 naval transports, 9 MT ships and a Depot Ship with another five liners to join from Liverpool making a total of 32 ships and therefore one of the largest of the WS series.

The naval forces required to support the Madagascar expedition had mostly to come from Force H at Gibraltar, comprising the battleship *Malaya*, cruiser *Hermione* with five destroyers and whose Rear-Admiral EN Syfret was appointed CinC of the entire operation. The carrier *Illustrious* recently returned from major repairs at Norfolk, Virginia, and embarked with two squadrons each of Martlets and Swordfish, was to add to the force and provide air cover for the convoy from the time of leaving the UK. The cruiser *Shropshire* and AMC *Alcantara* were to act as ocean escort for the convoy from the UK to Freetown.

The appointed Commodore of the convoy, Rear-Admiral AHC Candy CBE RNR on *Franconia* led the Clyde section out of the boom at 2030 on the 23rd and was followed during the night by *Illustrious*, *Shropshire*, *Alcantara* with destroyers *Pakenham*, *Lookout*, *Javelin* and *Inconstant*. *Clan Macdonald* was unable to sail due to engine defects but was then given priority berthing in the naval anchorage at the Tail of the Bank, close to the boating station and ready access to Kincaid's Engine Works, whose fitters worked around the clock on the twin B & W engines to allow the earliest departure of the ship to catch up the convoy, and having then proceeded non-stop from the Clyde, subsequently reached Capetown two days ahead of WS 17B.

The convoy proceeded at 10 knots towards the rendezvous 6 miles west of Orsay at 1000 next morning where the Liverpool section joined to form eight columns with another between columns 5 and 6 for the major escorts.[4] The SOE was Captain AG Talbot RN on *Illustrious* and SO A/S escort Captain EBK Stephens on *Pakenham*. The Master of *Franconia*, Captain Bertinshaw, accommodated the Commodore with his signals staff while Captain RW Tate of the Elder Dempster flagship *Abosso* acted as Vice Commodore.

Also at the rendezvous position the two Liverpool destroyers rejoined after refuelling at Moville with *Boadicea*, *Antelope* and *Grove* which had come down from the Clyde following the convoy conference, and at the same time *Keppel*, *Badsworth* and four of the Town class ex-US destroyers joined from 'Derry to provide an overall A/S screen of 15 escorts around the convoy.

A westerly course was maintained on the first day until 2300, when an alteration was made to the SW and in the early hours of the 25th the destroyers *Newport* and *Beverley* were in collision requiring the former to return to Liverpool. That evening a Swordfish on dusk patrol from *Illustrious* lost its way, the carrier made a wide diversion towards its position, fired starshell and sent *Javelin* and *Lookout* to search but were unsuccessful and all had to rejoin the convoy for protection purposes.[5] However the aircraft then reported having made a forced landing on the sea, giving a position 170 miles west of Londonderry. The incident was passed on to CinC WA who immediately ordered the destroyer *Viscount* with all despatch to its assistance. The aircraft was heard transmitting as late as 0530 next morning when *Viscount* was near to the given position. The weather being relatively calm with no wind, two Hudson aircraft joined the search in the forenoon but sadly the Swordfish and its three man crew were never located.

For this convoy *Abosso* and *Antelope* were fitted with HF/DF to assist in locating U-Boat transmissions and add to the warnings provided by the Admiralty. No U-Boat activity had been reported in the Western Approaches for the past five weeks but there were indications of their presence astern of the convoy as it progressed southwards on the 26th.

By the morning of the 27th the convoy was 700 miles west of Brest and beginning to cross the U-Boat tracks between their French Biscay bases and Atlantic patrol areas. At 0620 *Abosso* obtained a strong D/F bearing from a U-Boat on the port quarter and two hours later *Leamington* and *Grove* sighted one on the surface, were then joined by *Volunteer* and *Aldenham* which combined in depth charge attacks to sink *U 587*,[6] the first such sinking directly attributed to the use of HF/DF. The Admiralty then advised of another U-Boat believed to have been astern of the convoy that morning from which it appeared the convoy was being shadowed and reported. At 0900 *Badsworth* was detached to Plymouth and during that night reported a U-Boat on the surface which dived and was attacked but with inconclusive results. During the afternoon of the 27th, *Lookout, Aldenham* and *Grove* were detached ahead to refuel at Ponta Delgada then distant 500 miles, while *Keppel, Beverley* and *Volunteer* were detached to meet and escort the homeward convoy SL 103 of 45 ships to the UK.

The convoy was 100 miles east of Sao Miguel of the Azores group on the morning of the 29th when *Lookout* and *Grove* rejoined and allowed *Pakenham, Javelin* and *Inconstant* to detach to the island to refuel, and when *Aldenham* rejoined in the afternoon *Antelope* was similarly detached.

At 0915 on the 30th with the convoy 250 miles west of Madeira, *Boadicea* detached to Ponta Delgada and continued to the UK. That morning there was a tragic accident on *Illustrious* when one of the 4.5-inch guns fired directly into another turret causing casualties and damage.[5] *Pakenham* rejoined just after midday and at 1730 *Illustrious* left the convoy and proceeded ahead for Freetown with *Pakenham* and *Rockingham* as escorts, leaving *Shropshire* and *Alcantara* with the convoy. That evening, however, the Flag Officer West Africa (FOWA) signalled *Illustrious*, that an unidentified battlecruiser was steering towards the convoy from the SE at 20 knots and could intercept it at dawn.[7] *Illustrious* "despatched *Rockingham* at full speed to tell *Shropshire* to turn the convoy to the westward;"[5] the carrier rejoined WS 17 at 2200 and maintained air patrols overnight but by the next evening FOWA advised the battlecruiser had turned SSW and so the convoy resumed its S'ly course to pass between Cap Vert and the island group. *Illustrious* again left the convoy at 0930 on the 31st and proceeded at 18 knots for Freetown to arrive there on the morning of 3 April, having maintained dawn to dusk air

31. *Queen Elizabeth* anchored at Suez 18 July 1942 on arrival as convoy WS 19Y. (*IWM E 14726*)

32. WS 19 columns 1,2 and 3 viewed from air escort when approaching the Cap Vert gap, morning of 19 May 1942. L. to R. *Athlone Castle, Highland Brigade, Moreton Bay* with *Ormonde* (behind). *Clan Macarthur, Monarch of Bermuda*, Ocean escort *HMS Mauritius* in foreground. (*IWM A.10615*)

33. *Pasteur* of WS 19 leaving Freetown 26 May 1942 (*IWM A.10612*)

34. *Monarch of Bermuda* of WS 19 leaving Freetown 26 May 1942 (*IWM A.10611*)

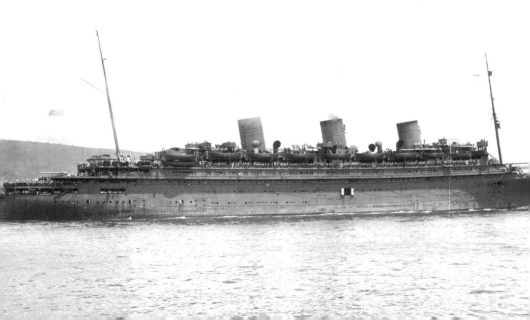

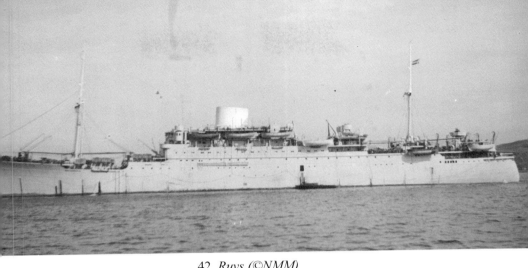

42. *Ruys (©NMM)*

43. *Sibajak (©NMM)*

44. *Highland Monarch (©NMM)*

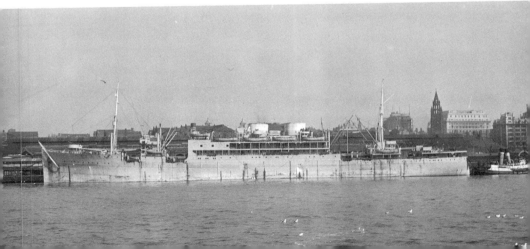

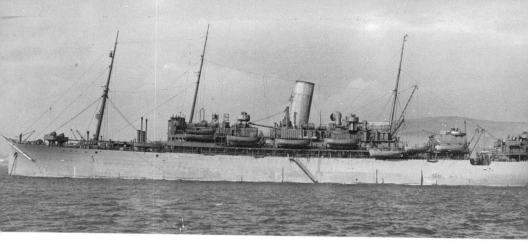

45. *Staffordshire* 15.4.43 *(©NMM)*

46. *Orduna (©NMM)*

47. *Ormonde (©NMM)*

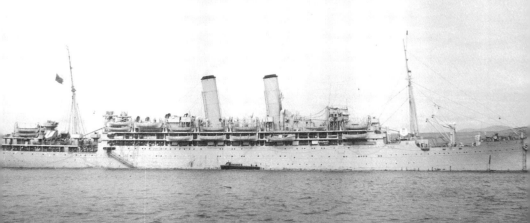

patrols for the convoy for most of its passage. A serious hangar fire occurred on the day before arrival Freetown which took six hours to extinguish and during which ten Swordfish were burnt out.

Soon after *Illustrious* left the convoy on the 31st, *Johan van Oldenbarnevelt* was reduced to 8 knots due to engine trouble and reported that 12 hours were required to make good. *Aldenham* was detached to escort the Dutch liner which rejoined on the morning of 3 April. The local escort destroyers, *Active, Anthony, Wild Swan* and two corvettes joined on 1st April and continued with the convoy to Freetown. The Cap Vert island gap was passed through during the night of 2/3 April and on the 4th, *Shropshire* heard U-Boat transmissions and ordered an emergency turn which was held for almost two hours. Sunderland air patrols were maintained around the convoy in daylight hours from the 3rd until arrival Freetown, and in failing to make an arrival before dark on the 5th, the convoy reversed course for five hours that afternoon. The convoy entered the searched channel at 0745 on the 6th, the Commodore anchored in Freetown at 1015 and the last of the 31 ships of WS 17, *Dunedin Star*, at 1630.

The official history best describes the scene while the ships of Force 121 were given priority for replenishment, "it was at Freetown that the naval and military commanders of the operation (i.e. assault on Diego Suarez) met for the first time,"[1] and as the various unit commanders were introduced to the senior naval and military officers aboard *Winchester Castle*, Brigadier Tarleton on *Oronsay* summoned his battalion commanders and warned them of their impending involvement in a combined operation for which they had received no training. As a consequence the two 17 Brigade liners and three MT ships were to proceed to Durban with those of Force 121 ahead of the main convoy.

Rear-Admiral Syfret with *Malaya, Hermione* and five destroyers of Force H arrived at Freetown from Gibraltar a few hours behind the convoy and as overall CinC of Operation Ironclad, now took part in the preliminary planning aboard the Brigade HQ ship. The whole of Force 121 and 17 Brigade ships sailed again on the 9th, together with *Dominion Monarch, Largs Bay, Windsor Castle*, three MT ships and with Force H, the cruiser *Devonshire* and eight destroyers as escort.[8] During the passage south a message was received that 13 Brigade (all on *Franconia* in the convoy following) was to join the expedition as a floating reserve, but for the troops of 17 Brigade the matter was more pressing as recorded by 2 Bn Northamptons on *Duchess of Atholl*: "for the next two weeks the ship was a hive of activity. To get the men fit, PT was intensified, route-marches were held around the decks in full equipment and to the horror of the ship's Captain, in boots. The organization of an LCA with a platoon aboard was practised in a mock craft built of planks and forms. The PT was to pay off later."[9]

On 18 April Force H detached with *Dominion Monarch* and the three MT ships into Capetown while the remainder of the convoy continued to Durban with *Devonshire* and were berthed alongside on the 22nd, closely followed by Admiral Syfret on *Illustrious* with the destroyers. *Malaya* had been ordered back to Freetown and was replaced by *Ramillies* of the Eastern Fleet now waiting in Durban. There was intense activity in the port throughout the next six days as the vehicles, guns and equipment of 17 Brigade had to be unloaded, the transport serviced and waterproofed, tanks retracked and landing craft refuelled and transferred to their assault ships while all the vehicles and equipment were restowed as for an operational basis. Also in Durban, the two companies of 2 Bn East Lancs on *Sobieski*, transferred to *Royal Ulsterman* which was to be the fifth assault ship for the landings.

Force 121 had been astute to send "service representatives ahead by air from Freetown to Durban to make preparations for the reception of the convoy....thus when the vessels arrived at Durban, all ships were berthed alongside and within a few hours of arrival, work on re-stowing them began."[1] The Impcon staff responsible for military movements in Durban also acknowledged "it would not have been possible to handle the various moves and transhipments of guns and equipment had there not been a Movement Control Group and Docks Operating Company with Force 121."[10]

There was also time to enjoy the hospitality offered by the people of Durban "we were given a royal welcome and entertained with unbelievable hospitality. The massed bands of the 1st and 2nd Battalions played on the seafront to huge audiences and were mobbed by excited fans at the end of the performances. The Scots Fusiliers, spotless in new khaki drill and with specially cleaned glengarries, were extremely popular in the town."[11]

The combined force of five assault ships and three troopships sailed from Durban on 28 April escorted by *Ramillies, Illustrious, Hermione* and six destroyers and made their landings on Madagascar from an anchorage in Courrier Bay to the west of Diego Suarez in the early morning of the 5th.[12] The approach to that part of Madagascar is influenced by a strong Equatorial Current and although a clear night with an almost new moon, the final 15 miles leading to Courrier Bay was through a myriad of unmarked reefs using the only available 1912 edition of a chart first published in 1892. Just after midnight *Winchester Castle* as HQ ship and with the other transports following, began the approach to an outer anchorage which was reached at 0200, and where the landing craft were lowered and set off to their appointed beaches. A passage ahead of the transports had been swept of mines and buoyed by the destroyer *Laforey*, yet would have remained a navigational challenge for any vessel in daylight never mind troop loaded transports in the dark. To the senior naval and military officers watching anxiously from the bridge of *Winchester Castle*, Captain Newdigate assured them "Its all right but I'm not sure my owners would approve of this!"[2] As an Extra Master and Captain RNR, Captain Newdigate was awarded the DSC for this part in the operation and remained in command of the ship for more landings until his retiral in 1945.

The assault phase was carried out as planned by No. 5 Commando and 29 Brigade; 17 Brigade began to land in the late forenoon and 13 Brigade next morning. The town of Diego Suarez was secured within 48 hours and *Ramillies, Hermione* and two destroyers entered the harbour that afternoon, followed by the personnel ships on the 8th and of which the five assault ships were retained for some weeks. The security of the sea route to India and the Middle East was meanwhile assured.

There now remained the question of moving all three brigades at Diego Suarez onwards to India as had been promised to Wavell who as CinC anxiously awaited their arrival. British and Indian forces were about to complete their long withdrawal from Rangoon by crossing the Chindwin and so brought the first stage of the campaign in Burma to a conclusion. 13 Brigade having been a reserve formation at Diego Suarez and not now required were therefore re-embarked on *Franconia* which sailed on the 20th with many of the troops having contracted malaria and dengue fever while on shore and others falling ill during the voyage to Bombay, which was reached on the 29th. The brigade moved to the cantonment at Ahmednagar and it was some time before they were fit for further service. *Franconia* left Bombay on 4 June, loaded on the Union Castle berth at Durban and Capetown, bunkered at Freetown and reached Liverpool to discharge and undertake routine drydocking before her next voyage in WS 22. Captain

Bertinshaw now left *Franconia* for a spell of home leave and subsequent appointment to *Scythia*. He was Mentioned in Despatches for his skilful and courageous handling of the ship when entering Courrier Bay on the morning of the assault landings. Meanwhile *Duchess of Atholl* and *Oronsay* were also released from the operation as their 17 Brigade troops were being retained on the island until relieved by 22 East African Brigade. Both liners left Diego Suarez on the 20th; the former loading in Durban and Capetown on the Harrison berth, *Oronsay* similarly on the Clan Line berth, both proceeded via Freetown to the Clyde and arrived on 27 and 30 June respectively and were next employed in WS 21P.

Winchester Castle and *Sobieski* remained in Diego Suarez for almost three weeks then proceeded to Mombasa to embark 22 East African Brigade, but on arrival there on the 26th found the port congested and the brigade not ready, so the ships were sent 70 miles south to wait in the relative calm and quietude of Manza Bay, returning to Mombasa four days later. 22 East African Brigade had served conspicuously throughout 1941 in the Somaliland and Abyssinian campaign and comprised three battalions of the King"s African Rifles with 9 Field Regiment RA and attached units under the command of Brigadier WA Dimoline. With embarkation of troops and stores complete, the two liners returned to Diego Suarez, a mere two day crossing from Mombasa and began the relief of 17 Brigade. After disembarking the East Africans, 17 Brigade HQ and 2 Northamptons embarked on *Winchester Castle*, 2 Royal Scots Fusiliers on *Keren* and 6 Seaforths on *Karanja*. All three liners sailed on 11 June for Bombay and reached there ten days later. 5 British Division was now complete in India but two months later moved to Iraq, then Persia, Syria, Egypt and subsequently landed as an assault formation in Sicily.

After ten days in Bombay, *Winchester Castle* returned home via Durban and Freetown, crossed to New York to load on the Furness Withy berth and with troops from Halifax reached the Clyde on the last day of August to begin preparations for the Torch landings in November. *Sobieski* remained at Diego Suarez over four weeks (see WS19) until joining *Keren* and *Karanja* at Bombay on 21 July, where they were to be used for training formations in amphibious landings. Only one of these exercises was carried out before all three ships were ordered home to prepare for Torch, the decision for that operation having been taken as late as 22 July. All three ships left Bombay on 9 August escorted by the AMC *Ranchi*, *Sobieski* proceeding via Mombasa, Durban and Capetown direct to the Clyde arriving on 4 September. The two naval transports were first directed to Capetown where they landed surplus landing craft, thence by Freetown to reach the Clyde on 20 September, all three sailing again in the Torch assault convoy on 26 October.

The remaining assault ship at Madagascar was the smaller *Royal Ulsterman*, which on 14 May was ordered back to the UK and proceeded via Durban, Port Elizabeth, Capetown and Pointe Noire (to complete an engine defect), then left Freetown on 8 July directed via Ponta Delgada to refuel. At this Azores port she hoisted the Red Ensign which allowed her to embark 101 survivors from *Avila Star* sunk in the vicinity twelve days earlier, and from where she was ordered to Penarth to begin a refit in preparation for Torch.

Two other liners were released on completing their outward voyages in WS 17A, the first being *Largs Bay* which fully disembarked in Durban and sailed on the 25th via Capetown to load on the Royal Mail berth on the Plate, returning via Freetown to Glasgow on 4 July and next sail in WS 21. From Capetown, *Dominion Monarch* continued independently to Bombay, arrived to disembark on 6 May but did not leave port again until the 15th, routed via Colombo, Fremantle and Sydney to load on her owners" berth in Auckland, whence she returned via Panama and Halifax to cross in NA 13 with Canadian troops to Liverpool, arriving on 29 July in time to discharge and next sail in WS 22.

In reverting to the balance of WS 17 following the departure of Force 121 at Freetown, this now comprised thirteen transports, five MT ships and *Adamant*, which sailed on 11 April as WS 17B, the first ship being the Commodore on *Franconia*, which passed the boom at 1300, followed by the others at four minute intervals. *Shropshire* as ocean escort followed an hour later and joined at 1830 at the outer end of the searched channel as did the local escort destroyers, *Wild Swan*, *Croome* and three corvettes (two being Free French), which had previously carried out an A/S sweep to seaward.[13]

Two ships had been torpedoed and sunk off the Ivory Coast the previous week, 500 miles distant from Freetown, so WS 17B was first given a wide diversionary route 400 miles SW, the convoy being formed into six columns with Captain Tate of *Abosso* as Vice Commodore at the head of column 1 and Captain HR Oulsram of *Samaria* as Rear Commodore in station 22. *Shropshire* and *Adamant* were between columns 3 and 4. An air escort was provided until darkness.

In the early hours of the 12th, the destroyer *Exmoor* joined as SO A/S escort and at 2200 the convoy turned six points to port on to the first of two long legs towards the Cape. The destroyer *Wild Swan* detached back to Freetown at 0700 on the 14th, by which time the convoy had barely averaged 8 knots during the past two days while crossing the Equatorial Current. Two of the corvettes detached at 1900 when the convoy recorded 12.5 knots for the past 12 hours.

At 1900 on the 15th, WS 17B was 200 miles east of Ascension and 550 miles NW of St Helena when *Exmoor*, *Croome* and the remaining corvette detached to meet and refuel from the *RFA Abbeydale*. Even by the 17th there were no reports of strong trade winds and that morning *Shropshire* had the convoy arranged in two columns for close-range AA practice firing and reformed on completion. By noon that day the convoy was 80 miles SW of St Helena and turned on to the second leg of almost 1,700 miles to the Cape. During that day and the next *Glaucus* began to falter and gradually brought the convoy speed down to 12.5 knots. The Commodore twice commented on the speed of *Glaucus* which was first given inadvertently to the Admiralty in the Master's absence at Liverpool as 14 knots, but at the Clyde conference "the Master said he would be able to maintain 13.5 knots, and I consider *Glaucus* did extremely well considering that she was outclassed in speed...there must have been a very good reason for her inclusion at such a price...a delay of one day in every twelve."[14] *Glaucus* was one of those lofty-funnelled Holt ships then 21 years old, but was turbine driven, burning oil fuel and a reliable steamer which survived until 1955.

The sloop *Milford* joined during the night of 18/19 April and *Shropshire* flew her Walrus on reconnaissance on the 21st as the convoy approached the land. On the morning of the 22nd the convoy was redisposed and the Capetown portion of fifteen ships plus *Adamant* was placed in charge of the Vice Commodore on *Abosso*. At 0500 on the 23rd the convoy reached a position 60 miles west of Capetown where the ships for that port were detached with *Milford* and on arrival the sloop and *Adamant* proceeded to Simonstown. The ten transports and five MT ships berthed in Capetown harbour on the morning of the 23rd to find the storeship *Clan Macdonald* awaiting them, having been unable to make the original departure date from the UK.

Shropshire continued around the Cape with *Franconia, Empress of Russia* and *Mataroa*, passing 70 miles south of Agulhas on the evening of the 23rd and 50 miles south of Cape St Francis next afternoon in avoiding both the Agulhas bank and current. At 0400 on the 25th the convoy was 40 miles SE of East London and 60 miles SE of Durban just after midnight. All ships were berthed in the harbour by 0600 when *Shropshire* proceeded to Maydon Wharf, an average speed of 12.3 knots having been maintained since detaching the Capetown section.

Whilst in Durban, *Franconia* had to re-stow much of 13 Brigade stores and equipment before continuing with the assault convoy on the 28th. *Mataroa* and *Empress of Russia* disembarked completely in Durban and due to pressure on berths, the former then moved down the coast to East London for twelve days engine repairs, before sailing via Capetown to load on the Blue Star berth on the Plate, returning via Freetown to Liverpool on 22 July for her next voyage in WS 22. *Empress of Russia* loaded small quantities of cargo at both Durban and Capetown on the Union Castle berth, and unusually returned home with calls at Pointe Noire and Freetown before reaching Liverpool on 6 June for 14 days in port before sailing again in WS 20.

These two transports together with *Largs Bay* which had arrived with WS 17A on the 22nd, disembarked 6,200 personnel who now re-embarked on the smaller *Khedive Ismail* and *Nova Scotia* for Bombay and on *Mendoza* and *Elisabethville* for Suez, which had been arriving in the port from the 9th and sailed onwards in WS 17B on 1st May. By 27 April the port of Durban was accommodating *Nieuw Amsterdam* and 19 other troopships, two Hospital ships and five major warships in addition to many general and bulk cargo ships discharging and loading. Many ships had to vacate their berths, some even to the outer anchorage to accommodate such large and valuable convoys but at no time were these formations delayed for want of anything in Durban or indeed any South African port during these years and was a tribute to the port organisation as a whole.

Of the ten transports of WS 17B which had berthed in Capetown on the 23rd, five were completely disembarked with 12,800 personnel of which half were accommodated in the newly built transit camp at Retreat, to await the arrival of *Nieuw Amsterdam* due in seven days time but first having to tranship POW to *Queen Elizabeth*.[15] *Nieuw Amsterdam* carried that half on to Suez and arrived there on the 25th, while the other half transhipped to *Mauretania* which berthed in Capetown a day behind the convoy, sailed on the 29th for Bombay and arrived there on 10 May. Both of these "Monster" sailings were made independently and without escort.

Abosso was the first of the disembarked liners at Capetown to depart, sailing on the 28th to load on her owners' berth at Freetown, Takoradi, Lagos, completed at Freetown and reached Liverpool on 6 June and next sailed in WS 20. *Orion* was dispatched on the 29th with some Union Castle cargo, fuelled at Freetown and docked in Liverpool on 19 May, also to sail again in WS 20. *Leopoldville* was also dispatched on the 20th but with Clan Line cargo, left Freetown on the 11th and reached the Clyde 13 days later and able to join WS 20. *Tamaroa* did not leave Capetown until 2nd May, loaded on the Houlder berth at Buenos Aires and after a quick call at Freetown was directed into Belfast Lough, then Loch Ryan and finally to Avonmouth where she docked to discharge on 18 June and subsequently drydocked in Cardiff before sailing again in WS 21. The last departure was *Arundel Castle* which loaded to capacity on her owners' berth and sailed on 7th May, proceeding direct to Loch Ryan arriving on the 22nd to land homeward personnel by tender to Stranraer and was then sent to Newport and grounded there at the river entrance on neap tides. She remained stuck fast for six days until refloated and able to dock in Avonmouth to discharge and drydock on 2 June. She sailed 15 days later in WS 20.

After four days in Capetown when the troops were exercised and allowed to refresh themselves ashore, the ongoing ships were watered and fuelled and sailed again as WS 17 in the late afternoon of 27 April comprising *Almanzora, Cameronia, Samaria, Johan van Oldenbarnevelt, Nieuw Holland* and the six MT ships. Escort was provided by the cruiser *Dauntless* newly returned from a Portsmouth refit, while *Adamant* rejoined from Simonstown. The convoy proceeded around the Cape without incident and on the morning of the 29th three US ships joined from Port Elizabeth, the ex Moore McCormack liner but now troopship *Brazil* on passage from New York and Charleston to Karachi and Bombay, the C3 cargo ship *Mormactide* also for Karachi and the smaller *Monterey* bound from New York to Basra, the first and last named carrying US troops.

Rendezvous was made at the outer end of the Durban searched channel at 1000 on the 1st May, with *Windsor Castle* now carrying Commodore Candy transferred from *Franconia*, with the smaller and slower Indian Ocean troopers embarked with those being on-carried, i.e. *Nova Scotia* and *Khedive Ismail* for Bombay via Mombasa, *Mendoza* for Suez via Mombasa and *Elisabethville* for Suez direct but whose low speed of 10.5 knots now dictated that of the convoy. The escort was strengthened by *Revenge* which had left Durban the previous day due to tidal constraints on the morning of the 1st. The convoy was now comprised nineteen ships and formed into six columns for passage towards the Mozambique Channel.[16]

As the convoy exited the north end of the Channel and passed between Comoro and Cape Delgado in the early morning of the 7th, British forces were then securing Diego Suarez 400 miles to the east and successfully concluding their first amphibious landings of the war to remain ashore and occupy the town and harbour, and having mounted the operation from the UK, 9000 miles distant, was hailed as a considerable achievement.

The depot ship *Adamant* originally intended for Trincomalee, was now being diverted to Mombasa to support surface warships and detached for that port at 1330 on the 7th. Weather conditions remained good during this passage and by 1600 on the 8th the convoy reached a position 70 miles due east of Mombasa where rendezvous was made with *Royal Sovereign*, the AMC *Corfu* and two destroyers from that port.[17] *Revenge* then parted company with the destroyers for Mombasa while the convoy altered to a NE'ly course to keep 50 to 100 miles off the Somali coast and so obtain maximum benefit from the north going current. At 1900 that same evening *Dauntless* detached with *Almanzora, Samaria, Cameronia, Mendoza, Khedive Ismail* and *Nova Scotia* for Mombasa where they arrived next morning, partly to mark time and prevent Bombay being congested with personnel ships at the onset of the SW monsoon.

By 10 May the convoy had experienced a 2 knot favourable current since *Royal Sovereign* joined, and meant that Bombay could be reached at 0630 on the 16th and was agreed to with some reluctance by the SOE, although believing this to be unsuitable in respect of tides. Heavy rain squalls were encountered early on the 11th and at 0800 *Elisabethville, Glaucus* and the two Ellerman ships detached with *Corfu* for Aden, while the remaining six transports and four storeships continued towards Bombay with *Royal Sovereign. Elisabethville* bunkered at Aden, called at Massawa and reached Suez on 22 May as the first of only three ships which carried WS 17 personnel to the Middle East.

The Chief Cook of *Nieuw Holland* died and was buried at sea on the 12th when that ship hauled out without orders and reduced speed to such an extent, that convoy speed had to be reduced to allow her to rejoin. On the morning of the 13th *Monterey* was detached for Basra and soon afterwards *Brazil* and *Mormactide* for Karachi, all unescorted. The convoy continued to experience a favourable current, the SOE estimating that 1130 on the 16th was a more suitable ETA[18] therefore reversed course for over six hours on the 14th to meet this. Paravanes were streamed next afternoon, *Clan Macdonald* stopped with engine trouble but regained station at 1930. WS 17 entered the Bombay swept channel at 0940 on the 16th and by 1315 *Royal Sovereign* had anchored west of Karanja Beacon. *Windsor Castle* with the Commodore picked up her Pilot at 1235 and berthed alongside Ballard Pier on arrival, but disembarkation was held over until the following morning.

At Bombay it took a month to discharge the three storeships which then dispersed to load homeward cargoes, *Clan Macdonald* in Australia and *Dunedin Star* in New Zealand. Of the three transports in this section of the convoy and despite the need for reinforcements in India, it took six days to clear *Windsor Castle* in Bombay which then sailed for Capetown, loaded there to capacity on her owners' berth and proceeded direct for the Clyde but was diverted to Liverpool where she arrived on 4 July and with 13 days in port to discharge was able to sail in WS 21P. *Nieuw Holland* left Bombay a day behind the *Castle* liner to load on the Ellerman berth at Durban and Capetown, and like all homeward liners at this time lifted personnel of every type at each port of call, military, RAF, RN, Indian crews, civilians including evacuees, DBS and other survivors. At Bombay 415 were embarked for South Africa and 66 for the UK, at Durban 252 embarked and on leaving Freetown there were 744 on board for the UK. *Nieuw Holland* reached Liverpool on 12 July for a next sailing in WS 22. *Johan van Oldenbarnevelt* loaded on the Ellerman berth at Bombay and Capetown and also embarked 188 mixed personnel at the former and 270 at the Cape, proceeding then direct to Liverpool arriving on 24 July also for WS 22.

The final section of the outward convoy, which had detached into Mombasa on 9th May, sailed again next day as WS 17B2 with the addition of the ex-French *Chantilly*, whose low speed held the convoy to 10.25 knots. A cruising order of four columns was formed with the appointed Commodore being the master of *Almanzora*, Captain FR Miles CBE, an Extra Master, Captain RNR and ADC to the King who was on his penultimate voyage to retiral.[19] The AMC *Ranchi* acted as escort on a passage devoid of incident, *Mendoza* and *Chantilly* were detached independently of one another after dark on the 14th for Aden and Suez, when *Nova Scotia* took station astern of *Samaria* and speed was increased to 13.5 knots. The remaining five transports arrived in Bombay on the 19th and were disembarked in turn at Ballard Pier. Taken with the subsequent onward movement of the three brigades from Madagascar, WS 17 landed nearly 50,000 in India and was a complete change in emphasis on the destination of WS personnel.

Samaria was the first of the WS liners to clear Bombay, sailing on the 23rd via Mombasa to Capetown for repairs and loading on the Clan Line berth, then making a brief call at Freetown to reach Liverpool on 15 July for inclusion in WS 21. *Almanzora* was scheduled to load on the BI berth in Bombay and Union Castle berth at Durban and Capetown; she sailed from the latter on 19 June for Freetown and the Clyde to arrive there on 14 July but then required six weeks repairs and was only able to make the next sailing in WS 22. *Cameronia* was delayed at Bombay for repairs, part loaded there, in South Africa and Halifax where she landed 600 German POW ex Raider crews carried from Bombay, after calling en route at Port Elizabeth, Capetown and Freetown. Leaving Halifax on 6 August she arrived in her home port on the 24th and was next employed on a round trip to Iceland prior to Torch. Captain George Kelly of Belfast had been Master of the ship almost without interruption since 1936 and was to continue without relief until 1946.

No better example can be given of Britain's maritime supremacy at that time, after three years of unremitting warfare on five oceans, as convoy WS 17 whose liners returned to the UK without loss or damage, having delivered 60,000 troops to destinations 12,000 miles distant and almost in the passing, landed and seized an important naval base astride the Indian Ocean.

WS 18 - sailed UK 15.4.42

Late in February the War Office gave notice that a second division would be sent abroad with the April convoy and for that departure 2 Infantry Division was selected. As early as October orders were issued to the divisional units for mobilization when Maj-General JML Grover was appointed to command but there the matter seemed to rest. 2nd Division was a regular formation comprised of 4, 5 and 6 Infantry Brigades which had served in France and Belgium from the outbreak of war and suffered grievous losses at St Omar and La Basse in the fighting withdrawal to Dunkirk, some of its battalions being virtually wiped out and having to be re-formed on return to the UK. In December 1941 the division moved from Yorkshire to the Cotswolds preparatory to embarkation which was then delayed until April.

It was also in February that the MOWT circulated a provisional list of seventeen liners for WS 18 having an estimated capacity then of 35,990, but allowing for "the inevitable casualties...might bring the total down to about 30,000 and with the increase due to extra fitting it looks as though WS 18 should be about 40,000,"[1] which agreed exactly with the 30% increase anticipated for all liners then being furnished with extra fittings.

It then happened, as befell most of the convoys, that four of the liners already listed were unable to make the sailing date set for 15 April, *Scythia* by reason of extended drydocking and repairs in Liverpool and *Narkunda* similarly held up in Durban. *Empress of Australia* and *Warwick Castle* both returning from WS 14 arrived too late for inclusion but were replaced by two other liners, *Nieuw Zeeland* brought home from Indian Ocean service where she had been exclusively employed since September 1940, and the P&O *Maloja*, one of the nine AMCs released by the Admiralty in July 1941, and since fitted out in Southampton with a capacity of 4,282, which was one-third above that of her sister *Mooltan* similarly converted ten months earlier. *Maloja* anchored in the Clyde to begin embarkation on 10 April, *Nieuw Zeeland* was drydocked and fitted for extra troop accommodation in Liverpool.

Seven of the allocated liners arrived in the UK during the three week period up to 2 April from previous voyages in WS 12, 12Z and 14, while *Rangitata* docked in Liverpool on 9 March from a voyage to Gibraltar, West Africa and the Plate, *Highland Chieftain* at Avonmouth on 12 March from the WS 8A voyage when damaged by collision with *Dominion Monarch*, the Dutch liners *Dempo* of Rotterdam Lloyd and *Marnix van St. Aldegonde* of the Nederland Line, both brought home from Indian Ocean routes for more gainful employment on the WS route; the former berthing in Liverpool on 2 April and the latter in Glasgow on 13 March but then sent to Liverpool for extra fittings. Finally to complete the personnel section of the convoy, the elderly PSNC sisters *Orbita* and *Orduna* , the former docking in Glasgow from Halifax in NA5 on 23

March and *Orduna* to the Clyde Anchorage from an Iceland trip only four days before the sailing date of the convoy.

Embarkation at Liverpool on *Empress of Japan*, *Reina del Pacifico* and *Rangitata* was completed on 12 April when they sailed for the Clyde Anchorage, and on *Duchess of Bedford* and *Dempo* two days later which then anchored in the Mersey to await *Capetown Castle*, *Marnix van St. Aldegonde* and *Nieuw Zeeland* which completed on the morning of the 15th. Embarked on *Reina del Pacifico* was 5 Brigade HQ, 2 Bn Dorsetshire Regiment, 7 Bn Worcestershire Regiment and 10 Field Regiment RA while the *Marnix van* carried 1 Bn Queen‚s Own Cameron Highlanders and other units of the same Brigade. Together with the storeships *Clan Lamont* and Holt's *Phemius* (a turbine driven oil fired steamer made famous by losing her lofty funnel in a West Indian hurricane), these five transports began leaving the Mersey at midday on the 15th, escorted by the destroyers *Lauderdale* and *Sabre*, to make rendezvous with the Clyde section next morning.

In Avonmouth, *Highlands Chieftain* and *Princess* embarked and sailed on the 14th with the storeships *City of Capetown* from Newport and Shaw Savill's *Waipawa* which had loaded in Swansea, all arriving at the Clyde Anchorage next morning. Embarkation and loading in the Clyde area was much reduced from the hectic activity which attended the previous departure of WS 17 carrying the assault forces for Madagascar. In Glasgow on 13 April the destroyer depot ship *Hecla*, which was sailing with the convoy to join the Eastern Fleet, sailed downriver from Princes Dock followed by the US carrier *Wasp* which had embarked Spitfires at 10 KGV Dock and sailed from the Clyde next day on her first ferry trip to Malta. Following close astern of *Wasp* was *Empress of Canada* which had embarked at No. 1 KGV, the 6 Brigade HQ, 1 Bn Royal Welsh Fusiliers, 2 Bn Durham Light Infantry, 99 Field Regiment RA and other units totalling 3,599. Next day *Orbita* completed embarkation at 4 KGV with 2 Bn Royal Norfolk Regiment, 1 Bn Royal Scots and A Coy 2 Bn Manchester Regiment all of 4 Brigade together with drafts of RAC, RAOC, RAMC and Royal Signals. (The remaining three companies of the Manchesters were spread between *Marnix van* and *Reina del* in Liverpool and *Empress of Canada* in Glasgow). To complete the Glasgow embarkations *Aorangi* left No. 2-3 KGV astern of *Orbita* and was anchored all ready for sea a mere two hours before the convoy began to depart. The P&O *Soudan* was the sole storeship loaded in Glasgow and was ready at the anchorage on the 11th, while the NZS passenger liner *Rimutaka* had loaded and embarked passengers for New Zealand at 4 KGV, followed *Soudan* downriver on the 11th and sailed that night in a slow convoy of 39 ships for Freetown and was thereafter included in WS 18.[2]

The total personnel embarked on the fifteen transports was 44,874 with a further 58 on the five storeships and 21 more on the two escorting cruisers. Seven of the liners were scheduled to disembark and return from South Africa, the remaining eight were for Bombay, none was actually proceeding to Suez which virtually followed the pattern established by the previous convoy. Almost half the total personnel on WS 18 were for "undecided destinations" and served to underline the uncertainties both in the Middle East and India, while less than a third of the personnel were then earmarked for Suez and nearly all of those were on ships being turned around in South Africa. In respect of personnel capacity, the emergency measures introduced in February were now having an even greater effect than forecast, with WS 18 showing an increase of 42%; the capacity of *Capetown Castle* having actually doubled but was exceptional. These and other measures adopted from the investigative trooping appreciation in February had the remarkable effect of doubling the numbers carried in the first six months of 1942, compared to the last six months of 1941, and with almost no change in the number of ships employed in the trooping fleet.

Ocean escort for WS 18 was provided by the cruisers *Gambia* (SOE) and *Frobisher*, the former being a recently completed addition to the Colony class while *Frobisher* of 1921 had refitted in Portsmouth; both had been working up at Scapa and came down to the Clyde to attend the convoy conference held in Gourock on the morning of the 14th. The destroyers *Salisbury* (SO A/S escort), *Boadicea* and *Georgetown* proceeded to 'Derry after the conference to top up with fuel and join at the morning rendezvous. Acting as A/S escorts as far as Freetown were the Hunt class *Tetcott* going around the Cape to join the Mediterranean Fleet and the newly completed Dutch *Van Galen* (ex *Noble*), which with the cruisers were en route to join the Eastern Fleet based in Mombasa. Rear Admiral CN Reyne was the appointed Commodore aboard *Empress of Canada* and had previously sailed in that capacity aboard *Tamaroa* of WS 5A when attacked by the *Hipper* (*q.v.*). The Master of *Duchess of Bedford*, Captain WG Busk-Wood was the appointed Vice Commodore.

The convoy began leaving the Clyde boom at 1800 on 15 April, comprising ten transports, three storeships and *Hecla* escorted by *Van Galen* and *Tetcott*. *Gambia* and *Frobisher* had left earlier for gunnery practice off Arran that evening with intent to join up at the morning rendezvous 6 miles west of Orsay, but found there only *Salisbury* and six other destroyers from 'Derry. It transpired that both the Clyde and Liverpool sections had been early at the rendezvous; they were sighted ahead at 0830 in the process of forming up which was completed by 1050 with all nine destroyers providing an A/S screen.[3] The convoy set off on a westerly course at 13 knots and with aircraft of Coastal Command making contact at frequent intervals during the first two days at sea.

At 0600 on the 17th course was altered to the SW and was held until 1600 next day when an alteration was made to SSW towards the less frequently used western passage through the Azores group. At 1530 on the 19th the destroyers *Badsworth*, *Lancaster* and *St. Mary's* were detached back to the UK and from that point onwards to Freetown, the convoy zigzagged during daylight hours or in moonlight. At 1900 that same evening destroyers *Volunteer* and *Boadicea* detached for the UK and one hour later *Van Galen* and *Tetcott* proceeded ahead to refuel at Ponta Delgada, then 450 miles distant, leaving two destroyers as A/S escort although no U-Boats were reported ahead.

WS 18 passed between the Azores islands of Faial and Flores without incident at 0200 on the 21st, and at 0800 the last two destroyers, *Salisbury* and *Georgetown* had to be detached to Ponta Delgada without waiting for their reliefs then being refuelled, as the CinCWA had changed their orders and were now required to rendezvous with *Wasp* and escort her to the UK. At midday course was altered to SSE to pass most unusually to the west of the Cape Verde islands which route had not been used since the passage of WS 7. During the absence of A/S cover, *Gambia* catapulted her aircraft for dawn and dusk patrols when conditions allowed recovery, but *Van Galen* rejoined at 1830 on the 22nd and the slower *Tetcott* next morning.

The reasonable weather enjoyed by this convoy was fully utilised by the personnel embarked: aboard *Orbita* (Captain EH Large) the Royal Scots found "every square yard of deck space was allocated to one unit or another for weapon training, PT or lectures in an effort to keep men fit and busy. To keep feet in marching condition boots were worn for part of the day and for washing the ration was often cut to half a pint per day."[4] It was also on *Orbita* that "all ranks had to shoot with light MGs at small barrels towed astern..while being distracted by kicking, rolled on, having buckets of water thrown on them and bugles blown in their ears. It was drastic training but taught the (Norfolks) steadiness...later shown in action against the Japs."[5] Similar training is recorded by the Dorsets and Worcesters on *Reina del Pacifico* (Captain Charles Stowe) where "a formidable assault course was rigged up on E deck...with the at first reluctant co-operation of the Captain who like all masters was averse to the wartime practice of wearing boots at sea."[6] The Royal Berks embarked on one of the Dutch liners reported "endless route marches around the deck until the Captain (Haan) pointed out there would soon be no deck left."[7] And for relaxation...on *Empress of Canada*, 2nd Lieutenant Jack Hawkins of stage and screen fame, devised a broadcast concert party over the ship's intercom system which he later developed for maintaining morale in the jungles of India and Burma.[8]

By 0800 on the 24th with the convoy 400 miles north of the Cape Verde islands, *Tetcott* had only 60% fuel remaining and insufficient to reach Freetown so *Gambia* transferred 58 tons successfully that afternoon. The convoy passed 100 miles west of the Cape Verde group during the night of the 25th and by 0930 next morning the local escorts *Wild Swan*, *Boreas* and *Petunia* joined from Freetown. The SSE course was continued until 0600 on the 27th when altered to the east direct for Freetown then distant 700 miles. No U-Boats were reported in the area since early April which remained quiet until mid July, although four ships were lost to an Italian submarine during the month of June. The convoy speed was increased in the afternoon of the 27th to make an early arrival on the 29th. From daylight on the 28th Sunderland aircraft from Freetown were intermittently in touch with the convoy which reached the outer end of the searched channel at 0900 next day, the ocean escort having entered and anchored first at 1000.

Although a homeward convoy had sailed from Freetown three days earlier, an outward one of 39 ships followed WS 18 into the harbour and within a day or so had 70 or 80 ships all requiring water and fuel. Priority attended the replenishment of the troop convoy which on this occasion shipped 7,820 tons of fresh water and 28,829 tons of oil fuel. Of personnel changes in Freetown, 621 disembarked from six of the transports while 29 embarked in lieu.

With temperatures of 100°F (38°C) recorded in some of the troopdecks while in harbour, everyone was relieved when the convoy began leaving Freetown at 0930 on 3 May, delayed at the gate by the entry of *Malaya* returning from WS 17. The NZS liner *Rimutaka* joined at Freetown, having arrived in the slow convoy astern of WS 18, and the US transport *Agwileon*, a 35 year old Caribbean trade passenger ship of 6,678 gross which had brought civil technicians and advisers to Freetown, and was now continuing to Capetown before returning to New York. The convoy was followed out of the harbour by the same two cruisers and destroyers as ocean escort, plus *Boreas* and *Wivern* as local escorts and with the seaplane tender *Albatross* carrying a Walrus squadron for the Eastern Fleet. Course was set to the SW to gain an offing of 200 miles from the land. The cruising order was considerably changed, to allow all but one of the twelve ships on the three port wing columns to detach off Capetown while the remainder continued to Durban.[9]

Once formed up and proceeding by zigzag at 13 knots it became evident that *Agwileon* never got in station and was soon lagging well astern. The SOE on *Gambia*, Captain MJ Mansergh CBE RN, ranged up alongside and "exhorted her Master through the loud hailer to further efforts. He informed me he was doing his utmost and from the dense clouds of smoke pouring from his funnel I believed him."[10] The convoy speed was reduced to 12 knots before dark to ensure his keeping in touch and was in fact still with the convoy next morning, when at 0800 course was altered six points to port on to a SE'ly course towards St Helena. Sunderland and Hudson aircraft provided air escort until dark on the 4th, the corvette *Hydrangea* joined the escort just after midday while *Boreas* and *Wivern* detached two hours later to return to Freetown.

The inclusion of *Agwileon* in the convoy was now causing concern to both the Commodore and Captain Mansergh, her speed had reduced that of the convoy by near-ly 3 knots and by increasing the length of the voyage would aggravate the fresh water situation in the transports. On the morning of the 5th, *Gambia* proceeded 50 miles clear of the convoy and signalled a proposal to the CinCSA at Simonstown. On rejoining at 1830 the SOE found that *Hydrangea* had detached to meet the AMC *Dunnottar Castle*, but of more importance, that *Agwileon* had in the interval advised the Commodore that due to a very foul bottom and dirty boilers, his fuel consumption was now so heavy as to prevent him reaching Capetown. Next afternoon a reply from the CinC instructed *Agwileon* to be detached with *Frobisher* as escort on reaching 12° South.

By the morning of the 8th the convoy was approaching 10° South where zigzagging ceased and the SE trades reached force 5 with a moderate swell. During the forenoon *Frobisher* refuelled *Tetcott* with some difficulty and at 1230 detached with *Agwileon*, not for Capetown but to Walvis Bay 700 miles less in distance. The convoy speed was then increased to 14 knots but later had to be reduced to 13.5 knots to allow the slower ships to keep up.

At 1000 on the 9th the convoy reached a position 70 miles NE of St. Helena, where course was altered 20° towards the Capetown approaches for an arrival there in six days time. During that same forenoon and with some difficulty in the fresh SE wind and swell, *Gambia* pumped 57 tons of fuel to *Van Galen* astern of her until the connections parted, both ships then detached at 20 knots to obtain a lee in the anchorage at St. Helena where *Van Galen* was able to berth alongside the cruiser and receive 155 tons. No one landed at St. Helena but fresh vegtables and potatoes were sent out to the ships in exchange for fresh meat. After three hours at anchor, *Van Galen* left independently for Simonstown, *Gambia* followed two hours later at 17 knots to rejoin the convoy which was achieved at 1600 on the 10th, the convoy having been left in charge of *Albatross* and *Tetcott*.

Speed was reduced on the afternoon of the 11th to 12.5 knots so as to make a dawn arrival at Capetown on the 15th, the delay caused by *Agwileon* having prevented that planned for the 14th. *Gambia* fuelled *Tetcott* during the forenoon of the 14th and at mid-day two South African whalers joined as additional escorts for the Capetown section of the convoy.

Two months earlier the liners of WS 16 narrowly missed encountering the mines laid by *Doggerbank* in the approaches to Capetown. Extensive minesweeping had been car-ried out since and although no losses had occurred since the middle of March, two ships were damaged in the first week of May which confirmed that mines remained. At Freetown the NCSO emphasized this with a warning that "the approaches to Capetown are dangerous owing to mines on both sides of the approach channel and it is advisable for the convoy to form single line ahead."[11] It was to prove singularly unfortunate and costly to WS 18 that none of the extensive mining of the waters off Cape Agulhas car-ried out by *Doggerbank* in March and April had yet been detected.

At 0300 on 15 May the convoy was in a position 60 miles west of Capetown where the ships for that port were detached with *Albatross*, *Tetcott* and the two whalers, i.e.

Empress of Canada, Reina del Pacifico, Orbita, Orduna, Marnix van', Dempo, Nieuw Zeeland, Rimutaka, Phemius and *Waipawa*, which berthed in the harbour soon after 0800 for replenishment and where *Rimutaka* continued independently to Australia and New Zealand. The remaining eight transports and three MT ships continued on course with *Gambia* and *Hecla* towards a position 70 miles SSW of Cape Agulhas well to the western edge of that bank, with Captain Busk-Wood of *Duchess of Bedford* now acting as Commodore.[12] By 0800 with the convoy 30 miles SW of Cape Point, the formation was redisposed from three columns of four ships to four columns each of three ships with *Gambia* stationed in the centre, and was then steaming on a broad front almost two miles wide.

At 1430 the convoy reached the alter course position off Agulhas and in making bare-ly 12 knots against the Agulhas current expected to cross the 100 fathom edge of the bank an hour later. At 1554 an explosion was heard aboard *Hecla* leading the starboard wing column, which then turned away, stopped and 15 minutes later reported being tor-pedoed although considered to have been mined. The convoy remained on course to the ESE and at 1630 *Gambia* detached to standby and assist *Hecla*, then at 1810 just before reaching the next alter course position, the storeship *Soudan* in the rear position of the port column reported being torpedoed or mined, quickly fell astern and broadcast a distress message. The convoy was then unescorted and having lost two ships the Commodore did not feel justified in sacrificing another to standby *Soudan* which soon flooded and sank although all 87 crew and gunners got safely away in three boats, two of which were picked up within 40 hours while the third, with the 2nd Officer and 31 others aboard was adrift for six days before being rescued by the *Clan Murray*.

Hecla had a fire in her CO_2 room with steering gear inoperative but main engines intact and at first asked for a tow, but by 1700 was proceeding at 12 knots by hand steer-ing towards Simonstown escorted by *Gambia*. The CinCSA meanwhile diverted the cruiser *Carlisle* to join the now unescorted WS 18, which was accomplished at 1030 next morning in a position midway between Mossel Bay and Port Elizabeth. The con-voy continued without further incident towards Durban and at 1800 on the 17th the Commodore detached *Empress of Japan* and *Capetown Castle* to proceed ahead at max-imum speed to help ease congestion in the port next morning, where WS 18 arrived just after midday.

It will be recalled that WS 16 was made aware of the mines laid by *Doggerbank* in the Capetown approaches in March, but remaining undetected then, were a further fif-teen mines close to Cape Agulhas. *Doggerbank* returned to this area on the night of 16/17 April and laid a further 80 mines near the southern edge of the Agulhas bank. WS 17 passed that way the very next day without harm but strangely WS 18, in using exact-ly the same route across the bank ran straight into them. No other ships were lost or damaged by mines on the Cape coast nor were any more mines found on the Agulhas Bank despite extensive sweeping by the Minesweeping Flotilla which continued until September.

Of the eight transports which berthed in Durban from WS 18, only *Capetown Castle* was continuing with the two MT ships to Bombay. The remaining transports disem-barked a total of 21,731 personnel of which 1,450 were for South Africa. Only two of the smaller Indian Ocean ships were then available for on-carriage so that 1,118 landed from the two *Highland* ships for East Africa were embarked with South African troops for Madagascar on *Empire Woodlark* and *Llandaff Castle* which thereafter joined the convoy. The remaining 19,163 were now destined for the Middle East comprising various workshop units and 18,000 in drafts (8,600 RAF, 7,500 Army and 1,900 Naval), one third of whom transhipped to *Mauretania* which arrived in Durban on the 22nd and left three days later independently and unescorted. Of the remainder, 6,500 were taken on by *Ile de France* on 12 June and 2,500 on *Nieuw Amsterdam* on the 27th of that month; having been accommodated in the interval at the Clairwood Transit Camp. Most of those left over were on-carried in the additional convoy CM 29 on 1st July.

The seven emptied transports were now given the fastest despatch in speeding up their return to the UK as a further result of the trooping appreciation conducted in February. *Empress of Japan* and *Maloja* were cleared in Durban within thirty hours, the former spending six days repairing at Capetown before proceeding direct to Halifax to load and embark 4125 Canadian troops and other personnel for the Clyde, crossing then with *Letitia* in NA 11 to arrive 23 June and next sailed in WS 21P. *Maloja* proceeded direct from Durban to Freetown, thence to New York where she loaded on the Cunard berth, embarked American troops and reached Liverpool in NA 12 on 12 July to sail again in WS 21. The remaining five liners left Durban two days ahead of the convoy, on 21 May, *Rangitata* and the two *Highland* ships sailing direct to the Plate to load there refrigerated meat cargoes on the Donaldson and Royal Mail berths, all three being in Buenos Aires together for over two weeks and sailing from Montevideo within the space of four days. *Highland Princess* docked in Avonmouth to discharge on 14 July, *Highland Chieftain* the following day at Swansea while *Rangitata* which returned via Freetown reached Liverpool on the 22nd, all three next sailing in WS 22. From Durban, *Duchess of Bedford* proceeded via Capetown and Freetown to New York, loaded there on the Cunard berth, embarked American troops and crossed in NA 12 with *Maloja* and *Aorangi* to reach Liverpool on 12 July and thereafter made a return crossing to New York in CT 20. Finally *Aorangi* was similarly despatched via Capetown, first to Hampton Roads, then loaded in New York on the Furness Withy berth and thereafter as above to Glasgow on 12 July for next sailing in WS 21. *Empress of Japan* had the shortest voyage time of all WS 18 liners having returned to the UK in under ten weeks including the North Atlantic troop crossing.

At Capetown almost all of the 19,212 personnel on seven transports were those of 2 Infantry Division whose destination had just been decided as India. The War Office had instructed the Impcon staff to arrange the maximum amount of exercise for the division during their time in port and with the permanent transhipment camp at Retreat not then complete,[13] it was decided to disembark all of the infantry and artillery units in rotation to spend 48 hours either at Retreat or Pollsmoor tented camp, altogether totalling 11,000 men who took with them the minium of kit and left the rest on the ships. Route march exercises were successfully carried out in fine weather and everyone finished with a most hospitable and enjoyable night on the town.

The onward passage of the convoy was resumed at 1500 on 19 May when the seven transports, two storeships and the utility tanker, *Bulkoil*, sailed from Capetown under escort of *Frobisher* and *Albatross* and with Commodore Reyne continuing on *Empress of Canada*, while Captain John V Langford, the Master of *Orduna* was appointed as Vice Commodore. The 2nd Divisional Commander, Maj-General Grover and his headquarters staff continued on the Dutch *Marnix van'* which had carried them thus far from Glasgow. Two hours after leaving harbour Holt's *Phemius* had to put back with a damaged paravane boom, otherwise the convoy formed up at the end of the searched channel and proceeded towards the Agulhas bank.

By midday on the 20th the convoy was 110 miles SSW of Cape Agulhas and maintained a clear distance south of the bank to avoid any possible mines until the early evening, when course was altered to ENE. Although clear of the mineable area this brought the convoy directly into the worst of the opposing Agulhas current and severely reduced the speed of advance. By midday on the 21st the convoy was 100 miles SW of Cape St. Francis having averaged only 9.8 knots in the past 24 hours and next day made good a mere 7.5 knots. By midday on the 22nd it was clear that WS 18 would be eight hours late for the rendezvous with the Durban ships and that afternoon Captain Langford assumed the duties of Commodore. At midnight the convoy was 170 miles SW of Durban where *Empress of Canada, Marnix van'* and *Nieuw Zeeland* proceeded ahead with *Albatross* as escort, to make a quick call at the Natal port where General Grover and his staff were hurriedly transferred to the *Empress* while *Nieuw Zeeland* landed an appendix case. At 1130 on the 23rd *Reina del Pacifico* also left the convoy to land an acute abdominal case at Durban, whence that liner and the *Empress* proceeded unescorted and independently at 18 knots direct to Bombay where they arrived on 2 June. This had the effect of allowing both General Grover and Brigadier Aldous of 5 Brigade five clear days to make arrangements for the arrival and deployment of the division, but the presence of enemy submarines in the Indian Ocean then prevented further independent WS sailings.

The Durban section of the convoy comprising *Capetown Castle, Empire Woodlark, Llandaff Castle, Nieuw Zeeland, Clan Lamont* and *City of Capetown* sailed in the morning of the 23rd for an appointed rendezvous with the Capetown portion at the end of the searched channel. They were then advised by the SOE on *Resolution*, i.e. the Vice Admiral commanding the 3rd Battle Squadron, Eastern Fleet, that the Capetown portion was eight hours late and the rendezvous altered, and in the absence of a convoy commodore (who had proceeded on the independent *Empress of Canada*) appointed Captain Thornton of *Capetown Castle* to act in this capacity until the two sections made junction.

The combined convoy of seven transports, three storeships and the fast tanker formed into four columns in a position 50 miles SE of Durban at 1400 on 23 May and set off towards the western half of the Mozambique Channel at a speed of 12.5 knots, the maximum of *Empire Woodlark*, escorted by *Frobisher* and *Resolution*.[14] Although no A/S escort was provided and probably not even available, the SOE warned of two reports of submarines in the channel which soon became evident.

Just before noon on the 24th, *Marnix van St. Aldegonde* with *Albatross* as escort caught up and rejoined, as did *Phemius* at 0200 on the 27th at the head of the Mozambique Channel which caused the SOE some anxiety and comment "that ships should be instructed not to join convoys at night even in bright moonlight".[15] By midnight that night the convoy was 120 miles east of Porto Mocambique, where *Llandaff Castle* was detached with *Frobisher* for Diego Suarez, and from where she continued to Mombasa before returning to Durban.

The convoy passed to the west of the Comoros during the evening of the 28th and at 1500 on the 30th, in a position 105 miles east of Mombasa, the cruisers *Emerald* and *Enterprise* joined the escort and relieved *Resolution* and *Albatross*, which then detached with *Empire Woodlark* to Mombasa. The Commodore noted that the average speed from Durban had been 11.5 knots but was then increased to 13.5. WS 18 continued up the Somaliland coast and at 0730 on the 31st, when 90 miles SE of Kismayu, the AMC

Worcestershire joined and relieved *Emerald* and by that evening the convoy was 70 miles SE of Mogadishu.

The pre-arranged split of the convoy took place in the afternoon of 2 June in a position 30 miles SE of Ras Hafun, when the Aden and Suez portion comprising *Waipawa*, *Phemius* and *Bulkoil* detached with *Worcestershire*, (*Bulkoil* became the tanker of the failed Vigorous convoy to Malta) while the six transports and two storeships altered to a more NE'ly heading towards Bombay with *Enterprise*. By the morning of the 3rd the Bombay section was 60 miles SE of the eastern end of Socotra and at midday on the 5th altered to ENE direct for Bombay then distant 530 miles. WS 18 reached the outer end of the searched channel at 0700 on 7 June and arrived in Bombay harbour two hours later having averaged 12.3 knots from Capetown in moderate winds and sea.

WS 18 had crossed the Indian Ocean just before the onset of the SW monsoon which arrived with a vengeance while the ships were in Bombay, and where disembarkation was more or less restricted to the use of a single berth at the Ballard Pier passenger terminal when not anchored uncomfortably in the open stream. There was no opportunity to disembark ships simultaneously as at the Cape ports and troops landing at Bombay had to entrain at the pier for destinations many miles inland. WS 18 had brought over 23,000 troops for India, Iraq and Ceylon.

The troops of 2nd Division entrained to concentrate mostly around Ahmednagar. Throughout the last of 1942 and all of 1943 2nd Division trained intensively in India for combined operations against the Andaman Islands which never took place, but later served conspicuously in the 1944 battles against the Japanese at Kohima, Mandalay and throughout the rest of the Burmese campaign to the end of the war.

Despite the two fast liners having been sent on ahead to reduce congestion and prepare for the divisional arrival in the port, *Empress of Canada* and *Reina del Pacifico* were still in Bombay when WS 18 arrived, but sailed on their homeward voyages next day. The *Empress* loaded a small quantity of cargo on the Ellerman berth, proceeded to Capetown which was heavily congested and was there redirected to wait in the remote anchorage of Saldanha Bay, 60 miles further north, which was in process of being brought into use as a relief anchorage. After five days at Saldanha, the *Empress* was able to berth in Capetown for eight days of repairs before sailing for Freetown to be delayed there a further nine days due to a stripped turbine. The *Empress* reached Liverpool on 4 August for two months extensive repairs and drydocking before next sailing in one of the Torch convoys to North Africa. *Reina del Pacifico* had a much smarter passage, loading on the Union Castle berth at Durban and Capetown and proceeding thereafter direct for the Clyde but diverted to her home port of Liverpool where she arrived on 16 July, also to be drydocked and surveyed and sailed again three weeks later on a round trip to New York.

Disembarkation and replenishment of the remaining six liners at Bombay was spread over a period of twelve days interspersed with the embarkation and despatch of five smaller transports with Indian troops for Basra. The first liner to clear the port was *Dempo* which sailed on the 13th with 167 commercial crews for South Africa and 200 RN, RIN, DBS and civilians for the UK. *Dempo* called at Durban in need of a repair berth but was redirected to Port Elizabeth where the commercial crews were landed and 34 days spent on machinery repairs, then sailed direct to Halifax with POW, then to New York for a month of drydocking, being fumigated, loading on the Anchor Line berth and embarking 2073 US Army for the UK. After calling at Halifax on 28 September, *Dempo* reached Liverpool on 7 October and next sailed in WS 24Q for Algiers.

The next departure from Bombay was *Capetown Castle* on 16 June, proceeding via Fremantle to Auckland where in nine days she loaded a full refrigerated and general cargo on the NZS berth, returning then via Panama and Halifax with US troops to Liverpool on 17 August, where she was drydocked over a six week period and next sailed in WS 23. *Nieuw Zeeland* left Bombay a day behind the Castle liner, having loaded on the Anchor Line berth but otherwise free of passengers, then completed on the Union Castle berth at Capetown where she also embarked 345 RAF, RN, Civilians and others for the UK. A further 239 mixed personnel were embarked at Freetown and all were landed by tender from Loch Ryan to Stranraer on 3 August. The *Zeeland* arrived at Swansea to discharge next day and after spending two months on extensive machinery repairs in Falmouth, next sailed on what became her last voyage on 26 October for the Torch landings; she was torpedoed and sunk on 11 November.

On 18 June *Orbita* and *Marnix van St. Aldegonde* left Bombay and were followed next day by *Orduna*. The homeward voyages of the PSNC sisters mirrored one another, the former having loaded on the Clan Line berth and *Orduna* for the Anchor Line; they were in Durban together for a couple of days and Capetown for five days, *Orduna* reached Freetown as *Orbita* left. They arrived in Liverpool a day apart on 9 and 10 August, *Orduna* next sailing in WS 22 and her sister in WS 24P for the Torch landings. The Dutch liner loaded on the Ellerman berth and embarked 154 mixed personnel for the UK then spent six weeks on engine repairs in Durban, sailing from there on 10 August direct for New York. Seven days later when almost halfway across the South Atlantic she was sighted and chased by the German raider *Michel*, reputedly of 18 knots as against the 16 knots of the *Marnix*, but either the raider had a foul bottom or the Dutch engineers under Captain Haan were able to coax addition r.p.m. out of the twin Sulzer diesels, sufficient to shake off the pursuit. Her best convoy speed was given as 16 knots and although built to maintain 17 knots in service could reach 19 knots as a maximum. The *Marnix* reached New York safely on 4 September for three weeks drydocking, cleaning and painting then embarked 3638 US Army and crossed with *Dempo* from Halifax to reach the Clyde on 6 October; her next voyage was in WS 24P for the Torch landings.

The two storeships took over four weeks for a complete discharge in Bombay, *Clan Lamont* then making a ballast voyage from Lourenco Marques to New York where a full cargo was loaded for Glasgow; *City of Capetown* made an exactly similar homeward voyage to Liverpool.

WS 18 was unique in that all of the transports disembarked without change at their original destinations, the convoy followed a changed route to Freetown, none of the transports proceeded to Suez and all but one of those calling at Durban were disembarked and turned around in that port. More significantly it was the only WS convoy to suffer loss although not of a troopship (*Anselm* was not in WS 9B when sunk). The MOWT could derive satisfaction in seeing some of their proposals to increase capacity on the route now bearing fruit: notably the rapid turnround of liners in Durban, fast liners being sent unescorted across the Indian Ocean and homeward ships loading in New York where they were also able to embark US troops for the UK.

Chapter 15

WS 19, 19W, 19P and 19Y

More reinforcements for Egypt as
8 Armoured and 44 Infantry Divisions leave the U.K.

WS 19 - sailed UK 10.5.42.
At the beginning of February 1942 the War Office sent a document to the MOWT detailing the numerous personnel movements envisaged throughout 1942 in which reference
was made to the four divisions being sent to the Middle East in the convoys between
February and May. This paper was passed on to the Sea Transport Department for
examination and as previously shown for WS 16, it was calculated that a shortfall of
115,000 personnel berths existed in these convoys between that which the War Office
wished to embark and the capacity that was actually available.

This matter soon caught the attention of the Prime Minister who referred to President
Roosevelt for help as he had done six months earlier. On 4 March Churchill wrote
explaining the shortfall and huge numbers being sent around the Cape in the next four
convoys which was only achieved by "scraping together every ton of man-lift shipping

we can lay our hands on and adopting every expedient to hasten the turn-round and increase the carrying capacity of the shipping."[1] Churchill asked for the loan of shipping to carry two complete divisions around the Cape (say 40,000 men), including their stores and equipment during the next critical four months. A further letter next day expanded the British position "where everything turns on shipping...with the immediate and decisive concern (being) the provision of troop carrying tonnage."[2]

The total British available trooplift in January 1942 was 286,000 compared to the American figure of 121,000 and which they only expected to increase to 205,000 by the middle of 1943. Despite this and their own commitments in the Pacific, Roosevelt quickly responded in the same generous manner as in 1941, "he would furnish the ships to move our two divisions with their equipment from Britain around the Cape."[3] To give effect to this two American transports were able to sail with WS 19 and five more with three storeships in the next following convoy: WS 19P three weeks later.

As early as 18 February the MOWT said the anticipated capacity of WS 19 sailing in mid May would be 31,000 but increased by the emergency measures to 38,000 and in later applying the one-third increase then adopted the figure would be 41,300. No ships were then specified but *Scythia* allocated for the previous convoy must have been top of the list and had been in Liverpool since early March for intensive repairs and dry-docking, while *Athlone Castle* arrived there early April and was also drydocked and provided with extra troop fittings. Four liners reached the UK in mid April allowing three weeks to discharge and prepare for WS 19, two having brought refrigerated cargoes from the Plate to Liverpool following outward CT trips to Halifax, i.e. *Highland Brigade* and *Moreton Bay*, the latter about to make her first WS voyage since conversion from an AMC. At Avonmouth *Highland Monarch* returned from WS 14 and the Plate, while *Pasteur* from WS 15 moored to a buoy at the Clyde Anchorage to allow the shut down of her boilers and machinery for overhaul. This Cunard managed liner had not been alongside in the UK since a visit to Glasgow eighteen months earlier. The remaining five British liners for WS 19 had little more than two weeks in port after returning from voyages in WS 15 and 16, *Ormonde* and *Monarch of Bermuda* at Liverpool while *Mooltan*, *Strathaird* and *Strathnaver* were berthed in Glasgow. The two American transports, *Borinquen* and *Orizaba* each of 7000 tons gross tons reached the Clyde Anchorage from Iceland on 2 May to provide additional capacity of 3,041 berths.

At the beginning of May 1942 as these liners prepared for embarkation, news of the landings in Madagascar and of other events in the war began to provide the Allies with a glimmer of hope that the relentless Axis tide against them might just be coming to an end. In Russia the German armies had failed to enter Moscow and were now embroiled in fighting to control Kharkov and the Crimea while Rommel was about to launch his offensive against the Gazala line that ended with a decisive halt at El Alamein. In Burma, Mandalay had fallen to the advancing Japanese army yet in the Pacific it was given its first check by the US Fleet in the Battle of the Coral Sea. In six months time the tide was to turn inexorably in favour of the Allies.

The two previous convoys had each carried an infantry division to India and now 8th Armoured Division was selected as the next formation for overseas. Confirmation was not given of their ultimate destination being the Middle East until they reached the Cape, but from the moment of embarkation none of its component units ever doubted their destination to be any other theatre of operations.

8 Armoured Division was formed in November 1940, mobilized for overseas in April 1942 and was inspected by HM The King at Cranleigh in Surrey on 1st May, prior to entraining to the ports of embarkation. The Division comprised 23 and 24 Armoured Brigades each of three regiments of the Royal Tanks and 8 Support Group of 5 Royal Horse Artillery, an Anti-Tank and Light AA Regiment. The motorized infantry units were 7 Bn. The Rifle Brigade attached to 23 Brigade who were embarked on *Mooltan* in Glasgow, 11 Bn. King's Royal Rifle Corps with 24 Brigade whose HQ and two of its regiments boarded *Scythia* in Liverpool, and 14 Bn. Sherwood Foresters with the Support Group who embarked by tender from Gourock on the US transport *Orizaba*. Also sailing in WS 19 were 3,000 RAF in drafts also bound for the Middle East. The total embarked was 41,541 of whom 15,250 landed directly at Suez and 8,400 at Bombay, the rest being transhipped to other ships in South Africa.

Three MT storeships carrying the divisional tanks, trucks and other vehicles were sailing with the convoy, *Clan Macarthur* and that company's *Lanarkshire* having loaded in Liverpool and *Sussex* of the Federal Company which loaded at 4 KGV Dock in Glasgow. The Shaw Savill passenger liner *Akaroa*, which remained on commercial service throughout the war years, loaded general cargo in Newport for New Zealand and also embarked a number of service personnel for Bermuda, Jamaica and Trinidad and was being included in the convoy as far as the Azores.

With embarkation complete at Avonmouth on 9th May, *Highland Monarch* locked out that afternoon and joined *Akaroa* from Newport off the Mumbles, where they set off for the Orsay rendezvous with the ex Isle of Man steamer *Tynwald* now acting as a fully commissioned AA escort. In Liverpool, *Monarch of Bermuda*, *Moreton Bay* and *Ormonde* embarked and completed for sea and anchored in the river on the 8th while *Athlone Castle*, *Highland Brigade* and *Scythia* embarked to complete in time for all six liners to leave the Mersey with the two storeships at 1800 on the 10th, escort to Orsay being provided by the destroyer *Volunteer*.

The Glasgow embarkation of *Mooltan* was completed by the evening of the 6th, the liner then leaving 6 KGV at 0545 next day to sail downriver to the anchorage and was followed by *Strathaird* 24 hours later from 2 - 3 berth, and by *Strathnaver* from No. 1 berth at 0830 on the 9th, preceded an hour earlier by *Sussex* to make the Glasgow sailings an exclusive P&O event. At the Clyde Anchorage the US transports *Borinquen* and *Orizaba* embarked by railway steamers from Gourock as did *Pasteur* which remained at her mooring buoy until departure.[4]

A convoy conference was held at Gourock on Sunday morning, 10th May, attended by the masters of the merchant ships and commanding officers of the escorts. The SO ocean escort was Captain WT Stephens RN of the cruiser *Mauritius* which had arrived from Scapa the previous day following a refit in Devonport, while the SO A/S escort was Commander JE Broome from the destroyer *Keppel*. The convoy commodore was Rear-Admiral AT Tillard DSO who had previously sailed in WS 15 and was now embarked with his staff on *Strathnaver* while Captain C Gudbranson USN of the US naval transport *Orizaba* was acting as Vice Commodore.

Following the conference the destroyers *Keppel*, *St Mary's* and *Churchill* (last two Town class) proceeded to Derry to top up with fuel. The Commodore led the seven ships of the Clyde portion out of the boom at 2330 that same evening and proceeded at 10 knots to arrive at the rendezvous 6 miles west of Orsay at 1100 on the 11th, where junction was made with the eight ships from Liverpool and two from the Bristol Channel and where the completed convoy formed into a cruising order of six columns and set off to the westward at a speed of 14.5 knots. The ocean escort comprising *Mauritius*, the AMC *Carnarvon Castle* and Hunt class destroyers *Belvoir* and *Hursley* (both destined for the Mediterranean) had left the Clyde seven hours earlier, the cruisers then taking station in a centre column while the Hunts joined the A/S screen with *Keppel* (SO), the Town class *St Mary's*, *Castleton* and *Leamington* while *Volunteer* joined shortly thereafter.[5]

Unusually for an AMC, *Carnarvon Castle* was embarked with an overflow of 1,044 Army and Naval personnel for West Africa, and had some difficulty adhering to the sailing date. Following a three month refit at Newport News, the AMC reached the Tail of the Bank on 7 April and spent the intervening period in feverishly rectifying electrical and mechanical defects and was only just able to complete by the sailing date.

By 0200 on the 12th the convoy was 200 miles west of Inishtrahull where it turned to the SW and then to a SSW course towards the Azores at 0400 next day. Shore-based air escort was present during the first two days at sea and WS 19 generally enjoyed a quiet passage in mainly fine weather until well south of the Azores, detaching *Keppel*, *Leamington* and *Volunteer* back to the UK just after midnight on the 13th, and the two Hunt class for Ponta Delgada at 1600 on the 14th when 400 miles north of these islands.

The Shaw Savill *Akaroa* was detached at 0100 on the 15th to proceed through the western Azores passage en route to Bermuda and by that evening the convoy was 130 miles east of Sao Miguel. Just after midnight *St Mary's* was detached for Ponta Delgada and the UK, and *Castleton* similarly at 1600 which left the convoy without A/S cover and *Mauritius* unable to operate her aircraft due to moderate SW headwinds. The Hunt class destroyers had been expected to rejoin by this time but were delayed on passage to the Azores by headwinds, suffering minor structural damage in consequence and when catching up were restricted to 15 knots by the need to conserve fuel. They rejoined at 1700 on the 17th and at which point the convoy was diverted 50° to port by Admiralty signal to pass inside the Cape Verde islands rather than the planned route outside the group, which saved 150 miles and eleven hours steaming on the remaining distance to Freetown.

Three U-Boats were known to have attacked the homeward SL 109 five days earlier and sank one ship some 300 miles SW of the diverted position of the convoy, but no other attacks or sightings then occurred and no U-Boats had been reported in the Freetown or Gulf of Guinea area since the beginning of April. In fact most of the U-Boats then at sea were operating in the more lucrative waters off the eastern seaboard of the United States.

Mauritius was able to catapult her two Walrus aircraft on the forenoon of the 18th for A/S patrols and recovered them at 1830. That same evening the Commodore ship *Strathnaver* fell astern, stopped and blacked out owing to water in oil fuel, *Carnarvon Castle* detached an hour later to assist but the liner was underway by 2300 and caught up overnight by which time *Scythia* fell astern with fuel pump trouble, the AMC remained in station astern of the convoy until *Scythia* rejoined at 0900 on the 19th.

The first of the local escorts, *Velox* from Bathurst, joined at 1030 on the 19th by which time the convoy was 200 miles NE of the Cape Verde group. Sunderland or Hudson aircraft began periodical visits over the convoy next morning as it passed through the Cap Vert gap while *Boreas* and *Wild Swan* from Freetown strengthened the A/S escort. Course was altered 70° to port direct for Freetown in the afternoon of the 20th and when 60 miles distant from Freetown on the morning of the 22nd, the starboard engine of *Highland Brigade* failed and caused that liner to straggle behind the convoy at 9 knots.

WS 19 was anchored in Freetown Harbour at 1130 on the 22nd; *Highland Brigade* arrived two hours later.

The breakdown of three large fully embarked liners was a source of some anxiety to both the Commodore and SOE on *Mauritius*, which "entailed reductions of speed, the temporary dispersion of escorts and undesirable signalling at night"[6]…"and usually means…volumes of black smoke."[7] The Commodore was advised that many of the ships had no refits since the beginning of the war, but further breakdowns elicited further comment on this subject later in the voyage.

WS 19 was in Freetown for the usual four days for replenishment of fuel and water. No comments are recorded in the regimental histories about the stopover but the Sherwood Foresters were not endeared to American style catering aboard their transport *Orizaba* which, "in spite of its variety and generous portions, British soldiers did not greatly appreciate American rations. Coffee instead of tea was regarded as a real hardship and the "tin and packet" system was not popular. They were not impressed by the high calorific value of food which many regarded as too unpalatable to eat."[8]

The convoy put to sea again in the afternoon of 26 May with the AMC *Alcantara* having replaced *Carnarvon Castle*, otherwise the ocean escort remained, with the SOE on *Mauritius*, the two Hunt class and local escorts provided by *Velox*, *Boreas* and the sloop *Milford*. Course was set to the SW for a distance of 250 miles until noon next day when the convoy carried out a wheel of 80° to port to steer towards St Helena where it was planned to refuel the Hunts. A local air escort was provided in daylight hours until that evening. This leg of the voyage began badly with another three breakdowns: *Strathnaver* suffered burst boiler tubes and condenser trouble on the first evening at sea and again next morning fell astern with fan trouble, while that afternoon *Highland Brigade* suffered another mechanical defect.

The local escort force remained until the convoy was 75 miles south of the equator where in the evening of the 28th, *Velox* was detached back to Freetown while *Boreas* left with *Highland Brigade* for Takoradi and Lagos, and after disembarking at these ports, the *Highland* liner proceeded to the Plate, loaded on her owners' berth and returned direct to the Clyde where she was re-directed to Avonmouth, docked there on 27 July and next sailed in WS 22.

During the night of the 28/29th, *Alcantara* and *Milford* went on ahead and next day the AMC transferred fuel to the sloop while her Seafox aircraft provided A/S protection in difficult weather. The convoy ceased to zigzag when reaching 5° South that evening. During the next night, 29/30th, *Alcantara* again went ahead with the Hunt class destroyers to fuel them in the lee of St Helena which proved most prudent as the SE trades on the 31st would not have allowed this in the open sea. The convoy was routed to pass south of St Helena but diverted to pass close north of the island where all three escorts rejoined after dark on the 31st. *Alcantara* detached on a South Atlantic patrol next aftenoon.

No other incidents occurred on passage to the Cape, two ships were spoken and identified on the 5th and just before noon that day, the cruiser *Shropshire* from Simonstown joined the escort in a position 180 miles west of Cape Columbine, and at 1700 *Shropshire* detached ahead with the Durban portion comprising *Orizaba* as Commodore, *Strathaird*, *Pasteur*, *Ormonde*, *Moreton Bay* and *Clan Macarthur*.

The remaining seven transports and two MT ships escorted by *Mauritius*, *Milford* and the two Hunts entered Capetown searched channel at 0800 on the 6th and berthed in the harbour later that morning while *Mauritius* parted company for Simonstown. Aerial photographs of Table Bay that afternoon show 43 ships anchored in Table Bay and at least ten in Capetown docks.[9] The Commodore reported the convoy as being well disciplined and the station keeping generally good but clearly unhappy to comment that 15 breakdowns involving eight ships had occurred since leaving the UK: three on *Strathaird*, two on *Strathnaver*, two on *Clan Macarthur*, one each on *Athlone Castle*, *Mooltan* and both *Highland* ships and no less than four occasions on *Scythia*.[7]

The Commodore doubtless elicited comments from the masters of these liners and particularly from Captain Starling who had served on *Strathnaver* almost continuously since 1936. From the outbreak of war that liner had enjoyed one four week overhaul but otherwise was never out of service for more than two or three weeks until the recent breakdowns necessitated drydocking and boiler repairs at Durban on the homeward voyage. It was widely recognized the demands of the Sea Transport Service were paramount in the national interests and although periodical drydockings were generally adhered to for the maintenance of speed, boilers and machinery were perhaps not allowed the attention they deserved. The period of liner overhauls certainly compared unfavourably with that recently allowed the AMC *Carnarvon Castle* which had been refitting out of service for nearly five months.

The liner *Queen Mary* arrived in Table Bay from the Clyde soon after WS 19 for fuel and water en route to Suez and is related below as convoy WS 19W. Meanwhile, as happened with the troops of 2nd Division in WS 18, the Impcon staff in Capetown had been instructed to ensure the maximum exercise for 8 Armoured Division who were duly disembarked to the temporary tented camp at Retreat. Unfortunately the camp "was virtually blown down and washed away in torrential rain by one of the Cape gales on the first night."[10] The Impcon staff arranged special trains to bring all the men into the city in the morning where they were taken "to various Turkish and swimming baths and laundries, borrowed for the purpose of drying the men's sodden clothes and equipment."[10] Amazingly the troops never complained "and the Camp staff were loud in their praises of their cheerfulness in such trying conditions."[10]

The Durban section of the convoy had an uneventful passage around the Cape with *Shropshire*, passing the Italian Reparation liners *Duilio* and *Giulio Cesare*, (then on charter to the Red Cross for evacuating personnel from East Africa) off Cape Agulhas in the afternoon of the 6th. *Shropshire* parted company as the liners approached Durban on the morning of the 9th and returned around the Cape to act as escort to the Capetown section. In Durban, *Ormonde* and *Pasteur* disembarked all of their 8087 personnel to Clairwood Camp for on-carriage in three weeks time, the earliest that Indian Ocean transports could be made available. *Ormonde* left Durban the day after arrival to load on the Union Castle berth at Capetown, proceeding then via Freetown to reach Glasgow on 18 July and was then used for a Halifax voyage preparatory to training for Operation Torch. *Pasteur* left Durban on the 16th and Capetown on the 22nd, proceeding via Freetown to New York where she embarked US troops for an independent voyage via Freetown and Durban to Suez; *Pasteur* then returned to New York for service on the North Atlantic route to the UK.

In Capetown all of the personnel on *Highland Monarch* were transhipped to the waiting BI trooper *Takliwa* for on-carriage to Suez. The *Highland* liner left Capetown on the morning of the 11th for Buenos Aires, loading there and at Santos and Rio, refuelled at Freetown, embarked RAF personnel at Bathurst and docked in Liverpool on 14 August where she remained for seven weeks for a next voyage in WS 23.

In the western desert Rommel's offensive had begun successfully two weeks earlier and increased the pressure to get 8 Armoured Division to that theatre as quickly as possible. Six transports and two storeships of WS 19 left Capetown in the early afternoon of the 11th and formed into three columns to set off at 12.5 knots under escort of the AMC *Cheshire* towards Durban.[11] Late on the previous evening it became clear that generator defects on *Scythia* would not allow that ship to sail before the 13th, but with Brigadier Kenchington's HQ and two regiments of 24 Armoured Brigade on that liner and urgently required as the leading divisional unit to land at Suez, alternative arrangements had to be made. *Nieuw Amsterdam* had recently arrived in Capetown and sailed on the 13th for Port Elizabeth to undergo boiler repairs. *Scythia* was able to patch up her generators sufficiently to make the passage to Port Elizabeth, where her troops transhipped to the Dutch liner but had to wait there three more days before going on to Durban to complete embarkation. The *Nieuw Amsterdam* continued as an independent to Suez where she arrived four days behind the main body of the convoy. *Scythia* meanwhile returned to Capetown to complete her generator repairs and was then sent to Durban to assist with the on-carriage of troops from that port on 1st July.

The eight ships of WS 19 passed around the Cape without incident, being joined by the cruiser *Shropshire* at midday on the 12th when 130 miles SSW of Agulhas and 25 miles clear of that bank and any possible mines. The two Hunt class destroyers from Simonstown caught up and joined on the morning of the 14th when 50 miles SE of East London. At 1100 next morning the convoy reached the outer end of the Durban searched channel where *Cheshire* and the two Hunts detached into that port, while the Durban section of seven ships joined with the cruiser *Emerald* as escort. The Durban section now comprised *Strathaird*, *Moreton Bay*, *Borinquen*, *Empire Woodlark*, with *Clans Macarthur*, *Mactavish* and *Macinnes*.

The re-formed fifteen ships of WS 19 set off not for the Mozambique Channel but an easterly course to pass south and east of Madagascar last used for troop convoys by WS 2. Japanese raiders and submarines had been active at both ends of the Mozambique Channel since the 5th June and sank eleven ships within a week. On 10 June the CinCEF directed that troop convoys and fast unescorted liners were now to pass east of Madagascar by accepting the risk of meeting raiders on that route.

On the first night at sea from Durban, the two Hunts caught up and rejoined while *Strathaird* reported to the Commodore that her fourth and last main boiler had started to leak, but hoped to maintain her present speed until repairs were completed on the others, otherwise her speed would be reduced to 5 knots.[7] *Clan Macarthur* then dropped astern to rescue three men from *Orizaba* but was only able to find one and did not rejoin until the following afternoon after an absence of eighteen hours. *Empire Trooper* being a late departure from Durban had caught up and joined at midday on the 16th.

The convoy was originally routed to pass 150 miles south of Madagascar, but on the morning of the 17th, the CinC signalled *Shropshire* that D/F bearings indicated the presence of a Japanese vessel to the SE of the route and ordered an immediate alteration to port away from that source of danger. The CinCEF believed that two Japanese raiders "lay SE of Madagascar, quietly waiting to refuel their submarines' then working in the Mozambique Channel.[12] *Shropshire* flew her Walrus on patrol for a few hours on the 18th but sighted nothing and at 1100 was relieved by *Mauritius* which appropriately had refuelled at her name island within the inhospitable and difficult of entry Grand Port on the SE coast. *Shropshire* now returned to Simonstown and without seeing any sign of the suspected Japanese raider, the convoy passed 15 miles south of Cape St Mary, the southern extremity of Madagascar at 1600 that day and thereafter passed up the eastern side between that island and Reunion. Very slow progress was then made against the Equatorial current and in the evening of the 21st came the news that Tobruk had fallen with the surrender of 33,000 seasoned British and South African troops. This news reached Churchill as he sat in conference with Roosevelt in Washington. He could not at first believe it, and was to write in his memoirs that "it was one of the heaviest blows I can recall during the war,"[13] while the official history states "The fall of Tobruk came as a staggering blow to the British cause."[14] It seemed that nothing could then prevent Rommel reaching the Suez Canal.

At 0900 on the 23rd when 230 miles SE of Diego Suarez, *Emerald* and the two Hunt class destroyers detached with the section for that port comprising *Moreton Bay*, *Empires Trooper* and *Woodlark* (carrying South African troops) and *Clans Mactavish* and *Macinnes*. The two *Empires* subsequently returned to Durban, *Moreton Bay* partially disembarked in Diego Suarez and landed the balance at Mombasa, from where she sailed on 4 July via Durban (for fuel) to the Plate, suffering heavy weather damage crossing the South Atlantic requiring repairs in Buenos Aires. *Moreton Bay* then loaded on the Blue Star berth and returned via Freetown to Liverpool on 14 September and was then employed in WS 23 two weeks later.

The convoy route passed east of the Farquhar islands then turned NW to clear the Seychelles group before again turning north for the Guardafui area 1,000 miles distant, and by the evening of the 26th, WS 19 was 370 miles east of Mogadishu where *Devonshire* joined and relieved *Mauritius* as ocean escort. At 1700 next day in a position 300 miles south of Ras Hafun, the AMC *Corfu* was met and at this point *Devonshire* detached NE direct for Bombay with *Orizaba*, *Athlone Castle* and *Strathaird*, where they arrived without further incident in the late afternoon of 1st July, 52 days after leaving the UK. Meanwhile *Corfu* with the remaining five transports and three storeships continued towards Guardafui, passing through that strait on the night of the 28th and reached Aden on the morning of the 30th where the convoy was finally dispersed and all ships entered harbour to refuel.

Independent passages were made from Aden to Suez, where *Monarch of Bermuda* arrived on the 4th, disembarked within two days and sailed for home via Mombasa, Diego Suarez, Durban (embarking there Italian POW), Capetown and Freetown to reach the Clyde on 27 August and Liverpool three days later where she began to prepare for Torch. *Mooltan* reached Suez a day behind the *Monarch* and left on the 7th for Aden, Durban, spent 16 days under repair at Capetown then via Freetown to Avonmouth and arrived on 7 September and later moved to the Clyde for Torch. *Strathnaver* also anchored in Suez on the 5th but after disembarking required to repair leaky boiler tubes before sailing on the 11th via Aden for Durban and drydocking over a twenty day period, she then refuelled at Capetown and Freetown and reached the Clyde on 7 September allowing five weeks prior to departure in the Torch convoy. Captain Starling now retired from the P&O Company's service after a lifetime at sea and was succeeded by Captain EM Coates brought back from service with the RNR. *Borinquen* returned around the Cape to New York, while the three storeships and *Takliwa*, (which had called en route at Massawa), reached Suez on the 11th, discharged within the space of three weeks and all being refrigerated carriers returned home with meat cargoes from the Plate. *Nieuw Amsterdam* reached Suez on the 9th with the troops on-carried from *Scythia* and was also disembarked and dispatched back to Durban within two days.

Of the three transports which arrived at Bombay, it was discovered that the Support Group troops on *Orizaba* should have gone to Suez; this liner sailed again on the 6th and reached its final destination twelve days later to complete the arrival of 8 Armoured Division in the Middle East. *Orizaba* then returned around the Cape via Recife to Norfolk.

Rommel's Afrika Corps had reached the Alamein line on 1st July and 8 Armoured Division was thrown piecemeal into defensive positions and tragically was never able to operate as a complete formation. 23 Brigade was committed to battle soon after receiving the last of their tanks from the base workshops on 17 July and were decimated in action within five days on Ruweisat Ridge. The KRRC of 24 Brigade lost all their vehicles when *Elysia* was sunk in the Mozambique Channel and the Support Group only disembarked on 18 July. All units of the division were attached to other formations in the desert until January 1943 when 8 Armoured Division was disbanded and ceased to exist.

At Bombay *Athlone Castle* partially disembarked and carried the balance of personnel on to Colombo, leaving there on 13 July as the last large troopship to use that port due to the proximity of the Japanese for fifteen months. Proceeding via Melbourne to Lyttelton, where a refrigerated cargo was loaded on the Port Line berth, *Athlone Castle* returned via Panama and Halifax to Liverpool on 7 October and next sailed in WS 24. *Strathaird* remained ten days at Bombay, loading there on the P&O berth and at Durban and Capetown on the Union Castle berth, to return via Freetown to Glasgow on 27 August and remained in the Clyde for twelve weeks preparing for Torch after being drydocked in the AFD off Greenock.

By the end of June with all the WS 19 liners approaching their destinations at Suez and Bombay, there remained at Clairwood Transit Camp in Durban 3,600 personnel from WS 18 and 8,000 from WS 19, for which arrangements had been made to move them onwards in an extra convoy CM 29 by using *Scythia* and four of the Indian Ocean troopers; *Dilwara* and *Dunera* having been especially taken off the Bombay/Basra service. The other two ships were *Llandaff Castle* and *Pulaski* both from the Durban/Red Sea route. These five ships embarked all 11,600 to clear the backlog and left Durban on 1st July with the storeship *Diomed* under escort of the cruiser *Frobisher*, netlayer *Guardian* and corvette *Fritillary*. The Japanese submarines were still active at both ends of the Mozambique Channel so CM 29 passed up the east side of Madagascar, where *Sobieski* joined from Diego Suarez on the 9th (having remained there for 33 days) and on reaching a position 400 miles east of Mombasa at 1700 on the 11th, *Royal Sovereign* from Mombasa joined as escort, as did *Khedive Ismail* from that port, both having separate destroyer escorts which then returned there with the remaining warships. *Royal Sovereign* continued towards Guardafui with the eight ship convoy until the afternoon of the 14th, when relieved by the AMC *Corfu* to allow the battleship to return to Mombasa. At about the same point south of Guardafui, *Sobieski*, *Dilwara* and *Dunera* detached NE for Bombay, probably with another cruiser as escort, and arrived there on the 21st.

The remaining five ships reached Aden on 17 July and were held there for three days to allow *Queen Elizabeth* and ten liners of WS 19P to be cleared at Suez. *Scythia* then arrived on the 25th, left again on the 27th with 1,393 Italian POW for the UK, loaded in Mombasa, then repaired in Durban, fuelled at Capetown and returned via Freetown to Liverpool on 29 September in time for much needed repairs before sailing in a follow-up convoy to Algiers. *Pulaski* reached Suez on the 27th and *Llandaff Castle* on the 30th, which completed the movement of all personnel carried in WS 18 and 19.

By the end of July the desert front line had stabilized along the Alamein line a mere 280 miles west of Suez, with the opponents exhausted, resting and regrouping while Eighth Army received reinforcements of men and materials with the arrival of each convoy, WS 20 being due within a week and WS 21 three weeks later. Lieut.-General BL Montgomery arrived two weeks later to take command of this army and immediately infused new life into it and from which it never looked back.

WS 19W - sailed Clyde 23.5.42.

It was shown earlier that Roosevelt replied to a request from Churchill at the beginning of March 1942 that "he would supply ships to move our two divisions from Britain round the Cape, the first convoy sailing about April 26 and the remainder about May 6."[1] However, large numbers of American troops were then being sent to the Pacific theatre, to Australia and to Northern Ireland and US troopships were much fewer in number than their British counterparts. Nevertheless, two small US transports had sailed with WS 19 on May 10 and five more with three storeships were being provided for WS 19P at the end of May, but their combined capacity was only 12,500 and therefore far short of the two convoys each estimated to lift 20,000 personnel.

Three divisions were sent around the Cape in each of the March, April and May convoys and three more were planned for the next convoys sailing at the end of May, June and July (WS 19P, 20 and 21). The entire WS fleet then of 81 ships was already committed to these convoys, in addition to assisting the movement of American troops to Northern Ireland by providing up to 15,000 berths per month by diverting homeward WS ships via New York.

Even allowing the measures already implemented to increase turnround and capacity on the WS route, there was insufficient to provide for the normal flow of drafts and the two divisions planned for June and July. On the Indian Ocean, however, the flow of Anzac troops to the Middle East had ceased in December 1941 with the outbreak of war with Japan which released the two *Queens* and *Aquitania* from this service. High level discussions ensued on the future use of these liners and was only settled at the end of March when the Admiralty agreed their use on the North Atlantic to carry US troops to the UK, beginning in July or August, but this date was advanced when the *Queen Mary* arrived at the Clyde Anchorage on 16 May with almost 10,000 US troops from New York. The MOWT and Admiralty in consultation with Cunard had by then decided to use that liner for a single voyage to the Middle East.

An earlier turnround of *Queen Mary* at the Clyde Anchorage in 1940,[2] the sole wartime UK port able to berth such giant liners,[3] handled 5,000 troops in each direction but even with double that number, four Clyde passenger steamers were now allocated as troop tenders and each able to land up to 2,000 per trip; the limiting factor was the ability of the railway to provide the necessary trains but was gradually overcome. The anchorage was also equipped with sufficient attendant craft to handle the necessary stores, provisions, cargo, fuel and fresh water.

Queen Mary was now embarked with 9,537 troops comprising 7,500 Army, 1,000 RAF and 900 Naval draft parties while 1,000 tons of military stores were loaded in her two holds. She sailed on 23 May as the single ship WS 19W "convoy" escorted only to the west of Ireland by the AA cruiser *Cairo* and destroyers *Keppel, Beagle, Douglas* and *Sardonyx*. Captain Bisset recorded his anxiety on this voyage, steaming at 28 knots over vast distances with 10,409 souls and no escort,[4] but he reached Freetown safely in seven days and therefore half the time taken by the usual WS convoys. He also noted that Freetown was "no place for such a big ship - a bad approach, strong currents, shoal water on the bar and the river congested with tankers, naval vessels and other ships."[4] There was, however, no alternative to Freetown.

A large homeward SL convoy was then assembling but priority attended replenishment of the liner which was able to sail next day and after another fast passage to the Cape was anchored in Table Bay for further replenishment six days later, where the first problems of the voyage began. Being unable to berth in Capetown docks and with oil and water tankers alongside in the bay, heavy weather rolled in from the westward which required the liner to shift round to the comparative shelter of Simons Bay where she anchored close to the naval base. Whilst the fuelling and watering was in progress, there was much conferring with the NCSO concerning the onward route to Suez, requiring as it then did the additional 500 miles to pass east of Madagascar by making a total distance of 6,167 miles, "the longest that ship ever made port to port. It was her absolute limit of endurance without replenishment,"[4] and being twice the North Atlantic passage for which she was designed, reflected very highly on the Naval Architects concerned.

Leaving Simonstown on 10 June under escort of the cruiser *Mauritius*, which remained until relieved by *Devonshire* off the Somali coast, various other escorts covered the liner through the Gulf of Aden and Red Sea to Suez Bay where she arrived on 22 June and anchored close north of Newport Rock, 31 days after leaving the Clyde. The last part of the voyage during one of the hottest months of the year in the Red Sea when the daily temperature reached 35°C, was particularly trying for the troops, especially at night when the ship was closed up to maintain blackout. Captain Bissett recalled "hundreds of improvised sea-water showers were rigged below decks for the sweltering troops...as many men as possible were allowed to sleep on deck. Despite these arrangements, there were many cases of heat prostration. The barber's shop, which was air-conditioned, was used as a temporary hospital. After a few hours in its cooled atmosphere, most of the sufferers recovered, but three men died and were buried at sea. The engine-room and kitchen staff suffered the torments of the damned."[4]

The *Queen Mary* had arrived at Suez twelve days ahead of WS 19, which left the UK two weeks ahead of her and fully justified the decision and risks of the voyage, most especially then as Tobruk was surrendered to the enemy the previous day. In the space of twelve hours on 22 June all of the troops were disembarked and the stores unloaded by means of barges and Nile ferry boats. Next day a mixed bag of 2,565 personnel embarked which included 1,398 German POW and 300 young Polish guard, and various homebound service personnel.

The liner left Suez on 22 June, called at Simonstown between 5 and 7 July where 610 mixed passengers were landed, then proceeded via Rio de Janeiro to dock in New York on 22 July. The ship was now prepared in earnest for North Atlantic service and sailed eleven days later for the Clyde with 15,125 US troops, "the greatest number of human beings that had ever embarked in one vessel for an ocean-crossing,"[4] but was later exceeded on more than one occasion.

WS 19P - sailed UK 31.5.42

Despite the ever increasing number of troops of all categories that were dispatched around the Cape in the first five convoys of 1942, by May it seemed the demand for more reinforcements for India, the Middle East and the northern front in Persia and Iraq was quite insatiable. Undoubtedly the much reduced prospect of a German invasion of the British Isles while their Armies were heavily engaged in Russia and the Desert, coupled with the increasing flow of US Army and Air Force personnel into the UK, allowed the release of many British troops for overseas service and most certainly was the basis for dispatching the four divisions beginning in March,[1] and for which WS 19P was to carry the last, (although two more were sent later).

The formation selected for inclusion in WS 19P was 44 (Home Counties) Infantry Division, comprised of first line Territorial battalions which had been in France for only two months in the spring of 1940 but was badly mauled with heavy casualties in the retreat from the River Escault to Dunkirk. The division then re-formed at Oxford and deployed to coast defences in Lincolnshire, until that October were moved first to Yorkshire then Kent and Surrey. In March 1942 the division was warned to mobilize for an undecided overseas destination and this was completed by the middle of May.

Beginning in April with WS 18, the interval between convoys was reduced from four or five weeks to three, as one means of increasing turnover and personnel capacity on that route. WS 19 sailed on 10 May and so WS 19P (the origin of the suffix letter being unknown) was due to sail at the end of that month, provided the necessary shipping was then available.

All but two of the liners allocated for the convoy were those which returned to the UK from WS 14 and 15 between the third week of April and 11 May, allowing *Laconia*, *Orontes*, *Strathallan*, *Andes* and *Orcades* about three weeks in their respective ports; *Arawa*, *Staffordshire*, *Christiaan Huygens* and *Otranto* almost four weeks, while *Britannic* and *Viceroy of India* had a week longer. *Warwick Castle* from WS 14 was six weeks in Glasgow during which time major machinery repairs were completed and her personnel capacity increased from 1,524 to 3,271. Two British and five American [2] additions to the WS route were provided to increase the capacity of the convoy, i.e. *Cathay* of P&O which had been converted from AMC service in Brooklyn and crossed in the 17 ship troop convoy AT 15 from Halifax to Belfast, then moved to Newport on 13 May for minor repairs and preparation for embarkation. Also taken from the same convoy was the Cunard *Aquitania*, previously employed on the US route until January 1942 when she crossed the Pacific to San Francisco and thereafter via Panama to New York and reached the Clyde Anchorage on 11 May. Five American transports from that convoy (two of which proceeded en route via Iceland) landed their troops in Belfast or the Clyde Anchorage and there prepared for embarkation, *Cristobal* and *JW McAndrew* first docking in Greenock's James Watt Dock to load military vehicles, guns and stores. *Mexico* and the Grace Line *Santa Elena* remained at the anchorage while *Santa Rosa* embarked in Liverpool.

The embarkation of 44 Division troops was spread over six liners in Liverpool, Glasgow and the Clyde Anchorage from 26 to 30 May. At No. 1 KGV Dock, Glasgow, the HQ of 131 Brigade with ʽ1/6 and 1/7 Bns The Queens Regiment were embarked on *Strathallan* which moved to the anchorage on the 27th, where 1/5 Bn The Queens embarked by tender on *Cristobal*. At Liverpool 132 Brigade HQ with 4 Bn Royal West Kents and 2 Bn The Buffs boarded *Laconia* which anchored in the river on the 29th, while 5 Royal West Kents and 6 Cheshires (the divisional machine-gun Bn) were on *Orontes* which anchored on the 30th. The remaining 133 Brigade embarked with their HQ and 4 Bn Royal Sussex on *JW McAndrew* at the Clyde Anchorage while 2 and 5 Bns Royal Sussex boarded *Santa Rosa* in Liverpool.

The first embarkations of other troops in the convoy which included eleven AA Regiments and other RA units, 3,000 Army and 2,800 RAF in drafts, was completed at Liverpool on *Viceroy of India* and *Arawa* which sailed for the Clyde Anchorage on the 27th, then on *Christiaan Huygens*, *Laconia* and *Santa Rosa* which anchored to await completion of *Andes* and *Orontes* on sailing day. Two ships embarked in the Bristol Channel, *Staffordshire* at Avonmouth and *Cathay* at Newport, both then sailed for the Clyde where they arrived on the 30th. Each of the transports were also loaded with various quantities of stores, guns, MT or ammunition, except *Britannic*, *Viceroy of India*, *Staffordshire*, *Cathay* and *Santa Elena* which carried only ballast.

In Glasgow, *Warwick Castle* embarked and moved to the anchorage from 4 KGV on the 26th, followed by *Strathallan* from No. 1 berth next day, while *Orcades* and *Otranto* from 2 and 3 KGV completed and moved down to the anchorage on the 29th. The remaining embarkations were on *Britannic*, *Aquitania*, *Mexico* and *Santa Elena* by tenders from Gourock to the Clyde Anchorage. The total embarked on the nineteen transports was 60,703,[4] with a further 42 on four storeships and 245 for West Africa taking passage on the battleship *Nelson*. This was the highest number carried of all the WS series while the gross tonnage of the transports at 342,358 was exceeded only once by WS 17. At the time of embarkation roughly one third of the total were each destined for the Middle East, India or simply listed as "undecided".

New Zealand Star and three Dutch Nederland motorships, the latter on US charters, were loaded as MT/storeships for the convoy, *Java* in Glasgow and *Talisse* with *Poelau Roebiah* and the Blue Star ship in Liverpool. Each carried military vehicles, guns, tanks, stores and ammunition and were capable of 15 knots, the slowest ship of the convoy being *Staffordshire* whose maximum was 14.5 knots. Each of the transports also carried a selection of guns and vehicles, except *Andes*, *Aquitania* and *Mexico* which were loaded only with stores.

This convoy left the UK with depressing news from the Western Desert where Rommel had launched a new offensive at Gazala and within a few days completely overran and virtually wiped out 150 Brigade of 50 (Northumbrian) Division, which then ceased to exist and never re-formed. The few survivors were visited by Rommel before passing into captivity; they had sailed out in WS 8A thirteen months earlier.

The escort provided for WS 19P was not large but included the battleship *Nelson* which the Admiralty had earlier advised Admiral Somerville, CinC Eastern Fleet, "was due to leave the Clyde in late May...and to reach Kilindini (Mombasa) on 7 July,"[3] but in fact she never joined that fleet until July 1945 while her sister, *Rodney*, also planned for that theatre of operations was otherwise engaged until finally de-commissioned. Both were initially required for the Pedestal convoy to Malta in August.

The Commodore of the convoy was another with previous experience of a WS convoy on *Britannic*, in September 1940, Rear Admiral (Rtd) KEL Creighton was this time sailing in *Orcades* and once again struck up a cordial relationship with that liner's Master, Captain Charles Fox and his officers. Captain JH Biggs of *Strathallan* was appointed Vice Commodore while Captain AE Nicholls of *Otranto* as Rear Commodore would also act for the Liverpool section until their junction with the main portion from the Clyde.

The Liverpool ships began leaving the Mersey at 1130 on 31 May, led by Captain Sharp in *Laconia* and followed at five minute intervals in the order: *Christiaan Huygens*, *Orontes*, *Andes*, *Poelau Roebiah*, *New Zealand Star*, *Talisse* and *Santa Rosa*. All AA guns were loaded and manned ready for instant action against approaching aircraft. Escort was provided by the Town class destroyers *Mansfield* and *Buxton* while the usual speed of 10 knots was maintained to the Orsay rendezvous.

From the Clyde and following the conference there, *Keppel* as Senior Officer with six other destroyers left for Moville to top up with fuel and had one missing when joining the convoy at Orsay. *Orcades* with the Commodore led the Clyde portion out of the boom at 1900 on 31 May, followed by the remaining fourteen liners and single store-ship. *Nelson* with the carrier *Argus* and destroyers *Beagle* and *Salisbury*, left at 2300 to join up at 0600 next morning off Orsay, where junction was made with both sections of the convoy which formed into a cruising order of seven columns with the two major warships in a centre one of their own.[5] The initial course was westerly until reaching the first position on the route at 0500 on the 2nd, where course was altered to SW. *Keppel* and eight other destroyers had joined at the rendezvous and *Mansfield* a few hours later to provide an Asdic screen of ten. The ordered speed of 13 knots could not be maintained in the W'ly head wind and sea and averaged less than 12 knots for the first day at sea. Reduced visibility also plagued the first four days and turned into fog on the morning of the 3rd when *Buxton* caught up from Moville and by the following morning as the weather began to clear, a SSE'ly course was set towards the eastern side of the Azores and at this point, *Keppel* and two destroyers detached for the UK.

At 0200 on the 5th *Nelson* obtained two radar contacts closing on the port bow, the convoy made an emergency alteration to port and three small vessels crossed the head of the columns. The Hunt class *Derwent* was sent to investigate and found two RN trawlers and an armed yacht. At 0530 *Wild Swan* from Ponta Delgada made rendezvous with the convoy and detached with *Argus* and *Beagle* for Gibraltar. The remaining destroyers *Douglas*, *Buxton*, *Blackmore* and *Derwent* were refuelled in turn as the convoy came abreast of the Azores next morning and *Derwent* caught up and rejoined that evening.

The destroyer *Wivern* joined to the SE of the Azores at midday on the 6th, by which date the convoy had reached 12.7 knots in steadily improving weather and course was then set to pass west of the Cape Verde islands. At noon on the 7th, *Aquitania* was detached unescorted to proceed ahead at her maximum speed of 25 knots as WS 19Q to Freetown, arriving there on the 11th and sailing next day for the Cape and Suez.

The convoy reached fine weather on the 8th, when steering due south for a position SW of the Cape Verdes where *Nelson* pumped 90 tons of fuel to *Wivern* before course was altered at 1400 on the 10th direct for Freetown. The warmer climes induced many to the open decks, not least on *Orcades* where Commodore Creighton recalled "a number of attractive young nursing sisters, mostly going to India...and playing deck tennis." From the bridge with Captain Fox "they derived a lot of innocent fun watching romances blossoming between the young army officers and the nurses."[6] In traditional naval style, the Commodore planned ahead for a party.

Velox from Freetown joined on the morning of the 11th and that day *Nelson* fuelled the other destroyers, it being doubtful if *Derwent* in particular had sufficient to reach that port. *Nelson* detached ahead early on the 13th and anchored in Freetown that morning closely followed by the 23 ships of the convoy which had enjoyed an uneventful passage averaging 13.08 knots free of any warnings or sightings of U-Boats or enemy aircraft.

Meanwhile *Aquitania* had left Freetown the previous day for the Cape, where she refuelled and in Diego Suarez and Aden before reaching Suez on 8 July to disembark; her return voyage began two days later with further calls at Diego Suarez, Table Bay and Freetown before drydocking in Boston on 14 August prior to a trip from New York to Suez.

It was at Freetown while the ships were busy watering and fuelling that Commodore Creighton arranged with Captain Fox on *Orcades*, for the temporary use of a sumptuous air-conditioned suite, normally reserved for millionaires, which maintained a comfortable temperature of 13°C in stark contrast to the sweltering conditions outside. Together they arranged a cocktail party and invited the nurses, army officers and ship's own officers. "Everyone chatted away happily and it seemed a great shame when it all had to come to an end and we ventured once more into the sweltering outer world."[6]

Of all the regiments represented in this convoy, a few acknowledged the renowned South African hospitality but had little to say about the voyage itself, other than The Queen's Regiment whose 1/5 Bn was embarked on the US Army Transport *Cristobal* where they took a long time to get used to American food and cooking. "Owing to the lack of space only two meals per day were served and these were eaten standing around mess tables, but the food was excellent and the absence of drink was borne philosophically."[7]

Three more US transports joined the convoy at Freetown where they had arrived with Army and Air Force personnel going east from the States, the largest being the ex Matson Liner *Mariposa* from Charleston carrying 4,000 while the smaller *Chateau Thierry* and Grace Line *Santa Paula* carried 900 and 2,400 respectively from New York. The enlarged convoy now comprised 21 transports and four storeships, while additional escort was being provided by the battleship *Rodney* with fleet destroyers, *Pathfinder*, *Penn* and *Quentin*, and may have impressed the Americans yet the reason is unclear as no German warships had taken part in ocean forays since March 1941 and although two disguised raiders were then believed to be operating in the South Atlantic such vessels generally avoided approaching convoys.

After six days in the steamy heat of Freetown, WS 19P was led out of harbour by the Commodore on *Orcades* at 0930 on 19 June, followed at four minute intervals by the remaining 24 ships to form into a revised cruising order of seven columns at the end of the searched channel two hours later. By 1330 the convoy was joined by *Nelson* and *Rodney* with five destroyers and set off for a position 270 miles SW at a speed of 14 knots, the battleships taking station between the two centre columns.[8] The alter-course position was reached at 0800 next day where the convoy undertook a wheel to port of 100° to steer initially into the Gulf of Guinea, rather than adopt the more usual St Helena-Cape route.

By the afternoon of the 21st the convoy was 240 miles SW of Cape Palmas on the Liberian coast where the destroyer *Velox* detached to rendezvous with the repair ship *Vindictive*. Zigzag was maintained until reaching latitude 5° South on the 24th, and that afternoon the Hunt class *Derwent* was detached to refuel at St Helena then distant 850 miles to the SW, from where she was to rejoin the battleships. It was also on this date that *Nelson* had to break W/T silence to obtain information from the CinCSA on the intended rendezvous with the cruiser, *Shropshire*, particularly as the convoy was now 70 miles astern of position due to the 2 knots adverse effect of the Equatorial Current. *Nelson* and *Rodney* refuelled the remaining destroyers *Pathfinder*, *Penn* and *Quentin* next day, prior to rendezvous with *Shropshire* at 1100 on the 26th. The convoy had now reached 12° South and was 330 miles west of Lobito on the Angolan coast where the battleships and destroyers detached to return to Freetown and Gibraltar, for subsequent service on the August "Pedestal" convoy to Malta.

From this point onwards the convoy steered SSE towards the Cape, maintaining a distance of 150 to 200 miles from the coast of South West Africa and completed this passage without incident. The AMC *Cheshire* was met on the morning of the 30th and at 1600 that day detached in a position 65 miles SW of Cape Columbine with the Vice Commodore on *Strathallan*, plus *Cathay, Laconia, Orontes, Staffordshire, Santa Elena, Santa Rosa, Mariposa, Mexico, JW McAndrew, Java* and *New Zealand Star* as the Capetown portion, where they arrived at daylight next morning and berthed in the harbour. *Shropshire* with the remaining thirteen ships including Commodore Creighton on *Orcades*, continued around the Cape to Durban, passing 130 miles south of Cape Agulhas and 15 miles clear of that bank, then east to a position 170 miles South of Cape St Francis before closing up the coast at 55 miles SE of East London, then from 50 miles south of the Bluff into the Durban Searched Channel where the convoy arrived at 0900 on 4 July but had to anchor outside as it was blowing hard from the SW.

The additional distance from Capetown to Durban by keeping so far outside the mineable waters of the Agulhas bank was almost 200 miles. Clearly it was the safest route but in passing through the worst of the Agulhas current reduced the speed of advance to 12.06 knots and prevented arrival at Durban on 3 July.

The continued shortage of trooping tonnage on the Indian Ocean allowed only three of the liners to disembark and turnround in Durban. Of the three "giant" liners used on the Durban/Suez shuttle, *Mauretania* was overhauling generators and main machinery in Port Elizabeth and thereafter proceeded to Newport News for drydocking, *Nieuw Amsterdam* was in the Red Sea en route to Suez leaving *Ile de France* arriving Durban on the 7th to provide most of the 8,630 berths required for on-carriage from *Andes, Arawa* and *Orcades*. Of these, 5,070 embarked and sailed on *Ile de France* as an independent sailing to Suez on the 17th, the remaining 3,560 embarked on *Yoma* and *Empire Trooper* which sailed as part of CM 30 on the 20th for Bombay. *Andes* and *Arawa* were despatched from Durban on the 6th, the former proceeding via Capetown to New York to load on the Furness-Withy berth and crossing from Halifax in NA 12 to Liverpool on 17 August for her next voyage in WS 22. *Arawa* spent a week repairing in East London and in Capetown embarked personnel and stores for the Meterological Station at Tristan da Cunha, (the station equipment having previously been landed from the AMC *Cilicia*). The Tristan party were put ashore on the 27th, *Arawa* then proceeding to load on the Plate and returned home via Freetown and Belfast to Avonmouth on 21 September, and having then to drydock in that port was not again available until sailing in WS 24.

It was in Durban that Commodore Creighton had to bid farewell to Captain Fox and his officers on *Orcades* by transferring to *Viceroy of India* for the remainder of the voyage to Suez. He made a pertinent note on the Capetown Searched Channel which "presents serious difficulties to large ships especially in convoy and during the winter months approaching from the westward,"[9] by having to turn into the wind and sea in a congested area with little or no way upon them and posed a serious risk of collision, grounding or loss of anchors. The Commodore recommended consideration of a route north and east of Robben Island, thus allowing convoys to approach the anchorage from that direction to give a clear view of the space available or alternately continue to seaward if conditions were unsuitable. Finally he suggested "the present channel was well known to the enemy" and should be changed.[9] *Orcades* left Durban on the 7th, loading small quantities of cargo there and at Capetown before proceeding via Freetown to New York where further cargo was loaded on the Cunard berth, and 5,000 US troops embarked for the UK. *Orcades* crossed from Halifax in NA 12 to reach Liverool on 17 August and next sailed in WS 22.

The arrival of WS 19P in South Africa coincided with a check on Rommel's advance at El Alamein which served to increase pressure for the earliest arrival of 44 Division in that theatre. It was decided to split the onward movement of the convoy, the first and fast section comprising the eight liners carrying that Division, i.e. *Laconia, Orontes, JW McAndrew, Mexico, Santa Elena* and *Strathallan* from Capetown with *Cristobal* and *Santa Rosa* from Durban. Two other fast liners added to this section were *Warwick Castle* fully embarked for East Africa and *Viceroy of India* for Suez.

The Capetown ships sailed on 4 July and made rendezvous with those from Durban at the end of that searched channel at 1100 on the 7th, forming into five columns with the cruiser *Mauritius* as ocean escort in a centre lane.[10] Speed was limited to the maximum 15 knots of *Laconia* and a course set to pass south and east of Madagascar. The Dutch cruiser *Heemskerck* joined as additional escort next morning but detached that same evening to relieve *Carnarvon Castle* then escorting the slower section following 300 miles astern. The ten ship convoy passed 180 miles south of Fort Dauphin at the SE tip of Madagascar before turning up the eastern side of the island; zigzag was maintained in daylight hours throughout as Japanese submarines continued their sinkings in the Mozambique Channel until the 8th July while their raider/supply ships were also believed to be supporting them from the area SE of Madagascar. *Mauritius* flew off her aircraft for A/S patrols when the weather permitted.

On board *Viceroy of India*, Commodore Creighton found he had been allocated a cabin "far from the bridge and deep in the bowels of the ship. This was crass stupidity, since as Commodore I needed to be on call at short notice."[6] It seems that he found Captain French and his officers less than amiable, "they did eventually deign to fix me up with a cot with a canvas screen round it on the lower bridge and this was really quite comfortable in the warm weather."[6] It was nevertheless a wretched way to accommodate an elderly, retired senior officer who had once served at Jutland and since 1939 voluntarily acted as Commodore on 25 ocean convoys.

At 0230 on the 11th, *Laconia* was detached by Admiralty instruction to join the following slow convoy, from which point speed was increased to 17 knots and by the afternoon of the 12th the convoy passed between the northern tip of Madagascar and the Farquhar group of islands, where course was altered NNW for a rendezvous with the cruiser *Caledon*. In the early afternoon of the 13th the convoy reached a point 450 miles east of Mombasa, where *Caledon* was duly met and detached with *Warwick Castle* to that port as her final destination. Course was now set NE towards Guardafui, the cruiser *Devonshire* relieved *Mauritius* next morning when 340 miles east of Kismayu. Convoy WS 19L passed through the Guardafui Strait at midday on the 16th and reached Aden 24 hours later where it was held to allow priority handling of the liner *Queen Elizabeth* (WS 19Y q.v.) at Suez. By the 19th all eight liners had continued up the Red Sea and anchored in Ashrafi Roads in the Gulf of Suez, 145 miles south of Suez and clear of possible German air attack. Each liner was then called forward singly to Suez anchorage in the order: *Strathallan, Orontes, Viceroy of India* and the five Americans.

We must now revert to the remainder of WS 19P left in South Africa to follow 19L as the slow section. From Capetown on 4 July, *Cathay, Staffordshire, Mariposa* with storeships *Java* and *New Zealand Star* sailed around the coast to the end of the Durban searched channel, where at 1030 on the 8th, they were joined by *Otranto, Christiaan Huygens, Santa Paula, Chateau Thierry* with storeships *Talisse* and *Poelau Roebiah.*

These eleven ships formed into a cruising order of four columns,[11] and set off towards the south of Madagascar at a speed of 13.5 knots under escort of the AMC *Carnarvon Castle* and two corvettes, the latter detaching again that evening. Captain ACG Hawker, the master of *Otranto*, acted as Commodore of this convoy which followed the same route as 19L some 300 miles ahead.

At 1230 on the 9th, distant 320 miles ENE of Durban, the AMC *Chitral* and Dutch cruiser *Heemskerck* relieved *Carnarvon Castle* as escort, and at 0630 on the 12th, on the east side of Madagascar, *Laconia* joined up, 28 hours after being detached from the faster convoy 19L. At midday on the 16th, the cruiser *Enterprise* joined as additional escort in a position 500 miles ENE of Mombasa and at 0600 next day *Heemskerck* was detached, while *Chitral* detached twelve hours later with *Laconia*, *Christiaan Huygens*, *Chateau Thierry* and three storeships for Aden and Suez, the split taking place 380 miles south of Ras Hafun. This section passed through Guardafui in the late afternoon of the 19th and reached Aden 24 hours later and Suez on the 25th and 26th as the last of the 19L liners were being disembarked.

Within a matter of weeks the troops of all three brigades of 44 Division were in position at Alam Halfa and served in that battle and at El Alamein in October, following which 131 Brigade moved to 7 Armoured Division and remained there until the end of the war in Northwest Europe. The other two brigades and 44 Division were disbanded in Egypt three months later when the battalions were dispersed to other formations.

The remainder of WS 19P continued towards Bombay with *Enterprise*. A man was reported overboard from Staffordshire on the morning of the 18th and despite assistance from the cruiser in searching, nothing was found. Two ships were met and identified during the next two days, one being the British tramp *Radwinter* which was lying stopped with engine trouble. By 0030 on the 22nd the convoy was 400 miles WSW of Bombay where *Mariposa* was detached north for Karachi and *Santa Paula* similarly at 0300, both being instructed to zigzag at their best speeds. The remaining four ships, i.e. *Otranto*, *Cathay*, *Staffordshire* and *Java* reached the Bombay searched channel at 0730 on the 23rd and arrived in the harbour later that morning.

The last liner of WS 19P to arrive at its destination was *Britannic*, delayed for ten days in Durban for engine repairs to her twin ten-cylinder B&W machinery. The opportunity was also taken to fumigate the ship, when all of the 4,500 personnel on board were temporarily accommodated in Clairwood Transit Camp along with the 8,000 awaiting on-carriage from the three liners which had fully disembarked. Although the camp could originally accept only 10,000, it was gradually expanded and at the beginning of July the War Office agreed with Impcon to increase its capacity to 30,000. After re-embarking, *Britannic* left Durban on 4 July and proceeded independently to Bombay where she arrived thirteen days later to find the three earlier arrivals of 19P still in port and not yet all disembarked.

The arrival of 15,000 additional troops at Bombay and 6,000 US Air Force personnel at Karachi was welcomed by Wavell as CinC but not by Gandhi's Indian Congress Party, who began to step up their civil disobedience campaign for Britain to withdraw from India, which that summer absorbed 57 infantry battalions in dealing with civil disturbances instead of training to fight the Japanese. Not much could be done on the Assam-Burma front during the height of the monsoon, but the opportunity was taken to form 77 Indian Infantry Brigade, the deceptively styled Chindits who penetrated the Burmese jungle to harass and destroy the Japanese wherever they found them.

The despatch of the first three liners from Bombay took place within four days from the 29th, when *Cathay* sailed to load small amounts of cargo at Durban and Capetown before returning via Freetown to the Clyde on 18 September. *Staffordshire* followed three days later by loading at Capetown then proceding via Pointe Noire and Matadi where native troops were embarked for Lagos and Takoradi, before returning via Freetown to Liverpool on 12 October. *Otranto* sailed on 2 August with some Ellerman cargo and completed to capacity in Durban, where she also embarked 1,801 Italian POW for the UK, then via Freetown to Liverpool, arriving on 25 September; all three were next employed on the Torch convoys to Algiers when *Cathay* was sunk.

Britannic was delayed at Bombay until 7 August for more engine repairs but also loaded there and at Durban and Capetown on the Clan berth, returning then via Freetown to Liverpool on 21 September to discharge and drydock. Extensive machinery repairs were also carried out over a period of sixty days when *Britannic* was sent to the Clyde Anchorage for a further four weeks before again sailing in WS 25.

At Mombasa, *Warwick Castle* disembarked the 2,475 troops destined for that port and part loaded there and in Capetown, from where she proceeded direct to Glasgow, arriving on 19 August to discharge and begin exercises preparatory to sailing in the Torch initial assault convoy, which proved to be her last voyage.

Meanwhile at Suez and despite the proximity of Rommel's Afrika Corps at Alamein and interference from the Luftwaffe, the five British and six US transports of WS 19P and L which arrived there in the five day period beginning on 21 July, all liners were turned around expeditiously, mostly within two days, and sailed again with mixed personnel but mostly POW; 882 Italians on *Christiaan Huygens* and 1,793 Italians and 200 Women on *Laconia*. *Strathallan* was the first away on the 23rd, refuelled at Aden, called at Durban, Capetown and Freetown before proceeding to New York to load on the Cunard berth and embark US troops for the UK, crossing from Halifax to reach the Clyde on 7 October. *Orontes* had a similar homeward voyage leaving Suez two days later and making the same calls and departure from New York and Halifax to reach Avonmouth also on 7 October, where she was drydocked, both were next employed in the follow-up convoys to Algiers.

Viceroy of India also left Suez on the 25th carrying a large number of women and children and wounded being evacuated to the UK due to the proximity of the enemy to the Delta bases. The *Viceroy* also refuelled at Aden, rejected 400 tons of cargo in Durban, refuelled and watered again in Capetown and Freetown before reaching Glasgow on 4 September and was soon engaged in exercises before sailing in the Torch assault convoy which like *Warwick Castle*, proved to be her last voyage.

It was during the voyage home on the *Viceroy* that Commodore Creighton decided to retire from that post after three years on ocean convoys on all manner of vessels from tramps to luxury liners. He was however, persuaded to accept a post as Commodore of Combined Operation Bases in the Middle East, and travelled out to Egypt on the *Marnix van St Aldegonde* in October 1943, only to be sunk en route but survived to complete his task as Director-General of Ports and Lights for Egypt.

During the week following the departure of *Viceroy of India*, the Luftwaffe made frequent visits to the area which closed the canal due to mines, but a number of mines and bombs were also dropped around the Suez anchorage although by good fortune the only casualty was a water boat.

The departure of *Christiaan Huygens* from Suez on the 27th was accompanied by some of the US transports which were all returning around the Cape to revert to US control on arrival on their eastern seaboard. The 'Huygens refuelled at Aden and disembarked the Italian POW and escort in Durban before spending three weeks undergoing engine repairs. Without cargo the 'Huygens then proceeded direct to Pointe Noire in the French Congo then Banana Creek inside the mouth of the Belgian Congo where 2,455 native troops were embarked for Lagos. At Takoradi 2,737 West African troops were embarked for Freetown and finally at Bathurst 53 service personnel and 386 civilians were embarked for the UK. The 'Huygens reached Liverpool on 2 November where she was drydocked in the space of eleven days and sailed in a follow-up convoy to Algiers.

The Cunard liner *Laconia* brought the last of the 44 Division personnel to Suez, having carried two of the battalions of 132 Brigade which was disbanded in Egypt in January 1943. The 4 Bn Royal West Kents were then sent to join 5 Indian Division in Iraq and then to India, serving in the Arakan until March 1944 when flown to Imphal, and by the end of that month arrived at Kohima to become the dominant unit in its defensive siege for fifteen consecutive days, repelling 25 major Japanese assaults before relief, which ultimately became the turning point of the war in Burma.

Laconia left Suez on 30 July, refuelled at Aden and loaded 3,000 tons of general cargo on the Union-Castle berth at Mombasa, Durban and Capetown, but unlike *Christiaan Huygens*, the 1,793 Italian POW on board were not landed in South Africa but were bound for the UK. *Laconia* left Capetown on 4 September carrying the above Italian POW, 103 Polish guard, 366 mixed passengers and 463 officers and crew under Captain Rudolph Sharp who had experienced the loss of *Lancastria* off St Nazaire two years previously.

Unfortunately, Doenitz had then decided to send his U-Boats to attack shipping off Capetown. It was their first foray south of the Equator: four and a supply U-Boat set out from Lorient in the second half of August and were to sink any shipping en route as far as 20° South. On 12 September *U-68* sank a Hain steamer just south of the Equator and that night *U-156* torpedoed the *Laconia* in 5° South, 850 miles almost due south of Freetown and 240 miles NE of Ascension.

Panic broke out among the prisoners, "the lighting failed and in the darkness and rough sea and with the ship's list, it was difficult to get the boats away. The U-Boat, waiting nearby for the ship to sink...became aware that some of the people in the water were Italian. At 0125 she reported by wireless to Headquarters and requested instructions."[12] U-Boat command instructed the other boats of that group to assist and asked the Vichy Government to send help from Dakar. While U-Boats were busy collecting survivors they were bombed by American aircraft, and this led to the issue by Doenitz of the order subsequently known as the "*Laconia* order", directing that survivors of ships sunk were not to be rescued, and has been extensively documented elsewhere and at the Nuremberg trials in 1946.[13]

The *Laconia* sank in just over an hour with her stern high in the air. It is not known how many boats got away from the ship, but most were collected by the French and interned in French West Africa. On the afternoon of the 17th, 51 survivors were packed into a lifeboat 700 miles from land, 39 days later when still 85 miles from land, four survivors were picked up by an RN trawler and taken to Freetown. Out of a total 2,725 persons reputed to be on board, only 975 were rescued of whom 137 were officers and crew but neither Captain Sharp nor the Staff Captain were among them. *Laconia* was the first troopship loss since the *Empress of Asia* at Singapore seven months earlier but was followed by another sixteen before the end of 1942.

An interesting story surrounding the sinking of *Laconia* was that some of the survivors said that Commander Hartenstein of *U-156* claimed "he had been waiting for one of the *Straths*, and that "he was in full possession of shipping movements and intended to torpedo the *Stratheden*, *Pasteur*, *Ile de France*, *Nieuw Amsterdam* and *Duchess of Atholl*."[13] Whether this was wishful thinking or simply good intelligence cannot be said, but note the raider *Stier* then in the South Atlantic had sighted and identified *Pasteur* which "she had been expecting...ever since Berlin had wirelessed that the liner had left Capetown (actually Durban) on the 30th August for Rio.[14] Roskill believed this "intelligence was possibly derived from careless talk about shipping movements of which there was a good deal in South African ports at this time.[14] It is a fact that *Laconia* left Capetown on September 4th, *Stratheden* on the 5th and *Duchess of Richmond* (sister of the *Atholl*) on the 9th. South Africans had always taken a genuine interest in the shipping which passed through their ports, and this could not be disguised even in wartime; nor could that information be suppressed from reaching erstwhile enemy Agents.

WS 19Y - sailed UK 17.6.42

This was another single ship, fast "convoy", being the liner *Queen Elizabeth* which had been employed for the previous year on the US route between Australia and the Middle East and was then drydocked at Esquimalt, near Vancouver, in February 1942. Her next voyage was with American troops from San Francisco to Sydney thence New York to the Clyde where she arrived on 9 June to disembark more Americans and prepare for a voyage to the Middle East.

The *Queen Elizabeth* embarked a total of 10,718 in drafts; 8,000 Army, 1,300 RAF, 800 Naval and 618 others and left the Clyde eight days later under the command of Captain EM Fall, a Liverpool man who held an Extra Master's Certificate and the rank of Captain RNR. Escort was provided for the first day only by the AA cruiser *Delhi* with destroyers *Boadicea*, *Keppel*, *Leamington*, *Salisbury* and *St Albans*.

Freetown was reached in the late afternoon of 25 June where rapid fuelling and watering allowed her early departure 24 hours later. Further replenishment was made in Table Bay and Simonstown from 2 to 5 July, and where the 1,300 RAF drafts were landed by Air Force Mission instructions received from the Middle East, to be held meantime in the Transit Camp until the Air Ministry considered their forward movement. Two days later the Impcon office in Capetown signalled the War Office that the Air Force Mission decided that RAF drafts were to proceed in the normal way, but the liner had already sailed and on-carriage had to be arranged by other means. Soon after sailing for the long haul to Suez, *Queen Elizabeth* passed the *Queen Mary* bound in the opposite direction outside the confines of Simons Bay.

As with her consort's voyage a month earlier, the troops and crew suffered from the intense heat inside the ship during the Red Sea passage when cabin temperatures of 125°F (!) were reported. Many of the troops slept on deck at night and hundreds of sea-water showers were improvised from the outlets of convenient fire-service mains.

Queen Elizabeth anchored in Suez Bay on 18 July and left again next day having disembarked all of the troops and embarked in lieu 2,000 German POW with Polish guard and some mixed passengers, leaving behind the last ferry load of POW due to the appearance of an enemy aircraft which caused the liner to hurriedly get underway for the return voyage.

No incidents occurred on the passage to Table Bay which was reached on 1st August where fuelling and watering began and the mixed passengers landed for on-carriage in other liners to the UK. The weather then deteriorated and necessitated moving the ship round to Simons Bay to complete replenishment, during which time some of the Germans jumped overboard and although a boat was lowered they were not recovered.

The liner left Simons Bay on 4 August and had a fine weather passage of five days to Rio Janeiro where she was topped up at the anchorage for the longer haul to New York. She arrived in the Hudson on 19 August to disembark the POW by ferry from the Quarantine anchorage under Canadian Army supervision, whence they entrained to camps in Canada. The liner then berthed at the Cunard Pier to prepare for continuous service between New York and the Clyde, which began twelve days later on 31 August; *Queen Elizabeth* subsequently made 39 crossings with American troops to the Clyde before the end of hostilities, and another ten to Southampton before completing war service in March 1946.

Chapter 16

WS 20, WS 21P, and WS 21

51 (Highland) Division and reinforcements for Alamein

WS 20 - sailed UK 21.6.42
During the short campaign in France and Belgium in the spring of 1940, fifteen British divisions were engaged in these operations of which all but 51 Highland Division were subsequently evacuated in whole or in part to recover and fight another day. From the very outset 51 Division operated with a French Corps and under their orders on the Saar front, far removed from the BEF, but successfully conducted a fighting withdrawal to the coast, south of the Somme, where it was hoped they could be evacuated from St Valery,but in that vicinity on 12 June the Division was forced to conform to the general surrender of the French units under which they served.

This whole Division thus went into captivity for the next five years and was an enormous blow to morale not only throughout the Highlands but in Scotland as a whole. A few small parties managed to slip away from the coast or through France and Spain to Gibraltar, and from these parties and men at the depots new battalions were immediate-

ly formed and from which a new 51 Highland Division began to take shape by the redes-
ignation of 9 Highland Division. Training was carried out in Scotland from the autumn
of 1940 until April 1942 when the division moved south to Hampshire and Surrey where
more realistic training was conducted with tanks and aircraft.

A War Office decision was taken at the beginning of May 1942 to send 51 Division
around the Cape and on the 8th of that month the Division began to mobilise when tropical kit and new vehicles were issued. The two convoys which sailed in May had carried 8 Armoured Division and 44 Home counties Division; 51 Division would sail in the
next convoy about the middle of June.

As early as 9 March the MOWT planned to provide 33,000 berths in WS 20 for a June
departure,[1] but allowing for the 30% increase by extra fittings this figure would reach
43,000 and eventually became 52,000 before adding two additional ships for Gibraltar
and West Africa. A classic example of the steady increase in capacity was that of *Orion*,
which two years earlier in WS 2 offered the same number of berths as in peacetime with
1,139 passengers, by August 1941 this had risen to 3,220, by March 1942 to 4,000 and
now for WS 20 provided for 5,285 troops.

Nineteen liners were eventually allocated for WS 20 including *Narkunda* for Gibraltar
only and *Batory* for West Africa. Three fast storeships were included of which the
Dutch motorship *Nigerstroom* was loaded with MT stores and 42 Spitfires for Australia
and was to be detached to proceed direct from the Cape. *Empress of Australia* and
Strathmore had been in Liverpool from WS 14 and 15 respectively from the middle of
April and both required extensive repairs and drydocking; the P&O liner also for turbine repairs. Eleven liners from WS 12Z, 14, 15, 16 and 17 arrived in UK ports within an eighteen day period from 10 May, of which two required drydocking, *Esperance
Bay* being handled at Avonmouth and a newcomer to the WS fleet, *Banfora*, which
arrived in the Clyde Anchorage from Halifax in NA 9 on 25 May.

As a Vichy French unit of the Fabre Line employed on their route between Marseilles
and West Africa, *Banfora* was intercepted and taken into Freetown in April 1941 and
there requisitioned by the Sea Transport Department of the MOWT. She arrived in
Liverpool in July 1941, transferred to the British flag and was placed under Elder
Dempster management while fittings were provided for 2,300 troops, her first employment being on the North Atlantic with six round trips to Iceland and Halifax. *Banfora*
was a twin screw steamer able for 14.5 knots, lately a coal burner with a consumption
of 90 tons per day and was presumably destined for the Indian Ocean routes. Four days
were first required alongside at Greenock for repairs, then returning to the anchorage for
three days, then to James Watt Dock for another five days of repairs and storing then to
the AFD for five days cleaning and painting from which she emerged in sufficient time
to prepare for embarkation.

The last arrivals in the UK were *Arundel Castle* at Avonmouth on 2 June which had
to be drydocked because of her grounding at Newport[2], *Abosso* and *Empress of Russia*
at Liverpool on the 6th from WS 17, *Empire Pride* on the same date in Glasgow from
WS 16 which also required drydocking, *Bergensfjord* also from WS 16 to Glasgow on
the 7th for drydocking, and finally the Polish *Batory* which reached the Clyde
Anchorage with Canadian troops from Halifax in NA 10, ten days prior to the sailing
date for WS 20. *Batory* had not been included in the WS series since WS 2, having
sailed exclusively to Gibraltar, Iceland, Halifax or on Operational Exercises in preparation for landings on the Atlantic islands.

Mobilisation of 51 Division was complete by 29 May on which date the MT parties left for their vehicle loading ports and shipment on a slow convoy towards Freetown. On 1 June the Division was inspected by HM The King, later by the Secretary of State for War and Chief of the Imperial General Staff, General Sir Alan Brooke, and by the third week of June all units entrained to their respective ports of embarkation.

At Avonmouth, 154 Brigade HQ with 1 Bn The Black Watch and 7/10 Bn Argylls were embarked with other divisional units on *Arundel Castle* and *Cuba*, while an independent unit entitled Task Force 122, numbering 1,643 officers and men, embarked on *Esperance Bay* for an undisclosed destination referred to later. These three liners locked out of Avonmouth on 17 and 18 June, sailed on the afternoon of the latter date and reached the Clyde Anchorage in the early morning of the 20th in time for their Masters to attend the convoy conference at Greenock.

Embarkations in Liverpool began on the 14th when 153 Brigade HQ, 1 Gordons, 5 Black Watch and a General Hospital boarded *Empress of Australia*, and with 6 Bn Grenadier Guards and various drafts on *Strathmore*,[3] both liners sailed for the Clyde on the 17th and anchored there next day. Other personnel in Liverpool boarded *Abosso*, *Durban Castle*, *Empress of Russia*, *Orion*, *Stirling Castle* (which included 9 Bn York & Lancaster Regt going out to India to join 25 Indian Division), and *Duchess of Richmond* which latter accommodated 152 Brigade HQ, 2 Seaforths, 5 Camerons and 127 Field Regiment RA; all six liners being complete to meet the sailing date on the 20th.

The first embarkations in Glasgow were on *Leopoldville* which carried 5/7 Gordons and sailed downriver from 2 KGV on the afternoon of the 16th, on *Empire Pride* which followed from the adjacent No. 3 berth on the 18th carrying 6 Bn Ox & Bucks and 98 Field Regt RA both for India, and on *Awatea* and *Stratheden* from Nos. 6 and 1 berths on the 19th; the last named carrying 51 Division HQ, 7 Black Watch and 1/7 Middlesex as the divisional Machine-Gun battalion.

Four liners embarked at the Clyde Anchorage including *Narkunda* and *Bergensfjord* which had moved downriver from their Glasgow berths at 10 KGV and Merklands on the 17th and 18th. The former was embarked with 7 Bn The Kings Own and drafts for Gibraltar, while *Bergensfjord* lifted 5 Seaforths and others, including eighty QARANS (Army Nurses). Of the two remaining liners, *Banfora* embarked 2,303 including another General Hospital while *Batory* carried 2,142 drafts and details for West Africa. Two storeships were included in the convoy of which Holt's *Adrastus* was for Bombay and the Royal Mail *Palma* for Suez; both were loaded with an assortment of stores, MT, tanks, guns and ammunition in addition to 77 personnel. An assortment of MT, stores, motor-cycles, guns and ammunition was also loaded on *Arundel Castle*, *Orion*, *Durban Castle*, *Strathmore* and *Stratheden*, most of it destined for Madagascar, and on *Esperance Bay* for the Falklands Islands and some stores and six Spitfires for Australia on *Stirling Castle*. The total embarked on the nineteen liners and two storeships was 57,094 [3] of which 22,476 were then for undisclosed destinations, 12,875 for India and 10,820 for Suez.

The astonishing increase in numbers of personnel carried in the WS convoys has been referred to previously and will be seen at a glance by reviewing the table in Appendix IV. [4] With a 25% increase in the number of transports but a decrease in the number of actual convoys, twice the number were carried in the first half of 1942 as in the same period of 1941, and was a remarkable achievement by the Sea Transport Department and all other responsible bodies.

All ships of WS 20 were ready to sail as arranged in the evening of 20 June, but fog in the Clyde and its approaches delayed the departure for fifteen hours until 1100 on the 21st, when the Commodore, Captain BWL Nicholson RN (Retd) on *Stratheden*, (whose Master, Captain AW Drew, held the rank of Commander RNR), led the thirteen liners out of the Clyde boom. The evening news by radio announced the fall of Tobruk, and as if to compound this depressing fact, fog and poor visibility prevailed but contact was made with the six transports from Liverpool at 2000 to the west of Orsay and where seven destroyers joined to provide an A/S escort as the sole protection for the first five days of the voyage.[5] The Dutch storeship *Nigerstroom* failed to join at Orsay and speed was reduced to 10 knots to allow her to catch up. A cruising order of seven columns was formed and Captain LJ Vestey, the master of *Orion*, acted as Vice Commodore.[6]

In accordance with instructions from the CinCWA, the route from Orsay was amended northwards to avoid the inward convoy SL 112 of 54 ships "which was not entirely successful as the port wing columns of both overlapped, or narrowly so during the night."[7] *Nigerstroom* joined with the destroyer *Vansittart* at 0230 on the 22nd when speed was increased to 13.5 and later to 14.5 knots as all ships could maintain that speed in the calm weather which prevailed all the way to Freetown. *Nigerstroom* later returned to the Clyde.

At 0800 on the 22nd the convoy turned to WSW, 24 hours later to SW and on reaching the latitude of Lands End on the morning of the 24th to a S'ly course towards the eastern side of the Azores and at this point the destroyers *Georgetown* and *Salisbury* detached back to the UK. By next morning on the latitude of Finisterre, *Boadicea* and *Ripley* were similarly detached leaving four destroyers as escort. Ten days earlier a U-Boat pack had attacked a homeward Gibraltar convoy in this area with some success, but were now believed to have moved west of the Azores for refuelling and indicates the high level of intelligence then held by the Admiralty.

By 0800 on the 26th the convoy was 120 miles east of Sao Miguel of the Azores, where the battleship *Malaya* joined from Gibraltar after taking part in the Harpoon convoy to Malta. Three destroyers which came out from Gibraltar with *Malaya* now detached back to that port with *Beagle*, *Wolverine* and *Narkunda*, where they arrived two days later. The Kings Own battalion on *Narkunda* there disembarked to spend the summer with 2 Gibraltar Brigade manning perimeter defences, and returned to the UK in September. *Narkunda* embarked homeward personnel of all services at Gibraltar, sailed on 6 July for the Clyde and arrived six days later for next employment in WS 21.

Four hours after *Malaya* joined the convoy, *St Albans* detached to meet and strengthen the escort of SL 113 from Freetown and that same evening *Brilliant* and *Blackmore* joined to bring the A/S escort back to three destroyers, which must have been some relief to the Commodore and SOE. The convoy with *Malaya* had proceeded for almost eight hours on the 26th with a single V and W class destroyer as A/S escort, despite the RN operators on the HF/DF guardship *Abosso* having detected enemy transmissions at this time which caused the convoy to make some necessary diversions.[8]

Shortly after midday on the 27th, by which time the convoy was 240 miles west of Madeira, a masthead report, confirmed by *Stratheden*, appeared to indicate the presence of a merchant ship accompanied by two small craft at extreme visibility on the starboard bow, but disappeared soon after sighting. A supply ship with two U-Boats was conjectured by *Malaya* but a comprehensive search by *Brilliant* and the battleship's two Walrus aircraft revealed nothing and was presumed to have been a mirage in the conditions of extreme visibility. Diversionary action was taken and a further sweep made before dark and again on the 28th but nothing was seen. It was at this point that *Malaya*, in consultation with the Commodore and considering the size of the convoy and the small escort, the known U-Boat situation and speed of advance, decided not to zigzag but maintain the highest convoy speed of 14 - 14.25 knots.[8]

Activities on the transports as they moved south into warmer climes was again typified by the experience of Lieut-Colonel RDMC Speirs commanding 5 Bn Cameron Highlanders on *Duchess of Richmond*, "training on the voyage consisted for the most part of PT, boxing and such individual and weapon training as was possible on the crowded deck space. Freetown was reached on 3 July where Maj-General DN Wimberley (commanding 51 Division) came aboard and inspected the battalion."[9]

The destroyer *Vimy* joined from Freetown at 0600 on the 28th when the convoy was 180 miles west of the Canaries, and half an hour later a collision occurred between *Awatea* and *Empire Pride*, in which both ships received substantial damage but fortunately all above the waterline without impairing their speed or seaworthiness in moderate weather. It transpired that *Awatea* had been on auto-steering which had cut out and allowed the ship to go hard-a-starboard before the Officer of the Watch was able to operate the telemotor. *Awatea* alarmingly crossed the bows of *Stirling Castle* in the next column and collided with *Empire Pride* in the next again. The Commodore rightly considered the use of auto-steering in convoy to be "quite inexcusable and the height of negligence,"[7] and immediately made a signal forbidding such usage. The Master of *Awatea*, Captain GB Morgan, was highly experienced and a DSC from the Great War who admitted having allowed the practice to be continued from the previous Master. Captain Fountain of *Empire Pride* made no comment although that ship suffered damage to two lifeboats and her superstructure that was not repaired until she returned to Liverpool five months later. The consequences could easily have been disastrous. The destroyer *Vansittart* being the last of the original escort detached back to Ponta Delgada that afternoon and was thereafter ordered to Gibraltar.

The convoy passed between the Cape Verde islands and Cap Vert on the morning of the 30th where rendezvous was expected with three destroyers from Freetown but not effected, due to low visibility, poor fixes and the high speed of advance. At 0800 on the 1st July *Boreas*, *Wivern* and *Velox* joined and at this point the convoy turned SE towards Freetown which was reached at midday on the 2nd, 24 hours ahead of the original ETA and having averaged 14.25 knots from the Clyde. It was found that "*Nigerstroom* had proceeded independently to her destination,"[7] presumably Freetown, but this ship did not continue with the convoy beyond that port.

Malaya appears to have refuelled the escorting destroyers en route rather than detach them to Ponta Delgada and this mode of refuelling warships of lesser endurance became an increasing facet of naval operations as the war progressed. *Malaya* commented "that the two *Empress* liners were frequent makers of smoke" and "extinguished lights in living quarters at night rather than closing deadlights" and recommended "this dangerous practice be brought to the notice of O.C. Troops concerned."[8]

WS 20 resumed its passage from Freetown when the Commodore on *Stratheden* led the same 20 ships out of the harbour at 1100 on 6 July, the last ship *Batory* clearing at 1216. Once beyond the searched channel a cruising order of six rather than seven columns was formed,[10] probably as the Commodore believed that zigzagging with a broad front was of little value. *Malaya* continued as ocean escort and with the destroyers *Brilliant*, *Blackmore*, *Boreas*, *Wivern* and *Velox* as A/S escorts, the battleship being disposed in a centre column between the 3rd and 4th. The convoy was first routed much as the previous two by passing 240 miles SW of Cape Palmas, but thereafter into the Gulf of Guinea to pass a similar distance off the mouth of the Congo before turning south and keeping 150 miles off Walvis Bay and thereafter towards the Cape. This divergence from the direct route may have been due to the known presence of two raiders then operating in the South Atlantic.

At midday on the 7th, *Batory* with *Blackmore* as escort was detached for Takoradi to disembark there and at Lagos, before returning around the coast to Freetown, whence she proceeded to New York and Halifax and crossed via Iceland to the Clyde on 25 August to prepare for service as an assault ship in Operation Torch.

Next day *Stratheden* and *Empress of Australia* went ahead and stopped to allow a surgeon from the Army General Hospital on the latter ship to transfer to *Stratheden* and remove a duodenal ulcer from a patient. The Commodore later commented on the two complete General Hospitals and equipment being wholly embarked on two ships, while *Stratheden* carrying a total of 4,967 troops and crew had no one on board capable of carrying out a major operation, which was nevertheless reported successful although the man died two days later.[7] Later that day *Blackmore* rejoined while *Boreas* and *Velox* detached back to Freetown. On the 13th *Empress of Australia* reported a man overboard from *Orion* on her port beam and *Blackmore* was sent to search astern but without sighting anyone; it later transpired that the man had previously attempted suicide. The convoy was then 200 miles west of Lobito on the coast of Angola and proceeding southwards towards the Cape and by the morning of the 16th the destroyers *Brilliant* and *Wivern* rejoined, probably having refuelled at Walvis Bay and later that day *Blackmore* fuelled from *Malaya*. On the 14th aboard *Cuba*, the Black Watch and Brigadier Houldsworth with his 154 Brigade HQ staff were treated to grand celebrations organized by the ship's French officers and crew on their National Day to mark the storming of the Bastille.[11]

By 0800 on the 17th the convoy reached a position 95 miles NW of Cape Columbine where the cruiser *Shropshire* from Simonstown was met and where *Brilliant* and *Wivern* detached ahead to refuel at that port. Also at this point *Malaya* and *Blackmore* detached with the Capetown portion being *Duchess of Richmond* (whose master, Captain T Jones, now acted as Commodore), *Empress of Australia*, *Abosso*, *Bergensfjord*, *Banfora*, *Esperance Bay*, *Leopoldville*, *Cuba*, *Empire Pride* with the two storeships *Adrastus* and *Palma*. These ships berthed at Capetown next morning to begin fuelling and watering and to allow the troops ashore for the customary exercise and recreation.

The remaining eight liners with *Shropshire* formed into four columns, increased speed to 16 knots and continued around the Cape for Durban, but at daybreak on the 18th when south of Agulhas, zigzag had to be abandoned due to a heavy quartering swell which caused all ships to yaw considerably with consequent difficulty in steering. The two destroyers from Simonstown did not rejoin as intended, however, the convoy arrived at the outer end of the Durban searched channel without further incident at 0730 on the 20th, where *Shropshire* detached back to Simonstown, while the Commodore led the eight liners into harbour at 1100 exactly 29 days since leaving the Clyde.

Of the eight liners which berthed in Durban, four disembarked there which allowed *Strathmore* and *Awatea* to sail on the 22nd and from Capetown four days later for Halifax, the former proceeding via Freetown and *Awatea* via Bermuda. Both embarked Canadian troops for the UK and sailed on 22nd August in convoy AT 20 which soon ran into fog. The US destroyer *Buck* apparently detected a U-Boat in the vicinity and while attacking with depth charges crossed the bows of *Awatea* with too fine a margin and "had her fantail knocked off."[12] The escort commander sent the destroyer *Ingraham* to investigate, which "was rammed by a tanker and blown up with the loss of all but eleven men of her crew."[12] *Awatea* had to return to Halifax, disembarked and was drydocked to effect collision damage repairs before sailing again on 29 September to reach the Clyde on 6 October. In Glasgow she was hurriedly converted to an LSI and sailed in the Torch assault convoy only to be bombed and sunk off Bougie on 11 November. *Strathmore* reached Glasgow safely on the 31st and next sailed on 1st November in a follow-up Torch convoy.

Durban Castle left her name port on 24 July, loaded in Capetown and sailed direct for the Clyde but was diverted en route to Avonmouth then to the Clyde and finally Liverpool where she arrived on 22 August also to become an LSI for the Torch assault convoy. *Empress of Russia* bunkered at the Bluff in Durban and left on the 31st with Italian POW for the UK, and from Capetown on 4 August, spent six days bunkering again in Freetown from where she was directed first to the Clyde then Liverpool where she arrived on 31 August and next sailed in WS 23.

Of the 4,010 personnel which embarked on *Stirling Castle* in Liverpool, 40 were for West Africa and a further 873 for South Africa. Also disembarked in Durban from this liner were 785 for the Middle East, 1138 for India (including 9 York & Lancs), 27 for Iraq and 7 for Ceylon to be on-carried in other ships. The balance of 873 on this liner were to be carried direct for Australia and New Zealand, and whilst in Durban these personnel and all of those on *Arundel Castle*, *Orion* and *Stratheden* appear to have disembarked to the transit camp where the mornings were spent on route marches through the city and neighbourhood while leave was granted till midnight each night. Much transhipment was required to accommodate the maximum number going forward from South Africa, the priority being the earliest arrival of 51 Highland Division whose destination was now confirmed as the Middle East.

At Capetown the situation was rather different as none of the liners were to disembark or to return from this port, although *Banfora* was unable to sail with the convoy due to engine trouble and was then delayed a further three weeks in Durban; her onward voyage is referred to later. The one liner which left the convoy in Capetown was *Esperance Bay*, whose destination, but not yet disclosed to the embarked troops of Task Force 122, was declared as the Falkland Islands. The liner had sailed on the 25th but was run into by an inbound US tanker which damaged the port bulwarks and lifeboats, necessitating a return alongside to effect repairs and finally sailed on the 28th with the AMC *Carnarvon Castle* as escort. Next day Lieut.Col. WH Hynes commanding the Task Force revealed the troops' destination, which proved a "bitter disappointment to a well trained battalion (11 West Yorks) thought to be bound for a battle front."[13] There was a raider scare when halfway across the South Atlantic (*Michel* and *Stier* were then operating in that area) but otherwise the passage was uneventful and both liners anchored in Port William, just outside Port Stanley harbour, which had insufficient room, on the forenoon of 11 August. *Carnarvon Castle*, which made five earlier visits to Port William that year in the course of routine South Atlantic patrols, then sailed in search of the raiders before returning to the Cape. The anchorage in Port William was 5 miles in length and provided good shelter from the prevailing winds from SW through West to North. Cloud cover was almost incessant, rain fell on twelve days per month and with August temperatures ranging from minus 4 to plus 9°C the weather proved similar to the UK winters and added to the despondency of the troops who had thought they were destined for the Middle East and were now consigned to a remote group of islands in 52°S latitude with little hope of relief.

The Task Force comprised 11 Bn West Yorkshires under Lieut.Col. WH Green, two static AA Batteries, a Construction Company of Royal Engineers and detachments of Signals, Ordnance, RASC and RAMC. Their task was to set up a camp and base from which they could defend the islands, half of whose population of 2,500 lived in Port Stanley. "In January anxiety was felt for the Falkland Islands where it was considered the Japanese might attempt a sudden landing, so the cruiser *Birmingham* and AMC *Asturias* were sent there for a time."[14] That visit was followed by another from the AMC *Cilicia* in March.

Arrangements were made to accommodate the troops from *Esperance Bay* through-out Port Stanley on a temporary basis while the camp was being built; disembarkation took place on the 13th on a cold and windy day, which soon became the norm and daily topic of conversation. One company of the West Yorkshires lived aboard the liner while the stores and equipment were laboriously unloaded by lighters which was not com-pleted until 10 September when the liner sailed for the Plate. The West Yorkshires and Task Force 122 remained in Port Stanley for nearly eighteen months. *Esperance Bay* loaded a full refrigerated cargo in Buenos Aires and Montevideo and returned via Freetown to Liverpool on 4 November and was next employed in WS 25 in December. The Master of *Esperance Bay*, Captain JW Johnson, who took command of the ship on return from her service as an AMC, was to remain until August 1946 but scarcely refers to the Falklands visit in the war history of the Shaw Savill company.

Meanwhile in Capetown the troops from the remaining eight liners enjoyed the cus-tomary morning route marches while the afternoons and evenings were given over to sightseeing and social enjoyment. After three days in a blissful blackout-free city, the seven liners and two storeships with almost 19,000 troops sailed again on 21 July and proceeded around the Cape coast under escort of the cruiser *Gambia*. In the forenoon of the 26th, at the outer end of the Durban searched channel the four liners from Durban joined up, having left that port under Commodore Nicholson on *Stratheden* at 0700, when a cruising order of five columns was formed, a speed of 14 knots adopted and course set to pass south and east of Madagascar.[15] The convoy was now zigzagged both by day and night as the moon was full. There had been no submarine attacks in the Mozambique Channel for nearly three weeks, the Japanese having retired from the area which kept the Cape waters quiet until the German raider *Michel* sank two ships in the South Atlantic in September. U-Boats however reached the Cape early in October.

When between Reunion and the east coast of Madagascar on the morning of the 30th, *Gambia* ordered an emergency turn due to a reported submarine contact but proved to be false, and at 0930 that same morning the cruiser *Frobisher* and AMC *Worcestershire* were met and took over the escort, while *Gambia* detached with *Stirling Castle* which she escorted as far as the vicinity of Mauritius. The Castle liner then continued inde-pendently direct to Melbourne where 867 were disembarked, before continuing for Auckland to load on the Blue Star berth. Returning via Panama and Halifax with Canadian troops to Liverpool on 7 October, *Stirling Castle* next sailed in WS 24.

On the 31st off the NE coast of Madagascar, the CinCEF ordered *Worcestershire* to part company as being unable to maintain the convoy speed leaving *Frobisher* as escort for the passage northwards between the Farquhar and Aldabra group of islands until the morning of 3 August, when the cruiser *Devonshire* was met in a position 300 miles east of Kismayu. At this point the Bombay portion comprising *Orion*, *Abosso*, *Empire Pride* and *Adrastus* detached NE with *Devonshire*, while the remaining seven transports and *Palma* continued up the Somali coast towards Guardafui, passed through that Strait in the late afternoon of the 5th and reached Aden 24 hours later where *Frobisher* dispersed the convoy.

All ships entered Aden to water and fuel and thereafter moved on to Suez by arrangement so that only two liners would be handled at that anchorage at any one time. The Commodore on *Stratheden* with *Duchess of Richmond* arrived on 11 August to allow 51 Divisional HQ together with most of the leading 152 Brigade to land first and proceed to Qassassin reception camp and thereafter to Tahaq camp to begin training in desert warfare.

The month of July ended with a stalemate in the desert, both sides exhausted and no prospect of resuming an offensive until the middle of September. On 13 August, however, as the second and third brigades of 51 Division were disembarking, Lieut-General BL Montgomery assumed command of Eighth Army and at once set about preparing defences against the next expected German attack. The arrival and disembarkation and training of 51 Division for the battles ahead was attended to with some urgency. *Arundel Castle* and *Cuba* arrived at Suez on the 12th, *Empress of Australia* next day, *Bergensfjord* on the 14th and *Leopoldville* on the 15th, which was also the last to clear the port on the 17th.

This Division was the sixth to reach the Middle East by the Cape route since the start of the WS convoys two years earlier. Their subsequent history and that of the component units has been well documented elsewhere and covered all the battles from Alamein to Tunis, the landings in Sicily and in Normandy and Northwest Europe from the Falaise pocket to the Rhine, and to a certain extent these exploits helped to offset the loss of the original 51 Division into captivity in June 1940.

The return of all liners to the UK was now a matter of great urgency as on 8 August, Eisenhower as the appointed CinC for the Expeditionary Force to land Allied forces in North Africa, had first proposed a date of 5 November for these landings and now confirmed these would take place on 8 November. Every possible liner would be required in the UK by the end of September and those to be fitted as LSI(L) much earlier, which meant their departure from the Cape by 10 September at the latest.

Duchess of Richmond left Suez on 13 August, loaded in Durban and Capetown on the Union Castle berth, fuelled in Freetown and reached Liverpool on 30 September. *Stratheden* and *Arundel Castle* left Suez a day later than the *Duchess*, the former also loading for Union Castle at three Cape ports, fuelled at Freetown and docked in Liverpool four days ahead of the CPS liner, having had a Halifax diversion cancelled. *Arundel Castle* first proceeded to Diego Suarez and embarked personnel for South Africa, also loaded at three Cape ports and with a similar homeward voyage reached the Clyde on 8 October. *Empress of Australia* cleared Suez on the 15th, embarked POW in Port Sudan, fuelled in Aden, repaired in Durban and also loaded there and at Capetown on the Clan berth before returning via Freetown to the Clyde on 10 October. These four liners were next employed in the Torch follow-up convoys.

The return voyages of the three remaining liners from Suez were rather different. *Bergensfjord* left Suez on 16 August, proceeding light via Aden to Basra in Iraq at the head of the Persian Gulf where Polish refugees were embarked for Durban, having escaped from Poland ahead of the Nazi onslaught and made their way with thousands of others through Russia and Iraq. They were now en route to joining the free Polish forces in the UK. From Durban, *Bergensfjord* was sent empty and direct to Ango-Ango and Boma in the Belgian Congo, where native troops under Belgian officers were embarked for Lagos, and at this port Nigerian troops were embarked in lieu for Takoradi, from where Gold Coast troops were carried around the coast to Freetown and Bathurst. *Bergensfjord* then proceeded in company with *Leopoldville* and under destroyer escort direct to the Clyde, arriving on 6 November when both were prepared for a Torch follow-up convoy.

The Belgian *Leopoldville* left Suez a day behind *Bergensfjord* and spent 26 days in Durban under repair before following the Norwegian liner to Matadi on the Congo, then similarly to Lagos, Takoradi, Freetown, Bathurst and Glasgow. The last departure from Suez was by *Cuba* on 19 August, having first carried out some vital repairs before proceeding via Aden and Durban to East London where another four weeks were spent on repairs. *Cuba* then made a similar voyage to the previous two liners via Capetown, Matadi, Pointe Noire, Takoradi, Lagos and Freetown to the Clyde where she arrived on 7 December but then proceeded to the Tyne where three months repair work was required to return the ship to service.

In reverting to the Bombay portion of WS 20 which detached from the main body of the convoy east of Kismayu on 3 August, good progress was made running before the SW monsoon across the north Indian Ocean, under escort of *Devonshire*, and all three liners and *Adrastus* arrived at Bombay on the 9th.

The disembarkation of *Abosso* and *Empire Pride* took place on arrival, the 6 Bn Ox & Bucks travelling then to the Madras Presidency to join 74 Indian Brigade and by March 1944 were engaged against the Japanese in the Arakan. Both liners sailed again on the 13th for Diego Suarez to take part in further operations in Madagascar, being joined there by *Dilwara* and *Dunera* which had left Bombay a day earlier. The two BI troopers and *Empire Pride* then sailed to Mombasa where they embarked the troops of 29 Independent Infantry Brigade who had led the earlier assault on Diego Suarez. All three liners sailed again on 5 September and made junction with the remaining forces south of the Comoro Islands four days later, comprising *Abosso*, *Llandaff Castle*, *Empire Woodlark* and *Khedive Ismail* which had embarked and sailed Diego Suarez on the 7th with the King's African Rifles troops of 22 East African Brigade. Ten storeships were attached to the force which was escorted by *Warspite*, *Illustrious*, six cruisers and several lesser warships.

The landings and capture of Majunga on the NW coast of Madagascar was successfully accomplished on 10 September, following which *Empire Pride*, *Dilwara* and *Dunera* repeated the process at Tamatave on the NE coast of the island and thereafter returned to Mombasa although the former ship made another trip to Diego Suarez and Tamatave before all three continued to Durban. The homeward passage of *Empire Pride* was made direct from Capetown to Liverpool where she arrived on 24 November in time for a North African convoy to Bone.

The return voyage of *Abosso* ended in her loss two days short of her home port. After the capture of Majunga, *Abosso* remained there for six days and returned some of the 29 Brigade troops to Mombasa, then loaded on the Ellerman berth at Durban and Capetown, leaving the latter on 9 October direct for Liverpool with 3000 tons of wool, 400 bags of mail and 189 passsengers. The crew numbered 161 in addition to 18 gunners and three RN W/T operators for the HF/DF equipment. All went well until the evening of 29 October by which time *Abosso* was 600 miles north of the Azores, when she was torpedoed twice by *U 575* and although the ship took almost an hour to sink, only five boats out of twelve, and at least two rafts seem to have got away.

No. 3 Boat in charge of one Quartermaster with 31 persons on board had lost sight of the remainder by next morning, and set off NE under sail towards Ireland over 1,200 miles distant. A second night at sea proved bitterly cold but by next morning the masts of a convoy were seen ahead. By the greatest stroke of luck the boat had almost sailed into the path of an outbound convoy. Red flares were fired and by the late forenoon all were safely rescued by the sloop *Bideford* on the starboard wing of convoy KMS 2 of 52 ships to North Africa. The survivors made up of 17 passengers and 14 crew were later landed at Gibraltar.

Both the Admiralty and the convoy had picked up the distress message from *Abosso* and so the escorts were on the lookout for ship's boats but no others were seen; *Bideford* said they had not seen flares from the boat but found the red sails conspicuous. The Quartermaster's boat proved to be the only survivors; Captain Tate with 146 officers and crew, all of the gunners, the RN operators and 172 passengers perished. It appears that Elder Dempster as owners took the matter up with the Admiralty, as a letter exists in the Company history from the CinCWA confirming that "immediate steps were taken to endeavour to find the remaining survivors...the importance of the convoy to which HMS *Bideford* was attached prohibited any search being made by escorts of this convoy, but the search was, in fact, continued with all the forces at our disposal for some days, unfortunately with no success."[16]

The homeward voyage of *Orion* from Bombay began by embarking Polish refugee families in Karachi, whence she sailed on 20 August, disembarking all at Tanga and Dar-es-Salaam where accommodation was built to house them. *Orion* then loaded on the Ellerman berth at Durban and Capetown, proceeding then via Freetown to Liverpool where she arrived on 9 October to begin a boiler survey and repairs which lasted four weeks before next employment in a Torch follow-up convoy.

The last liner to complete both outward and homeward sections of WS 20 was the Elder Dempster managed *Banfora* under the command of Captain Alec Smith, which was delayed for repairs at both Capetown and Durban, and finally left the latter port on 16 August in convoy CM 31. *Banfora* was embarked with her original complement, while five other Indian Ocean transports carried 7,622 personnel landed by WS 20 in Durban, the balance of 5,518 having been taken on to Diego Suarez and Mombasa by *Nieuw Amsterdam* on 3 August. CM 31 was escorted by the AMC *Worcestershire* and eventually split to allow *Nova Scotia* (carrying 9 Bn York & Lancs) and *Indrapoera* to proceed to Bombay where they arrived on 1 September, while *Banfora*, *Ascanius* (carrying 6 Bn Grenadier Guards rather uncomfortably), *Salween* and *Kosciuszcko* reached Suez on 7th, four weeks behind WS 20.

The convoy records are devoid of any complaint on the condition of *Banfora* for trooping but the OC Troops on board wrote several reports to the War Office that the ship had been hurriedly and inefficiently converted, was full of bed bugs and rats which entered the accommodation and ate the glue from the spine of books. He said the ship was unsuitable for trooping in the Western Ocean (i.e. North Atlantic) and then unfit for the tropics.[17]

The position of Officer Commanding Troops was a solitary one, responsible for the military personnel on a troopship much like the Master who had command of the whole ship and everyone on board. The War Office appointed permanent military staffs to troopships from the beginning of the war which included an Adjutant, Medical Officer, an RSM and several ORs to act as orderlies who remained for long periods much like the crew. The system was as good as the tact and tolerance between the Master and OC

Troops, the latter being responsible for the quantity of provisions and preparation of meals as issued to the troops, the cleanliness of the troopdecks and maintenance of good order amongst all the embarked personnel, even arrangements for exercise on the very limited areas of deck space. There was virtually no room for training. Leisure activities included organizing Housie-Housie, a cinema, deck sports, a library and records for playing over the inter-com...Even during homeward voyages, the OC Troops and staff were in charge of all embarked personnel including POW, civilians and DBS.

The homeward passage of *Banfora* was from Suez to Basra, from where she carried some of the 13,000 Polish families waiting there, first to Karachi, then Mombasa, and thereafter loaded in Lourenco Marques, East London and Capetown, proceeding via Pernambuco, Trinidad, Guantanamo Bay and New York to join convoy HX 221 for the Clyde where she arrived on 13 January 1943. After being drydocked and fumigated over a seven week period, *Banfora* was allocated to the KMF series of convoys to North Africa. Captain Smith thankfully transferred to the cargo fleet while the OC Troops was posted to the Dutch liner *Indrapoera*.

WS 21P - sailed UK 17.7.42

The departure of the previous convoy WS 20 on 21 June left only two serviceable liners in the UK: *Duchess of York* which arrived in Liverpool ten days earlier from Halifax and was then in the midst of five weeks of repairs, while *Tamaroa* had just begun discharging a meat cargo in Avonmouth and was due to follow this with a drydocking in Cardiff. There was in addition *Llangibby Castle* in Southampton undergoing major hull repairs following the torpedo damage sustained in WS 15, also the four AMCs released in January and now converting for trooping in three home ports and the first of the chartered Dutch KPM liners beginning a three month conversion for trooping in Liverpool.[1]

Since March 1942 the interval between the departure of WS convoys was reduced by agreement from four weeks to three[1] and would have indicated the July convoy, first estimated to provide 43,000 personnel berths, would sail on the 12th, i.e. three weeks after WS 20, and by which date another eleven WS liners had arrived in the UK. However, two of those were the remaining KPM liners requiring much attention, two other Dutch troopships, *Sibajak* and *Volendam*, required four or five weeks repairs, two other liners were discharging refrigerated cargoes while *Nea Hellas* required eight weeks for permanent repairs to the collision damage sustained in WS 16, but subsequently lasted three months. Taken overall only five of these nineteen liners could be made ready for a sailing close to 12 July which was then postponed until the 17th and allowed the most recent arrivals less than a fortnight for the business of turnround. All five liners were of minimum 17 knots, a further ten were ready for another convoy entitled WS 21 at the end of the month but were all of 14 - 15 knots maximum speed.

The reason for the decision to despatch two separate convoys demanding two separate escorts a mere two weeks apart is not clear, and may simply have been due to pressure on the War Office from the Chiefs of Staff who as never before, were urging further reinforcement of the Middle East. The situation there was that Rommel's attempt to break through at Alamein had been defeated by 5 July while repeated British attacks between 10 and 26 July ended indecisively with both sides exhausted. The need for more personnel in this critical theatre of operations was fourfold, of which the constant drain on manpower from battle casualties and a further 4 to 5,000 per month admitted sick to medical units, were the most obvious.[2] The administrative tail of Eighth Army was also increasing as it had to in maintaining the frontline formations in the field.

There were now many more transport companies for tanks, vehicles, water and petrol supplies, field maintenance centres and a new Corps of Royal Electrical and Mechanical Engineers created to be responsible for inspection and repair of guns and vehicles. In January 1942 the ration strength of Eighth Army was 88,000, in June it had risen to 100,000 and before Alamein in October reached 231,000.[3]

For some time past the Chiefs of Staff had been undecided as to whether to concentrate on the defence of India, or that of the northern front in Persia and Iraq or the Middle East, but on 12 July the Prime Minister said the prime task must be the defeat of Rommel and this policy was later endorsed by the Chiefs of Staff. It was also in July that the Prime Minister, President Roosevelt and their advisers were hammering out decisions which were to shape the rest of the war; all-out planning was ordered for an Allied landing in North Africa to take place at the end of October, codenamed "Torch", and which was ultimately to absorb half of the WS fleet.

The embarkation on the five liners of WS 21P took place in their ports of arrival in the UK from previous WS voyages, beginning in Glasgow on 12 July on *Empress of Japan* at 2 KGV Dock, on *Oronsay* at No. 1 berth and *Duchess of Atholl* at the adjacent Riverside berth, the last two having arrived at the end of June from the Madagascar landings and WS 17, while the *Empress* arrived from WS 18 to Durban. All three liners moved downriver fully embarked to the Clyde Anchorage in the early afternoon of the 14th. The appointed Commodore, Vice-Admiral FA Marten CB GCVO RNR, was accommodated and welcomed aboard *Empress of Japan* by Captain JW Thomas, while Captain JC Brown of *Windsor Castle* in the Liverpool section, an Extra Master and Commander RNR, was appointed Vice Commodore.

Embarkations at Liverpool on *Duchess of York* and *Windsor Castle*, the latter having returned from Bombay and WS 17 twelve days earlier, began on the morning of the 16th and both liners left the Mersey just before high water next afternoon and proceeded under escort of the destroyers *Buxton* and *Tjerk Hiddes*. The unfamiliar Dutch name was actually a newish unit of the Nizam class which had been purchased on the stocks, renamed, and was now on passage to join the Eastern Fleet. Four of the liners embarked in excess of 4,000 personnel, the total being 19,284,[5] all but 291 being for Suez.

The three liners of the Clyde section were led out of the boom at 2030 on the 17th by the Commodore on *Empress of Japan* with the cruiser *Orion* and destroyers *Nepal* and *Georgetown*. The cruiser was en route around the Cape to join the Mediterranean Fleet at Alexandria, *Nepal* was an Australian manned class-mate of *Tjerk Hiddes* also bound for the Eastern Fleet. *Georgetown* and *Buxton* were locally based ex US units of the Town class.

At 0500 on the 18th, junction was made with the Liverpool section six miles W of Orsay, when a cruising order of four columns was formed [6] and a westerly course and speed of 17 knots set under an air escort provided from 0830 to 1700. At 2100 course was altered to SW and at midnight on the 19th to SSW towards the eastern passage of the Azores.

This small and fast five ship convoy had an uneventful passage in fine weather to Freetown. *Buxton* was detached at 0800 on the 20th and *Georgetown* 24 hours later, leaving *Orion* and the two Nizam class destroyers as combined ocean and A/S escort. On the night of 21/22 July the convoy passed through the 75 mile wide gap of the Azores between Terceira and Sao Miguel and by 0800 was 40 miles west of Ponta Delgada on the latter island. A S'ly course was then set towards the Cape Verde group and at 1100 on the 24th course was altered to the SE to pass inside and east of that group, where at 0600 on the 25th to the NE of these islands, the V&W destroyer *Vimy* joined as local escort from Freetown.

During the night of 26/27 July the convoy reached a position 90 miles west of Freetown where course was altered directly for that port and where all ships arrived at 1600 on the 27th. The estimated speed of advance from the Clyde was reckoned as 15 knots but the convoy had actually averaged 16.6 knots, almost the speed of the slowest ship. Four U-Boats were known to be operating to the south and west of Freetown at this time and sank seven ships in the five days prior to arrival of the convoy, but none were believed to have been closer than 3-400 miles of its track.

The small size of WS 21P would normally have allowed a quick despatch from Freetown, certainly within 24 hours, but the convoy remained in port for five days, almost certainly due to the delayed and planned junction with nine US storeships for the Middle East. These had started out from the eastern seaboard of the States on 13 July as convoy AS 4 (America-Suez). Two were loaded with oil cracking-plants for the Persian Gulf, the remainder with 300 Sherman tanks and one hundred 105mm self-propelled howitzers for use as anti-tank weapons together with ammunition, all for the Eighth Army, "which President Roosevelt had given to Prime Minister Churchill on that black day in June when news reached them that Tobruk had fallen."[7] However even that was not the limit of American generosity as on 16 July one of the ships was torpedoed and sunk; this "loss was made good by sending 52 more tanks and by 11 September, 318 Shermans had arrived in the Middle East"[7] to take part in the Battle of Alamein on 23 October.

Unfortunately bad weather dogged the passage of AS 4 and on one of the ships, the American loaned but British commissioned *Empire Oriole*, (see also WS 14) three tanks in two separate holds had broken adrift, one being a 30 ton Sherman which nearly went through the ship's side. After heaving-to and securing the tanks as best the crew could manage in the seaway, *Empire Oriole* rejoined the convoy. Four other tanks were then found to be out of gear and arrangements were made for full securing and lashing to be carried out by shore labour in Pernambuco (now Recife) in NE Brazil[8] and where AS 4 arrived on the 26th, but the necessary work was not completed there until the 31st. Strictly speaking Brazil was then a neutral power and would hardly have wished to assist the belligerents, however, "since the early days of 1942 the Brazilian Government had shown itself to be favourably disposed towards the Allies" and the use of their ports "was greatly facilitated by Brazil's declaration of war against The Axis powers on 22 August."[9]

After disembarking 205 personnel in Freetown, the five liners of 21P left that port at 1100 on 1st August with the same ocean escort plus *Boreas*, and at first steered SW for a distance of 60 miles (rather than the 200 miles adopted by recent convoys), before turning SE that afternoon on a direct course for the Cape, which tends to negate an arrangement to join with AS 4. However, on the morning of the 3rd when 200 miles SW of Cape Palmas on the Liberian coast, the convoy altered course four points (45°) to starboard to make this junction in accordance with a signal from NCSO Freetown.

The two convoys finally merged at 1000 on the 5th in a position 200 miles east of Ascension. A cruising order of five columns was then formed,[10] course altered to ESE until the morning of the 6th when *Boreas* detached, and a direct course of SE adopted towards the Cape while the Free French patrol vessel, *Commandant Duboc*, joined the escort. The remaining passage was uneventful and the five liners and eight storeships reached Capetown at 1300 on the 13th, having averaged 12.83 knots from Freetown; the escorts meantime continued to Durban. The convoy remained three days in Capetown during which time the NCSO instructed *Santa Cruz* and *Mormacdale*, both 13.5 knots, and *American Manufacturer* 13 knots to be detached from WS 21P and to follow in a slower convoy beyond the scope of this work.

After replenishing with water, fuel and stores and disembarking a solitary unknown figure in Capetown, the five liners and five remaining storeships, the slowest being the *Norwegian Tarn* of 15.5 knots, sailed again at 1100 on 16 August escorted by *Shropshire* which was met at the end of the searched channel, having come round from Simonstown. The cruising order was amended to four columns[11] and the estimated speed of advance given as 14 knots.

The passage around the Cape was incident free while the ordered route took a wide sweep from the Natal coast to a position 165 miles ESE of Durban where at 1500 on the 19th, rendezvous was made with the earlier escort of *Orion*, *Nepal* and *Tjerk Hiddes* in relief of *Shropshire* which then proceeded to Durban. The waters around Madagascar had been free of enemy interference for the past six weeks and so the northward route reverted to using the Mozambique Channel, where in the evening of the 22nd, *Exhibitor* developed condenser trouble and detached into Mocambique distant 80 miles westward. *Nepal* and *Tjerk Hiddes* detached on the 24th for Mombasa to join the Eastern Fleet while *Orion* continued with the convoy which rounded Guardafui at dawn on the 28th and dispersed off Aden at 0500 on the 29th, having averaged 14.62 knots from Capetown.

All five liners entered Aden to water and fuel, the Commodore ship and *Duchess of Atholl* leaving again that same day and the remainder a day later to proceed independently to Suez. *Empress of Japan* was the first to arrive there on 1st September followed by *Duchess of Atholl* and *Oronsay* on the 2nd and the last two on the 3rd. Two days was the minimum to disembark personnel and stores at Suez anchorage so there was a period on the 4th when all five liners were in the bay inviting aerial attack from an enemy a mere 200 miles distant but strangely never occurred. "Except for fairly large raids nightly from 3-7 July and again between 25-30 July...the enemy showed no inclination to use his bombers to attack the sensitive spots in the British back area, i.e. the Canal, Suez, Alexandria etc...Mines were laid (in the canal) and bombs dropped among ships off Suez, but the only casualty was one water boat..the Germans and Italians seem not to have realised how important it was for them to dislocate the busy port of Suez, focal point for the arrival of British reinforcements of all kinds."[12]

Disembarkation of all five liners was complete on the 7th when *Windsor Castle* cleared the bay. *Empress of Japan* proceeded direct to Durban where she was loaded in six days on the BI berth and from there sailed direct to the Clyde arriving on 7 October having averaged 19 knots for this passage of 7,800 miles; her next voyage began three weeks later in WS 24.

On the homeward leg *Oronsay* refuelled in Aden and loaded on the Union Castle berth at both Durban and Capetown. She also carried priority personnel from one port to the other who were awaiting onward transhipment from Durban, and were to be embarked on the ships on WS 22 then replenishing in Capetown. *Oronsay* finally left Capetown on the last day of September for Freetown and the UK with 3,000 tons of oranges, 1,200 tons copper slabs and 130 passengers. She was due in Freetown on 10 October and was given a wide evasive route to approach that port from a position 500 miles WSW, where just before dawn on the 9th, she was torpedoed by the Italian submarine, *Archimedo*. Half an hour later a second torpedo struck the ship and Captain

Savage ordered "abandon ship." All passengers and crew were safely away in the boats when two more torpedoes struck home and the ship sank minutes later. The main party of survivors comprising 277 crew, 26 gunners and 105 passengers in nine boats under Captain Savage were sighted and picked up by a British escort vessel after eight days, having covered 247 miles towards the land and helped by the Counter Equatorial Current. Two other boats containing 37 crew, 25 passengers and a gunner were picked up by the enemy and became POW, but only five crew out of the total 476 persons on board were lost.

Captain Norman Savage, a Sunderland man then aged 49, had earlier survived the bombing and loss of *Orford* at Marseilles in June 1940 and had served as Master of *Oronsay* for the past seventeen months. He was awarded the OBE, took command of *Orontes* in December and continued to serve the Orient company until his retiral in 1953.

The CPS *Duchess* liners left Suez on 5 September, the *Atholl* going direct to Capetown where she loaded 3,500 tons general on the Harrison berth, embarked 534 passengers including 58 women and children and sailed on 3 October for Freetown and the UK. By the morning of the 9th when *Oronsay* was torpedoed 1,300 miles ahead of her, there were at least three other homebound liners spaced between, including *Nea Hellas* and *Andes* returning from WS 22 and *Windsor Castle* from 21P which had also left Capetown on the 3rd. The Italian submarine which sank *Oronsay* also claimed to have torpedoed *Nea Hellas* eighteen hours later in a position 24 miles SE, where that liner could certainly have been before turning east for Freetown but reported no such attack and may have had a lucky escape.

Duchess of Atholl was torpedoed by a U-Boat at 0635 next morning, the 10th, in a position 200 miles east of Ascension and 930 miles due south of Freetown. That torpedo struck the port side of the engine-room, killing four and extinguishing all of the lights. An SOS was transmitted but whether received or not was unknown. A second torpedo struck the same area twenty minutes later when Captain Moore ordered the women and children away in the boats. A third torpedo struck the port side forward of the bridge and as the ship began to settle in an upright condition, "abandon ship" was ordered and within twenty minutes all but four damaged boats out of 22 had been launched with 821 survivors aboard. *U-178* surfaced before the ship turned on her port side and sank at 0925.[14]

The loss of this liner occurred in the region of the westgoing South Equatorial Current, which might have carried the boats towards Ascension, or they might have missed the island to be faced with a voyage of 1,400 miles to the coast of Brazil. Mercifully the distress message had been picked up and the OBV *Corinthian* reached the scene at 0800 the next day and rescued all the survivors by 1330. They were landed at Freetown five days later and taken onwards by the AMC *Carnarvon Castle* which anchored at the Tail of the Bank on the 29th. Like the Master of *Oronsay*, Captain Harry Moore, whose father had also commanded in CPS, was awarded the OBE and later took command of *Duchess of Bedford* and reached retiral age at the end of the war.

The remaining two liners of WS 21P had comparatively uneventful homeward voyages, *Duchess of York* loading in Mombasa and Capetown on the Union Castle berth, leaving the latter during the afternoon of 6 October when observed but not attacked by *U-172* which was lying submerged 8 mls NW of the harbour entrance, quietly, noting the movements and routes of all shipping traffic; one of two U-Boats of the Eisbar group which had arrived in Cape waters two days earlier.[13] The *Duchess* was bound for

Freetown but diverted in lieu to Pernambuco and thence to the Clyde and Glasgow where she arrived on the 31st. It was here that Captain Sapsworth after four WS voyages in that ship and the earlier one in *Empress of Britain* now reached retiral on relief by Captain BL Leslie. The next voyage of *Duchess of York* was to Algiers.

Windsor Castle conveniently loaded general and fruit on her owners' berth at Durban, Port Elizabeth and Capetown, leaving the latter with a small number of passengers on 3 October and sailed direct to the Clyde, arriving on the 23rd to discharge at Merklands Wharf and also made her next voyage to Algiers.

Despite the relatively high speed during part of these voyages and a quick turnround in Suez, the overall voyage time of 81 days for *Empress of Japan* and 106 days for *Duchess of York* was not much improvement on the 90-111 days recorded by the liners of WS 4B nearly two years earlier, but was undoubtedly the best that could be obtained under war conditions.

WS 21 - sailed UK 30.7.42.

Reference was made at the beginning of WS 21P to a later and slower section of ten transports departing the UK at the end of July. These liners embarked a total of 28,290 personnel in reinforcement drafts of which half were destined for the Middle East, one third for Iraq, India and Ceylon, while a further 1,354 were for West Africa, 1,159 for South Africa, 2,181 for East Africa and 575 for Madagascar. This later convoy was simply numbered WS 21, which tends to suggest it having been planned as the original rather than an appendage to WS 21P, but in being six weeks behind WS 20 had doubled the established cycle of three-week departures. The next convoy WS 22 returned this cycle to four weeks and thereafter became erratic as the allocation of most WS ships was concentrated on the Allied landings in North Africa.

By the end of June four transports in the UK were allocated for WS 21 of which *Tamaroa*, *Sibajak* and *Volendam* were previously referred to[1] while *Rangitiki* docked in Liverpool on the 24th from a voyage out to Halifax which returned from the Plate and required drydocking on completion of her meat discharge. Six others reached home ports in the first half of July, beginning with *Largs Bay* from WS 17 which berthed at Glasgow's Plantation Quay from the Plate to discharge a Royal Mail refrigerated cargo on the 5th. Three liners arrived on the 12th, *Maloja* at Liverpool and *Aorangi* at Glasgow both from WS 18, and *Narkunda* at the Clyde Anchorage from a brief WS 20 trip to Gibraltar. On the 15th *Samaria* reached Liverpool from WS 17 and next day the Blue Funnel staff were able to welcome home *Antenor* which had been absent from the UK since June 1939 in service as an AMC in the Indian Ocean area. She was the last of the nine AMCs released in July 1941 and having decommissioned and converted for trooping in Calcutta, was loaded with an Anchor Line cargo in Bombay and now had twelve days to discharge and prepare for her first troop embarkation.

In the week before embarkation it became clear that another ex AMC, the modern Anchor Line motorship *Circassia* and first of the four released by the Admiralty in January, would complete conversion at Belfast in time to be included in WS 21 which allowed *Sibajak* to be released for a Gibraltar voyage in mid August which later extended to West Africa to join WS 22. *Circassia* completed at Belfast on the 24th and anchored in the Clyde next day to prepare for embarkation. On the 29th Captain David Bone came out of his brief retirement to take command in lieu of the Master who had suddenly taken ill. He was to remain on this ship to experience five assault landings in four years, being awarded the OBE in 1943, a Knighthood in 1946 and had reached the remarkable age of 72 when he finally brought the *Circassia* home in March 1946.

Only two ships embarked in Glasgow for this convoy, as all suitable berths in KGV Dock were occupied by fast cargo liners loading for the Operation Pedestal convoy to relieve Malta, which sailed three days behind WS 21. For embarkation and storing *Largs Bay* had to use the bare quayside at Berth 10, whence she moved downriver in the early afternoon of the 27th and was followed by *Aorangi* from Berth 2, 24 hours later. At the Clyde Anchorage the embarkations by tender were carried out on *Circassia*, *Narkunda* and *Tamaroa*, the latter having arrived from Cardiff on the morning of the 28th and barely 12 hours prior to the sailing time of the convoy. At the Tail of the Bank naval anchorage, the AMC *Ranpura* additionally embarked 785 personnel for West Africa.

In Liverpool, embarkations on *Antenor*, *Maloja*, *Rangitiki*, *Samaria* and *Volendam* were completed by the 28th when these liners sailed on the late forenoon tide under escort of the destroyer *Buxton* for the pre-arranged rendezvous off Orsay next morning. Also making their way up the Irish Sea under escort of the patrol vessel PC 74 were two storeships which had loaded in the Bristol Channel, the American *James Lykes* loaded with MT, tanks, guns, stores and ammunition for the Middle East and the Dutch flag *Curacao* similarly loaded and with ten Hurricanes and an MFV all for India. These two ships also carried an additional 72 personnel. Of the ten liners in the convoy, half were destined to disembark and turnaround in Durban, two each continuing to Bombay and Suez and one to Mombasa.[2]

The ocean escort for WS 21 was to comprise the cruiser *Hawkins*, AMC *Ranpura* and two newly completed and worked-up destroyers, the Hunt class *Catterick* and P class *Petard*, all four being sent out to join the Eastern Fleet then based in Mombasa. On 26 July, however, *Hawkins* which had refitted in Portsmouth and was completing workup at Scapa, was despatched with the battleship *Duke of York* to Iceland and only returned to the Clyde with sufficient time to refuel and sail with the convoy on the amended sailing date of the 30th.

With the departure thus delayed by 32 hours to the morning of the 30th, the Liverpool and Bristol Channel sections were diverted to the Clyde and there anchored on the morning of the 29th to join the others which completed the convoy ready for sea. The appointed Commodore EC Denison MVO RNR on *Narkunda* (Captain C Parfitt), with the respective Masters attended a conference at Marymount in Gourock, following which the destroyers *Keppel* (SO A/S escort and fresh from PQ 17), *Salisbury* and Hunt class *Bicester*, *Bramham*, *Lamerton*, *Ledbury* and *Wilton* proceeded to Moville to top up their fuel and rejoin at the Orsay rendezvous. The SOE was Captain GA French RN of *Hawkins* while Captain J Alder Smith of *Maloja* was appointed Vice Commodore.

Convoy WS 21 finally sailed from the Clyde as a complete formation of ten transports and two storeships at 0500 on 30 July, escorted by *Hawkins*, *Ranpura*, *Catterick* and *Petard*. Fog was experienced intermittently during the first three days and caused a number of unfortunate accidents but did not prevent the destroyers joining off Orsay that afternoon, when a cruising order of five columns was formed with the cruisers between columns 3 and 4.[3] A westerly course was set to take the convoy out to longitude 17°West. Spitfires and Ansons provided air cover during the daylight hours.

"At 0500 on the 31st the inward convoy HG 76 of seventeen ships was met in a thick fog. This convoy was not seen from *Narkunda*, but *Ledbury* on the port wing A/S screen collided with one of the HG 76 ships and had to return to base."[4] At 0800 in clear weather the Commodore signalled that ships could fire off a few rounds of machine-gun and 2 pdr ammunition into the air, and many ships did so that morning even when patches of fog were encountered. "At 1050 *Curacao* on the port wing reported having seen a plane crash into the sea at 1020, just 500 yards on her port beam, and had informed the nearest escort. They had heard the aircraft crew calling for help and saw the plane then explode and catch fire. The survivors picked up by one of the destroyers said the plane was shot down by tracer bullets from the convoy."[4] It was later concluded that this aircraft, a Sunderland, was brought down by *Aorangi's* Bren guns, firing at an unidentified aircraft which suddenly appeared out of the mist on the starboard bow. It appeared to be approaching the ship in a shallow dive at a height of about 150 ft as if to attack. About thirty rounds were fired, some witnesses stating that they saw bullets entering the port wing. No recognition signals were observed and no warning was received of any friendly aircraft being in the vicinity.[4]

In the early evening of that same day the convoy turned to a SW'ly course towards the Azores group leaving the option of passing through or on either side of these islands to a later decision dependent on the Admiralty's appreciation of the U-Boat situation. At 0608 on 1st August a Sunderland was seen flying around the convoy, very low at about 50 ft above the sea and several witnesses saw the aircraft drop a red and white Verey light, but was then lost sight of. At 0644 *Hawkins* which was 2 miles astern of the convoy and busy fuelling destroyers, reported that this aircraft had crashed into the sea and exploded. The weather was thick at the time, but two destroyers were seen to close the position with unknown results but no survivors were reported. "Both accidents were deeply regretted by the Commodore and the entire convoy."[4]

At 2100 on the 1st and on the latitude of the Scillies the destroyers *Petard* and *Catterick* detached ahead to fuel at Ponta Delgada in the Azores then distant 700 miles. At 0800 on the 2nd the convoy altered to a S'ly course to pass east of the Azores and at 1830 that day *Bramham* and *Wilton* detached for Gibraltar. No other incidents occurred until 0600 on the 4th, the convoy then being 85 miles east of Ponta Delgada, when *Petard* and *Catterick* rejoined and allowed the four remaining destroyers to detach for Gibraltar where the four Hunts were now to join the escort of the Pedestal convoy to Malta.

From the Azores the convoy continued on a S'ly course to pass east of the Cape Verde group, and at 2330 on the 6th and 360 miles north of these islands, the Portuguese passenger liner *Colonial* on a course of ENE, was identified and passed, brilliantly illuminated. On the morning of the 8th the convoy was 50 miles east of the nearest Cape Verde island, Boa Vista, where course was altered to the SE and held until midnight on the 9th when an E'ly course was adopted direct for Freetown. A Sunderland air escort visited the convoy briefly that morning and at 1100 the destroyer *Vimy* joined as additional A/S escort for the last few miles. The convoy was anchored in Freetown by 1435 on the heels of 51 ships of another outward convoy from the UK. The Commodore recorded an average speed of 13.15 knots from the Clyde, several contacts being obtained by aircraft escort south of the Azores but no submarines were sighted, although three U-Boats were then active and sinking ships some 120 miles west of the convoy route in the approaches to Freetown.

The convoy remained five days in Freetown to complete replenishment, and where also 569 personnel for West Africa were landed from *Circassia*, *Narkunda* and *Aorangi*, while others landed from *Ranpura* which then continued around the coast to disembark the remainder at Takoradi and subsequently rejoin the convoy. Also in Freetown three more storeships joined, which may have come out from the UK in a slow convoy, i.e. *Silverwalnut*, the 4-masted funnel-less Danish motorship *Erria* now under British and United Baltic management and the American flag *Lookout*, ex Danish *Anna Maersk*.

WS 21 thus enlarged to fifteen ships sailed again from Freetown at 0730 on 15 August, the ships now taking their departures on passing the fleet repair ship *Vindictive*, in lieu of the Hospital Ship *Oxfordshire* which had languished there at anchor for almost three years. Once clear of the searched channel a cruising order of six columns was formed,[5] and course set to the SW for a distance of 130 miles until 1900 when an alteration was made to the south towards Ascension and a rendezvous with a convoy from the United States, as occurred with the previous convoy WS 21P. *Hawkins*, *Petard* and *Catterick* remained as ocean escorts while an air escort on the first day was provided alternately by a Hudson, a Walrus and a Sunderland, while this latter aircraft also patrolled around the convoy for half an hour in the forenoon and afternoon of the 16th.

At 1330 on the 18th the convoy reached a position 120 miles north of Ascension where junction was made with two US storeships of convoy AS 6, i.e. *China Mail* and *American Press*, each carrying oil cracking plants for the Persian Gulf and reported to be of 16 and 14 knots respectively. They were escorted by the AMC *Alcantara* which then detached on patrol while the convoy altered to SE direct for the Cape. Next forenoon *Ranpura* rejoined from Takoradi and by which time the Commodore deduced that *American Press* could only manage 13 knots and was to break down on more than one occasion on the passage south; likewise *Lookout* listed as 13.75 knots also had considerable difficulty keeping up.

On the morning of the 20th in a position 220 miles NW of St Helena, *Catterick* detached ahead to fuel there from the RFA *Fortol* in the lee of the island and at midnight that night *Erria* detached with stores for the island but did not rejoin. By the morning of the 21st when 180 miles ESE of St Helena, *Catterick* rejoined which allowed *Petard* to detach and refuel in the same manner, rejoining 24 hours later.

There were no further incidents on the passage to the Cape which was accomplished "in perfect weather"[4] without mention of the SE trades. At 0600 on the 26th when 90 miles west of Robben Island, the Capetown portion comprising *Maloja*, *Aorangi*, *Antenor* and all six storeships detached with *Hawkins* and the two destroyers for Capetown, proceeding by a circuitous route going SE, then E, then NE in their approach to the searched channel but were unable to save daylight and had to spend another night at sea before arriving at daybreak on the 27th.

The remaining seven transports continued towards Durban under escort of *Ranpura* and were joined by the AMC *Corfu* at 1300 when 50 miles west of Cape Point. By 0200 the convoy ran into very strong headwinds and adverse current as it turned east for 90 miles keeping at a distance of 130 miles south of Cape Agulhas to ensure adequate clearance from the bank of that name. By the morning of the 29th the convoy was 75 miles to the east of East London where the corvettes *Thyme* and *Amaranthus* joined as A/S escorts. Speed was now reduced for a daylight arrival and by 0500 on the 30th the approach to the Durban searched channel was reached where *Corfu* detached while *Ranpura* and the transports entered the harbour. The average speed from Freetown was recorded as 12.11 knots and from the Clyde 12.56 while the adverse winds and current around the Cape, reduced the speed for this last leg from Capetown to 11.05 knots.

Five of the liners were entirely disembarked in Durban to allow their earliest return to the UK for inclusion in WS 24 or the follow-up convoys to North Africa. The first to complete were *Tamaroa* and *Narkunda*, which both left on the 31st with the latter proceeding up coast to Lourenco Marques in Portuguese Mozambique, where an exchange of envoys, consular officials and others was taking place between British and Japanese nationals under a diplomatic arrangement. The Japanese liner *Tatuta Maru* was already in port having brought British nationals from the Far East, while the ex-Egyptian liner *El Nil* and Ellerman's *City of Paris* brought Japanese from the UK and Bombay respectively. The last arrival was *City of Canterbury* with Japanese on 11 September from Melbourne. All ships were berthed alongside the quay to expedite the exchange of Japanese to *Tatuta Maru* while the main British party boarded *Narkunda* with a balance of 481 being carried to Durban on *City of Paris* for subsequent on-carriage to the UK. The ships were given safe conduct passages with their armaments temporarily neutralized, the word DIPLOMATIC and national flags painted on both sides. *Narkunda* replenished in Capetown on the 17th/18th and again at St Vincent in the Cape Verde islands rather than Freetown and reached Liverpool to disembark on 9th October. Her next voyage, which proved to be her last, began on 1st November bound for North Africa; she was bombed and sunk thirteen days later. Captain Parfitt survived this event, was awarded the DSC and Lloyds War Medal, went on to command the *Carthage* and retired in 1945.

From Durban, the refrigerated carriers *Tamaroa*, *Largs Bay* and *Rangitiki* were to have loaded on the Houlder, Royal Mail and Donaldson berths in Buenos Aires, but to expedite their homeward trips these arrangements were replaced by loading in lieu on the Union Castle berth in South Africa. *Tamaroa* loaded in East London and Capetown, leaving the latter on 16 September direct for the UK and first landing passengers in Loch Ryan (for Stranraer) on 8 October before proceeding to Avonmouth for discharge. *Largs Bay* loaded in Port Elizabeth and Capetown, leaving there on 15 September direct to Belfast Lough thence Avonmouth where she arrived to discharge on 14 October; both liners were next employed in WS 24.

Rangitiki loaded in both Durban and Capetown and from the former also embarked Italian POW with Polish guard for the UK. *Circassia* embarked a similar complement in Durban and both ships sailed on 7 September for Capetown where they completed loading on the 14th. They were then directed to an anchorage in Saldanha Bay to await the outcome of raider alarms from two ships sunk on the 10th/11th some 700 miles west of Capetown. On the 12th *Laconia* with nearly 1,800 Italian POW had been sunk near Ascension and clearly escort would now have to be found for such northbound liners.

On 18 September *Circassia* and *Rangitiki* left Saldanha Bay as convoy CF 5 (Cape-Freetown) under escort of the AMC *Corfu* conveniently due a refit after two years service. Captain Bone recalled this passage with the Poles and Italians, and some West African colour-sergeants returning to West Africa from the campaign in Abyssinia. Of the Polish guard, "not all were trained combatants, having assembled in India from refugee camps, been clothed and equipped in British battle-dress and shipped to South Africa as an intermediate halt on the way to Britain...they were inclined to be unnecessarily harsh with the Italians when on sentry duty..the prisoners gave no trouble...there was much song amongst them and with their many odd scraps of baggage brought from the wars in Ethiopia, were musical instruments that they played skillfully and well - even under the disapproving eyes of their stern northern custodians."[6] All three ships replenished at Freetown 29/30th and *Circassia* with *Corfu* reached the Clyde on 12 October. *Rangitiki* disembarked the Italians in Belfast Lough before continuing to Cardiff for discharge. Both liners were next employed in the Torch follow-up convoys while *Corfu* moved to Southampton for refit.

Of the personnel disembarked from WS 21 in South Africa, of which almost all were accommodated at Clairwood Transit Camp in Durban, 7,683 were for on-carriage to the Middle East and 2,508 for India, Iraq and Ceylon. Nearly 5,000 for the former destination were taken forward on *Pulaski*, *Elisabethville*, *City of Paris* and *City of Canterbury* which left Durban on 11 September and reached Suez between 10-12 October. The balance of 2,733 for the Middle East and those for India had to await the arrival of WS 22 on 29 September.

Having replenished to requirements in Capetown, the three transports were accompanied by seven storeships since the Dutch *Bantam* of Rotterdam Lloyd had joined, probably coming direct from the US with the balance of the promised Shermans for the Middle East. The convoy left by the searched channel at 1030 on 30 August under escort of *Hawkins* and formed into a cruising order of four columns.[7]

The passage around the Cape was without incident until the early morning of 2nd September and 60 miles SE of East London when *Hawkins* investigated a suspicious vessel which ultimately proved to be the Greek *Eleni*. That same forenoon with the convoy found to be 14 miles ahead of its intended position, *Hawkins* detached to locate the corvettes *Thyme* and *Amaranthus* which had been due to join, and eventually found them when 92 miles east of East London and ordered them to overtake and join at their best speed which was accomplished by 1730. The convoy was now considerably ahead of its next morning rendezvous with the Durban section and reduced speed accordingly.

Whilst in Durban, Commodore Denison transferred with his staff from *Narkunda* to *Samaria* where he was found appropriate accommodation by Captain HR Oulsram. *Samaria* and *Volendam* alone comprised the Durban section which left their berths at 0700 on 3 September and anchored outside the Bluff, while *Ranpura* sailed at 0800 to make contact with *Hawkins* and the Capetown section. This was effected at 0920,the two liners then got underway and by 1300 the whole convoy was reformed although remaining as four columns,[8] and set off on an E'ly course to pass south of Madagascar. *Hawkins* remained as SOE, *Ranpura* continued as additional escort while *Petard*, delayed leaving Durban, caught up and joined at 1530.

The basis for routing outside Madagascar is unknown. No enemy activity had been reported in the area for two months, other than a German raider believed to be in the central Indian Ocean, which later proved to be *Thor* which then moved to Batavia and blew herself up at Yokohama in November. By the early evening of the 6th the convoy was 180 miles SE of Fort Dauphin where course was altered to pass up the east side of Madagascar, and by the morning of the 9th was 210 miles SE of Diego Suarez, having made good 11.7 knots in the past 24 hours due to the adverse current and where *Petard* detached to fuel and rejoined next morning.

At 0400 on the 10th a position was reached 120 miles east of Farquhar Island, where course was altered NW to pass between that island and the southern extremity of the Seychelles group. This passage although 130 miles wide was subject to cross currents and required careful navigation of a convoy between "islands" which were in fact no more than very low isolated palm covered islets. *Petard* joined in the middle of this passage soon after midday and at 1800 when clear of the islet area the convoy was split. *Volendam* and the Bombay section detached on a W'ly course with *Hawkins* to meet *Enterprise*, which was achieved at 0700 on the 11th when *Volendam* and *Hawkins* continued on a W'ly course at 12 knots for Mombasa where they arrived on the morning of the 13th. The Bombay section comprising *Maloja*, *Antenor*, *Curacoa*, *China Mail* and

American Press under escort of *Enterprise* altered to a NE'ly course which carried them to a position 400 miles SE of Ras Hafun, where on the morning of the 14th course was altered direct for Bombay. On the 17th when 400 miles west of Bombay, *China Mail* and *American Press* were detached northwards to proceed independently to the Persian Gulf while the remaining three ships continued to Bombay where they arrived on the morning of the 19th.

This convoy had traversed the north Indian Ocean at the height of a particularly heavy monsoon in India without any mention in the Commodore's report. What is certain is that the personnel landed in Bombay for posting to whatever units they found themselves, could not help notice "the many administrative preparations and airfield construction programme...being pushed ahead as fast as the particularly severe monsoon conditions of 1942 and the supply of men and materials would permit. At the same time, Wavell was taking steps to improve the organization and training of the forces under his command."⁹ Preparations were also under way to mount the first Arakan offensive in Burma with a move towards Akyab being ordered on 21 September.

In such weather conditions the turnround of the two liners in Bombay could not be rapid, but after disembarking both loaded some homeward cargo, *Maloja* on her owners' berth, and left on the 27th for Karachi where a further batch of Polish refugee families were embarked and subsequently landed at Mombasa on 7 October and at Tanga the following day. *Maloja* then proceeded to Durban and Capetown, embarked mixed personnel and prepared to sail in a homeward convoy CF 7 with *Antenor* and two of the other liners from the same convoy. *Antenor* loaded in Bombay on the Anchor Line berth and left there on the 29th direct for Capetown with various personnel for the UK.

Meanwhile the Aden section of WS 21 had continued northwards after the split on 10 September, comprising *Samaria, Aorangi* and four storeships escorted by *Ranpura* and *Petard*. The equator was crossed in a position 200 miles SE of Mogadishu in the afternoon of the 12th when course was altered NE to follow the Somali coast and take advantage of the favourable current, which effectively increased the convoy speed over the next two days to 14.5 knots. In the late evening of the 13th, *Silverwalnut* hauled out of line reporting a fire in No. 3 shelter deck which contained 200 tons of smoke ammunition, but was got under control by daybreak with the release of CO_2 gas and by sealing the compartment; *Ranpura* kept station between her and the convoy until she rejoined. The convoy passed 40 miles east of Ras Hafun on the 14th and that night passed through the Guardafui Strait and into the Gulf of Aden, where unusually two destroyers joined to increase the A/S escort: *Hero* that morning and *Tetcott* in the late afternoon when also a Blenheim and Catalina provided air escort. The convoy arrived off the Aden searched channel at 1030 on the 16th where it was dispersed.

On conclusion of the convoy, Commodore Denison noted that *American Press*, listed as a 13.5 knots ship, could only manage 13 knots with great difficulty and broke down twice with engine trouble which further delayed the convoy. She also admitted by signal that her maximum speed was only 12.5 knots. *Lookout* also consistently broke down and delayed the convoy, while *Samaria, Silverwalnut* and *China Mail* also suffered breakdowns or steering defects but having sufficient speed were able to rejoin without reducing the convoy speed. The station keeping of *Tamaroa* (Captain W Dawson) was recorded as particularly good and that of *James Lykes* exceptional throughout the entire voyage, most of which that vessel was a column guide.⁴

Aorangi and *Samaria* both refuelled in Aden that day and continued independently to Suez, the former arriving on the 20th and *Samaria* next morning. Both disembarked their personnel to units busy training and preparing for the decisive Alamein battle which began four weeks later. They sailed south on the 24th, *Aorangi* loading on the BI berth at Durban whence she sailed on 21 October direct for the Clyde and arrived there on 16 November to discharge and spend three weeks under repair. This work must have revealed the necessity for more extensive work as *Aorangi* was then sent to the Mersey for drydocking and a major overhaul of her four 6 cylinder Sulzer diesels which the Fairfield company had built eighteen years earlier. The work lasted four months and *Aorangi's* next voyage was in WS 29 which began in April 1943. Of the four storeships which proceeded to Suez, the Dutch *Bantam* when discharged was taken over for the Stoneage convoy run from Alexandria to Malta in November.

Samaria loaded on the Clan Line berth at Durban and Capetown and also embarked a mixture of homeward personnel to join convoy CF 7, the final ship being *Volendam* which had disembarked 2,181 personnel in Mombasa and a further 575 in Diego Suarez. The Dutch liner then loaded in Durban and Capetown on the Clan berth and also embarked 114 mixed category personnel for the UK and three for West Africa, leaving Capetown independently on 4 October for Freetown where she arrived on the 28th to embark a further 504 and was then held for a week to await the arrival of the three liners of CF 7 which turned up with an escorting warship on 2nd November and thirteen days after leaving Capetown. The tragic loss of six valuable homeward liners on the North and South Atlantic during the seven week period up to the end of October seems to have prompted the Admiralty to insist on such liners being escorted when carrying numbers of personnel.

The four liners left Freetown under escort on 4 November and reached Liverpool on the 17th to disembark. All were quickly turned around to join the third "follow-up" convoy to North Africa ten days later. There was now a clear air of optimism in the country: Alamein had been won and Eighth Army was advancing across Libya, the Allies secured the ports in French North Africa and were moving into Tunisia, the Germans began their last major attack on Stalingrad while in the Pacific, control of the seas around Guadalcanal passed to the Americans. Only in Burma, British and Indian forces were thwarted in their advance into the Arakan by abnormal weather.

Chapter 17

Departures in August, September & October 1942 - WS 22, 23, and 24

The last complete formation, 56 (London) Division, moves to Iraq,
increasing Troopship losses in the South Atlantic and WS 24 refuels in Brazil.

WS 22 - sailed UK 28 August 1942

This convoy was the last of the series to move a complete division around the Cape and
was also the last of four to embark in excess of 50,000 personnel. There was now a
gradual change in the order of destination as only one of the liners in WS 22 actually
proceeded to Suez and coincidentally arrived there on the eve of the decisive Battle of
Alamein. The later success of Eighth Army in the desert campaign and of the Russians
at Stalingrad served to complement the Torch landings in North Africa, which in turn
allowed a gradual increase of the forces serving in India and Burma where the Japanese
continued to pose a major threat.

By the end of July there were thirteen WS type liners in the UK identified as being
available for the August WS 22 convoy, of which *Nea Hellas* in Glasgow and *Sibajak*

in Liverpool had been in the hands of repairers since the end of June, the former to make good collision damage suffered in WS 16 and *Sibajak* from the same convoy for dry-docking and extensive repairs to her twin Sulzer machinery. Also in Glasgow the Dutch KPM liners, *Ruys* and *Boissievain*, were being defensively armed and fitted out for 2,400 troops while Avonmouth was handling the discharge and repair of three Royal Mail Highland liners; Liverpool similarly handled *Nieuw Holland*, *Rangitata*, *Mataroa*, *Johan van Oldenbarnevelt* and *Dominion Monarch* while *Almanzora* was under repair in Glasgow. Four later arrivals in Liverpool were *Franconia* from WS 17 on 5 August, *Orduna* from WS 18 on the 10th while *Andes* and *Orcades* returned on the 17th from WS 19P carrying Canadian troops from Halifax, which allowed them barely a week to disembark, clean ship, re-store and prepare for the next embarkation. The capacity of WS 22 as estimated back in March was to be 45,000 but the number of berths finally provided was almost 51,000 which included 750 on the British and Irish Channel liner *Leinster* bound for Gibraltar.

The Dutch liner *Sibajak* had previously been intended for WS 21 but was held back for a special sailing to Gibraltar with RAF personnel who were displacing there a like number of army being moved around the Cape to India or the Middle East. *Sibajak* left the Clyde eight days ahead of the convoy and from Gibraltar continued to Freetown arriving there on 3 September to await and join WS 22. The liner selected to replace *Sibajak* was the Anchor Line's *California*, a near-sister of *Nea Hellas* (ex *Tuscania*), which completed conversion from an AMC at Southampton on 12 August under command of her pre-war Master, Captain Robert W Smart of Aberdeen, who was supported by Captain FM Henderson as Staff Captain and provided accommodation for 4,167 personnel which, when added to that of the KPM liners now increased the capacity of the WS fleet by almost 9,000.

The movement of 56 (London) Division overseas for the northern front in Iraq was first identified on 12 July[1] and four weeks later was listed under "reinforcements in sight for the Middle East."[2] This division was a first line Territorial formation composed entirely of those units and had first formed up in September 1939 as 1st London Division. It served solely in the UK and by November 1941 was stationed in Suffolk where orders were received to mobilize for overseas, tropical kit was issued and embarkation leave granted. Early in August the division was given the customary inspection by HM The King and between 21 and 23 August all units were entraining at Sudbury or Bury St Edmunds for their embarkation ports; those of 167 and 168 Brigades mostly to Gourock and 169 Brigade to Liverpool.

The embarkation of personnel at Liverpool began on *Dominion Monarch* (taking 7 Bn South Lancs Regiment to India for internal security duties) and three other liners on the 24th, with 56 Division HQ (Major-General EG Miles) and 2/6 Bn Queens Royal Regiment on *Franconia*, 169 Brigade HQ (Brigadier LO Lynne) with 2/5 and 2/6 Bns Queens, 113 Field Regiment RA and 11 Casualty Clearing Section on *Johan van Oldenbarnevelt*, while 1 Bn London Irish Rifles (of 168 Brigade and Territorial equivalent of Royal Ulster Rifles) were on *Orduna*, which liner anchored in the Mersey on the 26th. *Dominion Monarch*, *Franconia* and *J V Oldenbarnevelt* sailed that same day and anchored in the Clyde next morning to help relieve congestion in the Mersey. The remaining embarkations in Liverpool which included 9 Bn Royal Fusiliers (of 167 Brigade) on *Nieuw Holland*, were completed on the morning of the 28th on *Orcades* and *Andes* when these three liners with *Orduna* and storeship *Suffolk* left the Mersey at midday under escort of the destroyer *Chesterfield*, and proceeded at 11 knots for rendezvous with the main Clyde section next morning. Captain EA Bridges of *Andes* acted as Commodore of the Liverpool section and became Vice Commodore when the complete convoy formed up.

At Avonmouth, *Highland Brigade* embarked and locked out on the 24th followed by *Highland Chieftain* next afternoon when both sailed for the Clyde arriving on the morning of the 27th. Five liners had to be repositioned to the Clyde Anchorage for embarkation, i.e. *Rangitata* which moved from Liverpool to berth in Glasgow for six days to complete repairs and storing before moving downriver to the anchorage on the 24th. *California* arrived at the anchorage from Southampton on the 14th, *Highland Princess* from Avonmouth on the 16th which was embarking for West African ports only, *Almanzora* which came downriver from Glasgow on the 21st and *Mataroa* from Liverpool on the 24th. The relatively small *Leinster*, which was employed trooping between the Clyde and Iceland for the past twelve months although idle on the Clyde since the end of July, berthed alongside the railway terminus at Princes Pier, Greenock and embarked the RAF contingent for Gibraltar between 26 and 28 August.

The majority of 56 Division personnel arrived by trains at Gourock railway pier and transferred by Clyde steamers to the liners at the anchorage, 167 Brigade HQ (Brigadier KC Davidson) with 1 London Scottish, 10 Royal Berkshires, 90 Field Regiment RA, 140 Field Ambulance RAMC, 50 Field Company RE and 514 Company RASC all on *California* where also the appointed Commodore, Vice-Admiral AC Strutt RNR was accommodated in a very crowded ship. The London Scottish battalion, who were affiliated to the Gordons, noted that "the ship's officers were mainly Scots (the crew mostly from Southampton where the Articles were opened) and determined to do their utmost for the wellbeing of all ranks in the long weeks that followed, played their part nobly - particularly Captain Smart, Chief Officer Stormont, Purser Willoughby and Chief Steward Dickson."[3]

The last embarkations were made in Glasgow on *Boissievain* at 1 KGV and *Nea Hellas* at No. 4 berth, both sailing downriver in the early afternoon of the 27th, while *Ruys*, the final liner to complete the convoy, unusually left her berth at 2 KGV at 0230 on the 28th, under a full moon, and cleared the channel off Greenock at 0415 to begin compass adjustment, degaussing and engine adjustments in time to sail with the convoy that evening.[4] A single storeship from Glasgow was the brand new, first of class motor cargo ship *Canara* built by Barclay Curle for the BI company which completed trials on the 14th, loaded on the south side of Princes Dock and moved downriver in the early afternoon of the 28th to complete the Clyde section now comprising thirteen transports plus *Leinster* and *Canara*.

Although the preponderance of embarkations on WS convoys appeared to be in Liverpool, the total handled there by August 1942 was exceeded by that of the whole Clyde area which thereafter increased dramatically as the *Queens* and other "Monster" liners began operating a shuttle service between New York and the Clyde and continued until the cessation of European hostilities in May 1945.

Clyde Pilots were ordered and began boarding the ships spread around the anchorage at 1700 on the 28th, frequently a difficult task in an area which berthed 130 merchant and 45 naval vessels. The ships then began to get underway and *California* with the Commodore led the Clyde section out of the boom en route to sea at 1900 "in the failing light of a glorious summer day - it was the last look for some of their native shores for three years, and for some it was to be their last glimpse of that land![3] The guide ship was appropriately followed by *Nea Hellas*, whose Master, Captain JM Brown, was acting as Vice Commodore until junction with the Liverpool section. The remainder of the Clyde ships followed at four minute intervals until *Leinster* cleared the boom gate at 1956. Escort from the Clyde and also providing ocean cover to the South Atlantic was the cruiser *Aurora* (Captain HF Agnew) which had won fame in actions with Force K when based at Malta, the AMC *Carthage* fresh from a month long refit at the Tail of the Bank, and destroyers *Partridge* and *Quiberon*, the last named Australian manned. A speed of 11 knots was maintained overnight through the Firth of Clyde and North Channel.

A rendezvous was made as planned with the Liverpool section at 0600 29th in the usual position 6 miles west of Orsay, when a cruising order of seven columns was formed,[5] and with the addition of six destroyers from 'Derry an A/S screen of nine was provided and the convoy set off to the westward at the speed of 14 knots, the speed of the slowest ship *Orduna*, to give a speed of advance of 13 knots. Air escort was present in daylight hours until midday on the 30th.

Aboard *California* the London Scottish "settled down to the routine of life at sea where the lifejacket rather than the respirator became a constant companion, boat station drill was practiced by careful organization while the limitations of space consistent with the numbers on board meant that training (restricted to PT), lectures and discussions had all to be carefully arranged and staggered. A number of guards and fatigues had to be provided while the officers and NCOs supplemented the ship's own lookouts on anti-submarine watches. Both wet and dry canteen supplies were available and the food was invariably an improvement on the normal army diet. On the second and third days at sea rough weather claimed a number of victims from those in the crowded troop decks."[3]

No untoward incidents occurred until the evening of the 31st while steering SW towards the Azores, when the Polish destroyer *Blyskawica* reported abnormal fuel comsumption and was ordered back to base. At 2100 that same evening one of *Aurora's* best lookouts persistently reported a small object on the port bow horizon; an emergency turn to starboard was made but nothing more was seen and due to a misunderstanding this diversion was held until the morning of the 1st when another alteration to port was made to regain the route. Shortly after, at 0600, *Bulldog*, *Keppel* and *Zetland* were detached to return to base followed by *Bicester* at 1300 by which time the wind was NNE 7 on the port quarter and as the forecast was uncertain, the SOE on *Aurora* detached *Partridge* and *Quiberon* ahead for Ponta Delgada to refuel and rejoin on completion.

"On reaching warmer climes, battledress gave way to khaki drill and sun helmets, while off-duty, dress became as varied as it was scanty and the decks became crowded with sun-bathers throughout daylight hours. At night in the heat of the tropics the lack of adequate ventilation under enforced blackout conditions made life extremely difficult and many slept on deck."[3]

By the afternoon of the 2nd the convoy reached a position 240 miles NE of Sao Miguel in the Azores, where the destroyers *Laforey* and *Lookout* joined from Gibraltar and detached with *Leinster* for that port. Arriving there on the 5th, *Leinster* disembarked the RAF and re-embarked 7 Bn King's Own of 2 Gibraltar Brigade and returned with them to the Clyde on the 13th, remaining then in the Loch Long anchorage until sailing in the Torch assault convoy on 25 October.

From two signals received by *Aurora* on the 2nd, it seemed probable the convoy had been twice reported and therefore steered evasively after dark. The convoy was then approaching the eastern side of the Azores and although no U-Boats were subsequently reported in the area, these signals may have emanated from a U-cruiser acting as a refuelling stop for U-Boats on passage to and from their patrol areas.

After passing 130 miles east of Sao Miguel, *Partridge* and *Quiberon* rejoined from Ponta Delgada at 0930 on the 3rd, which allowed *Beverley* and *Chesterfield* to detach there for fuel and did not rejoin. By the early evening of the 5th the convoy was 400 miles SW of the Canaries when smoke was sighted to the SSW, *Aurora* went off to investigate and at 1930 came up with and identified the Spanish steamer *Indauchu*, probably bound for Brazil, and rejoined at dusk. By the afternoon of the 6th in a position 240 miles NE of the Cape Verde islands, the destroyer *Antelope* joined from Freetown as additional A/S escort. The convoy was now 50 miles ahead of its plotted position which required *Aurora* to break W/T silence and report accordingly. By 1300 on the 7th, the Cape Verde island of San Tiago, the largest and most populous of the group, was passed at a distance of 120 miles where the Greek ex Hunt class destroyer *Pintos* joined the A/S screen. There were no further incidents on this passage, *Aurora* passed inside the Freetown Boom at 1230 on the 9th and all ships were anchored in the harbour shortly afterwards. The Commodore noted that the station keeping and convoy discipline of all ships was excellent although *Orduna* and *Almanzora* (both 28 years old) frequently made excessive smoke while the new *Canara* broke down twice for short periods.

In reviewing the passage of this convoy in the third year of war it is worth noting the scale of armament on the liners of WS 22. Each were fitted aft with either a 4-inch, 4.7 or 6-inch gun; all had at least one high angle gun, some had two while the largest ships had three. Every ship had a number of machine-guns, most having ten although three had twelve while *Andes* and *Nieuw Holland* had fourteen.

The convoy remained in the hot and sticky conditions of Freetown for four days fuelling and watering, and in contrast to WS 16 when nineteen liners shipped almost 25,000 tons of fuel, only seven ships of WS 22 lifted 6,245 tons while fourteen took 9,745 tons of fresh water. The sharp reduction in bunkering was to comply with an instruction from the DoST "that bunker oil liftings at Freetown be reduced to the absolute minimum until further notice"[6] and was doubtless due to the increased sinkings of tankers supplying Freetown from the Caribbean.

The Queen's Royal Regiment historian on *J.V.Oldenbarnevelt* noted "the harbour contained over a hundred ships, no troops were allowed ashore and time was spent watching the fuel and water tenders and the bumboats selling fruit. Rain fell steadily and it was very hot, so everyone was glad to sail again."[7] It was at Freetown that *Sibajak* joined the convoy and while some personnel disembarked from *Highland Princess*, 112 others embarked on *Rangitata* and three other liners and during all this activity, Commodore Strutt made an arrangement with Captain Smart to entertain Captain Agnew and his officers to dinner aboard *California*; this hospitality being returned next day.

WS 22 sailed from Freetown with the Commodore on *California* passing the fleet repair ship *Vindictive* at 0645 on 13 September, followed at four minute intervals with *Highland Princess* being last at 0801. Pilots were not employed leaving Freetown, there being no difficulty in leaving the harbour with the fairway buoy immediately beyond the boom which also marked the inner end of the 10 mile searched channel running due west from Cape Sierra Leone Light. The ships proceeded through this channel two columns abreast and thereafter formed into seven columns but with the convoy completely reorganized.[8] *Aurora*, *Partridge* and *Quiberon* continued as ocean escorts, the

AMC *Alcantara* now replaced *Carthage* while four other destroyers provided additional A/S cover, *Antelope* and *Boreas* from the local escort force and the Hunt class *Derwent* and *Pindos*, the former having taken part in the recent Pedestal convoy to Malta and now proceeding around the Cape to join the Mediterranean Fleet in Alexandria.

Late in the evening after departure a signal was received from FOWA ordering an alteration of the route to close up the African coast and steer into the Gulf of Guinea, before turning south for the Cape and this was complied with by 0100 next morning. It transpired that six ships had been torpedoed and sunk to the south and east of Freetown in the two weeks prior to the departure of the convoy; the most recent being the Swedish ship *Lima* early on the 13th close to the intended route, which necessitated the change to pass 100 miles SE of Cape Palmas.

At 1410 on the 14th, a lifeboat under sail was sighted, *Antelope* went to investigate and recovered 28 survivors from the *Lima* torpedoed 38 hours earlier. This boat had sailed 105 miles in the interval, half the distance towards the African coast and was fortunate to have begun its journey under the influence of the favourable Guinea Current rather than the Equatorial variety which carried so many ships" boats into the open ocean. Four U-Boats were responsible for the recent sinkings, two being from the Eisbar group en route to the Cape and one of the ships lost was *Ocean Might* bound for the Middle East with a full military cargo which included vehicles intended for 56 Division.

The troops on *California* were certainly made aware of the submarine alarms but the Entertainment Committee diverted attention with a full programme of concerts and sing-songs to occupy the leisure hours, while the "Pipes and Drums of the London Scottish alternated with the Drum and Fife Band of the Royal Berkshires playing 'Retreat', and never failed to attract large audiences."[3]

By 1800 on the 15th the convoy was 300 miles SE of Takoradi where *Highland Princess* was detached with *Boreas* for that port while *Antelope* detached back to Freetown. The *Highland* liner reached Takoradi on the afternoon of the 16th, disembarked there and at Lagos where other service personnel were embarked for return to Freetown, whence she sailed on the 28th for the Plate, loading refrigerated meat on her owners" berth at Buenos Aires and Montevideo before proceeding via Belfast Lough to reach Avonmouth on 20 November and was next employed on WS 25.

On the morning of the 16th the convoy altered course to the SE in following the Bight of Africa and at 1800 *Alcantara*, whose aircraft had provided dawn and dusk A/S patrols ahead of the convoy, detached with *Derwent* and *Pindos* to fuel at Pointe Noire and rejoined 48 hours later in a position 340 miles WSW of that port. The Commodore at this point formed the convoy into two columns and ordered ships to conduct AA practice firing on smoke bursts from the destroyers. At 1800 on the 19th *Aurora*, *Partridge* and *Quiberon* passed down the lines being cheered by the troops and detached to Pointe Noire for fuel and subsequently returned to Freetown before taking part in the Torch assault on North Africa.

Cooler weather south of the Equator brought sports events to the programme while training continued with the emphasis on desert warfare. Khaki drill shorts gave way to battledress blouses and with the approach to the Cape all ranks busied themselves with letters and airgraphs which kept the Security Staff hard at work on censorship tasks.

There were no other incidents on the passage south until 0645 on the 24th when the convoy reached a position 160 miles NW of Cape Columbine, the usual peacetime landfall on the trade route to Capetown, where the cruiser *Shropshire* was met and detached with the Durban portion comprising *Orcades* with Captain Fox acting as Commodore, *Rangitata, Sibajak, Boissievain, Mataroa, Suffolk* and the two *Highland* liners. A cruising order of three columns was formed, no incidents occurred on the passage around the Cape until the early morning of the 28th when the convoy reversed course for seven hours to suit a morning arrival at Durban. *Shropshire* had signalled ahead giving an ETA in the late afternoon of the 28th but was advised in reply the convoy could not then be berthed due to congestion. The Durban searched channel was reached at 0245 on the 29th and the ships were berthed in the harbour that morning. Meanwhile the remaining eleven ships with the Commodore on *California* had arrived Capetown at 0900 on the 25th.

As always the morning arrival in the bright and colourful South African ports greatly impressed the troops and was graphically described by the regimental historians of 56 Division whose six liners docked in Capetown, especially the Ox & Bucks battalion on *Almanzora* "who rushed to the port side when Table Mountain was sighted even before Reveille...to see the sun just rising behind the mountain...topped with a few golden cirrus clouds."[9] The battalion was given shore leave that night amongst the brilliantly lit streets and buildings which surprised them all, while the SAWAS handed out free bus, train and cinema tickets and civilians provided car transport to just about anywhere including their own homes. As with all the troops who passed through Capetown, all units retained fond memories of the Del Monico Bar and Restaurant and the Mount Nelson Hotel. The next two days being a weekend were spent by all the troops enjoying surf bathing, visiting Table Mountain or driving around with new-found friends. On Monday morning all battalions disembarked for a route march and next morning the ships were being prepared for sea.

However, it was not beer and skittles for everyone. Until reaching Capetown, 56 Division units assumed their destination to be the Middle East, where attention was focused on the armies facing one another at Alamein. Now, it seemed, or so it was rumoured, 56 Division was proceeding to Iraq via Bombay. Vehicles of all types awaited their arrival in the Middle East delta base while others had been lost in the *Ocean Might*. There was no transport to spare in Iraq and so the War Ofice instructed the Impcon staff to disembark the driver parties numbering about 5,000 and sail them on an independent voyage of *Nieuw Amsterdam* to Suez, where they would collect the necessary divisional vehicles and drive them overland to Iraq. To fill some of the berths thus vacated, 1,409 priority personnel awaiting on-carriage from Durban were brought to Capetown on *Oronsay* returning home from WS 21P (*qv*). *Nieuw Amsterdam* completed boiler cleaning in Durban and reached Capetown on 1 October, embarked a total of 6,409 and left two days later for Suez where she arrived on the 17th five days ahead of *Orduna*, the only liner of the original convoy to proceed there.

The personnel of 56 Division on *Orduna* were now exchanged with non-divisional Middle East personnel from the other five liners, so that a General Hospital which included 80 QARANS and 1 Bn London Irish on *Orduna* transferred to *California*. The Impcon staff noted "there was hardly an hour of daylight on any of the four days while this convoy was in port that bodies of men were not marching from one ship to another or entraining or detraining from the transhipment camp."[10]

All of the liners at Capetown were now bound for Bombay, except *Orduna* for Suez and *Andes* with *Nea Hellas* which disembarked completely and loaded for return to the UK, the former on the Union Castle berth and sailed direct for Liverpool where she arrived on 19 October to be next employed for a single trip to Oran before transferring to North Atlantic service. *Nea Hellas* was short loaded in Capetown and left on the same day as the convoy, proceeding via Freetown to the Clyde and arrived on 29 October and was then engaged on four round trips to North Africa.

At Durban, only two of the liners were continuing with WS 22 while *Orcades*, *Sibajak*, *Mataroa* and the two *Highland* liners disembarked a total of 12,368 for on-carriage to Suez. With a mere two days in port, *Mataroa* and *Highland Brigade* left on 1 October, the former loading a small quantity of Union Castle cargo at Capetown before proceeding to complete in New York, where also US troops embarked for Belfast; *Mataroa* finally docked in Avonmouth to discharge on 27 November. *Highland Brigade* loaded to capacity in Capetown and also embarked homeward personnel, sufficient to merit inclusion in convoy CF 7 with *Antenor*, *Maloja* and *Samaria* (from WS 21), which sailed for Freetown on 20 October and allowed the *Highland* liner to begin discharge at Avonmouth on 18 November and was next employed with *Mataroa* in WS 25.

Highland Chieftain and *Sibajak* left Durban on 2 October, the former proceeding to Capetown to load stores, equipment and mail for the recently established army base on the Falklands, where she arrived on the 17th to spend fifteen days laboriously discharging at Port Stanley, before continuing to the Plate to load meat on her owners' berth and returning direct to Liverpool on 10 December for discharge and drydocking. *Sibajak* loaded on the Harrison berth at Port Elizabeth and Capetown, being delayed there over four weeks for Sulzer machinery repairs, and then sailed direct for the Clyde but was diverted to Liverpool and arrived on 16 December. Both these liners were next employed on WS 26.

Orcades was the last of the disembarked liners to leave Durban behind the convoy itself on 3 October and proceeded to Capetown, loading there 3,000 tons of general on the Union Castle berth and after embarking 712 mixed passengers for the UK, sailed on the afternoon of 9 October bound for Liverpool direct. Unfortunately the four U-Boats of the Eisbar group directed to attack shipping in the Capetown approaches, had arrived in the area three days earlier and had by then sunk eleven ships to the south and west of the port. *Orcades* was first routed evasively to the SW in an attempt to avoid these dangers but soon ran into the view of *U 172* at dawn next morning. The U-Boat had great difficulty getting into a firing position, losing sight of the liner in more than one rain squall but obtained two hits in the late forenoon, followed by a third torpedo which brought the ship to rest. The boats were lowered, one capsizing in the rough sea prevailing which drowned all the occupants but the remainder got away while Captain Fox and 51 volunteers remained aboard to try and save the ship. *Orcades* was got underway and began to proceed slowly towards Capetown, distant 210 miles ENE, and had covered about 15 miles when struck again by three more torpedoes and had to be abandoned, just before she sank at 1400; Captain Fox being the last to leave and having to swim for it. The distress messages from *Orcades* had been received in Capetown and three destroyers were despatched to assist, which might conceivably have provided A/S escort and prevented this loss. The survivors numbering 1,021 including 694 passengers, some being women and children, were picked up by the Polish steamer *Narwick* that afternoon and taken back to Capetown.

The loss of this fine modern liner so close to the Cape and within 24 hours of *Oronsay* and *Duchess of Atholl* being sunk further north and of *Laconia* a month earlier, all homeward from the Cape, was a major blow to those involved in the operation of British troopships and naturally suggested a leak in security arrangements although this may not have been the case. South African harbours were in the public domain and shipping movements widely discussed in peacetime as many of the ships and their crews were well known to the local population and could hardly be suppressed in wartime. On his eventual return home, as a survivor, Captain Fox had a spell of home leave before making several voyages on *Orion* lasting into 1944 and became her regular Master in 1945. He was awarded the CBE and Lloyds War Medal in 1943.

Of the personnel disembarked in Durban, 2,527 plus 3,832 remaining from WS 21 were now embarked on the only Indian Ocean troopships then available, the ex-French but Bibby managed *Felix Roussel* and BI *Ekma* which had arrived from Fremantle and the Dutch *Indrapoera* from Mombasa. These liners all for Suez together with *Boissievain* for Bombay and *Rangitata* for Mombasa and Diego Suarez now comprised the Durban section of the convoy, the storeship *Suffolk* having proceeded independently to Diego Suarez and was later to feature in the December convoy to Malta.

The Capetown portion was made up of *Orduna* for Suez, the 56 Division transports *California*, *J.V. Oldenbarnevelt*, *Almanzora*, *Franconia* and *Nieuw Holland*, together with *Dominion Monarch* and *Ruys* all for Bombay, plus storeship *Canara* for Karachi, and sailed at midday on 29 September under escort of the AMCs *Ranchi* and *Alcantara* to form into a cruising order of four columns with one of the AMCs on either bow. There were no incidents passing around the Cape, apart from two days of rough blustery weather which helped to dampen the spirits of the 56 Division personnel having left behind such splendid hospitality and now being sent to the backwater of Iraq rather than the action front of Egypt. About midday on the 3rd at the end of the Durban searched channel, *Alcantara* detached and proceeded into that port on being relieved by the cruiser *Devonshire* which became SOE after bringing out the Durban section. The combined convoy of fourteen ships now formed a cruising order of four columns and proceeded at 14 knots to give a speed of advance of 12.5 knots.[11]

As with the previous convoy, WS 22 proceeded south and east of Madagascar and then passed between Cape Amber at its northern tip and the Farquhar islands and by 1030 on the 10th, was 160 miles north of that Cape where rendezvous was made with the cruiser *Hawkins* from Mombasa, which then became SOE. *Devonshire* then detached with *Almanzora* and *Rangitata* for that port where they arrived on the morning of the 13th, the former to fuel and water having insufficient to reach Bombay, and *Rangitata* to part disembark before moving on to complete at Diego Suarez. *Almanzora* sailed again on the same day under escort for Bombay and arrived there on the 21st four days behind the main convoy.

At 0800 on the 11th the convoy was 320 miles west of Mahe in the Seychelles where it split into two, *Ranchi* continuing ahead with *Orduna* and the three Indian Ocean liners for Aden and Suez, while the main convoy of eight transports, *Canara* and *Hawkins*, altered course NE direct for Bombay. A number of ships were met and identified while crossing the northern Indian Ocean in fine weather, while AA firing practice was carried out on one occasion at a target provided by *Hawkins*. *Canara* was detached at 1930 on the 15th to proceed independently to Karachi and the convoy arrived in Bombay at 0800 17th when *Hawkins* as SOE berthed in the Alexandra Dock with a single comment that *Franconia* made smoke throughout the voyage.[12]

The Aden section obtained daylight air cover from the 14th onwards, when also the Hunt class destroyers *Beaufort* and *Tetcott* joined as A/S escorts until reaching Aden on the 16th where the convoy was dispersed. All four liners refuelled in Aden, *Felix*

Roussel and *Indrapoera* continuing that same day for Suez where they were disembarked by the 23rd. The former then proceeded to Basra to embark Polish troops for Durban while *Indrapoera* carried 327 civilians from Suez to Massawa and 834 mixed personnel from Aden to Durban where she remained for ten weeks undergoing extensive engine repairs to her Sulzer machinery. The Dutch liner then embarked 400 Italian PoW, loaded there and at Capetown on the Union Castle berth and left that port on 27 January 1943 in convoy CF 11 for Freetown and Liverpool, arriving on 27 February and was thereafter employed on the KMF route to North Africa.

From Aden, *Ekma* and *Orduna* followed a day behind the other two liners up the Red Sea and were disembarked at Suez by the 24th, *Ekma* then working her way back to Durban via many ports while *Orduna* carried civilians to Berbera, refuelled in Aden, then moved East African troops to Diego Suarez and South Africans from Tamatave to Durban, by which time Eighth Army was advancing on Tripoli. *Orduna* then loaded in Durban and Capetown on the Union Castle berth, leaving the latter on 29 November and proceding via Freetown to Gibraltar where she joined the homeward MKF 5 convoy from Algiers to reach the Clyde Anchorage for discharge on the last day of 1942 and was next employed on WS 26.

The return voyage of *Rangitata* began from Diego Suarez on 26 October, when a troop detachment was carried to Mauritius to replace a Royal Engineer Fortress Company which had been disbanded, and was the sole visit of a WS ship to the island. *Rangitata* then proceeded direct to the Plate, loading at La Plata and Buenos Aires then sailing via Trinidad to embark US troops in New York, crossing in HX 222 to Belfast where she arrived on 21 January and subsequently discharged in Avomouth before next employment on a North African trip.

The eight liners of WS 22 which reached Bombay in the fine weather season was the largest both in number of ships and personnel carried since WS 18 arrived with the onset of the SW monsoon in June. Almost 25,000 were now to be disembarked of which half were those of 56 Division being transhipped to smaller Indian Ocean liners for on-carriage to Basra at the head of the Persian Gulf, the actual destination only now being confirmed to the troops although the battalion COs had been informed at Capetown.

As always the berthing and disembarkation of so many liners at Bombay was a protracted affair, restricted by suitable berths and exacerbated by the need to tranship the maximum number directly to the smaller ships and entrain the balance to transit camps up country. *California* after waiting in the stream for five days then berthed at Ballard Pier to allow the troops two days shore leave, and then berthed within Alexandra Dock where on the 25th, the London Irish battalion marched around the dock with all their kit to re-embark on the Dutch KPM *Melchior Treub*, while the HQ 168 Brigade, the London Scottish, 10 Royal Berks and 93 General Hospital similarly transferred to the BI *Neuralia*, where Lt. Col. Ian Baird of the Royal Berks was appointed O.C. Troops. From *Almanzora* the HQ 167 Brigade and 7 Bn Ox & Bucks transhipped to the BI *Santhia*, while 169 Brigade HQ and 2/7 Queens moved to *Nieuw Holland* which was allocated to assist the movement and finally 8 Royal Fusiliers and other units boarded the BI *Ellenga* and ex French but Ellerman managed *Cap St Jacques*. These six ships left Bombay on 26 October carrying the first 8,600 personnel and arrived at the mouth of the Shatt of Arab on 2 November and thereafter moved upriver in stages the 88 miles to disembark alongside at Basra where disembarkation began on the 5th. From Basra all six battalions moved by train 335 miles to Baghdad, where they changed stations to a narrower gauge railway for the final 265 miles to Kirkuk amongst the oilfields in northern Iraq, a defensive situation re-created by US troops 61 years later.

The remaining three battalions and other units of 56 Division were disembarked at Ballard Pier from *J.V. Oldenbarnevelt, Franconia* and *Nieuw Holland* and moved by train 100 miles inland to Deolali Transit Camp to await the assembly of more shipping. They returned to Bombay on the 23rd where embarked with 113 Field Regiment RA on the BI liners *Rajula, Rohna* and *Erinpura*, and Bibby's *Lancashire*, which sailed in convoy on 3 November and reached Basra from the 9th onwards. A final batch of 3,300 was carried from Bombay on the 16th by *Devonshire* and *Ellenga*, these units joining the Division at Kirkuk in the last week of November having been fourteen weeks in transit since leaving Suffolk.

56 Division remained in Kirkuk until March 1943 when relieved by Polish troops and then travelled overland a distance of 3,300 miles in 31 days to reach Enfidaville in Tunisia where they saw action in the last few weeks of the fighting there. Thereafter they took part in the landings at Salerno and Anzio and in the Gothic Line battles in June 1944 suffered 6,000 casualties before ending the war near Venice.

Both Freetown and Bombay lie on the western coasts of large continents in the northern tropical zone and have a similarity in climate although Freetown suffers from a higher humidity, but the troops now landed found conditions in India very hot and sticky after the relative comfort of cooler sea breezes. Those not with 56 Division were soon dispersed to reinforce units in NE India where 14 Indian Division, which included 10 Lancashire Fusiliers from WS 14 (qv) began to move south for the first Arakan offensive after being immobilized from movement during the monsoon.

The first liner to clear Bombay for the return voyage to the UK was the refrigerated *Dominion Monarch* which left on 24 October for Fremantle and Sydney before loading on her owners' berth at Auckland in eleven days, proceeding then via Panama to begin discharge in Liverpool on 28 December and was next employed on WS 26. The Dutch *Ruys* left Bombay on the 26th with 82 Army and 249 RAF for Karachi, and there embarked 754 Polish refugees for East Africa, landing them at Tanga and thereafter loading at Durban and Capetown, leaving there on 23 November with passengers in convoy CF 8 with *Franconia* and escorted by *Alcantara* to Freetown, the Clyde and Glasgow where she docked on 15 December and next sailed in WS 26.

On 26 October *Boissievain* and *J.V. Oldenbarnevelt* left Bombay with small amounts of general cargo, the former picking up another 1,000 tons in Capetown and then sailed direct for the Clyde arriving on 8 December to be transferred thereafter to the KMF route. The '*Oldenbarnevelt* had embarked 326 passengers for the UK but had to disembark them at Durban as fifteen days were spent there on machinery repairs and a further four weeks in Capetown before embarking mixed personnel and sailing on 19 December in CF 10 with *Almanzora*. After Freetown this convoy was directed to Gibraltar where on 7 January junction was made with MKF 6 and the Clyde reached on the 15th whence this liner also transferred to the KMF route.

The last three liners to clear Bombay were *California, Franconia* and *Almanzora* on 29 October, the former having loaded on her owners' familiar berth in Alexandra Dock then embarking Polish refugees in Karachi which were landed in Mombasa on 9 November. From there *California* proceeded for Durban and when 180 miles east of that port on the morning of the 15th, by which date three U-Boats of the Eisbar group were operating in these waters, she was sighted and pursued on the surface by *U-177* but having also observed the U-Boat, Captain Smart asked the engineers for maximum speed which prevented the U-Boat closing the distance for an attacking position and finally abandoned the chase after five hours. *California* berthed in Durban next morning and loaded there and in Capetown, leaving on the 26th for Freetown and the Clyde where she arrived on 20 December and was next employed in WS 26.

Franconia also loaded on the Anchor Line berth in Bombay and completed in Durban and Capetown, sailing thence with *Ruys* (above) to reach Liverpool on 16 December and then transferred to the KMF route. *Almanzora* loaded on the Clan berth in Bombay, Mombasa and Durban but then had to spend 24 days on rudder repairs at Port Elizabeth before joining CF 10 (above) at Capetown and reached the Clyde 14 January and was next used on WS 27.

Despite having to continue to Basra, *Nieuw Holland* was by no means the last home. After disembarking 1,963 troops and baggage at the Iraqi port, the Dutch liner embarked 5 RN and 522 Polish evacuees with 2 QARANS and sailed on 1 November for Tanga, where the Poles were landed. Cargo was loaded there and at Durban and Capetown whence the homeward passage via Freetown was completed at Liverpool on 18 December and thereafter the liner proceeded to Falmouth for five weeks repairs before next sailing in KMF 10 to North Africa.

Of the eighteen liners which left the UK at the end of August in WS 22, exactly half completed the round voyage in 3.5 months, while the two which turned round at Capetown did so within eight weeks and three of the refrigerated meat carriers were home within three months. Machinery repairs to three others delayed their return to five months and was the inevitable result of almost constant steaming, the shortage of spares, materials and skilled labour.

WS 23 - sailed Liverpool 30 September 1942

As the summer of 1942 turned to autumn the WS fleet then comprised ninety-six liners including two commissioned transports of which two-thirds at any one time were engaged on WS voyages or returning from them. A further seven were retained to supplement services in the Indian Ocean area (two involved in Madagascar movements) while the remainder were in UK ports discharging, repairing, converting, fitting or otherwise being held for WS 23 or the forthcoming Torch expedition to North Africa. All the transports for this major operation were to depart from the Clyde, beginning on 26 October, the first three convoys absorbing more than half the WS fleet. In addition to this major effort to prepare the great Torch convoys, each of the existing frontline areas in the Middle East, Burma and Persia/Iraq required a steady flow of reinforcements to keep pace with casualties and so demanded the monthly cycle of WS convoys to be maintained. The August convoy was certainly the last of the large formations in that series and WS 23 was the first of those on a much reduced scale as more emphasis was placed on the establishment of the British and American armies in North Africa.

Whilst there had never been a quiet period at the Clyde Anchorages since the outbreak of war, the amount of shipping berthing there by September 1942 had clearly reached the point that previously considered overflow anchorages, rejected as being too remote, would now have to be brought into use. The Tail of the Bank area offered the best holding ground but was widely used by all classes of warships for repairs, the battlecruiser *Renown* of the Home Fleet being present for ten days in September, two of the US lease-lend escort-carriers were undergoing major modifications, the AMC *Queen of Bermuda* spent the whole month under refit while new warships were constantly using the area as a trials base. To add to the pressure on space and attendant services, the Cunard *Queens* began in August to bring 15,000 US troops per trip to the anchorage to be landed by tenders and entrained to destinations in the south of England. In the Merchant Ships' anchorages, many of the liners and storeships for the Torch convoys began to assemble there to increase congestion from the middle of September.

Doubtless due to the berthing situation on the Clyde, all the ships for WS 23 were embarked and loaded entirely in Liverpool, where *Highland Monarch* and *Capetown Castle* had been berthed since mid August, *Empress of Russia* arrived on the 31st and *Moreton Bay* on 14 September, the CPS and Union Castle liners requiring drydocking in addition to voyage repairs. Four storeships were accompanying the transports each carrying tanks, guns, stores, MT and ammunition with three destined for the Middle East and one for Karachi and Basra. In addition those ships carried 16 Anson aircraft and two MFVs for South Africa and eight Hurricanes for Karachi.

Embarkation began on the four liners on the 25th and by the 27th, 9,779 were aboard with another eighteen on the storeships, while 1,918 personnel for West Africa embarked at the Tail of the Bank on the AMC *Queen of Bermuda* as her refit was hurriedly completed on the 30th to allow her departure as part of the ocean escort. All but 59 of the 4,018 personnel embarked on *Capetown Castle* were for India and included 12 Bn Sherwood Foresters (Lt.Col. RM Ingall) and 7 Bn Royal Leicesters (Lt.Col. PDS Palmer). Almost half the total embarked was for India and one-fifth each for West Africa, South Africa and the Middle East.[1]

Commodore OH Dawson RNR and his staff were accommodated on the Union Castle Company's flagship *Capetown Castle*, whose Master, Captain EH Thornton and himself a Commander RNR, held command of that liner from January 1939 until July 1946 and was knighted for his war service in 1944. *Capetown Castle* was fully embarked by the 28th when she anchored in the Mersey, the remaining three liners completed and were ready for sea by the morning of the 30th, as were the storeships *Port Jackson*, *Kina II* (ex Danish under United Baltic management) and Dutch KPM *Straat Malacca*. The Silver Line's *Silversandal* for Karachi was delayed due to engine defects but was able to join later and with *Empress of Russia* were the two slowest ships of the convoy at 14 knots. Captain JB Smith of the latter ship was acting as Vice Commodore of the convoy.

Capetown Castle led the seven ships out of the Mersey, passing the Rock Light at 1400 on 30 September and was followed at five minute intervals in the order *Kina II*, *Highland Monarch*, *Empress of Russia*, *Port Jackson*, *Moreton Bay* and *Straat Malacca*, the convoy proceeding under escort to meet the ocean escort of *Queen of Bermuda* from the Clyde and aged cruisers *Durban* and *Despatch* from work-up at Scapa. *Durban* had recently completed five months of repairs in New York and Portsmouth; *Despatch* was in refit at Chatham and the Tyne since May and was now assigned to West Africa command. A late inclusion in the convoy was the NZS liner *Rimutaka* on a commercial freight voyage to Australasia which was also carrying passengers for South Africa and the Antipodes. On arrival of the convoy at the forming up point off Orsay at 0630 on 1st October, "it was directed to return to Belfast Lough"[2] where it arrived and anchored shortly after midday.

The reason for this about-turn and subsequent delay of three days at anchor was not revealed amongst the convoy records. However, a later signal sent by the DoST to Freetown and Capetown[3] soon after the final departure showed that all ships unusually left the UK with sufficient bunkers to reach the Cape, other than *Empress of Russia* which required 3,000 tons of coal, and two liners in need of fresh water at Freetown. It seems that the crippling loss of 216 tankers in the Caribbean and western Atlantic in the first six months of 1942 was now affecting fuel supplies at Freetown, but for WS 23 would be offset by topping up to capacity on all ships whilst anchored in Belfast Lough. The DoST fresh water calculation was based on 36 days consumption of 5 gallons per head per day, the passage to Durban being estimated at 32 days including a four day stopover in Freetown.

The eight ships of WS 23 were joined in Belfast Lough by *Silversandal* and sailed at 1645 on 4 October to rendezvous with the A/S escort off Orsay that night, where strong headwinds and a short steep sea were encountered which came aboard *Straat Malacca* and smashed one of the crated Anson aircraft on her foredeck. The destroyer screen which had come out from Moville comprised *Beagle* (SO), *Wrestler*, with Hunt class *Bicester*, *Zetland*, *Puckeridge* and Greek *Kanaris* (ex *Hatherleigh*) but later that afternoon the Asdic of *Wrestler* broke down to leave an effective screen of five. The cruising order of four columns was formed and a WNW course set to the first position at a speed of 13 knots[4]. The ocean escort may have been stationed between the convoy columns.

The initial route followed the usual pattern by steering out to the westward for 24 hours before turning SW for the next two days then south towards the eastern side of the Azores. A German R/T home station was heard by the escort on the morning of the 6th speaking to six other stations or ships, otherwise there were no incidents until the early evening of the 8th when *Beagle* left to return to the UK and *Bicester* took on the duties of SO A/S escort. At about this time with the convoy on the latitude of Finisterre and 300 miles north of the Azores, *Durban*, *Kanaris* and *Puckeridge* detached ahead to fuel at Ponta Delgada.

When 60 miles NE of Sao Miguel in the late afternoon of the 9th, *Durban* rejoined when *Despatch* left for Ponta Delgada and two hours later the two Hunt class destroyers rejoined from that port. In the early hours of the 10th, *Zetland* detached to return to the UK while *Bicester* and *Wrestler* detached back to Ponta Delgada and thereafter also returned to the UK which left the two remaining Hunts as A/S escort. *Despatch* rejoined that evening and no further incidents were reported until *Antelope* from Freetown joined in the morning of the 13th by which time the convoy was NE of the Cape Verde islands. *Velox* joined 24 hours later and next morning *Kanaris* and *Puckeridge* detached ahead for Freetown where the convoy arrived at 0800 on the 16th.

Neither the Foresters nor Leicesters on *Capetown Castle* made any reference to the call at Freetown which had by now become well known throughout military circles simply as a hot and sticky non-landing replenishment port. The Commodore commented that the four days spent there were dependent on the time taken to laboriously coal *Empress of Russia*.

The convoy sailed again from Freetown at 1740 on 20 October with the same nine ships and formed into the same cruising order but with the escort provided by *Durban* (SO), the AMC *Carthage* in lieu of *Queen of Bermuda* detached to South Atlantic patrols, the Hunt class *Avon Vale* and *Kanaris* and corvette *Tamarisk*. The route laid down passed 60 miles SW of Cape Palmas on the 22nd where a U-Boat had unsuccessfully attacked a coastal convoy ten days earlier, was depth-charged by the escort but escaped to join a consort for a reconnaissance of the area around the Congo.

On the 23rd while heading ESE into the Gulf of Guinea, the cruiser *Despatch* and sloop *Milford* caught up and joined the escort which allowed *Avon Vale* to detach, and on the morning of the 25th, when 200 miles WSW of the Portuguese island of Sao Tome, the corvette *Amaranthus* joined to relieve *Tamarisk*. Later that same day, with the convoy heading to close the coast near Pointe Noire in two days time (to facilitate fuelling of escorts), the Admiralty ordered a wide diversion of 70° on to a southerly heading "in consequence of a submarine reported off Pointe Noire."[2] In fact the cruiser *Phoebe* had been torpedoed there on the 23rd and suffered damage that required her being sent to the United States for repair. The two U-Boats otherwise found nothing else of interest and then moved to the Gulf of Guinea. *Amaranthus* was detached on the 26th and did not rejoin.

The convoy received a report on the 29th of having been sighted by a U-Boat but nothing transpired. Otherwise the remaining passage to the Cape was free of incident, the convoy having been missed by the U-Boats near the Congo and later by those of the Eisbar group off the Cape. The Admiralty warned of the southward movement of these latter boats on 21 September but was unable to have sufficient escorts in place before they arrived in the first week of October and by the end of that month had sunk 24 ships, although their U-supply cruiser had also been sunk.

On the 30th when 120 miles SW of Cape Frio at the northern edge of South West Africa, the A/S escort was considerably strengthened by the Australian manned destroyer *Norman* with corvettes *Rockrose* and *Thyme*, and next day *Despatch* and *Milford* were detached when 100 miles abreast of Walvis Bay. By this date two of the Eisbar U-Boats were in the South Atlantic making their way homewards while the remaining two were about to follow in completing operations to the south of Port Elizabeth.

At 0900 on 2 November the convoy reached the Cape coast in a position 28 miles west of Cape Columbine and later that day detached the AMC *Carthage* to Capetown. By 1700 the formation was passing close to Cape Point and began to prepare paravanes for crossing the Agulhas Bank which was now considered safe from the mines laid by *Doggerbank* eight months earlier.[5] By the early hours of the 3rd the convoy had rounded Cape Agulhas and next morning was 45 miles south of East London and steering up the Natal coast for Durban. At 0900 on the 5th WS 23 was 32 miles south of the Bluff and by 1330 all ships were berthed within the harbour where the troops had their first opportunity to stretch their legs since embarkation at Liverpool 41 days earlier.

The arrival of just four transports in a port which had witnessed the arrival of so many larger convoys, would create no great stir, but it coincided with the peak of negotiations for the capitulation of the Vichy French on Madagascar which had been dragging on ever since the first landings six months earlier. There was much speculation amongst the Leicester battalion of being sent to that island and was only dispelled when news of the complete and final surrender reached Durban on the 6th.

The transhipment programme in Durban was relatively simple as only *Moreton Bay* was completely disembarking her complement of 1,825, which included 810 for the Union, and when added to those transhipping from *Highland Monarch* and *Empress of Russia* meant that on-carriage was required for 643 destined for East Africa, 462 for India, 55 for Madagascar and 20 for the Middle East. There were in addition others waiting in Clairwood Transit Camp, but only one of the Indian Ocean transports was available to assist the movement for which the BI *Dilwara* reached Durban from Tamatave on 25 October and now began to embark personnel for Bombay. The balance of those awaiting on-carriage from Durban was carried forward in convoy CM 35 which left on 13 November comprising, *Sontay, Empire Woodlark* and *Empire Trooper* carrying 6,000 for Suez and *Dunera* with 2,000 for Mombasa and Bombay.

Moreton Bay left both the convoy and Durban on the 9th, proceeding direct to Buenos Aires and loaded a refrigerated meat cargo there and in Montevideo, from where she returned home via Trinidad, Guantanamo Bay in Cuba to join a convoy for New York where she embarked US troops. Crossing in the 41 ship convoy HX 223 to Belfast, *Moreton Bay* sustained deck damage due to heavy weather on this 19 day passage, disembarked in Belfast Lough and began discharge in Avonmouth on 2 February 1943, being next engaged for a trip to North Africa before reverting to the WS route. The NZS liner *Rimutaka* also left the convoy in Durban and proceeded independently to Melbourne and Wellington before returning via Panama to Avonmouth on 25 February.

During the convoy conference in Durban, Captain JB Smith of *Empress of Russia* stated his misgivings of having sufficient coal for the ensuing passage to Bombay without bunkering en route, if the convoy speed fell below 13.5 knots and therefore prolonged the voyage. The Commodore pointed out the distance, planned to go east of Madagascar, was actually the same as that from Freetown to Durban when the *Empress* had not encountered any problem of endurance, but in the event Captain Smith's estimate proved to be correct.[2]

The revised eight ship convoy sailed from Durban at 1400 on 9 November with the cruiser *Dauntless*, AMC *Carthage* and unspecified A/S escort vessels. Four columns were again formed, the Commodore remaining on *Capetown Castle* while Captain RH Robinson of *Highland Monarch*, who had served as Master since 1914 and was now on his last voyage before retiral, became Vice Commodore and would later act as Commodore of the Aden section after the convoy split.

U-Boats of the Eisbar group had been present and sinking ships in the Mozambique Channel up until the first week of November when they began to turn for home, but necessitated the convoy route going south and east of Madagascar. When two days out of Durban, *Dauntless* and the A/S vessels were relieved by the cruiser *Hawkins*, and by this time it was evident the speed of *Empress of Russia* was reduced by 2 knots to a maximum of 12.5 knots due to bad coal shipped at Durban. By the following night as the convoy rounded the SE tip of Madagascar and began to experience the adverse effect of the Equatorial Current, Captain Smith informed the Commodore he was anxious about the consumption of coal, reckoned as 240 tons per day, and believed he would have insufficient to reach Bombay and had always to retain 700 tons for stability purposes. The Commodore then consulted with the SOE on *Hawkins* and suggested shortening the route by half a day and making an allowance for fine weather as expected, and to consider water ballasting the *Empress*, but even at that Captain Smith said he could not reach Bombay.[2] Every effort was made to maintain a convoy speed of 13.5 knots, which was zigzagging continuously, by allowing the *Empress* to steer a steady course in the rear.

By the morning of the 16th the convoy was 100 miles north of Cape Amber, the northern tip of Madagascar, where *Hawkins* was relieved by *Mauritius* and allowed the former to detach with *Empress of Russia* for Mombasa and arrived there on the 18th. The convoy meanwhile altered to a N'ly course towards Guardafui and by next afternoon was 350 miles west of Mahe in the Seychelles, where at 1500 course was altered NE direct for Bombay while *Highland Monarch*, *Port Jackson*, *Kina II* and *Straat Malacca* detached with *Carthage* as escort for Aden, where they arrived on the 21st and were dispersed to continue independently to Suez.

The Commodore on *Capetown Castle* continued NE with *Dilwara*, *Silversandal* and the cruiser *Mauritius* towards Bombay and at 0600 on the 21st, in the middle of the Indian Ocean, met and were passed by *Mauretania* escorted by *Devonshire*, crossing from the Gulf of Aden to Colombo and carrying Australian troops homewards from the

Middle East. At this point the convoy altered to a NNE heading until midday on the 22nd when *Silversandal* was detached ahead and unescorted for Karachi and subsequently to Basra. The remaining two ships of the convoy altered course to ENE for the remaining 500 miles to Bombay and *Mauritius* streamed paravanes at 1600 next afternoon as the ships approached the 100 fathom line in the approaches to that port where all three ships arrived at 0830 on the 24th. During the passage from the north of Madagascar, aircraft from *Mauritius* carried out daylight A/S patrols on the first four days and again on the day prior to arrival at Bombay.

The two liners disembarked 6,200 personnel in Bombay including 32 for on-carriage to Australia and New Zealand, while the *Castle* liner also discharged a quantity of stores, guns and military vehicles before sailing on the 29th for Capetown to refuel, thence Halifax where Canadian troops and RAF were embarked for the UK. *Capetown Castle* reached Liverpool on 14 January for a six week period of engine overhaul, drydocking and extra fittings before sailing again in WS 27. *Dilwara* re-embarked in Bombay and sailed on 4 December for Basra while *Empress of Russia*, delayed after bunkering in Mombasa for repairs, only reached Bombay on the 6th.

The troops were soon dispersed with the Sherwood Foresters posted to Bhopal State where they were to become a jungle training battalion for the rest of the war. The 7 Bn Leicesters transferred to the smaller BI *Varsova* and sailed three days later for Karachi where they began training and conversion into two columns for Wingate's famous Chindits. They were flown into Burma in March 1944 and extricated five months later so decimated by disease, sickness and under-nourished that the battalion was disbanded, leaving 159 fit survivors transferred to the 2nd Bn of the same regiment which had also been engaged in Chindit operations.[7]

After disembarking all 2,000 personnel in Bombay, *Empress of Russia* was delayed for 18 days further repairs and after first being ordered to load at the Cape, then Bombay which changed again to New York, none of these were achieved when she proceeded first to Mombasa for bunkers, then in Durban embarked 500 Italian PoW for the UK. She finally left Capetown on 27 January and proceeded via Freetown to Gibraltar where the homeward slow convoy MKS 8 from North Africa was joined and reached the Clyde Anchorage on 2 March. After drydocking in the AFD at the Tail of the Bank, the *Empress* spent a further ten weeks under repair in Glasgow before making one trip each to North Africa, New York and a special PoW exchange voyage to Gothenburg. She then made seven round trips to Iceland before being assigned to Overlord and retained at Spithead for four months as a Depot Ship for tug crews. In October 1944 she was laid up unwanted in the Gareloch for seven months until sent to Barrow in June 1945 for an extensive refit, suitable for returning Canadian troops and families from Europe, but on 8 September was gutted by fire, declared a total loss and broken up where she lay, an ignominious end for a splendid liner which had given 32 years service to her owners and country in two world wars, but as a prodigious coal-burner to the end, really belonged to another age.

In reverting to the *Highland Monarch* at Aden, this liner left the next day for Suez where she arrived on the 26th to disembark and discharge military stores and her unusual outward cargo of seed potatoes. The *Monarch* then embarked the first batch of returning South African 1st Division troops, who were to be reorganized in the Union as 6 South African Armoured Division and return to Italy in the following spring. *Highland Monarch* left Suez on 12 December, refuelled in Aden and arrived in Durban to a tumultuous welcome on New Year"s Day 1943. A half-holiday was declared in the city as the troops landed and marched through the streets behind two bands, the atmosphere almost being like the end of the war.

At Durban, *Highland Monarch* embarked 100 German PoW and 50 RN escort for Canada, the first of five batches being carried on returning refrigerated ships proceeding first to New York from where the POW moved by train to their ultimate destinations.[8] The passage to New York began on 20 January and occupied thirty days; a mixed cargo was then loaded on the Furness berth, 772 US troops embarked and were landed in Belfast Lough on 17 March before the *Monarch* continued to Avonmouth to begin discharge and was next engaged in WS 29. It was here that Captain Robinson left the ship for retirement after a lifetime at sea with the Nelson Line and Royal Mail.

WS 24 - Sailed UK 29 October 1942

This convoy was planned and assembled in the shadow of the great Torch expedition to North Africa which involved nine separate convoys of personnel ships, storeships, LSTs, tugs, colliers etc., all being at sea between the UK and Azores/Gibraltar area during the last week of October, while two further follow-up personnel convoys sailed in the first two weeks of November. Altogther fifty of the WS fleet were then allocated to that operation leaving less than half on WS voyages or returning from them. In respect of escorts for the Torch convoys, "about 160 in all, could only be provided by removing a substantial part of the Home Fleet's strength, by stopping the Russian convoys, by reducing our Atlantic escort forces and by temporarily suspending the mercantile convoys running between Britain and the South Atlantic."[1] The last northbound convoy of the SL series left Freetown on 16 October while the last southbound one dispersed south of the Azores on the 9th and left the Freetown base bereft of escorts and clearly implied the need to replenish WS 24 elsewhere.

Despite the shortage and pressure for escorts, the WS series was to continue on a monthly cycle by sailing WS 24 at the end of October, the necessity being dictated by the need to maintain a steady flow of reinforcements to three frontline areas accessible only by the sea route around the Cape. Six liners not then required for the Torch operation were allocated for WS 24, principally Union Castle's *Athlone* and *Stirling Castle* which arrived in Liverpool from Halifax and WS 19 and 20 voyages on 7 October, and *Empress of Japan* which reached the Clyde Anchorage on the same date from WS 21P to Suez where she was officially and appropriately re-named *Empress of Scotland* three days later; the nameboards being fitted after berthing in Glasgow on the 17th. The other selected liners were of the "intermediate freezer" type best suited for homeward meat cargoes from the Plate and were all berthed in Avonmouth, where *Arawa* arrived on 21 September from WS 19P while *Tamaroa* and *Largs Bay* both from voyages in WS 21, arrived on the 9th and 14th October respectively. A single storeship allocated to this convoy was the ex-French motorship *Indochinois* dating from 1939 and having been built for the CGT was later taken over by the MOWT, placed in Canadian Pacific management and registered in Liverpool. *Andes* was to have been included in this convoy but having only reached Liverpool from WS 22 on 19 October, was then delayed by voyage repairs and extra fittings which were not completed until 12 November.

Embarkations began at Avonmouth on 26 October on *Arawa* and *Tamaroa* which locked out of the Royal Edward Dock at 0800 on the 27th and proceeded to Barry Roads for compass adjustment and Oerlikon gun trials, thereafter anchoring on completion. *Largs Bay* from Avonmouth and *Indochinois* from Newport locked out of these ports twelve hours later and joined the other two ships in Barry Roads. These four ships were underway again at 0100 on the 28th, Captain TV Roberts of *Arawa* acting as Commodore of this Bristol Channel portion which proceeded at 9 knots in single line ahead to the Helvig Light Vessel where speed was increased to 11.5 knots. Under escort of the destroyer *Skate,* these ships continued up the Irish Sea to join the rest of the convoy off Orsay on the morning of the 29th.

At Liverpool, embarkation on the two *Castle* liners began on the morning of the 27th while the Commodore, Rear Admiral AHC Candy RNR boarded *Stirling Castle* (Captain WD Roach). The Master of *Athlone Castle*, Captain A Alderson, was to act as Vice Commodore of this two ship section which was ready to leave the Mersey at midday 28th to proceed at 10 knots towards the rendezvous, but were prevented from sailing by thick fog. This did not clear until these two liners were able to depart at 1030 on the 29th under escort of the destroyer *Sardonyx*, with orders to proceed at 17 knots to overtake and join the convoy, and were joined off Orsay by *Skate* which had fuelled at Derry.

As the single ship from the Clyde, *Empress of Scotland* embarked at 1 KGV Dock in Glasgow and sailed downriver in the afternoon of the 27th to the Clyde Anchorage. [2] Proceeding again next evening, the *Empress* passed out of the boom at midnight under escort of the destroyers *Rotherham* and *Holcombe* and continued at 15 knots to the rendezvous 6 miles west of Orsay where at 0730 junction was made with the four ships from the Bristol Channel, which had detached *Skate* to refuel while *Onslow* (Captain D17), *Oribi* and *Offa* joined to provide an A/S screen of five destroyers. Also joining from Derry at this time was the small US seaplane tender *Barnegat* and referred to later. Captain FSW de Winton RN (Captain D11) of the John Brown built and newly completed, first of class *Rotherham*, was SOE while Captain JW Thomas of *Empress of Scotland*, to be Vice Commodore of the complete convoy was meantime acting as Commodore pending the joining up of Commodore Candy on *Stirling Castle*.

Amongst the Army personnel embarked on this convoy were three Royal Armoured Corps regiments recently converted from territorial infantry battalions, i.e. 6 South Wales Borderers, 9 Royal Sussex and 10 Gloucestershires, all being posted to India to join newly forming Indian Armoured Brigades. Of the total 18,213 embarked on the six liners of WS 24, 7,525 were destined for the Middle East, 4,017 for India and Ceylon and 2,948 for Iraq. *Tamaroa* for Freetown and Takoradi only carried 1,755.

Off Orsay the convoy formed into cruising order and set off to the WSW at 14 knots for the first position on the prescribed route which was similar to that of other recent WS convoys. However, the area beween the NW approaches and the Azores was then almost "congested" by the Torch convoys and so WS 24 was given a route inshore and 90 miles to the east of them but would later have to cross them to the north of the Azores. By midday on the 30th, the convoy turned to the SW and in the early hours of the following morning *Oribi* on the starboard wing of the A/S screen sighted a darkened ship which on investigation proved to be the Norwegian tanker *Frontenac*, torpedoed three days earlier in the homeward convoy HX 212 and was making progress NE'wards at 5 knots (and safely arrived at Lamlash on 4 November).

In the afternoon of the 31st *Onslow*, on the port wing screen obtained a contact and later sighted a periscope. The convoy carried out an emergency turn to port while *Rotherham* joined the U-Boat hunt and also obtained a contact. Seven separate attacks were made during which time the U-Boat went very deep and remained there until about 1720 when contact was lost, and although both destroyers carried out a further search, contact was not regained. Although these attacks were made in fine, clear weather with a light WNW breeze, *Rotherham* concluded the U-Boat was almost certainly not sunk, so *Onslow* remained in the vicinity until after dark while *Rotherham* rejoined the screen.[3] It was during this U-Boat hunt that the two liners from Liverpool with *Skate* and *Sardonyx* were seen to be overtaking the convoy and did in fact join up to make the planned cruising order of five columns at 2100.[4] The two S class destroyers then detached for Derry, *Skate* being diverted en route to locate and escort *Frontenac* into the North Channel. At this point the convoy turned SSW towards the Azores and had expected the cruiser *Despatch* to join the escort but was re-arranged to join at the Equator.

Soon after forming up the SOE on *Rotherham* expressed disquiet on the five column arrangement as being unsuitable for screening by five destroyers and requested the Commodore to reduce to four columns which was complied with. However Commodore Candy did not believe this to be the safest disposition for troop-laden transports and had previously referred to this in his report on convoy WS 17 (*qv*).

A new route was given to the convoy on 1st November and that afternoon the Canadian corvette *Louisbourg* was spoken when crossing the track en route to Gibraltar. At 0300 on the 2nd when 300 miles north of the Azores, *Rotherham* detached ahead for Ponta Delgada to refuel and at midday *Barnegat* was detached "under secret orders" which turned out to be joining the US Assault Force about to land at Casablanca; the seaplane tender was then employed in providing base support for two Catalina squadrons flown into Port Lyautey for patrol service. At the point where *Barnegat* detached, 160 miles north of Sao Miguel, the convoy crossed the stern track of the first two Torch convoys then heading SE towards the Strait of Gibraltar. Altogether with the US Task Group heading towards Morocco, the homeward SL 125 convoy and the numereous British Torch convoys, over 300 Allied merchant ships were in the immediate vicinity with nearly 230 escort vessels.

The convoy continued south, zigzagging at 13.25 knots and during the evening of the 2nd as it approached the Azores, wide evasive alterations were made 40° to port then 64° to starboard and a further 21° to starboard, all due to a U-Boat reported 70 miles eastward. The convoy passed through the 75 mile wide gap between Terceira and Sao Miguel at 0200 on the 3rd and thereafter steered a SW'ly course for the next 24 hours. The destroyer *Holcombe* was detached to Ponta Delgada as the convoy passed through the Azores and was subsequently ordered independently to Bathurst. During the afternoon of the 3rd, *Rotherham* rejoined the escort as did the AMC *Queen of Bermuda* which came up from the south.[5] Two hours later *Onslow*, *Oribi* and *Offa* detached back to Ponta Delgada and thereafter rejoined the Home Fleet leaving *Rotherham* as the sole A/S escort. In the early hours of the 4th another evasive alteration of 35° to port was made and held for nearly five hours when a S'ly course was adopted towards the western side of the Cape Verde islands.

Unlike the previous convoys in the series, WS 24 was to use Bahia in Brazil as a replenishment port rather than Freetown, almost certainly due to the allocation of escorts for Torch but also as Brazil had recently joined the Allies and was visited by the Rear Admiral West Africa to make arrangements with his US counterpart for mutual operations against Axis ships.[6] The Admiralty decision to use Bahia cannot have been taken lightly, involving as it did an additional 1,500 miles and five days steaming on the voyage between the UK and Durban. Using the western side of the South Atlantic brought the convoy into the US sphere of influence but in the event provided only Catalina air escorts on the four days prior to arrival at Bahia; the choice of that port rather than the larger and more convenient Pernambuco (now Recife) may simply have been due to the facilities then available.

By the morning of the 4th, WS 24 was steering a S'ly course towards the western side of the Cape Verdes, zigzagging for the next four days while wide evasive alterations were made each night as the Admiralty reported that three U-Boats were believed to be moving in from the SW during the three days prior to the 5th. The homebound *Aorangi* was passed on the morning of the 7th, and by that evening the convoy was 350 miles west of the Cape Verde group where a U-Boat reported its presence and two hours later, *Indochinois* dropped astern with engine defects. The convoy with a single A/S escort was unable to help nor could the Commodore afford to slow down and despite written orders to the contrary, *Indochinois* repeatedly called on W/T which remained unanswered but finally reported the engine trouble had been made good.

In the early hours of the 8th, RAWA instructed a wide alteration of 97° to reach a new route which was achieved in three stages by 0200. Meanwhile, *Queen of Bermuda* was sent ahead and used her Seafox aircraft to successfully locate the A/S whaler *Southern Pride*, which then detached with *Tamaroa* at 1230 for Freetown where they arrived on the morning of the 12th. The liner disembarked all her mainly RAF personnel at Freetown and Takoradi before proceeding to load at Buenos Aires and Montevideo, returning home via Trinidad and New York. After embarking US troops in the latter port, *Tamaroa* crossed in HX 223 to reach Belfast on 31 January 1943 and Avonmouth two days later; her next two voyages were to North Africa before joining WS 32 in West Africa. *Queen of Bermuda* rejoined in the evening of the 8th.

The RAWA ordered another alteration to avoid U-Boats in the early hours of the 9th, and during that forenoon *Queen of Bermuda* was detached to search for *Indochinois* which the SOE on *Rotherham* considered would be 60 to 100 miles to the westward due to the several diversions from the original route. In mid-afternoon a welcome addition to the A/S escort was made by the destroyer *Ilex*, newly worked up at Key West after six months extensive repairs at Charleston Navy Yard. Another evasive alteration on the morning of the 9th was to take the convoy east of St. Paul's Rocks due to U-Boats reported cruising to the west of these islets, and yet another that afternoon precluded any possibility of reaching Bahia on the 14th, speed was therefore reduced to 12.5 knots, but that evening *Largs Bay* for the third time on the voyage had a breakdown on one engine which reduced her speed to 9 knots and to which the convoy suitably complied. This proved a critical speed for the Union Castle motorships until 12 knots was resumed by all five liners next morning.

At noon on the 12th the convoy reached latitude 5° South where course was altered in three stages to a SW'ly one towards Bahia, and during that afternoon a US Catalina began to provide A/S patrols around the convoy during daylight hours which continued until arrival. A landfall was made on Itapua Light at 0500 on the 15th and three hours later all ships were anchored north of Bahia breakwater, the escorts soon after berthing alongside to begin fuelling and watering.

The Commodore commented on a "perfect landfall due entirely to the precise and untiring attention to navigation"[7] (of the Commander and 1st Officer of *Stirling Castle*). The passage of 5,299 miles had been accomplished in eighteen days at an average speed of 12.99 knots, and was half as much again as the distance to Freetown. The many prudent diversions ordered by the Admiralty had kept the convoy safe from at least eight U-Boats reported on or near to the original route.

In the 1940s, Bahia (now Salvador) was a substantial city of 400,000 inhabitants situated on the Brazilian coast, 800 miles north of Rio de Janeiro in 13° South latitude and with a climate very similar to Freetown but only half its rainfall. The port of Bahia offered easy access being a mere 3 miles from the open sea (a disadvantage from the protection viewpoint) and provided good anchorage adjacent to the harbour breakwaters, within which were extensive wharves with sufficient depths alongside to berth two transports simultaneously. There was a resident British Consul, provisions were plentiful and minor repairs could be attended.

In normal times Bahia could only supply water to a single ship at the rate of 10 tons per hour, but during the first day in port when *Athlone Castle* and *Empress of Scotland* berthed alongside for fuel and water, the local appliances were supplemented by every available means so that by midnight two ships could be supplied simultaneously at a rate of 60 to 70 tons per hour. *Stirling Castle* took the berth occupied by her sister, *Athlone*, on the 16th, *Largs Bay* that of the *Empress* on the 17th and finally *Arawa* on the 18th so that all five liners were complete by 0900 on the 19th when it was decided to sail the convoy at 1530 leaving the AMC *Queen of Bermuda* to complete and sail that evening and overtake next forenoon.

Soon after the arrival of the convoy, the British Consul boarded *Stirling Castle* at the anchorage to confer with the Commodore about landing the troops ashore for a route march. This was readily agreed to and with great enthusiasm from the Consul, the proposal was then placed before Captain de Winton, SOE, who had similar views and since "the troops presence could not be hidden it was considered beneficial for them to land and in the event proved to be good propaganda with an extremely good moral effect on the populace."[3] Together with the COs of *Despatch* and *Ilex* all five then called upon the City Mayor, the Acting Governor of the district and local military commander who also enthusiastically approved the route marches "for the health of the troops who had been living in cramped conditions for three weeks."[7] There would not be parades and a special request was made to prevent any press reports being made and this was strictly adhered to.

As each transport berthed alongside, the troops were organised for a 6 mile route march, the ships carrying more than 2,000 doing so in two sections, and only those on *Arawa* were unable to participate as not until the last day did that ship ask for 380 tons of water and therefore berthed overnight. Each of the troop contingents received a great ovation, especially the women's ATS who were given a tremendous reception and loudly cheered. "Having so recently joined the Allied cause, the sight of British troops was most beneficial to the morale of the public!"[7] Battle-dress was worn throughout.

One aspect which caused the SOE some anxiety was the exposed position of the transports at anchor, there being no anti-submarine measures in place. The months of November and December 1942 were the worst months for sinkings off the Brazilian coast, nine merchant ships being sunk in November and twelve in December."[8] Although continuous daylight air patrols were flown over a considerable distance to seaward, as soon as *Ilex* completed fuelling, that destroyer was detached to establish an A/S patrol during the dark hours to seaward of the transports.

Including that supplied to HM ships, a total of 7,180 tons of fresh water was graciously supplied free gratis by the City Water Board as a small contribution towards the war. The liners were supplied with 2,300 tons of fuel. Undoubtedly the British Consul and his staff, together with the Brazilian authorities were most helpful in assisting the passage of the convoy while the untiring efforts of Commander Hamilton RN, the

British Routing and Liaison Officer and Lieut. Commander Sabon, US Naval Observer, performed wonders in getting all ships completed with fuel and water in the space of four days."[7]

With the troops exhilarated by the ardent welcome of the populace and refreshed by their route marches, the convoy sailed from Bahia at 1600 on 19 November escorted by *Despatch*, *Rotherham* and *Ilex*. That evening *Queen of Bermuda* completed with fuel and sailed to overtake the convoy, which was joined at 1500 next day. The initial course for the first three days was ESE until midday on the 22nd when reaching 19° South and 25° West when an alteration was made to SE. At this point a PO Telegraphist on *Rotherham* sustained a serious accident when fencing and was transferred to *Queen of Bermuda* for X-Ray but sadly died on the 25th and was buried at sea.

In contrast to the passage out to Bahia with so many evasive U-Boat diversions, none occurred on the leg to Durban despite the arrival of four new large U-Boats on the South African coast in October and November; of which one was promptly sunk. The remainder operated around the coast and into the Mozambique Channel sinking 26 ships before departing for home just before Christmas. As WS 24 approached the Cape coast on the last day of November, one of the U-Boats was already on its way home but the other two were still sinking ships off Lourenco Marques.

The passage across the South Atlantic was otherwise without incident, *Ilex* detached on the morning of the 23rd to return to Bahia and *Despatch* that evening for Pernambuco. By midday on the 26th the convoy reached a position 270 miles NE of Tristan where course was altered to due east for the next four days towards Cape Point. By daybreak on the 27th the zigzag zone was reached but poor visibility and heavy rain squalls made this precarious until the weather later cleared, and as *Arawa* and *Largs Bay* were only capable of 13 kts, those two liners maintained a straight course in the centre column while the four ships on the outer columns carried out a zigzag. The AMC *Alcantara* joined on the morning of the 28th when 800 miles west of Cape Point and took station on the port wing column in a cruising order of four columns.[9] On the following morning the RAN destroyer *Norman* joined as additional escort, by which time the convoy was 400 miles west of the Cape.

By daybreak on the 30th the convoy was 170 miles from Cape Point where two Venturas arrived to provide air escort and that afternoon a quantity of wreckage was passed, followed by survivors clinging to broken boats and rafts. *Rotherham* picked up seven and *Norman* eleven which were transferred to the former and turned out to be the Master, Chief Officer, Chief Engineer and fifteen others from the Greek *Argo* torpedoed and sunk by an Italian submarine the previous night. *Rotherham* then sighted three RN trawlers and directed them to search for a further 18 survivors but these were never found. The corvettes *Thyme* and *Rockrose* joined during the recovery of survivors, also the RAN *Nepal* escorting the errant *Indochinois* from Capetown and took station 12. Having ben absent from the convoy for 26 days, *Indochinois* was to be the subject of an inquiry following arrival in Durban. By 1800 *Rotherham* had detached for Simonstown to refuel and land the Greek survivors and reached that port at 2030.

The convoy was now steering ESE for a position 10 miles south of Cape Agulhas, which was duly passed at 0330 on 1st December and by 1800 that day *Rotherham* rejoined and detached the two corvettes to return to Simonstown. WS 24 maintained a relatively close distance off the coastal headlands and by 0900 on the 2nd was 8 miles off Cape Recife and that evening abeam of the bright lights of East London while heading up the Natal coast towards Durban.

At 0930 on the 3rd the convoy ceased zigzag and turned four points to port to close the land near Port St Johns and confirm its position as the weather turned increasingly hazy. An ETA Durban had been given for 0500 next day, but an Admiralty message then forbade arriving within 15 miles of that port during darkness so at 1600 the convoy reversed course for 1.5 hours to waste time, only to receive a message at 1900 from the Commodore of the Port instructing arrival off the entrance at 0500 which effectively cancelled that from the Admiralty. Speed was increased accordingly but at 0400 the visibility rapidly decreased to almost 0.25 miles, the next ship being hardly discernible, and speed was reduced to 9 knots and the course held until daylight.

The visibility remained poor and the Commodore again reversed the course of the convoy until D/F bearings obtained at 0630 allowed a turn to the NE to stem the current, until further D/F bearings at 0700 confirmed the position and allowed the convoy to form single line ahead, and with the visibility at 0.5 miles Pilots were picked up allowing the Commodore to lead the entrance into the harbour where the visibility was found to be quite good. By 0930 *Stirling Castle* was secured alongside with the other four liners and *Indochinois* following astern. The distance from Bahia was recorded as 4,331 miles and the average speed for the 15 day passage was 12.34 knots.

Commodore Candy commented on the timely arrival of the convoy off Durban despite the poor visibility, being "due entirely to the local knowledge of Captain Roach and his Radio Officers which emphasised the value of detailing a Commodore ship familiar with the ports of call on the convoy route".[7] An ideal situation but seldom achievable.

The transhipment programme in Durban was fairly straightforward. *Empress of Scotland* and *Largs Bay* were disembarked completely to allow their return to the UK, landing 4,264 for the Middle East, 992 for Iraq, 417 for India and 60 for East Africa, to which was added 1,656 for the Middle East and 170 for Mombasa from the two *Castle* liners which alone were continuing to Bombay. *Arawa* with 1,655 for Suez was to continue with four of the Indian Ocean troopers, BI's *Aronda* and *Ekma*, Blue Funnel *Ascanius* and Bibby-managed *Felix Roussel*, the last named only reaching Durban with Polish refugees on the 6th and first to be cleaned, stored, fuelled and watered.

All of the transhipped personnel for Iraq and India re-embarked on *Athlone* and *Stirling Castle* which sailed on 6 December as WS 24B under escort of the cruiser *Frobisher*. By this date one U-Boat was 200 miles SE of Durban working its way homewards while the last of that group remained off Lourenco Marques until the 13th, and by next day was to the SE of Durban and clear of South African waters a week later. Neither *Frobisher* nor the Commodore appears to have lodged a report of this section of the voyage, which certainly proceeded east of Madagascar and thereafter almost in a direct line towards Bombay. On the morning of the 12th in a position 200 miles SE of Mahe, *Frobisher* was relieved by *Mauritius* which continued as escort to destination. There were no incidents crossing the north Indian Ocean, two British ships were passed en route, one being *City of Canterbury* bound for Durban from Bombay. Paravanes were streamed by all three ships as the convoy approached soundings before dark on the 16th, and just before midnight a small radar echo picked up by *Mauritius* was illuminated by starshell to reveal an innocent dhow. The convoy arrived at the entrance to the Bombay searched channel at 0630 on the 17th and arrived in the stream later that morning, having averaged just over 16.5 knots for the passage from Durban.

Despite the apparent simplicity of fully disembarking two liners in Bombay, both remained there for a week, having to await three of the smaller troopers required to on-carry the 2,948 personnel bound for Iraq, which did not leave Bombay until the 22nd. Of the three RAC regiments landed to join Indian Armoured Brigades, it was soon found there was not enough requirement for armoured units and all reverted to their infantry status and later served in Burma until the end of the war.

Athlone and *Stirling Castle* left Bombay on Christmas Eve, not for their usual destination in the Antipodes, but via Durban to New York where they arrived on 1 February, the former to drydock and her sister to change a broken piston. Both then embarked US troops, *Athlone* sailing in USF 5 for Casablanca and returned to Liverpool on 15 March in MKF 10A from Gibraltar with 750 personnel; her next voyage was in WS 29. *Stirling Castle* crossed in AT 37 to Liverpool, arriving on 19 February and after almost four weeks voyage repairs, proceeded to New York for a US troop voyage to Oran.

The return voyage of the two liners which disembarked in Durban began on 9 December, *Empress of Scotland* having had instructions to load on the Cape coast cancelled. Proceeding direct to New York, US troops were embarked there and the *Empress* crossed in AT 33 to reach the Clyde on 13 January, and thereafter continued on the North Atlantic route until October 1944. *Largs Bay* also proceeded to New York, refuelling in Capetown and Freetown, loading on the Furness berth and embarking US troops to cross in HX 225 to Liverpool on 13 February. Four months were then spent in that port undergoing much needed re-blading of her turbines, before resuming service on the KMF route in June 1943.

The final section of WS 24 started out from Durban at 1315 on 13 December, when *Arawa* (as WS 24A) and the four Indian Ocean troopers (as CM 36) sailed as a combined convoy for Suez under escort of the cruiser *Capetown*, AMC *Chitral* and destroyers, *Rotherham, Norman, Nepal* and *Inconstant*. This must have been the strongest A/S escort given to any convoy in the area and was due to the scale of recent U-Boat activity, albeit the last of the group was moving south that very day and may just have missed encountering this valuable convoy carrying nearly 8,500 troops.

The SOE was on *Capetown* which took the convoy to the south and east of Madagascar but at 0900 on the first morning at sea, *Inconstant* was detached north towards Lourenco Marques where a ship had been torpedoed and sunk late on the 12th. The destroyer and a corvette picked up all the survivors but did not locate the U-Boat which was by then well south of Durban and clear of the convoy route.

When nearing the northern tip of Madagascar on the morning of the 19th and well clear of the U-Boat area, *Rotherham* and *Nepal* detached ahead for Mombasa to join the Eastern Fleet and at midday *Norman* detached to Diego Suarez. By next morning when the convoy was 250 miles SE of Mombasa, Henderson's *Salween* joined from that port carrying troops for Berbera and with the cruiser *Ceres* as escort which relieved *Capetown*, which then detached with *Ekma* carrying the East African contingent to reach Mombasa next morning.

The remaining combined convoy, (which may also have included *Indochinois*), now comprised *Arawa, Aronda, Ascanius, Felix Roussel* and *Salween*, escorted by *Ceres* and *Chitral*, which continued up the East African coast to reach Aden where it was dispersed on the 27th, *Salween* having detached to Berbera. *Aronda* and *Ascanius* sailed again that day and were cleared at Suez on the 3rd and 4th January, *Felix Roussel* left Aden on the 28th to reach Suez on the 2nd and was cleared by the 5th while *Arawa* was dealt with last, not leaving Aden until the 30th and was at Suez for five days from the 3rd, her voyage out from Avonmouth having lasted sixty-eight days.

The return voyage of *Arawa* began from Suez on 8 January 1943 by carrying Italian POW to Mombasa, following which five days were spent on repairs in Durban before loading refrigerated meat in Buenos Aires and Montevideo. *Arawa* then proceeded to Freetown and joined SL 126 to reach the Clyde and Glasgow on 3 April with a round voyage time of over five months; her next sailing was on 19 May to North Africa.

Chapter 18

WS 25, WS 25W and WS 26

Serious Troopship losses, the last independent WS departure and first of those
sailings in combination with KMF North African convoys.

WS 25 - sailed UK 18.12.42

WS 25 and the single ship "*Queen Mary* convoy" which left the UK five days later,
were not only the last of the series to depart in the calendar year 1942 but the last to
leave these shores as independent formations. All successive WS convoys were combined with KMF North African troop convoys and sailed as such with the WS portion
stationed on the starboard wing columns. On reaching a convenient splitting position to
the west of Gibraltar, the WS section detached for Freetown while the KMF portion
headed for the Mediterranean. This system helped to ease the critical shortage of escorts
on both these routes.

In the first six days of the Torch landings, the troopship fleet suffered grievous and
irreplaceable losses of seven ships and so reduced their availability for both the KMF
and WS routes.[1] If the monthly cycle of WS sailings had been maintained, WS 25
would have sailed during the last week of November, at which date *Britannic* was the

sole liner then in readiness, having anchored in the Clyde from Liverpool on the 21st, and so the departure date had to be postponed until the third week of December.

Soon after the readiness of *Britannic*, three of the intermediate refrigerated liners arrived at Avonmouth from their voyages in WS 22, i.e. *Mataroa* with *Highland Brigade* and *Princess* each requiring two to three weeks to discharge and effect voyage repairs. On 3 December, *Orion* and *Rangitiki* reached Liverpool from their first Torch voyages to Algiers and Oran respectively; both were allocated for WS 25 while *Esperance Bay*, which had been in Liverpool from 4 November after her Falklands voyage in WS 20, had left the Mersey on 13 December to embark on the Clyde but was in collision with the Belgian *Jean Jadot* next day and had to return to Liverpool for repairs. These were hurriedly completed in time to begin embarkation on the 16th.

By 8 December the convoy sailing date had been fixed for the 17th and necessarily sandwiched one week each side of KMF 5 and 6. This required strict adherance to the embarkation and sailing programme of all three convoys to prevent overlapping and may have hastened the need to combine their departures from the UK. Embarkation on *Mataroa* and *Highland Princess* at Avonmouth was complete by the morning of the 15th when these two liners with an empty *Highland Brigade* locked out on the midday tide and proceeded on passage to the Clyde Anchorage escorted by the new frigate *Jed*. On arrival there next afternoon, *Highland Brigade* was embarked with 1,882 US technicians transhipped from *Queen Mary* recently arrived from New York. The *Highland* liner was loaded with 650 tons commercial stores for West Africa, where the US party were to assist in expanding their air route to the east.

At Liverpool, *Rangitiki* completed embarkation and anchored in the river on the 15th, while *Orion* and *Esperance Bay* completed on the 17th. Also sailing from Liverpool were the MT ships *City of Lincoln*, a veteran of three Malta convoys and now loaded with tanks, guns, stores and ammunition for Basra, and the Norwegian Wilhelmsen motorship *Tarifa* carrying stores, ammunition, vehicles and ten Hurricanes for Bombay. All five ships sailed on the 1900 tide on the 17th, escorted by the Hunt class destroyer *Rockwood*, and proceeded at 12 knots to make rendezvous with the Clyde portion off Orsay at 1000 on the 18th.

The great North African expedition had exerted extreme pressure on all the west coast ports but nowhere more so than on the Clyde which in addition to docks and riverside quays, had a vast and safe anchorage with nearby access to all necessary facilities which could not be matched by any other port in the UK. Prominent amongst the warships then berthed in the naval anchorage off Greenock was the aircraft carrier *Victorious* at the flagship buoy, having recently returned from supporting the Torch landings and now preparing to depart for the US en route to joining the Pacific Fleet. Also at this anchorage were three AMCs under orders to act as ocean escort to WS 25, i.e. *Cheshire* having newly completed repairs at Belfast after being torpedoed in August, *Carnarvon Castle* newly out of Belfast refit and *Cilicia* also out of Liverpool refit but bedevilled by minor defects which could not be completed by the convoy sailing date and so was held over to sail with WS 26. The AMCs were most useful in providing berths for personnel which could not be accommodated on the transports, 806 were embarked on the *Castle* liner and 109 on *Cheshire* all destined for West Africa.

The largest merchant ship then in the Gourock anchorage was of course *Queen Mary* which together with her consort had been engaged on North Atlantic service carrying US troops to the Clyde since August 1942. Embarkation on the Clyde for WS 25 was confined to *Britannic*, the two AMCs and the transhipment to *Highland Brigade* referred to above. Commodore AT Tillard RNR, who had previously sailed on *Strathmore* in WS 15, was now accommodated with his staff on *Britannic*, which Captain DS Robinson had recently been appointed to command after being temporarily released from RNR service. Captain LJ Vestey of *Orion* was to act as Vice Commodore of the nine ship convoy. The total number embarked, including those on the AMCs and nine on *City of Lincoln*, was 21,304 of all services in drafts and details of which 6,748 were for India, 5,148 for Iraq, 3,758 for the Middle East, 2,835 for West Africa, 1,279 for South Africa and 1,536 for destinations in East Africa, Madagascar, Ceylon and Australia.[2] Embarked on *Mataroa* from Avonmouth was the 7 Bn Kings Own Regiment en route to India. They were subsequently landed at Durban where they remained for six weeks providing guard parties for POW passing through the port, until "on-carried" on the liners of WS 26 to Bombay.[3]

The Clyde portion of the convoy comprising *Britannic*, the two *Highland* liners and *Mataroa* passed out of the Clyde boom at 0200 on the 18th, to proceed at 14 knots under escort of *Carnarvon Castle*, *Cheshire* and the newly completed destroyer leader *Quilliam* which was making the passage to join the 4th Destroyer Flotilla in the Eastern Fleet. The SOE was the commanding officer of *Quilliam*, Captain SH Curtiss Karbill DSO. Rendezvous was effected off Orsay at 1000 that morning where the destroyers *Badsworth*, *Haydon* and *Wolverine* joined from Derry while *Rockwood* from the Liverpool section made the A/S screen up to a total of five. The convoy here formed into five columns [4] and set off to the westward at a speed of 13 knots until midnight, when course was altered to the SW. With the reduction and frequent absence of the Luftwaffe in the Western Approaches, the long diversionary westerly courses into the Atlantic were now being appropriately reduced.

Heavy weather was experienced on the 20th when the convoy made good only 8.5 knots and 9 knots next day by which time it was steering towards the centre of the Azores group. At noon on the 22nd a S'ly course was adopted to pass east of the Azores and about this time *Quilliam* and *Rockwood* detached ahead to fuel at Ponta Delgada, which was abeam at 2300 on the 23rd at a distance of 68 miles. These two destroyers rejoined next afternoon allowing *Badsworth*, *Haydon* and *Wolverine* to similarly detach and thereafter proceeded to Gibraltar.

It may be noted that WS escorts frequently refuelled at the neutral Portuguese port of Ponta Delgada and whilst the exactitudes of providing a belligerent power with these facilities is beyond the scope of this work, they were ongoing since first granted to *Challenger* and three corvettes in July 1941.[5] Whatever arrangements prevailed, they were discreetly applied to a once only visit of any escort and was accomplished by allocating to WS convoys only those destroyers on passage to foreign stations beyond the North Atlantic. The visits were of short duration only for fuelling and watering but the opportunity was usually taken to obtain fresh provisions and for the officers to make courtesy calls upon any Portuguese warships then in harbour. In respect of air bases for A/S patrols from the Azores, these were not established until October 1943 after "the British and Portuguese Governments had been negotiating on the matter for two years".[6]

At 1800 on the 24th course was altered SSE to an unusual position 140 miles west of Cap Blanc in the Spanish Sahara, close to the border with the French colony of Mauritania, and presumably to obtain shore-based air escort, where the destroyer *Ilex* joined at 0800 on the 27th and course again altered for a position 100 miles east of the Cape Verde islands which was reached 24 hours later. A S'ly course was then maintained until 0100 on the 30th, when a wide alteration of nine points to port brought the convoy on to an E'ly course direct for Freetown and then distant 500 miles. The corvettes *Crocus* and *Woodruff* joined as local escorts at 1300 and the convoy anchored in Freetown at 1500 next day, 31 January, having averaged 12.4 knots from the Clyde. The passage was completed free of enemy sighting or interference.

Freetown was then lacking the customary surfeit of shipping from outward and homeward convoys, which had been suspended due to the number of escorts required for Torch, and did not resume until March 1943. Nonetheless, three full days were occupied in replenishing the nine ships of WS 25 while 953 personnel were disembarked from the two AMCs, *Orion* and *Britannic*; the US party on *Highland Brigade* being destined for Takoradi. The AMC *Carnarvon Castle* left the convoy in Freetown to undertake South Atlantic patrols and was replaced by *Alcantara* recently arrived from the Cape escorting convoy CF 10.[7]

Both the Commodore and SOE commented most unfavourably on the unusual deterrent camouflage painted on each side of *Mataroa* and the two *Highland* liners consisting of extrememly conspicuous white shapes in the form of a destroyer or corvette. "No matter how misleading this....might be when viewed through a periscope,...from a surface ship at night it is..definitely undesirable..and were especially visible in moonlight".[9] At the Freetown conference "the Masters of all three ships expressed themselves strongly in disfavour of such camouflage and that "it was a point of aim on the engine room".[9] An interesting photograph of *Highland Princess* in this condition appears in the Royal Mail history.[8]

Britannic led the same nine ships out past the Freetown boom at 1500 on the 3 January with the AMCs *Alcantara* and *Cheshire* as ocean escorts while *Quilliam* (SOE) and *Rockwood* continued as A/S escorts with the locally based *Crocus*. At 1630 while still in the searched channel, *Quilliam* closed *Alcantara* to pass a hand message by the latter's crane but was drawn into the AMC's starboard quarter, resulting in damage to mast and yards and buckling of the upper deck abreast the after superstructure, but fortunately did not affect her watertight integrity.[9] By 1815 the convoy formed into a revised cruising order and with the AMCs between columns 3 and 4,[10] set off on a SW'ly course at 13.5 knots in calm conditions and extreme visibility. At 2300 course was altered to SSW and soon after a darkened ship was sighted ahead but identified as *Rockwood* which had missed the turn; at 2330 a S"ly course was adopted. No U-Boats had been reported in the Freetown or West African area for some time but this evasive course to clear the land was held until 1430 next day when two wide alterations brought the convoy round to ESE and was retained until the evening of the 6th, and at which point the Catalina or Hudson daylight air escort was dispensed with. As with some of the recent WS convoys, Cape Palmas on the Liberian coast was passed at a distance of 90 miles.

At midday on the 6th the RIN minesweeping sloop *Baluchistan* and a French corvette (not of the Flower class) joined the escort and both detached seven hours later with *Highland Brigade* for Takoradi, where that liner arrived at noon on the 7th, disembarked the US technicians and sailed again the same day, light ship, for Buenos Aires. The Highland liner loaded there on her owners' berth and at Montevideo and Rio de Janeiro, returning home via Bermuda and New York to Liverpool on 14 March where she was discharged and drydocked prior to sailing again in WS 29.

An hour after detaching *Highland Brigade*, at 2000 on the 6th, WS 25 was now 180 miles SW of Cape Three Points on the Gold Coast, where course was altered SE to cross the Gulf of Guinea. During the evening of the 7th, *Cheshire* reported a radar contact astern which *Rockwood* investigated but found nothing, and the following evening *Quilliam* searched astern with the same negative result. The SE trades were first encountered that day from the SSE force 3 and blew at force 4 for the next three days when the weather became calm and thereafter SSW or SSE 3 until reaching the Cape.

At 0430 on the 9th *Alcantara* went ahead at 17 knots, followed two hours later by *Quilliam* at 20 knots, to a rendezvous where the AMC pumped 200 tons of fuel to the destroyer by the astern method. At 0915 during the interval the convoy altered course SSE direct for the Cape and at the same time *Crocus*, being short of fuel, was detached to Pointe Noire distant 450 miles ENE. *Quilliam* completed fuelling from *Alcantara* at 1300 whereupon *Rockwood* took her place and completed at 1915 when the AMC detached independently for Trinidad where she was to form part of the escort for the towage of *AFD 24* to Freetown.

There were no other incidents on the passage towards the Cape, the two destroyers carrying out various exercises between 10 and 12 January including dummy attacks and night encounters. By midday on the 12th, WS 25 was 160 miles WNW of Walvis Bay and next morning encountered the British tramp *Tilsington Court* bound for Bahia and later that forenoon Ellerman's *City of Agra* bound for Freetown.

The convoy reached a position 80 miles west of Cape Columbine on the South African coast at 1830 on the 14th where the destroyer *Express* was met and relieved *Quilliam*, which detached to refuel at Simonstown and arrived there at 0845 next morning. By the forenoon of the 15th the convoy had Cape Point in sight abeam and shortly after, the corvette *Genista* relieved *Rockwood* which also proceeded to Simonstown to refuel and thereafter continued to Suez to join the Mediterranean Fleet.

By 1600 that same day *Quilliam* rejoined, detached *Genista* and three hours later the convoy rounded Cape Agulhas at a distance of 8 miles and began steering for Cape St Francis on a coastline reported free of U-Boats since December. When to the south of Mossel Bay on the morning of the 16th, the convoy had to reduce to 8 knots for a time to allow *Rangitiki* to carry out repairs to one engine. Port Elizabeth and Cape Recife were passed at a distance of 7 miles that evening and East London with a similar offing at 0530 on the 17th. Identities were passed to Durban port signal station 24 hours later, the convoy formed single line ahead at 0700 and began entering harbour where *Quilliam* and *Express* secured alongside an oiler. The average speed from Freetown was recorded as 12.8 knots while the passage from the Clyde had occupied 31 days.

When WS 25 left the UK it was intended to disembark the four refrigerated liners in Durban and despatch them direct to New York where they would load for the UK while providing much needed extra lifting capacity for US troops crossing on that route. *Britannic* and *Orion* were either to disembark in Durban or continue to Bombay, but during the outward voyage of the convoy all these plans were overtaken by a decision to move further batches of Italian and German POW to the UK and Canada. At the end of September 1942 there were 226,500 of those POW scattered throughout the UK, India, South Africa, Australia, East Africa and Canada, and by the year end it was agreed to move more than half of those already in South Africa, i.e. 44,000 to the UK during 1943.[11]

Without encroaching into the refrigerated-carrying spaces, it was arranged to embark each of these four liners with 100 German Other Ranks POW and 50 RN guard in South Africa, all for Canada, which matched their New York destinations where the prisoners would complete their journey by train, and was a follow-on for those already embarked and sailed on *Highland Monarch* returning from WS 23.(*qv*) In the event only *Highland*

Princess and *Esperance Bay* proceeded to New York, the other two ships being loaded on the Plate.

On completion of disembarkation in Durban, *Highland Princess* embarked the POW and guard and sailed light ship on the 21st direct for New York, where they were landed and entrained to Canada. The *Highland* liner then loaded on the Cunard berth and crossed with US troops to reach Belfast on 11 March and Avonmouth two days later, and like her sister *Highland Brigade* made her next voyage in WS 29.

Rangitiki left Durban on the 24th followed two days later by *Mataroa*; both liners called at Capetown to embark their POW parties and cleared that port on the 28th and 30th respectively for New York, but were not to proceed by the direct route. "The opening of the North African campaign caused..a proportion of ships from South Africa (to be) routed through the Magellan Straits, up the west coast of South America and then by the Panama Canal to the Atlantic".[12] Arrangements were made for a refuelling stop roughly halfway between Capetown and Panama at Punta Arenas in the Magellan Straits, however, after twelve days at sea and approaching the northern side of the Falklands, these plans were cancelled and both liners were re-directed to load on the Plate and reached Montevideo on the 11th and 13th of February.

An Admiralty signal of 28 January permitted those liners with POW to call at any colonial or South American port other than those in the Argentine.[13] *Mataroa* was to load at the Argentine capital of Buenos Aires, and so while at Montevideo in Uruguay, transferred her complement of POW temporarily to *Rangitiki* while the former ship proceded up river to load and re-embark the POW on completion, before sailing for Freetown to join convoy SL 126 of 36 ships. This was heavily attacked by U-Boats and lost four ships before reaching Liverpool on 2 April. The next voyage of *Mataroa* was in WS 30. *Rangitiki* only began loading in Montevideo on the departure of *Mataroa* but sailed on 10 March for Freetown where she joined SL 127 and reached Liverpool without encountering the enemy on 24 April. Her next voyage was in WS 31. The last of this group to leave Durban was *Esperance Bay* on 27 January, and having loaded a part cargo there and in Capetown where the POW embarked, finally left the Cape in convoy CF 11 on 11 February.

Whilst WS 25 was on passage to Durban, the DoST decided to turn *Britannic* and *Orion* at the Natal port, embark on them 6,000 Italian POW for the UK and use the balance of trooping space for RAF Training Scheme personnel awaiting return to the UK, and to load both ships in South Africa to comply with a sailing date of 23 January.[14] These plans were modified just before the convoy reached Durban when the CinCSA decided to reverse the priorities by first embarking all those RAF, RN or MN personnel awaiting passage and to use the balance of space for POW on a revised scale of 4,000.[15] Both liners were accordingly embarked and loaded, partly in Durban and Capetown: *Britannic* on the Clan Line berth and *Orion* under Union Castle. Both left Durban with *Esperance Bay* as convoy CF 11 on 30 January and reached Freetown on 11 February, where they were joined by *Indrapoera* returning from WS 22 and carrying 400 Italian POW. All four ships left Freetown three days later and during the passage north detached *Esperanace Bay* for New York to land the German POW for entraining to Canada. The *Bay* liner then completed loading in New York and crossed with US troops in HX 229 to reach Liverpool on 26 March where she disembarked, discharged, drydocked and thereafter made a round trip to New York before again sailing in WS 32.

The remaining three liners of CF 11 reached the UK on 26 February, *Britannic* going to Liverpool and after 17 days in port next sailed in WS 28. *Orion* was directed to the

Clyde Anchorage to disembark, discharged at 1 KGV Dock, Glasgow and next sailed in KMF 11 to Algiers. *Indrapoera* disembarked in Liverpool and made her next voyage in KMF 13 also to Algiers.

There remains for WS 25 the on-carriage of all 17,181 personnel landed in Durban for other destinations and for which only one third could then be accommodated, while the balance was sent to Clairwood Transit Camp. The only liner then available was the "monster" class *Nieuw Amsterdam*, about to make her last trip on the northward shuttle service from Durban by embarking to capacity 6,000 for Suez, i.e. all of the 3,758 originally destined for the Middle East plus 2,242 re-directed from Iraq. The Dutch liner sailed the day following arrival of WS 25 and reached Suez on the 30th.

Three of the smaller Indian Ocean troopers arrived at Durban within ten days of WS 25, i.e. *Aronda*, *Ascanius* and *Ekma* which then embarked 5,000 for Bombay, and together with *Pulaski* then completing repairs embarked all 1,289 for Madagascar and East Africa. These four ships sailed on 1 February, refuelled and detached *Pulaski* at Diego Suarez and reached Bombay on the 20th where 2,900 were transhipped to other ships for the Persian Gulf and disembarked at Basra between 28 February and 2 March. The final on-carriage of 5,000 were embarked on *Felix Roussel* and *Yoma* which sailed from Durban on 14 February and reached their Bombay destination on 3 March.

WS 25W - sailed UK 23.12.42

Whilst *Britannic* of the previous convoy WS 25 was preparing to begin embarkation at the Clyde Anchorage, *Queen Mary* arrived from New York on her fourth crossing with US troops and the first since the fateful collision with the AA cruiser *Curacao*. Captain Bisset had then been relieving on the *Queen Elizabeth* but returned to her consort at New York in mid November and having previously voyaged to Suez on the *Queen Mary* as WS 19W, was about to repeat that experience with another single ship sailing of that same liner as WS 25W.

The *Queen Mary* anchored in the Clyde on 14 December with 10,389 US troops from New York, after a crossing which Captain Bisset modestly described as "a passage in severe winter weather, with north-westerly gales, which made the ship roll heavily for four days".[1] His reserve on the degree of rolling was not supported by the facts, which record that in some of "the broadside waves the ship rolled (alarmingly) to within 4° of capsize",[2] and caused weather damage which took four days to repair at the Clyde Anchorage while the ship was disembarked, replenished and re-embarked with 10,669 personnel which included British troops, 2000 RAF men and 160 women and US Airforce all bound for the Middle East.

The great ship left the Clyde two days before Christmas 1942 and five days behind the nine ships of WS 25 but overtook this convoy in the vicinity of the Cape Verde islands on the 28th and reached Freetown next day. An AA and A/S escort was provided for the first day out from the Clyde, thereafter the ship proceeded alone. Captain Bisset graphically describes conditions on the liner on that Christmas Day, "we were 600 miles to the westward of Ireland, and headed southwards in a NW gale with mountainous seas, most of the troops were seasick or at least decidedly uncomfortable. The Chief Steward and his staff worked hard to prepare a slap-up Christmas Dinner of turkey and plum pudding, but most of it went to waste".[3]

After being refuelled and watered in Freetown, the *Queen Mary* left on the 30th for Capetown where she arrived without incident six days later and was again replenished while at anchor in Table Bay between 5 and 7 January 1943. The next leg of the voyage took the liner around Cape Agulhas and in passing as before to the east of Madagascar, reached Aden on the 15th, was refuelled there at the outer anchorage and finally anchored in Suez Bay on the 18th, 26 days after leaving the Clyde.

At Suez the liner was disembarked, stored and re-embarked with 9,995 Australian troops being returned to their homeland to help stem the Japanese advance in the western Pacific. Together with *Aquitania*, *Ile de France*, *Nieuw Amsterdam* and the AMC *Queen of Bermuda*, these "monster" liners formed the "Pamphlet" convoy with Captain Bisset acting as Commodore and proceeded towards Fremantle and Sydney under escort of the cruisers *Gambia* and *Devonshire*. After reaching Sydney safely on 27 February, the *Queen Mary* proceeded to Capetown where 4,050 Italian POW and 4276 mixed military, naval and airforce passengers were embarked for the UK.[4] Sailing again from Capetown on 10 April, and after fuelling at Freetown on the 15th/16th, the liner reached the Clyde Anchorage on 22 April and thereafter resumed service on the North Atlantic shuttle service which was continued without interruption for the next three years until the end of September 1946.

WS 26 - sailed UK 24.1.43

This was the first convoy of the series to leave the UK in unison with a similar type KMF convoy for North Africa, which altogether involved 23 transports and three storeships being embarked and loaded in four ports for seven destinations spread over two continents. Not surprisingly this resulted in some of the records, certainly those concerning the assembly and dispatch of this convoy to be less than complete and somewhat misleading.

The allocation of liners for WS 26 was spread over a six week period from the beginning of December as they arrived in UK ports from voyages in WS 22: *Dominion Monarch*, *Highland Chieftain* and *Sibajak* in Liverpool; *California*, *Ruys* and *Orduna* in Glasgow. To these were added nine others returning from KMF voyages; *Mooltan*, *Dempo*, *Volendam* and *Duchess of Richmond* in Liverpool; *Maloja* in Avonmouth, and *Arundel Castle*, *Antenor*, *Empress of Canada* and *Stratheden* in Glasgow. The KMF 8 component of the combined convoy was allocated *Circassia*, *Durban Castle*, *Dunnottar Castle*, *Letitia* and *Strathnaver* in Glasgow; *Duchess of York*, *Empire Pride* and *Samaria* in Liverpool. Three storeships to accompany WS 26 were the newly completed BI *Chyebassa* with Dutch cargo liners *Rembrandt* and *Tawali* although the latter failed to make the sailing date.

There is evidence to suppose the original sailing date of the combined convoy was to be 20 January, on which date nine of the liners left the Mersey on the morning tide but with three of the Glagow embarkations only just beginning, the Liverpool ships were diverted to the Clyde Anchorage to await their completion. From Avonmouth, the fully embarked *Maloja* locked out on the afternoon tide of the 16th and next day departed Barry Roads with one of the storehips with escort for the Clyde where they anchored on the 18th. The final embarkations in Glasgow were completed on *Orduna* and *Circassia* at 7 and 2 KGV Dock respectively, from where they moved downriver on the late forenoon of the 21st; and on *Dunnottar Castle* at 1 KGV next morning. The Clyde portion was now ready for sea and due to sail at 0100 on the 23rd but was delayed by fog for a further 24 hours. *Duchess of York* was the last ship to complete in Liverpool and left the Bar in the evening of the 23rd to make rendezvous with the main body off Orsay. The final embarkations amounted to 31,802 in Liverpool, 19,500 at the Clyde Anchorage, 18,000 in Glasgow and 4,305 in Avonmouth, or a grand total of 73,607 and one fifth more than the previous highest number embarked on WS 19P in May 1942.[1] One third of the personnel in the combined convoy were bound for North Africa, one third for Bombay of which a small proportion were there on-carried to Iraq, and the remainder for Madagascar and the Middle East. Amongst those carried on WS 26 were 20 Bn The Royal Fusiliers, 100 Anti-Tank Regiment (converted from 8 Bn Gordon Highlanders), 158 Regiment RAC (ex 6 Bn South Wales Borderers), 118 Light AA Regiment and 136 Field Regiment RA, all of these units proceeding to India while 68 Field Regiment were destined for Iraq.[2]

The ocean escort allocated for WS 26 was the AMCs *Canton* and *Cilicia*, both proceeding to the Cape, the former having completed a four month refit in Southampton while *Cilicia* was similarly handled in Liverpool. Also continuing to the Cape was the Fleet Repair ship *Wayland* (ex *Cunard Antonia*) which had gone out to Gibraltar with KMF 7 but returned immediately to sail again with WS 26 en route to join the Eastern Fleet at Mombasa, as were the newly completed destroyers *Quadrant* and *Relentless*. The carrier *Argus* ferrying aircraft to North Africa was included in the escort for KMF 8.

Commodore Sir Raymond Fitzmorris of the combined convoy on *Durban Castle* (Captain RF Bayer) was to continue as such with KMF 8, while the Vice Commodore, Rear Admiral CN Reyne on *Stratheden* (Captain AW Drew) would become Commodore of WS 26 on reaching the splitting position. (Rear Admiral Reyne had previously acted as Commodore of WS 5A and WS 18.) The Acting Vice Commodore and Rear Commodore of the combined formation were the Masters of *Dunnottar Castle* (Captain LP Wilkie) and *Duchess of Richmond* (Captain T Jones) respectively. The Master of *Arundel Castle* (Captain RT Smailes) was to act as Vice Commodore of WS 26 after splitting from the KMF section.[3]

The Clyde section of 22 transports and two storeships, which almost completed the convoy, began passing out of the Clyde boom at 0100 in the waning moonlight of 24 January, led by the Commodore on *Durban Castle* and with the AMCs *Canton*, *Cilicia*, repair ship *Wayland*, carrier *Argus* and destroyer escort, proceeded at 10 knots towards the rendezvous position. By 0800 the single line formation was passing 4 miles south of the Mull of Kintyre and by midday was joined off Orsay by *Duchess of York* from Liverpool; the A/S screen then consisting of the destroyers *Quadrant*, *Relentless*, *Adrias* and *Miaoulis* (both Greek flag Hunt class), French sloop *Savorgnan de Brazza*, ex US coastguard cutters, *Banff* and *Fishguard* and finally the River class frigate *Test*. A cruising order of eight colums was formed with the two AMCs, *Wayland* and *Argus* comprising column 5, following which the convoy steered out to the westward for 150 miles in foul weather until the following morning when course was altered to the SW towards the Azores.[4]

The southgoing route of this convoy was laid out to keep within the range of air cover and by the evening of the 26th, when 200 miles west of Mizen Head, the Greek *Miaoulis* and French sloop were detached, probably with *Antenor* which had to depart at 1730 to return to the Clyde with engine trouble thought to be due to contaminated fuel oil. The convoy was beset by dirty and adverse weather until the forenoon of the 27th when it reached the latitude of the Scillies, having averaged a mere 8.2 knots from the Orsay rendezvous. The weather then gradually improved and by next morning the convoy altered course to the SE towards Cape St Vincent and passed 300 miles west of Cape Finisterre rather than the minimum 650 miles previously maintained by WS convoys off that headland.

In the early afternoon of the 29th, *Empress of Canada* had a breakdown of steering gear lasting an hour but miraculously collisions were avoided. By the evening of the 29th the convoy reached the latitude of Lisbon, where *Banff*, *Fishguard* and *Test* were detached and by 0800 next morning was in a position 75 miles SW of Cape St. Vincent, where course was altered to an easterly heading towards Gibraltar and passed 40 miles south of Sagres in the early afternoon. At 1600 the convoy reached the splitting position, 120 miles west of Cape Spartel on the African coast, where the first two ships in column 3 and all those in columns 4 to 8 detached as WS 26 by turning away nine points to starboard to steer for a position 100 miles west of Casablanca. The ships of KMF 8 continued eastward and reached Oran and Algiers on 1st February. WS 26 reached the Casablanca position at 0800 next morning, 31 January, where the destroyers, *Quality*, *Quiberon*, *Racehorse* and *Redoubt* joined the escort; course was then altered to steer towards the Canary Islands group which had never previously been approached by a WS convoy.

During the evening of the 1st the convoy passed through the 30 mile wide gap between Teneriffe and Gran Canaria and at 1900 next day altered to a S'ly heading to pass inside the Cape Verde group, the Greek *Adrias* was detached on the 3rd and at midday on the 4th, when 80 miles NW of Cap Vert, the Belgian flag trooper *Leopoldville* was overhauled and joined the convoy while on passage from Gibraltar but detached again that evening for Bathurst and did not rejoin.

WS 26 passed 60 miles west of Cap Vert that same afternoon, 3rd February, and although most of these troop convoys had used the 300 mile wide channel between the Cape Verde islands and Cap Vert, their route was never less than 150 miles distant from that Cape and the French naval base at Dakar which lay behind it. Towards the end of November 1942, however, improved Anglo-American relations with the French forces in North Africa allowed facilities in French West Africa to become available to the Allies, which included "airfields for flying boats..and a sorely needed naval air base..at Dakar, (which port) could also be used as an advanced base for the escorts..instead of Freetown".[5] Unfortunatley the diversion of the convoy route into the Gibraltar approaches rather offset the revised shortened route to Freetown but the advantage of continuous air cover all the way from the UK was a major gain in the overall protection of these convoys.

At 0800 on the 5th the convoy altered to a SE"ly heading direct for Freetown then distant 350 miles, and arrived there safely at 1030 on the 6th, having averaged 13 knots from the Clyde. It was a quiet period in the area very much lacking in U-Boat activity, until an Italian submarine reached the waters to the south of Freetown early in March. Little comment was made on this voyage by the complete units known to be embarked, other than 100 Anti-Tank Regiment RA (ex 8 Bn Gordons) under the command of Lt. Colonel RWF Johnstone, whose historian simply noted an uneventful voyage without identifying the ship, although there was "practically daily training and firing of 6 pounders on board. All ranks did PT and, (at Freetown), by request of the Commodore, the Gordon pipes and drums played the departing convoy out of the roadstead".[6]

In contrast to these brief military accounts, a lengthy but most apposite report was lodged with the Flag Officer Commanding West Africa station, by the CO of *Cilicia* and compiled by a Naval Signals Lieutenant taking passage on that ship to Freetown. This highlighted a "very dangerous lack of W/T discipline among the convoy escorts "[7] and gave several examples of "almost negligible effort to maintain W/T silence".[7] The practice was held to be widespread and with a considerable risk of interception by the enemy "it is suggested that more attention be given to the matter by shore authorities before the departure of convoys".[7] The report was to be destroyed by fire when complied with.

After the customary three days of replenishment in the heat of Freetown, the convoy sailed again without change at 1000 on 9 February for the Cape, forming into a cruising order of six columns beyond the searched channel and with the three HM ships as column 3.[8] The same two AMCs continued as ocean escort with destroyers *Quality*, *Quiberon*, *Quickmatch*, *Racehorse*, Greek *Adrias* and OBV *Corinthian*. The number of long range A/S escorts was significant; another group of U-Boats was then believed to be heading for South African waters and confirmed as WS 26 was leaving Freetown when a US liberty ship was torpedoed and sunk 400 miles south of St Helena that same day. Two days later two ships were sunk 12 miles SW and SE of Agulhas and Cape St Francis respectively. These proved to be victims of the U-Boat Group Seehund and the third such group to reach Cape waters within four months.

Unlike previous convoys which usually gave the West African coast a wide berth, WS 26 exited Freetown channel and turned SE to keep within 50 miles of the Liberian coast and when off Cape Palmas at daybreak on the 11th, altered course ESE towards a position 70 miles south of Cape Three Points and Takoradi on the gold Coast, where it was intended to detach *Leopoldville* for that port, but having only reached Freetown from Bathurst as WS 26 was departing, this liner was unable to be included.

In the early afternoon of the 12th, course was altered SE to cross the Gulf of Guinea towards Pointe Noire where the smaller escorts could be refuelled. On the 13th *Corinthian* and *Adrias* detached while the French sloop *D'Estienne D'Orves* joined. The destroyer *Relentless* joined next day and at 1500 on the 15th when 80 miles SW of Pointe Noire, course was altered south for the Cape while the destroyers may have detached in turn to refuel or receive this from the AMCs. During the forenoon of the 18th when 100 miles SW of Cape Frio on the South West African border, course was altered SSE towards Luderitz Bay and when 30 miles SW of that port in the afternoon of the 20th, *Quality* detached when relieved by *Blackmore*.

Once again unlike previous convoys, WS made a landfall 12 miles west of Cape Columbine at 0500 on the 22nd, and at 0630 when abreast of Saldanha Bay the Capetown portion was detached by the Vice Commodore on *Arundel Castle*, with *California*, *Duchess of Richmond*, *Highland Chieftain*, *Orduna*, *Ruys*, *Sibajak* and *Chyebassa*, where they arrived just before midday. The remaining seven transports with *Rembrandt* and the Commodore on *Stratheden* continued around the Cape for Durban, detaching *Canton* off Cape Point at 1300 for Simonstown. Cape Agulhas was rounded at 2100 and by next morning, 23rd, the convoy was 70 miles SE of Mossel Bay where the destroyer *Racehorse* was detached.

By the morning of the 24th the convoy was 50 miles SE of East London and entered Durban at noon next day after a passage of 32 days from the Clyde. Commodore Reyne reported that station-keeping and signalling of all ships was good, but noted bad whistles on *Maloja* and *Moolton*, "for which the company have a saying - as weak as a P & O whistle".[9] The convoy had arrived in Cape waters with the five U-Boats of Group Seehund widely dispersed between Capetown and East London and well clear of the entire coastal route to Durban; no enemy had been encountered on the voyage from the UK.

The transhipment plan for WS 26 in South Africa called for all 9,144 personnel on *Duchess of Richmond*, *Ruys* and *Sibajak* in Capetown to be disembarked and accommodated in Retreat Transit Camp for three weeks while awaiting on-carriage to their destinations. These three liners then sailed on the 25th as empty ships and reached Lagos eight days later. Here they were embarked with miscellaneous personnel of all three services being moved to the Middle East as the changed attitude in the neighbouring French colonies had removed the threat to West African bases and concurrently allowed the rundown of the Lagos air transit base. All three ships left Lagos on 13 March to join WS 27 at sea (q.v.)

At Durban on 25 February *Empress of Canada* and *Volendam* transhipped 4,200 of their 6,268 personnel to three waiting Indian Ocean troopers, *City of Paris*, *Lancashire* (completing drydocking) and *Dilwara* completing engine repairs. To this number were added 800 being 7 Bn King's Own Regiment who had been enjoying six weeks in Clairwood Camp since disembarking from *Mataroa* in the previous convoy. Much of their time was spent in providing parties "for seaching POW in Durban docks, as each POW disembarking had to be searched to secure forbidden articles or an unreasonable amount of tobacco or cigarettes".[10] The balance of 2,140 personnel were sent to Clairwood Camp to await on-carriage four weeks later in a nine ship Indian Ocean convoy to Bombay and Suez. Of the personnel landed in Capetown from WS 26, 7,000 were embarked on *Devonshire*, *Dilwara*, *City of Canterbury* and *Khedive Ismail* which left the port on 16 March for Durban and there became part of the nine ship convoy departing on the 22nd.

Whilst in Durban, *Empress of Canada* loaded 800 tons sugar on the Ellerman berth, plus military baggage, and embarked a mixed group of passengers which included Italian POW, Polish Army (including 70 women), three nationalities of naval personnel and a number of all three British Services altogether totalling 1,434. The *Empress* left Durban on the same day, 1st March, as the ongoing convoy, and turned south to pass around the Cape bound for the UK via Freetown. She was almost certainly sighted by *U-160* between Durban and Port Shepstone who observed (amongst other ships) "a passenger ship but could not pursue, being too near the land...a ship travelling fast with a flying-boat and two escort vessels in attendance and another passenger ship"[11], all this on the first two days of March.

The *Empress* avoided all the Group Seehund U Boats and being given a wide evasive route was not due at Freetown until 14 March, but on the 11th when in the vicinity of St Helena, Captain Goold received "orders to proceed to Takoradi and giving me a new route". Next day a further message changed that route while yet another on the afternoon of the 13th instructed the *Empress* "to proceed direct to Takoradi".[12] Just before midnight the ship was torpedoed on the starboard side abreast the after boiler-room, causing the loss of power and lighting, the main engines and steering-gear. The ship took an immediate heavy list to starboard and within sixteen minutes the Master had to order "Abandon Ship". A further torpedo forty minutes later caused the ship to sink rapidly with the loss of 44 crew, 8 armed guard and 340 passsengers of which 196 were Italian POW. Fortunately an SOS had been picked up and just before sunset that same day, the survivors' boats were found by a searching Catalina. Next evening the destroyer *Boreas* and corvettes *Crocus* and *Petunia* reached the scene and picked up 1,360 (MOWT records show 1,496 survivors) who were landed at Freetown on the morning of the 18th. There were suggestions of suspicious circumstances surrounding the loss of this ship, one claiming that an Italian Army Doctor POW had actually signalled the Italian submarine *Leonardo da Vinci* which sank the ship and later picked him up. After the war a German Radio Officer claimed the messages to change course had been sent by German radio; it seems unlikely these claims can now be corroborated.

The tragic loss of *Empress of Canada* in a position 480 miles NE of Ascension and 360 miles SW of Cape Palmas and not far from where *Laconia* and *Duchess of Atholl* suffered the same fate had proved a valuable hunting ground for Axis submarines. More importantly it was the irreplaceable loss of yet another WS liner and regrettably not the last. Capable of 20 knots this fine liner had sailed in six WS convoys around the Cape, another two from the Antipodes, the Spitzbergen raid and two of the KMF convoys to North Africa. Captain Goold, who had been Master in CPS since 1922, was sent on survivor's leave before appointment to his previous ship *Empress of Russia* where he remained until November 1945 and retired a year later.

The departure of *Volendam* from Durban was delayed until 6 March by nine days of engine repairs during which time cargo was loaded on the Clan berth. Proceeding direct to Freetown, *Volendam* there joined the homeward convoy SL 127 (with *Rangitiki* of WS 25) to reach Liverpool on 24 April, where 58 days were spent on repairs and a boiler survey before making an Iceland trip prior to KMF 20 for North Africa.

In reverting to the Durban transhipment to the smaller and slower Indian Ocean troopers, *City of Paris* arrived from Bombay on 22 February to disembark a mixed collection of 600 personnel. The DSTO asked the Master, Captain Percival, if his ship "could be ready to sail on 1st March fully embarked with Europeans in a 13 knot convoy (i.e. WS 26) for Bombay".[13] In normal circumstances *City of Paris* with a capacity of 1,500 could maintain almost 14 knots given good fuel, but Herbert Percival was an experienced Ellerman Master who had commanded their passenger ships since 1932, and cautiously agreed the DSTO's request subject to obtaining good quality bunker coal. The ship's destination was then changed to Suez, which required a considerable adjustment in storing the ship, but trouble with the Indian crew then nearly prevented the ship from sailing. Three firemen were prosecuted in Durban for insubordination during the passage to that port and on the day of arrival, a riot broke out between the firemen and saloon (catering) crew, which resulted in both sides refusing to sail and was only resolved by the timely intervention of the Deck Serang. The balance of the personnel for Suez and Bombay were carried forward in a nine ship CM convoy which sailed from Durban on 22 March and reached Bombay and Suez on 8 and 13 April respectively.

At Capetown the four liners and *Chyebassa* continuing with the convoy sailed from that port at midday on 26 February with the escort unspecified but most likely the cruiser *Ceres* which had recently refitted in Simonstown. During the coastal passage to the Durban rendezvous the convoy narrowly escaped contact with the Group Seehund U-Boats, one of which was then cruising close-in to Agulhas and two others similarly deployed in the vicinity of East London where they sank the Dutch Submarine Depot Ship *Colombia* on the 27th.

The Durban portion now comprising *Stratheden, Maloja, Mooltan, Dominion Monarch, Dempo, Lancashire, Dilwara, City of Paris*, Fleet Repair Ship *Resource* and storeships *Rembrandt* and *Selandia*; the latter ex Danish being operated by the South African government for supplying their bases in the Middle East, left the Natal port at 1630 on 1st March and made rendezvous with the Capetown section one hour later at the end of the searched channel, where a cruising order of five columns was formed.[14] Escort was provided by the cruisers *Birmingham* and *Ceres* (which cruised between columns 2 and 3) destroyers *Relentless, Blackmore, Catterick*, corvettes *Jasmine, Freesia, Nigella*, French patrol vessel *Commandant Duboc* and RIN Bangor class minesweeper *Carnatic*. Whilst the convoy was busily engaged in forming up and setting off initially towards a position 200 miles to the SE, *U-160* was a mere 40 miles down the coast and blissfully unaware of this priceless prize, but sank four ships and damaged two others in a coastal convoy two days later.

The revised convoy now of twelve transports and three storeships was carrying 18,500 personnel for Bombay and 18,000 for Suez. During the first night at sea *Nigella* dropped astern with an overheated bottom-end bearing and soon afterwards *Dilwara* straggled with engine trouble. *Carnatic* was detailed to remain with *Dilwara* and in the early hours of the 2nd, *Nigella* was ordered back to Durban. On reaching the alter-course position at 0800 *Birmingham* flew off her Walrus to contact *Dilwara* and similarly order that ship to return to Durban escorted by *Nigella*, while *Carnatic* caught up and rejoined the convoy which was now steering ENE towards the south of Madagascar. Late that same afternoon *Jasmine* and *Freesia* were detached to join a southbound convoy and at daybreak on the 4th, with WS 26 now judged clear of U-Boats, *Relentless*, *Blackmore* and *Catterick* were detached. That same evening with the convoy 100 miles south of Cape St Mary on Madagascar, *Carnatic* was detached to proceed independently to Diego Siuarez due to shortage of fuel.

Air escort was provided until the morning of the 5th when the convoy turned NNE to pass up the east side of Madagascar. At 1600 *Birmingham* sighted a merchant ship 16 miles ahead and increased speed to 22 knots to investigate. On closer approach the ship turned away and also increased speed whereupon *Birmingham* went to action stations and loaded main armament while ordering her to stop. The ship ignored this order and made the raider alarm by W/T. A warning shot brought a ready response but the ship then turned towards *Birmingham* sending unreadable morse by lamp and hoisting indistinguishable flags on her halliards. *Birmingham* circled the ship zigzagging at 8,000 yards range (4.5 miles) while endeavouring to establish her identity. Everything suggested this was a raider as she continued to turn slowly but keeping *Birmingham* broad on her starboard bow. She had a derrick unusually topped up and a large launch on deck which could have concealed guns or an E-boat. Flying the US flag this ship was finally identified as the *Robin Doncaster* on passage from Capetown to Aden and proved to be one of the C2 class loaned to Britain in 1941 as the *Empire Curlew*.

During the afternoon of the 6th, *Lancashire* with *Comm. Duboc* detached to the NW for Tamatave where she arrived next morning to part disembark, and thereafter continue with the balance to Diego Suarez, Mombasa and Suez. At daylight next morning the convoy overhauled the MOWT standard type *Ocean Gypsy* which replied correctly when challenged by *Ceres* but failed, like many other ships to hoist her signal letters. The *Ocean Gypsy* was on her maiden voyage from New York with military stores for Abadan and had been routed via Panama, down the west coast of South America and around Cape Horn to Durban; she was also the penultimate ship of the type to be completed by the Todd-Bath yard at Portland, Maine.

At 0800 on the 8th *Ceres* detached for Diego Suarez at which point the convoy had averaged 11.5 knots from Durban. Course was set to pass 90 miles NE of Cape Amber at the north tip of Madagascar between that island and the isolated islets of the Farquhar group. At 0800 on the 9th the cruiser *Hawkins* joined as SOE to relieve *Birmingham*, which then detached with *Resource* for Mombasa distant 660 miles WNW and where they arrived on the 11th; the latter to take station with the Eastern Fleet while *Birmingham* was proceeding home for refit in Devonport.

At 1100 on the 10th the cruiser *Frobisher* joined from Mombasa to become SOE, by which time the formation had exchanged *City of Paris* with *Mooltan* while *Chyebassa* moved from 53 to 33. Next forenoon the convoy reached the splitting position 350 miles east of Kismayu, where *Hawkins* detached NE for Bombay with *Stratheden, California, Dominion Monarch, Dempo, Mooltan* and *Chyebassa*, while *Frobisher* continued NNE towards Ras Hafun with *Arundel Castle, Highland Chieftain, Maloja, Orduna, City of Paris* and the two storeships for Suez.

The Suez portion passed through the Guardafui Strait at midnight on the 13th and reached Aden at 1300 on the 15th, where it was dispersed after all ships entered that harbour to refuel, sailing again as independents between the 16th and 18th and anchoring at Suez between the 20th and 22nd with a voyage time of 55 days. The area was now bereft of enemy activity, the front line in the desert being 1,300 miles to the west with that campaign nearing its end. The Bombay section encountered no incidents on the fine weather passage across the northern Indian Ocean, detaching *Chyebassa* for Colombo on the 14th while the convoy of five troopships reached Bombay at 1130 on the 17th. Of the complete units landed by this convoy in Bombay, the 7 Bn King's Own were posted to Lahore and 20 Royal Fusiliers to Allahabad both for internal security duties, 158 RAC went to Poona, 138 Field and 100 Anti-Tank Regiments to Ahmednagar and subsequently Burma, while 68 Field Regiment were on-carried to Iraq in a seven ship Indian Ocean type convoy on the 23rd.

The return voyages of the liners fom Suez followed much the same pattern as earlier convoys; *City of Paris* and *Orduna* being clear of the port on the 23rd, the former embarked with a very mixed bag of about 1,000 passengers including women of all three services plus Yugoslavs and Poles, and at Massawa additionally embarked 600 Italian internees. All of these people were landed at Durban from which the Ellerman liner was retained on Indian Ocean service. Captain Percival remained on the *City of Paris* until August 1944 when relieved in Suez and sent home on leave. He was awarded the O.B.E. for war services when commanding *City of Canterbury* during the evacuation from Greece in 1941. The homeward voyage of *Orduna* was an extended one lasting 97 days calling at thirteen ports almost entirely round Africa, beginning at Djibouti and completing at Casablanca and Gibraltar, from where she returned to Liverpool on 28 June for seven weeks drydocking and repairs before next sailing in the KMF section of the final WS convoy in August.

Arundel Castle and *Maloja* left Suez on 24 March, both refuelled in Aden, landed personnel and part loaded in Mombasa, completing in Durban and Capetown all on the Union-Castle berth. *Arundel Castle* also embarked some 1,250 Italian POW in Capetown for the UK, sailed on 29 April direct for the Clyde but directed to Liverpool where she arrived on 20 May and remained for four weeks before next sailing in KMF 19. At Capetown, *Maloja* joined with her sister *Mooltan* which left Bombay with some P&O cargo on the 27th and called at Diego Suarez before completing on the Union Castle berth at the Cape. The two sisters left that port on 29 April, called at Pointe Noire on 4 -5 May and then proceeded to Takoradi where they found *California* awaiting them. The Anchor liner was the last of the group to leave Bombay, on 29 March, having loaded there some cargo to her owners account before proceeding via Capetown to the Gold Coast port. It was here that all three liners were embarked with mainly RAF personnel being moved to Casablanca and Gibraltar at the start of a general rundown of the extensive Takoradi air route base.[15] A special convoy, SR 4F took the liners to refuel in Freetown, thence Casablanca (*Mooltan*) and Gibraltar from where they returned by MKF 15 to the UK and arrived on 4 June, *Maloja* at Liverpool and the other two on the Clyde. *Mooltan* also brought a batch of German POW to disembark at KGV Dock in

Glasgow. The P&O liners sailed again six weeks later in the combined WS 32/KMF 20 convoy while *California* set out on her final voyage on 7 July.

The last of the WS 26 liners from Suez was *Highland Chieftain* which had been delayed by engine repairs and sailed on 1 April with orders to load in the Plate on her owners' berth. After fuelling at Aden, the Royal Mail liner was delayed seven days in Durban, four due to further engine repairs. En route to the Plate she called at the Falkland Islands on 6 May with stores and mail for the garrison there, and loaded only in Montevideo before sailing direct for the UK, calling at Belfast and docking at Avonmouth on 17 June to discharge and undertake survey before sailing two weeks later in WS 32.

The first liner to leave Bombay and urgently required in the UK for WS 31 was *Stratheden*, which part loaded on her owners' berth and sailed on 24 March with a number of service personnel and families for the UK. Capetown was reached on 5 April and next morning *Queen Mary* anchored in Table Bay en route from Sydney to the Clyde and was due to be followed by *Aquitania* four days later. Prior arrangements had been made to embark several ships at that time with Italian POW being moved from the Transvaal to the UK, of which 4,000 were intended for *Queen Mary*, 2,726 for *Aquitania*, 1,750 on *Stratheden*, 1,250 on *Arundel Castle* (as above) and 2,000 on *Britannic*. A very heavy swell in the bay prevented embarkation on *Queen Mary* during the 6th, 7th and 8th by which time all but two of the special trains had left the Transvaal so arrangements were made to accommodate 3,000 overnight on the P&O liner. Next day the swell subsided and *Queen Mary* completed and sailed early on the 10th while *Stratheden* moved to Saldanha Bay for a few days to allow the liners of WS 28 to berth in the port. *Stratheden* finally left Capetown with *Britannic* as convoy CF 12 on the 19th and after fuelling in Freetown reached the Clyde on 10 May in sufficient time to make the sailing of WS 31 three weeks later.

Dempo and *Dominion Monarch* left Bombay on the same date as *Mooltan*, 24 March, the former having part loaded on the Ellerman berth and proceeded via Durban to Capetown where the ship was delayed for 23 days repairs to her twin 10 cylinder diesel engines. Sailing again on 4 May, *Dempo* proceeded direct to Liverpool arriving on the 26th and after seven weeks further repairs sailed again in KMF 20.

The homeward voyage of Shaw Savill's *Dominion Monarch* was rather more protracted and she did not reach home waters until September. Being known throughout the Company as the "*Dom*", this liner had orders to load refrigerated produce in New York, proceeding there via Durban, the Magellan Straits and Panama due to the U-Boat situation on the western side of the South and North Atlantic. After a brief call at Durban, the *Dom* made a passage across the South Atlantic, entered the Magellan Straits and refuelled at Punta Arenas on 12 April, as had been intended for the two "Freezer" ships from WS 25. Somewhere along the way, *Dominion Monarch* was ordered not to New York but to Wellington, after first disembarking the Magellan Straits pilot at Valparaiso. After a few days waiting time at Hobart in Tasmania, the *Dom* embarked 3,509 New Zealand reinforcements at Wellington for 2 NZ Division in the Middle East, sailed on 14 May and proceeded via Fremantle and Aden to Suez where she arrived on 11 June. She then returned south via Colombo to Capetown to load on the Union Castle berth for the UK, which included a move to Saldanha for a few days. Leaving Capetown on 4 August, the *Dom* returned home via Freetown and Gibraltar to join MKF 22 and reached Liverpool on 9 September after a voyage lasting 7.5 months. She was discharged, drydocked by Cammell Laird at Birkenhead and next sailed in KMF 25.

The routing of six WS 26 liners to call and embark at West African ports for destinations in other theatres was an additional burden on those priceless ships which featured in many of the later convoys in the series. It was partly the result of improved relations with neighbouring French African colonies, but also the successful Allied campaigns in Tunisia and the Western Desert which led to the re-opening of the through Mediterranean route to the east in May 1943.

Chapter 19

WS 27, WS 28 and WS 29

WS 27 moves British personnel from West Africa to the Middle East,
WS 28 becomes the Eastern Assault Force for Sicily and WS 29 carried an advance
party of West Africans to India.

WS 27 - sailed UK 24.2.1943
WS 27 was scheduled to leave the UK one month behind the previous convoy and in
conjunction with KMF 10A as far as the split position somewhere west of Gibraltar. Six
liners were allocated to the convoy, while six others would join in West Africa where
the Takoradi and Lagos air transport bases serving the air route to the Middle East, had
begun to run down on being replaced by a new route established through Casablanca.
Many of the personnel in these West African bases, mostly RAF, were now being moved
to the Middle East at the start of a build up to launch the eastern section of the invasion
of Sicily. With the British First Army still engaged with the enemy at Kasserine in
Tunisia, and being relatively easily supplied by KMF convoys taking nine days to reach
Algiers, Eighth Army could still only be reached from the Delta base after the long voy-
age around the Cape, as did British forces in Iraq, Persia, India and the Arakan.
   Three of the liners allocated for WS 27 arrived in UK ports in the second half of
January from voyages in WS 22, 23 and KMF 6: *Almanzora* and *Strathaird* in Glasgow,

Capetown Castle in Liverpool. To these were added *Strathmore* returned from KMF 2
to spend ten weeks with her builders at Barrow and *Christiaan Huygens* also spending
ten weeks repairing in Liverpool after returning from KMF 3, finally Holt's *Antenor*,
which had put back to Glasgow from WS 26 and remained at 7 KGV dock throughout.

Embarkation was completed at Liverpool on *Capetown Castle* and *Christiaan
Huygens* on 23rd February when both liners anchored in the river, while that on
Strathmore was delayed for a further 24 hours. In Glasgow, *Almanzora* embarked and
sailed downriver from 10 KGV dock soon after midday on the 23rd, and was followed
by *Antenor* 24 hours later. At the Clyde Anchorage *Strathaird* completed on the morn-
ing of the 23rd and of the liners sailing in KMF 10A, *Franconia* alone embarked in
Liverpool, *Boissievain* and *Letitia* in Glasgow and the remainder, *Circassia*, *Batory* and
Nieuw Holland at the Clyde Anchorage. The total embarked in both convoys was
36,099 and of those in WS 27, 8,953 were for Suez, 4,740 for on-carriage from South
Africa, 4,236 for Bombay and 2,670 for East Africa.[1]

For the first time in nine months a battleship was sailing with the convoy as far as
Freetown, *Malaya* having recently completed workup after a refit and was being accom-
panied by more of the Q and R class destroyers being deployed to the Eastern Fleet.
Captain JWA Waller of *Malaya* would act as SOE, the convoy Commodore was Sir AJ
Davies KBE CB RNR on *Circassia* (Captain DW Bone) acting for the combined con-
voys and later as Commodore of the KMF section. The combined Vice Commodore
and later Commodore of WS 27 after the split was Comm. JH Taylor DSC RNR on
Almanzora (Captain A Watts).[2] No storeships were attached to either convoy.

The original sailing date from the UK was scheduled for 23rd February, but was put
back 24 hours to allow *Strathmore* to be included rather than sail at a later date on completion of embarkation and be left with the problem of catching up. The combined
Liverpool section of *Capetown Castle*, *Christiaan Huygens*, *Franconia* and *Strathmore*
with the destroyer *Raider* as escort cleared the Bar Light Vessel at 1900 on the 24th,
while the Clyde section began passing out of the boom at 2330, led by the Commodore
on *Circassia* and followed at four minute intervals in the order: *Batory*, *Boissievain*,
Letitia, *Almanzora*, *Nieuw Holland*, *Antenor* and *Strathaird*. The Clyde escort of
Malaya, *Queenborough* and *Quail* left in the early hours of the 25th to join up in the
forenoon.

Rendezvous was made with both sections of the convoy and ocean escort, 6 miles
west of Orsay, at 1000 hours and where also the 44th Escort Group joined from Moville
comprising the sloops *Egret*, (SO A/S escort), *Erne*, cutter *Fishguard*, destroyers *Clare*
and *Wolverine*. At this point the combined convoys formed into a cruising order of five
columns[3] and set off for a position 200 miles to the westward, where course was altered
to the SSW and held for the next two days. This allowed the convoy to pass even closer to the Irish Coast than the route of WS 26, i.e. 60 miles west of Eagle Island on the
County Mayo coast (compared to 100 miles) and 90 miles west of Valencia rather than
180 miles.

During the five day passage to the split position near Cape St Vincent, *Malaya* commented on the low speed of advance at 11.5 knots which was therefore "an uncomfortably low speed during the first two days of the voyage..in the more dangerous submarine areas".[2] The speed quoted was 2.5 knots less than that of the slowest ship but was
said to be that required, allowing a reasonable margin for weather, to arrive at the dividing point at the pre-arranged time, where escorts were to meet and continue with the WS
section.

By the morning of 1st March the convoy was heading SE towards the intended split position 70 miles SW of St Vincent and at 1100 hours *Queenborough* and *Wolverine* detached for Casablanca to refuel, then 480 miles distant. At 1800 *Quadrant* joined the screen at the same time as the convoy was sighted by an aircraft said to be a Focke-Wulf Condor. The Admiralty ordered an immediate diversion to a more southerly course and moved the split position 130 miles westward to conform to this route. This position, 200 miles SW of St Vincent, was reached at 1100 on the 2nd without enemy interference when KMF 10A with five escorts of the 44th Escort Group turned eight points to port for the Straits of Gibraltar, which were passed through next afternoon and the convoy anchored safely off Oran at daybreak on the 4th.

WS 27 meanwhile re-formed into three columns[4] and continued on its southerly route. *Queenborough* and *Wolverine* rejoined from Casablanca soon after midnight and at 0800 on the 3rd, when 80 miles west of Cape Ghir on the Moroccan coast, course was altered to SW to pass through the 55 mile wide passage between Fuerteventura of the Canary group and Cape Juby on mainland Africa that night. *Malaya* provided 40 tons of fuel each to *Quadrant* and *Raider*, the former destroyer detaching ahead at midday 4th for Bathurst.

By 0800 on the 5th the convoy was 60 miles west of Cap Blanco and heading south, when *Malaya* received "two signals ordering *Almanzora* to Dakar and of either a storecarrier or oiler being sent up from Freetown and of *Almanzora* being sent to Freetown later".[2] The SOE felt this odd and referred to the Commodore on *Almanzora* who explained they had on board 200 MN officers and crew for (French) ships taken over in Dakar, and later added that 1100 tons of fuel and 600 tons of water were required at Dakar while "23 tons POW clothing may be landed at Freetown".[2] *Almanzora* was accordingly detached ahead at 1800 that evening for Dakar with *Quail* as escort, but may only have had 1.5 knots in excess of the convoy.

At 0800 6th, the convoy passed 25 miles west of Cap Vert and during the next 24 hours made good only 130 miles, presumably having reversed course for some hours while awaiting *Almanzora* and *Quail* to rejoin. The southerly course was resumed and maintained until the evening of the 7th when an alteration was made to ESE direct for Freetown where the convoy was led into the anchorage by *Malaya* at 0930 on the 8th. The average speed for the passage was recorded as 12.81 knots, the Commodore (who may have transferred at sea to *Antenor*) noting only that fine weather was experienced throughout while the SOE commented that the conduct of both convoys was excellent in all respects.

Whilst in Freetown, *Malaya* handed over the duties of SOE to the cruiser *Sussex*, and waiting at the anchorage were three more transports, *Bergensfjord*, *Leopoldville* and *Orbita*. Each had previously gone out to Algiers in KMF 7, and thereafter carried mixed personnel between Gibraltar, Casablanca, Dakar and Bathurst before reaching Freetown during the first nine days of February. They were then engaged for two round trips each, first to Takoradi then Lagos before arriving in Freetown three days ahead of and ready to join WS 27, fully embarked with 7,000 British and West African personnel for the Middle East.

The convoy now of nine liners sailed again from Freetown on 11 March, with Commodore Taylor embarked on *Antenor*, the first ship passing through the boom gate at 0830 and were preceded down the swept channel by the A/S escorts *Queenborough*, *Quail*, *Raider*, *Crocus* and *Petunia* carrying out a sweep to seaward. *Sussex* sailed an hour behind the convoy and joined up as it formed into four columns and set off on a

SW'ly heading for 75 miles to clear the 100 fathom line, before turning SE to follow the Liberian coast at a distance of 50 miles offshore.

Whilst the convoy was forming up, *Raider* reported an enemy submarine transmission which was relayed to FOWA at Freetown. This may have emanated from the Italian *Leonardo da Vinci* which was then in the area moving south and soon to encounter the *Empress of Canada*. At midnight on the first day out *Quail* was detached to meet the US Army transport *James Parker* (built 1939 as the *Panama*) at Marshall on the Liberian coast, thereafter escorting her to join WS 27 which was effected at 1300 on the 12th.

At 0800 on the 13th the convoy reached a position 90 miles south of Cape Palmas where course was altered to due east, and at 0200 on the 14th *Quail* detached with *James Parker* for Takoradi, distant 150 miles NE, where the destroyer was to refuel. Three hours later the corvettes *Crocus* and *Petunia* were detached by an "Immediate" Admiralty order to proceed to the assistance of *Empress of Canada* having been torpedoed 500 miles to the SW.[5] At 1800 that same day the Lagos section of the convoy joined up with the corvettes *Bellwort* and *Armeria*, comprising *Duchess of Richmond*, *Ruys* and *Sibajak* carrying a further 9,000 service personnel being moved to the Middle East, the three liners having previously turned round at Capetown in WS 26. (*q.v.*) At midnight the convoy turned SE towards Pointe Noire.

There was considerable activity of the escort during the next three days while crossing the Gulf of Guinea: at 1300 on the 14th *Quail* rejoined from Takoradi and five hours later *Raider* detached WNW at 20 knots to carry out an A/S sweep in view of a submarine reported 500 miles in that direction and 150 miles SW of Cape Three Points. Next morning *Raider* reported an HF/DF bearing of a U-Boat to a patrolling aircraft but rejoined the convoy next evening without further result and then detached ahead to refuel at Pointe Noire. *Sussex* meanwhile had refuelled both *Quail* and *Queenborough*. At daybreak on the 17th and 150 miles WNW of Pointe Noire the convoy altered to a southerly heading towards Cape Frio, *Raider* rejoined that evening while the two corvettes were detached.

By 0900 on the 20th WS 27 was 150 miles SW of Cape Frio and adopted a course of SSE towards the Cape. *Sussex* detached from the convoy that evening to transmit a message to the CinCSA of the intention to keep outside 200 fathoms, due to eight ships not having paravanes and rejoined at 0700 on the 21st when an air escort arrived and maintained day air cover until arrival at Durban.

No further incidents occurred on this passage, although the convoy was approaching South African waters with the Group Seehund U-Boats still operating in the area. During the night of the 21st/22nd, the convoy crossed the latitude of Luderitz Bay and in the early hours inadvertently passed 40 miles astern of *U-516* then heading home. *Sussex* detached ahead for Capetown at 0530 23rd and berthed in the Duncan Dock five hours later. At 0830 the convoy was 26 miles abeam of Cape Columbine, at a time when *U-509* was cruising in the area but poor visibility that morning fortunately obscured the convoy from his view. *U-160* was 150 miles to the westward also heading home while *U-182* was cruising to the east of Durban but never approached the route of the convoy which therefore passed through unscathed. At 1300 when 8 miles NW of Robben Island the Capetown portion was detached, comprising *Almanzora* (although turning round at Durban) and the six liners which joined in West Africa; all were berthed alongside by 1430. Meanwhile *Sussex* had refuelled and sailed again to catch up the remaining five ships of the Durban section which had been joined by *City of Bristol* from Capetown, and at 1500 by *Sydney Star* from Simonstown. The three destroyers were at this time relieved by *Foxhound, Quilliam* and *Racehorse*.

At midnight on the 23rd, WS 27 passed 5 miles south of Cape Agulhas and at 2045 the following night was 30 miles south of Cape Francis where the Ellerman and Blue Star cargo liners detached for Port Elizabeth, then distant 65 miles NE and arrived there next morning. *Sussex* entered Durban harbour at 0900 on the 26th ahead of the convoy which followed in the order: *Strathmore, Strathaird, Christiaan Huygens, Capetown Castle* and *Antenor*, the voyage from Liverpool having taken 29.5 days.

After three nights and days of hospitality and other delights in Capetown and without change to the personnel embarked, the same seven liners and three escorting destroyers left that port at 1600 on the 26th with the Commodore now on *Duchess of Richmond*. Cape Point was passed at 2000 and by 0300 next day the convoy was 5 miles south of Agulhas on an Easterly course. No incidents occurred on the coastal passage and by 0900 on the 29th the convoy was 32 miles south of the Durban Bluff, having made a mere 11.9 knots in the past 24 hours in the worst of the adverse Agulhas current.

By midday on 29 March, the seven liners were 12 miles SE of the Bluff where *Almanzora* and the three destroyers detached for Durban, to be replaced by *Capetown Castle* (whose Master, Captain EH Thornton, was acting as Vice Commodore), *Strathaird, Strathmore* and *Christiaan Huygens* escorted by the cruiser *Frobisher* and destroyers *Foxhound, Napier, Rotherham* and *Catterick*. A cruising order of four columns was formed and the revised WS 27 set off for a position 300 miles south of Madagascar where course would be altered to pass up the east side of the island but was later radically amended.[6]

Whilst in Durban, *Antenor* disembarked completely as did *Almanzora* which arrived on the 29th, leaving 4,740 in the transit camp to await on-carriage four weeks later when the Indian Ocean troopers *Aronda, Dunera* and *City of Paris* became available, the first spending four weeks repairing in Durban while *Dunera* spent two weeks in Port Elizabeth. *City of Paris* was available almost on the day of her arrival from Suez on 13 April, but utilized the time for coal bunkering, storing and having ten oerlikon gun-nests erected by DEMS, only to be demolished and rebuilt in Bombay on two separate occasions. The three ships were joined by *Christiaan Huygens* returned from Mombasa and sailed as a DB convoy on 25 April to reach Bombay on 11 May and from where the Dutch liner continued to Suez to join the Sicily assault.

The return voyages of the disembarked ships in Durban are simply related, *Almanzora* sailing on 1st April and after a brief call at Capetown reached Lagos on the 17th, Takoradi on the 20th and Freetown six days later having embarked advance parties of 81 West African Division at each port before joining WS 29 (*q.v.*). *Antenor* left Durban on the 8th and Capetown a week later before proceeding homewards via Takoradi and Freetown, sailing then in convoy SR 4F to Gibraltar and finally in MKF 15 to reach the Clyde on 4 June for five weeks repairs before sailing again in KMF 22.

When WS 27 left the Durban rendezvous there was news of a U-Boat near the south end of Madagascar, hence the unusually wide berth being given to the island. Subsequent D/F bearings showed this submarine (possibly *U-182* lost on her homeward voyage) to be moving south towards the path of the convoy, and so the CinCEF ordered the convoy to divert up the Mozambique Channel, but this signal was not received by *Frobisher* until 1800 on the 30th and when deciphered there was barely 45 minutes of daylight remaining to wheel the convoy eight points, but was "well carried out and...a great credit to the Masters of all ships".[7]

The convoy continued up the centre of the Mozambique Channel, the first to pass this way since WS 18 in May 1942, without incident until the forenoon of 1st April when *Rotherham* went off to investigate a contact to port, the convoy following with an emergency turn of 45° in that direction. *Catterick* joined *Rotherham*, both dropped depth-charges, while the patrolling Catalina ahead of the convoy was also sent to assist but *Rotherham* concluded the contact to be only a possible submarine and insufficient to warrant an enemy report. At 1900 that evening on the latitude of Beira, *Catterick* was detached back to Durban and the remaining destroyers two hours later.

The forenoon of the 3rd found WS 27 passing 30 miles west of Comoro Island where course was altered to NNE towards Guardafui and at 1500 the AMC *Carthage* joined the escort. At 0300 on the 4th, *Christiaan Huygens* detached independently for Mombasa distant 370 miles NW where she arrived next morning, disembarked and immediately returned to Durban for the on-carriage section to Bombay.

The remaining nine liners, all for Suez, continued northwards in fine weather and by 0830 5th, were 360 miles ESE of Kismayu, where the cruiser *Durban* joined and relieved *Frobisher* as SOE which then detached. There were no incidents on this passage which was made at an average speed of advance of 13.5 knots. The absence of any raider or U-Boat reports allowed *Durban* to carry out range and inclination exercises, to calibrate her radar and make dummy torpedo attacks on *Carthage*. The Guardafui Strait was approached on the evening of the 7th and by 1000 on the 8th the convoy was 20 miles NE of the lighthouse. Aden was reached at 1830 on the 9th when the convoy dispersed to proceed independently to Suez, the Commodore noting that the voyage was made without incident, in fine weather throughout and an excellent formation to handle.

All ships refuelled in Aden and continued to Suez between the 10th and 14th, *Capetown Castle* and the two *Straths* being disembarked first and re-embarked with POW for Bombay where they all arrived on the 26th. From here the Union Castle liner was ordered to New York to load on the Cunard berth and embark US troops for the UK, and because of the U-Boat situation in the Atlantic narrows, as with *Dominion Monarch* in WS 26 (*q.v.*), was directed to proceed the long way round via the Magellan Straits and Panama, an additional distance of 3,300 miles adding nine days to the voyage. Calls were made at Durban (3 days) and Capetown (5 days) before further refuelling stops at Punta Arenas and of course the Panama Canal. The small Chilean port of Punta Arenas is situated 110 miles within the eastern entrance to the Magellan Straits and requires careful navigation to reach it, but thereafter the remaining 200 miles to gain the open Pacific is fraught with steep sided mountainous narrow passages, where gales, heavy squalls of rain or snow and indifferent visibility are the norm. The western end is noted for heavy snowstorms or rain and low cloud, which frequently reduce the visibility of the lights. In the month of June there is barely eight hours of daylight. It was a waterway hardly if ever used by British shipping since the PSNC abandoned that route to the west coast in 1920. The *Capetown Castle* was drydocked in New York over a ten day period and reached Liverpool on 8 July to follow that voyage with four round trips between these two ports.

The CPS *Duchess of Richmond* was the only other liner of WS 27 to return directly homewards, leaving Suez on 20th April and Aden four days later to load on the Union Castle berth at Durban and Capetown. The passage north was made via Takoradi and Freetown to Liverpool where she arrived on 15 June after an absence from the UK of six months. Captain Tom Jones then transferred to the *Empress of Australia* where he remained until retiral five months later. The *Duchess* was next employed for an Iceland trip and thereafter KMF 22.

From Bombay the two *Strath* liners made a two ship convoy to Durban arriving there on 18 May to embark for the on-carriage of personnel from WS 29 and were retained in the Indian Ocean for two similar voyages in July and August. Also *Ruys*, *Sibajak*, *Bergensfjord*, *Leopoldville* and *Orbita* all returned via Aden to Durban between 4 and 5 May to await the arrival of WS 29; *Orbita* alone going on to embark at Capetown where she berthed on the 10th.

The shortage of tonnage which had afflicted the WS route in 1941 had now spread to the Indian Ocean ships of which there never was more than forty. By the spring of 1943 nearly a quarter of them were employed, not in the Indian Ocean at all but in the Mediterranean operating a shuttle service for Eighth Army between Alexandria and Tripoli. Three more were then taken up to serve as LSIs for the Sicily assault while a further demand for a Bay of Bengal service, to supply Fourteenth Army through Chittagong from Madras and Calcutta began in January 1943 with a single ship and by the end of the year this service employed eleven. Nor was there any slackening of demand between Bombay and Basra which engaged thirteen of the Indian Ocean fleet to maintain four Indian and two Polish divisions then in Iran and Iraq. With some ships inevitably under repair, no more than nine remained to cover all of the on-carriage demands including UDF troops from South Africa to East Africa, India and the Middle East, and from May onwards was exacerbated by the transfer of the three "Monster" liners from the Durban-Suez shuttle to the North Atlantic route.

WS 28 - sailed UK 16.3.43.

During the three years of WS convoys which ended in the summer of 1943, only one of the entire series of fifty-one convoys ever contained more than twenty transports and so were relatively small formations compared to the Atlantic trade convoys which often comprised eighty or more ships and occasionally over one hundred. What set the WS convoys apart from all others was the sheer scale of personnel carried and safely delivered over extremely long distances. As the very last of the "larger " WS convoys, WS 28 comprised eleven liners, all but one being fitted as LSIL to later act as the Eastern Task Force to assault Sicily.

As far back as the autumn of 1941, the British Chiefs of Staff had contemplated an invasion of Sicily to exploit the victory which they hoped to win by the Crusader offensive begun in the Western Desert that November. Such invasion was later judged to be impracticable, but a year later the successful exploitation of the Torch landings into Tunisia led to an outline plan being prepared to invade Sicily, whereupon Churchill and Roosevelt arranged "to meet at Casablanca in January 1943 to shape future strategy".[1] The Americans, with the notable exception of the President, came to that conference strongly opposed to further military ventures other than a cross-channel invasion of Europe, and it was the British Chiefs of Staff who had to persuade them otherwise, "to exploit Torch within the Mediterranean by invading Sicily or Sardinia".[2] The choice eventually fell on Sicily as it contributed "towards completely opening up the Mediterranean and..the target date was fixed for the favourable July moon".[3]

Eight months earlier the first overseas landing at Diego Suarez was made by 13,000 troops carried in seven troopships, four being fitted with their own landing craft, i.e. Landing Ships Infantry Large (LSIL). For subsequent landings on the east side of Madagascar three more liners were fitted as LSIL and the experience gained in these operations proved invaluable for the Torch expedition when 68,500 troops were landed from twenty LSIL and eight other troopships. Five of the LSIL were lost during the Torch operations while the remainder was retained on KMF service to and from North Africa, where they could be readily called upon should further landings be required, rather than release them to extended WS voyages.

The early planning for Sicily in November 1942 dictated the need for a Western Task Force to be launched from the UK as a KMF convoy with lesser ships and landing craft crossing over from Tunisia. A separate Eastern Task Force would simultaneously be launched from the Middle East and for which the necessary ships would have to come from India or around the Cape from the UK. At this time the MOWT stated they would "require three months to assemble ships in the Eastern Mediterranean",[4] which allowed barely a month to train the troops already in that theatre for assault landing techniques from these ships and their landing craft, and meant their latest departure from the UK must be towards the end of March 1943.

The Casablanca conference on 23 January issued a directive confirming that the attack on Sicily would be launched in July, and following this five more liners began conversion to LSIL to replace those lost on Torch, three being the Indian Ocean class fitted out in Bombay. All of these liners were allocated to the Eastern Task Force while three more began conversion in the spring in sufficient time to join the Western Task Force as convoy KMF 18.

The two British Infantry Divisons (i.e. 5th and 50th) with 231 Independent Brigade selected as the Eastern Assault Force were already in the Middle East and had first to be refitted before training for beach landings at Kabrit on the Great Bitter Lake, but could not practise the ways and means of transferring from ship to landing craft until the liners of WS 28 reached Suez and disembarked the 31,000 personnel brought out from the UK.

The allocation and fitment of the ten LSIL to sail in WS 28 was ongoing since the first liners returned to the UK from the Torch landings in November. Some required modification and repairs, others needed extra fittings and many of their attached landing craft (LCA) carried on the lifeboat davits had been damaged and needed replacement. The process was a gradual one as only a few liners could be handled in the repair yards simultaneously without denuding the KMF flow of reinforcements to North Africa.

The first liners taken out of KMF service were the HQ ship *Winchester Castle* and HMS *Keren* (ex BI *Kenya*); both anchored in the Clyde in late November and apart from short spells repairing in Glasgow and Liverpool respectively, spent all of the intervening weeks there or at moorings in the sheltered waters of the Gareloch which proved the most convenient area for shipment and for practise-handling their LCA. Other liners were then fitted or re-equipped to serve as LSIL whenever they became available; *Tegelberg* came into the Clyde on 23 December after a collision with *Llangibby Castle* in KMF 4 and required nine weeks in Glasgow to make good the damage, while *Orontes* arrived from KMF 6 on 14 January and later moved to Glasgow for repair and refit. Four liners arrived from KMF 7 on 26 January, *Duchess of Bedford* and *Otranto* in Liverpool, *Sobieski* and *Reina del Pacifico* to the Clyde whence the last named later proceeded to Liverpool. *Strathnaver* arrived on 9 February from KMF 8 to spend most of her time in the Gareloch and finally *Monarch of Bermuda* reached Liverpool from KMF 9 on 24 February and four days later moved to the Clyde to ship her LCA. Also sailing in WS 28 were three HM ships, *Bulolo*, *Largs* and *Ulster Monarch* all previously having been in the Torch assault. The one liner included in the convoy but not for Sicily was Cunard"s *Britannic* having returned to Liverpool on 26 February from WS 25.

By the first week of March eight of the LSIL were in the Gareloch receiving or exercising the LCA crews. *Monarch of Bermuda* and the three HM ships plus *Keren* remained at the Clyde Anchorage and on the 9th the two Orient liners and *Duchess of Bedford* left for Liverpool to begin embarkation at the Princes Stage, followed by *Monarch of Bermuda* two days later. On that same date *Reina del Pacifico* shifted to the Clyde Anchorage, followed by *Strathnaver* on the 13th and again by *Sobieski*, *Tegelberg* and *Winchester Castle* on the 14th; all nine LSIL plus HM ships then began embarkation which was completed with all ships ready for sea on the 15th.[5] Amongst the personnel embarked were reinforcement details for all three Services but more importantly many of the Army and RAF administrative units which were to land behind the assault troops to set up and operate such services as the Field Maintenance Centres for rations, petrol, water, ordnance, ammunition, engineers, medical stores, a transit camp, a post office and POW cage. The 2nd Survey Regiment (RA) en route to India were among those known to be embarked on *Britannic*. Three storeships were included in the convoy, *Empire Might* (Blue Star) and *Perthshire* (Clan Line) which both loaded in Glasgow, while Shaw Savill's *Waipawa* loaded in Liverpool.

WS 28 sailed as a combined convoy with the eight liners of KMF 11 for which *Nea Hellas*, *Banfora*, *Orion* and *Ormonde* embarked in Glasgow, *Windsor Castle* at the Clyde Anchorage, *Cuba* and *J.V.Oldenbarnevelt* in Liverpool and *Rangitata* in Avonmouth; the total lift being 24,910 all for Algiers although *Windsor Castle* was destined never to reach that port. The Commodore of the combined convoys and of WS 28 was Rear Admiral DMT Bedford on *Strathnaver* (Captain EM Coates) while the Vice Commodore RHR Mackay on *Nea Hellas* (Captain JM Brown) would later act as Commodore of KMF 11.

The first movement of this combined 25 ship convoy was that of *Rangitata* which completed embarkation in Avonmouth and sailed on the midday tide of the 14th for the Clyde where she anchored next afternoon. The eight ships of the Liverpool section began clearing the Bar Light Vessel at 2300 on the 15th and proceeded towards the ordered rendezvous with *Woodpecker* as escort, while the Clyde portion began passing out of the boom at 0500 16th led by the Commodore on *Strathnaver*, escort being given by the destroyer *Skate*. Both sections were due to meet 6 miles west of Orsay at 1500 that afternoon, but fog at intervals during the morning delayed this junction by half an hour while *Skate* with a steering defect was relieved by *Woodpecker* at 1400. By 1600 the completed convoy had formed into seven columns [6] and set off to the WSW at 9 knots under escort of the sloops *Wren* (SO) and *Woodpecker*, destroyers *Douglas*, *Goathland*, *Eggesford*, *Whaddon*, *Badsworth* and *Krakowiak*. By 1700 speed was increased to 13 knots while at 1930 the Admiralty altered the course slightly northward, presumed to avoid a reported U-Boat. No AMC or cruiser accompanied this convoy.

Several adjustments were made to the ordered route over the next two days, at 0530 17th course was altered to SW and half an hour later to due south in a westerly swell and SW wind force 4. At noon course was again altered by Admiralty order to SSE to pass 40 miles east of a reported U-Boat, the speed increased to 13.5 knots and at 2100 when in position 60 miles west of Valencia, a SW course was resumed. Next morning the weather deteriorated with reduced visibility of 4-5 miles and strengthening wind from the SSE 4-5 causing anxiety for the LCA slung overside from the davits of the LSIL, some of necessity being at very low levels. However, with a Fortress air escort in sight, course was altered to south at 0830 and held for the next two days. That same afternoon *Keren* and *Largs* hauled out of line for a time to effect engine repairs and by 1730 with the wind increased to SE 5-6 and a rough sea, speed had to be reduced to 12 knots then 10 knots on instructions from SOE for the benefit of the five Hunt class destroyers, but the wind moderated that same evening when a speed of 13.5 knots was resumed. Conditions for the personnel on all ships gradually improved, and fortunately no damage was reported to the overside LCA.[7]

By dawn on the 19th the wind eased further to SE 3 when the cruiser *Newfoundland* with destroyer escort was sighted ahead for a time but in providing distant cover for more than one convoy, including WS 28, did not join up. A Sunderland air escort was present most of that morning and three of the destroyers were sent on ahead to refuel in Gibraltar.

Next morning, 20th, in a light breeze and smooth sea the convoy reached latitude 40° North and being 240 miles west of the Portuguese coast, altered course to SE for the pre-arranged split position. At 1500 *Reina del Pacifico* at the head of column 6 reported a German aircraft to the south (presumably a Condor), some ships fired a couple of rounds of 12 pdr but the aircraft was out of range. The convoy was then 200 miles west of Lisbon and the aircraft 700 miles from its base at Bordeaux-Merignac but had a range extending to 900 miles. The SOE on *Wren* claimed the aircraft had not been identified but during the next hour first *Ulster Monarch* reported enemy aircraft in sight and opened fire, followed by *Krakowiak* who then reported that aircraft as friendly but another one as hostile and confirmed this 20 minutes later, followed by a further signal from the SOE stating the aircraft had not been identified but no further incidents occurred. The air escort provided by Catalina, Sunderland or Fortress aircraft was now present in daylight hours all the way to Freetown.

At 0725 on the 21st, the split position 75 miles SW of Cape St Vincent was reached, where *Malcolm* (SO), *Wolverine*, *Witch* and *Quadrant* joined as the new A/S escort for WS 28 and 20 minutes later KMF 11 parted company with *Wren* and remaining escorts for Gibraltar, plus *Largs* and *Ulster Monarch* for that port and reasons unknown but later continued to Freetown to rejoin WS 28. The KMF section safely passed into the Mediterranean at midnight that same day but in the early hours of the 23rd *Windsor Castle* was torpedoed by an enemy aircraft in bright moonlight when a mere 100 miles short of her destination. Fortunately she did not sink until 15 hours later by which time two destroyers had rescued all but one of a total complement of almost 3,000; the rest of KMF 11 reached Algiers safely that morning.

From the split position WS 28 turned five points to starboard to steer towards Cape Ghir as followed by the previous convoy WS 27. The formation basically remained unchanged with *Otranto* and *Orontes* taking up stations 31 and 32, while the Commodore exchanged positions with *Bulolo* to retain his position in the centre of the convoy. Before 1100 the Tribal class *Ashanti* (one of four survivors of a class of 18) joined up and speed increased to 14 knots.

The weather continued fine with extreme visibility for the remainder of the passage and by noon on the 22nd the convoy was 90 miles SW of Cape Ghir where course was altered to SW for the channel between Fuerteventura and the African mainland. Late that afternoon *Empire Might* reported a fire in her stokehold, *Ashanti* was detached to assist and when only 10 knots could be obtained both were ordered to Dakar distant 1,020 miles ahead, where they arrived on the 26th. After eleven days making repairs, *Empire Might* resumed her voyage and reached Freetown on 9 April by which date the convoy had almost reached the Cape. Eleven weeks were spent in Freetown while the adjacent hold was flooded to extinguish the smouldering fire and a considerable amount of cargo discharged to reach the adjoining bulkhead. By the time all this was made good the Mediterranean had been re-opened for fast cargo ships so *Empire Might* returned north to use that route and reached Port Said on 4 July.

Meanwhile WS 28 passed 20 miles east of Fuerteventura at midnight 22nd at reduced speed of 13.5 knots due to boiler trouble on *Perthshire* which caused a further reduction to 12.5 next morning but resumed 13.5 that same afternoon. Daylight air cover continued and by noon 24th the convoy was 60 miles due west of Cape Blanco where a direct S'ly course was set towards Cap Vert. At 0800 25th *Malcolm* and *Wolverine* detached ahead to refuel at Dakar then 120 miles distant and rejoined that same evening which allowed *Witch* to detach for Bathurst. During the 26th an arrangement was made between the Commodore and SOE to follow an amended route outside the 100 fathom line and as agreed by the Admiralty. At noon course was altered to SE and in the late evening to ESE direct for Freetown. By 0600 27th the convoy was 65 miles distant from the port; single line ahead was formed at 0900 when *Otranto* (Captain ACG Hawker) took guide and reached the Fairway Buoy at noon. All ships were anchored in the harbour shortly after 1300 having averaged 12.94 knots from the Clyde over a distance of 3,433 miles, the Commodore simply noting that *Stathnaver* was an excellent ship for that purpose.

There was cause for some rejoicing as the ships lay in Freetown when news was received of Eighth Army breaking through the Mareth Line to set the scene for what everyone then knew to be the final encounter with Axis forces in North Africa. In Russia a massive offensive had retaken Rostov, Kharkov and Kursk from German occupation while in the Pacific, Australian and US troops were engaged with the Japanese in New Guinea and the Solomons. Only in Burma, where British and Indian forces were retreating from the Mayu peninsula before the onset of the monsoon, were the Allies suffering reverses.

Whilst the ships were fuelling and watering in the oppressive heat of Freetown, *Largs* and *Ulster Monarch* arrived independently from Gibraltar to rejoin the convoy although the latter ship was unable to complete in sufficient time by the ordered sailing time. The cruiser *Kenya* also joined in Freetown being on passage from the Home to the Eastern Fleet. At 1130 on 30 March the Commodore on *Strathnaver* led the 15 ships through the boom gate with an escort provided by *Kenya*, *Malcolm*, *Redoubt*, *Quadrant*, *Witch* and *Wolverine*, to reach the end of the swept channel at 1300 where a course of SW was adopted and a speed of 9 knots maintained while the convoy formed into a completely revised cruising order of five columns.[8] Speed was then increased to 12 and then 13.5 knots and by late evening the convoy was 95 miles SW of the Liberian coast, where an alteration of course was made in three stages from SW to SE to maintain a like distance off that coastline.

The weather remained very warm with a calm sea and barely a ripple when *Ulster Monarch* caught up at 0200 31st and took station 44. Later that day *Largs* developed engine trouble causing the convoy to reduce speed for an hour. Soon after midnight course was altered to ESE and at 0800 1st April when 100 miles south of Cape Palmas, an easterly course was adopted to follow the favourable Guinea Current on a route similar to that of the previous convoy. However, that evening the FOCWA instructed a sharp alteration to SE to avoid a U-Boat reported by aircraft to be 20 miles south of the convoy's intended track. No further reports were made but this may have been an

Italian submarine known to be operating to the south and west of Freetown at that time. The danger was judged to be passed soon after midday on the 2nd when a course of ESE was laid off towards Pointe Noire; that evening *Ulster Monarch* detached ahead for that port to refuel, distant 900 miles, while daylight air cover continued across the calm condition of the Gulf.

A frequent change of destroyers occurred as the convoy neared Pointe Noire; *Witch, Wolverine* and *Malcolm* detaching entirely to be replaced by *Racehorse* and *Relentless*, while *Redoubt* and *Quadrant* were refuelled and rejoined for the passage to the Cape. By midday 5th the convoy was 60 miles west of Pointe Noire and at 1330 altered to due south towards Cape Frio on the southern Angolan border.

The noon position on the 6th showed the convoy to have averaged 14 knots during the previous 24 hours and by next evening was 40 miles west of Cape Frio, from which point onwards the course line generally followed the shape of the coastline at a distance of about 60 miles. That same evening *Winchester Castle* reported a radar echo 13 miles to port which *Kenya* sent a destroyer to investigate and found the British steamer *Benalder*, under tow of two Admiralty tugs from Takoradi to Capetown; this ship having her machinery disabled when torpedoed off the West African coast five months earlier.

By the afternoon of the 8th Walvis Bay was 60 miles distant to the SE, at which point daylight air cover was resumed and continued until reaching the Cape Coast when it was provided both by day and night. *Britannic* was astern with engine trouble for three hours that evening. A S"ly breeze sprang up on the 9th with a moderate head sea and extreme visibility and that evening paravanes were streamed as the convoy approached soundings. At 0300 11th the convoy was 20 miles SW of Cape Columbine and by dawn at 0700, Table Mountain was in sight. One hour later, when 10 miles south of Dassen Island, the Vice Commodore (and Master) of *Duchess of Bedford*, Captain HA Moore, detached with the Capetown portion, i.e. *Monarch of Bermuda, Winchester Castle, Tegelberg, Britannic* and *Waipawa*, escorted by *Kenya, Relentless, Redoubt* and all arrived in port later that morning.

Meanwhile the ten remaining ships continued for Durban under escort of *Quadrant* and *Racehorse*, detached *Largs* and *Ulster Monarch* at 1130 off Cape Point for Simonstown and soon after *Foxhound* and *Rotherham* joined and relieved the other two destroyers. It was during this period that speed had to be reduced for five hours due to further boiler trouble on *Perthshire*. The convoy passed 5 miles south of Cape Agulhas at 1800 and by noon next day was 50 miles south of Cape St Francis and two hours later 60 miles off Cape Recife, by which time the wind freshened from the East to become 4-5 with a moderate head sea.

From Recife onwards the convoy began to close up to the coast but keeping 20-30 miles offshore. By noon 13th the position was 30 miles SE of East London in a NNE wind force 5 with a rough sea and speed down to 10 knots in the adverse Agulhas current, but next morning as the Natal coast was approached the wind backed to WSW 4. The Durban Bluff was sighted to the NW at 0620 14th and half an hour later the convoy was ordered to proceed into harbour, having averaged 12.87 knots from Freetown. In respect of U-Boat activity, WS 28 reached Cape waters six days after the last of the Group Seehund boats had left these waters heading home.

There were no transhipment or disembarkations in Durban, other than for exercise and recreation, but a very complex situation arose in Capetown where WS 28 had arrived in the aftermath of a large complement embarked on the *Queen Mary* at the Table Bay anchorage, which included POW all for the UK. *Aquitania* was in the Duncan Dock similarly embarking while *Britannic* disembarked all of her complement to the transit camp and therafter embarked 2,500 including POW, DBS, service personnel and families for the UK (WS 26 q.v.). In addition to the personnel exercising ashore from the four liners of WS 28, movements increased further when *Dempo* arrived from Bombay to embark two special train loads of service families for the UK, and on the 12th *Felix Roussel* also homebound had to land all her passengers to effect temporary repairs to weather damage incurred in a cyclone on the Indian Ocean. "Matters were further complicated when the War Office changed the destination of units for transhipment even after *Britannic* arrived, but all was accomplished within a week when the Impcon staff estimated having handled 35,000 of all categories".[9] About half of the number landed from *Britannic* were RAF for training in South Africa, the remainder waited six weeks for on-carriage on *Orbita* to Bombay.

After four days and nights in Capetown, the four transports and storeship *Waipawa* sailed again at 0800 15th with *Kenya*, *Quadrant*, *Redoubt* and *Relentless* as escorts, and were joined off Cape Point by Largs but not Ulster Monarch. No incidents were reported during the coastal passage to the Durban approaches, and from that port the Commodore on *Strathnaver* with the four other transports plus *Bulolo*, *Keren* and *Perthshire* moved from the harbour to the outer anchorage at 0830 18th to await the Capetown section. The Durban ships were underway again at 1100 and proceeded down the searched channel to meet and form up with the Capetown section into five columns,[10] very similar to that used from Freetown. The convoy, now of 14 ships with the cruiser *Kenya* at the head of column 4, set off at 1300 with a speed of 14 knots towards a position off the south tip of Madagascar. The destroyer escort was strengthened off Durban by *Raider* and RAN manned *Napier*, in relief of *Quadrant* which detached into that port.

The initial course of ENE towards Madagascar was deliberately set to retain the option of proceeding east or west of that island. The latter was eventually instructed by the Admiralty and at 0230 20th the convoy turned to NNE to steer towards the western shore of the island rather than the usual route in the centre of the Mozambique Channel. Very light winds with extreme visibility were experienced on this passage, all four destroyers were detached at 2100 that evening and by next morning the convoy was 70 miles NW of Cape St Vincent on the Madagascar shore where the course was altered to north towards mid channel. Daylight air cover was maintained during most of the passage to the north exit, which was reached early on the 23rd when the convoy was 20 miles west of Comoro and resumed a course of NNE.

A rendezvous position 300 miles east of Mombasa was reached at 1000 on the 24th, where *Kenya* detached on relief by the ex P&O AMCs *Chitral* and *Canton* which took station on either bow. Course was then altered to NE to maintain a distance of 200 miles from the Somali coast while the two remaining ships in column 4 each moved up one place and were joined by *Largs* from column 5.

The convoy was now gaining the effects of the Somali current and maintained almost 14 knots for the next two days which were free of incident until the evening of the 26th when course was altered to NNE for the Guardafui Strait. Ten hours later the course reverted to NE to pass eastward and around the north of Socotra for reasons unknown. Air cover resumed from the afternoon of the 27th and by 2300 that day the convoy was 60 miles east of Socotra and turned NW, at which point *Chitral* detached in pursuit of previous orders.

The passage into the Gulf of Aden was made at 13.25 knots and was free of incident; at 1050 29th the convoy re-organised into three columns and into single line ahead at 0530 next morning 30th April. *Monarch of Bermuda* then took guide and the speed reduced to allow a tanker convoy into Aden ahead of WS 28. The Fairway Buoy was reached at 0800 where all ships anchored to await their turn for entering to refuel and water. The average speed from Durban was recorded as 13.56 knots. The AMC *Canton* also refuelled in Aden and departed on 4 May for Bombay to remain on the East Indies station until March 1944 when she became the last of that class of warship to be released for conversion into troopship.

After refuelling and watering in Aden, all ships of the convoy continued independently to Suez where they arrived between 4 and 6 May to disembark and thereafter be "held in readiness for operations", as yet unknown to the officers and crews but deemed to be within the Mediterranean. Both MT storeships were passed through the canal to discharge at Alexandria and from where, as refrigerated carriers, they proceeded in ballast to the Antipodes and returned to the UK five months later.

The task of the nine liners and three HM Ships of WS 28 was to remain at Suez anchorage and prepare to receive the troops of the six brigades selected as the Eastern Assault Force for Sicily, and to train them in the previously developed techniques of transferring from ship to LCA and thereafter land on a hostile shore. The troops were already disengaged from offensive operations and were now being refitted and trained in the use of LCA for beach landing at the Combined Operations Centre at Kabrit on the Great Bitter Lake.

On 14 May the liners at Suez were joined by *Ulster Monarch* which had followed independently from Simonstown, by *Devonshire*, *Dilwara* and *Dunera* from Bombay towards the end of the month, by *Christiaan Huygens* on 1st June also from Bombay and finally *Ruys* and *Bergensfjord* which arrived as WS 29 from Durban on 12 June. The Eastern Assault convoy of 18 ships was now complete and from the first week of June a first group of four liners embarked their assault troops and proceeded to the Gulf of Aqaba to practise landings. When all ships and troops had been similarly exercised, a full scale rehearsal involving the entire force was arranged to take place at Safaga on the Egyptian Red Sea coast but bad weather caused a postponement, the plans were changed and the troops landed instead at Aqaba, at the head of that Gulf and now a favoured Jordanian holiday resort. *HMS Largs* meanwhile passed into the Mediterranean to act as HQ ship for the assault forces setting out from Sfax in Tunisia.

On the last day of June and 1st July all the ships passed through the canal and berthed at Port Said fully embarked and ready for sea, from where they departed as assault convoy MWF 36 on 5 July for Sicily. Following the successful landings there without loss of any ships, eight of the liners returned to the UK in MKF 18, *Bulolo* and *Keren* left Suez on 4 August for Bombay to form the nucleus of an assault force preparing for landings in the Bay of Bengal, and were joined there by *Winchester Castle* in September and by *Sobieski* in November.

In less than two months from the date of the Sicilian landings the troops of Eighth Army secured a lodgement on the toe of Italy from where the land war was carried into Southern Europe, and by this same time the Mediterranean was once again open to shipping of all types although the last of the WS convoys was then en route to West Africa to embark troops for Bombay via the Cape.

WS 29 - sailed UK 15.4.43

This convoy left the UK exactly a month behind WS 28 comprising seven storeships and five transports, plus another for detachment to the US, and while at first glance it appeared to conform to the typical WS pattern, certain changes were introduced which continued one way or another until the end of the entire series in August 1943.

The drastic depletion of the trooping fleet in the Torch landings and its aftermath brought their total loss for the six month period ending in March 1943 to 21 British operated troopships, of which 14 were of the WS type with a combined personnel capacity of 45,000 and could not be replaced. Not only did this affect the WS, KMF and North Atlantic routes, but the coincident shortage of the Indian Ocean ships by their diversion to the Mediterranean and other theatres, meant the on-carriage flow from South Africa could only be maintained by one of two means, i.e. to allow more WS ships to continue beyond Durban, or retain some of them there to operate a shuttle service from that port as previously given by the three "Monsters". The latter option was chosen and resulted in seven liners of WS 27 being held for Indian Ocean service on their arrival in that area in May 1943.

A further demand for WS liners was soon to arise from the decision taken in February 1943, with the War Office approval.. "to send 81st West African Division to India if shipping could be found during the summer and autumn, and to bring the East African force already in Ceylon up to the strength of a division by the dispatch of the [2] additional brigades from East Africa when they were ready".[1] It was Wavell as CinC India who first suggested at the end of 1942 the use of African troops for operations in Burma and elsewhere in the Far East, "for it seemed to him that West African formations, used to tropical jungles and to moving with porter transport would be invaluable in parts of Burma and Malaya".[1] However, the logistical problem of moving that Division bore no resemblance to that of moving a British infantry division which then had a war establishment strength of about 18,000. The West African divisions were organized on a man-pack basis for the jungle with neither animals nor vehicles. Soon after their arrival in India, General Slim inspected 81 West African Division training near Bombay and was struck "by the horde of unarmed porters who were needed to carry supplies, ammunition, baggage and the heavier weapons, and by the large number of white men in a unit, 50 or 60 to a battalion".[2] All this brought the strength of the West African Division,complete with Base, Admin., Non-Divisional and Reinforcement Troops up to about 45,000 and proved a severe strain on WS capacity for a period of five months which repeated itself in 1944 when 82nd West African Division was moved to Burma.

Four of the liners allocated for WS 29 had been in UK ports for periods of four weeks on return from WS 23, 24 and 25, *Athlone Castle* and *Highland Brigade* in Liverpool were drydocked for survey and overhaul, *Highland Princess* and *Monarch* at Avonmouth. A week before the convoy was due to depart *Orion* berthed in Glasgow from KMF 11 and also from that convoy *Nea Hellas* which managed barely two days in Glasgow for storing. One other liner due to sail with the convoy was the New Zealand *Aorangi* which had returned to Liverpool from WS 21 to be drydocked and have her quadruple 6 cylinder Sulzer machinery overhauled, all of which lasted four months. *Aorangi* left the Mersey on 10 April for extensive trials and anchored in the Clyde three days later with many defects and was unable to make the sailing date.

The embarkation programme for WS 29 began in Glasgow with *Orion* which sailed downriver with 5284 troops aboard from 1 KGV Dock on 12 April, on which date *Nea Hellas* also moved to the anchorage to embark a small number of personnel for the

United States. At Avonmouth *Highland Princess* completed and moved down channel on the midday tide of the 13th to anchor in Barry Roads, followed by *Highland Monarch* next day, when both sailed (with the storeship *Straat Malacca*) for the Clyde, but anchored again due to embarkation delays on the KMF 13 ships sailing in the combined convoy. In Liverpool *Athlone Castle* and *Highland Brigade* completed on the 14th and anchored in the river.

Of the liners allocated to KMF 13, *Cuba* and *Dunnottar Castle* embarked in Glasgow and moved to the Clyde Anchorage on the 13th and 14th respectively to join *Banfora*, *Boissievain* and *Nieuw Holland* embarking there, which were in turn joined by *Franconia*, *Duchess of York* and *Staffordshire* which arrived on the 13th fully embarked from Liverpool. The final embarkations on the Mersey were made on *Indrapoera* which completed and anchored in the river on the 13th to await *Empire Pride* and *Ormonde* which were ready to sail by midday on the 15th.[3]

The conference for this combined convoy was held at Marymount, Gourock on 15 April, following which three of the A/S escorts proceeded to Moville to top up with fuel and where also an escort conference was held aboard *Weston* as SO 42nd Escort Group. The first movements began at 0200 on that day when the three ships of the Bristol Channel portion escorted by *Shikari* left Barry Roads for the Orsay rendezvous, and at 1930 *Athlone Castle* (Captain A Alderson) led the five transports and storeships *Pardo*, *Troilus*, *Silverwalnut*, *Gloucester*, and *City of Edinburgh* passed the Rock Light to similarly proceed towards Orsay, escorted by the Bangor class minesweeper *Shippigan*. The Clyde portion of nine transports began passing out of the boom at 0200 16th led by Commodore AT Tillard on *Orion* (Captain C Fox, late of *Orcades*) with the storeship *Empire Kamal*, a P&O managed ex German motorship *Hohenfels*. Escort from the Clyde was by the destroyer *Rapid* while the cruiser *Newcastle* sailed independently to exercise and join up later as the ocean escort. The Vice Commodore EO Cochrane was on *Franconia* and would later act as Commodore of KMF 13.

At 1400 on the 16th all three sections made rendezvous 6 miles west of Orsay into a cruising order of seven columns with a lane between columns 3 and 4 for the ocean escort[4], while the A/S escort was provided by the sloops *Weston* (SOE), *Wellington*, destroyers *Rapid*, *Venomous*, *Lauderdale*, frigate *Ness* and cutter *Totland*.[4] The local escort from the Mersey and Bristol Channel detached into Derry. A speed of 12.25 knots was set on the initial course out to the westward and at 1730 the cutter *Gorleston* joined from Derry and half an hour later *Newcastle* took station within the columns as ocean escort.

The convoy followed a route very similar to that of the previous two convoys and in the early hours of the 17th the frigate *Exe* caught up and joined from Derry having been delayed there fitting a new radar set. By 0700 that morning a course of SSW was set for the next 24 hours and thence South to pass 250 miles west of Finisterre. The cruiser *Charybdis* joined at 1500 on the 18th on the latitude of the Scillies to provide additional AA protection against enemy interference but none was encountered. Shortly after midday 19th an Admiralty message stated that an enemy aircraft had reported a convoy at 1205 and was thought to be either WS 29 or MKS 11. No avoiding action was taken as the convoy was due to alter course two points to port that evening which was considered a sufficient diversion from the original line of advance. This alteration was made at 2130 when on the latitude of Finisterre and soon afterwards to SE towards the split position 35 miles SW of Cape St Vincent.

By the afternoon of the 20th the convoy was 140 miles west of Lisbon when *Rapid* detached ahead for Casablanca to refuel and at 2100 *Nea Hellas* detached independently for New York but was diverted enroute to Norfolk (Virginia) where she arrived safely ten days later. *Charybdis* detached soon after *Nea Hellas* as the convoy was now out of range of the Condors based at Bordeaux. At daybreak on the 21st course was altered to ESE towards the Straits of Gibraltar and at 1000 the amended split position was reached, 30 miles south of St Vincent, where the destroyers *Malcolm, Witch* and *Wolverine* joined and detached nine points to starboard with the nine liners and seven storeships of WS 29 towards Cape Ghir. The eleven liners of KMF 13 continued towards the Straits and arrived at Algiers on the morning of 23rd after detaching *Dunnottar Castle* for Gibraltar while *Boissievain* and *Nieuw Holland* proceeded to Oran.

Meanwhile WS 29 continued SSE with *Newcastle* and three destroyers while *Rapid* rejoined from Casablanca[5]. In the early hours of the 23rd course was altered to SW and by 0900 Fuerteventura was abeam 30 miles to starboard. At 0530 on the 24th *Gloucester* was detached independently for Panama en route to New Zealand and at midday course was altered to South towards Cap Vert. That headland was passed 60 miles off at 0900 26th where the US storeship *China Mail* joined from Dakar and where course was altered to SSE. There were no further incidents on the passage to Freetown; in the early afternoon of the 27th course was altered to ESE direct for that port, the convoy entered the searched channel at 0645 28th and anchored in the harbour at 1030 where all ships were to remain in the usual hot and sticky conditions for the next seven days.

The unusual delay at Freetown was partly to allow *Aorangi* to catch up, having sailed four days later than the main convoy as WS 29A (*q.v.*) but also the result of renewed U-Boat activity in the Freetown area. "In April six U-Boats and a 'milch-cow' arrived in the waters off Freetown, 'the old battle-ground' where the enemy had so often found easy targets in earlier phases. Five independents were quickly sunk and then, on the 30th April convoy TS 37 (Takoradi-Sierra Leone), of eighteen ships escorted by a corvette and three trawlers, was attacked when approaching Freetown. The SOE had picked up U-Boat transmissions and merely passed the information through a patrolling Hudson, which in turn only included the message in its report and so did not reach the FOWA until after the convoy was attacked that evening, when four ships were sunk 70 miles south of the end of Freetown Swept Channel".[6] "Three destroyers were at once sent out to reinforce the escort, but they did not arrive until after a second attack early on the 1st May"[7] when three more ships were sunk a mere 50 miles SW of the Swept Channel, a total of seven claimed by one U-Boat. "The enemy kept an average of four U-Boats off Freetown until the end of May, but they did not repeat their previous success".[7] In fact they sank ten more ships in the area during the rest of May and first week of June. Clearly WS 29 would be held in Freetown until the situation was stabilized and so this convoy remained in port for seven hot uncomfortable days.

WS 29A - sailed Clyde 20.4.04

With the machinery defects made good *Aorangi* embarked at the Clyde Anchorage when it was arranged to sail her with the storeship *Clan Lamont* which completed loading for the Middle East in Glasgow and moved downriver on 19 April. Both ships were due to have sailed that evening but a late signal postponed this to 1100 on the 20th when the two ship convoy cleared the boom escorted by *Anthony* (SO) and *Lewes* with the Master of *Aorangi* (Captain AT Toten) acting as Commodore.

Most unusually and presumably to save time, this small convoy was routed down the Irish Sea and was joined by the destroyer *Brissenden* outside Milford Haven at 0800 21st when a course was set out to the SW but later that day the route was altered by signal from SOE. During the night of 23/24th the convoy passed 220 miles west of Finisterre and next day was reported by an enemy aircraft but no attack developed, and by 0900 26th both ships anchored in Casablanca roadstead where *Brissenden* and *Anthony* detached while *Lewes* refuelled and was joined by *Boreas* as SO. The two ships sailed again at 1930 that evening, at 0800 28th passed 12 miles SE of Fuerteventura and thereafter followed the route of the main convoy, but anchored off Dakar at 1000 on 1 May for reasons unknown, sailed at 0800 next day and reached Freetown 0700 4th to join the main convoy. Captain Toten reported the "voyage was made under fine weather conditions and without incident, with the exception of the report by enemy aircraft on the 25th when 100 miles west of Cape St Vincent when evasive alteration of course was accordingly made that night.[8]

Awaiting the arrival of the convoy in Freetown was *Almanzora*, which had previously sailed in WS 27 to Durban and then returned to Lagos where she embarked the Nigerian advance parties of 81 West African Division. This was followed by the Gold Coast contingent at Takoradi and finally the Sierra Leone and Gambia sections when she arrived at Freetown on the 26th.

The reconstituted convoy now of seven liners and six storeships sailed from Freetown at 0600 on 5 May (without *China Mail*) and by midday was clear of the swept channel and continued out to the SW for 200 miles before turning SE to maintain a distance of 250 miles off the Liberian Coast as a U-Boat had sunk a ship 100 miles offshore that morning. Escort was continued by *Newcastle* which had recently refitted in Devonport and was en route to become flagship of the 4th Cruiser Squadron Eastern Fleet. The A/S escort was initially provided by *Malcolm*, *Rapid*, *Wolverine*, *Lewes*, *Boreas* and *Witch*, the heaviest then given to a WS convoy in that area. A cruising order of four columns was formed for the passage to the Cape.[9]

By the morning of the 7th the convoy reached a position 30 miles SW of Cape Palmas where course was altered to ESE in the general direction of Pointe Noire, quite unlike the route followed by recent convoys which had taken advantage of the Guinea Current deep into that Gulf. At 1800 that day, *Highland Princess*, *Troilus* and *City of Edinburgh* detached for Takoradi under escort of *Boreas* and *Witch*. The Ellerman ship had a fire in one of her holds and was sent into that port where they all arrived on the morning of 9th. The fire was extinguished, damaged cargo discharged and *City of Edinburgh* resumed her voyage on the 22nd, proceeding via Walvis Bay and Capetown to her ultimate destination of three ports in India.

At Takoradi *Highland Princess* disembarked the balance of the personnel not landed in Freetown and thereafter made two return trips between Takoradi and Lagos before embarking RAF personnel for the air base being established at Casablanca. Leaving Freetown on 4 June and Dakar four days later, she reached Casablanca six days later to disembark there and at Gibraltar, where she joined the homeward XK 9 convoy to reach the Clyde on 28 June. Berthing in Glasgow next day to disembark troops and passengers, she next sailed out in KMF 20.

Meanwhile the convoy continued towards Pointe Noire and on the morning of 11th, *Racehorse*, *Relentless* and *Rotherham* joined from that port and relieved *Malcolm*,

Rapid and *Wolverine* which then detached to refuel there distant 270 miles ahead. At this point the convoy turned to the SE and maintained this course for the next 24 hours when a S'ly course was adopted to generally follow the Angolan/SW Africa coastline keeping at least 60 miles offshore.

It was during this passage with West African troops to Bombay that caused the OC Troops on *Almanzora*, Colonel W Boyle, to record his impressions on their faith and simplicity. On one forenoon a man remarked he had malaria and was not getting better. "See that my wife gets my money"[10], he then leaped overboard and his friends watched him drift astern and only two hours later was the incident made known. "The fatalism shown was unique and difficult to handle; and seemed to be almost ingrained in their nature despite so many affirmative and excellent qualities".[10] The Africans also "bought Brylcreem from the ship's canteen and used it as butter, while hairdressing was done "by the corner of a safety razor blade ploughing through the tonsorial undergrowth until a straight bare line of skull appeared".[10]

The latitude of Walvis Bay was reached on the night of the 15th/16th and during the 16th *Quadrant* joined and relieved *Rotherham*. By 0800 on the 18th the convoy was 17 miles SW of Dassen Island and 35 miles NW of Capetown where the section for that port comprising *Athlone Castle*, *Almanzora*, *Silverwalnut*, *Pardo* and *Empire Kamal* detached with *Newcastle*, *Racehorse*, *Relentless* and *Lewes* on being relieved by *Norman* and *Redoubt*. All ships were berthed in Capetown harbour before noon. The remaining ships, i.e. *Orion*, *Highland Brigade*, *Highland Monarch*, *Aorangi*, *Clan Lamont* and *Straat Malacca* continued around the coast with the three destroyers escort passing Cape Agulhas just before midnight and at 0300 20th were 20 miles south of Cape Recife. By 0800 21st the convoy was 110 miles south of Durban and arrived there at 1930 that day.

Awaiting the arrival of the convoy in South Africa were six liners which had gone to Suez in WS 27 (*q.v.*): *Orbita* was at Capetown where she embarked 2,800 of the personnel landed from *Britannic* in WS 28, while *Bergensfjord*, *Ruys*, *Leopoldville*, *Strathmore* and *Strathaird* were berthed in Durban. The two *Straths* embarked all of the 9,049 personnel transhipped from *Orion* and the two *Highland* liners, which were turning round in that port, while the other three liners embarked 8,000 South African troops and Air Force units for the Middle East, where twelve SAAF squadrons were now preparing to carry the war on to Sicily.

From Durban the three disembarked liners sailed on the 30th (the same date as the continuing convoy), *Orion* having part loaded on the Union Castle berth, proceeded direct via Freetown to Liverpool where she arrived on 26 June to be next employed in KMF 20. The two *Highland* liners proceeded light to Lagos, embarking mixed units there for transfer to Freetown where they arrived on 25 June and began preparing to join WS 31 with West African troops (*q.v.*).

The U-Boat situation while the convoy was in South Africa was such that one was 200 miles south of Agulhas heading east but doubled back and sank two ships off that headland on the 28th. One was known to be cruising between Port Elizabeth and East London, another was upcoast from Lourenco Marques and two others working in the Durban approaches or between that port and East London, one of which *U-198*, sighted a convoy of ten ships 200 miles SE of Durban on 26 May which might well have been WS 29.

In Capetown, the convoy was joined by the American storeship *Alcoa Pioneer* and by *Llanstephan Castle*, the latter having left the Clyde in a slow convoy on 26 March en route to India to become an LSIL for the Royal Indian Navy. Calls were made at Freetown, Takoradi, Lagos and Walvis Bay before arriving at the Cape one day ahead of WS 29, which began leaving that port at 0930 on the 22nd led by the Commodore, Captain Alderson of *Athlone Castle*, followed by *Alcoa Pioneer*, *Orbita* (whose Master, Captain EH Large), was acting as Vice Commodore, *Almanzora*, *Llanstephan Castle*, *Pardo*, *Silverwalnut* and *Empire Kamal*. The Commodore was due to pass Robben Island half an hour later but there was a delay due to engine trouble on *Empire Kamal* while that ship was still alongside. Escort was provided by *Relentless*, *Racehorse* and *Rotherham* and once outside the swept channel a cruising order of three columns was formed.[11] By midnight 22nd, the convoy was passing Cape Agulhas where two ships had been sunk by *U-177* that day and 24 hours later was off Port Elizabeth where *U-178* reported seeing a convoy close inshore. This may have been WS 29 but no attack was made.

The Durban section began leaving that harbour at midday 25th led by Commodore Tillard now transferred to *Strathmore* (Captain JK Chaplin), with *Strathaird*, *Bergensfjord*, *Ruys*, *Leopoldville*, *Straat Malacca*, *Selandia* (South African forces store-ship) and *Clan Lamont*, whose Master was acting as Vice Commodore. Escort from Durban was given by the cruiser *Kenya* and destroyers *Norman*, *Quadrant* and *Redoubt* and after proceeding down the searched channel met the Capetown portion now of six ships which at 1430 when 35 miles south of Durban had detached *Empire Kamal* and *Llanstephan Castle* for Durban, the former with serious engine trouble and the *Castle* liner to join a slow on-carriage convoy departing on the 30th. Two destroyers, *Relentless* and *Rotherham*, were also detached into Durban. It seems clear that the Capetown portion was narrowly missed by *U-198* as it crossed 20 miles astern off the Natal coast on the 25th, while *U-196* was also cruising in the Durban approaches that day but never reported sighting the convoy.

The afternoon of the 25th was largely spent reorganizing the convoy into six columns.[12] *Silverwalnut* broke down at 1600 and returned to Durban. *Aorangi* was delayed in Durban by engine repairs when Captain Toten who was to act as Vice Commodore devolved this task to *Clan Lamont*. The New Zealand liner eventually continued her voyage on 9 June, proceeding via Mombasa and Colombo to Bombay where she arrived on 2 July and after loading homeward cargo there and at Capetown, called at Freetown and Casablanca before reaching the Clyde on 7 September to sail again in KMF 25A.

The reconstituted convoy now of 8 transports and 5 MT ships was embarked with 7,500 South African personnel for Suez and almost 20,000 others for Bombay, which included the advance party of 2890 West Africans destined for Burma. The initial course was ESE until 1330 next day when this was altered to ENE towards the south end of Madagascar. At 0900 on the 28th the convoy was 160 miles SW of Cape St Mary where course was altered to east and *Norman* was detached later that day and by next morning the convoy was 160 miles SE of Fort Dauphin and altered to NNE to pass up the east side of Madagascar. The last two destroyers, *Quadrant* and *Redoubt*, detached at 1100 that day and at 1800 *Almanzora* was detached ahead independently to Diego Suarez to refuel, arriving there late afternoon 31st.

On the morning of 1 June the convoy was steering NNW from a position 100 miles east of Diego Suarez and during the ensuing night passed through the gap between Cape Amber and the Farquhar group of islands. *Almanzora* rejoined at 0600 on the 2nd and three hours later by which time the convoy was 600 miles ESE of Mombasa, the AMC

Chitral joined as ocean escort, course was altered NNE towards Guardafui and at 1300 *Kenya* detached for Mombasa to join the Eastern Fleet. By the morning of the 3rd the AMC *Alaunia* joined the escort and course was altered towards the eastern side of Socotra. At 0900 on the 5th course was altered NE for Bombay and shortly after mid-day when still 350 miles south of Guardafui, *Alaunia* detached with the Bombay section comprising the Commodore on *Strathmore* with *Athlone Castle*, *Almanzora*, *Orbita*, *Strathaird* and *Straat Malacca*.

There were no incidents on the passage across the northern Indian Ocean which was made at an average speed of 12.3 knots. *Straat Malacca* was detached for Karachi on the morning of the 9th and the convoy arrived at Bombay at 0700 on the 10th. After disembarking half their personnel in that port, the two *Straths* sailed again on the 13th with *Alaunia* to land the remainder at Colombo where they arrived on the 15th. Leaving again five days later they returned to Bombay and thence to Durban which they reached on 10 July to prepare for a further on-carriage trip with personnel from WS 30.

Of the three remaining transports which arrived at Bombay, *Orbita* disembarked and sailed on the 15th for Suez, followed three days later by *Almanzora*. Both then prepared to embark British troops for the Sicily follow-up convoy, MWF 37, which sailed from Alexandria on 9 July for Syracuse. The Royal Mail liner then returned to the Clyde in MKF 19 but *Orduna* was retained in the Mediterraneaan and did not return to Liverpool until September and thereafter both continued on the KMF route.

Whilst in Bombay, *Athlone Castle* was ordered to load homewards on the Cunard berth in New York and at the same time the PSTO Capetown arranged with the Admiralty that she should also embark 500 German POW in Durban for passage to the U.S. The Castle liner left Bombay on the 22nd and shortly after the PSTO reduced the number of POW to 400 but on the 27th, it became evident that *Athlone Castle* had embarked in Bombay a mixed collection of passengers including civilians which made it undesirable to add POW. The Durban call was therefore cancelled and the ship called at Capetown to embark priority personnel for the UK up to the limits of her passenger certificate. Sailing from the Cape on 9 July *Athlone Castle* arrived at New York 16 days later, loaded refrigerated cargo and crossed as convoy AT 58A to reach Liverpool on 17 August for further employment in KMF 24 three weeks later.

Meanwhile the Middle East section of the convoy comprising *Bergensfjord*, *Leopoldville*, *Ruys* with the storeships *Clan Lamont*, *Pardo*, *Selandia* and *Alcoa Pioneer* continued under escort of *Chitral* after detaching the Bombay section on the morning of 5 June. The island of Socotra was given a wide berth to the eastward and northward two days later and this seven ship convoy reached Aden to water and refuel at 0900 on the 9th where it was dispersed to proceed independently to Suez. *Bergensfjord* and *Ruys* arrived there on the 12th and after disembarking, re-embarked British troops and joined the assault convoy MWF 36 for Sicily whence *Ruys* returned to the Clyde on 23 July while the Norwegian liner remained on Mediterranean service until returning to the Clyde at the beginning of September. *Leopoldville* disembarked in Suez on 14 June and was then employed on the Sicily follow-up convoy MWF 37 and like *Beregensfjord* was also retained on cross-Mediterranean routes until arriving in the Clyde early September; all three thereafter continued on the KMF service.

There were now 30 troopships and LSIL in the Suez area making the final preparations to embark the assault and follow-up troops for the landings in Sicily. In previous times such a congested anchorage would have been an excellent and high priority target for enemy bombers, but with the German armies being steadily pushed back on the

Russian front and now expelled from the North African shores, the enemy now had other priorities to attend.

Chapter 20

WS 30, WS 31 and the Faith Convoy

The decline of the WS route, more West Africans for India and the
lamentable loss of another two Troopships.

WS 30 - sailed UK 19.5.43

All Axis resistance in Tunisia ceased on 13th May and brought to an end three years of
desert warfare by the Eighth Army and six months for the First Army in the mountains
between Algiers and Tunis. This prize yielded 250,000 prisoners of war who might otherwise have escaped to fight again in Italy and was the second German Army to capit-
ulate; Stalingrad three months earlier having surrendered 90,000 to the Russians.

Not only did the clearance of enemy from the North African shores pave the way for
the next phase of the war by allowing the Allies to land on Sicily at the southern tip of
Europe, but more importantly for the WS fleet and the reinforcement of British and
Indian troops in India and Burma, a direct passage through the Mediterranean would
soon become possible with a consequent saving of three weeks on the passage to reach
these theatres and six weeks or more on a round voyage. The early provision of a
mineswept channel through the Sicilian Narrows allowed the first convoy of four fast
cargo liners to reach Tripoli and Alexandria from Gibraltar two weeks after the end of
the Tunisian campaign. Others soon followed and the first troop convoy to continue

eastwards beyond Sicily was KMF 22 which left the UK on 16th August, even although personnel sailings had been operating internally at both ends of the Mediterranean since the Sicilian landings on 10th July.

The WS series meanwhile continued to leave the UK at roughly four or five weekly intervals, but on a very much reduced scale of personnel capacity which had been declining steadily, apart from WS 26 and 28, since preparations began for Operation Torch in October 1942. Less than 11,000 personnel embarked on the five liners of WS 30 of which four were American and none proceeded beyond Durban because of their urgent requirement elsewhere.[1]

The sole British liner available for this convoy was *Mataroa* having returned to Avonmouth on 2 April from WS 25 to discharge a refrigerated cargo from Buenos Aires. Drydocking and boiler cleaning was then carried out in that port before embarkation was completed to allow departure in the afternoon of 16 May for a coastal passage to the Clyde Anchorage where she arrived on the morning of the 18th. Already waiting there and completing embarkation were the American troopships *Argentina*, *Siboney* and *Sloterdyk*, which together with the *HF Alexander* which embarked at 3 KGV Dock, Glasgow, and came downriver that forenoon, had a combined capacity of 9041 and was a classic example of Anglo-American co-operation in the overall trooping programme when all but one of the British managed 'Monsters' were operating to American account. All four of the US transports had previously crossed the Atlantic carrying American troops to Oran and thereafter joined the UK bound convoy MKF 13 which arrived in the Clyde on 2nd May to add to a very congested anchorage but which nevertheless always seemed able to accommodate more than the number of allotted berths. Hidden then in the sheltered waters of the Gareloch were the LSIL exercising their landing craft in preparation for the western assault on Sicily, while the naval anchorage at the Tail of the Bank had the *Warspite* and *Indomitable* also preparing to support these landings in addition to five escort carriers, two AMCs, six warships on builders' trials and a general plethora of escort vessels, while the liner *Queen Elizabeth* anchored in the midst of all this for five days disembarking 15,000 US troops and embarking in lieu various personnel bound for New York.

Of the American transports in WS 30, most notable was the *Argentina*, one of three 20,000 ton sisters formerly operated by Moore McCormack Lines on a service to South America. Both *HF Alexander* and *Siboney* were much smaller of 8,358 and 6,927 tons gross, both built during the First World War and now showing their age, but nevertheless able to manage 15-16 knots. The Dutch *Sloterdyk* was a twin-screw motor cargo liner of the Holland America Line converted for trooping with a capacity for 1,714 personnel. Two British cargo liners *Brisbane Star* and the Royal Mail *Deseado* were also being included in WS 30 for their protection until detachment but were not carrying military cargoes.

The KMF 15 component of the combined convoy comprised eleven liners of which *JV Oldenbarnevelt*, *Samaria*, *Duchess of York* and *Stirling Castle* embarked in Liverpool and moved thereafter to the Clyde Anchorage where they arrived between 15 and 17th May, and on *Franconia*, *Staffordshire* and *Ormonde* which completed ready to leave the Mersey on the 19th. Moving downriver from Glasgow on the 13th were *Arawa* and *Letitia* which then embarked at the Clyde Anchorage, while *Boissievain* and *Indrapoera* embarked at KGV Dock in Glasgow and moved downriver on the 16th and 17th respectively. Also sailing in the Clyde section of KMF 15 were the small commissioned LSI sisters, *Royal Scotsman* and *Ulsterman* returning to the Mediterranean theatre after short refits and having their LCAs replaced at Southampton and Barry respectively.[3] All five liners of WS 30 and eight of KMF 15 were ready on the Clyde by the 17th awaiting the completion of those in Liverpool, a total of 46,478 personnel were embarked in the combined convoy.[2]

Few U-Boats were at this time active in the Western Approaches but a heavy escort was nonetheless provided including the cruiser *Suffolk* (SOE) recently worked up at Scapa after a four month refit on the Thames, the AMC *Corfu* also out of a five month refit in Southampton, the new repair-carrier *Unicorn* ferrying Beaufighters to Gibraltar, destroyers *Active*, *Boadicea* and *Cleveland* allocated to WS 30 and seven units of the 42nd Escort Group with KMF 15 i.e. sloops *Weston* (SO), *Wellington*, *Lowestoft*, frigates *Exe* and *Ness*, and cutters *Totland* and *Gorleston*. The Polish Hunt class *Slazak* was also included for the Mediterranean Fleet. Commodore Sir CG Ramsay KCB RNR of the combined convoy was on *Siboney*, while the Vice Commodore DA Casey CBE DSO RD RNR on *Samaria* would later act as Commodore of KMF 15.

WS 30/KMF 15 began leaving the Mersey at 1030 on 19 May when *Staffordshire* (Captain RS Evans) passed the Rock Light, followed by *Ormonde*, *Franconia* and *Brisbane Star* to proceed up the Irish Sea escorted by *Sardonyx* where they were joined by *Deseado* from the Bristol Channel and continued towards the appointed rendezvous with the main section from the Clyde, which began passing out of the boom there at 1800 that day led by the Commodore on *Siboney*.

Rendezvous was effected with the Liverpool section 6 miles west of Orsay at 0530 on the 20th, where *Sardonyx* returned to base and the combined convoy formed into a cruising order of seven columns [4], less *Royal Ulsterman* which caught up and joined that afternoon. The usual W'ly course was first adopted before turning SW then SSW to a position 400 miles west of Ushant on the morning of 22nd, when course was altered to South and held for the next two days, passing 300 miles west of Finisterre on the morning of the 23rd. The escort dropped depth charges on 21st and 23rd without result and at 1800 that evening *Boadicea* detached to fuel. On the 24th there was more depth charging as the convoy steered SE towards the split position, and that afternoon for an hour and a half a Focke-Wulf was seen on and off presumed to be spotting and homing for U-Boats. *Siboney* and other ships fired a few rounds at extreme range while *Unicorn* was favoured with some near misses and flew off a Seafire to intercept, but seemed unable to make contact although the enemy was in sight of the convoy.[5]

At 1045 on 25th the split position was reached, 90 miles south of Cape St Vincent, where KMF 15 of eleven troopships and two HM LSILs detached with *Unicorn* and 42 EG plus *Active*, *Cleveland* and *Slazak* for Gibraltar and subsequently detached *Letitia* to Gibraltar, *Staffordshire* and *Stirling Castle* to Oran, while the remainder continued to Algiers arriving on the 27th. Eight of these liners returned to the UK on 4 June in MKF 15 while *Arawa*, *Staffordshire* and *Stirling Castle* left Gibraltar on 31st May in convoy to Dakar and Freetown to embark West African troops and join WS 31 bound for Bombay.

At the split position WS 30 as a three column formation [6] still escorted by *Suffolk* and *Corfu* were joined by an A/S escort of *Bulldog*, *Foxhound* and *Catterick*, and where also Captain WHP Jackson of *Mataroa* began to act as Vice Commodore. The convoy then turned ten points to starboard by stages to steer a SSW'ly course towards Cap Ghir on the Moroccan coast. *Boadicea* rejoined seven hours after the split. Also detached at the split position were the two cargo liners proceeding thereafter independently, *Brisbane Star* to Panama and Australia: *Deseado* to the River Plate.

The convoy passed between Fuerteventura and the African mainland in the early hours of the 27th and 50 miles west of Cap Vert and Dakar at midnight 29th. Continuous fine weather was experienced throught the passage to Freetown which was reached without further incident in the last of the daylight on 1st June.

In Freetown the five liners of WS 30 were joined by *Nieuw Holland* which with *Cuba*, both from KMF 13, had been escorted from Gibraltar on 3rd May to Dakar and Freetown arriving there on 16 May. *Nieuw Holland* remained at anchor to embark West African troops while *Cuba* went on to similarly embark at Lagos and Takoradi. These were the leading brigade advance parties of 81 West African Division following on from the first batch carried by *Almanzora* in WS 29 and now almost arriving in Bombay.

After a mere 36 hours for fuelling and watering in Freetown, the convoy sailed again at 0700 on 3 June with *Suffolk* and *Corfu* continuing as ocean escorts but strengthened by the AMC *Carnarvon Castle* which had been based at Freetown for South Atlantic patrols since the beginning of January. Five destroyers provided the A/S screen: *Wolverine* (SO), *Boadicea*, *Rapid*, *Witch* and *Catterick*. At least four U-Boats were then known to be operating in the Freetown area; one ship was sunk 90 miles south of the port on the day before the arrival of the convoy and two more while it lay in Freetown. The initial course took WS 30 out to a position 200 miles SW of the Liberian coast before turning ESE to pass 60 miles south of Cape Palmas where on the morning of the 5th course was altered to east.

At 1500 on the 6th the convoy reached a position 90 miles south of Cape Three Points where the French liner *Cuba* escorted by *Witch* joined from Takoradi carrying the Nigerian and Gold Coast contingents destined for India and Burma. The convoy now turned SE across the Gulf of Guinea towards Pointe Noire and that evening *Corfu* and *Boadicea* parted company; the former continuing South Atlantic patrols until November when sent into Simonstown for repairs. *Catterick* was detached ahead for Pointe Noire to refuel in the late evening of 8th and next day at 1700 the convoy was 75 miles NW of Pointe Noire where *Wolverine* and *Witch* detached on relief by *Norman*, *Quadrant* and *Redoubt*. Course was then altered to south towards Cape Frio and three hours later *Catterick* rejoined and *Rapid* parted company to fuel and rejoined at a later date.

At 0900 13th the convoy was 60 miles west of Walvis Bay, where the French sloop *Savorgnan de Brazza* joined with the US cargo liners *Exceller* and *Santa Barbara* but the sloop detached again that evening. There were no incidents on the passage south, at 1230 on 15th the convoy was 22 miles abeam of Cape Columbine, at 1400 the destroyer *Nizam* joined when *Suffolk* and *Catterick* detached. At 1800 all seven liners arrived at Capetown with the AMC *Carnaravon Castle* and destroyers *Redoubt*, *Norman*, *Quadrant* and *Nizam*.

This convoy of seven transports and two US storeships had a very short stay of fourteen hours in Capetown which probably allowed no shore leave and would certainly have applied to the West Africans on *Cuba* and *Nieuw Holland'*. WS 30 sailed again at 0900 on the 16th June, continuing with *Carnarvon Castle* and the same four destroyers as A/S screen. Seven U-Boats of a new group had been operating off South Africa since the end of May with poor results; one had since returned home with engine trouble and by the time WS 30 reached Capetown, the remainder were making for a supply ship rendezvous 700 miles east of Durban due to begin on 21st, and were therefore well clear of the convoy route between Capetown and Durban.

Cape Agulhas was passed 5 miles off in the late evening of 16th November, where another US cargo liner *Exiria* joined from Capetown. By 0900 18th the convoy was 10 miles south of Cape Recife and Port Elizabeth where *Carnarvon Castle* was detached to return to Simonstown for seven weeks refit, and at 1730 that evening the Dutch liner *Sibajak* joined from Port Elizabeth where she had been undergoing extensive machinery repairs. Soon after daylight on the morning of 19th when the convoy was midway between Bashee Light and Port St Johns and 12 miles offshore, convoy DC 31 bound in the opposite direction was met directly ahead. The Commodore ordered emergency turns to avoid it and duly commented on the need or otherwise of having routed two opposite convoys so close to one another and known to be zigzagging. Had it been the dark hours, a collision would have been inevitable. By 2100 that evening the convoy could have approached the end of the Durban Searched Channel but as the port and its approaches were closed at night a suitable reduction in speed was made to allow arrival at daylight next morning where all ships were soon berthed within the harbour.

All five liners which had come out from the UK now disembarked all of their 10,938 personnel, of which 2444 transhipped to *Sibajak* while the remaining 8494 were sent to Clairwood Camp to await on-carriage five weeks later on *Strathmore* and *Strathaird* making a further return voyage to Bombay and Colombo, after that in WS 29 as no Indian Ocean tonnage was available. Commodore Ramsay now transferred from the American *Siboney* to the Dutch *Nieuw Holland*, and commented on the unsuitability of the former ship for a Commodore, "although the Master and all officers were most courteous and did everything in their power for my comfort, the cabin provided was a long way from the bridge...consequently (I was) condemned to sleep on a short settee in the Master's cabin as the best and most convenient cabins were occupied by junior American naval and military officers permanently attached to the ship".[5]

Following disembarkation in Durban, *Siboney* returned to New York via Rio, Trinidad and Guantanamo Bay while the other three US ships made the voyage to New York via Casablanca. *Mataroa* was scheduled to load in New York on the Furness Withy berth and left Durban on 2 July to proceed there via Bahia, Trinidad, and Guantanamo Bay (for convoy). Having loaded a full cargo in the space of fourteen days she crossed to Avonmouth to begin discharge on 16 September and was thereafter continuously employed on round trips between the UK and New York until April 1945.

Several signals from the CinC EF were received by Commodore Ramsay of WS 30 whilst the convoy was on the South African coast; the first advising that *Exceller* and *Exiria* were to be detached for Beira and that their Durban discharge should be expedited to ensure they were able to sail with the convoy, the first named was actually included on the sailing list but neither were able to do so. The BI mail ship *Karagola* then employed on the Durban/East Africa/Bombay service was to be included in the convoy and later detached for Mombasa. Two other cargo ships included were the Norwegian (ex US C1 class) *General Fleischer* bound for Suez and the neutral Swedish *Sagoland* for Mombasa. A final signal on the 24th one day prior to sailing stated that the AMC *Canton* to join later would replace the cruiser *Suffolk* as ocean escort.

The revised convoy now styled WS 30B of three transports, one mailship and two cargo ships began moving out of Durban harbour to the Outer Anchorage on 25 June, led by the Commodore on *Nieuw Holland* at 0600, *Karagola* at 1300 and finally *Cuba* at 1500 with *Sibajak* close behind where they joined *Santa Barbara*, *General Fleischer* and *Sagoland* already at anchor. The whole convoy was underway at 1600 and after proceeding 8 miles SE down the searched channel then formed into a cruising order of three columns[8] and with the destroyers *Norman*, *Quickmatch* and *Rotherham* as escorts set off on a direct course of NE towards the Mozambique Channel. At 0430 26th the convoy was 15 miles SE of Cape St Lucia on the Zululand coast and at 0800 28th reached the latitude of Beira where AMC *Canton* joined as ocean escort.

On the night of the 29th the convoy exited the north end of the Mozambique Channel where all three destroyers were detached; *Norman* at 2000 and the other two at 0200 on 30th and by 0600 WS 30B was 40 miles west of Comoro Island where course was altered NNE towards Guardafui. At 0900 on 1st July when 330 miles ESE of Mombasa, the AMC *Alaunia* joined and relieved *Canton* which then detached with *Karagola* and *Sagoland* for Mombasa.

There were no other incidents until the early hours of the 3rd, when 200 miles east of Mogadishu, where *Santa Barbara* was detached to proceed independently direct for Colombo. By 1100 next morning the five ships were 170 miles south of Ras Hafun where *Sibajak* and the Norwegian cargo ship were detached independently for Aden; the former passed 20 miles east of Guardafui at 0300 5th and reached Aden at 0500 on the 6th, sailed again the same day and reached Suez on the 10th. After disembarking there *Sibajak* returned south via Aden and Mombasa to Durban on the 6th August to await a further on-carriage trip to Suez.

After detaching *Sibajak*, the Commodore now with a convoy of two ships with *Alaunia* as escort altered course to NE towards Bombay. No incidents were reported crossing the north Indian Ocean and the convoy reached Bombay at 0700 on the 9th July, 12 hours ahead of the original ETA. Following disembarkation, the 4,000 West Africans entrained to establish base camps in the Ranchi area and prepare for the arrival of the three brigades of 81 West African Division.

On conclusion of his Report of Proceedings, Commodore Ramsay made some pertinent comments on the French liner *Cuba* whose station keeping had been very erratic and got steadily worse, and particularly her Master, Captain Deschatres, who "appeared to take no interest in station-keeping and was full of excuses for not doing so... a most unsatisfactory ship to have in convoy".[5] The average speed recorded from Durban to Bombay was 12.45 knots.

In Bombay, *Cuba* was delayed for two months under repair and left that port on 13 September for Suez and was thereafter employed for five months on cross-Mediterranean routes before proceeding to the West Indies and eventually reached the Clyde on 11 November 1944 after a voyage lasting 1.5 years. *Nieuw Holland* had two weeks under repair in Bombay before returning to Durban on 6 August and was retained in the Indian Ocean for a voyage from Mombasa to Colombo and another from Mombasa to Suez, being thereafter retained in the Mediterranean until November and returned to the Clyde on 9 December.

WS 31 - Sailed UK 19.6.43

For this brief period of the war as the Anglo-American assault forces began making their final preparations by employing almost half of the WS fleet for the major amphibious operation against Sicily, it is strange to note that no other British or Commonwealth land forces were then actually engaged with the enemy, other than those of the Australian divisions battling against the Japanese in New Guinea and not served by the WS route. In Burma the failed first Arakan offensive found the British and Indian forces back where they had started six months earlier, while those of the First Chindit operation had also returned to India. Lieut.-General Slim had since been given command of all these forces, but with the monsoon now descended upon the area little could then be done but draw up plans for a renewed offensive in the autumn.

By the middle of 1943 the Indian Army had expanded ninefold since the outbreak of war to reach a strength exceeding two million men of which 145,500 were British. A further expansion planned for 1943 had to be modified due mainly to a shortage of British personnel and a lack of appropriate Indian recruits. Nonetheless, expansion continued despite a shortage of certain types of personnel and by the end of the war the strength of the British component had risen to 240,613 in addition to which there were 131,907 RAF in India[1]. Thus the need to maintain a steady flow of reinforcements to meet both expansion and losses never diminished although the re-opening of a Mediterranean passage soon allowed this traffic to pass from the WS to the KMF route.

Of the eleven transports allocated for the combined WS 31/KMF 17 convoy, five were American and continued to highlight the Anglo-American shipping alliance which had grown steadily from the beginning of 1942. In respect of trooping capacity the U.S. was now suffering the same critical shortages which afflicted the British WS route in 1941. After eighteen months at war the U.S. trooping fleet, including sixteen new vessels fitting out, amounted to 129 ships with a combined capacity for 264,301 personnel but was then only 70 per cent of the British controlled fleet. Massive building programmes begun in 1943 could not improve the situation in the short term and with the expansion of the 'Bolero' movement of US troops to Britain, most of that traffic had to be met by British tonnage of the Monster and WS class. In 1942, 250,860 US troops were brought to the UK of which 61 per cent were carried in British troopships, a further 983,000 were scheduled to cross in 1943 in addition to 227,400 Canadian and RAF personnel.[2]

The arrival of convoy MKF 15 in UK ports on 5 June provided six of the transports scheduled to sail in WS 31/KMF 17 two weeks later, of which five were American. With the North African campaign now at an end, they brought with them the first batch of German POW who disembarked at the NW berths of KGV Dock in Glasgow, the ships then re-storing before returning downriver three days later to embark at the Clyde Anchorage. The US transports were *John Ericsson* (ex Swedish America *Kungsholm*), *Cristobal* (ex Panama Railroad *Ancon*), *JW McAndrew* (ex *Deltargentino* of the Mississippi Co.) and *George W Goethals* (one of four similar C3 class troopships built in 1942); the first and last named having been selected for inclusion in WS 31 and the others with *Santa Rosa* of the Grace Line which turned round at the Clyde Anchorage for KMF 17.

The British component of WS 31 was *Stratheden* which berthed in Glasgow on 10 May, having returned from WS 26 to Bombay, and *Rangitiki* which had sailed in WS 25 to Durban and returned with a meat cargo from Montevideo to Liverpool on 24 April, and where also drydocking and extensive repair to her twin five-cylinder Sulzers was carried out over an eight week period. *Rangitkiki* embarked in Liverpool only personnel bound for West Africa; *Stratheden* and the five US transports embarked at the Clyde Anchorage. Three cargo liners with general cargo for South African ports were included in the convoy: *City of Lincoln* and *Clan Macaulay* having loaded in Birkenhead and *Clan Macarthur* in Glasgow's Yorkhill Basin; the last two being sister ships.

In addition to the American transports in KMF 17, *Britannic* from WS 28, *Samaria* from KMF 15 and *Largs Bay* from WS 24 were embarked in Liverpool while *Tamaroa* from KMF 10B embarked in Avonmouth. A single storeship, *Silverteak*, was loaded and sailed in the Liverpool section. A total of 14,432 personnel were embarked on the four liners of WS 31, all but those on *Rangitiki* being destined for India, while 18,979 were on the ships of KMF 17 for Algiers.[3]

As had occurred with the previous convoy, congestion in the west coast ports was extreme in the weeks prior to the departure of the western assault forces for Sicily during the third week of June, and more so at the Clyde Anchorages, where in addition to all the naval traffic, five convoys for that operation as well as WS 31/KMF 17 were assembling during that month, comprising 50 storeships, 24 transports and LSIL, 14 LST together with their accompanying escorts. The Tail of the Bank anchorage had also to provide for a six day visit of the *Queen Elizabeth*, repairs on the battleships *Warspite* and *Malaya*, carriers *Indomitable*, *Argus*, *Archer*, *Activity* and *Battler*, monitors *Roberts* and *Abercrombie*, cruisers *Uganda* and *Sheffield* and all manner of lesser vessels including RFA oilers and new ships undergoing sea trials.

Tamaroa locked out of Avonmouth on the morning tide of 19 June and proceeded under escort of *Saladin* from the Bristol Channel and through the Irish Sea towards the rendezvous with the Liverpool section comprising *Britannic* carrying the Vice Commodore, Captain LG Crabbe, with *Samaria*, *Largs Bay*, *Rangitiki* and storeships *City of Lincoln*, *Clan Macaulay* and *Silverteak*, which cleared the Bar Light Vessel at 2100 that evening and with the River class frigate *Mourne* as escort, proceeded to the rendezvous at a speed of 12 knots. The Clyde section was led out of the boom by the Commodore, Sir AJ Davies, on *Stratheden* (Captain JH Biggs) at 2200, followed by *George W Goethals*, *John Ericsson* and *Clan Macarthur* of WS 31, and by *Cristobal*, *JW McAndrew* and *Santa Rosa* of KMF 17. Escort was given by the destroyer *Amazon* and while a speed of 12 knots was ordered, a mere 9.7 knots was averaged to the rendezvous point at 0900 next morning. Also included in the convoy was the netlayer *Guardian* proceeding from the Clyde to Gibraltar.

As the combined convoy formed up to the west of Orsay, 6 columns were formed while the almost new cruiser *Uganda* joined and took station between columns 3 and 4, while no less than twelve destroyers provided the A/S escort, i.e. seven Hunts, *Mendip* (SO), *Blencathra*, *Hambledon*, *Brecon*, *Brissenden*, *Blankney*, *Ledbury* and of the older classes, *Wallace*, *Viceroy*, *Woolston*, *Arrow* and *Witherington*.[4] *Uganda* and nine of the destroyers were bound for the Mediterranean to take part in Operation Husky for the landings in Sicily. The convoy of eleven transports, four storeships and *Guardian* set off initially to the westward with a speed of advance of 12.5 knots but by 1700 altered to the SW and overnight passed 40 miles NW of Eagle Island on the Connemara coast.

Dirty weather dogged this convoy for the first two days when speed had to be reduced for a few hours for the destroyers. By the morning of the 21st the convoy was steering SSW and 24 hours later on reaching the latitude of the Scillies, a S'ly course was adopted and held for the next two days. At 1700 on 22nd the convoy was 225 miles West of Finisterre, the closest yet given to that headland by the WS series, but similar to the route adopted during the past six months. It provided these convoys with continuous air cover but also allowed the enemy a similar advantage for the Focke Wulf Condors based at Bordeaux, although no enemy interference or action developed. The latitude of 40° was reached in fine weather on the morning of the 24th where course was altered SE towards St Vincent, and with a speed of 12.5 knots being maintained the convoy was 75 miles SW of that Cape on the morning of the 25th when course was then altered to ESE towards the Straits of Gibraltar. This should have been the split position but was moved 104 miles eastward by Admiralty instruction to accommodate destroyers being sent from Gibraltar to take over the escort of WS 31. During the late afternoon the destroyers *Amazon*, *Blackmore*, *Bulldog* and *Foxhound* accordingly joined the WS 31 section which detached by turning away to starboard almost ten points towards the

Fuerteventura channel. The KMF 17 section continued towards the Straits with *Uganda*, *Guardian* and remaining destroyers and reached Algiers safely on the morning of the 27th. The American transports then returned to the States and *Samaria* to Liverpool while *Britannic*, *Tamaroa* and *Largs Bay* proceeded independently on differing dates to Freetown to embark West African troops and join WS 32.

WS 31 continued to the SSW in the same formation with the columns renumbered 1 to 3. Fair weather with a following wind and some favourable current was experienced all the way to Cape Vert. The convoy passed to the east of Fuerteventura during the afternoon of the 27th and continued on the same SW'ly course until the following evening when this was altered to South for Cap Vert. The evaporator on *Amazon* broke down on this passage but *Stratheden* was able to supply her with 9 tons of fresh water in 1.5 hours by gravity feed while the destroyer was held alongside in the slight swell in a very seamanlike manner.[5]

The convoy was 80 miles west of Cap Vert at daybreak on the 30th when the French AMC *Quercy* (converted from a fruit carrier) joined the escort and soon after course was altered to SE. At midnight the Admiralty reported a submarine near the track of the convoy and the route was changed to keep outside the 200 fathoms line as only three ships were fitted with paravanes[5] The convoy reached Freetown free of interference at 1830 on 1st July.

Already languishing in the Freetown anchorage were five liners allocated to embark the leading 6 West Africa Infantry Brigade for Bombay: *Stirling Castle*, *Arawa* and *Staffordshire* which had arrived almost three weeks earlier from Gibraltar and KMF 15 (*q.v.*), *Highland Brigade* and *Highland Monarch* from Durban (WS 29 *q.v.*) via Lagos on 25 June. This West Africa Brigade comprised one battalion each from the Gambia, Sierra Leone and Nigeria, and together with their attached porterage numbered a total force of 12,000 men. As *Stirling Castle* was too large to berth in Lagos, all her complement was embarked in Freetown, while a number of mixed personnel brought out from the UK in *Rangitiki* were transhipped to the remaining four liners for on-carriage to Lagos. They left Freetown in a special coastal convoy on 2 July and were at Lagos for four days until embarkation was completed there in the evening of the 10th.

After fuelling and watering in Freetown, the same seven ship convoy was joined by *Stirling Castle*, and by the AMC *Corfu* as ocean escort and were due to sail on the morning of the 5th to meet the other four liners off Lagos, but these latter ships were delayed arriving there by the low speed of *Staffordshire* (11.5 knots) and *Arawa* (12 knots) due to dirty bottoms. Steps were taken to have their propellers scraped by divers whilst berthed in Lagos, which improved their speeds by half a knot. However, the low speed and longer voyage to the Cape required the two American ships to obtain extra provisions and stores while at Freetown.

The Freetown approaches had been devoid of U-Boat activity since early June. However during the time that WS 31 was in port, the homeward *Empire Kohinoor* was torpedoed and sunk some 230 miles to the WSW by *U-618*. This was an isolated U-Boat, which later joined a group of six patrolling the Ivory and Liberian coasts but they neither sighted nor sank any further victims in the area before returning home.

WS 31 eventually sailed from Freetown at 0800 on 6 July with *Corfu*, the cruiser *Despatch*, French *Quercy* and destroyers *Wolverine*, *Foxhound*, *Bulldog* and *Blackmore* as A/S escorts. A wide sweep of 120 miles was initially made to the SW and at 1300 soon after clearing soundings when about to turn to the South, a ship's lifeboat was recovered containing 27 survivors from the *Empire Kohinoor* sunk four days earlier.

This boat had already covered half the distance to Freetown with an increasing chance of being picked up. On the morning of the 7th the convoy turned to the SE to follow the Liberian coast at a distance of 180 miles and at the same time *Rangitiki* was detached independently for the Plate to load there on the Donaldson berth. This liner returned via Freetown and convoy SL 136 to Liverpool on 24 September and was next employed for seven round trips to New York, carrying not only homeward refrigerated produce but military personnel and were therefore much more profitable voyages than those to the Plate.

Course was altered to East on the morning of the 8th to pass 100 miles south of Cape Palmas, while *Despatch* was detached ahead to refuel at Takoradi, and 24 hours later the course became ENE to approach that port which was reached on the 10th where *Corfu* was detached, while *Despatch* rejoined with the corvette *Armeeria*. Also near this rendezvous *Bulldog* and *Blackmore* detached to fuel on relief by *Witch*. Commodore Davies later complained about closing Takoradi as it had taken the convoy through 80 miles of waters with depths of less than 200 fathoms and although paravanes were streamed, four ships were not so fitted.[5]

At midday 11th the convoy was 75 miles south of Lagos where *Arawa*, *Staffordshire*, *Highland Brigade* and *Highland Monarch* joined with the Nigerian contingent of 6 West Africa Brigade, escorted by *Rapid*, *Bulldog* and *Blackmore* which in turn relieved the three remaining destroyers. The convoy now formed into a cruising order of four columns[6] and turned SSE to cross the Gulf of Guinea and Bight of Biafra towards Pointe Noire, and in the early hours of the 13th passed 30 miles west of the little known Portuguese island of Sao Tome and then detached *Despatch* and *Rapid* ahead to fuel at the French held port.

In the late afternoon of the 14th, WS 31 was 60 miles west of Pointe Noire where *Despatch*, *Rapid*, *Redoubt* and *Quadrant* joined and relieved the three remaining destroyers and *Quercy* which did not rejoin. The convoy now turned south and maintained this heading for the next three days while daylight air cover was restored and continued all the way to the Cape.

Cape Frio was passed at a distance of 60 miles during the forenoon of the 17th when thick fog was experienced for six hours while the course of the convoy thereafter generally followed the coastline at a like distance off. Walvis Bay was passed on the afternoon of the 18th and Luderitz Bay 24 hours later. The morning of the 20th found the convoy 200 miles NW of Capetown having to reduce speed to make a daylight arrival on the 21st, where all eight transports arrived that morning after detaching the three storeships into Saldanha Bay to reduce congestion in Table Bay. They subsequently discharged general cargoes on the Cape Coast but *Clan Macarthur* was sunk en route to Mauritius on 12 August.

WS 31 arrived at Capetown having averaged 11.73 knots from Freetown and was a classic example of the passage time wasted for such liners as *Stratheden* capable of 18 knots and *Stirling Castle* 21 knots which could have completed that leg in ten rather than 15 days. The problem was widely known and continued to be the penalty for convoying ships of widely divergent speeds. Commodore Davies criticized the time wasted when entering Capetown, "much delay...by Examination Drifter going alongside each ship of the convoy only to tell them 'go and pick up pilot'. This and a secret flag hoist he considered "can be signalled to the Commodore for all ships of the convoy".[5]

In Capetown, all of the 7,437 personnel on the US transports *John Ericsson* and *George W Goethals* were landed ashore for the transit camp to await on-carriage at a later date as no other ships were then available. The personnel for India on *Stratheden* enjoyed four days and nights of South African hospitality which was denied the West Africans aboard the other five liners, because of the very definite colour bar then in vogue. "They were however exercised daily by route marches and they were a colourful sight headed by their own bands .. and extremely well disciplined .. Armed guards for the gangways of these ships were supplied from the white personnel on other ships of the convoy, for the sight of armed natives would incite feeling and was contrary to Union Government policy"[7]. The high incidence of cerebro spinal meningitis and lobar pneumonia amongst those native troops caused the Medical embarkation staffs considerable work and worry.

Following disembarkation, both US transports returned to New York, the *Goethals* embarking 800 German POW and guard originally intended for *Athlone Castle* (WS 29 *q.v.*). The remaining convoy now of six transports sailed from Capetown at 1100 on 26 July under escort of *Despatch*, *Quadrant* and *Redoubt*; the Commodore continuing on *Stratheden* and it was quickly noted the speed of *Arawa* and *Staffordshire* had increased to 13.5 knots as a result of South African divers scraping the propellers and brushing the ships' bottoms. A cruising order of three columns was formed.[8]

There was considerable anxiety for the subsequent safe passage of this convoy due to further U-Boat activity in South African waters where six were known to be cruising in mid July. Three were active in the Mozambique Channel and two working to the south and east of Madagascar, while another was in the Mauritius and Reunion area. These U-Boats sank twelve ships in the first two weeks of July and appeared to cover every route between the Cape and Bombay. From the outset therefore WS 31 was routed far south into bad weather with heavy rain squalls (which prevented air cover) to a distance of 180 miles from Cape Agulhas in latitude 38° South, and from this point at noon the next day altered to an ESE heading to continue increasing distance from the Cape coast. By noon on the 28th the convoy was 280 miles south of Cape St Francis, course was altered to east and next day to ENE whilst the speed of advance was recorded as 12.5 knots.

During the 31st, *Staffordshire* developed a defect on one of her engines which had to be stopped for eleven hours. This reduced her speed and that of the convoy to 8.5 knots but was efficiently repaired and the speed of 13.5 knots resumed. By the morning of 1st August the convoy was 500 miles south of Madagascar where it altered course to NE and at noon on the 4th was 250 miles SSE of Mauritius where the cruiser *Frobisher* joined and relieved *Despatch* and the destroyers, which then detached. The convoy then began to steer towards Rodriquez and maintained a distance of 250 miles from Mauritius where *U-181* sank another ship that day.

In the afternoon of the 5th the convoy passed 50 miles west of Rodriquez and altered course to NNE to pass eastward of the Nazareth and Saya de Malha Banks and thereafter a Northerly course to pass west of the Chagos Archipelago and the Maldive Islands. By the 6th the convoy was clear of the U-Boat zone but continued to experience strong E'ly trade winds with a favourable SW'ly current until the 9th when the Equator was crossed and speed increased to 13.7 knots which caused *Arawa* to smoke badly due to dirty oil fuel. By midday 11th the convoy was 300 miles west of Minicoy, no further incidents occurred and all six transports arrived in Bombay harbour at 1300 on the 13th, having averaged 12.63 knots from Capetown. It was the only convoy of the series to have followed such a wide diversionary route across the Indian Ocean.

On completion of this passage the SOE on *Frobisher* commented that "only one day passed without an African soldier dying, generally from pneumonia or common colds. *Stirling Castle* had five such deaths and *Highland Monarch* three"[9]. From the operational aspect the passage was devoid of incident with seasonal SW monsoon weather towards Bombay and only one ship sighted being an American Liberty ship bound from Hobart to Aden.

Arriving in Bombay two hours ahead of the convoy was the Polish LSIL *Batory*, which had taken part in the Sicily assault landings four weeks earlier and was now to act as an exercise ship for troops preparing for operations in the Bay of Bengal. Significantly *Batory* had come down the Red Sea direct from the Mediterranean and three days later on 16 August the first through convoy of transports left the UK for Suez which effectively ended the need for continuing the lengthy WS route around the Cape.

Not long after the troops of 6 West Africa Brigade disembarked and established themselves in the jungle training camp near Bombay, General Slim flew there and after spending a few days with them, wrote "their discipline and smartness was impressive, and they were obviously more at home in the jungle than any troops I had yet seen".[10] Two brigades of the division moved into the Arakan against the Japanese while the third brigade was selected to join Special Force (i.e. Chindits).

The dispersal of the six liners from Bombay now required three to be retained for further service on the Indian Ocean. It had earlier been intended to dispatch *Arawa*, *Stirling Castle* and the two *Highland* liners homeward via Australia and Panama and to use them en route to carry 500 each Italian POW to Australia[11], but this entire movement had to be cancelled. *Arawa* and *Highland Monarch* were selected in lieu to load homewards from the Plate, both left Bombay on 19 August, refuelled in Durban and left Buenos Aires two days apart. The *Highland* liner returned direct from Rio to Belfast and Avonmouth arriving on 7 November to discharge and drydock before joining the KMF route to the Mediterranean. *Arawa* was routed via Freetown and convoy SL 139 to Gibraltar and did not reach Glasgow to discharge until 16 December where she too was drydocked, surveyed and overhauled before commencing seven round trips to New York.

Stratheden, *Highland Brigade* and *Stirling Castle* were now required for on-carriage from Durban to Bombay and Suez as an additional convoy CM 45, the first two leaving Bombay on the 19th, while the *Castle* liner left on the 23rd and was drydocked on reaching Durban for cleaning and survey. All three were ready to begin embarkation on 13 September. *Staffordshire* was drydocked and part loaded in Bombay before sailing on 25 August to proceed home via Suez and convoy MKF 24 to Liverpool, where she arrived on 7 October to begin service on the KMF route.

Convoy Faith/The California Convoy - Sailed UK 8.7.43

The planned movement of the leading infantry brigade of 81 West Africa Division to India on five liners of WS 31 was to be continued by embarking the second brigade on WS 32 and the third and last on WS 33. However, as happened with WS 31, the logistics of sending empty liners to West Africa either from South Africa or from KMF North African convoys which operated on a monthly frequency, inevitably meant some of these valuable ships reached Freetown well in advance of the embarkation date to wait there for periods of up to four weeks, simply to join the next WS convoy. Not only was this a waste of valuable shipping time, but allowed ships' bottoms to become foul and reduced both their own speed and that of the ongoing convoy.

The personnel lifting of West African troops on WS 32 due to call at Freetown on 31 July was expected to be similar to the 12,000 embarked on the previous convoy. Prior arrangements were made accordingly with *Britannic*, *Largs Bay* and *Tamaroa* already anchored there with a combined capacity of 8,528, having previously gone out to Algiers in KMF 17 (with WS 31 *q.v.*). The balance was to be found by sailing *California* (capacity 4,200) direct from the Clyde as an empty ship to embark on the West African coast.

After almost three years service as an AMC and having completed two trooping voyages to Bombay in WS 22 and 26, *California* returned to the Clyde in MKF 15 from Gibraltar on 4 June and moved upriver to a lay-by berth at 58 Stobcross three days later. Voyage repairs originally expected to last a fortnight were not completed until 4 July when she moved to 2 KGV Dock to prepare for embarkation of 470 personnel mainly RN but also some Army, civilians including clergy all for West Africa. In the adjacent No. 1 berth the CPS *Duchess of York* was concurrently embarking 600 RAF and a few civilians also for West Africa. The *Duchess* had recently completed six round trips to North Africa and returned to the Clyde with *California* in MKF 15 but unlike the latter carried a large number of German POW which were disembarked at the NW side of KGV Dock on 8 June. She then moved across the dock and embarked for a further trip to North Africa and shifted to the Clyde Anchorage on the 19th ready to sail in KMF 17 but was unable to do so by electrical problems. The troops remained on board while shore electricians worked aboard at the anchorage but were unable to complete the work until the 29th. It was then decided to use the *Duchess* for the West African troops to Bombay and utilize *California* for more of the West African personnel moving from bases in West Africa to the Middle East.

Duchess of York left her berth at 1600 on 7 July and was followed half an hour later by *California*; both liners remained at the Clyde Anchorage overnight and sailed out past the boom at 0800 on the 8th. At the usual Orsay rendezvous they were joined by the storeship *Port Fairy* bound for the Antipodes via Panama and being included for her protection as far as Freetown. Escort was provided initially by the destroyer *Douglas* and frigate *Moyola*. It is believed that the Master of *Duchess of York*, Captain WG Busk-Wood, acted as Commodore of this three ship convoy which passed a mere 26 miles off Eagle Island next morning steering to the SW. Captain Busk-Wood was a Liverpool man, a Commander RNR who had been Master of the *Duchess of Bedford* from pre-war until transferring to the *York* in November 1942.

The route given to this convoy was very similar to that followed by the most recent WS/KMF formations but of course had a very much reduced escort consistent with the number of ships and personnel embarked. By the morning of the 10th the convoy was 350 miles west of the Scillies where the Canadian Tribal class *Iroquois* joined the escort and course altered to due south which was to be held for the next two days by maintaining a distance of 285 miles west of Finisterre. The speed made good to the morning of the 10th was 13.75 knots but for the next 24 hours increased to 15 knots. During the 11th as the small convoy came abreast of Finisterre the frigate *Swale* joined up to make an A/S escort of four which was doubtless considered adequate.

Unfortunately the perceived danger to this convoy was not to arise from underwater but from the air. By the evening of the 11th the ships were 300 miles west of Oporto and still steering south when an unidentified aircraft was sighted at 2000 hours. Soon after two Focke Wulf Condors were sighted, flying at about 15,000 feet and began to attack through an intense barrage of AA fire from all ships. The *California* caught a near miss "which blew open the ship's hull for a length of about 100 feet. The second plane then attacked and got two direct hits, one in No. 2 hatch and one between the funnel and the bridge; another near miss blew a hole in the starboard side in the vicinity of No. 7 hold. The ship was now badly on fire and No. 1 hold was flooded. The engines were stopped and the order given for the lifeboats to get away with the passengers while the crew remained on board to fight the fires. Eventually, when it became clear that nothing more could be done to save her, the Master rang 'Finished with engines' and gave the order to abandon ship".[1] Captain Henderson, who was relieving Captain Smart for that particular voyage, was taken off by a cutter from one of the destroyers. A destroyer later tried to play hoses on the blazing ship but had to give up due to exploding ammunition. Sadly this fine ship had to be torpedoed and sunk by one of the destroyers at 0045 on the 12th.

Meanwhile the *Duchess of York* received similar punishment from the Luftwaffe Condors, soon being hit by a stick of bombs when "the centre of the ship quickly became a raging inferno and communication between the bridge and other parts of the ship became impossible, and while the guns continued to fire at the five aircraft (*California* reported six), ... efforts were made to control the fire, but without success; the ship had to be abandoned".[2] Captain Busk-Wood and his Chief Engineer were the last to leave the ship at 2240. *Douglas* fired a torpedo at the burning hulk in order to reduce the risk of the convoy being found by submarines.

There are differing records of the casualties on both liners; that provided by the Admiralty to the MOWT states the *Duchess* had a complement of 908 of whom 819 were saved which included 270 crew, 112 civilians and 537 RAF. On the *California* there were 765 on board with 739 saved including 272 crew, 253 RN, 49 Army and 165 civilians. Considering the ferocity of the attacks and rapid spread of fire, the total loss of life at 115 was remarkably small and most certainly related to the limited number embarked at 25 per cent of the stated capacity. Had the ships been fully embarked to their maximum capacities each of 4,000, the losses would inevitably have been much greater but on the other hand, if so heavily embarked, their departure would most likely have been delayed for inclusion in the next WS convoy.

The survivors of both ships were picked up by the two destroyers and *Moyola* which then proceeded to Casablanca where they were safely landed and from where the crews were sent home on *Arundel Castle* one week later. All of the personnel for West Africa were at the same time taken on to their destinations by *Nea Hellas* of KMF 19 (see WS 32).

Following these tragic sinkings, the unharmed *Port Fairy* continued towards Casablanca with *Swale* where the escorts were due to have refuelled. During the evening of the 12th, however, these two ships were attacked by a single Condor which made a series of bombing runs at a high altitude. The *Port Fairy* "received a direct hit aft which pierced the maindeck and blew a hole in the ship's hull".[3] This started a fire which rapidly spread but was extinguished by assistance from *Swale* at 2300. With her steering gear damaged *Port Fairy* made it safely to Casablanca by steering on her main engines alone and when repairs were completed resumed her voyage.

After returning home for survivor's leave, Captain Henderson was appointed to the Anchor Line's *Castalia* where he remained until the end of the war. Captain Busk-Wood reverted to his previous command on *Duchess of Bedford* for one short voyage to Phillipville but then retired and died in 1946. He was Mentioned in Despatches and awarded the OBE for his part in the Torch operation in 1942.

It seems that complacency may have been responsible for prescribing a route for these liners which had allowed the most recent convoys a passage free of enemy interference. The previous convoys, however, were able to offer a massive firepower, including that of a cruiser as a deterrent against interference from marauding Condors. By comparison the 'California' convoy was a target they could hardly resist.

Chapter 21

WS 32, CM 45 and WS 33

The second and third Brigades of West Africans move to India
and termination of the WS route.

WS 32 - Sailed UK 19.7.43

The loss of two well managed high capacity liners from the Faith convoy one week
before the sailing of WS 32 which they had been scheduled to join in West Africa was
a severe blow to all involved in the operation of British troopships. This came at a time
when the severe losses sustained during and after the Torch operation just might in some
small measure be overcome by negotiations taking place between the MOWT and the
US Maritime Commission for the charter of thirteen C1 class ships fitted out as LSIL.
These ships each had capacity for about 1,200 personnel but the first were not delivered
until October 1943 and all were subsequently earmarked for the Normandy landings.

The rapid destruction of two high profile liners by precision bombing from a high altitude and on such a highly utilized route must have raised more than a few eyebrows
amongst the Admiralty and Coastal Command of the RAF. It was certainly a sobering
thought to realise that the Germans, despite their ejection from North Africa, their
reverses in Russia and now in Sicily were able to mount such a crippling loss to our
trooping fleet so close to home. The immediate affect was to move the route further

westward to keep 500 miles off Finisterre and so increase the distance from the Focke-
Wulf Condor base at Bordeaux-Merignac, indeed almost beyond the limit of their
endurance.

In respect of WS 32, the first priority of the MOWT was to find a replacement for
Duchess of York and able to reach West Africa in sufficient time to embark the West
Africans and join WS 32. The answer was simply met by utilizing *Nea Hellas* which
had just arrived at Algiers in the outward KMF 19 convoy. After disembarking and
fuelling at Gibraltar, she called at Casablanca to uplift the survivors from *California* and
the *Duchess* destined for West Africa, and left there on the 19th to reach Freetown on
the 25th and from there continued to Takoradi to begin embarking the Gold Coast contingent. The movement of the personnel planned for *California* to the Middle East was
now postponed until WS 33.

Apart from *Maloja* which returned to Liverpool on 5 June for boiler re-tubing and
drydocking after the WS 26 voyage to Suez, the availability of liners for WS 32 was
wholly confined to the intermediate refrigerated class all of which would be turned
around in Durban to load homeward meat cargoes from the Plate. *Rangitata* docked in
Liverpool from New York on 28 May to spend seven weeks under engine repairs. The
sisters *Esperance* and *Moreton Bay*, docked in Avonmouth from New York on 10 June
to discharge and have additional armament fitted while *Highland Chieftain* arrived at
that same port one week later to discharge from Montevideo. Three storeships were
accompanying WS 32, the sisters *Rochester* and *Rowallan Castle*, the first named allocated as a Rescue Ship, and the Belgian flag motorship *Copacabana*.

Embarkation on the two *Bay* class liners was completed in Avonmouth on 16 July;
both ships locked out that evening and proceeded towards the Clyde, joining with four
others which had embarked and sailed from Liverpool at 1000 on the 17th, i.e. *Maloja*
and *Rangitata* of WS 32 and *Orion* and *Dempo* of KMF 20. All six anchored in the
Clyde soon after daybreak on the 19th which allowed the Masters to attend the local
convoy conference later that morning. On the Clyde, *Mooltan* was the only ship to
embark in Glasgow and came downriver from 1 KGV on the 16th, followed by
Highland Princess next day and *Highland Chieftain* on the 18th to join *Volendam*
recently arrived from Iceland and turning round to sail in KMF 20.[1]

The appointed Commodore WAB Magee DSO RNR on *Maloja* led the ten liners out
of the Clyde boom at 2030 on 19 July and proceeded towards the rendezvous off Orsay,
where at 0700 next day junction was made with the storeship *Rowallan Castle* and five
others which had sailed from the Mersey anchorage at 1000 on the 19th; *Rochester
Castle* and the Belgian *Copacabana* also for WS 32, while *City of Bristol*, *Chyebassa*
and the Dutch *Rembrandt* were for the KMF section. *Rochester Castle* by now famous
in having survived the Pedestal convoy to Malta, was allocated as a Rescue Ship, possibly one result of the *California* convoy although her station in the convoy hardly
reflected that task.

The combined convoy formed into a cruising order of six columns[2] screened by the
1st Support Group from Derry comprising the sloops *Pelican* (S), *Egret* and River class
frigates *Wear*, *Rother* and *Jed*, reinforced by the destroyer *Beagle* and frigates *Tay*, *Kale*
and *Derg*, the latter three being part of a group of seven being sent to South African
waters. The Vice Commodore HA Baxter DSC on *Mooltan* would later act as
Commodore of KMF 20. The Master of *Highland Chieftain*, Captain RB Hill was
appointed Rear Commodore.

The convoy set off at the nominated speed of 13.5 knots for a short distance to the westward of Tory Island before turning SW on a course which was held for the next three days. At 1830 on the 21st the latitude of the Scillies was crossed where the cruiser *Charybdis* joined as extra surface and air protection and remained all the way to Gibraltar. Less than two hours later a Junkers 88 was sighted but reckoned to be a meteorological aircraft. Shortly after midday on the 22nd as the convoy passed to the west of Biscay a Focke-Wulf Condor shadowed for an hour which was reported to the Admiralty and a diversion ordered to keep further from the enemy aircraft bases. The SO A/S escort on *Pelican* expected bombers to appear on the next two days but most fortunately cloud cover precluded high level bombing and no enemy aircraft were sighted.[3]

On the morning of the 23rd the convoy reached a position 500 miles west of Finisterre where it turned south and next morning altered to SE and during that day probably reached the limit of enemy aircraft endurance. That night *Pelican* had to stop and go astern to release a 6 ft. diameter decomposed turtle which had become lodged on her A/S dome. By the morning of the 25th the convoy was 360 miles WSW of Cape St Vincent and 120 miles NE of Madeira where course was altered to East. At midday *Douglas*, *Ness* and the sloop *PC 74* joined from Gibraltar and two hours later *Beagle* detached ahead to fuel at Casablanca. By 1800 the convoy reached the split position 240 miles SW of St Vincent, KMF 20 altered to ENE towards the Straits of Gibraltar with *Charybdis* and the 1st Support Group, from which *Pelican* had to detach with leaking tubes in both boilers. The Straits were passed through at midnight on the 26th and KMF 20 reached Algiers safely without incident at 0900 on the 28th. *Mooltan*, *Volendam* and *Highland Princess* then returned to the Clyde with POW in MKF 22, *Orion* returned from Oran also in MKF 20 while *Dempo* was sent from Gibraltar to Freetown but then returned to the Clyde in MKF 22.

Meanwhile WS 32 adopted a four column formation[4] and altered to ESE to close the Moroccan coast to expedite the fuelling of escorts at Casablanca, until the following morning when a SSW heading was adopted towards the Fuerteventura Channel. This was passed through in the early afternoon of the 27th on a SW course, which was held until next morning when *PC 74* detached and a S'ly heading was adopted and held for the next three days. At 1015 on the 30th the convoy was 30 miles NW of Cap Vert where three more storeships joined from Dakar, Holt's *Melampus*, the US *Delaires* and the MOWT owned but Elder Dempster managed *New Northland* permanently engaged in trooping on the West African coast.

There were no further incidents on this passage which was made in fine weather throughout. Course was altered to SE direct for Freetown on the morning of the 31st and all ships were anchored in the harbour 24 hours later. The average speed made good from the Clyde was 12.54 knots. An air escort of Catalinas or Sunderlands was provided almost continuously throughout by aircraft based in the UK, at Gibraltar, Port Lyautey or Bathurst. Commodore Magee, as others had done before him on *Maloja*, commented that the accommodation was good but on four decks below was too far from the bridge although there was a telephone connected to the wheelhouse.[5]

Awaiting the arrival of WS 32 in Freetown was *Britannic* which, with *Tamaroa* and *Largs Bay* had gone out to Algiers in KMF 17 and were then ordered to Freetown for the West African movement and arrived there independently between 8 and 14 July. The last two named then made a round trip to Lagos before returning there via Takoradi to begin embarking the Nigerian section of 5 West Africa Brigade on 4 August. They were followed to West Africa by *Nea Hellas* from KMF 19 which replaced *Duchess of York*, and this liner began embarking the Gold Coast section at Takoradi on 2 August. *Britannic* remained at Freetown throughout to embark the Gambia and Sierra Leone sections, the whole force totalling 12,453 men.

There was no reported U-Boat activity in the Freetown or West African coastal area at this time, and after fuelling and watering to capacity, the revised convoy of six transports and four storeships (*Melampus* and *New Northland* having detached) sailed again at 0930 on 5 August for the Cape. The A/S escort was continued by *Beagle, Tay, Kale, Derg, Douglas* and *Bulldog* and when clear of the swept channel at 1145 the convoy formed into four columns and proceeded out to the SW before turning SE to follow the Liberian coast at a distance of 40 miles. *Rowallan Castle* was detached at 1800 next day for Ascension and by the early hours of the 7th the convoy was round Cape Palmas and heading for Takoradi.

The convoy was off the Gold Coast port at 0900 on the 8th where *Copacabana* and *Delaires* detached and where *Nea Hellas* under escort of *Wolverine* joined up while *Beagle* and *Douglas* refuelled. Course was then laid off for the Lagos area and when 30 miles south of that port at 1430, on the 9th, *Tamaroa* and *Largs Bay* joined to form the enhanced convoy of nine transports and a single storeship.[6] Course was now altered to SE to cross the Gulf of Guinea towards Pointe Noire and during the night of 10/11th August the convoy passed to the west of Sao Tome island. The three frigates detached ahead at noon on the 11th to refuel at Pointe Noire.

At 1000 on the 12th the convoy was 60 miles south of the French colonial port where *Beagle, Douglas* and *Wolverine* detached on relief by the modern destroyers *Norman, Relentless* and *Quiberon*. The convoy now turned to the SSW and six hours later *Bulldog* was replaced by *Rapid*. Air escort either by Catalinas, Wellingtons, Venturas or Ansons provided continuous daylight cover all the way from Freetown to the Cape.

Late on the 13th the Admiralty signalled *Norman* that the convoy originally bound for Durban was to anchor in Table Bay en route. All ships were then given the opportunity to obtain fuel, fresh water and provision should the weather permit while in Table Bay. *Nea Hellas* requested 1650 tons and *Tamaroa* 1,000 tons of fuel.

There were no other incidents on the passage south, the convoy was 60 miles off Cape Frio on the morning of the 15th and as with previous recent convoys maintained a similar distance off the coast as it progressed towards the Cape to pass abeam of Walvis Bay on the morning of the 16th. A landfall was made on the Cape Coast early on the 18th and by 0300 the convoy was 20 miles SW of Cape Columbine light. *Rochester Castle* was bound for Capetown while all nine transports actually for Durban proceeded as instructed into Table Bay and anchored there at 1500 that same day to await further orders.

The U-Boats which had caused such a wide diversion of WS 31 when passing through South African waters, were still around in the first half of August when they sank six more ships. Although the official history states "in mid-August the U-Boats were all on their way or about to return home",[7] this was not yet the case as WS 32 approached the Cape on the 17th. Intensive air and surface attacks on *U-196* east of Durban between the 14th and 16th were unsuccessful and allowed that boat to escape, while *U-197* which sank a ship south of Madagascar on the 17th, initiated further searches resulting in her destruction by a Catalina on the 20th.

After remaining in Table Bay overnight the convoy was allowed to proceed and got underway at 1000 on the 19th with the same A/S escort for Durban. The three frigates were detached at midday when 15 miles south of Cape Point while the four destroyers continued. By 1800 the convoy had passed Agulhas and next morning was 80 miles west of Cape St Francis. No further incidents occurred on this passage, East London was passed at a distance of 10 miles at 0700 on the 21st and the convoy reached Durban the following morning having averaged 12.67 knots from Freetown to Capetown and 11.87 knots to Durban.

The transhipment plan for this convoy allowed for all four of the intermediate refrigerated carriers of the original convoy from the UK to disembark entirely in Durban and proceed to the Plate to load meat and produce cargoes for the UK. Thus, 7,763 personnel were landed to Clairwood Transit Camp to await subsequent on-carriage as no other liners were then immediately available. This was in addition to 7,439 landed in Capetown from WS 31 four weeks earlier, but nearly a third of the total was to be lifted on *Strathmore* which reached Durban from Bombay on the 24th to make a third on-carriage trip since arriving in WS 27. The balance of waiting personnel was moved on CM 45 three weeks later(*q.v.*).

Rangitata was the first ship released from Durban sailing on the 24th for Montevideo, via Capetown and Tristan da Cunha, where mails and stores were landed for the RN Meteorological Station. Loading on the Plate was on the Donaldson berth at Buenos Aires completing at Montevideo, whence she proceeded to Freetown to join convoy SR 6 for Gibraltar and finally MKF 25 to reach Liverpool to discharge on 5 November; her next employment was six round trips to New York. *Highland Chieftain* and *Esperance Bay* left Durban on the 26th, called at Capetown and both loaded on the Royal Mail berth, the former at Buenos Aires and the *Bay* liner at La Plata completing at Montevideo. The *Highland* liner proceeded direct via Belfast to reach Swansea for discharge on 16 October. *Moreton Bay* sailed from Durban on 4 September and after a quick call at Capetown loaded on the Blue Star berth solely at Montevideo, whence *Rangitata* and the two *Bay* liners left within the space of a day for Freetown to join the same homeward convoys, *Moreton Bay* discharging in Avonmouth and *Esperance Bay* in Cardiff. This was the last occasion that homeward WS liners returned around the Cape, all four were subsequently employed on North Alantic round trips to New York.

After fuelling and storing in Durban, the four liners carrying 5 West Africa Brigade, plus *Maloja* all for Bombay and *Strathmore* bound for Suez were ready to sail on the morning of 28 August, at which point *Nea Hellas* was unable to proceed due to repairs to a dynamo which could not be completed in time and was later included in CM 45 (*q.v.*). The remaining five liners were led out of the harbour by the cruiser *Hawkins* acting as SOE at 1200 on the 28th and when clear of the swept channel formed into three columns[8] and set off to the NE towards the Mozambique Channel. The A/S escort was provided by *Norman*, *Rapid* and *Quiberon*.

The northward passage of this convoy through an area now devoid of the enemy was made without incident. Commodore Magee remained on *Maloja* while Captain GE Cove, the Master of *Britannic*, acted as Vice Commodore. At 1800 on the 30th course was altered to NNE for the centre of the channel and at 0700 on 2nd September the convoy passed 70 miles west of Comoro Island and continued on a course direct for Guardafui. At 0900 on the 3rd a position was reached 270 miles ESE of Mombasa where *Emerald* joined from Mombasa in relief of *Hawkins* which then detached to that port with the three destroyers.

The passage towards Guardafui continued uneventful, at 1600 on the 6th the convoy was 60 miles SE of Ras Hafun where course was altered to NE direct for Bombay, while

Strathmore detached independently for Aden, passing 15 miles off Guardafui at 0100 on the 7th and reaching that port by the evasive route directed at 0800 on the 8th. The P&O liner was there fuelled and watered and sailed again that evening for Suez where she arrived to disembark on the 12th. Four days later she passed through the canal to join the homeward convoy MKF 24 and reached Liverpool on 7 October. After 19 days in port the *Strathmore* sailed again in KMF 25A for Bombay via Suez, the Mediterranean route being then fully reopened.

Meanwhile the main convoy of four liners continued free of incident to Bombay where they arrived at 1800 on 10 September after a voyage of 53 days from the Clyde, the average speed from Durban being recorded as 12.91 knots. The disembarkation of *Maloja* and *Britannic* were handled first, the British personnel from the UK on the P&O liner being dispersed to multifarious units throughout India while the troops and porters of 5 West Africa Brigade went to join their compatriots in the jungle training camp. From the historical viewpoint *Maloja* and WS 32 were the last in the series to carry personnel entirely from the UK around the Cape.

As always these liners were urgently required back in the UK, and with the complete Mediterranean passage re-opened for troopships by KMF 22 in August, the long return route around the Cape was no longer necessary. There was however a need to connect with the departures of MKF convoys from Port Said which like their outward counterparts ran on a monthly cycle. *Maloja* and *Britannic* left Bombay on the 23rd, refuelled in Aden and anchored at Suez on 2 and 3 October respectively to wait there for MKF 25 sailing from Port Said on the 17th; both reached Liverpool on 5 November whence the Cunarder was disposed to New York round trips while *Maloja* reverted to the KMF route. *Tamaroa* and *Largs Bay* followed these liners three days later, were also included in MKF 25 and were directed to Avonmouth and Cardiff respectively, the former then beginning New York trips while the *Bay* liner continued on KMF service.

Although WS 32 was the last of the established and renowned WS series which had so successfully carried the war around the Cape for more than three long years, one other convoy was run from West Africa to complete the movement of 81 West Africa Division in India, but sandwiched in between these sailings was the important on-carriage of personnel in South Africa landed from WS 31 and 32.

CM 45 - sailed Durban 14.9.43

The need for this sailing and the further use of the only available tonnage was explained above. *Stratheden* returned to Durban on 30 August from WS 31 to Bombay; similarly *Highland Brigade* on 3 September and *Stirling Castle* to drydock two days later. *Sibajak* which had been under engine repairs in Durban since 6 August was also to be included in the convoy having been retained in the area since her Lagos to Suez voyage in WS 27, and finally *Nea Hellas* which completed dynamo repairs and was now able to continue to Bombay with the Gold Coast troops of 5 West Africa Brigade.

The U-Boat situation in South African waters had now changed, the previous group had left the area only to be replaced by five boats of Gruppe Monsun which on 11 September made rendezvous with a supply tanker and depot ship 450 miles south of Mauritius. They were instructed to operate in the northern Indian Ocean while an Italian submarine and one Japanese would work the Mozambique Channel. Six ships were sunk in September and convoys were introduced on routes between Durban, Mombasa, Aden, Bombay and Colombo. The Eastern Fleet now based at Colombo had some knowledge of these submarines and provided a strong A/S escort for CM 45.

All five liners sailed from Durban on 14 September embarked with 6,779 British and South African personnel for Suez, plus 6,199 British and 3,661 West Africans for Bombay, a total of 16,635. Escort was provided by the battleship *Ramillies* and fleet destroyers *Nepal*, *Napier*, *Roebuck* and *Relentless*. No details of the cruising order or the convoy Commodore or indeed the initial route have survived but it is believed this was similar to that followed by WS 32 up the Mozambique Channel.

On reaching the latitude of Mombasa on the 20th, *Ramillies*, *Nepal* and *Napier* were relieved by the cruisers *Frobisher* and *Durban*, destroyer *Quadrant* and next day by *Quickmatch* which brought *Salween* and *Nieuw Holland* out from Mombasa to join up en route to Suez. *Durban* detached on the 22nd and in the early evening of the 23rd the convoy divided to the south of Ras Hafun, *Stratheden*, *Sibajak* and the two 'joiners' continuing towards Guaradfui and Aden where they arrived on the 27th to refuel and thereafter continued to Suez, anchoring there to disembark on 1st October. *Sibajak* and *Nieuw Holland* then continued first to Alexandria, then Taranto, the former and *Stratheden* joining MKF 25 for the homeward passage to the Clyde where they arrived on 4 November. Both were next employed on KMF 27.

Meanwhile the Bombay section of three liners crossed the Indian Ocean without incident. *Quickmatch* was detached on the 25th and the three remaining destroyers on the day prior to arrival, this being the first WS type convoy to cross these waters with an A/S escort. *Frobisher* arrived safely with the convoy on the morning of 28 September. Seven days were occupied in disembarking and replenishing the liners one after the other at Ballard Pier, and due to the possible presence of submarines, all three liners left Bombay in convoy on 5 October and after fuelling in Aden proceeded independently to Suez; *Stirling Castle* arriving with three days to spare for joining MKF 25 and continued beyond Algiers to New York and Boston, crossing to Liverpool on 16 December. *Nea Hellas* just missed the cut for MKF 25 but joined an additional MKF 25A convoy and reached the Clyde on 24 November, both liners resumed service on the KMF route. *Highland Brigade* was required at Suez for personnel returning to Mombasa and thereafter for a further CM 48 voyage from Durban on 27 November to Suez, and proved to be the last such voyage by a WS liner. Passing through the canal on 28 December, the *Highland* liner called at four Mediterranean ports before returning to Avonmouth in MKF 28 on 8 February to complete a voyage which lasted ten months. Her next employment was for five round trips to New York.

WS 33 / KMF 22 - sailed UK 16.8.1943

WS 33 the final convoy of the series departed the UK a month behind the previous convoy comprising six liners, three each being embarked and destined for Gibraltar and Algiers as part of KMF 22. Beyond these ports the liners were to proceed to West Africa and there embark the third and last brigade to complete the assembly of 81 West Africa Division in India. WS 33 was therefore quite different from its predecessors by having no ships sailing direct from the UK to Freetown, although some of those going via Gibraltar may also have carried personnel for West Africa. KMF 22 was also notable in being the first convoy to send troopships all the way through the Mediterranean, five were bound for Port Said and Suez while another was continuing to Mombasa and Durban in direct opposition to the WS route which it was now replacing.

The first liners allocated for the WS section of the convoy were *Antenor*, *Boissievain* and *Indrapoera* which arrived in the Clyde with MKF 15 on 4 June, the last two named disembarking German POW at the NW side of KGV Dock in Glasgow and thereafter returned to the Clyde Anchorage to await embarkation orders. *Antenor* spent five weeks at a repair berth in Glasgow before returning to the anchorage on 18 July, altogether these three liners were virtually unemployed on the Clyde for ten weeks prior to their departure in WS 33.

Johan de Witt arrived in the Clyde from New York on 6 July and was in Glasgow for three weeks engine repairs and storing, before she too occupied a berth at the anchorage on 4 August. *Ormonde* was the next liner to be allocated on reaching the Clyde on 30 July in MKF 19, moving upriver on 4 August she remained in Glasgow to embark at No. 2 KGV Dock and return downriver on the 14th. The final allocation was *Duchess of Richmond* which reached the anchorage from an Iceland trip on 8 August, and may have been a replacement for the *California* convoy. The *Duchess* moved upriver four days later to embark at 1 KGV, and preceded *Ormonde* to the anchorage on the 14th, where the other four liners were now completing embarkation and preparing for sea.

Some of the twelve liners allocated for KMF 22 had also been in UK ports for extended periods; *Empress of Australia* in Liverpool since 5 March repairing collision damage sustained with *Ormonde* in KMF 6, and *Orduna* in Liverpool from 28 June for dry-docking after a voyage in WS 26. Eight of the remainder arrived on 23 July in MKF 18 and the last two in MKF 19 seven days later. The embarkation of these liners was completed on *Durban Castle* at 1 KGV in Glasgow on 12 August, on *Marnix van St Aldegonde* and *Ruys* next day at adjacent KGV berths and on *Cameronia*, *Otranto* and *Duchess of Bedford* at the Clyde Anchorage. At Avonmouth on the 14th *Arundel Castle* completed and sailed to join the main group on the Clyde, as did *Orontes* and *Monarch of Bermuda* from Liverpool on that same date, while *Empress of Australia*, *Orduna* and *Tegelberg* completed and sailed as the Mersey section on the 16th with the single MT storeship *Glenartney* bound for Bombay via Suez.[1]

The appointed Commodore of WS 33, Rear Admiral Sir OH Dawson KBE was embarked on *Duchess of Richmond* (Captain HS Knight), who led the Clyde section of fifteen liners out through the boom at 1800 on 16 August, to make rendezvous with the three liners and single storeship from Liverpool which left the Princes Stage and Mersey anchorage eight hours earlier. Junction was made 6 miles west of Orsay at 0500 on the 17th when the convoy formed a cruising order (unknown) and set off on a westerly course at a speed of 13 knots.[2] Perhaps to deter possible interference from enemy aircraft as befell the *California* convoy, WS 33 was accompanied by the fighter carrier *Hunter* en route to Malta to support the Salerno landings. The Australian cruiser *Shropshire* was acting as ocean escort en route to Sydney for attachment to the US Seventh Fleet. The A/S escort was provided by the destroyer *Wrestler*, sloops *Chanticleer*, *Narbada*, *Weston*, cutter *Totland* and frigates *Barle*, *Ettrick* and *Usk*.

At 1300 on the 17th course was altered to SW and held until the latitude of Finisterre was reached on the morning of the 20th, at a distance of 400 miles, where the cruiser *Charybdis* joined as an additional deterrent to enemy interference and course was then altered to south and held on that direction to maintain possible German aircraft at their maximum range.

Reference was previously made to the British contribution to the American trooping programme and particularly the 'Bolero' movement of US troops crossing the Atlantic to the UK. It was fortunate that complete co-operation prevailed between the War Office, Washington and Canada in planning these moves as many signals were exchanged throughout the summer of 1943 when circumstances changed with the release of WS liners on the cessation of that route. The bulk of the US movement was carried in AT convoys by five of the Monster class supported by *Andes*, *Pasteur* and *Empress of Scotland*. The Americans had withdrawn much of their trooping tonnage to the Pacific where they had enormous commitments and were given British assistance when *Nieuw Amsterdam* made two trips from San Francisco later in the year. Even this proved insufficient, the War Office had to decline a request for two of the WS class for the Pacific theatre, but provided six in late August with a lift of 25,000 to help run a subsidiary North Atlantic service of UT convoys, but when further WS liners were asked for, the War Office could not help further.. "It is unlikely we can boost UT 3 by replacing small US ships with large British ships as KMF 22 and UT 2 cleans us out and we may be stretched to produce a complete KMF in September. Probable however that we can provide 30,000 lift for UT 4 early October".[3] These were surely classic examples of the great Anglo-American shipping alliance.

No enemy interference occurred on the passage south and at 1900 on the 21st the convoy reached a position 450 miles WSW of Cape St Vincent, where a wide alteration of 80° was made towards the Straits of Gibraltar. The convoy passed through in the late forenoon of the 23rd, detaching *Antenor*, *Boissievain*, *Johan de Witt* of WS 33 and *Cameronia* of KMF 22 into Gibraltar, while the remainder continued eastwards and detached *Duchess of Richmond*, *Indrapoera* and *Ormonde* of WS 33 and *Duchess of Bedford*, *Otranto* and *Orontes* of KMF 22 into Algiers where they arrived at 1900 on the 24th. The balance of nine ships continued through the Mediterranean, *Durban Castle* and *Marnix van St Aldegonde* detaching into Phillipville on the 25th, while the remaining six liners and single storeship reached Port Said safely on the 29th.

On completion of disembarkation in Algiers, the three liners of WS 33 returned to Gibraltar on the 29th to find six liners of the homeward MKF 22 just arrived (four from Alexandria and two from Freetown); these six were then joined by *Cameronia* and that convoy sailed for the UK on 1st September. Meanwhile the six liners of WS 33 were delayed at Gibraltar for some reason but sailed again at 0100 on the 3rd under escort of a very mixed group comprising the destroyer *Bulldog*, sloop *Weston*, cutter *Totland*, corvette *Hydrangea* and frigates *Bann* and *Ness*.

The convoy passed through the Fuerteventura channel in the early hours of the 5th and continued on a SW'ly course until the morning of the 6th when a S'ly heading was adopted towards Cap Vert. That headland was passed at a distance of 25 miles at 2100 on the 7th and on the following morning when the destroyer *Douglas* joined, the convoy altered to the SE towards the Freetown approaches, and being 70 miles west of the port next morning arrived at 1500 that day. The area was then believed to be free of U-Boats.

On the West African coast, the process of embarking the third and last flight of 81 West Africa Division was an extremely complex one lasting two weeks, the reasons for which must remain unclear. It is unlikely that many or indeed any troops were embarked in Freetown as 3 West Africa Brigade now moving to India was almost wholly composed of Nigerian units, other than additional porter units originating from the Gold Coast. *Duchess of Richmond* alone was embarking RAF West African units, being moved from bases at Takoradi and Lagos to relieve British units in the Middle East. The other five liners were embarking solely West African troops for India.

All six liners left Freetown on the morning of 14 September escorted by *Beagle*, *Boadicea*, *Bulldog*, *Wolverine* and *Bann* to follow the same close-to route followed by WS 32 to Takoradi, where *Duchess of Richmond*, *Ormonde* and *Boissievain* arrived at 0800 on the 17th, while the remaining three liners continued and reached Lagos 24 hours later. After three days in Lagos, *Antenor* and *Johan de Witt* returned to Takoradi where on the 22nd they took the place of *Boissievain* and the Commodore on *Duchess of Richmond* which in turn arrived at Lagos on the 23rd. Next day *Antenor* and *Johan de Witt* left Takoradi and returned to Lagos on the 25th to join the *Duchess*, *Boissievain* and *Indrapoera*, the latter having remained there throughout as had *Ormonde* at Takoradi.

The *Duchess* was now embarked with 4,000 mainly RAF while the others carried the three Nigerian battalions and supporting units with porters totalling 11,838 men. *Ormonde* left Takoradi in the afternoon of 29 September to steam along the coast where at 1500 next day the five liners from Lagos joined up and presumably formed a cruising order of three columns. Escort was now provided by four of the River class frigates, *Bann* , *Plym*, *Teviot* and *Trent* on passage to join three others which had taken WS 32 out to the Cape. September being almost the hottest month of the year in West Africa, everyone on these six liners and four escorts must have been relieved to get back to sea.

The initial SE course of the convoy passed 50 miles west of Sao Tome in the early morning of 2 October, and by 0800 course was altered towards Pointe Noire where at midday on the 3rd, and 50 miles SW of that port, a S'ly course was adopted for the next three days. On the morning of the 6th the convoy reached a position 100 miles SW of Cape Frio from where a course of SSE was steered until 90 miles south of Luderitz Bay on the morning of the 8th. The course was then adjusted towards Cape Columbine and at 0900 next morning the convoy was 43 miles NW of that point and 110 miles from Capetown where all ships arrived at 1800 that day, having averaged 12 knots for the past three.

After fuelling and watering in Capetown the same six liners and escorts sailed again next day and had an uneventful passage around the coast to Durban where they arrived at daybreak on the 14th, the speed for the first two days having averaged a mere 9 knots. Waiting to join the convoy in Durban was *Orduna* which had been part of the KMF 22 section going to Port Said and having continued via Mombasa, arrived in Durban on 20 September, five weeks ahead of the west coast convoy. *Orduna* disembarked personnel, re-embarked others for the Middle East and Union Castle cargo for the UK and was ready for sea when WS 33 arrived. Also joining the convoy here was the coal-burning Polish *Pulaski* bound for Suez. WS 33 remained in Durban for six days during which time there was some interchange of British personnel between *Duchess of Richmond* and those in Clairwood Transit Camp with priority being given to those for the Middle East and Italy.

The same six liners plus *Orduna* and *Pulaski* sailed from Durban at 0600 on 20 October escorted by the AMC *Chitral*, destroyer *Rapid* and frigates *Bann*, *Teviot* and *Trent*, on which date the Italian submarine *Ammaraglio Cagni* arrived in port to take advantage of the Italian armistice declared on the 8th. A month had now passed from the Gruppe Monsun U-Boats arriving in the area since when the boats took up cruising stations in the Gulf of Aden, the south coast of Arabia, the Seychelles area, Chagos Archipelago and Indian coast south of Bombay, but the seven River class frigates lately arrived were to greatly enhance the A/S capabilities of escorts in the area. The U-Boats sank four ships in October, the Japanese two and by the end of that month Gruppe Monsun had withdrawn to Penang for refit. It was fortunate their arrival in the Indian Ocean was almost matched by the impending closure of the WS route and major troop movements from South Africa across that ocean.

WS 33 followed the usual route up the Mozambique Channel and was clear of that area on the morning of the 25th when passing 40 miles west of Comoro. Course was continued NNW towards Mombasa which the convoy entered for a few hours at 0600 on the 27th to coal *Pulaski* and fuel the escorts, but sailed again soon after midday to continue NE up the Somali coast by keeping a minimum distance of 50 miles offshore. At 0500 on the 31st the convoy divided in a position 130 miles south of Ras Hafun, the Bombay section of five liners now re-styled CM 46B proceeding ENE towards that port under escort of *Chitral* and *Bann*, where they arrived at daybreak on 5 November.

The disembarkation of the three Nigerian battalions and supporting troops and porters of 3 West Africa Brigade from each of the five liners in turn occupied eight days. Unlike the other two brigades which formed 81 West Africa Division, 3 West Africa Brigade was sent immediately to the Central Provinces to join five British brigades for intensive training and conversion to Long Range Penetration columns, i.e. the Chindits, for operating behind Japanese lines in Burma. The West Africans spent five months in this role in 1944 while the other two brigades moved into the Arakan with their division in November 1943. The division was re-united at Chiringa in February 1945 and repatriated to West Africa by January 1946.

From Bombay, *Antenor*, *Boissievain* and *Ormonde* sailed on the 13th in convoy to Aden, and thereafter independently to Suez and through the canal to join MKF 27, which proceeded via Taranto, Algiers, Naples and Oran before reaching the Clyde on 4 January where all three continued service on the KMF route. *Johan de Witt* followed from Bombay on 17 November and also joined MKF 27, but was retained in the Mediterranean until January when sent back to Bombay and did not return to Liverpool until 16 March. *Indrapoera* was delayed at Bombay until 2 December, joined MKF 27 at Augusta but then spent seven weeks broken down in Algiers, had to be towed to Gibraltar for three months repairs and then brought a party of Madeirans from Funchal to the fortress. Finally *Indrapoera* made a further trip from Freetown via the Mediterranean to Karachi and did not return to Liverpool until 14 September from a voyage which had lasted thirteen months.

In reverting to the remaining section of WS 33, which from the split position south of Ras Hafun on 31 October, *Duchess of Richmond* with *Orduna* and *Pulaski*, now re-styled CM 46A and under escort of *Rapid*, *Trent* and *Teviot*, passed Guardafui in the early hours of 1 November and reached Aden at 1300 on the 2nd to water and fuel. Sailing again later that afternoon, the *Duchess* and *Orduna* continued to Suez, the former arriving just before dark on the 5th and *Orduna* next morning. *Pulaski* was coal bunkered in Aden and only reached Suez on the 7th.

Duchess of Richmond disembarked at Suez and waited until the 15th to pass into the canal with *Orduna* and join MKF 26 at Port Said; both reached Liverpool on 9 December, *Orduna* continuing on the KMF route while the *Duchess* crossed to New York to join UT 6 with US troops for the UK. The arrival of *Duchess of Richmond* at Suez and of the other five liners at Bombay was the ultimate end of the WS route which had been in operation from beginning to end for three years and four months. Strictly speaking *Maloja* in WS 32 was the last to convey British personnel from the UK around the Cape but even so this P&O liner completed only four WS sailings. *Highland Brigade* sailed in nine WS convoys although only once went all the way to Suez. *Monarch of Bermuda* was in eight of the convoys with five going to Suez, likewise *Otranto* with seven convoys also went five times to Suez.

The initial achievements of the WS convoys in providing the means by which British and Empire troops were able to defend Egypt cannot be denied, and yet have remained wholly unsung. From early beginnings the service was expanded to reinforce Iraq, India, even up to the eleventh hour, Singapore. Thereafter all effort was spent in increasing and reinforcing our forces in the Middle East and India, including West African units carried there to fight in Burma.

Fifty-two separate convoys sailed around the Cape in which 458 troopships carried 1,173,010 British and Allied personnel of all services over a distance of 13,000 miles. Bad weather initially, twice through the tropics, the delights of South African hospitality and ultimate arrival in a desert waste after two months at sea was the common experience of all who travelled on these ships. There were occasional encounters with the enemy en route but overall it is astonishing that the passage of these convoys was never seriously challenged throughout the three and a quarter years in which they operated.

With the termination of the 'Winston Specials', the liners were simply switched to other routes and continued to serve the Allied cause long after hostilities ended in August 1945. Millions of service personnel and displaced civilians had then to be returned to their homelands or carried abroad to a brighter world across the sea. The last of the 'liner troopships' was not released from Government Service until the end of 1948. No official figure of the number carried by these liners has been found by this author, but an exhaustive analysis arrives at a figure just exceeding 40 million persons of all categories.

The unsung heroes of these liners must be their Masters, Navigating and Engineer Officers, Senior Ratings and skilled crews which in wartime required of them "a continuously active courage, never ordinarily asked of civilians in war".[4] They had neither the uniform, training or discipline of the Armed Services they were expected to carry, yet never failed to serve them in the manner that befits their calling. Of the ships themselves, it is thanks to our greatest wartime Ally that the great *Queen Mary* lies preserved in Los Angeles as the sole survivor and living testimony to all who travelled around the Cape in these dangerous years. It is still possible to view the pleasing sheer and curves of this ship so devoid of modern cruise liners. Witness also the wide teak-laid promenade decks which carried so many army boots, the accommodation alleyways and public rooms where once stood tiers of standee bunks and the working alleyways on the lowermost deck where lay the working innards of the ship. A fitting monument to all WS troopships of WW2.

CHAPTER NOTES

Chapter 1 - The British Passenger Fleet in 1939.

1.   Behrens. *Merchant Shipping & the Demands of War*. HMSO, 1955 p.39.
2.   Table in Appendix One.
3.   Fifteen more were lost in the second half of 1940.

Chapter 2 - Early troop moves from the UK and Dominions.

1.   *The North African Campaign 1940-43*, Orient Longmans 1956, pp 35 and 516.
2.   *Queen's Own Cameron Highlanders 1932-48*, Wm. Blackwood 1952.
3.   PRO ADM 199/20 Reports of Heron Convoy.
4.   Conversation between author and ex BISN officers.
5.   PRO ADM 199/11, 199/18 and 199/20. Reports of CG 1 Convoy.
6.   PRO ADM 199/20. Report of SO 10 Convoy.
7.   PRO ADM 199/20. Report of SOE, SO 10 Convoy.
8.   Sir James Bissett, *Commodore*, Angus & Robertson, 1961 p.300.
9.   PRO ADM 199/20. Reports of K 6 Convoy.
10.   PRO ADM 199/20. Reports of First Cavalry Convoy.
11.   Churchill, *The Second World War Vol. 2,* p.509, Vol. 3 pp 560/1.
12.   PRO ADM 199/17. Reports by *HMS Resolution and HMS Furious*, TC 1 Convoy.
13.   Roskill, *The War at Sea Vol 1*, HMSO 1954 p.89.
14.   PRO ADM 199/17. Report by HMS *Furious*, TC 1 Convoy.
15.   PRO ADM 199/17. Report by HMS *Revenge*, TC 2 Convoy.
16.   Bushell, *Eight Bells*, Trade & Travel Pubs. 1950, pp 72/3.
17.   McClymont, *2 NZEF to Greece*, 1959, pp 1-24.
18.   *Australia in the War, To Benghazi*, 1952 p. 69.
19.   *Australia in the War, To Benghazi*, 1952, p. 71.
20.   PRO MT 40/43, Correspondence between DoST and Ministry of Shipping.
21.   PRO ADM 199/18, Report of HMS *Ramillies*, US 2 Convoy.

Chapter 3 - Changes in Europe and first convoys around the Cape.

1.   PRO MT 40/35, Letter to Director General, MoS, February 1940.
2.   Derry, *The Campaign in Norway*, HMSO 1952 Chapters 2 and 3.
3.   Erskine, *The Scots Guards 1919 - 55*, Wm. Clowes 1956.
4.   Fitzgerald, *Irish Guards in WW2*, Gale & Polden 1953.
5.   Griffen, *History of the Tenth Foot 1919-50*, Gale & Polden 1953.
6.   Hingston, *The King's Own Yorkshire Light Infantry 1919-42*, (Vol.5) Lund Humphries, 1950.
7.   Bissett, *Commodore*, Angus & Robertson 1961, pp 312 et sec.
8.   Kerr, *Business in Great Waters*, Faber & Faber 1951, pp 44/5.
9.   Grattidge, *Captain of the Queens*, Richard Collier, Chapter 12.
10.   PRO ADM 199/18, Report of Commodore, US 3 Convoy.

11.   Bean, *Strangers in our midst*, Howard Timmins 1970 p. 70.
12.   McClymont, *2 NZEF to Greece*, 1959.
13.   McClymont, *2 NZEF to Greece*, 1959. (Quoted by General Sir Bernard Freyberg).
14.   Churchill, *The Second World War, Vol. 2*, pp 45, 110, 1127-8, 133, 135.
15.   PRO ADM 199/20, Commodore"s Report, BC Convoy
16.   PRO ADM 199/20, Report of HMS *Cornwall*, BC Convoy.

Chapter 4 - The early convoys - WS 1, RS 5, WS 2, AP 1 and AP 3.

1.   Churchill, *The Second World War, Vol 2*, pp 45, 110, 127-8, 133, 135.
2.   Butler, *Grand Strategy, Vol 2*, HMSO 1957, p. 299.
3.   Churchill, *The Second World War, Vol 2*, p. 127.
4.   See Appendix Two, Convoy Cruising Order.
       Also ADM 199/1136, Reports of WS 1 Convoy
       ADM 199/19, Reports of BN 3 Convoy.
5.   Harrison, *Grey & Scarlet*, Hodder & Stoughton, 1944.
6.   Butler, *Grand Strategy Vol 2*, HMSO, 1957, p. 306.
7.   Behrens, *Merchant Shipping*, HMSO, 1955, p.217.
8.   Bissett, *Commodore*, Angus & Robertson, 1961.
9.   Est. embarkations WS 2: *EoBritain* 3600; *Strathaird* 2900; *Otranto* 2900; *MoBermuda* 2000; *Aska* 1000; *Ormonde* 1600; *Stratheden* 1050; *Batory* 900; *Orion* 1100; *Andes* 2500; *EoCanada* 2000; *Franconia* 2900: Totals 24,450.
10.   WS 2 Cruising Order 5-8.8.40: 11 *Clan Macaulay*; 12 *Waiwera*; 21 *Stratheden* (C); 22 *Otranto*; 23 *Batory*; 31 *EoCanada*; 32 *Andes*; 33 *Franconia*; 41 *Ormonde*; 42 *MoBermuda*; 43 *Aska*; 51 *EoBritain*; 52 *Strathaird*; 53 *Lanarkshire*; 61 *Suffolk*; 62 *Memnon*.
       Also PRO ADM 199/1136. Reports of WS 2 convoy.
11.   PRO ADM 199/17. Report of Paddy convoy.
12.   Saunders, *Valiant Voyaging*, Faber & Faber 1948 pp. 64/5.
13.   Poolman, *The Scourge of the Atlantic*, Macdonald & Jones, 1978, pp 25-34.
14.   These were convoys AP 1 and 2 (*q.v.*).
15.   Bushell, *Eight Bells*, Trade & Travel Pubs., 1950, p.74
16.   Roskill, *The War at Sea, Vol. 1*, HMSO, 1954, p. 351.
17.   Playfair, *The Mediteranean & Middle East, Vol. 1*, HMSO, 1954, pp. 190-192.
18.   Churchill, *The Second World War, Vol. 2*, p. 456.
19.   Est. embarkations AP 3 convoy, *Britannic* 2600; *Dom. Monarch* 1482; *Athlone Castle* 1500; *Durban Castle* 468: totals 6,050.
20.   Cruising order AP 3 10.9.40: 11 *Brisbane Star*; 12 *Imperial Star*; 21 *Athlone Castle*; 22 *Durban Castle*; 23 *HMS Ulster Prince*; 31 *Britannic* (C); 32 *Dom. Monarch*; 33 *Glaucus*; 41 *Clan Macarthur*; 42 *Clan Campbell*.
21.   Creighton, *Convoy Commodore*, Wm. Kimber, 1956, pp. 115-126.

Chapter 5 - Departures October and November 1940,

WS 3S and F, WS 4A and WS 4B

1.   PRO ADM 199/1136 - Report of *Highland Brigade.*
2.   One cable being one-tenth of a nautical mile i.e. 600 ft.
3.   Embarkations WS 3F - *Oronsay* 2,500; *Winchester Castle* 700; *Georgic* 2,500; *Capetown Castle* 800; *Orontes* 2,000; *Duchess of York* 2,500; *Monarch of Bermuda* 2,000: Total 13,000 (estimated).
4.   PRO ADM 199/1136 - Report of HMS *Ottawa.*
5.   Such position being 470 miles west of Tory Island was not repeated as a rendezvous in subsequent convoys.
6.   PRO ADM 199/1136 - Report of HMS *Kenya.*
7.   Cruising order WS 3F from Freetown to Cape - 11 *Orontes* (C); 12 *Monarch of Bermuda*; 13 *Duchess of York*; 21 *Georgic*; 22 *Capetown Castle*; 23 *Winchester Castle.*
8.   Combined cruising order after amalgamation 3.11.40 - 11 *Monarch of Bermuda*; 12 *Dorset*; 13 *Highland Brigade*; 14 *Khedive Ismail*; 21 *Orontes* (C); 22 *Perthshire*; 23 *Port Chalmers*; 24 *Erinpura*; 31 *Georgic*; 32 *Duchess of York*; 33 *Oropesa.*
9.   PRO ADM 199/1136 - Report of Commodore WS 3F.
10.   Churchill, *The Second World War, Vol. 2*, p.385.
11.   Embarkations WS 4A - *Stirling Castle* 1,529; *Scythia* 1,323; *Almanzora* 1,848; *Highland Monarch* 800: Total 5,500.
12.   The small island of Orsay with its lighthouse lies at the extreme SW tip of Islay and was singularly referred to in Admiralty documents as Oversay. The routing of shipping close to this point maintained a distance of 25 miles from the northern coast of neutral Eire.
13.   Cruising order WS 4A sailed UK 1.11.40 - 11 *Malancha*; 12 *Clan Lamont*; 13 AMC *Salopian*; 21 *City of Manchester*; 22 *Highland Monarch*; 23 *Clan Chattan*; 24 *Akaroa*; 31 *Stirling Castle* (C); 32 *Port Wyndham*; 33 *Almanzora*; 41 *Scythia* (VC); 42 *Martand*; 43 *Warwick Castle*; 44 *Duchess of Richmond*; 51 *Dunedin Star*; 52 *Delius*; 53 *Abosso.*
14.   PRO ADM 199/11 - Report of Commodore WS 4A.
15.   Mc Corquodale, *The King's Dragoon Guards 1938-45*, McCorquodale, 1950, pp 14-17.
16.   Cruising order WS 4A (Fast) after split 11.11.40: 21 *Warwick Castle*; 22 *Highland Monarch*; 31 *Stirling Castle* (C); 32 Port Wyndham; 41 *Scythia*; 42 *Clan Lamont*; 51 *Dunedin Star*; 52 *Clan Chattan.*
17.   Cruising order WS 4A sailed Durban 5.12.40: 11 *Highland Monarch*; 12 *Clan Lamont*; 13 *Clan Chattan*; 21 *Stirling Castle* (C); 22 *Port Wyndham*; 23 *City of Manchester*; 31 *Dunera* (VC); 32 *Delius*; 41 *Dunedin Star*; 42 *Malancha*; 43 *Martand.*
18.   PRO ADM 199/1136 - Report of Commodore WS 4A.
19.   Kerr, *Business in Great Waters*, Faber & Faber, 1950, pp 76-78.
20.   Daniell; *4 Queen's Own Hussars 1685-1958*, Gale & Polden, 1959
21.   PRO ADM 199/1136 - Report of Commodore WS 4B.

22.   Embarkations WS 4B - *Andes* 2,550, *Reina del Pacifico* 2,200; *Orcades* 2,000;
        Strathallan 3,050; *Strathnaver* 3,050; *Duchess of Atholl* 2,000; *Strathaird*
        3,050; *Otranto* 3,250; *Empress of Canada*, 2,000; *Viceroy of India* 1,050.
        Estimated total 24,200 all for Middle East.
23.   Cruising order WS 4B sailed UK 17.11.40: 11 *Strathnaver*; 12 *Strathaird*;
        21 *Strathallan*; 22 *Viceroy of India*; 31 *Duchess of Atholl* (C); 32 *Empress of
        Canada*; 41 *Orcades*; 42 *Andes*; 51 *Reina del Pacifico*; 52 *Otranto*.
24.   History 2/10 Australian Battalion history A.I.F.
25.   On completing a three month voyage to Suez in WS 2, *Strathaird* was a mere
        three days discharging South African cargo in Glasgow and then despatched to
        Belfast to carry troops to the Clyde; these were disembarked three days later
        and with no time for cleaning was sent upriver to Glasgow next day, to begin
        embarkation for WS 4B, sailing three days later on another voyage to Suez.
26.   McCorquodale, *The King's Dragoon Guards 1938-45,* McCorquodale, 1950,
        pp 19-20.
27.   PRO ADM 199/1136 - Report of HMS *Norfolk.*
28.   Report of Commodore WS 4B; the quantities of fuel required by each ship
        varied from 450 tons for *Strathallan* to 2,600 tons for *Empress of Canada*,
        while fresh water requirements varied from a mere 200 tons for *Orcades* to
        1,300 tons each for the two liners.
29.   PRO ADM 199/11 - Correspondence between the Admiralty and MOWT.
30.   Cruising order WS 4B Freetown to Durban sailing 1.12.40: 11 *Andes*;
        12 *Strathallan*; 21 *Viceroy of India*; 22 *Strathaird*; 31 *Duchess of Atholl* (C);
        32 *Empress of Canada*; 41 *Orcades*; 42 *Reina del Pacifico*; 51 *Otranto*;
        52 *Strathnaver*.
31.   Behren's quotes an approximate figure of 77,000 while the *'Mediterranean &
        Middle East Vol.1'* states 76,000 made up of 28,000 in complete British
        combatant units; 15,500 in administrative units (e.g. hospitals, workshops,
        depots, engineer, supply, ordnance, transportation units); 19,300 in drafts and
        details; 7,500 RAF; 5,000 Australians and 700 New Zealanders.
32.   PRO ADM 199/1136 - Report of HMS *Ceres.*

Chapter 6 - WS 5A and WS 5B

WS 5A

1.   WS 5A embarkations (estimated): *Orbita* 1719, *Tamaroa* 1220, *City of London*
        1226; *Anselm* 1088; *Elisabethville* 909; *Neuralia* 1610; *City of Canterbury*
        1480; *Empire Trooper* 2351; *Costa Rica* 1078; *Rangitiki* 1130. Total 13,811.
2.   Churchill, *The Second World War, Vol. 2*, 1949, p.409.
3.   PRO MT 40/43, Corrrespondence papers between War Office and MOWT.
4.   PRO ADM 199/1136 and 266, Report of HMS *Argus*, WS 5A.
5.   PRO ADM 199/1136 and 266, Report of HMS *Naiad*, WS 5A.
6.   Report of Captain Percival to Ellerman City Line
7.   Report of Captain Longstaff to Ellerman City Line.
8.   Holman, *In Danger's Hour*, Hodder & Stoughton, 1948, p. 85.
9.   Waters, *Ordeal by Sea*, New Zealand Shipping Co., 1949, pp. 55/6.

10.	Roskill, *The War at Sea Vol. 1*, HMSO, 1954, pp. 263, 291.

11.	Roskill, *The War at Sea Vol. 1*, HMSO, 1954, p.369.

12.	WS 5A Cruising Order from Durban 29.1.41:
	11 *Settler*, 12 *Bhutan*, 13 *Delane*, 21 HMS *Atreus*, 22 *Orbita*, 23 *Rangitiki*, 31 *City of London*, 32 *Elisabethville*, 33 *Nieuw Holland*, 34 *Adviser*, 41 *Tamaroa* (C), 42 *Costa Rica*, 43 *Neuralia*, 44 *Barrister*, 51 *City of Canterbury*, 52 *Anselm*, 53 *Talamba*, 54 *Stentor*, 61 *Menelaus*, 62 *City of Derby*, 63 *Arabistan*, 64 *Benrinnes*.

13.	PRO ADM 199/1136, Report of HMS *Enterprise*, WS 5A.

14.	PRO ADM 199/1136, Report of Commodore, WS 5A.

15.	Noted on Ship Movement Cards of MOWT.

WS 5B

16.	*Pilsudski* lost 26 Nov. 1939 (Chap.3); *Chrobry* lost 15 May 1940 (Chap. 4); the others were *Batory*, *Sobieski*, *Pulaski* and *Kosciuscko*.

17.	Belgian *Elisabethville*, *Thysville* and *Leopoldville* (lost 24 Dec. 1944).

18.	Norwegian *Oslofjord* lost 1 Dec. 1940, *Bergensfjord* survived.

19.	Embarkations WS 5B: *Athlone Castle* 1409; *Britannic* 2658; *Duchess of Richmond* 2904; *Samaria* 2857; *Windsor Castle* 1133; *Empress of Australia* 2230; *Pasteur* 3335; *Franconia* 2606; *Pennland* 2030; *Arundel Castle* 1153; *Durban Castle* 989; *Highland Chieftain* 1046; *Capetown Castle* 1032; *Nea Hellas* 1824; *Cameronia* 2931; *Ormonde* 2476; *Empress of Japan* 2621; *Winchester Castle* 1048; *Highland Princess* 1042; *Monarch of Bermuda* (empty); and *Duchess of Bedford* 2783. The total number was reduced to 37,267 by the breakdown of *Pasteur*.

20.	By including those which came downriver from Glasgow that afternoon, ten liners had spare accommodation for 2262.

21.	PRO MT 40/43. Letter from Ministry of Shipping to War Office; 18 Jan. 1941.

22.	One of the Germans was Cmdr. Jenisch of *U-32*, who had sunk *Empress of Britain* ten weeks earlier. Captain Sapworth of that liner was now Master of *Duchess of York*.

23.	See Appendix II showing Convoy Formation.

24.	WS 5B Cruising Order sailed UK 12.1.41: 11 *Winchester Castle*; 12 *Monarch of Bermuda*; 13 *Highland Chieftain*; 21 *Duchess of Bedford*; 22 *Highland Princess*; 23 *Nea Hellas*; 31 *Windsor Castle*; 32 *Duchess of Richmond*; 33 *Britannic*; 41 *Athlone Castle* (C); 42 *Empress of Australia*; 43 *Samaria*; 51 *Empress of Japan*; 52 *Franconia*; 53 *Arundel Castle*; 61 *Ormonde*; 62 *Cameronia*; 63 *Duchess of York*; 71 *Durban Castle*; 72 *Capetown Castle*; 73 *Pennland*.

25.	The morning watch is between 0400 and 0800.

26.	PRO ADM 199/1136, Report of HMS *Naiad*, WS 5B.

27.	Bone, *Merchantman Rearmed*, Chatto & Windus, 1949, pp. 83, 84-86.

28.	Bissett, *Commodore*, Angus & Robertson, 1961, p. 346.

29.	Various communications between the author and Lt.Col. FL Carroll RE during 1974.

30.   Turner, *War in the Southern Oceans*, Oxford University Press, Capetown, 1961, p. 64.

Chapter 7 - WS 6

1.   PRO MT 40/43, Letter from War Office to Ministry of Shipping 8 Jan. 1941.
2.   PRO MT 40/43, Letter from Ministry of Shipping to War Office and others 20 Dec. 1940.
3.   PRO MT 40/43, Discussion at Admiralty 30 Dec. 1940.
4.   See WS 5B, three liners damaged during air raids in Liverpool.
5.   Zigzag reduced the actual speed of advance by 1 or 2 knots.
6.   PRO MT 40/43, Letter from Ministry of Shipping to War Office lst Jan. 1941.
7.   PRO MT 40/43, Convoy Memo by C.I.G.S. 2 Jan. 1941.
8.   PRO MT 40/43, Meeting in Ministry of Shipping 5 Jan. 1941.
9.   PRO ADM 199/1136, Letter from VCNS dated 4 Feb. 1941.
10.   WS 6 embarkations (estimated): *Llandaff Castle* 900; *Ascanius* 1,700; *Thysville* 900; *Burma* 1,400; *Nova Scotia* 1,000; *Yoma* 1,300; *Scythia* 2,950; *Rangitata* 1,600; *Mataroa* 1,550; *Leopoldville* 1,400; *Salween* 1,375; *Almanzora* 2,000; *Highland Brigade* 800; *Llangibby Castle* 950; *Bergensfjord* 2,000; *Ruahine* 1050. Total estimate 22,875. MT ships were *City of Athens*, *City of Marseilles*, *Consuelo*, *Mulbera*, *Opawa*, *Cape Horn*, *Burdwan*, *Bellerophon*, *Manchester Citizen*, *Port Alma*, *Benvannoch*, Danish *Kina II*. (Admiralty records state that *City of Pittsburgh*, *Mahseer*, *City of Corinth*, *City of Hankow*, *Dalesman* and *Logician* were also included as MT ships, but neither a confirmed list of ships or cruising order was found for WS 6.)
11.   WS 6B embarkations (estimated) - *Llanstephan Castle* 1,000; *Northumberland* 1,500. Total 2,500. (Plus *Burma* and *Yoma* already allowed in WS 6 above.)
12.   Cruising Order WS 6B sailed U.K. 18.2.41 - 11. *Yoma*; 12. *Adda*; 21 *Llanstephan Castle* (C); 22. *Burma* (VC); 31 *Northumberland*; 32. AMC *Cilicia*.
13.   The total on both sections of WS 6 were now 800 for West Africa and 23,175 for Middle East.
14.   PRO ADM 199/1136, Report of HMS *Cornwall*, WS 6.
15.   PRO ADM 199/1136, Report of HMS *Birmingham*, WS 6.
16.   PRO ADM 199/1136, Report of DoST dated 30 April 1941.
17.   Report of Captain Percival to City Line Ltd.
18.   PRO ADM 199/710, Report of Commodore and SOE   SW 6. SW6 Cruising Order - 21. *Scythia* (C); 22. *Cameronia*; 23. *Talamba*; 31 *Bergensfjord*; 32. Nova Scotia; 33. *Leopoldville*.

Chapter 8 - WS 7

1.   Playfair, *The Mediterranean & Middle East, Vol 2,* HMSO, 1956, p.224.
2.   WS 7 embarkations (estimated) *Duchess of York* 3,000; *JV Oldenbarnevelt* 1,506, *Duchess of Atholl* 2,700; *Andes* 2,600; *Viceroy of India* 2,500; *Strathallan* 3,100; *Orion* 3,100; *Dempo* 1,481; *Strathmore* 3,000; *Warwick*

Castle 1,400; *Highland Monarch* 1,100; *Stratheden* 3,000; *Orcades* 2,400; *Pasteur* 3,500; *Stirling Castle* 1,440; *Otranto* 3,300; *Strathaird* 3,100; *Empress of Canada* 2,000; *Strathnaver* 3,100; *Orontes* 3,213; *Reina del Pacifico* 2,200; plus *Georgic* for Halifax with 3,000. Total embarked 55,740, less 3,100 by return of *Strathaird*, i.e. 52,640.

3. PRO ADM 199/1138, Report by HMS *Somali*, WS 7.
4. PRO ADM 199/1138, Report by Captain EE Spradbrow, Master of *Stirling Castle*.
5. Cruising Order WS 7 25.3.41 - 11. *Duchess of York*; 12. *Viceroy of India*; 13. *Andes*; 14. *Georgic*; 21 *Stirling Castle* (VC); 22. *Denbighshire*; 23. *JV Oldenbarnevelt*; 24. *Dempo*; 31. *Duchess of Atholl*; 32. *Orion*; 33. *Strathallan*; 34. *Orontes*; 41. *Empress of Canada* (C); 42. *Stratheden*; 43. *Pasteur*; 44. *Highland Monarch*; 51 *Warwick Castle*; 52. *Strathnaver*; 53. *Strathmore*; 61. *Otranto*; 62. *Orcades*; 63. *Glenorchy*. (Had it not been for the collision involving *Strathaird*, this would have been the only WS convoy to involve all five P&O Straths and the two modern Orient liners.)
6. PRO ADM 199/1138, Report by HMS *Nelson*, WS 7.
7. PRO ADM 199/1138, Report by Commodore, WS 7.
8. PRO ADM 199/1138, Admiralty Report on WS 7.
9. Gardiner, *Camera at Sea 1939-45*, Conway Maritime Press, 1978, pp. 154/5.
10. Behrens, *Merchant Shipping and the demands of war*, HMSO, 1955, P. 211.
11. PRO ADM 199/710, Report by Commodore, Convoy SW 7.
12. PRO ADM 199/710, Cruising Order SW 7 - 11. *Duchess of Atholl*; 12. *Empress of Australia*; 21. *Strathnaver* (C); 22. *Strathmore*; 31. *Viceroy of India*; 32. *Orontes*.
13. PRO ADM 199/710, Cruising Order SW 7A - 11. *Otranto*; 12. *Duchess of York*; 21 *Strathnaver* (C); 22. *Strathmore*; 31. *Viceroy of India*; 32. *Orontes*.

Chapter 9 - WS 8A, WS 8B, WS 8C, WS 8X and the HP Convoy

WS 8A

1. See Chapter 7 - Allocation of shipping for WS 6.
2. Churchill, *The Second World War, Vol. 3*, p. 193.
3. WS 8A embarkations (estimated) - *Strathaird* 3,100; *Sobieski* 2,100; *Aronda* 1,500; *Reina del Pacifico* 2,500; *Dominion Monarch* 1,700; *Highland Chieftain* 1,200; *Empress of Asia* 2,400; *Empress of Russia* 2,500. Total: 17,000.
4. WS 8A sailed U.K. 26.4.41 - 11. *Highland Chieftain*; 12. *Empress of Asia*; 21. *Dominion Monarch*; 22. *Reina del Pacifico*; 23. *Empress of Russia*; 31. *Strathaird* (C); 32. *Sobieski*; 33. New Zealand Star; 41. *Clan Campbell*; 42. *Clan Lamont*; 43. *Abbekerk*; 51. *Aronda*; 52. *Empire Song*; 53. AMC *Pretoria Castle*; (*Clan Chattan* and *Imperial Star* omitted)
5. John Nicolson, Article in *Sea Breezes*, July 1988.
6. PRO ADM 199/1138, Report by HMS *Beagle*, WS 8A.
7. PRO ADM 199/1138, Report by HMS *Hurricane*, WS 8A.
8. PRO ADM 199/1138, Report by Admiralty on WS 8A.

9.   PRO ADM 199/1138, Report by HMS *Mauritius*, WS 8A.
10.   Clay, The Path of the 50th, Gale and Polden, 1950.
11.   WS 8A cruising order Freetown to Durban - 11. *Imperial Star*; 12. *Abbekerk*;
          21. *Reina del Pacifico*; 22. *Aronda*; 23. *Dominion Monarch* (VC);
          31. *Strathaird* (C); 32. *Empress of Asia*; 41. *Empress of Russia*; 42. *Sobieski*.
          (Captain WG Summers of *Dominion Monarch* acted as Vice Commodore.)
12.   WS 8A cruising order from Durban 31.5.41 - 11. *Sobieski*; 12 *Aronda*;
          21. *Strathaird* (C); 31. *Empress of Russia*; 32. *Abbekerk*.
13.   Musk, *Canadian Pacific*, David & Charles, 1981, pp. 134-137.
14.   PRO ADM 199/682 - Report by HMS *Carthage*.

HP Convoy

15.   PRO ADM 199/682, Report of HP Convoy.

WS 8B

16.   Embarkations WS 8B - *Almanzora* 2,009; *Duchess of Bedford* 3,100; *Orduna*
          2,161; *Georgic* 3,135; *Duchess of Richmond* 3,081; *Christiaan Huygens*
          1,592. Total 15,078.
17.   WS 8B sailed U.K. 25.5.41 - 11. *Christiaan Huygens*; 12. *Abosso*;
          21. *Georgic* (C); 22. Martand; 31. *Duchess of Richmond* (VC); 32. *Almanzora*;
          41. HMS *Argus*; 42. *Orduna*.
18.   Lowden & Duffy, *Elder Dempster 1852 - 1985*, 1986.
19.   PRO ADM 199/1138, Report of HMS *Exeter* / Report of Commodore.
20.   WS 8B sailed Freetown 6.6.41. - 11. *Almanzora*; 12. *Orduna*; 21. *Georgic*
          (C); 31. *Duchess of Richmond*; 32. *Martand*.
21.   Bushell, *Eight Bells*, Trade-Travel Publications, 1950, pp. 76/7.
22.   *Sea Breezes*, Article by JH Isherwood, July 1973.
23.   Aitken, *In time of War*, Aitken, 1980, pp. 129-134.

WS 8X

24   WS 8X sailed U.K. 31.5.41 - 11. *Port Wyndham*; 21. *Duchess of Bedford* (C);
          31. AMC *Esperance Bay*; 41. *Waiwera*.
25.   PRO ADM 199/1138, Report of HMS *Norfolk*.
26.   *Orduna* homeward voyage - see WS 8B.
27.   PRO ADM 119/682, Report of Commodore, convoy CF 2.
28.   Cruising Order CF 2 - sailed Capetown 26.8.41 - 11. *Durban Castle* (C);
          12. *Nieuw Zeeland*; 21. *Duchess of Bedford*; 22. *Sobieski*.

Chapter 10 - WS 9A and WS 9B.

WS 9A

1.   Part of a group of six fast cargo liners loaned to Britain by the U.S. in
          November 1940 but recalled after Pearl Harbour in December 1941.

2. WS 9A estimated embarkations - *Capetown Castle* 1,568; *Durban Castle* 979; *Franconia* 3,052; *Llangibby Castle* 1,154; *Empress of Japan* 2,993; *Mooltan* 3,200; *Orbita* 2,358; *Samaria* 3,084; *Highland Brigade* 1,231; *Eastern Prince* 1,200. Total embarked 20,819.

3. Cruising Order WS 9A sailed U.K. 3.6.41 - 11. *Capetown Castle*; 12. *Highland Brigade*; 13. Aagtekerk; 21. *Samaria*; 22. *Eastern Prince*; 23. *Empire Condor*, 31. *Empress of Japan* (C); 32. *Mooltan*; 33. *Empire Curlew*; 41. *Durban Castle*; 42. *Orbita*; 43. *Empire Egret*; 51. *Franconia* (VC); 52 *Llangibby Castle*; 53. *Empire Widgeon*.

4. PRO ADM 199/1138, Report by Master, *Empire Widgeon*.

5. Roskill, *The War at Sea, Vol. 1*, HMSO, 1954, p. 479.

6. Martin, *History of The Essex Regiment 1929-50*, 1952.

7. PRO ADM 199/1138, Report of Commodore WS 9A.

WS 9B

8. WS 9B estimated embarkations: *Athlone Castle* 1,676; *Anselm* 1,309; *Monarch of Bermuda* 2,201; *Rangitata* 1,919; *Oronsay* 3,089; *Pulaski* 1,160; *Tamaroa* 1,450; *Mataroa* 1,450; *Arundel Castle* 1,200. Total 15,454.

9. WS 9B Cruising Order sailed U.K. 28.6.41 - 11. *Tamaroa*; 12. *Pulaski*; 13. HMS *Corinthian*; 14. HMS *Galatea*; 21 *Oronsay* (C); 22. *Athlone Castle*; 23. *Monarch of Bermuda*; 24, *Ceramic*; 31. HMS *Edinburgh*; 32. AMC *Moreton Bay*; 33. AMC *Cathay*; 34 AMC Chitral; 41. *Clan Forbes*; 42. *Arundel Castle*; 43. *Mataroa*; 51. *Pampas*; 52. *Rangitata*; 53. *Elisabeth Bakke*.

10. PRO ADM 199/496, Report of Captain Elliott, Master of *Anselm*, WS 9B.

11. PRO ADM 199/496, Report by HMS *Cathay*, WS 9B.

12. PRO ADM 199/496, Report by HMS *Challenger*, WS 9B.

13. Captain Elliott was a Lincolnshire man who held an Extra Master's Certificate. He was awarded the OBE in 1945 and remained in command with the Booth Line until his retiral in 1947.

14. PRO ADM 199/1138, Report of HMS *Galatea*, WS 9B.

15. WS 9B Cruising Order Freetown to Cape - 11. *Tamaroa*; 12. *Pulaski*; 13. HMS *Galatea*; 21 *Oronsay* (C); 22. *Athlone Castle*; 23. *Monarch of Bermuda*; 24. *Ceramic*; 31. *Clan Forbes*; 32 *Arundel Castle*; 33. *Mataroa*; 41 *Pampas*; 42. *Rangitata*; 43. *Elisabeth Bakke*.

16. PRO ADM 199/1138, Report of Commodore Knowles, WS 9B.

17. PRO ADM 199/1138, Report by HMS *Queen of Bermuda*, WS 9B.

18. WS 9B Cruising Order Capetown to Durban 30.7.41 - 11. *Clan Forbes*; 12. *Pulaski*; 21. *Pampas*; 22. *Elisabeth Bakke*.

19. See also homeward voyage of *Capetown Castle* from WS 9A.

Chapter 11 - WS 10 and WS 10X

WS 10

1. PRO MT 40/45 - Statement from Ministry of Shipping 1.7.41.

2.   This is presumed to have been *Oronsay*.
3.   See WS 7 arrival at Suez and subsequent return voyages, Chapter 7.
4.   PRO MT 40/45 - Statement by Ministry of Shipping 4.7.41.
5.   Behrens, *Merchant Shipping and the demands of War*, HMSO, 1955, p.224.
6.   Embarkations WS 10 sailed U.K. 2.8.41 - *Britannic* 2,747; *Strathallan* 3,256;
         Windsor Castle 1,167; *Nea Hellas* 3,164; *Cameronia* 3,131; *Volendam* 2,172;
         Indrapoera 1,377; *Andes* 3,076; *Stirling Castle* 1,700; *Orcades* 3,190; *Reina
         del Pacifico* 2,478; *Warwick Castle* 1,548; *Highland Monarch* 1,215;
         Rangitiki 1,779. Totals 32,000.
7.   Cruising Order WS 10 Clyde to Freetown - 11. *Phemius*; 12. *Diomed*;
         13. *Indian Prince*; 21. *Andes*; 22. *Rangitiki*; 23. *Indrapoera*;
         31. *Orcades* (C); 32. *Britannic*; 33. *Highland Monarch*; 34. *Manchester Port*;
         41. *Strathallan* (VC); 42. *Volendam*; 43. *Cameronia*; 51. *Reina del Pacifico*;
         52. *Stirling Castle*; 53. *Nea Hellas*; 61. *Windsor Castle*; 62. *Warwick Castle*;
         63. *Nigerstroom*.
8.   HF/DF - High Frequency Direction Finder bearings.
9.   PRO ADM 199/1138 - Report by HMS *Gurkha*, WS 10.
10.   The lack of a proper fogbuoy on *Strathallan* which was now making her third
         WS voyage appears to indicate the shortage of these items.
11.   DG i.e. Degaussing Coils as defence against magnetic mines.
12.   PRO ADM 199/1138 - Report of HMS *London*, WS 10.
13.   Cruising Order WS 10 Freetown to Cape - 11. *Windsor Castle*; 12. *Phemius*;
         21. *Britannic*; 22. *Indrapoera*; 23. *Nigerstroom*; 31. *Stirling Castle*;
         32. *Strathallan*; 33. *Volendam*; 41. *Orcades* (C); 42. *Highland Monarch*;
         43. *Cameronia*; 44. *Manchester Port*; 51 *Andes*; 52. *Rangitiki*;
         53. *Nea Hellas*; 61. *Reina del Pacifico*; 62. *Diomed*; 63. *Indian Prince*.
14.   PRO ADM 199/1138 - Report of HMS *Edinburgh*, WS 10.
15.   PRO ADM 199/1138 - Commodore's Report of WS 10.
16.   Cruising Order WS 10B Durban to Bombay - 11. *Strathallan*; 21. *Aronda*
         (C); 22. *Stirling Castle*; 31. *Britannic*; 32. *Windsor Castle*.
17.   Cruising Order CM 17 Durban to Aden 11.9.41. - 11. *Rangitiki*; 12. *Indian
         Prince*; 13. *Indrapoera*; 21 *Dunera* (C); 22. *Nigerstroom*; 23. *Manchester
         Port*; 31. *Nea Hellas*; 32. *Volendam*; 33. *Phemius*; 41. *Diomed*.

WS 10X

1.   Playfair, *The Mediterranean & Middle East, Vol 2*, HMSO, 1956, p. 256.
2.   PRO MT 40/45 - Statement 3.8.41 and ADM 199/2229 - Reports.
3.   Embarkations WS 10X sailed U.K. 16.8.41 - *Orion* 3,220; *Strathnaver* 3,198;
         Strathmore 3,586. Total 10,004.
4.   Cruising Order WS 10X Clyde to Freetown - 11. *Strathnaver*; 12. *Palma*;
         21. *Strathmore* (C); 22. *Brisbane Star*; 31. *Orion*; 32. *Port Jackson*.
5.   PRO ADM 199/1138 - Report by Commodore Willan, WS 10X.
6.   Cruising Order WS 10X Capetown to Aden - 11. *Strathnaver*; 12. *Palma*;
         13. *Brisbane Star*; 21. *Strathmore* (C); 22. *Orion*; 23. *Port Jackson*.
7.   Playfair, *The Mediterranean & Middle East, Vol. 3*, HMSO, 1960, p.5.

Chapter 12 - WS 11, WS 12, WS 12X and WS 12Z

WS 11

1. See Chapter 11, WS 10.
2. PRO MT 40/45, Letter from DoST 5 July 1941.
3. Embarkations WS 11 sailed U.K. 30.8.41 - *Abosso* 1,013; *Otranto* 3,211; *Empress of Australia* 2.548; *Northumberland* 1,593; *Viceroy of India* 2,539; *Duchess of York* 3,055; *Mooltan* 3,233; *Orontes* 3,244; *Scythia* 3,130; *Largs Bay* 864. Total 24,430 (6,474 for Middle East; 6,363 Iraq; 5,062 India; 2,569 West Africa; 2,319 Malaya). Additionally *Largs Bay* carried 94 guns and vehicles plus 1648 tons stores for Malaya, *Duchess of York* 24 guns for India, *Otranto* 69 guns also for India, *Scythia* 88 guns for Middle East and *Orontes* 72 guns and 76 tons stores for India.
4. Barclay, *The Duke of Wellington's Regiment 1919-52*, Wm. Clowes, 1953.
5. Sheffield, *The York & Lancaster Regiment, 1919-53*, Gale & Polden, 1956.
6. Churchill, *The Second World War, Vol. 3*, pp. 460, 676, etc.
7. Cruising Order, WS 11, sailed UK 4.9.41 - 11. *Kina II*; 12. *Bhutan*; 13. *Barrister*; 14. *Glaucus*; 21. *Mooltan*; 22. *Empress of Australia*; 23. *Northumberland*; 24. *Abosso*; 31. *Orontes*(C); 32. *Scythia*; 33. *Viceroy of India*; 41. *Otranto*; 42. HMS *Guardian*; 43. *Duchess of York*; 44. *Largs Bay*; 51. *City of Edinburgh*; 52. *Glenorchy*; 53. *City of Manchester*; 54. *Manchester Progress*.
8. PRO ADM 199/1138, Report of HMS Derbyshire, WS 11.
9. PRO ADM 199/1138, Report of Commodore, WS 11.
10. Cruising Order WS 11 from Durban 8.10.41 - 11. *Dilwara*; 12. *City of Canterbury* 13. *Pulaski;* 21. *Mooltan;* 22. *Eastern Prince;* 23. *Manchester Progress;* 31. *Llandaff Castle*; 32. *Nieuw Holland*; 33. *City of Manchester*; 34. *Bhutan*; 41. *Orontes*; 42. *City of Edinburgh*; 43. *Nieuw Zeeland*; 44. *Barrister*; 51. *Glenorchy*; 52. *Viceroy of India*; 53. *Largs Bay*; 54. *Johan de Witt*; 61. *Otranto*; 62. *Duchess of York*; 63. *Kina II*; 64. *Glaucus*.
11. Behrens, *Merchant Shipping and the demands of War*, HMSO, 1955, p.241.
12. WS 11X Cruising Order from Bombay 27.10.41 - 11. *Glaucus*; 12. *Kina II*; 13. *Johan de Witt*; 21. *Orion*; 22. *Nieuw Zeeland*; 23. *Largs Bay*. (From 1.11 *Ellenga* took 14.)
13. See *Rangitiki* in WS 10 and *Orion* in WS 10X.

WS 12

14. Roskill, *The War at Sea, Vol. 1*, HMSO, 1954, pp. 453/4
15. PRO MT 40/45. MOWT Note of 19.8.41.
16. Churchill, *The Second World War, Vol. 3*, p. 382.
17. Roskill, *The War at Sea, Vol. 1*, HMSO, 1954, p. 380.
18. Embarkations WS 12 sailed U.K. 30.9.41 - *Mendoza* 1,369; *Franconia* 3,094; *Samaria* 3,062; *Dominion Monarch* 1,732; *Duchess of Richmond* 3,045; *Almanzora* 2,034; *Strathaird* 3,070; *Empire Pride* 2,015; *Empress of Canada* 1,968; *Empress of Russia* 2,544; *Leopoldville* 1,528; *City of Paris* 1,590; *Ormonde* 2,464; *Narkunda* 1,836; *Highland Brigade* 1,225: totals

	21,002 for Middle East; 4,027 Iraq; 3,265 Malaya; 1,890 West Africa; 1092 South Africa; 872 Aden and 403 other destinations, total embarked 32,576.
19.	See WS 7.
20.	Cruising Order WS 12 U.K. to Freetown - 11. *Clan Campbell*; 12. *Empire Trust*; 13. *Highland Brigade*; 14. *Sarpedon*; 21. *Perseus*; 22. *Almanzora*; 23. *Empire Pride*; 24. *Leopoldville*; 31. *Strathaird* (C); 32. *Empress of Russia*; 33. *Empress of Canada*; 34. *Narkunda*; 41. *City of Paris*; 42. *Ormonde*; 43. *Samaria*; 44. *Franconia* (RC); 51. *Mendoza*; 52. *Duchess of Richmond* (VC); 53. *Dominion Monarch*; 54. *Highland Princess*; 61. *Prince Baudouin*; 62. *Royal Ulsterman*; 63. *Clan Lamont*; 64. *Perthshire*.
21.	*The 10th Royal Hussars 1939-45*, Gale & Polden, Aldershot, 1948.
22.	Beddington, *The Queen's Bays 1939-45*, Warren & Son Ltd., Winchester, 1954.
23.	See WS 8X.
24.	Bright, *The 9th Queen's Royal Lancers, 1936-45*, Gale & Polden, Aldershot, 1951.
25.	*Empress of Russia* and *Sarpedon* could only burn coal. *Almanzora* and *Mendoza* were fitted only for oil, while *City of Paris*, the two Clans and *Perthshire* could burn either mode of fuel.
26.	Woodburn Kirby, *The War against Japan, Vol. 1*, HMSO, 1957, p. 173.
27.	Bowen, *The Flag of the Southern Cross*, Shaw Savill, 1947, p.23.
28.	Bissett, *Commodore*, Angus & Robertson, 1961, p.351.

WS 12X

29.	Churchill, *The Second World War, Vol. 3*, p.384
30.	Four from WS 10, one from WS 9B and another from WS 8A.
31.	For CF 2 see WS 9A homeward voyages.
32.	Estimated embarkations CT 5 (for WS 12X at Halifax) - *Oronsay* 3,076; *Warwick Castle* 1,501; *Orcades* 3,196; *Reina del Pacifico* 2,485; *Andes* 3,089; *Duchess of Atholl* 3,129; *Sobieski* 2,092; *Durban Castle* 966, totals 19,534.
33.	Cruising Order CT 5 sailed U.K. 30.10.41 - 11. *Sobieski*; 12. *Warwick Castle*; 21. *Duchess of Atholl*; 22. *Orcades*; 23. *Andes*; 31. *Durban Castle*; 32. *Oronsay*; 33. *Reina del Pacifico*.
34.	Estimated embarkations WS 12X at Halifax, *West Point* - 5,623; *Mount Vernon* 5,120; *Wakefield* 4,600; *Orizaba* 1,578; *Joseph T Dickman* 1,194; *Leonard Wood* 1,419, totals 19,534.
35.	Barclay, *The Sherwood Foresters 1919-57*, Wm. Clowes, 1959.
36.	Nicholson, *The Suffolk Regiment 1928-46*, The East Anglian Magazine, 1947.
37.	Morison, *The Battle of the Atlantic, Vol.1*, 1939-43, Little Brown & Co., Boston, 1962, pp.109-112.
38.	Various communications between the author and Lt.Col. FL Carroll RE during 1974.
39.	Woodburn Kirby, *The War against Japan, Vol. 1*, HMSO, 1957, pp. 253-260.
40.	PRO ADM 199/1138 Report of *Dorsetshire*; WS 12X.

WS 12Z

41. Churchill, *The Second World War, Vol. 3*, p. 645.
42. Embarkations WS 12Z - *Capetown Castle* 1,902; *Duchess of Bedford* 3,012; *Empress of Asia* 2,344; *Monarch of Bermuda* 2,287; *Orduna* 2,145; *Mataroa* 1,436; *Aorangi* 2,449; *Arundel Castle* 1,204; *Narkunda* 2,144; *Empress of Japan* 2,844, totals South Africa 1,210; Middle East 8,077; Iraq 10,660; India 1,283; Malaya 295; Other areas 242: total embarked 21,767.
43. Cruising Order WS 12Z sailed UK 12.11.41 - *11.Adrastus*; 12. *Empire Star*; 13. *Sussex*; 21. *Mataroa*; 22. *Duchess of Bedford*; 23. *Empress of Asia*; 31. *Narkunda* (C); 32. *Empress of Japan*; 33. *Aorangi*; 34. *Arundel Castle*; 41. *Orduna*; 42. *Monarch of Bermuda*; 43. *Capetown Castle*; 51. *Deucalion*; 52. *Abbekerk*; 53. *Rimutaka*.
44. Howard & Sparrow, *The Coldstream Guards 1920-46*, Oxford Univiersity Press, 1951.
45. PRO ADM 199/1138 Report of *Royal Sovereign*, WS 12Z.
46. PRO ADM 199/1138 Report of Commodore, WS 12Z.
47. Signal to CinC SA 18.11.42 held in Naval Historical Branch, MOD.
48. Various communications between the author and Lt.Col. FL Carroll RE during 1974.
49. Cruising Order WS 12Z sailed Durban 24.12.41 - 11. *Orduna*; 12. *Aronda*; 13. *Eastern Prince*; 14. *Nieuw Amsterdam*; 21. *Capetown Castle*; 22. *Deucalion*; 23. Adrastus; 31. *Duchess of Bedford*; 32. *Empress of Japan*; 33. *Indrapoera*; 34. Empire Star; 41. *Narkunda*; 42. *Aorangi*; 43. *Abbekerk*; 44. *Sussex*.
50. *Ordeal by Sea*, The New Zealand Shipping Coy. Ltd., London, 1949, p.107.

Chapter 13 - WS 14 and WS 15.

WS 14

1. See WS 12X
2. PRO MT 40/45 Estimated Trooping requirements.
3. WS 14 estimated embarkations (P&O/Orient figures confirmed) - *Abosso* 1013; *Scythia* 3127; *Oronsay* 3093; *Reina del Pacifico* 2510; *Andes* 3396; *Orcades* 3545; *Strathallan* 3459; *Empress of Australia* 2559; *Esperance Bay* 1502; *Durban Castle* 1330; *Warwick Castle* 1524; *Athlone Castle* 1845; *Cameronia* 3155; *Duchess of Atholl* 3112; *Highland Princess* 1458; *Highland Monarch* 1520. Totals for Middle East 17,369; India/Iraq 13,441; South Africa 2978; West Africa 1013; Malaya 3347. Total embarked 38,148.
4. PRO ADM 199/1138. Crusing Order WS 14 sailed U.K. 8.12.41. - 11. *Troilus*; 12. *City of Pretoria*; 13. *Empire Curlew*; 21. *Warwick Castle*; 22. *Empress of Australia*; 23. *Empire Oriole*; 24. *Empire Condor*; 31. *Orestes*; 32. *Scythia*; 33. *Oronsay*; 34. *Andes*; 41. *Abosso*; 42. *Esperance Bay*; 43. *Reina del Pacifico*; 44. *Orcades*; 51. *Duchess of Atholl* (C); 52. *Strathallan*; 53. *Cameronia*; 54. HMS *Engadine*; 61. *Durban Castle*;

62 *Athlone Castle*; 63 *Empire Peregrine*; 71. *Highland Princess*; 72. *Highland Monarch*; 73. *Empire Egret*; 74. *Empire Widgeon*; 81. *Empire Pintail*; 82. *Clan Cameron*; 83. AMC *Cilicia*.

5. PRO ADM 199/1138. Admiralty instructions for organization of WS 14.
6. PRO ADM 199/1138. Report of SOE on *Ramillies*.
7. Signal from DoST to STO Freetown 14.12.41.
8. Various communications between the author and Lt.Col. FL Carroll RE during 1974.
9. PRO ADM 199/980. Letter from PSTO Simonstown to DoST London, 18.1.42.
10. Churchill, *The Second World War, Vol. 4.*, p. 92.
11. PRO MT 40/47 - Meeting of priority Movements Committee 3.12.41.
12. Report of Captain H Percival to owners, Ellerman Lines Ltd.
13. Cruising Order WS 14 from rendezvous outside Durban 13.1.42. - 11. *Orestes* (VC); 12. *Empire Oriole*; 13. *Empire Pintail*; 21. *Highland Monarch*; 22. *Empire Egret*; 23. *Thysville*; 31. *Nova Scotia*; 32. *Esperance Bay*; 33. *Clan Cameron*; 41. *Dunera* (C); 42. *Empire Condor*; 43. *Empire Curlew*; 51. *Dilwara* (RC); 52. *Empire Peregrine*; 53. *Empire Widgeon*; 61. *Warwick Castle*; 62. *Troilus*; 63. *Malancha*; 71. *Empress of Australia*; 72. *City of Pretoria*; 73. *City of Canterbury*.
14. Roskill, *The War at Sea, Vol 2*, HMSO, 1956, p.12.
15. Gill, *The Royal Australian Navy 1939-42,* Canberra, 1957, p. 528.
16. Woodburn Kirby, *The War against Japan, Vol. 1*, HMSO, 1957, Introduction p. xix.
17. Musk, *Canadian Pacific*, David & Charles, 1981, p. 136.
18. Dean, *The Loyal Regiment 1919-1953*, The Loyal Regiment 1955.
19. PRO ADM 199/980 Letter from PSTO Simonstown to DoST London, 18.1.42.

WS 15

1. PRO ADM 199/1211. report of FOIC Greenock.
2. Embarkations WS 15 - sailed U.K. 11.1.42. - *Arawa* 1509; *Britannic* 2887; *Empire Woodlark* 1384; *Letitia* 2232; *Orontes* 3265; *Otranto* 3250; *Stirling Castle* 1725; *Christiaan Huygens* 1575; *Laconia* 3035; *Llangibby Castle* 1157; *Strathmore* 3545; *Strathnaver* 3060, *Viceroy of India* 2557; *Pasteur* 3538; Staffordshire 2211; on 7 storeships 913. Totals for Middle East 19,326; Malaya 7247; Iraq 4998; India 3562; Others 2710: total embarked 37,843. (Behrens gives MOWT figure as 37,841.)
3. PRO ADM 237/268, Signals concerning WS 15.
4. Cruising Order WS 15 Clyde to Freetown sailed 11.1.42. - 11. *Port Chalmers*; 12. *Melbourne Star*; 13. *Elisabeth Bakke*; 21. *Empire Woodlark*; 22. *Otranto*; 23. *Orontes*; 24. Awara; 31. HMS *Resolution*;* 32. AMC *Cheshire*; 33. AMC *Ascania*; 34. HNMS *Heemskerk*; 41. *Strathmore*(C); 42. *Britannic*; 43. *Laconia*; 44. *Stirling Castle*; 51. *Staffordshire*; 52. *Viceroy of India*; 53. *Strathnaver*; 54. *Pasteur*; 61 *Autolycus*; 62. HNMS *Colombia*; 63. *Christiaan Huygens*; 64. *Letitia*; 71. Pardo; 72. *Dorset*; 73. *Llangibby Castle*;* 74. Aagtekerk. *These ships joined later.

5.   PRO ADM 199/1211, Report of VA 3, HMS *Resolution*, WS 15.
6.   PRO ADM 237/268, Report of Master, *Llangibby Castle*, WS 15.
7.   The Seaforths were a draft going to join their 1st Battalion in India.
8.   Cruising Order WS 15 from Durban 16.2.42. - 11. *Melbourne Star*,
        12. *Laconia*; 13. *Dorset*; 21. *Orontes* (VC); 22. *Otranto*; 23. *Viceroy of India*;
        24. *Pasteur*; 31. *Strathnaver* (C); 32. *Strathmore*; 33. *Britannic*; 34. HNMS
        Colombia; 41. *Stirling Castle*; 42. *Empire Woodlark*; 43. *Christiaan
        Huygens*; 44. *Port Chalmers*; 51. *Staffordshire*; 52. *Pardo*; 53. *Aagtekerk*;
        54. *Autolycus*.
9.   Cruising Order DM 3 formed 22.2.42. - 11. *Port Chalmers*; 12. *Autolycus*;
        13. HNMS *Colombia*; 21. *Strathnaver* (C); 22. *Empire Woodlark*;
        23. *Christiaan Huygens*; 31. *Staffordshire*; 32. *Pardo*; 33. *Aagtekerk*.
10.   PRO ADM 199/1211, Report of Commodore Tillard on *Strathnaver*.
11.   PRO ADM 199/1211. Report of HMS *Worcestershire*.

Chapter 14 - WS 16, WS 17 and WS 18.

WS 16 - sailed U.K. 16.2.42.

1.   PRO MT 40/45 - General Trooping Appreciation 1942.
2.   Churchill, The Second World War, Vol. 4, pp. 146-156.
3.   See MOWT correspondence relative to WS 5B, 6 and 7 and WS 10 and 11
4.   M. Murray, Union Castle Chronicle 1853-1953, Longmans, 1953.
5.   Embarkations WS 16 - sailed U.K. 16.2.42. - *Duchess of Richmond* 4050;
        Monarch of Bermuda 2500; *Mooltan* 4288; *Strathaird* 4202; *Awatea* 2480;
        Cuba 2100; *Sibajak* 2440; *Volendam* 2502; *Empire Pride* 2290; *Duchess of
        York* 4180; *Bergensfjord* 2600; *Nea Hellas* 4010; *Ormonde* 3564; *Stratheden*
        4134, totals 45,340. (Behrens quotes War Office figure of 45,339.)
6.   Roskill, The War at Sea, Vol. 2, HMSO, 1956, p.49.
7.   Cruising Order WS 16 sailed U.K. 16.2.42: 11. *Denbighshire*; 12. *City of
        Lincoln*; 13. *Port Jackson*; 21. *Monarch of Bermuda*; 22. *Strathaird*;
        23. *Awatea*; 31. *Delftdyk*; 32. *Duchess of Richmond*; 33. *Mooltan*;
        34. *Sibajak*; 41. *Stratheden* (C); 42. *Nea Hellas*; 43. *Empire Pride*; 44. *Cuba*;
        51. *Volendam*; 52. *Duchess of York*; 53. *Ormonde*; 54. *Bergensfjord*;
        61. *Potaro*; 62. *City of Edinburgh*; 63. *Brisbane Star*. The major warships
        were formed in column between 3 and 4.
8.   PRO ADM 199/1211. Report of HMS *Formidable*, WS 16.
9.   Turner, *War in the Southern Oceans,* Oxford University Press, 1961, pp. 118-
        124.
10.   *Doggerbank* was originally the Bank Line's *Speybank*, one of an easily
        recognized class of 25, which had been taken in prize in January 1941 and
        converted for minelaying. She was mistakenly sunk by *U-43* in March 1943.
11.   PRO ADM 199/1211, Report of Commodore WS 16.
12.   Cruising Order WS 16 sailed Durban 25.3.42: 11. *Nea Hellas* (VC);
        12. *Bergensfjord*; 13. *Volendam*; 21. *Duchess of Richmond*; 22. *Duchess of
        York*; 31. *Stratheden* (C); 32. *Awatea*; 33. *Sibajak*; 41. *Empire Pride*; 42. *Port
        Jackson*; 43. *Delftdyk*; 51. *Brisbane Star*; 52. *Denbighshire*; 53. *Potaro*.

13.   Woodburn Kirkby, *The War against Japan, Vol. 2*, HMSO, p. 106.
14.   Various communications between the author and Lt.Col. FL Carroll RE during 1974.

WS 17 sailed U.K. 23.3.42.

1.   Woodburn Kirby, *The War against Japan, Vol. 2*, HMSO, p.133/134.
2.   Murray, *Union Castle Chronicle 1853-1953*, Longmans, 1953.
3.   Embarkations WS 17: *Oronsay* 4389; *Duchess of Atholl* 4114, *Dominion Monarch* 3446, *Nieuw Holland* 1938; *Abosso* 2035; *Arundel Castle* 2753; *Leopoldville* 2216; *Empress of Russia* 2547; *JV Oldenbarneveldt* 3418; *Samaria* 4086; *Mataroa* 1916; *Largs Bay* 1730; *Windsor Castle* 2397; HMS *Keren* 1500; HMS *Karanja* 1500; *Almanzora* 2031; *Franconia* 4000; *Orion* 4,000; *Cameronia* 3849; *Winchester Castle* 1500; *Sobieski* 2105; *Tamaroa* 1760: estimated Totals 59,230, which largely agrees with MOWT figure of 59,231.
4.   Cruising Order Clyde to Freetown: 11. *Glaucus*; 12. *Port Wyndham*; 13. *Kina II*; 14. *Dunedin Star*; 21. *Leopoldville*; 22. *Samaria*; 23. *JV Oldenbarneveldt*; 24. *City of Lincoln*; 31. *Abosso* (VC); 32. *Empress of Russia*; 33. *Oronsay*; 34. *Arundel Castle*; 41. *Tamaroa*; 42. *Duchess of Atholl*; 43. *Dominion Monarch*; 44. *Winchester Castle*; 51. *Franconia* (C); 52. *Orion*; 53. *Windsor Castle*; 54 *Nieuw Holland*; 61. *Almanzora*; 62. *Cameronia*; 63. HMS *Karanja*; 64. HMS *Keren*, 71. *Mataroa*; 72. *Sobieski*; 73. HMS *Adamant*; 81. *Largs Bay*; 82. *Bhutan*; 83. *Rembrandt*; 84. *City of Edinburgh*.
5.   PRO ADM 199/1211, Report of *Illustrious*, WS 17.
6.   Wynn, *U-Boat Operations of Second World War, Vol. 2*, Chatham Publishing, p. 59.
7.   As no such German warships were then at sea this warship was probably from the French base at Dakar.
8.   WS 17A sailed Freetown 9.4.42: *Winchester Castle*; *Sobieski*; *Keren*; *Karanja*; *Duchess of Atholl*; *Oronsay*; *Dominion Monarch*; *Largs Bay*; *Windsor Castle*; *Bhutan*; *Port Wyndham* and *Rembrandt*. (Cruising Order unknown.)
9.   Jervois, *The Northamptonshire Regiment 1934-48*, Regimental History Committee, 1953.
10.   Various communications between the author and Lt.Col. FL Carroll RE during 1974.
11.   Kemp, *The Royal Scots Fusiliers 1919-59*, Maclehose & Co., 1963, p.65.
12.   Assault Convoy sailed Durban 28.4.42: *Winchester Castle*; *Sobieski*; *Keren*; *Karanja*; *Royal Ulsterman*; *Oronsay*; *Duchess of Atholl*; *Franconia*.
13.   WS 17B sailed Freetown 11.4.42: 11. *Abosso* (VC); 12. *Kina II*; 13. *Dunedin Star*; 21. *Tamaroa*; 22. *Samaria* (RC); 23. *Empress of Russia*; 31. *Glaucus*; 32. *Leopoldville*; 33. *JV Oldenbarneveldt*; 41. *Franconia* (C); 42. *Orion*; 43. *Nieuw Holland*; 51. *Mataroa*; 52. *Cameronia*; 53. *Arundel Castle*; 61. *Almanzora*; 62. *City of Edinburgh*; 63. *City of Lincoln*.
14.   PRO ADM 199/1211. Report of Commodore WS 17B.
15.   For details of this transfer see under WS 16.

16. WS 17 Cruising Order sailed Durban 1.5.42: 11. *Almanzora*; 12. *Nova Scotia*; 13. *Khedive Ismail*; 21. *Samaria*; 22. *Cameronia*; 23. *Mendoza*; 31. *Glaucus*; 32. *City of Lincoln*; 33. *City of Edinburgh*; 41. *Windsor Castle*; 42. *Kina II*; 43. *Dunedin Star*; 51. *JV Oldenbarneveldt*; 52. *Elisabethville*; 53. *Nieuw Holland*; 61 *Brazil*; 62. *Monterey*; 63. *Mormactide*; 64. *Clan Macdonald*.

17. *Arrow* and Dutch *Isaac Sweers*.

18. See WS 10. Pilots required arrival 45 minutes before HW to allow berthing at Ballard Pier on the first of the ebb.

19. Cruising Order WS 17 B2 sailed Mombasa 10.5.42: 11. *Mendoza*; 12. *Chantilly*; 21. *Samaria*; 31. *Almanzora* (C); 32. *Nova Scotia*; 41. *Cameronia*; 42. *Khedive Ismail*.

WS 18

1. PRO MT 40/45.

2. Embarkations WS 18 sailed U.K. 5.4.42.: *Nieuw Zeeland* 1311; *Marnix van St Aldegonde* 3557; *Rangitata* 2603; *Reina del Pacifico* 3130; *Empress of Japan* 4329; *Duchess of Bedford* 3606; *Dempo* 1844; *Capetown Castle* 3932; *Highland Chieftain* 1900; *Highland Princess* 1884; *Empress of Canada* 3600; *Aorangi* 3126; *Orbita* 2871; *Orduna* 2899; *Maloja* 4282: Totals 44,874.

3. Cruising Order WS 18 from the U.K.: 11. *Phemius*; 12. *Clan Lamont*; 13. *Soudan*; 21. *Orduna*; 22. *Duchess of Bedford* (VC); 23. *Capetown Castle*; 24. *Dempo*; 31. *Rangitata*; 32. *Reina de Pacifico*; 33. *Empress of Japan*; 34. *Marnix van St Aldegonde*; 41. *Empress of Canada* (C); 42. *Maloja*; 43. *Highland Chieftain*; 44. *Highland Princess*; 51. HMS *Hecla*; 52. *Aorangi*; 53. *Nieuw Zeeland*; 61. *Orbita*; 62. *City of Capetown*; 63. *Waipawa*.

4. Muir, *The First of Foot*, Royal Scots History Committee, 1961.

5. Kemp, *The Royal Norfolk Regiment 1919-51*, Regimental Association, 1953.

6. White, *Straight on for Tokyo, the 2nd Dorsets 1939-48*, Gale & Polden, 1948.

7. Blight, *History of The Royal Berkshire Regiment 1920-47*, Staples Press 1953.

8. Kemp, *The Red Dragon, Royal Welch Fusiliers 1919-45*, Gale & Polden, 1960.

9. Cruising Order sailed Freetown 3.5.42: 11. *Orbita*; 12. *Phemius*; 13. *Waipawa*; 14. *Agwileon*; 21. *Orduna* (RC); 22. *Reina del Pacifico*; 23. *Marnix van St Aldegonde*; 24. *Rimutaka*; 31. *Empress of Canada* (C); 32. *Dempo*; 33. *Nieuw Zeeland*; 34. *City of Capetown*; 41. *Rangitata*; 42. *Maloja*; 43. *Empress of Japan*; 44. *Aorangi*; 51. HMS *Hecla*; 52. *Duchess of Bedford* (VC); 53. *Capetown Castle*; 54. *Highland Chieftain*; 61. *Clan Lamont*; 62. *Highland Princess*; 63. *Soudan*.

10. PRO ADM 199/1211, report of HMS *Gambia*, WS 18.

11. PRO ADM 199/1211, Signal of NCSO Freetown to Commodore WS 18, 2.5.42.

12. Cruising Order Durban section 15.5.42: 11. *Aorangi*; 12. *City of Capetown*; 13. *Soudan*; 21. *Rangitaka*; 22. *Maloja*; 23. *Empress of Japan*; 31. *Duchess*

of *Bedford* (C); 32. *Capetown Castle*; 33. *Highland Chieftain*; 41. HMS Hecla;
42. *Clan Lamont*; 43. *Highland Princess*.

13.　　Various communications between the author and Lt.Col. FL Carroll RE during 1974.

14.　　The cruising order is unknown until off Mombasa on 30.5.42, when it became:
11. *Waipawa*; 12. *Phemius*; 13. *Bulkoil*; 21. *Orbita*; 22. *Marnix van St Aldegonde*; 31. *Orduna* (C); 32. *Dempo*; 33. *Nieuw Zeeland*; 41. *Capetown Castle*; 42. *Clan Lamont*; 43. *City of Capetown*.

15.　　PRO ADM 199/1211 - Report of HMS *Resolution*, WS 18.

Chapter 15 - WS 19, WS 19W, WS 19P and WS 19Y.

WS 19

1.　　Churchill, *The Second World War, Vol. 4*, pp. 146/7.
2.　　Churchill, *The Second World War, Vol.4*, p. 149.
3.　　Churchill, *The Second World War, Vol. 4*, p. 151.
4.　　Embarkations WS 19: *Athlone Castle* 4240; *Monarch of Bermuda* 4024; *Scythia* 4160; *Ormonde* 3587; *Highland Brigade* 1895; *Moreton Bay* 1825; *Highland Monarch* 1883; *Mooltan* 4299; *Strathaird* 4202; *Strathnaver* 3885; *Pasteur* 4500; *Borinquen* 1368; *Orizaba* 1673; (the last two having embarked in Iceland). Total 41,541.
5.　　Cruising Order WS 19 sailed U.K. 10.5.42: 11. *Lanarkshire*; 12. *Clan Macarthur*; 21. *Monarch of Bermuda*; 22. *Ormonde*; 23. *Highland Brigade*; 31. *Moreton Bay*; 32. *Scythia*; 33. *Athlone Castle*; 41. *Strathnaver* (C); 42. *Strathaird*; 43. *Pasteur*; 51. *Mooltan*; 52. *Orizaba* (VC); 53. *Boringuen*; 61. *Akaroa*; 62. *Highland Monarch*; 63. *Sussex*.
6.　　PRO ADM 199/1211, Report of HMS *Mauritius*, WS 19.
7.　　PRO ADM 199/1211, Report of Commodore Tillard, WS 19.
8.　　Barclay, *The Sherwood Foresters 1919-57*, Wm. Clowes, 1959.
9.　　Turner, *War in the Southern Oceans*, Oxford University Press, p. 164.
10.　　Various communications between the author and Lt.Col. FL Carroll RE during 1974.
11.　　Cruising Order WS 19 sailed Capetown 11.6.42: 11. *Athlone Castle* (VC); 12. *Lanarkshire*; 13. *Sussex*; 21. *Strathnaver* (C); 22. *Mooltan*; 23. *Orizaba*; 31. *Monarch of Bermuda*; 32. Takliwa.
12.　　Turner, *War in the Southern Oceans*, Oxford University Press, 1961, p.139.
13.　　Churchill, *The Second World War, Vol. 4*, p. 297.
14.　　Playfair, *The Mediterranean & Middle East, Vol. 3*, HMSO, 1960, p. 274.

WS 19W

1.　　Churchill, *The Second World War*, Vol. 4, p.150.
2.　　See WS 2.
3.　　PRO MT 40/47, Ports able to accommodate giant liners 23.12.41.
4.　　Bisset, *Commodore*, Angus & Robertson, 1961, pp. 373-5.

WS 19P

1. Churchill, *The Second World War, Vol. 4*, p. 75.
2. Refer to WS 19.
3. Roskill, *The War at Sea, Vol. 2*, HMSO, 1956, p. 29.
4. Embarkations WS 19P: *Viceroy of India* 3512; *Arawa* 1663; *Christiaan Huygens* 2670; *Laconia* 3728; *Andes* 3499; *Orontes* 3641; *Santa Rosa* 2502; *Warwick Castle* 3271; *Otranto* 4207; *Orcades* 4131; *Strathallan* 4397; *Britannic* 5083; *Aquitania* 5811; *Cristobal* 1234; *Mexico* 1193; *JW McAndrew* 2080; *Santa Elena* 2187; *Staffordshire* 2181; *Cathay* 3713: Totals 60,703.
5. WS 19P Cruising Order sailed U.K. 31.5.42: 11. *Poelau Roebiah*; 12. *Mexico*; 13. *New Zealand Star*; 21. *Orontes*; 22. *Laconia*; 23. *Christiaan Huygens*; 24. *Santa Rosa*; 31. *Arawa*; 32. *Viceroy of India*; 33. *Strathallan* (VC); 34. *Andes*; 41. *Orcades* (C); 42. *Britannic*; 43. *Aquitania*; 44. *Warwick Castle*; 51. *Staffordshire*; 52. *Cathay*; 53. *Otranto*; 54. *Santa Elena*; 61. *Talisse*; 62. *JW McAndrew*; 63. *Cristobal*; 64. *Java*.
6. Creighton, *Convoy Commodore*, Wm. Kimber, 1956, pp. 170/1.
7. Foster, *The Queen's Royal Regiment Vol. 8*, 1924-48, Gale & Polden Ltd., 1953.
8. Cruising Order sailed Freetown 19.6.42: 11. *New Zealand Star*; 12. *Mexico*; 13. *Java*; 21. *Strathallan* (VC); 22. *Laconia*; 23. *Santa Rosa*; 24. *Cathay*; 31. *Orontes*; 32. *Mariposa*; 33. *JW McAndrew*; 34. *Santa Elena*; 41. *Orcades* (C); 42. *Britannic*; 43. *Warwick Castle*; 44. *Staffordshire*; 51. *Andes*; 52. *Otranto*; 53. *Chateau Thierry*; 54. *Arawa*; 61. *Viceroy of India* (RC); 62. *Christiaan Huygens*; 63. *Santa Paula.*; 71. *Cristobal*; 72. *Talisse*; 73. *Poelau Roebiah*.
9. PRO ADM 199/1211, Report of Commodore, WS 19P.
10. Cruising Order WS 19L from Durban 7.7.42: 11. *Warwick Castle*; 12. *Santa Elena*; 21. *Viceroy of India* (C); 22. *Santa Rosa*; 23. *JW McAndrew*; 31. *Orontes*; 32. *Mexico* 33. *Cristobal*; 41. *Strathallan*; 42. *Laconia*.
11. Cruising Order WS 19P from Durban 8.7.42: 11. *Chateau Thierry*; 12. *New Zealand Star*; 13. *Poelau Roebiah*; 21. *Christaan Huygens*; 22. *Talisse*; 23. *Mariposa*; 31. *Otranto*(C); 32. *Santa Paula*; 33. *Java*; 41. *Cathay* (VC); 42. *Staffordshire*.
12. Turner, *War in the Southern Oceans*, Oxford University Press; 1961, pp. 161-5.
13. Goldsmith, *The Sinking of the Laconia*, Paul Watkins, Stamford, 1994.
14. Roskill, *The War at Sea, Vol. 2*, HMSO 1956 pp. 265/6.

Chapter 16 - WS 20, WS 21P and WS 21.

WS 20 - sailed U.K. 21.6.42

1. PRO MT 40/54, Document attached to General Trooping Appreciation 1942.
2. See WS 17, homeward voyages.

3. Embarkations WS 20: *Abosso* 2039; *Duchess of Richmond* 4038; *Orion* 5285; *Durban Castle* 2280; *Empress of Australia* 3768; *Empress of Russia* 2630; *Stirling Castle* 4010; *Strathmore* 4726; *Bergensfjord* 2559; *Narkunda* 2,708; *Banfora* 2303; *Batory* 2142; *Awatea* 2485; *Leopoldville* 2216; *Stratheden* 4470; *Empire Pride* 2506; *Arundel Castle* 2959; *Cuba* 2113; *Esperance Bay* 1770; Storeships 77: Total 57,094.
4. See Appendix IV.
5. It was by then known that German warships had abandoned forays into the Atlantic, which would have been suicidal, nor indeed was it German policy. (Roskill, *The War at Sea, Vol. 2*, HMSO, p.176.)
6. WS 20 Cruising Order, Clyde to Freetown: 11. *Abosso*; 12. *Durban Castle*; 13. *Palma*; 21. *Duchess of Richmond*; 22. *Orion* (VC); 23. *Batory*; 31. *Empress of Russia*; 32. *Empress of Australia*; 33. *Strathmore*; 41. *Stratheden* (C); 42. *Bergensfjord*; 43. *Adrastus*; 51. *Banfora*; 52. *Awatea*; 53. *Narkunda*; 61. *Esperance Bay*; 62. *Leopoldville*; 63. *Stirling Castle*; 71. *Arundel Castle*; 72. *Cuba*; 73. *Empire Pride*.
7. PRO ADM 199/1211, Report of Commodore, WS 20.
8. PRO ADM 199/1211, Report of HMS *Malaya*, WS 20.
9. *Queen's Own Cameron Highlanders, 1932-95*, Wm. Blackwood, 1952.
10. WS 20 Cruising Order Freetown to Cape: 11. *Abosso*; 12. *Durban Castle*; 13. *Palma*; 21. *Duchess of Richmond*; 22. *Orion* (VC); 23. *Stirling Castle*; 31. *Empress of Russia*; 32. *Empress of Australia*; 33. *Strathmore*; 34. *Cuba*; 41. *Stratheden* (C); 42. *Bergensfjord*; 43. *Adrastus*; 44. *Batory*; 51. *Banfora*; 52. *Awatea*; 53. *Empire Pride*; 61. *Arundel Castle*; 62. *Leopoldville*; 63. *Esperance Bay*.
11. Fergusson, *The Black Watch and the King's Enemies*, Collins, 1950.
12. Morison, *Battle of the Atlantic, Vol. 1*, Boston, 1962, p. 327.
13. Sandes, *From Pyramid to Pagoda*, Regimental Association, 1951.
14. Roskill, *The War at Sea, Vol. 2*, HMSO, 1956. p. 176.
15. WS 20 Cruising Order Durban onwards 26.7.42: 11. *Empress of Australia*; 12. *Palma*; 21. *Duchess of Richmond*; 22. *Leopoldville*; 23. *Empire Pride*; 31. *Stratheden* (VC); 32. *Bergensfjord*; 33. *Cuba*; 41. *Orion* (VC); 42. *Adrastus*; 43. *Abosso*; 51. *Arundel Castle*; 52. *Stirling Castle*.
16. Cowden & Duffy, *Elder Dempster Fleet history 1852-1985*. 1986, p. 224.
17. Correspondence with Brigadier W R Shilstone, 1974/75.

WS 21P - sailed U.K. 17.7.42.

1. See WS 16.
2. Playfair, *The Mediterranean & Middle East, Vol. 3*, HMSO, 1960, p. 372.
3. Playfair, *The Mediterranean & Middle East, Vol. 4* , HMSO, 1966, p. 16.
4. PRO ADM 199/1211, Report of Commodore WS 19P.
5. Embarkations WS 21P: *Duchess of Atholl* 4114; *Empress of Japan* 4337; *Oronsay* 4335; *Duchess of York* 4004; *Windsor Castle* 2494: Total all for Suez 19,284.
6. WS 21P Cruising Order sailed U.K. 17.7.42: 11. *Windsor Castle* (VC); 21. *Oronsay*; 31. *Empress of Japan* (C); 32. *Duchess of York*; 41. *Duchess of Atholl*.

7. Playfair, *The Mediterranean & Middle East, Vol. 4*, HMSO, 1966, p. 6.
8. PRO ADM 199/122, Report of Commanding Officer; *Empire Oriole.*
9. Roskill, *The War at Sea, Vol. 2*, HMSO, 1956, pp.202/3.
10. Cruising Order from Ascension 3.8.42: 11. *Windsor Castle* (VC); 12. *Empire Oriole*; 21. *Oronsay*; 22. *Tarn;* 23. *Hawaiian Shipper*; 31. *Empress of Japan* (C); 32. *Duchess of York*; 33. *Santa Cruz*; 41. *Duchess of Atholl*; 42. *Zaandam*; 43. *Mormacdale*; 51. *Exhibitor*; 52. *American Manufacturer.*
11. Cruising Order from Capetown 16.8.42: 11. *Windsor Castle* (VC); 12. *Empire Oriole*; 21. *Oronsay*; 22. *Exhibitor*; 23. *Hawaiian Shipper*; 31. *Empress of Japan* (C); 32. *Duchess of York*; 33. *Tarn*; 41. *Duchess of Atholl*; 42. *Zaandam.*
12. Playfair, The Mediterranean & Middle East, Vol. 4, HMSO, 1966, pp. 337-8.
13. See WS 22.
14. Musk, *Canadian Pacific*, David & Charles, 1981.

WS 21 - sailed UK 30.7.42.

1. See WS 21P
2. Embarkations WS 21: *Antenor* 1833; *Maloja* 4314; *Rangitiki* 2604; *Samaria* 4086; *Volendam* 2769; *Circassia* 2509; *Tamaroa* 1760; *Narkunda* 2752; *Aorangi* 3090; *Largs Bay* 1716: Total 28,290 which includes 785 for West Africa on AMC *Ranpura* and 71 on Storeships.
3. Cruising Order from Clyde sailed 30.7.42: 11. *James Lykes*; 12. *Curacao*; 21. *Circassia*; 22. *Largs Bay*; 23. *Aorangi*; 31. *Narkunda* (C); 32. *Tamaroa*; 41. *Maloja* (VC); 42. *Rangitiki*; 43. *Volendam*; 51. *Antenor*; 52. *Samaria.*
4. PRO ADM 199/1211, Report of Commodore WS 21.
5. Cruising Order from Freetown 15.8.42 and Ascension 18.8.42: 11. *China Mail*; 12. *American Press*; 21. *James Lykes*; 22. *Curacao*; 23. *Lookout*; 31. *Maloja* (VC); 32. *Antenor*; 33. *Volendam*; 41. *Narkunda* (C); 42. *Tamaroa*; 43. *Silverwalnut*; 51. *Circassia*; 52. *Rangitiki*; 53. *Samaria*; 61. *Aorangi*; 62. *Largs Bay*; 63. *Erria.*
6. Bone, *Merchantmen Rearmed*, Chatto & Windus, 1949, pp. 138/9.
7. Cruising Order from Capetown 30.8.42: 11. *Aorangi*; 12. *Lookout*; 21. *James Lykes*; 22. *Silverwalnut*; 23. *Bantam*; 31. *Maloja* (VC); 32. *Antenor*; 33. *Curacao*; 41. *China Mail*; 42. *American Press.*
8. Cruising Order from Durban 3.9.42: 11. *Aorangi*; 12. *Volendam*; 13. *Lookout*; 21. *James Lykes*; 22. *Bantam*; 23 *Silverwalnut*; 31. *Samaria* (C); 32. *Maloja* (VC); 33. *Antenor*; 41. *China Mail*; 42. *Curacao*; 43. *American Press.*
9. Woodburn Kirby, *The War against Japan, Vol. 2*, HMSO, 1953, p. 282.

Chapter 17 - Departures in August and October 1942 - WS 22, WS 23 and WS 24.

WS 22 - sailed U.K. 28 August 1942.

1. Playfair, *The Mediterranean & Middle East, Vol. 3*, HMSO, 1960, p. 364.

2.   Playfair, *The Mediterranean & Middle East, Vol. 3,* HMSO. 1960, p. 365n.
3.   Barclay, *The London Scottish 1939-45,* Wm. Clowes, 1952.
4.   Estimated embarkations WS 22 sailed U.K. 28.8.42: *Nieuw Holland* 1951; *Orcades* 4372; *Orduna* 2912; *Andes* 3729; *Dominion Monarch* 3556; *Franconia* 4162; *JV Oldenbarneveldt* 3454; *Rangitata* 2616; *Highland Princess* 1930; *California* 4167; *Mataroa* 1920; *Almanzora* 2802; *Boissievain* 2400; *Nea Hellas* 4023; *Ruys* 2374; *Highland Brigade* 1750; *Highland Chieftain* 1902; *Leinster* 750: Total embarked 50,770.
5.   Cruising Order WS 22 sailed U.K. 28.8.42: 11. *Suffolk*; 12. *Nieuw Holland*; 21. *Orduna*; 22. *Orcades*; 23. *Leinster*; 31. *Almanzora*; 32. *Andes*; 33. *Boissievain*; 41. *California*; 42. *Nea Hellas*; 43. *JV Oldenbarneveldt*; 51. *Rangitata*; 52. *Dominion Monarch*; 53. *Highland Princess*; 61. *Mataroa*; 62. *Franconia*; 63. *Ruys*; 71. *Highland Brigade*; 72. *Highland Chieftain*; 73. *Canara*.
6.   PRO ADM 199/980 - Troop and Military Convoys.
7.   Foster, *History of the Queen's Royal Regiment, Vol. 8,* 1924-48, Gale & Polden Ltd., 1953.
8.   Cruising Order from Freetown 13.9.42: 11. *Nieuw Holland*; 12. *Suffolk*; 13. *Highland Princess*; 21. *Orduna*; 22. *Dominion Monarch*; 23. *Ruys*; 31. *Almanzora*; 32. *Franconia*; 33. *JV Oldenbarneveldt*; 41. *California* (C); 42. *Nea Hellas*; 43. *Sibajak*; 51. *Rangitata*; 52. *Orcades*; 53. *Boissievain*; 61. *Andes* (VC); 62. *Mataroa*; 63. *Canara*; 71. *Highland Brigade*; 72. *Highland Chieftain*.
9.   Neville, *The Oxfordshire & Buckinghamshire Light Infantry Chronicle, Vol. 3,* Gale & Polden, 1951.
10. Various communications between the author and Lt.Col. FL Carroll RE during 1974.
11. Cruising Order from Durban 3.10.42: 11. *Orduna*; 12. *Ekma*; 13. *Felix Roussel*; 21. *Dominion Monarch*; 22. *JV Oldenbarneveldt*; 23. *Boissievain*; 24. *Rangitata*; 31. *California* (C); 32. *Nieuw Holland*; 33. *Canara*; 34. *Indrapoera*; 41. *Franconia* (VC); 42. *Ruys*; 43. *Almanzora*.
12. PRO ADM 199/1211, Report of HMS *Hawkins*, WS 22.
13. Cruising Order Aden section from 11.10.42: 11. *Orduna*; 12. *Felix Roussel*; 21. *Indrapoera*; 22. *Ekma*.

WS 23 - sailed U.K. 4.10.42.

1.   Embarkations: *Capetown Castle* 4018; *Highland Monarch* 1883; *Empress of Russia* 2053; *Moreton Bay* 1825; MT ships 18; AMC *Queen of Bermuda* 1918: Total 11,715.
2.   PRO ADM 199/1211, Report of Commodore WS 23.
3.   Signal of 6.10.42 from DoST to RAWA, CinCSA and CinCEF.
4.   WS 23 Cruising Order sailed U.K. 4.10.42: 11. *Silversandal*; 12. *Port Jackson*; 21. *Kina II*; 22. *Empress of Russia* (VC); 31. *Capetown Castle* (C); 32. *Highland Monarch*; 33. *Rimutaka*; 41. *Moreton Bay*; 42. *Straat Malacca*.
5.   See WS 18, Chapter 14.
6.   Cruising Order sailed Durban 9.11.42: 11. *Kina II*; 12. *Straat Malacca*; 21. *Highland Monarch* (VC); 22. *Port Jackson*; 31. *Capetown Castle* (C);

32. *Empress of Russia*; 41. *Dilwara*; 42. *Silversandal*.
7.   Underhill, *The Royal Leicestershire Regiment 1928-56*, Underhill, 1957.
8.   PRO ADM 199/996, Prisoner of War Part I, 1941-44.

WS 24 - sailed U.K. 29.10.43.

1.   Roskill, *The War at Sea, Vol. 2*, HMSO, 1956, p. 315.
2.   Embarkations WS 24: *Arawa* 1660; *Tamaroa* 1755; *Largs Bay* 1723; *Stirling Castle* 4332; *Athlone Castle* 4437; *Empress of Scotland* 4306: Total 18,213.
3.   PRO ADM 199/1211, Report of *Rotherham*, WS 24.
4.   Cruising Order WS 24 from 31.10.42: 11. *Tamaroa*; 21. *Athlone Castle*; 22. *Arawa*; 31. *Stirling Castle* (C); 41. *Indochinois*; 42. *Empress of Scotland* (VC); 51. *Largs Bay*.
5.   Amended Cruising Order from 11.11.42: 21. *Arawa*; 22. *Indochinois*; 31. *Stirling Castle* (C); 32. *Athlone Castle*; 41. AMC *Queen of Bermuda*; 51. *Empress of Scotland*; 52. *Largs Bay*.
6.   Roskill, *The War at Sea, Vol. 2*, HMSO, 1956, p. 383.
7.   PRO ADM 199/1211, Report of Commodore, WS 24.
8.   Roskill, *The War at Sea, Vol. 2*, HMSO, 1956, p. 385.
9.   WS 24 Cruising Order 28.11.42: 11. AMC *Alcantara*; 21. *Stirling Castle* (C); 22. *Athlone Castle*; 31. *Arawa*; 32. *Largs Bay*; 41. AMC *Queen of Bermuda*; 42. *Empress of Scotland*.

Chapter 18 - WS 25, WS 25W and WS 26.

WS 25 - sailed U.K. 17.12.42.

1.   Troopship losses off North Africa between 11 and 15 November 1942 were *Cathay, Nieuw Zeeland, Viceroy of India, Awatea, Narkunda, Warwick Castle* and *Ettrick* totalling 107,421 grt.
2.   Embarkations: *Esperance Bay* 1805; *Orion* 5313; *Rangitiki* 2598; *Highland Princess* 1930; *Mataroa* 1897; *Britannic* 4955; *Highland Brigade* 1882; AMCs 915; MT ship 9: totals 21,304.
3.   Cowper, *The King's Own, Vol 3, 1914-50*, Gale & Polden, 1957.
4.   Cruising Order WS 25 sailed UK 17.12.42: 11. *Tarifa*; 21. *Rangitiki*; 22. *City of Lincoln*; 31. *Britannic* (C); 32. *Orion* (VC); 41. *Esperance Bay*; 42. *Mataroa*; 51. *Highland Brigade*; 52. *Highland Princess*.
5.   See WS 9B.
6.   Roskill, *The War at Sea, Vol. 3, Part I*, HMSO, 1960, pp. 46/7.
7.   See homeward voyages of *Almanzora* and *JV Oldenbarneveldt* in WS 22.
8.   Bushell, *Eight Bells*, Trade & Travel Publications Ltd., 1950, p. 100.
9.   PRO ADM 199/1211, Report of Commodore and SOE (HMS *Quilliam*).
10.   Cruising Order WS 25 sailed Freetown 3.1.43: 11. *Highland Brigade*; 21. *Tarifa*; 22. *Highland Princess*; 31. *Rangitiki*; 32. *City of Lincoln*; Escort column; 41. *Britannic* (C); 42. *Orion* (VC); 51. *Esperance Bay*; 52.*Mataroa*.

11. PRO ADM 199/996 Prisoners of War 1941-44, Letter from Admiralty to ACNBF, dated 20.9.42.
12. Roskill, *The War at Sea, Vol. 2*, HMSO, 1956, p. 214.
13. PRO ADM 199/996 Prisoners of War 1941-44. Letter from Admiralty to CinCSA dated 28.1.43.
14. PRO ADM 199/996 Prisoners of War 1941-44. Letter from DoST to PSTO Capetown dated 8.1.43.
15. PRO ADM 199/996 Prisoners of War 1941-44. Letter from CinCSA to Admiralty dated 17.1.43.

WS 25W - sailed U.K. 23.12.42.

1. Bisset, *Commodore*, Angus & Robertson, 1961, p. 385.
2. Table of Abnormal Wave ship incidents compiled by Em. Professor Douglas Faulkner of Naval Architecture at the University of Glasgow, in which the wave height was estimated as 80 ft. and almost level with *Queen Mary*'s Sports Deck.
3. Bisset, *Commodore*, Angus & Robertson, 1961, p. 386.
4. See WS 26, homeward voyage of *Stratheden*.

WS 26 - sailed U.K. 24.1.43.

1. Embarkations WS 26: *Dempo* 1859; *Dominion Monarch* 3456; *Duchess of Richmond* 4000; *Highland Chieftain* 1900; *Mooltan* 4311; *Sibajak* 2444, *Volendam* 2797; *California* 4200; *Ruys* 2700; *Stratheden* 4643; *Antenor* 1850; *Arundel Castle* 2965; *Empress of Canada* 3471; *Orduna* 3912; *Maloja* 4305: Totals 48,813. (On KMF 8 - 24,794; total both convoys 73,607).
2. Joslen, *Orders of Battle, the Second World War 1939-45, Vol. 2*, HMSO, 1960.
3. PRO ADM 199/720 and ADM 199/1026, Commodore's Report of Proceedings KMF 8 and WS 26.
4. Cruising Order from U.K. 24.1.43: 11. *Empire Pride*; 12. *Letitia*; 21. *Dunnottar Castle*; 22. *Strathnaver*; 23. *Duchess of York*; 24. *Circassia*; 31. *Highland Chieftain*; 32. *Sibajak*; 33. *Volendam*; 34. *Samaria*; 41. *Durban Castle* (C); 42. *Duchess of Richmond*; 43. *California*; 44. *Orduna*; 51.-54. HM Ships; 61. *Stratheden* (VC) ; 62. *Maloja*; 63. *Mooltan*; 64. *Dominion Monarch*; 71. *Arundel Castle*; 72. *Empress of Canada*; 73. *Ruys*; 74. *Dempo*; 81. *Chyebassa*; 82. *Rembrandt*; 83. *Antenor*.
5. Roskill, *The War at Sea, Vol. 2*, HMSO, 1956, p. 339.
6. Miles, *The Gordon Highlanders 1939-45*, Aberdeen University Press, 1961.
7. PRO ADM 199/1026, Report by CO HMS *Cilicia* to FOWA 7.2.43.
8. Cruising Order from Freetown 9.2.43: 11. *Highland Chieftain*; 12. *Sibajak*; 13. *Volendam*; 21. *Arundel Castle* (VC); 22. *California*; 23. *Orduna*; 24. *Rembrandt*; 31. HMS *Wayland*; 32. AMC *Canton*; 33. AMC *Cilicia*; 41. *Stratheden* (C); 42. *Ruys*; 43. *Chyebassa*; 51. *Duchess of Richmond* (RC); 52. *Maloja*; 53. *Empress of Canada*; 61. *Mooltan*; 62. *Dempo*; 63. *Dominion Monarch*.
9. PRO ADM 199/1026, Report by Commodore WS 26.

10.   Cowper, *The King's Own, Vol. 3, 1914-50*, Gale & Polden, 1957.
11.   Turner, *War in the Southern Oceans*, Oxford University Press, 1961, p.210.
12.   Musk, *Canadian Pacific*, David & Charles, 1981, p. 141.
13.   Master's Report to Ellerman City line 1.10.44.
14.   Cruising Order from Durban 1.3.43: 11. *Orduna*; 12. *Arundel Castle*;
       13. *Rembrandt*; 21. *Maloja* (VC); 22. *Selandia*; 23. *Highland Chieftain*;
       31. *Stratheden* (C); 32. *Dominion Monarch*; 33. *Lancashire*;
       34. HMS *Resource*; 41. *City of Paris*; 42. *Mooltan*; 43. *Dilwara*;
       51. California; 52. *Dempo*; 53. *Chyebassa*.
15.   See also under WS 27.

Chapter 19 - WS 27, WS 28 and WS 29.

WS 27 - sailed U.K. 24.2.43.

1.   Embarkations: *Capetown Castle* 4236; *Christiaan Huygens* 2670;
      Strathmore 4763; *Strathaird* 4190; *Almanzora* 2890; *Antenor* 1850:
      Total 18,749* (on KMF 10A 15,500, combined convoys - 34,249)
      *excluding *Antenor* 1850 counted in WS 26.
2.   PRO ADM 199/1026 Reports of Commodore and SOE on HMS *Malaya* WS
      27.
3.   Cruising Order from U.K: 11. *Letitia*; 12. *Nieuw Holland*; 21. *Boissievain*;
      22. *Batory*; 31. *Circassia* (C); 32. *Franconia*; 33. *Strathmore*;
      41. *Almanzora*; 42. *Strathaird*; 43. *Capetown Castle*; 51. *Antenor*;
      52. *Christiaan Huygens*.
4.   Cruising Order WS 27 from 2.3.43: 11. *Almanzora* (C); 12. *Strathaird*;
      21. HMS *Malaya*; 22. *Capetown Castle*; 23. *Strathmore*; 31. *Antenor*;
      32. *Christiaan Huygens*.
5.   See WS 26.
6.   Cruising Order from Durban 29.3.43: 11. *Leopoldville*, 12. *Strathmore*;
      21. *Duchess of Richmond* (C); 22. *Capetown Castle* (VC); 23. *Strathaird*;
      31. *Orbita*; 32. *Ruys*; 33. *Sibajak*; 41. *Christiaan Huygens*; 42. *Bergensfjord*.
7.   PRO ADM 199/1026 Report of HMS *Frobisher*, SOE WS 27.

WS 28 - sailed U.K. 16.3.43.

1.   Molony, *The Mediterranean & Middle East, Vol. V*, HMSO 1973, p.2.
2.   Playfair & Molony, *The Mediterranean & Middle East, Vol. IV*, HMSO,
      1966, p. 261.
3.   Playfair & Molony, *The Mediterranean & Middle East, Vol. IV*, HMSO, 1966,
      p. 263.
4.   Molony, *The Mediterranean & Middle East, Vol. V*, HMSO, 1973, p.6.
5.   Embarkations: *Britannic* 5050; *Duchess of Bedford* 4000; *Monarch of
      Bermuda* 3433; *Orontes* 3940; *Otranto* 4684; *Reina del Pacifico* 3130;
      Sobieski 2105; *Strathnaver* 4293; *Tegelberg* 2620; *Winchester Castle* 1158;
      HMS *Keren* 1158; *Bulolo* 258; *Ulster Monarch* 110: Total 36,089. (On KMF
      11 - 25,502: combined convoys - 61,591.)

6.   Cruising Order from U.K.: 11. *Rangitata*; 12. *Banfora*; 13. *Cuba*; 21. *Winchester Castle*; 22, *Orion*; 23. *Ormonde*; 31. *Nea Hellas*; 32. *Otranto*; 33. *Orontes*; 34. *JV Oldenbarneveldt*; 41. *Strathnaver* (C); 42. HMS *Keren*; 43. HMS *Largs*; 44. HMS *Ulster Monarch*; 51. HMS *Bulolo*; 52. *Duchess of Bedford*; 53. *Britannic*; 54. *Sobieski*; 61. *Reina del Pacifico*; 62. *Monarch of Bermuda*; 63. *Tegelberg*; 64. *Winchester Castle*; 71. *Perthshire*; 72. *Empire Might*; 73. *Waipawa*.

7.   It was indeed remarkable that ships in wartime safely carried their overside LCA throughout vast ocean distances without apparent damage, a somewhat unseamanlike procedure which in peacetime conditions would hardly have been contemplated.

8.   Cruising Order from Freetown 30.3.43: 11. *Duchess of Bedford*; 12. *Monarch of Bermuda*; 13. *Winchester Castle*; 21. *Reina del Pacifico*; 22. *Otranto*; 23. *Tegelberg*; 31. *Strathnaver* (C); 32. *Orontes*; 33. *Britannic*; 34. *Sobieski*; 41. *Bulolo*; 42. *Keren*; 43. Largs; 51. *Perthshire*; 52. *Waipawa*.

9.   Various communications between the author and Lt.Col. FL Carroll RE during 1974.

10.   Cruising Order from Durban 18.4.43, as above but with *Sobieski* 33; HMS *Kenya* 41; *Bulolo* 42; *Keren* 43; *Largs* 53.

WS 29 - sailed U.K. 15.4.43.

1.   Woodburn Kirby, *The War against Japan, Vol. 2*, HMSO, 1958, p.361.

2.   Viscount Slim, *Defeat into Victory*, Cassell, 1956, p. 165.

3.   Embarkations: *Athlone Castle* 5000; *Highland Brigade* 1882; *Orion* 5284; *Aorangi* 3090; *Highland Princess* 1930; *Highland Monarch* 1883: Total 19,069. (On KMF 13 - 29,823: combined convoys 48,892.)

4.   Cruising Order 16.4.43: 11. *Troilus*; 12. *Silverwalnut*; 13. *Empire Kamal*; 21. *Banfora*; 22. *Cuba*; 23. *Staffordshire*; 24. *Dunnottar Castle*; 31. *Franconia* (VC); 32. *Duchess of York*; 33. *Ormonde*; 34. *Boissievain*; 41. *Orion* (C); 42. *Empire Pride*; 43. *Indrapoera*; 44. *Nieuw Holland*; 51. *Highland Monarch*; 52. *Athlone Castle*; 53. *Gloucester*; 61. *Highland Princess*; 62. *Highland Brigade*; 63. *Nea Hellas*; 71. *City of Edinburgh*; 72. *Pardo*; 73. *Straat Malacca*.

5.   Cruising Order after split 21.4,43: 11. *Highland Monarch*; 12. *Troilus*; 13. *Silverwalnut*; 21. *Orion* (C); 22. *Athlone Castle*; 23. *Glouccester*; 31. *Highland Princess*; 32. *Highland Brigade*; 33. *Empire Kamal*; 41. *City of Edinburgh*; 42. *Pardo*; 43. *Straat Malacca*.

6.   Roskill, *The War at Sea, Vol. 2*, HMSO, 1956, p.371.

7.   Roskill, *The War at Sea, Vol. 2*, HMSO, 1956, p. 372.

8.   PRO ADM 199/1026, Report by Master *Aorangi*.

9.   Cruising Order from Freetown 5.5.43: 11. *Pardo*; 12. *Straat Malacca*; 21. *Athlone Castle*; 22. *Almanzora*; 23. *Silverwalnut*; 31. *Orion* (C); 32. *Highland Brigade*; 33. *Clan Lamont*; 41. *Highland Monarch*; 42. *Aorangi*; whilst the stations of *Troilus, Empire Kamal, Highland Princess* and *City of Edinburgh* are unknown.

10.   Bushell, *Eight Bells*, Trade & Travel Pubs. Ltd., 1950, p. 77.

11. Cruising Order from Capetown 22.5.43: 11. *Alcoa Pioneer*; 12. *Llanstephan Castle*; 13. *Empire Kamal*; 21. *Athlone Castle* (C); 22. *Almanzora*; 23. *Silverwalnut*; 31. *Orbita* (VC); 32. *Pardo*.

12. Cruising Order from Durban 25.5.43: 11. *Alcoa Pioneer*; 12. *Selandia*; 21. *Clan Lamont*(VC); 22. *Bergensfjord*; 23. *Silverwalnut*; 31. *Ruys*; 32. *Leopoldville*; 33. *Pardo*; 41. *Strathmore* (C); 42. *Almanzora*; 51. *Strathaird*; 52. *Athlone Castle*; 61. *Orbita*; 62. *Straat Malacca*.

Chapter 20 - WS 30, 31, Faith Convoy

WS 30 - sailed U.K. 19.5.43.

1. Table of embarkations, Appendix II.
2. Embarkations WS 30: *HF Alexander* 1803; *Argentina* 4323; **Siboney** 1201; *Sloterdijk* 1714; *Mataroa* 1897: Total 10,938. (Embarked on KMF 15 - 35,540: total combined convoys 46,478.)
3. Both *Royal Scotsman* and *Royal Ulsterman* had taken part in Torch.
4. WS 30/ KMF 15 combined Cruising Order from U.K. 19.5.43: 11. *Arawa*; 12. *Indrapoera*; 13. *Staffordshire*; 21. *Ormonde*; 22. *Franconia*; 23. *Royal Scotsman*; 31. *Samaria* (VC); 32. *Duchess of York*; 33. *Royal Ulsterman*; 41. *Stirling Castle*; 42. *JV Oldenbarneveldt*; 43. *Boissievain*; 51. *Siboney* (C); 52. *Argentina*; 53. *Letitia*; 61. *HF Alexander*; 62. *Sloterdijk*; 63. *Deseado*; 71. *Mataroa*. 72. *Brisbane Star*.
5. PRO ADM 199/1026, Report of Commodore, WS 30.
6. WS 30 after split 25.5.43: 11. *Siboney* (C); 12. *Argentina*; 21. *HF Alexander*; 22. *Sloterdijk*; 23. *Deseado*; 31. *Mataroa* (VC); 32. *Brisbane Star*.
7. On account of the colour bar in South Africa, the West Africans were not allowed shore leave, but see also WS 31.
8. Cruising Order from Durban 25.6.43: 11. *Sibajak*; 12. *General Fleischer*; 21. *Nieuw Holland* (C); 22. *Cuba*; 23. *Santa Barbara*; 31. *Karagola*; 32. *Sagoland*.

WS 31 - sailed UK 19.6.43.

1. *Expansion of (Indian) Armed Forces and Defence Organisations*, Orient Longmans, 1956.
2. Behrens, *Merchant Shipping and the demands of War*, HMSO, 1955, p. 329.
3. Embarkations WS 31: *Rangitiki* 2598; *Stratheden* 4397; *John Ericsson* 5461; *George W Goethols* 1976: Total 14,432. (Embarked on KMF 17 - 18,979: total combined convoy 33,411.)
4. Combined Cruising Order 20.6.43: 11. *Largs Bay*; 12. *JW McAndrew*; 21. *Britannic* (VC): 22. *Cristobal*; 23. *Silverteak*; 31. *Santa Rosa*; 32. *Samaria*; 33. *Tamaroa*; 41. *Stratheden* (C); 42. *John Ericsson*; 43. *Clan Macarthur*; 51. *George W Goethols*; 52. *Rangitiki*; 53. HMS *Guardian*; 61. *City of Lincoln*; 62. *Clan Macaulay*.
5. PRO ADM 199/1026 Report of Commodore, WS 31.

6.   Cruising Order from Lagos 11.7.43: 11. *John Ericsson*; 12. *George W Goethols*; 13. *Staffordshire*;   21. *Stratheden* (C); 22. *Stirling Castle*; 23. *Clan Macarthur*; 31. *Highland Monarch*; 32. *Highland Brigade*; 33. *Arawa*; 41. *City of Lincoln*; 42. *Clan Macaulay*; 43. *Quercy*.
7.   Various communications between the author and Lt.Col. FL Carroll RE during 1974.
8.   Cruising Order from Capetown 26.7.43: 11. *Stirling Castle*; 12. *Arawa*; 21. *Stratheden* (C); 22. Staffordshire; 31. *Highland Monarch*; 32. *Highland Brigade*.
9.   PRO ADM 199/1026 Report of HMS *Frobisher*, WS 31.
10.   Viscount Slim, *Defeat into Victory*, Cassell, 1956, p. 165.
11.   PRO ADM 199/996, Prisoners of War 1941 - 44.

Convoy Faith - sailed 8.7.43.

1.   McLellan, *Anchor Line 1856-1956*, Anchor Line, 1956, pp. 126/7.
2.   Musk, *Canadian Pacific*, David & Charles, 1981, pp. 174/5.
3.   Russell, *Port Line*, London, 1985, pp. 80/81.

Chapter 21 - WS 32, CM 45 and WS 33.

WS 32 - sailed U.K. 19.7.43.

1.   Embarkations WS 32: *Maloja* 4249; *Rangitata* 2618; *Highland Chieftain* 1902; *Esperance Bay* 1572; *Moreton Bay* 1671: Total 12,012. (Embarked on KMF 20 - 16,872. Total combined convoys 28,884.)
2.   Combined Cruising Order WS 32/ KMF 20 sailed 19.7.43: 11. *City of Bristol*; 12. *Chyebassa*; 21. *Highland Princess*; 22. *Volendam*; 23. *Rembrandt*; 31. *Mooltan* (VC); 32. *Orion*; 33. *Dempo*; 41. *Maloja* (C); 42. *Rangitata*; 43. *Esperance Bay*; 51. *Highland Chieftain*; 52. *Moreton Bay*; 53. *Rowallan Castle*; 61. *Rochester Castle*; 62. *Copacabana*.
3.   PRO ADM 199/1026 Report of SO A/S escort, HMS *Pelican*, KMF 20.
4.   Cruising Order WS 32 from 25.7.43: 11. *Esperance Bay*; 12. *Rowallan Castle;* 21. *Maloja* (C); 22. *Rangitata*; 31. *Highland Chieftain*; 32. *Moreton Bay*; 41. *Rochester Castle*; 42. *Copacabana*.
5.   PRO ADM 199/1026 Report of Commodore, WS 32.
6.   Cruising Order from Lagos 9.8.43: 11. *Esperance Bay*; 12. *Nea Hellas*; 21. *Maloja* (C); 22. *Britannic*; 23. *Tamaroa*; 31. *Highland Chieftain*; 32. *Moreton Bay*; 33. *Largs Bay*; 41. *Rochester Castle*; 42. *Rangitata*.
7.   Turner, *War in the Southern Oceans*, Oxford University Press, 1961, p. 234.
8.   Cruising Order from Durban 28.8.43: 11. *Maloja*; 12. *Tamaroa*; 21. HMS *Hawkins*; 22. *Strathmore*; 31. *Britannic*; 32. Largs Bay.

WS 33 - sailed U.K. 16.8.43.

1.   Embarkations WS 33 - sailed 16.8.43 (part Algiers, Gibraltar and W. Africa): *Duchess of Richmond* 4000; *Ormonde* 3700; *Antenor* 1850; *Boissievain*

2400; *Indrapoera* 1973, *Johan de Witt* 1915. Total: 15,838. (Embarked on KMF 22 - 37,324: total combined convoy 53,062.)

2. WS 33 17.8.43: *Duchess of Richmond, Antenor, Boissievain, Indrapoera, Johan de Witt, Ormonde*; KMF 22 - *Arundel Castle, Cameronia, Duchess of Bedford, Durban Castle, Empress of Australia, Marnix van St. Aldegonde, Monarch of Bermuda, Orduna, Otranto, Tegelberg, Orontes, Ruys, Glenartney*. (Cruising Order unknown)

3. PRO ADM 199/991 War Office Telegram to Washington 4.8.43.

4. Behrens, *Merchant Shipping and the demands of War,* HMSO, 1955, p. 172.

ABBREVIATIONS USED IN TEXT

A/A	Anti-Aircraft
ACNBF	Australian & Commonwealth Naval Board, Fremantle.
AFD	Admiralty Floating Dock
AMC	Armed Merchant Cruiser: In most instances AMCs are listed as such, although they were fully commissioned as HM ships. This is to clear ly distinguish them as partially converted passenger ships rather than cruisers designed and built as such.
Anzac	Australian and New Zealand
A/S	Anti-Submarine
ATS	Auxiliary Territorial Service
Bde	Brigade
BEF	British Expeditionary Force
BI	British India Steam Nav. Co. Ltd.
Bn	Battalion
BTC	BritishTanker Co. (later BP)
Cable	One-tenth of a nautical mile (600 ft.)
CinC	Commander-in-Chief
CIGS	Chief of Imperial General Staff
CM	Cape - Mombasa
CO	Commanding Officer
CPS	Canadian Pacific Steamships
DBS	Distressed British Seamen (usually Survivors)
DG	De-gaussing (against mines)
DOST	Department of Sea Transport
DSTO	Divisional Sea Transport Officer
EF	Eastern Fleet
EG	Escort Group
EI	Eastern Indies
ESO	Embarkation Staff Officer
FOIC	Flag Officer in Charge
FOWA	Flag Officer West Africa
grt	Gross Registered Tons
HF/DF	High Frequency Direction Finder, which allowed a bearing to be taken of a U-Boat transmission
HNMS	Her Netherland Majesty"s Ship
Impcon	Imperial Movement Control
IWM	Imperial War Museum
KDG	King"s Dragoon Guards
kts	Knots (i.e. nautical miles per hour)
KRRC	King"s Royal Rifle Corps
LCA	Landing Craft Assault
LSI	Landing Ship Infantry and LSIL (Large)
Lt Col	Lieutenant Colonel
ME	Middle East

mls	Nautical Miles (of 6080 ft.)
MN	Merchant Navy
MOMP	Mid Ocean Meeting Point
MOS	Ministry of Shipping
MOWT	Ministry of War Transport (succeeded MOS)
MT	Military Transport (i.e. Storeships not Troopships)
NB	New Brunswick
NCO	Naval Control Office
NCSO	Naval Control Service Officer
NMM	National Maritime Museum
NOIC	Naval Officer in Charge
NS	Nova Scotia
NZS	New Zealand Shipping Co. Ltd.
OBV	Ocean Boarding Vessel
OC Troops	Officer in Charge of Troops (aboard ship)
ORs	Other Ranks
POW	Prisoners of War
PSNC	Pacific Steam Nav. Co. Ltd.
PSTO	Principal Sea Transport Officer
QARANS	Queen Alexandra"s Royal Army Nursing Service
RA	Royal Artillery
RAN	Royal Australian Navy
RAOC	Royal Army Ordnance Corps
Regt	Regiment
RIN	Royal Indian Navy
RNZN	Royal New Zealand Navy
RSM	Regimental Sergeant Major
Rtd	Retired (or RD)
RTR	Royal Tank Regiment
SA	South Atlantic
SAAF	South African Air Force
SAWAS	South African Women"s Auxiliary Service
SNOL	Senior Naval Officer Landings
SOE	Senior Officer Escort
STO	Sea Transport Officer
UDF	Union Defence Force (of South Africa)
VA	Vice Admiral (or Virginia in United States)
VCNS	Vice Chief of Naval Staff
WA	Western Approaches or West Africa
W/T	Wireless Telegraphy (i.e. Morse)

The customary nautical reference to the general direction of wind or swell is used throughout, i.e. NW for Northwest, SE - Southeast, etc.

APPENDIX I

BRITISH & DOMINION PASSENGER SHIPS 1939

Trade Route	Ships	Gross Tons	Passenger Capacity
North Atlantic	38	864,427	56,420
Australia & New Zealand	40	683,867	27,810
South America & West Indies	33	485,300	15,511
South, West & East Africa	39	482,486	15,271
Near & Far East	47	494,785	11,442
Pacific & Indian Ocean Cross Trades	42	336,461	10,912
Total Build Ocean-Going	239	3,347,326	137,366
Government owned	9	92,124	13,864
Australian owned	23	149,859	6,216
Canadian owned	23	122,773	14,662
New Zealand owned	8	76,843	5,046
Total British & Dominion	302	3,788,925	177,154
Short-sea/Cross Channel	72	191,058	94,522
Total Passenger Ships	374	3,979,983	271,676

APPENDIX II

Mercantile Convoy
Direction of Advance

CONVOY........

Port **Cruising order** **Starboard**

Column No.	1	2	3	4	5	6
Ship Number Name						
Ship Number Name						
Ship Number Name						
Ship Number Name						
Ship Number Name						

APPENDIX III

PERSONNEL EMBARKED FROM U.K. IN WS CONVOYS

Convoy	Sailed UK	Transports	MT	Total Ships	Gross Tonnage Transports	Speed Slowest Ship	Personnel Embarked (10)	Days to Suez	Landed in M.E. (11)
WS 1	29.6.40	3	-	31	61,299	22	11,500	*55	8,280
RS 5	24.7.40	1	1	2	17,702	15.5	2,000	42	2,000
WS 2	5. 8.40	12	5	17	259,280	14	24,450	42	17,000
AP 1	22. 8.40	1	3	5(1)	20,123	16.5	2,000	32	2,000
AP 3	10. 9.40	4	5	10(2)	97,050	14	6,050	42	5,582
WS 3S	3.10.40	2	4	6	28,252	14.5	3,086	44	3,086
WS 3F	7.10.40	7	-	71	57,358	17.5	13,000	40	9,000
WS 4A	1.11.40	4	8	16(3)	75,001	11	5,500	51	4,852
WS 4B	17.11.40	10	-	10	216,422	17	24,200	41	24,200
WS 5A	17.12.40	10	12	28(4)	108,038	11.5	13,811	61	12,201
WS 5B	12.1.41	20	-	21(5)	398,291	15	37,267	50	28,894
WS 6	7.2.41	16	17	33	182,871	8.5	22,875	73	22,400
WS 6B	17.2.41	2	1	5(6)	38,859	11.5	2,500	62	5,400
WS 7	24.3.41	21	2	23(7)	457,751	16	52,640	43	33,093
WS 8A	26.4.41	8	7	15	135,053	15	17,000	48	17,000
HP	6.5.41	1	1	2	14,133	15	1,200	64	11,978
WS 8B	22.5.41	6	1	7	95,126	13.5	15,078	47	1,042
WS 8X	31.5.41	1	2	3	20,123	16.5	(8)	45	3,100
WS 9A	3.6.41	10	5	15	183,810	13.5	20,819	61	15,239
WS 9B	28.6.41	9	3	13(9)	140,980	12.5	15,454	55	12,469
WS 10	2.8.41	14	5	19	252,500	13	32,000	58	18,654
WS 10X	16.8.41	3	3	6	69,082	14	10,004	46	9,900
WS 11	30.8.41	10	8	18	179,388	14	24,430	55	6,569
WS 12	30.9.41	15	5	20	248,830	14	32,576	67	21,022
WS 12X	30.10.41	8	-	8	155,529	15.5	19,534	-	-
WS 12Z	12.11.41	10	5	15	193,628	14	21,767	60	8,077

Convoy	Sailed UK	Transports	MT	Total Ships	Gross Tonnage Transports	Speed Slowest Ship	Personnel Embarked (10)	Days to Suez	Landed in M.E. (11)
WS 14	9.12.41	16	11	27	305,391	15	38,148	66	17,369
WS 15	11.1.42	15	7	22	281,702	13.5	37,843	54	15,654
WS 16	16.2.42	14	7	21	234,217	14	45,340	54	25,766
WS 17	23.3.42	22	9	31	360,677	14	59,230	60	9,600
WS 18	15.4.42	15	5	20	274,515	14	44,874	50	20,281
WS 19	10.5.42	13	3	16	234,099	15	41,541	56	24,792
WS 19W	22.5.42	1	-	1	81,2352	8	9,537	31	9,537
WS 19P	31.5.42	19	4	23	342,358	14.5	60,703	50	37,857
WS 19Y	17.6.42	1	-	1	83,673	28	10,718	31	10,718
WS 20	21.6.42	19	2	21	313,832	14.5	57,094	51	26,843
WS 21P	18.7.42	5	-	5	105,356	17	19,284	48	19,284
WS 21	30.7.42	10	2	12	155,697	14	28,290	53	14,226
WS 22	28.8.42	18	2	20	296,180	14	50,770	55	8,522
WS 23	30.9.42	5	5	10	72,142	15	11,715	57	1,642
WS 24	29.10.42	6	1	7	118,224	14.5	18,213	68	7,755
WS 25	18.12.42	7	2	9	121,955	14	21,304	43	6,000
WS 25W	23.12.42	1	-	1	81,235	28	10,669	26	10,669
WS 26	24.1.43	15	3	18	269,847	14	48,813	55	20,686
WS 27	24.2.43	6	-	6	110,670	14	18,749	51	13,000
WS 28	16.3.43	14	3	17	219,240	15	36,089	50	31,039
WS 29	15.4.43	6	7	13	108,914	15.5	19,069	58	7,459
WS 30	19.5.43	5	2	7	57,529	14.5	10,938	52	2,444
WS 31	19.6.43	4	3	7	69,065	14	14,432	85	4,763
FAITH	8.7.43	2	1	3	36,813	15	1,056	SUNK	
WS 32	19.7.43	5	3	8	80,183	14	12,012	74	6,779
WS 33	16.8.43	6	-	6	81,611	14	15,838	-	4,000 *(12)*
Totals									
52		456	185				1,173,010		659,723 (56%)

*   Via Ceylon and India
(1)   Includes one transport for Gibraltar.

(2)	Includes *Ulster Prince* for Middle East
(3)	Includes four commercial passenger ships
(4)	Includes five storeships for Piraeus and Med. and HMS *Atreus* for East Indies
(5)	Includes one transport for Halifax.
(6)	Includes two transports returned from WS 6
(7)	One transport returned to sail in WS 8A
(8)	Included under WS 8B
(9)	Includes one passenger ship
(10)	Refers to Table in Appendix IV
(11)	These figures are based on known transhipments but can only be regarded as approximate.
(12)	Embarked in West Africa

APPENDIX IV

**PERSONNEL NUMBERS EMBARKED ON WS CONVOYS
IN EACH HALF-YEAR PERIOD
JUNE 1940 - JULY 1943**

Period	Number of Convoys	Number of Transports	Personnel embarked from UK	Average per Ship	Landed in Middle East
June - Dec 1940	10	54	105,597	1,956	88,201
Jan - June 1941	10	93	184,833	1,989	150,615
July - Dec 1941	7	76	178,459	2,348	81,591
Jan - June 1942	9	119	366.880	3,076	181,048
July - Dec 1942	7	51	160,245	3,142	68,098
Jan - Dec 1943	9	63	176,996	2,810	89,726
Totals	52	456	1,173,010	2,572	659,179

Two sets of figures for the numbers embarked on Convoys WS 10 to 24 inclusive are quoted in Behrens p.244, one set for the MOWT and the other from the War Office. The numbers given for the remaining convoys have been extracted from various sources and where none was found, the stated capacity of the ships involved has been used to determine the totals.

APPENDIX V

WS CONVOYS - U.K. PORTS OF EMBARKATION

Convoy	Transports	Liverpool	Clyde Anchorage	Glasgow	Bristol Channel	Totals
WS 1	3	6,350	5,150		*(1)*	11,500
RS 5	1	2,000				2,000
WS 2	12	17,050	2,900	4,500		24,450
AP 1	1	2,000				2,000
AP 3	4	6,050				6,050
WS 3S	2	3,086				3,086
WS 3F	7	6,500	3,200	3,300		13,000
WS 4A	4	2,852		2,648		5,500
WS 4B	10	14,850	3,050	6,300		24,200
WS 5A	10	6,162	3,429	3,090	1,130 A	13,811
WS 5B	20	13,191	7,824	11,379	2,783 N	
					2,090 A	37,267
WS 6	16	7,200	8,875	5,750	1,050 A	22,875
WS 6B	2		2,500			2,500
WS 7	21	22,987	14,400	9,840	5,413 A	52,640
WS 8A	8	10,300	1,500	5,200		17,000
HP	1	1,200				1,200
WS 8B	6		9,969	5,109		15,078
WS 8X	1					*(2)*
WS 9A	10	5,515	8,551	6,753		20,819
WS 9B	9	7,105	4,249	1,450	1,450 A	
					1,200 N	15,454
WS 10	14	13,207	17,014		1,779 A	32,000
WS 10X	3	3,198		3,586	3,220 A	10,004
WS 11	10	13,959	3,994	6,477		24,430
WS 12	15	12,302	13,945	5,104	1,225 A	32,576
WS 12X	8	10,271	6,187		3,076 A	19,534
WS 12Z	10	13,126	2,844	5,797		21,767
WS 14	16	16,684	10,374	8,112	2,978 A	38,148
WS 15	15	20,862	5,749	10,319	913 MT	37,843
WS 16	14	22,060	11,572	11,708		45,340
WS 17	22	30,942	9,043	17,485	1,760 A	59,230
WS 18	15	24,312	7,181	9,597	3,784 A	44,874

Convoy	Transports	Liverpool	Clyde Anchorage	Glasgow Channel	Bristol	Totals
WS 19	13	19,731	4,500	12,386	1,883 A	
					3,041 *(3)*	41,541
WS 19W	1		9,537			9,537
WS 19P	19	21,215	17,588	16,006	2,181 A	
					3,713 N *(4)*	60,703
WS 19Y	1		10,718			10,718
WS 20	19	28,776	9,712	11,677	6,852 A	
					77 MT	57,094
WS 21P	5	6,498		12,786		19,284
WS 21	10	15,606	7,021	4,806	785 AMC	
					72 MT	28,290
WS 22	18	24,136	14,185	8,797	3,652 A	50,770
WS 23	4	9,779			1,918 AMC	
					18 MT	11,715
WS 24	6	8,769		4,306	5,138 A	18,213
WS 25	7	9,716	6,837		3,827 A	
					915 AMC	
					9 MT	21,304
WS 25W	1		10,669			10,669
WS 26	15	20,767	11,543	12,198	4,305 A	48,813
WS 27	6	11,669	4,190	2,890 *(5)*		18,749
WS 28	14	21,107	14,982			36,089
WS 29	6	9,972		5,284	3,813 A	19,069
WS 30	5		7,238	1,803	1,897 A	10,938
WS 31	4	2,598	11,834			14,432
FAITH	2			1,056		1,056
WS 32	5	6,867	1,902		3,243 A	12,012
WS 33	6		8,138	7,700		15,838
Totals		532,527	314,094	245,199	81,190*(6)*	1,173,010

(1)   A refers to Avonmouth and N for Newport.
(2)   Included in WS 8B.
(3)   Embarked in Iceland.
(4)   Plus 245 on HMS *Nelson* for WA and 47 on MT ships.
(5)   Plus 1850 for *Antenor* included in WS 26.
(6)   Avonmouth 65,746; Newport 7,696; embarked on AMCs 3618; MT 1089 and on US ships from Iceland 3041.

APPENDIX VI

BRITISH OPERATED WS CLASS TROOPSHIPS
JUNE 1940 - AUGUST 1943

Name	Grt	Spd	Passenger Capacity 1939	Full Requisition	Capacity 1943	Remarks
Queen Elizabeth	83,673	28	2,283	24.09.40	12,468	
Queen Mary	80,774	28	2,139	06.03.40	11,509	
Aquitania	44,786	22	1,725	21.11.39	7,200	
Ile de France	43,450	23	1,645	08.11.40	9,600	
Empress of Britain	42,348	23	1,153	21.11.39	8,000	Sunk 28.10.40
Nieuw Amsterdam	36,287	20	1,203	14.10.40	7,823	
Mauretania	35,739	22	1,378	06.03.40	6,500	
Pasteur	29,253	23	751	20.08.40	4,500	
Georgic	27,759	18	1,604	13.04.40	5,000	CTL 14.07.41
Dominion Monarch	27,155	19	517	25.11.40	3,781	
Capetown Castle	27,002	18	800	12.11.40	4,236	
Britannic	26,943	18	1,542	24.08.40	5,050	
Empress of Japan	26,032	21	1,115	26.11.39	4,337	
Andes	25,689	21	520	26.11.39	4,100	
Athlone Castle	25,564	18	780	03.07.40	4,711	
Stirling Castle	25,550	19	790	14.10.40	4,332	
Strathallan	23,722	18	986	14.10.40	4,632	Sunk 21.12.42
Stratheden	23,722	18	980	14.10.40	4,643	
Orcades	23,456	19	1,140	14.10.40	5,000	Sunk 10.10.42
Strathmore	23,428	19	984	30.07.40	4,763	
Orion	23,371	19	1,139	29.11.39	5,449	
Monarch of Bermuda	22,424	18	860	22.11.39	3,433	
Strathnaver	22,283	18	1,166	27.10.40	4,293	
Strathaird	22,281	18	1,166	29.08.39	4,190	
Empress of Australia	21,833	18	1,139	11.09.39	3,789	
Empress of Canada	21,517	18	1,770	29.11.39	3,929	Sunk 13.03.43
Mooltan	20,952	15	656	04.02.41	4,311	ex AMC
Maloja	20,914	15	656	06.11.41	4,305	ex AMC
Franconia	20,341	16	1,650	12.09.39	4,162	
Duchess of Bedford	20,123	17	1,559	10.08.40	4,000	
Duchess of Atholl	20,119	17	1,559	30.10.40	4,114	
Warwick Castle	20,107	18	699	14.10.40	3,271	Sunk 14.11.42
Orontes	20,097	18	991	14.09.40	3,940	
Orford	20,043	19	991	21.11.39	4,300	Sunk 02.06.40
Oronsay	20,043	18	1,836	09.04.40	4,335	Sunk 09.10.42
Otranto	20,026	17	1,836	21.11.39	4,831	
Duchess of Richmond	20,022	18	1,559	12.11.40	4,112	
Duchess of York	20,021	18	1,559	04.09.40	4,208	Sunk 11.07.43

Name	Grt	Spd	Passenger Capacity 1939	Full Requisition	Capacity 1943	Remarks
Winchester Castle	20,012	18	699	12.11.40	3,790	
Orama	19,840	18	1,836	28.05.40	4,300	Sunk 08.06.40
Scythia	19,761	16	1,768	23.10.40	4,160	
Laconia	19,695	16	1,768	26.09.41	3,728	Ex AMC Sunk 12.9.42
Viceroy of India	19,627	17	415	04.11.40	3,512	Sunk 11.11.42
Samaria	19,597	16	1,768	12.12.40	4,086	
Marnix van St Aldegonde	19,355	16	683	07.05.41	3,557	Sunk 07.11.43
J.V.Oldenbarnevelt	19,429	16	683	13.01.41	3,694	
Windsor Castle	19,191	19	604	30.10.40	2,510	Sunk 23.03.43
Arundel Castle	19,118	19	580	23.12.40	2,965	
Oslofjord	18,650	17	1,000	23.10.40	3,000	Sunk 01.12.40
Reina del Pacifico	17,702	19	888	29.08.39	3,130	
Aorangi	17,491	15	970	18.07.41	3,090	
Durban Castle	17,388	17	540	24.08.40	2,573	
Felix Roussel	17,083	17	1,198	12.09.40	3,165	
Dempo	17,024	16	623	10.01.41	2,550	Sunk 17.03.44
Nea Hellas	16,991	15	1,982	26.11.40	4,023	
Empress of Asia	16,909	15	1,180	02.12.40	2,600	Sunk 05.02.42
Empress of Russia	16,810	16	1,180	28.11.40	2,630	
California	16,792	16	1,131	09.04.42	4,167	ex AMC Sunk 11.7.43
Rangitata	16,737	14	419	21.12.40	2,618	
Rangitiki	16,698	14	419	13.11.40	2,598	
Narkunda	16,632	15	674	19.04.41	2,752	Sunk 14.11.42
Westernland	16.479	15	550	09.07.40	2,500	Released 3.1.43 Repair Ship
Pennland	16,381	15	550	01.08.40	2,500	Sunk 25.04.41
Cameronia	16,297	15	1,419	12.11.40	3,849	
Christiaan Huygens	16,287	16	600	06.08.40	2,683	Sunk 26.08.45
Lancastria	16,243	15	1,580	15.04.40	3,600	Sunk 17.06.40
Almanzora	15,551	15	1,390	01.11.40	2,890	
Orduna	15,507	14	878	14.03.41	2,912	
Arandora Star	15,500	16	400	15.05.40	2,500	Sunk 02.07.40
Orbita	15,495	14	878	12.11.40	2,871	
Volendam	15,434	14	1,175	10.05.41	2,797	
Cathay	15,225	15	335	10.11.41	3,713	ex AMC Sunk 11.11.42
Dunnottar Castle	15,007	16	484	27.07.42	2,763	ex AMC
Ormonde	14,952	16	777	28.05.40	3,700	
Arawa	14,491	15	292	28.08.41	1,600	ex AMC
Pilsudski	14,294	17	759	21.11.39	2,000	Sunk 26.11.39
Batory	14,287	17	759	30.11.39	2,142	

Name	Grt	Spd	Passenger Capacity 1939	Full Requisition	Capacity 1943	Remarks
Esperance Bay	14,204	15	512	08.09.41	1,805	ex AMC
Moreton Bay	14,193	15	540	10.09.41	1,825	ex AMC
Largs Bay	14,182	14	550	02.08.41	1,723	
Ruys	14,155	16	430	24.04.42	3,127	
Tegelberg	14,150	16	433	30.07.42	2,755	
Highland Monarch	14,139	15	528	29.10.40	1,883	
Highland Chieftain	14,135	15	528	04.11.40	1,902	
Highland Brigade	14,134	15	528	01.10.40	1,882	
Boissievain	14,134	16	435	25.03.42	3,209	
Highland Princess	14,133	15	528	04.11.40	1,930	
Oropesa	14,118	15	632	14.09.40	2,500	Sunk 16.01.41
Ascania	14,013	15	1,700	21.09.42	2,358	ex AMC
Empire Trooper	13,994	14	1,131	04.12.40	3,083	
Antonia	13,867	15	1647	12.10.40	2,500	Released 10.11.40 Conv. Fleet Repair Ship
Letitia	13,595	15	1,306	28.11.41	2,232	ex AMC
Awatea	13,482	21	430	04.09.41	2,485	Sunk 11.11.42
Tamaroa	12,405	14	130	19.11.40	1,755	
Mataroa	12,390	14	130	04.12.40	1,897	
Sibajak	12,226	16	450	18.04.41	2,444	
Llangibby Castle	11,951	15	450	12.11.40	2,000	
President Doumer	11,892	16	270	02.08.40	2,000	Sunk 30.10.42
Derbyshire	11,660	15	275	14.03.42	3,085	ex AMC
Slamat	11,636	17	400	06.08.40	2,500	Sunk 27.04.41
Northumberland	11,588	13	-	13.12.40	1,650	Reverted cargo 27.12.41
Leopoldville	11,509	15	500	01.10.40	2,248	Sunk 24.12.44
Cuba	11,420	15	448	25.05.41	2,253	Sunk 06.04.45
Llanstephan Castle	11,348	13	429	06.01.41	2,000	
Abosso	11,330	14	550	24.08.41	2,039	Sunk 30.10.42
Antenor	11,174	15	135	21.10.41	1,864	ex AMC
Circassia	11,136	16	300	06.03.42	2,509	ex AMC
City of Benares	11,081	15	219	10.09.40	2,500	Sunk 17.09.40
Nieuw Zeeland	11,069	15	155	07.08.40	2,000	Sunk 11.11.42
Nieuw Holland	11,066	15	155	06.08.40	2,004	
Sobieski	11,030	16	904	23.11.39	2,105	
Chrobry	11.030	16	904	05.10.39	2,100	Sunk 15.05.40
Bergensfjord	11,012	15	745	11.11.40	2,559	
Indrapoera	10,825	14	393	07.08.40	2,004	
Staffordshire	10,683	14	273	30.05.41	2,181	
Johan de Witt	10,474	15	353	06.08.40	1,915	

Name	Grt	Spd	Passenger Capacity 1939	Full Requisition	Capacity 1943	Remarks
Karanja	9,891	16	240	29.03.40	1,158	HMS from 23.07.41. Sunk 12.11.42
Kenya	9,890	16	240	23.05.40	1,158	HMS *Keren* from 23.07.41
Banfora	9,472	14	307	04.07.41	2,303	
Empire Pride	9,248	16	-	14.05.41	2,506	
Empire Woodlark	7,793	14	500	19.05.41	1,700	
Anselm	5,954	13	290	08.11.40	1,500	Sunk 05.07.41

Note:The table includes those liners suitable for inclusion in WS convoys although lost by enemy action prior to service on the route. It excludes those of the Indian Ocean type used for a single positioning voyage to that zone.

*The column of troop capacities are those stated by the MOWT in mid 1943 and in the case of ships lost before that date, the capacities are those that would have been reached by that time.

APPENDIX VII

MAPS

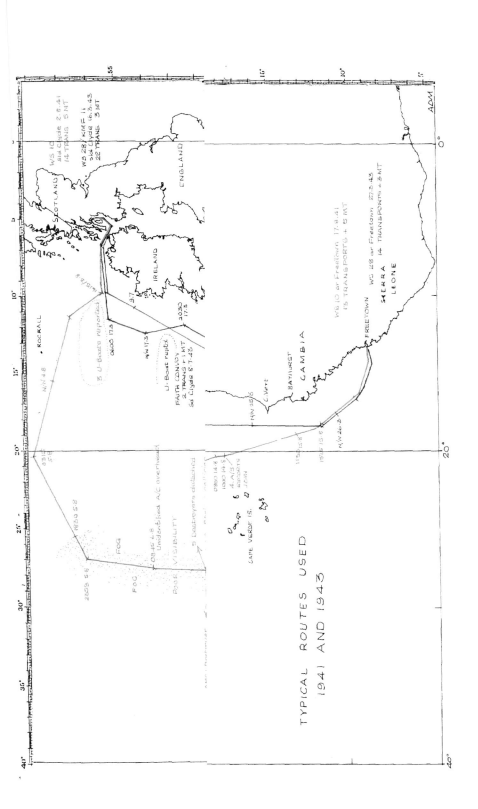

TYPICAL ROUTES USED
1941 AND 1943

ADM

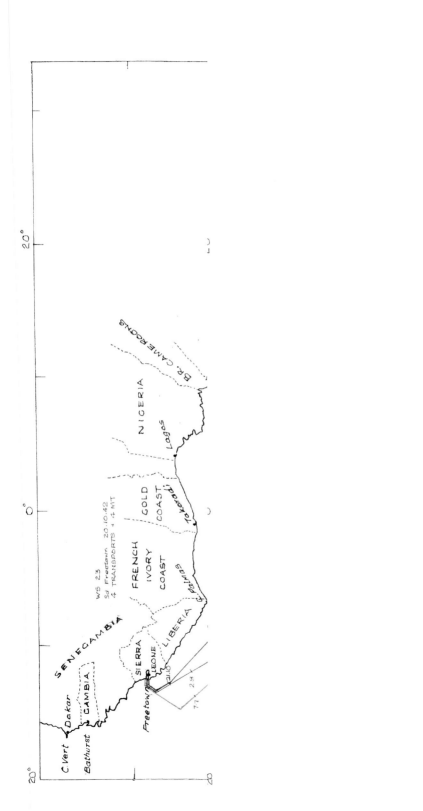

C.Vert
Dakar

SENEGAMBIA

Bathurst

GAMBIA

SIERRA
LEONE
Freetown

WS 23
Sd Freetown 20.10.42
4 TRANSPORTS + 4 MT

LIBERIA

FRENCH
IVORY
COAST

C Palmas

GOLD
COAST

Takoradi

NIGERIA

Lagos

Br.N. CAMEROONS

20°

0°

20°

21.10

23

21

20°

0°

20°

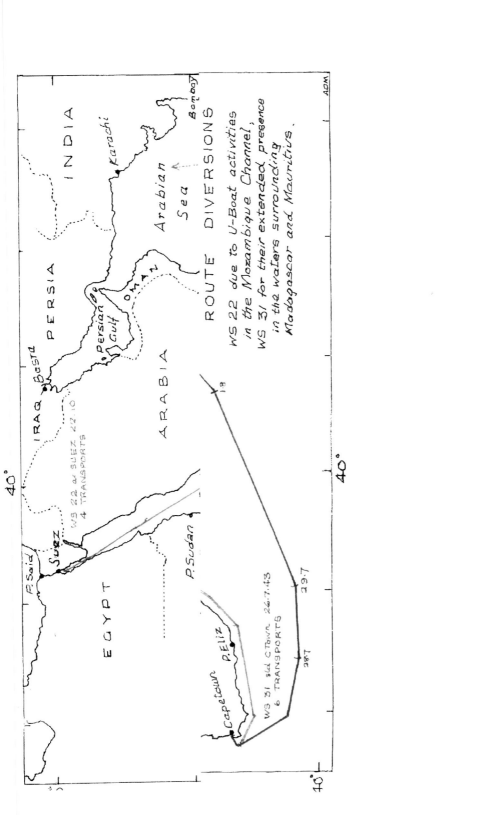

ROUTE DIVERSIONS

WS 22 due to U-Boat activities in the Mozambique Channel,
WS 31 for their extended presence in the waters surrounding Madagascar and Mauritius.

INDIA

Karachi

Bombay

Arabian Sea

PERSIA

OMAN

Persian Gulf

Basra

IRAQ

WS 22 or SUEZ 22.10
4 TRANSPORTS

ARABIA

P. Said

Suez

EGYPT

P. Sudan

Capetown

P. Eliz.

WS 31 sld C.Town 26.7.43
6 TRANSPORTS

18

29.7

28.7

40°

40°

AOM

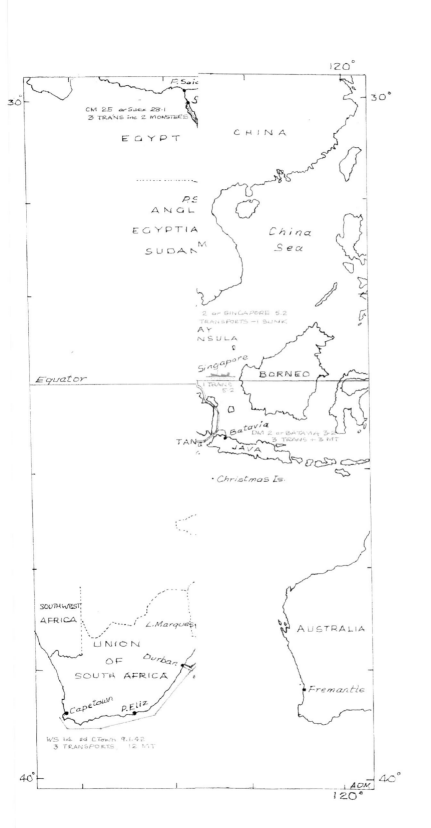

120°

30°   30°

P. Said

CM 25 or Suez 28·1
3 TRANS inc 2 MONSTERS

EGYPT   CHINA

P.S.
ANGL
EGYPTIA
SUDAN M   China
                 Sea

2 or SINGAPORE 5.2
TRANSPORTS —1 SUNK
AY
NSULA

Singapore   BORNEO

Equator

1 TRANS
5.2

Batavia   DM 2 or BATAVIA 3·2
TAN   3 TRANS + 3 MT
     JAVA

· Christmas Is.

SOUTHWEST
AFRICA   L.Marques

UNION   AUSTRALIA
OF   Durban
SOUTH AFRICA

Capetown   P.Eliz   · Fremantle

WS 14 ed CTown 9.1.42
3 TRANSPORTS, 12 MT

40°   ADM   40°
120°

Index

With innumerable references to ships or units in any one chapter or page, it proved unwieldy to provide an index based simply on page numbers. The complete lack of an index would be inexcusable, so a compromise was reached by referring names to convoy numbers with their respective chapters in brackets. It should be noted, however, that such reference to a convoy number does not necessarily mean that a ship or person joined that convoy at the outset, or even at intermediate ports along the way. The actual composition of each convoy will be found in the comprehensive chapter notes, where the first of the two figures bracketed after each ship's name, indicates the column number (from port or left) while the second figure shows the position in each column reading from the front, as shown by plan in Appendix II.

Capetown BM1(4) WS5A(6) US9.5(6)
WS24A(17)
Carlisle SW2(4) AP3(4) SW2A(4) WS3(5)
  WS4A(5) WS4B(5) BS11.25(5) SW4B(5)
  WS18(14)
Carnarvon Castle AP3(4) WS4A(5) WS7(8)
  WS10(11) WS19(15) WS19P(15)
  WS20(16) WS21P(16) WS25(18)
  WS30(20)
Carnatic(RIN) WS26(18)
Carthage RS5(4) SW2(4) AP3(4) WS3(5)
  WS7(8) CM11(8) SW10(11) WS22(17)
  WS23(!7) WS27(19)
Castleton WS9B(10) WS19(15)
Cathay SL59(6) WS6(7) WS9B(10)
  WS12(12)
Catterick WS21(16) WS26(18) WS27(19)
  WS30(20)
Centurion WS8B(9)
Ceres WS2(4) AP3(4) SW4B(5) WS5A(6)
  SW6(7) SW7(8) WS10X(11) WS11(12)
  WS12(12) WS14(13) WS24A(17)
  WS26(18)
Chakdina RS5(4)
Challenger WS9B(10)
Chanticleer WS33(21)
Charybdis WS29(19) WS32(21) WS33(21)
Cheshire WS3(5) CF2(9) CF2(12) WS15(13)
  WS16(14) WS19(15) WS19P(15)
  WS25(!8)
Chesterfield WS22(17)
Chitral WS9B(10) WS19P(15) WS24A(17)
  WS28(19) WS29(19) WS33(21)
Churchill WS5B(6) WS19(15)
Cilicia AP3(4) WS6(7)   CF2(9)-(10)
  WS14(13) WS19P(15) WS20(16)
  WS25(18) WS26(18)
Cimarron(US) WS12X(12)
Clare WS27(19)
Clematis WS5A(6) HP(9)
Cleveland WS30(20)
Clover WS12Z(12)
Colombia(Du) WS15(13)
Colombo WS7(8) SW7(8) WS12Z(12)
  WS15(13) WS16(14)
Comm. Domine(Fr) WS14(13)
Comm.Duboc(Fr) WS21P(16) WS26(18)
Corfu WS5B(6) WS14(13) WS14B(13)
  WS15(13) WS17(14) WS19(15)
  WS21(16) CF5(16) WS30(20) WS31(20)
Corinthian WS9B(10) WS21P(16) WS26(18)
Cornwall GC1(2) CM(3) BC(3) WS2(4)
  WS4A(5)   WS5B(6) WS6(7) WS12Z(12)
Cossack WS8B(9) WS9A(10)

Coventry WS2(4) AP1(4)
Crocus WS25(18) WS26(18) WS27(19)
Croome WS16(14) WS17(14)
Cumberland US3(3) WS1(4) WS3(5)
  WS4B(5)
Curacao WS21(16) WS25W(18)
Cyclamen WS10(11)

D'Est D'Orves(Fr) WS26(18)
Danae BM12(13)
Dauntless WS17(14) WS23(17)
De Ruyter(Du) DM1(12)
Delhi WS19Y(15)
Demirhisar(Tuk) WS15(13)
Derbyshire WS11(12) WS12(12) WS14(13)
Derg WS32(21)
Derwent WS19P(15) WS22(17)
Despatch WS23(17) WS24(17) WS31(20)
Devonshire WS4B(5) WS5A(6) WS12(12)
  WS12X(12) BM12(13) WS20(16)
  WS17(14) WS19(15) WS19P(15)
  WS19W(15) WS22(17) WS23(17)
Dorsetshire US3(3) WS2(4) WS3(5)
  WS5B(6) WS6(7) WS10X(11)
  WS12X(12) WS14(13)
Douglas WS3(5) WS19W(15) WS19P(15)
  WS28(19) Faith(20) WS32(21) WS33(21)
Douro(Por) WS15(13)
Dragon BC(3) WS2(4) WS12V(12)
  BM11(12) BM12(13)
Duke of York WS6(8) WS21(16)
Dulverton WS12Z(12)
Duncan WS7(8) WS8B(9) WS16(14)
Dunedin WS5A(6)
Dunkerque(Fr) TC2(2)
Dunnottar Castle WS9A(10) WS10X(11)
  WS12(12) WS15(13) WS16(14)
  WS18(14)
Durban WS5B(6) WS9AX(10) DM1(12)
  BM11(12) BM12(13) WS16(14)
  WS23(17) WS27(19) CM45(21)

Eagle GC1(2) US1(2) WS16(14)
Eclipse WS7(8)
Edinburgh WS4B(5) WS7(8) WS9B(10)
  WS10(11)
Effingham Nor(3)
Eggesford WS28(19)
Egret GC1(2) WS27(19) WS32(21)
Emerald TC1(2) WS2(4) WS5B(6) WS10(11)
  WS12Z(12) DM1(12) DM2(13)
  WS18(14) WS19(15) WS32(21)
Encounter WS11(12) CM25(13)
Engadine WS14(13)

Laforey WS16(14) WS17(14) WS22(17)
Lamerton WS15(13)
Lancaster WS18(14)
Lance WS10(11) WS10X(11)
Largs WS28(19)
Lauderdale WS18(14) WS29(19)
Laurentic WS4A(5)
Lavender WS9B(10)
Leamington WS17(14) WS19(15)
   WS19Y(15)
Leander US1(2) US3(3) BN3(4)
Ledbury WS21(16) WS31(20)
Legion WS8X(9) WS10(11)
Leopard(Fr) WS5B(6)
Lewes WS29A(19)
Lightning WS16(14)
Lincoln WS5B(6)
Liverpool GC1(2) US2(2)
London WS8X(9) WS10(11)
Lookout WS17(14) WS22(17)
Louisbourg WS24(17)
Lowestoft KMF15(20)

Malaya TC3(2) WS16(14) WS17(14)
   WS18(14) WS20(16) WS27(19)
   WS31(20)
Malcolm WS28(19) WS29(19)
Maloja K6(2) RS5(4)
Malvernian WS8X(9)
Manchester Heron(2) K4(2) NP1(3)
Manoora BM1(4)
Mansfield WS19P(15)
Maori WS8B(9) WS9A(10) WS9B(10)
   WS12Z(12)
Margeurite WS8B(9)
Mauritius WS6(7) WS8A(9) WS9AX(10)
   WS11X(12) WS19P(15) WS19(15)
   WS19W(15) WS23(17) WS24B(17)
Mendip WS31(20)
Miaoulis(Gk) WS26(18)
Milford WS5A(6) WS12Z(12) WS15(13)
   WS16(14) WS17(14) WS19(15)
   WS23(17)
Monowai WS8A(9) – (10)
Moreton Bay HP(9) WS9B(10)
Mourne WS31(20)
Moyola Faith(20)

Naiad WS5A(6) WS5B(6) WS8A(9)
Napier WS6(7) WS27(19) WS28(19)
   CM45(21)
Narbada WS33(21)
Nelson WS1(4) WS7(8) WS19P(15)
Nepal WS21P(16) WS24(17) CM45(21)

Neptune WS8X(9)
Ness WS29(19) KMF15(20) WS32(21)
   WS33(21)
Nestor WS11(12) WS14(13)
New Mexico(US) CT5(12)
Newark WS12X(12)
Newcastle WS7(8) CF2(9) WS16(14)
   WS29(19)
Newfoundland WS28(19)
Newport WS17(14)
Nigella WS16(14) WS26(18)
Nizam WS30(20)
Norfolk WS4B(5) WS8X(9)
Norman WS15(13) WS23(17) WS24(17)
   WS29(19) WS30(20) WS32(21)

Offa WS24(17)
Onslow WS24(17)
Oribi WS24(17)
Orion WS20(16)
Ottawa WS3(5) WS4A(5) WS6(7) HP(9)
   WS8B(9) WS9A(10)

Pakenham WS17(14)
Paladin WS16(14)
Panther WS16(14)
Partridge WS22(17)
Pathfinder WS19P(15)
Patroclus WS4A(5)
PC74 WS21(16) WS32(21)
Pelican WS32(21)
Penn WS19P(15)
Perth WS4A(5)
Petard WS21(16)
Petunia WS9B(10) WS18(14) WS26(18)
   WS27(19)
Philadelphia(US) CT5(12)
Phoebe WS5B(6) WS6(7) WS23(17)
Pintos(Gk) WS22(17)
Piorun(Pol) WS8B(9) WS8X(9) WS9B(10)
   WS10(11) WS10X(11)
Plymm WS33(21)
Pretoria Castle CM(3) WS4A(5) WS8A(9)
Prince David CF2(9)
Prince of Wales WS11(12) WS12(12)
   WS12X(12)
Prince Robert WS8A(9)
Puckeridge WS23(17)

Quadrant WS26(18) WS27(19) WS28(19)
   WS29(19) WS30(20) WS31(20)
   CM45(21)
Quail WS27(19)
Quality WS26(18)

Trent WS33(21)
Tynwald WS19(15)

Uganda WS31(20)
Ulster Monarch WS12(13) WS28(19)
Ulster Queen WS14(13)
Unicorn WS30(20)
Usk WS33(21)

Valiant TC3(2) AP1(4)
Vampire BM12(13)
Van Galen(Du) WS18(14)
Vanoc WS15(13)
Vanquisher WS9B(10) WS12Z(12) WS15(13)
Vansittart WS9B(10) WS10(11) WS15(13)
    WS20(16)
Velox WS5B(6) WS8X(9) WS9A(10)
    WS9B(10) WS10(11) WS12Z(12)
    WS19(15) WS19P(15) WS20(16)
    WS23(17)
Venomous WS29(19)
Verity WS3(5) WS15(13) WS16(14)
Veteran WS8A(9)
Viceroy WS31(20)
Victorious WS5B(6) WS8B(9) WS8X(9)
    WS25(18)
Vidette WS6(7) WS7(8)
Vimy WS12Z(12) WS15(13) WS20(16)
    WS21P(16) WS21(16)
Vincennes(US) WS12X(12)
Vindictive WS19P(15) WS21(16) WS22(17)
Viscount WS17(14)
Volunteer WS15(13) WS17(14) WS18(14)
    WS19(15)

Walker WS15(13) WS16(14)
Wallace WS31(20)
Wanderer HP(9)
Warspite TC1(2) East Africa(16) WS30(20)
    WS31(20)
Wasp(US) WS18(14)
Wayland WS26(18)
Wear WS32(21)
Wellington WS5A(6) WS29(19) KMF15(20)
Wells WS9B(10)
Westcott US1(2)
Weston WS29(19) KMF15(20) WS33(21)
Westralia BM1(4)
Whaddon WS28(19)
Whitehall WS3(5) WS10(11) WS10X(11)
Wild Swan WS9B(10) WS16(14) WS17(14)
    WS18(14) WS19P(15)
Wilton WS21(16)
Winchelsea WS9B(10) WS10(11)

Wishart WS7(8)
Witch WS5A(6) WS10(11) WS10X(11)
    WS28(19) WS29(19) WS30(20)
    WS31(20)
Witherington WS5B(6) WS15(13) WS16(14)
    WS31(20)
Wivern WS9B(10) WS18(14) WS19P(15)
    WS20(16)
Wolfe AP3(4)
Wolverine Nor(3) WS9B(10) WS20(16)
    WS25(18) WS27(19) WS28(19)
    WS29(19) WS30(20) WS31(20)
    WS32(21) WS33(21)
Woodpecker WS28(19)
Woodruff WS25(18)
Woolston WS31(20)
Woolwich WS3(5)
Worcestershire WS10(11) WS15(13)
    WS16(14) WS18(14) CM31(16)
    WS20(16)
Wren WS28(19)
Wrestler WS10(11) WS11(12) WS23(17)
    WS33(21)

Yarra BM12(13)
York AP1(4)
Yorktown(US) CT5(12)

Zetland WS22(17) WS23(17)
Zulu WS8B(9) WS9A(10)

Warships (Axis)

Admiral Hipper(Ge) Nor(3) WS5A(6)
    WS6(7)
Admiral Scheer(Ge) SW3(5) WS4A(5)
    WS4B(5) WS5A(6) WS5B(6)
Amaraglio Cagni(It) WS33(21)
Archimedo(It) WS21P(16)
Atlantis(Ge) WS1(4) WS2(4) WS5A(6)
    WS5BB(6) - (10) WS12X(12)

Baden(Ge) WS5A(6)
Bismarck(Ge) WS8B(9)

Charlotte Schliemann(Ge) WS16(14)

Doggerbank(Ge) WS16(14) WS18(14)
    WS23(17)

Eisbar Group(Ge) WS22(17) WS23(17)

Chateau Thierry(US) WS19P(15)
Christiaan Huygens(Du) SW2(4) WS8B(9)
　　WS9A(10) -(11) TC15(12) WS12Z(12)
　　WS15(13) WS19P(15) WS27(19)
　　WS28(19)
Chrobry(Pol) TC2(2) TC3(2) Nor(3)
Circassia WS16(14) WS21(16) CF5(16)
　　KMF8(18) KMF10A(19)
City of Canterbury WS5A(6) WS6(7)
　　WS11(12) WS14(13) WS21(16)
　　WS24B(17) WS26(18)
City of London WS5A(6) WS6(7)
City of Paris WS11(12) WS12(12) WS21(16)
　　WS26(18) WS27(19)
Costa Rica(Du) WS5A(6) WS6(7)
Cristobal(US) WS19P(15) KMF17(20)
Cuba(Fr) WS7(8) WS16(14) WS20(16)
　　KMF11(19) KMF13(19) WS30(20)

Dempo(Du) WS7(8) WS8B(9) WS18(14)
　　WS26(18) WS28(19) KMF20(21)
Devonshire lstCC(2) 2ndCC(2) 3rdCC(2)
　　CM(3) BN3(4) BP15(11) BP-(12)
　　BP-(17) WS26(18) WS28(19)
Dilwara 1stCC(2) 2ndCC(2) 3rdCC(2)
　　CM(3) BN3(4) WS6(7) WS11(12)
　　WS14(13) CM29(15) WS20(16)
　　WS23(17) WS26(18) WS28(19)
Dominion Monarch AP3(4) WS8A(9)
　　WS12(12) WS17(14) NA13(14)
　　WS22(17) WS26(18)
Duchess of Atholl Med(2) Norw(3) WS4B(5)
　　SW4B(5) WS7(8) SW7(8) WS10(11)
　　WS11(12) CT5(12) WS12(12) TC15(12)
　　WS14(13) AT12(13) WS17(14)
　　WS19P(15) WS21P(16) WS22(17)
　　WS26(18)
Duchess of Bedford GC1(2) TC1(2) AP1/2(4)
SW2(4) WS5B(6) WS8B(9) WS8X(9)
CF2(9) WS12Z(12) CF2(12) BM11(12)
　　WS18(14) NA12(14) WS28(19) Faith(20)
　　KMF22(21)
Duchess of Richmond WS4A(5) WS5B(6)
　　WS8B(9) WS9A(10) WS12(12)
　　WS16(14) WS19P(15) WS26(18)
　　W27(19) WS33(21)
Duchess of York Norw(3) Bisc(3) WS3(5)
　　SW3(5) WS5B(6) WS7(8) TC12(11)
　　WS11(12) WS16(14) NA10(14)
　　WS21P(16) KMF8(18) KMF13(19)
　　KMF15(20) Faith(20) WS32(21)
Dunera US1(2) US2(2) WS4A(5) WS8A(9)
　　WS10(11) SW10(11) CM17(11)

　　WS14(13) CM29(15) WS20(16)
　　CM35(17) WS27(19) WS28(19)
Dunnottar Castle WS16(14) KMF8(18)
　　KMF13(19)
Durban Castle GC1(2) AP3(4) WS5B(6)
　　CF2(9) WS9A(10) CT5(12) TC15(12)
　　WS14(13) WS20(16) KMF8(18)
　　KMF12(21)

Eastern Prince WS8B(9) WS9A(10) -(11)
　　WS11(12) WS12Z(12)
Edinburgh Castle WS4B(5)
Egra WS1(4)
Ekma WS1(4) WS22(17) WS24(17)
　　WS25(18)
El Nil WS21(16)
Elisabethville(Be) WS5A(6) WS6(7)
　　WS17B(14) WS21(16)
Ellenga WS2(4) WS11X(12) BP-(17)
Empire Pride WS11(12) WS12(12)
　　WS16(14) WS20(16) KMF8(18)
　　KMF13(19)
Empire Trooper WS5A(6) WS5B(6) -(11)
　　WS19(15) CM30(WS19P)(15) CM35(17)
Empire Woodlark WS10(11) WS15(13)
　　WS18(14) WS19(15) EA(16) CM35(17)
Empress of Asia WS8A(9) WS12Z(12)
　　BM12(13) WS19P(15)
Empress of Australia SO10(2) TC1(2) TC3(2)
　　Norw(3) WS5B(6) US9.5(6) WS7(8)
　　SW7(8) WS11(12) WS14D(13)
　　WS18(14) WS20(16) KMF22(21)
Empress of Britain TC1(2) TC3(2) Norw(3)
　　US3(3) WS2(4) SW1(4)
Empress of Canada US1(2) US3(3) WS2(4)
　　SW1(4) WS4B(5) SW4B(5) WS7(8)
　　TC12(11) WS11(12) WS12(12) NA5(12)
　　WS18(14) WS26(18) WS27(19)
Empress of Japan/Scotland US1(2) US3(3)
　　SW2(4) WS3(5) WS5B(6) WS9A(10)
　　WS12Z(12) BM11(12) WS18(14)
　　NA11(14) WS21P(16) WS24(17)
　　WS33(21)
Empress of Russia WS8A(9) WS12(12)
　　WS17(14) WS20(16) WS23(17)
Erinpura WS1(4) WS3(5) BP-(17)
Esperance Bay WS12(12) WS14(13)
　　WS20(16) WS25(18) WS32(21)
Ethiopia WS1(4) BP-(12)
Ettrick US2(2) Bisc.(3) WS6(7) WS8A(9)
　　WS8C(9) WS10(11)

Felix Roussel BM12(13) WS22(17)

WS5(6) WS5B(6) WS9B(10)-(11)
WS12Z(12) WS16(14) WS19(15)
WS29(19) KMF22(21)
Montcalm GC1(2)
Monterey(US) WS17(14)
Mooltan WS8B(9) WS9A(10) WS11(12)
WS14(13) WS16(14) WS19(15)
WS26(18) KMF20(21)
Moreton Bay WS12(12) CT8(13) (seeWS15)
WS19(15) WS23(17) WS32(21)
Mount Vernon(US) WS12X(12) WS12Z(12)
DM1(12)

Narkunda WS8A(9) WS8C(9) WS10(11)
WS12(12) WS12Z(12) DM1(12)
WS18(14) WS20(16) WS21(16)
Nea Hellas WS5B(6) -(8) WS10(11)
SW10(11) WS16(14) WS21P(16)
WS22(17) KMF11(19) WS29(19)
Faith(20) WS32(21) CM45(21)
Neuralia US2(2) WSA(6) BP15(11)
Nevasa US2(2) BP(12) WS14(13)
Nieuw Amsterdam(Du) WS5B(6) -(9) -
(10) CM15(10) CM18(11) WS12(12
WS12Z(12) WS15(13) WS16(14)
WS17B(14) WS18(14) WS19(15)
WS19P(15) WS20(16) WS22(17)
WS25(18) WS25W(18) WS33(21)
Nieuw Holland(Du) SW2A(4) WS5A(6)
WS5B(6) WS11(12) WS17(14)
WS22(17) KMF10A(19) KMF13(19)
WS30(20) CM45(21)
Nieuw Zeeland(Du) WS9.5(6) HP(9)
WS8B(9) CF2(9) WS11(12) WS18(14)
Northumberland WS6B(7) WS11(12)
Nova Scotia WS6(7) SW6(7)-(11) WS12(12)
WS14(13) WS17B(14) CM31(16)

Orama TC2(2) Norw(3)
Orbita WS5A(6) WS5B(6) -(8) WS8A(9)
WS8B(9) WS9A(10) WS12(12) NA5(12)
WS18(14) WS27(19) WS28(19)
WS29(21)
Orcades GC1(2) US1(2) WS4B(5) SW4B(5)
WS7(8) WS10(11) CT5(12) TC15(12)
WS14(13) WS19P(15) NA12(15)
WS22(17)
Orduna WS8A(9) WS8B(9) WS12Z(12)
WS18(14) WS22(17) WS26(18)
KMF22(21) WS33(21)
Orford GC1(2) Med(2) US1(2) Norw(3)
Orion GC1(2) US1(2) Norw(3) CM(3)
SW2(4) BS11.25(5) WS7(8) WS10X(11)
WS11X(12) NA4(13) WS17(14)

WS20(16) WS25(18) KMF11(19)
WS29(19) KMF20(21)
Orizaba(US) WS12X(12) WS12Z(12)
WS19(15)
Ormonde TC2(2) Norw(3) Bisc(3) WS2(4)
SW2(4) WS5B(6) WS8A(9) WS8C(9)
WS10(11) WS12(12) WS16(14)
WS19(15) KMF11(19) KMF13(19)
KMF15(20) WS33(21)
Oronsay Norw(3) Bisc(3) WS3(5)
WS9B(10)-(11) CT5(12) TC15(12)
WS14(13) WS17(14) WS21P(16)
WS22(17)
Orontes WS3(5) SW3(5) WS7(8) SW7(8)-(9)
WS11(12) WS15(13) WS19(15)
WS28(19) KMF22(21)
Oropesa WS3(5)
Otranto Med(2) US1(2) Bisc(3) SW1(4)
WS2(4) WS4B(5) SW4B(5) WS7(8)
WS11(12) WS15(13) WS19P(15)
WS28(19) KMF22(21)

Pasteur WS4B(5) WS5B(6) WS7(8)
WS10(11) WS11(12) WS15(13)
WS19(15) WS19P(15) WS33(21)
Pennland(Du) WS5B(6)
Pilsudski(Pol) US1(2)
President Doumer(Fr) WS5B(6)-(9)
Pulaski(Pol) WS6(7) WS8A(9) WS9A(10)
WS9B(10) WS11(12) CM29(15)
WS21(16) WS25(18) WS33(21)

Queen Elizabeth WS4A(5) WS5B(6)
US10(8)-(10) -(12) WS16(14)
WS17B(14) WS19(15) WS19P(15)
WS19Y(15) WS30(20) WS31(20)
Queen Mary US2(2) US3(3) WS1(4)
WS4B(5) WS5B(6) US10(8) -(10) -(12)
WS16(14) WS19(15) WS19W(15)
WS25(18) WS25W(18) WS26(18)
WS28(19)
Queens (Monsters) WS22(17) WS23(17)

Rajula 1stCC(2) 2ndCC(2) 3rdCC(2) BC(3)
BN(4) BP(17)
Rangitata US1(2) WS6(7) WS9B(10)
WS12Z(12) WS18(14) WS22(17)
KMF11(19) WS32(21)
Rangitiki WS5A(6) WS10(11) WS11X(11)
WS17(14) WS21(16) CF5(16) WS25(18)
WS31(20)
Reina del Pacifico GC1(2) TC2(2) Norw(3)
CM(3) RS5(4) WS4B(5) WS7(8)
WS8A(9) WS10(11) CT5(12) TC15(12)

Other Merchant Ships

Aagtekerk(Du) WS9A(10)   WS15(13)
Abbekerk(Du) WS8A(9) WS12Z(12)
    DM1(12)
Abbeydale(RFA) WS16(14) WS17(14)
Adrastus WS12Z(12)   WS20(16)
Adviser WS5A(6)
Akaroa WS4A(5) WS19(!5)
Alcoa Pioneer(US) WS29(19)
American Manufacturer(US) WS21P(16)
American Press(US) WS21(16)(AS6)
Arabistan WS5A(6)
Argo(Grk) WS24(17)
Arraiz(Sp) WS8A(9)
Athelking WS5A(6)
Autolycus WS15(13)
Avila Star WS17(14)

Baharistan WS8A(9)
Bantam(Du) WS21(16)
Barnegat(US) WS24(17)
Baron Belhaven WS5A(6)
Barrister WS5A(6) WS11(12)
Bayano HP(9)
Beaverford WS4A(5)
Bellerophon WS6(7)
Benalbanach HP(9)
Benalder WS28(19)
Benarty -(4)
Benmohr WS16(14)
Benrinnes WS5A(6)
Benvannoch WS6(7)
Bhutan WS5A(6) WS11(12)   WS17(14)
Brisbane Star AP3(4) SW3(5) WS10X(11)
    WS16(14) WS30(20)
British General WS3(5)
Bulkoil WS18(14)
Bullmouth WS12Z(12)
Burdwan WS6(7)

California Star SW1(4)
Campas(Sp) WS12(12)
Canadian Cruiser WS5B(6)
Canara WS22(17)
Cap Norte(Ge) WS5A(6)
Cape Horn WS6(7)
Casanare WS4A(5)
Castalia Faith(20)
Ceramic WS9B(10)
China Mail(US) WS21(AS6)(16) WS29(19)
Chyebassa WS26(18) KMF 20(21)
City of Agra WS4A(5) WS25(18)
City of Athens WS6(7)

City of Bristol WS27(19) KMF20(21)
City of Capetown SW3(5) WS18(14)
City of Derby WS5A(6)
City of Edinburgh WS11(12) WS16(14)
    WS17(14) WS29(19)
City of Florence WS7(8)
City of Hong Kong WS10X(11)
City of Lille WS3(5)
City of Lincoln WS16(14) WS17(14)
    WS25(18) WS31(20)
City of Manchester WS4A(5) WS11(12)
City of Marseilles WS6(7)
City of Nagpur WS8A(9)
City of Pretoria WS14D(13)
City of Sydney WS8B(9)
Clan Cameron WS14(13)
Clan Campbell AP3(4) WS8A(9) WS8B(9)
    WS12(12)
Clan Chattan (WS4A(5) WS8A(9)
Clan Cumming WS4A(5)
Clan Ferguson RS5(4)
Clan Forbes WS9B(10)
Clan Lamont WS4A(5) WS8A(9) WS12(12)
    WS18(14) WS29A(19)
Clan Macarthur AP3(4) WS5A(6) WS19(15)
    WS31(20)
Clan Macaulay WS2(4) WS31(20)
Clan Macdonald WS5A(6) WS17(14)
Clan Macinnes WS19(15)
Clan Mactavish WS19(15)
Clan Murray WS18(14)
Colombia(Du) WS26(18)
Colonial(Port) WS21(16)
Consuelo WS6(7)
Copacabana(Be) WS32(21)
Curacao(Du) WS21(16)

Delaires(US) WS32(21)
Delane WS5A(6)
Delftdyk(Du) WS16(14) WS17(14)
Delius WS4A(5)
Denbighshire AP1(2) WS7(8) WS16(14)
Deseado WS30(20)
Deucalion WS12Z(12)
Dingledale(RFA) WS12Z(12)
Diomed WS10(11) CM29(15)
Dorset WS3(5) WS15(13)
Duilio(It) WS19(15)
Dumana -(11)
Dunedin Star WS4A(5) SW4B(5) WS17(14)

Eibergen(Du) WS9A(10)
Eleni(Grk) WS21P(16)
Elisabeth Bakke(No) WS9B(10) WS15(13)

Rimutaka WS12Z(12) WS18(14) WS23(17)
Robin Doncaster(US) WS26(18)
Rochester Castle WS8A(9) WS32(21)
Roslin Castle HP(9)
Rowallan Castle WS32(21)

Sagoland(Sw) WS30(20)
Santa Barbara(US) WS30(20)
Santa Cruz(US) WS21P(16)
Sarpedon WS10X(11)
Selandia WS26(18) WS29(19)
Silversandal WS23(17)
Silverteak KMF17(20)
Silverwalnut WS21(16) WS29(19)
Soudan WS18(14)
Speybank WS5A(6)
St Anselm WS9B(10)
Stentor WS5A(6)
Straat Malacca(Du) WS23(17) WS29(19)
Suffolk WS2(4) SW1(4) WS22(17)
Susan V Luckenbach(US) WS16(14)
Sussex DM1(2) WS12Z(12) WS19(15)
Sydney Star AP1(2) SW2(4) WS27(19)

Talisse(Du) WS19P(15)
Tarifa(No) WS25(18)
Tarn(No) WS21P(16)
Tatuta Maru(Jap) WS21(16)
Tawali(Du) WS26(18)
Thames(Du) WS15(13)
Tilsington Court WS25(18)
Troilus WS5A(6) WS14D(13) WS29(19)

Umona WS7(8)

Waiotira AP1(2) SW2(4)
Waipawa WS18(14) WS28(19)
Waiwera WS2(4) WS8X(9)

Zamzam(Eg) SW4A(5)

Military Formations and Units

Divisions

1st Armoured WS11(12) WS12(12)
1st Cavalry   France(2)
1st Canadian TC1/2/3(2)
2nd Armoured WS4A&B(5)
2nd Infantry WS18(14)
2nd NZ US1(2)
2nd South African WS7(8)
5th Infantry WS17(14) WS28(19)

6th Australian WS4B(5)
7th Armoured WS4A(5)
7th Australian WS4B(5)
8th Armoured WS19(15)
18th Infantry CT5/WS12X(12)
44th Home Counties WS19P(15)
50th Northumbrian WS8A&B(9) WS9A(10)
    WS28(19)
51st Highland WS20(16)
56th London WS22(17)
81st West Africa WS27(19) WS29(19)

Brigades

1st Armoured WS4A(5) WS4B(5)
2nd Armoured WS12(12)
3rd Armoured WS4A(5)
22nd Armoured WS10X(11) WS12(12)
23rd Armoured WS19(15)
24th Armoured WS19(15)
1st Support Grp WS12(12)
2nd Support Grp WS4B(5)
8th Support Grp WS19(15)
4th Cavalry 3rd CC(2)
5th Cavalry 2nd CC(2)
6th Cavalry 1st CC(2)
4th Infantry WS18(14)
5th Infantry WS18(14)
6th Infantry WS18(14)
13th Infantry WS17(14)
15th Infantry WS17(14)
17th Infantry WS17(14)
24th Guards Norw(3)
29th Independent WS17(14) EA(16)
53rd Infantry WS12X(12)
54th Infantry WS12X(12)
55th Infantry   WS12X(12)
69th Infantry WS8B(9) WS9A(10)
131st Infantry WS19P(15)
132nd Infantry WS19P(15)
133rd Infantry WS19P(15)
146th Infantry Norw(3)
148th Infantry Norw(3)
150th Infantry WS8A(9)
151st Infantry WS8B(9)
152nd Infantry WS20(16)
153rd Infantry WS20(16)
154th Infantry WS20(16)
161st Infantry   WS2(4) WS5A(6) WS9A(10)
167th Infantry WS22(17)
168th Infantry WS22(17)
169th Infantry WS22(17)
231st Independent WS28(19)
4th New Zealand US1(2)

1st Lon Irish WS22(17)
5th Loyals CT5/WS12X(12) BM12(13)
2nd Manchester WS18(14)
1/7th Middsx WS20(16)
2nd Ox & Bucks BC(3)
6th Ox & Bucks WS20(16)
7th Ox & Bucks WS22(17)
1st Camerons WS18(14)
2nd Camerons Heron(2)
5th Camerons WS20(16)
4th RW Kent WP19P(15)
5th RW Kent WP19P(15)
1/5th Queens WS19P(15)
2/5th Queens WS22(17)
2/6th Queens WS22(17)
1st Rifle Bde WS12(12)
7th Rifle Bde WS19(15)
1st Tower Hamlets WS4A(5)
10th R Berks WS22(17)
9th R Fusiliers WS22(17)
20th R Fusiliers WS26(18)
2nd R Innisks WS17(14)
1st R Norfolk BC(3)
2nd R Norfolk WS18(14)
4th R Norfolk CT5/WS12X(12)
5th R Norfolk CT5/WS12X(12)
6th R Norfolk CT5/WS12X(12)
9th R. Nmbld Fus CT5/WS12X(12)
1st Royal Scots WS18(14)
1st R Scots Fus BC(3) WS17(14)
2nd R Scots Fus WS17(14)
2nd R Sussex WS19P(15)
4th R Sussex WS19P(15)
5th R Sussex WS19P(15)
9th R Sussex WS24(17)
1st R Ulster R BC(3)
1st R Welch Fus WS18(14)
2nd R Welch Fus BC(3) WS17(14)
2nd Seaforths WS20(16)
5th Seaforths WS20(16) WS15(13)
- Seaforths WS15(13)
1/5th Sh.Foresters CT5/WS12X(12)
14th Sh.Foresters WS19(15)
2nd S Lancs BC(3) WS17(14)
7th S Lancs WS22(17)
2nd S Staffs BC(3)
2nd S Wales Bords Norw(3)
6th S Wales Bords WS24(17) WS26(18)
4th Suffolk CT5/WS12X(12)
5th Suffolk CTS/WS12X(12)
11th W Yorks WS20(16)
2nd Wilts WS17(14)
7th Worcest WS18(14)
1st York&Lancs WS17(14)

7th York&Lancs WS14(13)
9th York&Lancs WS20(16)
10th York&Lancs WS11(12)
Hallams Norw(3)
2/10th Australian WS4B(5)
2/9th Queensland WS4B(5)
Capetown High WS5B(6)
Kings African Rifles WS12(12) WS17(14)
   WS20(16)
11th Nigeria WS9A(10)

Other Units

No. 5 Commando WS17(14)
Task Force 122 WS20(16)
West African troops WS12(12)

Miscellaneous

SAWAS US3(3)
Indian Expeditionary Force France(2)
Focke Wulf Condors AP1&2(4) WS2(4)
   WS3F(5) WS5A(6) WS8B(9) WS11(12)
   WS12(12) WS15(13) WS27(19)
   WS28(19) WS29(19) WS30(20)
   WS31(20) Faith(20) WS32(21)
IMPCON WS5A(6) WS6(7) WS8A(9)
   WS12X(12) WS12Z(12) WS14(13)
   WS15(13) WS17(14) WS18(14)
   WS19(15) WS22(17)
Clairwood Transit Camp WS1(1)
   WS5A&B(6) WS6(7) WS9A(10)
   WS18(14) WS19(15) WS23(17)
   WS25(18) WS26(18) WS30(20)
   WS32(21) WS33(21)
Pollsmoor Transit Camp WS18(14)
Retreat Transit Camp WS18(14) WS19(15)
Pointe Noire WS11(12) WS12Z(12)
   WS22(17) WS23(17) WS25(18)
   WS26(18) WS27(19) WS28(19)
   WS29(19) WS30(20) WS31(20)
   WS32(21)
St Helena WS16(14) WS18(14) WS19(15)
   WS19P(15) WS21(16)

Personnel

Alderson, Capt. A (Union Castle) AP3(4)
   WS24(17) WS29(19)
Aldous, Brigadier JRT, WS18(14)
Alexander, HV, First Lord of the Admiralty
   AP3(4)
Almond, Captain JG (NZS) WS5A(6)